ORDINARY PRUSSIANS

This book gives voice, in unprecedented depth and immediacy, to ordinary villagers and landlords (Junkers) in the Prussian–German countryside, from the late middle ages to the nineteenth century. In their own words, preserved in the rich archives of the Brandenburg lordship of Stavenow, the trials and fortunes of everyday life come into view—in the family, the workplace, in many humble men's and women's private lives, in courtroom and jailhouse, and under the gaze of the rising Prussian monarchy's officials and army officers. What emerges is a many-dimensioned, long-term study of a rural society, inviting comparisons on a world-historical level.

Amid current debates between skeptics and optimists, the book puts to a new test the possibilities of empirical historical knowledge at the microhistorical or 'grass-roots' level. But it also reconceptualizes, on the scale of Prussian–German and European history, the rise of agrarian capitalism, questioning views widespread in the economic history literature on the common people's living standards. It presents massive new documentation on women's condition, rights, and social roles. It challenges deep-rooted views on the triangular relationship between state, landed nobility, and village farmers in the history of Prussia, on which current understandings of authoritarianism in modern German history still depend.

WILLIAM W. HAGEN is Professor of History, University of California, Davis. His previous publications include *Germans, Poles, and Jews: The Nationality Conflict in the Prussian East, 1772–1914* (Chicago, 1980).

NEW STUDIES IN EUROPEAN HISTORY

Edited by

PETER BALDWIN
University of California, Los Angeles
CHRISTOPHER CLARK
University of Cambridge
JAMES B. COLLINS
Georgetown University
MIA RODRIGUEZ-SALGADO
London School of Economics and Political Science
LYNDAL ROPER
Royal Holloway, University of London

This is a new series in early modern and modern European history. Its aim is to publish outstanding works of research, addressed to important themes across a wide geographical range, from southern and central Europe, to Scandinavia and Russia, and from the time of the Renaissance to the Second World War. As it develops the series will comprise focused works of wide contextual range and intellectual ambition.

ORDINARY PRUSSIANS

Brandenburg Junkers and Villagers, 1500–1840

WILLIAM W. HAGEN

CAMBRIDGE
UNIVERSITY PRESS

PUBLISHED BY THE PRESS SYNDICATE OF THE UNIVERSITY OF CAMBRIDGE
The Pitt Building, Trumpington Street, Cambridge, CB2 1RP, United Kingdom

CAMBRIDGE UNIVERSITY PRESS
The Edinburgh Building, Cambridge, CB2 2RU, UK
40 West 20th Street, New York, NY 10011-4211 USA
477 Williamstown Road, Port Melbourne, VIC 3207, Australia
Ruiz de Alarcón 13, 28014 Madrid, Spain
Dock House, The Waterfront, Cape Town 8001, South Africa
http://www.cambridge.org

© William W. Hagen 2002

First published 2002

Printed in the United Kingdom at the University Press, Cambridge

Typeface Baskerville Monotype 11/12.5 pt.   *System* Quark   [TB]

A catalogue record for this book is available from the British Library

Library of Congress Cataloguing in Publication data

Hagen, William W.
Ordinary Prussians: Brandenburg Junkers and Villagers, 1500–1840 / William W. Hagen.
p.   cm. – (New Studies in European History)
Includes bibliographical references and index.
ISBN 0 521 81558 4 hardback
1. Brandenburg (Germany) – Social conditions.
2. Nobility – Germany – Brandenburg – History.   3. Brandenburg (Germany) – Rural
conditions.   4. Prussia (Germany) – Rural conditions.   5. Prussia (Germany) – Social
conditions.   6. Villages – Germany – Prussia – History.
7. Nobility – Germany – Prussia – History.
8. Agriculture and state – Germany – Prussia – History.   I. Title.   II. Series.
DD801.B687 H34 2002   2002017502
943′.15 – dc21

ISBN 0 521 81558 4 hardback

Contents

v

Illustrations

MAPS

Acknowledgments

This book is the harvest of long seasons of work, both in German archives and at home. The research in Germany was an education in many things besides puzzling out a myriad of provincial handwritings and centuries-old mentalities. Its funding flowed from the Alexander von Humboldt-Stiftung, which supported two stays in Berlin, lasting sixteen months altogether. Also essential to my work in Germany were short-term grants from the Deutscher Akademischer Austauschdienst and annual faculty research grants from the University of California, Davis. In this country, I gained a year's leave to work on this project in the agreeable atmosphere of the Institute for Advanced Study in Princeton, New Jersey, supported by grants from the Institute's School of Historical Studies, the National Endowment for the Humanities, and the University of California.

Vital to my thinking about this work was cooperation with the research group on east-Elbian agrarian societies at the University of Potsdam, about which this book's introduction has more to say. The group's funding by the Max Planck-Gesellschaft benefited me through participation in its path-breaking conferences and resulting book projects, and through a grant supporting a four-month residency in 1994. Similarly important was my 1992–8 tenure as director of the Center for History, Society, and Culture at the University of California, Davis. This interdisciplinary program of research and graduate instruction in the historical social sciences was the crucible of the thinking about historical scholarship and method informing these pages. It helped me grasp more firmly, through reflection on other modes of approaching time-bound human experience, the great and irreplaceable strengths of the discipline of history, not as its past practitioners conceived them, but as they appear in contemporary light.

Among the many people whose professional services supported this project, I am indebted to the archivists and photocopyists of the

Geheimes Staatsarchiv Preußischer Kulturbesitz, in former West Berlin, who upheld the highest standards of friendly efficiency and expertise. Christopher L. Brest expertly drew the map of the Stavenow lordship in its regional setting. Other maps and illustrations display the skills of UC Davis specialists. For invitations to present talks on this project (whether skeptically or assentingly received) I thank, in Germany, the Historische Kommission zu Berlin, the Freie Universität Berlin, Bielefeld University, and the Max Planck-Gesellschaft work group at Potsdam University; in Britain, the universities of East Anglia, Manchester, and London; and, in the United States, Cornell and New York University and the universities of Chicago, Michigan at Ann Arbor, and Oregon. Among those colleagues and friends who assisted my stays in Germany, discussed this project, and hosted me at their universities, I would like to remember here historians John Boyer, Thomas Brady, Otto Büsch, Geoff Eley, Lieselott Enders, Rolf Engelsing, Richard J. Evans, Hartmut Harnisch, Hartmut Kaelble, Edgar Melton, David Sabean, and Hans-Ulrich Wehler. For their friendly reception I thank Professor Peter Paret at the Institute for Advanced Study and all the participants in the Potsdam group, especially its director, Professor Jan Peters, and his associates Heinrich Kaak and Axel Lubinski. I am mindful of many others who have taken an interest in this work. My thanks also to Dr. Hamish Scott for encouraging me to submit this work to him and his colleagues for review for publication by Cambridge University Press, and to History Editor William Davies for steering it forward.

This book is, in part, a product of the post-1945 era of German division. The Stavenow lordship lay in a region that, before 1990, formed part of the German Democratic Republic. A stay there in the 1980s with hospitable Blüthen village pastor Karl Gross and his wife Gerlinde enabled me to hand-photograph the parish register, as well as Pastor Gross's laborious statistical analysis of it, and acquaint myself with the spirits of the locality, including those hovering around the lordship's ruins. On that trip I also met others who took an interest in Stavenow, among them schoolteacher Franz Giese, who wrote an unpublished history of Premslin village, of which, unfortunately, I never managed to obtain a readable copy. This and later post-1990 visits to Brandenburg's Prignitz district, along with numerous other travels in the east German countryside, have left me with a strong visual impression of the rural world which the pages below conjure up, and with a sense for the worthy people who embody its traditions now and for their predecessors, of whom I write in these pages. I would like to think they will recognize something of themselves in this book. After 1990 I worked briefly in the Brandenburgisches Landesarchiv in Postdam, and made copies of valuable unpublished photographs in the Perleberg Museum. From these and other sources more could be added to the present work, but the Geheimes Staatsarchiv's 728 Stavenow document files formed a mountain of evidence that required all available time and energy to scale and explore.

Though grateful for all help tendered in this enterprise, I bear responsibility for these pages' arguments and analysis. The friends and relatives who witnessed my labors distinguished themselves by their benevolence. Ulla, who lived it all, deserves a crown.

Currencies, weights, and measures employed in the text

CURRENCIES

1. The Reichstaler (Rt.) = 24 groschen (1 groschen = 12 pfennigs): early modern German silver-based money of account.
2. The Rhenish gulden (fl.) = 18 groschen: another early modern German money of account. In the sixteenth and seventeenth centuries, the Brandenburg gulden = 18 groschen at 12 pfennigs = 24 Lübeck schillings.
3. The Brandenburg "current taler" (Courant Taler): real coinage minted from one "Imperial Mark" Of silver (234 grams) according to these proportions: pre-1667: 9 talers per Mark; 1667–90: 10.5 talers; 1690–1750: 12 talers; 1750–1821 and beyond: 14 talers. To 1738 the Imperial German Reichstaler numbered 10.5 talers to the silver Mark and after 1764 12 talers. From this money of account the coinages of the various German states more or less diverged, as the just-cited silver equivalencies of the Brandenburg taler show. The Brandenburg currency was temporarily devalued during the Seven Years War (8 talers Saxon = 3.5 current talers = 100:44). In 1821 Prussia revised its coinage, retaining the Brandenburg taler in the silver value established in 1750 and reconfirmed in 1764 (whereby 14 talers were struck from a 234-gram Mark of silver). But now the taler counted 30 "silver groschen" (*Silbergroschen*) rather than the previous 24.

AREAL MEASURES

1. The Brandenburg (*kurmärkischer*) *Morgen* (400 square German rods [*Ruten*] = 0.57 hectares = 1.4 Anglo-American acres): the standard areal measure until displaced in the late eighteenth century by the Magdeburg *Morgen* (180 square rods or 0.26 hectares = 0.62 acres). One hectare = 2.5 acres.

2. The Brandenburg hide of land (*Hufe*) = 30 "large" (Brandenburg) *Morgen* = 17 hectares = 42.5 acres.
3. One German mile = 5 English miles.
4. The *Gebind* (*Verbind*) – space, approximately 7 feet, between upright timbers by which buildings were measured.

HOLLOW AND LIQUID MEASURES, AND WEIGHTS

1. The Brandenburg bushel (*Scheffel*) approximated 1.5 modern Anglo-American bushels and varied in weight by grain type and in volume (slightly) by region. Modern equivalents of eighteenth-century weights of the Berlin bushel of grain (similar or identical to that in use at Stavenow) were: rye: 40–5 kilograms (88–99 lbs); barley: 33–8 kg (73–84 lbs); oats: 24–6 kg (53–7 lbs). The bushel in use at Berlin markets retained virtually constant size in the years 1682–1868. After the metric system's 1868 adoption, the previously prevailing Berlin bushel yielded to the "new bushel" with a hollow volume of 50 liters or 0.5 hectoliters; the earlier bushel held 55 liters.
2. Wagonloads, measured in *Fuder:* normatively, 1 *Fuder* = ca. 20 Prussian hundredweights (*Zentner*); 1 *Zentner* = 110 German lbs (*Pfund*) = 51.5 kilograms (113 lbs). The wider "manorial wagonload" carried a load (*Knechtsfuder*) twice as heavy as that borne by the narrower "villagers' wagonload" (*Bauernfuder*).
3. The stone weight (*Stein*), measuring especially wool: the heavy stone weighed 22 German or English pounds, the light stone half as much.
4. 1 quart = 0.87 liter; 1 liter = 1.06 US liquid quarts; 1 barrel (*Tonne*) = 100 quarts = 87 liters = 92 US quarts or 23 gallons; *Oxschaft* (High German: *Oxhaupt/Oxhoft*) = oxhead = (anno 1808) 180 quarts.

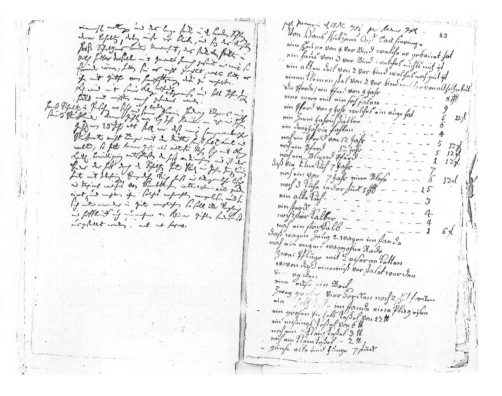

1 Pages from the Stavenow lordship's seigneurial court transcripts recording an amicable farm transfer from retiring elders to the possessor's step-son, 1751. On left: seigneurial judge Johann Erdmann Hasse's entries. On right: farm inventory ("Von Hans Schultzens Hoff Tacksierung"), in the hand and words of Blüthen village farmer Johann Guhl. Geheimes Staatsarchiv Preußischer Kulturbesitz.

2 Prussian (Pomeranian) farmers traveling near the Oder river with artist Daniel Chodowiecki, 1773.

3 Chodowiecki dining with traveling companions. From left: innkeeper (telling tales of robbery and murder), carriage-driver, merchant, the artist, butcher's apprentice, unidentified woman, and child.

4   The Stavenow manorial residence (*Schloß*) and church tower ca. 1900.

5   Stavenow from across the Löcknitz stream, ca. 1900.

6   The Stavenow tower (earlier housing the dungeon) and courtyard, ca. 1900.

7 Prignitz farmer and wife sitting before their house, ca. 1900. They are probably the progeny of the last generation of subject farmers figuring in this book.

8 Young Prignitz farmer's living room (*Bauernstube*), 1905.

9 Prignitz farmhouse and outbuildings, ca. 1900.

10 and 11   Prignitz farmhouses and outbuildings, ca. 1900.

12   Prignitz farmstead, ca. 1900.

13   Perleberg, ca. 1910, from church tower. Market square, with late medieval statue
of Roland, enforcer of honesty, lower right.

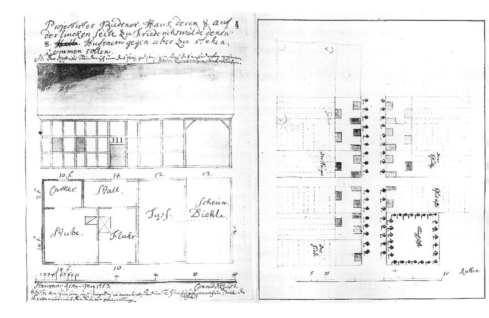

14 Conrad von Kleist's design of cottager's house and street plan, Dargardt village settlement, 1753. The house includes a living room, bedroom, entry-hall and kitchen, livestock stall, and adjoining barn. The street plan displays the farmsteads and houses of fullholders, innkeeper, schoolmaster, and livestock herder, and the cemetery.

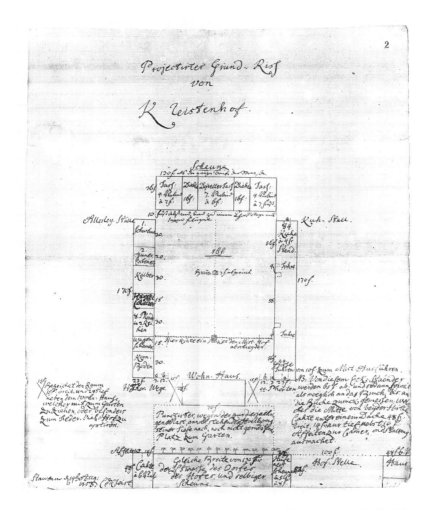

15 Conrad von Kleist's seigneurial manor-farm design, Dargardt, 1755. Behind the
dwelling-house, livestock stalls extend on two sides back to the barn. They enclose a
manure and compost pile that "a picket fence could separate" from the house.
Dimensions in German feet.

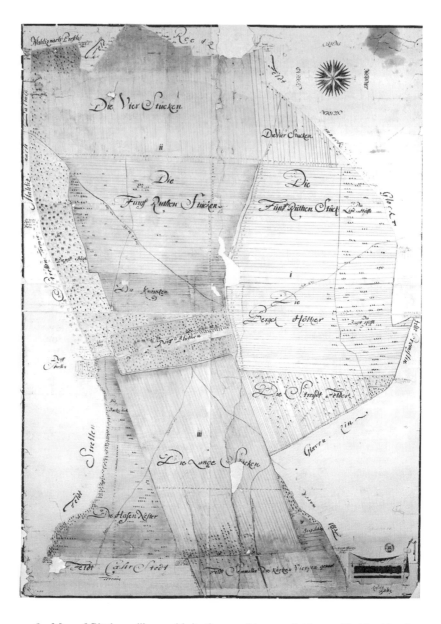

16   Map of Blüthen village, with its three arable open fields, smallholders' land,
pasture, and woodlands, ca. 1726.

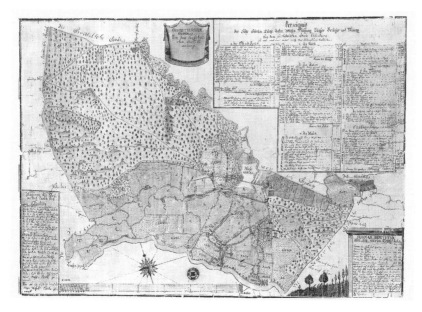

17 "Geometrical Ground-Plan of the Most Noble Eldenburg Estate," ca. 1750, displaying seigneurial arable, pastures, woods, and other appurtenances, all self-enclosed and separate from the village land.

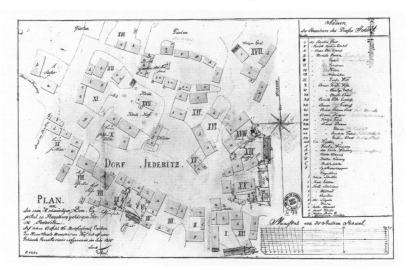

18 Diagram of Prignitz village Jederitz, 1800, subject to the Havelberg Cathedral Chapter, commissioned by State Minister (and future Stavenow owner) Otto von Voss, including farmhouses (a), barns and stalls (b), retirement quarters (c), and day laborers' dwellings (1–11).

19   Daniel Chodowiecki, *Frederick II*, 1777: a picture free of heroization.

20 Major General Friedrich Wilhelm Gottfried Arndt von Kleist (1724–67), of the
Stavenow Kleist line and Frederick II's celebrated hussar commander ("Green
Kleist") during the Seven Years War. He possessed a reputation for "humanitarianism" (*Menschenfreundlichkeit*). A subordinate described him as "a very agreeable man
who issued his orders with a light and fine touch."

21   Detail of late medieval–Renaissance grave memorial of a Prignitz nobleman (d. 1570), Havelberg Cathedral.

22　Von Quitzow altar, Kletzke village, Prignitz. Early seventeenth-century Baroque style.

Grand narratives, ordinary Prussians

The historical realm this book conjures up, though now mostly vanished from the western world, casts a long shadow. It was the agrarian regime of subordinate villages and powerful landlords, as old as Egypt. Into it, until the eighteenth and nineteenth centuries, most Europeans and many North Americans were born, and only recently did it cease to be the prime site of life and death for the rest of humanity.

In this study it is also Prussia – in most minds, a vague and distant, troubling or even menacing concept. It is, more precisely, a Prussia that looms large in explanations of the unstable and violent course of modern German history: the Prussia of the landed nobility and their subject villagers, from the late middle ages to the nineteenth century. But from these pages an unexpected picture will emerge, both of villages and manors, state and society, soldiers and civilians. Some reigning views on German and central European history will fall out of focus, and a new passage will appear across the early modern European world to the twentieth century's much-debated modernity. This work is also an essay in historical envisioning amid present-day debates between philosophical pessimists and optimists, "constructivists" and "objectivists," over the possibilities of historical knowledge. It aims also to illuminate in the mind's eye various groups of people invisible in histories of high culture and politics, or hidden behind conventionalized identities assigned them by modern social science. And, though this study's landscape is German, it communicates by many paths with the larger world.

Prussia was a north German state, embracing an array of provinces centered on Brandenburg, with Berlin as princely residence (map 1). From the fifteenth to the nineteenth century it expanded both to west and east, until it stretched from the Rhine river and the North Sea across the Baltic plains to Imperial Russia. Under the Hohenzollern dynasty, Brandenburg-Prussia emerged, plundered and ravaged from

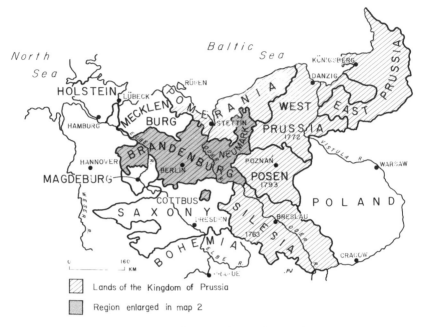

Map 1   East-Elbian Germany in the eighteenth century

the great European conflagration of the Thirty Years War (1618–48), to
become an archetypal "absolutist monarchy," distinguished, admired,
and feared for its large standing army. The landed nobility officered this
force, while a mushrooming bureaucracy of mostly commoner origins
collected royal taxes financing it. In the age of Frederick II, "the Great"
(ruled 1740–86), Prussia laid claim not only to European major-power
status, but to eighteenth-century Reason. Despite its imperfections,
Frederick's "enlightened absolutism" helped strengthen an emergent
bourgeois civil society which, both in his day and in the nineteenth century, proved a hothouse of educational and cultural attainment and
capitalist growth. These qualities, paired with military strength, supplied Chancellor Otto von Bismarck with the tools to hammer the
numerous other German states, excepting defeated Austria, into the
Prussian-dominated German Empire of 1871.[1]

---

[1] The vast literature on pre-Napoleonic Prussia tends to offer a celebratory-nostalgic view (from
conservative German pens) or a critical-condemnatory perspective (from left-liberal and
Marxist authors, both German and Anglo-American). For bibliography and critique see
William W. Hagen, "The Descent of the *Sonderweg*. Hans Rosenberg's History of Old-Regime
Prussia," *Central European History* (hereafter: *CEH*) 24 (1991): 24–50. A modern masterwork is
Reinhart Koselleck, *Preussen zwischen Reform und Revolution: Allgemeines Landrecht, Verwaltung und*

World War I destroyed this state, toppling the Hohenzollerns. Its successor was the democratic Weimar Republic of 1918–33, among whose many enemies were Prussian conservatives, especially those with ties to the prewar high bureaucracy, army officer corps, and large landowning class. Symbolized and even embodied in the second Weimar president and World War I field-marshal Paul von Hindenburg, Prussian conservatism was instrumental in crippling Weimar democracy and bringing Hitler and the National Socialists to power in 1933. Although Prussia had also been since the nineteenth century a stronghold of middle-class liberalism, working-class socialism and, later, communism, the Nazi avalanche crushed them.

soziale Bewegung von 1791 bis 1848 (Stuttgart, 1981). Cf. Jonathan Sperber, "State and Civil Society in Prussia: Thoughts on a New Edition of Reinhart Koselleck's *Preussen zwischen Reform und Revolution.*" *Journal of Modern History* (hereafter: *JMH*) 57 (1985): 278–96. Valuable in English is C. B. A. Behrens, *Society, Government, and the Enlightenment. The Experiences of Eighteenth-Century France and Prussia* (New York, 1985). Cf. Reinhold Dorwart, *The Prussian Welfare State before 1740* (Cambridge, MA, 1971). Stimulating still is Henri Brunschwig, *Enlightenment and Romanticism in Eighteenth-Century Prussia* (Chicago, 1974 [French original, 1947]). The single-volume political-history classic in German is Otto Hintze's (not wholly uncritical) *Die Hohenzollern und ihr Werk* (Berlin, 1916), which should be supplemented by the strong recent scholarship displayed in Philip G. Dwyer, ed., *The Rise of Prussia: Rethinking Prussian History, 1700–1830* (London, 2001); the special issue on "Prussia from Rossbach to Jena," ed. H. M. Scott, *German History* (hereafter: *GH*) 12 (1994): 279–394, and Wolfgang Neugebauer, "Zur Staatsbildung Brandenburg-Preußens: Thesen zu einem historischen Typus," *Jahrbuch für brandenburgische Landesgeschichte* (hereafter: *JBL*) 49 (1998): 183–94. Valuable too is the five-volume catalog to the 1981 Berlin exhibition, *Preußen – Versuch einer Bilanz* (Reinbek bei Hamburg, 1981), especially vol. II: Manfred Schlencke, ed., *Preußen – Beiträge zu einer politischen Kultur* and vol. III: Peter Brandt, ed., *Preußen – Zur Sozialgeschichte eines Staates.* Useful is Wolfgang Menge and Emanuela Wilm, *So lebten sie alle Tage. Bericht aus dem alten Preußen* (Berlin, 1984). Measured is Rudolf von Thadden, *Prussia: The History of a Lost State* (Cambridge, 1987 [German original, 1981]). Vitriolic, and characteristic of widespread liberal opinion, is Hans-Ulrich Wehler, "Preußen ist wieder chic . . . Der Obrigkeitsstaat im Goldrähmchen," in H.-U. Wehler, *Preußen ist wieder chic . . . Politik und Polemik* (Frankfurt/Main, 1983), 11–18 and passim. Attractively presented is Hans Kathe, *Preußen zwischen Mars und Musen. Eine Kulturgeschichte von 1100 bis 1920* (Munich, 1993). Valuable perspectives from the German Democratic Republic are offered in Günter Vogler and Klaus Vetter, *Preußen: Von den Anfängen bis zur Reichsgründung*, third edn (Berlin, 1974) and Ingrid Mittenzwei and Erika Herzfeld, *Brandenburg-Preußen, 1648 bis 1789: Das Zeitalter des Absolutismus in Text und Bild* (Cologne, 1987). For a valuable study of the Prussia Reform Era (1807–19) and its aftermath, see Mathew Levinger, *Enlightened Nationalism. The Transformation of Prussian Political Culture, 1806–1848* (New York, 2000). Interesting popular treatments include Giles MacDonogh, *Prussia. The Perversion of an Idea* (London, 1994) and James C. Roy, *The Vanished Kingdom. Travels through the History of Prussia* (Boulder, Co., 1999). On Frederick II: Theodor Schieder, *Friedrich der Große. Ein Königtum der Widersprüche* (Berlin, 1983) and Ingrid Mittenzwei, *Friedrich II. von Preußen. Eine Biographie* (Berlin, 1983). On the Mark Brandenburg: Ingo Materna and Wolfgang Ribbe, eds., *Brandenburgische Geschichte* (Berlin, 1995). For the wider German context: Rudolf Vierhaus, *Deutschland im Zeitalter des Absolutismus, 1648–1763* (Göttingen, 1978); James Sheehan, *German History, 1770–1866* (Oxford, 1989); Thomas Nipperdey, *Deutsche Geschichte 1800–1866. Bürgerwelt und starker Staat* (Munich, 1985); Lutz Niethammer et al., *Bürgerliche Gesellschaft in Deutschland* (Frankfurt/M., 1990); David Blackbourn, *The Long Nineteenth Century. A History of Germany, 1780–1918* (Oxford, 1997).

Many of Hitler's generals were Prussian aristocrats, and while some of them participated in the 1944 plot to assassinate him, at World War II's end the Prussian legacy, tied so intimately to German militarism, stood profoundly discredited. At the postwar 1945 Potsdam Conference, Truman, Churchill, and Stalin approved cession, mainly to war-terrorized Poland, of all the once-Prussian German lands to the east of the Oder–Neisse river line, but forty miles in Warsaw's direction beyond Berlin. The German population there largely fled before the Soviet army or was evacuated to German soil farther west. In 1947 the Allied Control Council in occupied Germany pronounced Prussia's death sentence in a decree abolishing it as a territorial concept and entity. Today there are few people still alive who would describe themselves as Prussians, unless they descend from the former far-distant Baltic province of East Prussia. The Hohenzollerns had once ruled most of the lands comprising the ill-fated German Democratic Republic (1949–90), but these regions, such as Brandenburg, have reverted to provincial identities that never ceased to be significant.

Such are the associations the concept of Prussia conjures up in most minds today, even in Germany itself. Inseparable from it are the qualities of loyalty, discipline, and order, which the state instilled in its inhabitants through the army, the state-dependent Protestant church, and schools. While, in the realm of stereotype and prejudice, Catholic Austria and south and west Germany sometimes evoke amiable disorder (*Schlamperei*), Prussia often summons the idea of unquestioning obedience, even "cadaver-obedience" (*Kadaver-Gehorsam*), a nineteenth-century epithet for Prussian army discipline. Above all, Prussia is linked to the idea of dominated subject, rather than self-determining citizen. The German word for subject is *Untertan*, and it looms large in these pages.[2]

---

[2] For a recent presentation of these images, see Lonnie R. Johnson, *Central Europe. Enemies, Neighbors, Friends* (New York, 1996), 111ff. Influential, though weakened by the premise that top-down disciplinization went unchallenged, is Otto Büsch, *Military System and Social Life in Old-Regime Prussia: The Beginning of the Social Militarization of Prusso-German Society, 1713–1807* (Atlantic Highlands, NJ, 1997 [German original, 1962]). Extreme is Emilio Willems, *A Way of Life and Death. Three Centuries of Prussian-German Militarism. An Anthropological Approach* (Nashville, 1986). Peter Paret offers a realistic view of the pre-1806 Prussian army in *Yorck and the Era of Prussian Reform, 1807–1815* (Princeton, 1966). A valuable synthesis is Dennis Showalter, "Hubertusberg to Auerstädt: The Prussian Army in Decline?", *GH* 12 (1994): 308–33. For recent challenges to the social militarization thesis, see Peter Burschel, "Von Prügel und höherer Kultur. Über eine Quellensammlung zur Sozialgeschichte des preußischen Militärs," *Forschungen zur brandenburgischen und preußischen Geschichte, Neue Folge* (hereafter: *FBPG-NF*) 3 (1993): 251–4; Ralf Pröve, "Zum Verhältnis von Militär und Gesellschaft im Spiegel gewaltsamer Rekrutierungen (1648–1789)," *Zeitschrift für Historische Forschung* (hereafter: *ZHF*) 22 (1995): 191–223. Useful, but also exaggerating the Prussian state's repressive apparatus, is Alf Lüdtke, *Police and State in Prussia, 1815–1850*

There is no more widespread explanation of the modern German catastrophe than the argument that, between the French Revolution of 1789 and the National Socialist power-seizure in 1933, Germany failed to develop a democratic political culture based on morally autonomous citizens. Otherwise, the Weimar Republic's fall and widespread popular acquiescence in Nazi dictatorship and crimes would not have occurred. The prime impediment to democratization was the survival into the twentieth century of the Prussian monarchy and the conservative-authoritarian institutions it fostered and shielded. Though the 1848 Revolution bequeathed constitutional and parliamentary government to Prussia, and though the German Empire of 1871 rested on universal male suffrage, at the level of society and culture the Prussian lands remained, as this argument holds, a stronghold of the subject mentality. Its inhabitants deferred to those who "wore the king's coat" and harkened to the commands of "the state," a historical actor whose moral and civilizational role enlightened absolutism's defenders, and after them the philosopher Hegel, apostrophized.[3]

Many nineteenth-century German liberals, and not only Protestants, followed Hegel in placing trust in the progressive potential of the Prussian state, which one of them, the historian Friedrich Dahlmann, described in conservative pre-1848 years as "the magic spear which heals as well as wounds."[4] Yet in the twentieth century this perspective grew unfamiliar. It is also usually thought that the industrial capitalism which came to flourish in Prussian Germany assumed harshly authoritarian forms, reinforcing the dominant political culture's anti-democratic tendencies. Bismarck's rebaptism of the Prussian monarchy in the ideological and psychological

(Cambridge, 1989 [German original, 1982]). Cf. Mary Lee Townsend, *Forbidden Laughter: Popular Humor and the Limits of Repression in Nineteenth-Century Prussia* (Ann Arbor, 1992).

[3] The most forceful and authoritative formulations of this view flow from Hans-Ulrich Wehler's pen. See his *Das Deutsche Kaiserreich, 1871–1918* (Göttingen, 1973 [English translation, 1985]), *Deutsche Gesellschaftsgeschichte*, 3 vols. (Munich, 1987–95), and "A Guide to Future Research on the Kaiserreich?", *CEH* 29 (1996): 541–72, which marked another stage in a debate sparked by David Blackbourn's and Geoff Eley's neo-Marxist critique of Wehler's work in *The Peculiarities of German History. Bourgeois Society and Politics in Nineteenth-Century Germany* (Oxford, 1984). See Eley's reply, "Problems with Culture: German History after the Linguistic Turn," *CEH* 31 (1998): 197–227. Wehler drew inspiration from Max Weber, who expressed biting liberal criticism of the Prussian conservative elites in his essays, well known to social scientists, "Capitalism and Rural Society in Germany" (1906) and "National Character and the Junkers" (1917), in H. H. Gerth and C. Wright Mills, eds., *From Max Weber: Essays in Sociology* (Oxford, 1946), 363–95. On intellectuals and the state, see Leonard Krieger, *The German Idea of Freedom* (Chicago, 1957) and Bernhard Giesen, *Die Intellektuellen und die Nation. Eine deutsche Achsenzeit* (Frankfurt/M., 1993).

[4] Quoted by T. C. W. Blanning in "The Commercialization and Sacralization of European Culture in the Nineteenth Century," in T. C. W. Blanning ed., *The Oxford Illustrated History of Europe* (Oxford, 1996), 143.

waters of nineteenth-century German nationalism, with its frustrated
yearning for state unity and national prestige, yielded explosive effects,
especially once ruthless war for European and world hegemony broke out
in 1914. The spread in the war's aftermath of a vengeful right-wing
extremism opened the path to mass murder and genocide whose execution depended on ordinary Germans' readiness to follow orders.

This is the basic story of the German *Sonderweg* or "separate path" to
the misshapen and destructive modernity of National Socialism, rather
than the comparatively benign modernity of the western liberal-
democratic welfare state. The same argument holds that, among
Prussianism's pillars, none was mightier than the nobility. This numerous
class, whose scions – including Bismarck himself – figured so prominently in the government and army, was economically anchored in possession
and self-management of large landed estates, occupying much of the
agricultural land in Prussia's heartlands east of the Elbe river.[5]

The Prussian nobility emerged from German medieval eastward
expansion. Because many of their founding members were west
German noble families' sons, they came to be known, as they settled in
the east, as "Junkers" (*Junker*), a contraction of the term "young lord"
(*junger Herr*). Eventually, especially in the nineteenth century, the term
Junker acquired strongly polemical and pejorative meaning, which it
retains today, though the word has lost any contemporary referent. It
evokes coercive and even brutal masters of landed estates and dependent villages who, when clothed in the uniform of army officer, county
administrator, police president, or high official, translated the habits of
landlordly or seigneurial domination into the state's realm. Junker
authority perpetuated and spread the mentality of the subject or
Untertan – a term originally describing feudal vassals, including villagers
subordinated to noblemen – throughout Prussian-dominated Germany,
which by 1871 encompassed most of the German Empire.[6]

[5] The *Sonderweg* argument is still pervasive at the textbook level (and in popular thinking). See Rob
Burns, ed., *German Cultural Studies: An Introduction* (Oxford, 1995). It is usefully problematized as
an interpretive approach in Mary Fulbrook, ed., *German History since 1800* (London, 1997); in
Blackbourn's above-cited *Long Nineteenth Century*; and in Hermann Beck, *The Origins of the
Authoritarian Welfare State in Prussia. Conservatives, Bureaucracy, and the Social Question, 1815–70* (Ann
Arbor, MI, 1995); and persuasively challenged in Margaret Lavinia Anderson, *Practising
Democracy: Elections and Political Culture in Imperial Germany* (Princeton, NJ, 2000).

[6] On liberal and Marxist critiques of the Junkers, see Hagen, "Descent of the *Sonderweg*" and
William W. Hagen, "Village Life in East-Elbian Germany and Poland, 1400–1800: Subjection,
Self-Defense, Survival," in Tom Scott, ed., *The Peasantries of Europe from the Fourteenth to the
Eighteenth Centuries* (London, 1998), 145–90. In the English-language literature, this perspective is
familiar by way of Max Weber's above-cited essays, which helped shape Barrington Moore's
influential argument in *Social Origins of Dictatorship and Democracy. Lord and Peasant in the Making of*

Thus the most deep-rooted and influential interpretation of modern German history leads directly to the Junkers' doorstep. Historians have shown how, in the aftermath of the French Revolution of 1789, but especially after 1871, the Prussian nobility and their intellectual partisans raised their voices against democratization in Prussia. They occupied strongholds at court, and in army and state administration, and dominated powerful conservative political parties and pressure groups. The Junkers' weighty influence on economic policy, from seigneurialism's abolition in the early nineteenth century to tariff protection after 1879 and ruthless special-interest lobbying in the Weimar Republic, is a well-told story.[7]

Yet, except for old-fashioned genealogical and literary works often bathed in sentimental or apologetic light (which falls too on the great novelist Theodor Fontane's pages), the modern historical literature on the Prussian nobility as estateowners and seigneurial village overlords is sparse, though in the hands of present-day historians in Germany it is experiencing efflorescence. The classic English-language political histories, written in the liberal spirit in World War II's aftermath and dealing sternly with the Junkers, have little to say about them as country gentry. The shelves remain empty of archivally based English-language studies, though important historiographical and synthetic works have recently appeared.[8]

Apart from stressing the Prussian nobility's political power, the historical literature assumes that a prime avenue of "Junker domination" (*Junkerherrschaft*) ran from manor-house to village, and thence via internal migration to burgeoning nineteenth- and twentieth-century towns. Thus the Prussian subject mentality radiated widely through modern Germany. Yet if studies of the Junkers in their rural setting are scant,

---

the *Modern World* (Boston, 1966). Still influential syntheses underpinning the *Sonderweg* argument are Francis L. Carsten, *The Origins of Prussia* (Oxford, 1954) and Hans Rosenberg, *Bureaucracy, Aristocracy, and Autocracy. The Prussian Experience, 1660–1815* (Boston, 1958). Cf. F. L. Carsten, *History of the Prussian Junkers* (Brookfield, VT, 1989 [German original: 1988]) and Walter Görlitz, *Die Junker: Adel und Bauer im deutschen Osten* (Glücksburg, 1957).

[7] See Wehler's above-cited works; Hanna Schissler, *Preußische Agrargesellschaft im Wandel. Wirtschaftliche, gesellschaftliche und politische Transformationsprozesse von 1763 bis 1847* (Göttingen, 1978); Hans-Jürgen Puhle and Hans-Ulrich Wehler, eds., *Preußen im Rückblick* (Göttingen, 1980); Robert M. Berdahl, *The Politics of the Prussian Nobility. The Development of a Conservative Ideology 1770–1848* (Princeton, NJ, 1988). For an alternative perspective, and additional bibliography: William W. Hagen, "The German Peasantry in the Nineteenth and Early Twentieth Century: Market Integration, Populist Politics, Votes for Hitler," *Peasant Studies* 14 (1987): 274–91.

[8] Edgar Melton, "*Gutsherrschaft* in East Elbian Germany and Livonia, 1500–1800: A Critique of the Model," *CEH* 21 (1988): 315–49; "The Decline of Prussian *Gutsherrschaft* and the Rise of the Junker as Rural Patron, 1750–1806", *GH* 12 (1994): 286–307.

works on the rural common people living in east-Elbian Prussian villages are rarer still, though older local histories retain value and scholars in the German Democratic Republic carried out important research. More recently, the east-Elbian nobility's and villagers' life on the land, and their complex and conflictual relationship, have been themes of a Max Planck Society research center established, following German reunification in 1990, at the University of Potsdam – the Prussian Versailles. Its members have written and continue to produce innovative monographs. I have benefited from working with them, and the pages below are in part conceived as a contribution to a common project. The Max Planck Institute of History in Göttingen has also generated research on west and south German agrarian society of major significance which, together with important related studies in English, informs the present work.[9]

---

[9] The Max-Planck-Gesellschaft Arbeitsgruppe in Potsdam, directed by Professor Jan Peters, bore the name "Ostelbische Gutsherrschaft als sozialhistorisches Phänomen" ("East-Elbian Manorial Lordship as Social-Historical Phenomenon"). Its work, and that of colleagues engaged in similar projects elsewhere in central and eastern Europe, appears in the following important, large-scale collective volumes: Jan Peters, ed., *Konflikt und Kontrolle in Gutsherrschaftsgesellschaften. Über Resistenz und Herrschaftsverhalten in ländlichen Sozialgebilden der frühen Neuzeit*, Veröffentlichungen des Max-Planck-Instituts für Geschichte (hereafter: *VMPIG*), vol. cxx (Göttingen, 1995); Jan Peters, ed., *Gutsherrschaft als soziales Modell*, published as *Beiheft* 18 of the *Historische Zeitschrift* (hereafter: *HZ*) (Munich, 1995); Jan Peters, ed., *Gutsherrschaftsgesellschaften im europäischen Vergleich* (Berlin, 1997); Axel Lubinski, Thomas Rudert, and Martina Schattkowsky, eds., *Historie und Eigen-Sinn. Festschrift für Jan Peters zum 65. Geburtstag* (Weimar, 1997). Among Peters' own works, especially relevant to the present study are "Eigensinn und Widerstand im Alltag. Abwehrverhalten ostelbischer Bauern unter Refeudalisierungsdruck," *Jahrbuch für Wirtschaftsgeschichte* (hereafter: *JfWG*) (1991/2): 85–103 and his contribution to *Märkische Bauerntagebücher des 18. und 19. Jahrhunderts. Selbstzeugnisse von Milchviehbauern zu Neuholland* (Weimar, 1989), co-authored with Lieselott Enders and Hartmut Harnisch; see also his essays in the above-cited edited volumes, and articles cited below. Among Enders' works, see especially *Die Uckermark. Geschichte einer kurmärkischen Landschaft vom 12. bis zum 18. Jahrhundert* (Weimar, 1992). Harnisch's important works are cited below. A valuable study of nineteenth- and twentieth-century historiography on east-Elbian agrarian society is Heinrich Kaak, *Die Gutsherrschaft. Theoriegeschichtliche Untersuchungen zum Agrarwesen im ostelbischen Raum* (Berlin, 1991). Written with the support of the Max-Planck-Institut für Geschichte in Göttingen were the following important microhistorical studies of the south and northwest German regions: David Warren Sabean, *Power in the Blood. Popular Culture and Village Discourse in Early Modern Germany* (Cambridge, 1984); David Warren Sabean, *Property, Production, and Family in Neckarhausen, 1700–1870* (Cambridge 1990); David Warren Sabean, *Kinship in Neckarhausen, 1700–1870* (Cambridge, 1998); Jürgen Schlumbohm, *Lebensläufe, Familien, Höfe. Die Bauern und Heuerleute des Osnabrückischen Kirchspiels Belm in proto-industrieller Zeit, 1650–1860, VMPIG*, vol. cx (Göttingen, 1994); Hans Medick, *Weben und Überleben in Laichingen 1650–1900. Lokalgeschichte als Allgemeine Geschichte, VMPIG*, vol. cxxvi (Göttingen, 1997). Similarly important and innovative are the microhistorical works of Silke Göttsch, *"Alle für einen Mann . . ." Leibeigene und Widerständigkeit in Schleswig-Holstein im 18. Jahrhundert* (Neumünster, 1991); Rainer Beck's study of Bavaria, *Unterfinning. Ländliche Welt vor Anbruch der Moderne* (Munich, 1993); and historical anthropologist Palle Christiansen's *A Manorial World. Lord, Peasants and Cultural Distinctions on a Danish Estate 1750–1980* (Copenhagen, 1996). On other relevant German literature, including from the German Democratic Republic, see discussion and citations in Hagen, "Descent

In the older literature, east-Elbian villagers appear as their noble lordships' victims, coerced into silent submission and demoralization. Like the Junkers, they bestride the German historical stage as one-dimensional figures, even caricatures. In Hans Rosenberg's righteous words, they suffered at their landlords' hands "legal and social degradation, political emasculation, moral crippling, and destruction of [their] chances of self-determination." The absolutist Prussian rulers "confirmed and enlarged" the Junkers' "customary fiscal, economic, and social privileges and [their] *de facto* freedom to tyrannize the tillers of the soil and the rural craftsmen . . . In consequence, the basic social institution of agrarian Prussia, peasant serfdom, increased in severity until the latter part of the eighteenth century." "Abject poverty" and "helpless apathy" were the common people's fate. In F. L. Carsten's widely accepted formulation, the founder of Prussian absolutism used "the Junkers' class interests to win them over to an alliance with the crown . . . The peasant-serfs were too down-trodden to revolt, and anyhow they were more oppressed by their [Junker] masters than by the government."[10]

But just as other social classes, along with ethnic and religious groups, are ceasing to figure in modern thinking as homogeneous bodies possessing one or another set of essential(ized) characteristics, so is time past due for a nuanced depiction in the English-language literature of the east-Elbian countryside's inhabitants that does not strip them of their capacity to act in their own interests and self-defense. Here the Potsdam school's work on east Elbia, and the historical literature in both German and English on west and south German rural society, offer inspiration.[11] Especially vital, in view of the central role

of the *Sonderweg*," "Village Life in East-Elbian Germany and Poland, 1400–1800," and "Capitalism and the Countryside in Early Modern Europe: Interpretations, Models, Debates," *Agricultural History* 62 (1988), 13–47. Other recent English-language works on south and west Germany are cited below.

[10] Hans Rosenberg, "Die Ausprägung der Junkerherrschaft in Brandenburg-Preussen, 1410–1618", in Hans Rosenberg, *Machteliten und Wirtschaftskonjunkturen. Studien zur neueren deutschen Sozial- und Wirtschaftsgeschichte* (Göttingen, 1978), 82; Rosenberg, *Bureaucracy, Aristocracy, and Autocracy*, 45, 48; Carsten, *Origins of Prussia*, 275, 277.

[11] See Werner Troßbach's valuable synthesis (with extensive bibliography): *Bauern 1648–1806*, Enzyklopädie deutscher Geschichte, vol. xix (Munich, 1993). The above-cited *Peasantries of Europe*, ed. Tom Scott, offers the best recent account of European village society in its many national and regional forms. Among English-language monographs, apart from David Sabean's above-cited works, see: Hermann Rebel, *Peasant Classes. The Bureaucratization of Property and Family Relations under Early Habsburg Absolutism, 1511–1636* (Princeton, NJ, 1983); Thomas Robisheaux, *Rural Society and the Search for Order in Early Modern Germany* (Cambridge, 1989); Peter K. Taylor, *Indentured to Liberty. Peasant Life and the Hessian Military State, 1688–1815* (Ithaca, NY, 1994); John Theibault, *German Villages in Crisis: Rural Life in Hesse-Kassel and the Thirty Years' War, 1580–1720* (Atlantic Highlands, NJ, 1995); and David Luebke, *His Majesty's Rebels. Communities, Factions and*

assigned the subject mentality in modern German history, is the study of east-Elbian villagers, for it was this large population that originally embodied, in historians' view, Prussian authoritarianism's defects. They most thickly populate the following pages, though much in evidence too are their noble lordships and the many other social groups, privileged and unprivileged, who inhabited the Prussian countryside. Fundamental is the question of subordination and insubordination toward seigneurial authority in the villagers' lives. This aligns the book with the strongest post-1945 trend in worldwide studies of village society, emphasizing resistance and rebellion against higher powers.[12]

Rural Revolt in the Black Forest, 1725–1745 (Ithaca, NY, 1997). See also the chapters on early modern Austria and south and western Germany by Rebel and Robisheaux, respectively, in Scott, *Peasantries of Europe*, 191–226, 111–44. For comparisons of Brandenburg-Prussian rural society with its counterparts to west and east, see William W. Hagen, "Der bäuerliche Lebensstandard unter brandenburgischer Gutsherrschaft im 18. Jahrhundert. Die Dörfer der Herrschaft Stavenow in vergleichender Sicht," in Peters, *Gutsherrschaft als soziales Modell*, 178–96; Hagen, "Village Life in East-Elbian Germany and Poland, 1400–1800." Cf. Joseph Gagliardo, *From Pariah to Patriot. The Changing Image of the German Peasant 1770–1840* (Lexington, KY, 1969).

[12] Widely influential is James Scott, *Weapons of the Weak. Everyday Forms of Peasant Resistance* (New Haven, CT, 1985). Cf. Forrest D. Colburn, ed., *Everyday Forms of Peasant Resistance* (London, 1989); Andreas Suter, "Informations- und Kommunikationsweisen aufständischer Untertanen," in Peters, *Gutsherrschaftsgesellschaften*, 55–68. From the large general European literature, see Yves-Marie Bercé, *Revolt and Revolution in Early Modern Europe: An Essay on the History of Political Violence* (Manchester, 1987 [French original, 1980]). German historians, faced with interpreting the German Peasants' War of 1525 (probably the largest rural uprising in European history before the 1789 French Revolution) and many other early modern rural conflicts, have authored an important literature. See, apart from relevant above-cited works, Peter Blickle, *Deutsche Untertanen: Ein Widerspruch* (Munich, 1981); *The Revolution of 1525: The German Peasants' War from a New Perspective* (Baltimore, 1981 [German original, 1975]); and Peter Blickle, ed., *Aufruhr und Empörung. Studien zum bäuerlichen Widerstand im Alten Reich* (Munich, 1980). Cf. also the chapters relevant to Germany in Winfried Schulze, ed., *Bäuerlicher Widerstand und feudale Herrschaft in der frühen Neuzeit* (Stuttgart, 1980) and *Europäische Bauernrevolten der frühen Neuzeit* (Frankfurt, 1982). From the German Democratic Republic see, *inter alia*, Hartmut Harnisch, "Klassenkämpfe der Bauern in der Mark Brandenburg zwischen frühbürgerlicher Revolution und Dreissigjährigem Krieg," *Jahrbuch für Regionalgeschichte* (hereafter: *JbfRG*) 5 (1975), 142–72. Cf. William W. Hagen, "The Junkers' Faithless Servants: Peasant Insubordination and the Breakdown of Serfdom in Brandenburg-Prussia, 1763–1811," in Richard Evans and W. R. Lee, eds., *The German Peasantry. Conflict and Community in Rural Society from the Eighteenth to the Twentieth Centuries* (London, 1986), 71–101.

For further contributions to the ongoing German debate, see Robert von Friedeburg, "'Kommunalismus' und 'Republikanismus' in der frühen Neuzeit? Überlegungen zur politischen Mobilisierung sozial differenzierter ländlicher Gemeinden unter agrar- und sozialhistorischem Blickwinkel," *ZHF* 21 (1994): 65–91; Peter Blickle, "Begriffsverfremdung. Über den Umgang mit dem wissenschaftlichen Ordnungsbegriff Kommunalismus," *ZHF* 22 (1995): 246–53; Robert von Friedeburg, "'Reiche', 'geringe Leute' und 'Beambte': Landesherrschaft, dörfliche 'Factionen' und gemeindliche Partizipation, 1648–1806," *ZHF* 23 (1996): 219–65; Andreas Suter, "Regionale politische Kulturen von Protest und Widerstand im Spätmittelalter und in der frühen Neuzeit. Die schweizerische Eidgenossenschaft als Beispiel," *Geschichte und Gesellschaft* (hereafter: *GG*) 21 (1995): 161–94; Andreas Würgler, "Das Modernisierungspotential von Unruhen im 18. Jahrhundert. Ein Beitrag zur Entstehung der politischen Öffentlichkeit in Deutschland und in der Schweiz," in ibid., 195–217; Luebke, *Rebels*.

These pages also address capitalist development in the Prussian countryside, including the clash of interests in play during seigneurialism's dismantling after 1807.[13] Still more important is the study of ordinary people's everyday lives, at the manor but especially in the villages. The effects of domination, and of resistance, are discernible in villagers' incomes, material culture, health, and longevity. A crucial issue is the degree of autonomy that men and women alike wielded in their personal, marital, and familial lives, and in pursuit of communally important social and cultural values. The practices of conflict resolution and dealing with dissenters, rebels, and the socially weak speak eloquently, especially of a society's preeminent tensions and clashes, which in these pages were not only those between lordship and village. Collective protest and judicial practice loom large here, mainly at local level, though increasingly royal courts intervened decisively.

This work's chronological scope is wide, since the system of commercialized large estates producing for markets near and far with dependent villagers' labor arose in the early sixteenth century. Junkers' seigneurial powers and villagers' subjection ended in the nineteenth century, though large estates survived, often growing stronger economically, until their destruction in World War II and subsequent communist land reform. I have devoted previous studies to this agrarian social system's rise, and concentrate here on the era following 1648 to village emancipation after 1807.[14] Large estate–village relations in the later nineteenth and twentieth

---

[13] On the Prussian lands specifically, see Wilhelm Treue, *Wirtschafts- und Technikgeschichte Preussens* (Berlin, 1984); William W. Hagen, "Prussia," in Joel Mokyr, ed., *The Oxford Encyclopedia of Economic History* (forthcoming); Hartmut Harnisch, *Kapitalistische Agrarreform und industrielle Revolution* (Weimar, 1984); Eric Dorn Brose, *The Politics of Technological Change in Prussia: Out of the Shadow of Antiquity, 1809–1848* (Princeton, 1993); and, for Prussia–USA comparisons, Terence J. Byres, *Capitalism from Above and Capitalism from Below: An Essay in Comparative Political Economy* (London, 1996) and Shearer David Bowman, *Masters and Lords: Mid-19th-Century U.S. Planters and Prussian Junkers* (New York, 1993).
On the early modern German economy: Wilhelm Abel, *Geschichte der deutschen Landwirtschaft* (Stuttgart, 1962); *Agrarkrisen und Agrarkonjunktur: Eine Geschichte der Land- und Ernährungswirtschaft Mitteleuropas seit dem hohen Mittelalter*, third edn (Hamburg, 1978); *Massenarmut und Hungerkrisen im vorindustriellen Europa* (Hamburg, 1974); Hermann Aubin and Wolfgang Zorn, eds., *Handbuch der deutschen Wirtschafts- und Sozialgeschichte*, 2 vols. (Stuttgart, 1971–6); Friedrich Lütge, *Geschichte der deutschen Agrarverfassung* (Stuttgart, 1963); Günther Franz, *Geschichte des deutschen Bauernstandes* (Stuttgart, 1970). More recently: Shilagh Ogilvie and Bob Scribner, eds., *Germany: A New Social and Economic History, 1450–1800*, 2 vols. (London, 1996); Walter Achilles, *Landwirtschaft in der frühen Neuzeit*, Enzyklopädie deutscher Geschichte, vol. x (Munich, 1991); Peter Kriedte, *Peasants, Landlords and Merchant Capitalists. Europe and the World Economy, 1500–1800* (Cambridge, 1983 [German original: 1980]); Hagen, "Capitalism and the Countryside"; Robert Duplessis, *Transitions to Capitalism in Early Modern Europe* (Cambridge, 1997).
[14] See, together with other articles cited above, William W. Hagen, "How Mighty the Junkers? Peasant Rents and Seigneurial Profits in Sixteenth-Century Brandenburg", *Past and Present*

centuries are an important theme that remains surprisingly unexplored at the level of daily reality and subjective experience. But it requires research in sources other than those deployed here.

The questions this study poses are central to understanding noble landlords and villagers in Prussia and comparable lands between the sixteenth and nineteenth centuries. The argument is framed in light of the existing historical literature as it ranges across east Elbia. The method applied is microhistory, a genre that has richly repaid the energy early modern European historians have invested in it. Yet it is an approach not without pitfalls. The marriage of microlevel "thick description," in Clifford Geertz's inescapable phrase, with macrolevel theorization and generalization characteristic of historical social science is in some ways ill-matched and in constant danger of breakup. The temptation to proclaim the universal in the particularities discovered by ethnographic method has led more than one author to overstrain the interpretive bow, with sometimes shattering effect. No one can object if historians' prime object is to reformulate broad generalizations in the light of locally based research designed exclusively to test them, as occurs in economic and demographic history. But microhistory overly anxious to establish its macrolevel relevance can inadvertently neglect its own strengths, which are to bring the voices of ordinary people back within hearing, their lifeworlds within sight, their existential logics within grasp.[15]

(hereafter: *PP*) 108 (1985): 80–116; "Seventeenth-Century Crisis in Brandenburg: The Thirty Years' War, the Destabilization of Serfdom, and the Rise of Absolutism", *American Historical Review* (hereafter: *AHR*) 94 (1989): 302–35; "Working for the Junker: The Standard of Living of Manorial Laborers in Brandenburg, 1584–1810", *JMH* 58 (1986), 143–58.

[15] Martin Dinges, "'Historische Anthropologie' und 'Gesellschaftsgeschichte'. Mit dem Lebensstilkonzept zu einer 'Alltagskulturgeschichte' der frühen Neuzeit?", *ZHF* 24 (1997): 179–214; Richard van Dülmen, "Historische Kulturforschung zur Frühen Neuzeit: Entwicklung – Probleme – Aufgaben," *GG* 21 (1995): 403–29. Cf. Edward Muir and Guido Ruggiero, eds., *Microhistory and the Lost Peoples of Europe* (Baltimore, MD, 1991). Related to microhistory, but not identical with it, is "the history of everyday life" (*Alltagsgeschichte*), discussed and exemplified in Alf Lüdtke, ed., *The History of Everyday Life. Reconstructing Historical Experiences and Ways of Life* (Princeton, NJ, 1995 [German original, 1989]). Many of the works of the Potsdam and Göttingen schools, cited above, are cast in the microhistorical or *Alltagsgeschichte* vein, including, in English, Sabean's *Power*. Exemplary also are: Giovanni Levi, *Das immaterielle Erbe. Eine bäuerliche Welt an der Schwelle zur Moderne* (Berlin, 1986 [Italian original: 1985]), and Richard J. Evans, *Szenen aus der deutschen Unterwelt. Verbrechen und Strafen, 1800–1914* (Reinbek, 1997). For broad overviews: Sigrid and Wolfgang Jacobeit, *Illustrierte Alltagsgeschichte des deutschen Volkes, 1550–1810* (Leipzig, 1986); Richard van Dülmen, *Kultur und Alltag in der frühen Neuzeit*, 2 vols. (Munich, 1990–2). These genres have come under criticism from practitioners of Weberian macro-oriented historical social science. See Lüdtke's editor's introduction, *History of Everyday Life*, 3–40; Geoff Eley, "Labor History, Social History, *Alltagsgeschichte*: Experience, Culture, and the Politics of the Everyday – A New Direction for German Social History?," *JMH* 61 (1989): 297–343; and Thomas Welskopp, "Die Sozialgeschichte der Väter. Grenzen und Perspektiven der

Map 2   Brandenburg in the seventeenth and eighteenth centuries

This study's microhistorical stage is the noble lordship of Stavenow. Lying in the Prignitz District of Brandenburg near the Elbe river northwest of Berlin, it comprised a once-fortified noble castle or manor-hall, a group of large-scale seigneurial manor (or demesne) farms, and eight villages with their own extensive lands cultivated by family farmers (see maps 1–3). Such lordships were vital centers of life in pre-modern Germany and Europe alike, both because of the landlordly authority manor-houses exerted over villages and because of the importance in everyone's lives of the judicial powers noble lordships wielded in the name of princely power or state.[16] Exceptionally, the Stavenow lordship's archive, comprising 728 packets thick and thin of manuscript documents ranging from the fifteenth to the nineteenth centuries, survived the conflagration of noble country houses at World War II's end that consumed many similar collections. In the 1920s, Stavenow and its estates fell to the one non-nobleman who ever owned them, a Saxon shoe manufacturer. Practically minded, he donated the Stavenow

Historischen Sozialwissenschaft," *GG* 24 (1998): 173–98; William W. Hagen, review essay on Hans Medick, *Weben und Überleben in Laichingen*, *CEH* 32 (1999), 453–9.

[16] For a recent European-wide perspective on early modern noble lordship, see Jonathan Dewald, *The European Nobility, 1400–1800* (Cambridge, 1996).

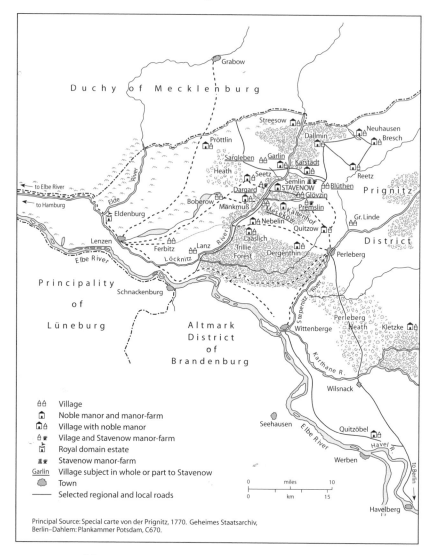

Map 3   The Stavenow lordship and surroundings, 1770

papers' greater part, reaching up to the 1840s, to Berlin's Prussian State
Archive. During World War II, as German laborers were put under
arms, Stavenow, like many other large estates, came to depend on east
European captive workers. When the Soviet army moved onto Prussian

soil, rebellions of such workers, paired with fighting and plundering by the advancing Soviet army, destroyed a myriad of estates, amid the flight or murder of many of their inhabitants. The great house at Stavenow burned, while its master and mistress retreated into the forest, where they perished, seemingly by suicide.

In the 1980s I began studying the voluminous Stavenow documents. A 1959 dissertation charted the lordship's familial and institutional history, but passed over the massive records concerning villagers' lives and fortunes, seigneurial economy, and quarrels and legal confrontations between lordship and subject farmers.[17] The archive proved to house a nearly unbroken set of seigneurial court transcripts, recording all cases of adjudication involving the rural common people themselves, whether amicable or hostile, civil or criminal, from the 1720s to the 1760s. Further documentation of lengthy manor–village court battles in the years 1767–97, mediated by Prussian officialdom, and the records of seigneurialism's liquidation after 1807, together make possible a triangular study of nobility, state, and village from Thirty Years War's end to the early nineteenth century. Drawing on such sources, including household inventories and parish registers of births, marriages, and deaths, these pages reconstruct and analyze both villagers' individual, household, and communal lives and manor–village relations. Documentation is dense and rich not only on central actors – lordship and its officials, on one side, and, on the other, landholding village farmers – but also on women, youth, the elderly, and other social groups.[18] Such a many-dimensioned study of the Brandenburg-Prussian countryside does not exist in the English-language literature, nor even yet in German.[19]

This book straddles the early modern period's post-1648 end-phase and the modern period's beginning, conventionally dated from the eighteenth century. Few any longer would think to divide German or European history into two self-sufficient realms of interpretation and

---

[17] Joachim Sack, *Die Herrschaft Stavenow* (Cologne/Graz, 1959).

[18] For wide-ranging studies on women, see Heide Wunder, *"Er ist die Sonn', sie ist der Mond." Frauen in der Frühen Neuzeit* (Munich, 1992); Ute Frevert, *Women in German History. From Bourgeois Emancipation to Sexual Liberation* (Oxford, 1989 [German original, 1986]); Merry Wiesner, *Women and Gender in Early Modern Europe* (Cambridge, 1993); Isabel V. Hull, *Sexuality, State, and Civil Society in Germany, 1700–1815* (Ithaca, NY, 1996); Marion W. Gray, *Productive Men, Reproductive Women. The Agrarian Household and the Emergence of Separate Spheres during the German Enlightenment* (New York, 2000).

[19] For an expertly researched, microhistorically informed regional portrait, encompassing the urban as well as rural sphere, see Lieselott Enders' *Uckermark* and her below-cited articles, foreshadowing a similar book on the Prignitz District.

thought, divided at 1789 or any other date.[20] Yet among early modern German historians, Brandenburg-Prussia is sometimes marginalized in favor of concentration on west and south Germany. These older-established, more urbanized, and richer regions were indeed prime theaters of German religious, cultural, and political history, particularly before the Thirty Years War. From this perspective, Prussia's emergence in the east appears as a harbinger of the end of the radically decentralized, pre-industrial world represented by the structurally intricate "Holy Roman Empire of the German Nation," with its precarious federalism and hundreds of principalities.

Against this backdrop Prussia's rise can appear as a negative process: centralizing, militarizing, absolutizing, imperializing, rationalizing. A recent synoptic view of early modern Germany reassured its readers that "even in Brandenburg-Prussia a totalitarian absolutism never prevailed."[21] The temptation is not always resisted of romanticizing pre-modern, non-Prussian Germany as a not yet disenchanted world, innocent of modernity's dangerous knowledges. This is the old, deeply ideological form of thinking embedded in the dichotomous German sociological language of pre-modern "community" (*Gemeinschaft*) set against modern "society" (*Gesellschaft*), which blocks the subtle explanations of modernity's origins in pre-modernity that are needed.[22] Conversely, historians arguing that German history in the nineteenth and twentieth centuries followed a "separate path" or *Sonderweg* leading not to liberal democracy but to militarism and fascism customarily explain this outcome by "pre-industrial" or "traditional" "authoritarian structures'" survival. Under their weight, German society could not

---

[20] See, for example, the important synthesis of Christoph Dipper, "Übergangsgesellschaft. Die ländliche Sozialordnung in Mitteleuropa um 1800," *ZHF* 23 (1996): 57–87.

[21] Ogilvie and Scribner, *Germany: A New Social and Economic History*, vol. II, 222. For more sophisticated discussion see, alongside relevant works cited above and in note 23, below, James Van Horn Melton, "Absolutism and 'Modernity' in Early Modern Central Europe," *German Studies Review* (hereafter: *GSR*) 8 (1985): 383–98; Charles Ingrao, "The Problem of 'Enlightened Absolutism' and the German States" and Eberhard Weis, "Enlightenment and Absolutism in the Holy Roman Empire: Thoughts on Enlightened Absolutism in Germany," *JMH* 58 (Supplement, 1986): 161–97; and Diethelm Klippel, "Von der Aufklärung der Herrscher zur Herrschaft der Aufklärung," *ZHF* 17 (1990): 193–210. Cf. also James Van Horn Melton, *Absolutism and the Eighteenth-Century Origins of Compulsory Schooling in Prussia and Austria* (Cambridge, 1988).

[22] Mack Walker's influential *German Home Towns: Community, State, and General Estate, 1648–1871* (Ithaca, NY, 1971) is not free of this tendency. His perspective is modified, in a forceful analysis of modern liberalism's emergence from the social-political dynamics of early modern urban society in Württemberg, in Ian McNeely, "*Writing, Citizenship, and the Making of Civil Society in Germany, 1780–1840*" (Ph.D. dissertation, University of Michigan, Ann Arbor, 1998).

realize modernity's emancipatory potential, unlike the British, French, and North Americans, who by revolutionary means shook off feudalism's fetters. Though the most fateful "pre-industrial" structures were Prussian, it is the broader legacy of the early modern period, widely (and paradoxically) seen by early modern historians as free of modernity's curses, that explains the twentieth-century German catastrophe. Awareness of this problem doubtless reinforces interpretations of Brandenburg-Prussia as a negative case in early modern historiography.

Yet the now-dominant tendency among historians of early modern Brandenburg-Prussia is to emphasize its commonalities with other contemporary German societies and political cultures. This is especially evident in their downscaling of Prussian absolutism's power and success. In this view, Prussia, like other German states, was a "society of estates" in which a landed nobility jealous of its autonomy from the crown predominated, and in which among the populace at large mentalities were shaped far more by allegiances to religion, community, trade or profession, and narrow local "fatherlands" than by self-identification as Prussians. The efficacy of Prussian absolutism's centralizing and modernizing policies is cast so far into doubt that the term itself, never very satisfactory, is often placed in ironical quotation marks. Insofar as Prussia's rise as a military-bureaucratic power-state must be acknowledged, this is seen (and deplored) as an instance of a larger European state-building process.[23] Still, the view persists of Prussia as an atypical early modern state and society which, instead of yielding to more liberal forms, robustly survived into the twentieth century, with highly unfortunate consequences. The long-prevailing explanation stressed perpetuation of the Prussian "subject mentality" (*Untertanengeist*), which Junker authoritarianism, translated into state practice, instilled in the population. But it is an open and weighty question whether research into the everyday experience of the inhabitants, privileged and unprivileged, of old-regime, pre-1807 Prussia will buttress this approach or call it into question.

These pages measure, at grass-roots level, the noble and state coercion and popular deference and obedience which figure so centrally in accounts of Germany's "separate path." They also engage a major

---

[23] On literature downscaling the accomplishments of Prussian absolutism, see, with above-cited works, Peter Baumgart, "Wie absolut war der preussische Absolutismus?" in Manfred Schlenke, *Preussen. Beiträge zu einer politischen Kultur*, 89–105; Klaus Deppermann, "Der preussische Absolutismus und der Adel. Eine Auseinandersetzung mit der marxistischen Absolutismustheorie," *GG* 8 (1982): 538–53; Peter-Michael Hahn, "Landesstaat und Ständetum im Kurfürstentum Brandenburg während des 16. und 17. Jahrhunderts," in Peter Baumgart, ed., *Ständetum und Staatsbildung in Brandenburg-Preussen* (Berlin, 1983), 41–79.

debate in the early modern field, addressing the extent and success of the "social discipline" that educated elites sought to impose from top down during and after the Protestant and Catholic Reformations. Its aims included both institutional "confessionalization," whether Protestant or Catholic, and state-building and economic development. Prussian experience usually figures as prime evidence for social-disciplining processes' efficacy. But these pages will cast doubt on any simple version of this view, supporting instead the approach of those many historians, particularly of west and south Germany, who emphasize the capacity for resistance among common people, and resultant clashes between them and the authorities. These shaped historical development in ways controllable neither by governing elites nor subjects, though channeled by aspirations and aversions of both.[24]

It might be objected that this book's findings are limited to the Stavenow lordship. There are three responses. First, I have weighed Stavenow evidence in the light both of the monographic literature on other individual lordships and the broader literature on east-Elbian Germany and Europe. The Stavenow lordship, though comparatively large, wealthy, and well managed, was neither exceptionally rich nor poor, neither notably oppressive nor permissive, and, from villagers' standpoint, neither heaven nor hell.[25] Second, in the construction of a historical portrait of the Brandenburg-Prussian countryside based on primary-source documentation, a mostly recent enterprise, any generalizations about the society as a whole will need to account for all important cases. In the folk-tale, the blind men needed to comprehend the elephant in its various characteristic parts. In this sense, every significant case is vital, offering a perspective on the whole. Finally,

---

[24] Jürgen Schlumbohm, "Gesetze, die nicht durchgesetzt werden–ein Strukturmerkmal des frühneuzeitlichen Staates?", *GG* 23 (1997): 647–63. For an overview: Ronald Po-chia Hsia, *Social Discipline in the Reformation: Central Europe, 1550–1750* (London, 1989). An important early statement was Gerhard Oestreich, "Strukturprobleme des europäischen Absolutismus" (1969), translated in Gerhard Oestreich, *Neostoicism and the Early Modern State* (Cambridge, 1982). Cf. Winfried Schulze, "Gerhard Oestreichs Begriff 'Sozialdisziplinierung in der Frühen Neuzeit,'" *ZHF* 14 (1987): 265–302, and Richard Gawthrop, *Pietism and the Making of Eighteenth-Century Prussia* (Cambridge, 1993). See also Norbert Elias: *The Civilizing Process*, 2 vols. (New York, 1978 [German original, 1938]), and *The Court Society* (Oxford, 1983 [German original, 1969]). Bernd Roeck, *Lebenswelt und Kultur des Bürgertums in der frühen Neuzeit*, Enzyklopädie deutscher Geschichte, vol. ix (Munich, 1991); Manuel Frey, *Der reinliche Bürger. Entstehung und Verbreitung bürgerlicher Tugenden in Deutschland, 1760–1860* (Göttingen, 1997); Michael Maurer, *Die Biographie des Bürgers. Lebensformen und Denkweisen in der formativen Phase des deutschen Bürgertums (1680–1815)* (Göttingen, 1997).

[25] See the local and regional studies of Brandenburg-Prussian noble lordships, villages, and crown estates cited in the bibliography.

there are not many estate archives of the sheer denseness, chronological sweep, and thematic multidimensionality that Stavenow documents possess. It is a broad vein of evidence that, though I mined it in Berlin's Prussian State Archive for two years, neither these pages nor earlier articles exhaust.

The line of analysis commences in chapter 1 with an account of the Stavenow lordship and its villages in the sixteenth and seventeenth centuries, set against the backdrop of medieval east-Elbian German rural society. It treats the sixteenth-century emergence of what is here conceived as early capitalist commercialized manorialism as symbiotic with, rather than destructive of, the villagers. Before the Thirty Years War, Stavenow's noble landlords, successful though they were in establishing production-raising and profit-bearing large landed estates, were hard-pressed to maintain a competent and adequate labor-force, and made important investments, including in wages, to hold their workers, whether freely or compulsorily recruited. In 1648, amid the great war's still smoking ruins, the lordship's fortunes hung perilously on its decimated villages' recovery.

Chapter 2 encompasses the crisis-ridden, turbulent early era of absolutist state-building, from 1648 to the 1730s. The landlords needed, long after the war, to make major concessions to rebuild and hold their farmers in place. The villagers played crown off against manor-house. In 1700–2 they staged, throughout Brandenburg's Prignitz District, a centrally organized protest movement against seigneurial efforts to raise rents. This dramatic action, unknown to the historical literature, engulfed the Stavenow villages along with some one hundred others. It reveals attitudes, both in villages and country towns, toward aggressive landlords and crown officials partial to them, as well as the authorities' views and treatment of the protesters. At Stavenow, the seigneurial rent offensive faltered, and after 1717, as the lordship passed into the possession of a militarily distinguished branch of the von Kleist lineage (perfectly embodying the new absolutist service nobility), important concessions to the villages seemed necessary if the Kleists' ambitious plans for raising manorial production and profits, and for disciplining their workforce, were to succeed.

The next two chapters break the narrative flow to investigate everyday life in the villages during the eighteenth and the early nineteenth centuries. Chapter 3 focuses on family, household organization, kinship networks, and women's and children's guardianship, as well as on everyday conceptual terminology employed to discuss them. It shows too

what landholding villagers' legal subjection to the lordship meant to
them, both in theory and practice, and what manner of property rights
they possessed in their farms. These are matters either unknown, or
routinely misunderstood, in the historical literature. This chapter also
addresses courtship, marriage, and remarriage among landed villagers.
It discusses dowries and marriage portions – vital assets of the young
and important measures of parental households' well-being. The influence of parents, and the seigneurial lordship, on villagers' marital decisions comes to light, along with cultural practices surrounding marriage. This chapter looks too at relationships between husbands and
wives and parents and children, siblings among themselves, and of
retired elders to younger couples who replaced them as household
heads. The elaborate arrangements made to support elders in retirement figure here, as do village rituals of death. Emotional bonds and
tensions among villagers are central issues, as they are throughout the
book. Chapter 4 turns to village farmers' economic practices, incomes,
and assets; their material culture, including housing, household
goods, and dress; and their physical well-being as reflected in diets,
longevity, and causes of death. It raises the neglected question of payments from parental farm to retired parents, and offers unanticipated
findings on this rural society's mortality regime. On village living standards' strengths and deficiencies I reject simple pessimism and optimism, emphasizing contingencies, both within the familial life-cycle
and beyond, spelling relative well-being or deprivation.

Chapter 5 examines the eighteenth-century seigneurial household
and economy, particularly in the years of Kleist management
(1717–1803). The costs of living nobly, and the social-political ambitions
of master and mistress, intensified the search for profit, resulting in
technological improvements, heightened output, and rising asset values
amounting to a kind of eighteenth-century "agricultural revolution."
The chapter looks also at noble marriages, inheritance settlements, and
money-lending practices and strategies. It examines the Stavenow
estates' management in the mid-eighteenth century, when a noble
widow possessed them, affording a view of lordship exercised by a
woman, working with stewards, lawyers, and sons. These pages display,
contrary to economic historians' assumptions about east-Elbian backwardness, a sophisticated large-estate economy, oriented toward
profitable investment and innovation, however much constrained by
pre-liberal property rights and other legal hindrances. It shows,
too, that villagers' refractoriness and self-defense against seigneurial

exactions continued to hold labor costs far higher than the lordship found acceptable.

Chapter 6 musters commoner notables and others standing between noble lordship and village farmers. These included estate stewards and occasional bourgeois leaseholders of one or more seigneurial manor-farm. They were figures of considerable rural stature, as were the dairy-men, millers, and university-trained clergy. Humbler but important in the villages were tavernkeepers, independent shepherds, blacksmiths, and sextons-tailors-schoolmasters. This was true also of the lordship's lesser officials, especially hunter-foresters. Many in these groups formed a web of seigneurial patronage distancing them from ordinary villagers. They also pioneered new bourgeois modes of consumption and behavior, parading before their lesser neighbors' eyes possibilities not lost on them. Chapter 7 descends the social scale to the landless workers' realm, including unmarried laborers hired by village farmers and their counterparts on manorial estates. The lordship also employed married servants, and maintained a growing cadre of wage laborers living with their families in rented cottages. These workers' employment and general life-condition displayed the lot of the humblest among this society's settled and able-bodied members. They revealed the fruits, both sour and sweet, of seigneurial patronage, and held up to subject farmers' eyes the fate of all those, including landed families' numerous non-inheriting children, possessing no hereditary farms of their own.

Chapter 8 addresses power structures overarching and dominating the villages. Preeminent was the lordship's seigneurial authority, exercised through its court and police organs. These pages investigate land-lordly violence and coercion, including lashings and other physical punishments, whose disciplining effects are central to the thesis of top-down Prussian authoritarianism. The chapter weighs seigneurially appointed village mayors' and local clergymen's disciplinary powers. It looks too at the Prussian army's role in villagers' lives, and at their attitudes toward it and royal authority generally, arriving at conclusions questioning the prevailing social militarization thesis. It also discusses judicial practices upholding village social and cultural codes, especially those governing sexual behavior, which come to light in cases of pre-marital pregnancy, adultery, and (alleged) incest. It examines honor and dishonor among country people, especially in connection with insults, libel, and witchcraft charges. Villagers' claims to reputation and respectability emerge as important motives for self-assertion and refractoriness.

Chapter 9 charts deepening eighteenth-century manor–village conflicts. These issued after 1763 in three decades of escalating courtroom strife, accompanied by clamorous strikes and low-level violence of considerable symbolic importance. Conflict resolution required the forceful intervention of royal judicial officials and Berlin courts, whose mediation led, in the 1780s and 1790s, to the negotiation and signature of a comprehensive, legally binding contract (Urbarium) between lordship and subject farmers. This outcome signaled "feudal lordship's" end as an attribute primarily of noble property rights and ancient common law. The chapter offers a study in "judicialization" of landlord–village conflict under enlightened absolutism, with results at odds with prevailing views.

Finally, chapter 10 analyzes the contentious transformation, in the early nineteenth century, of the villages into freeholders' settlements and Stavenow lordship into a large-scale agrarian capitalist venture. After Napoleon's armies in 1806 hammered the post-Frederickian state to its knees, initiating the 1807–19 Prussian Reform Era, Stavenow's villagers again, as they had a century earlier, joined their Prignitz District neighbors in mounting a strike against feudal rents. It set the stage on which the Stavenow lordship – now owned by Baron von Voss, one of the Prussian nobility's most influential conservative leaders – negotiated the end of its claims on its villagers' resources and labor power. The subject farmers emerged as struggling small property-owners in an age of dawning liberal capitalism, while the lordship shifted entirely to the employment of wage labor, adapting itself aggressively and profitably to new technologies and markets. Voss, his officials, and the villagers offer blunt testimony on the psychological and material stakes in this final round of their centuries-long tug-of-war. The argument stresses all parties' lack of sentimental attachment to the fast-receding pre-Napoleonic old regime and their hard-headed struggle for advantage under free-market conditions that their eighteenth-century experience had prepared them for better than the historical and economic literature supposes.

The conclusion highlights the book's findings and weighs its implications for a history of Germany and central Europe that will accommodate the picture drawn here of the east-Elbian rural world. About the book's structure in general: its large stories are mostly constructed of small ones. In historical documentation of ordinary people's lives, sustained and complex self-representations, voiced by the subjects themselves, survive mainly to the extent that judicial inquests recorded them. Other documents offer but a myriad of momentary glimpses into common people's thoughts and feelings, households and bedrooms, private social worlds and workplace experiences. To project a vivid and vocal picture, both of the villages' various social types and the manor-hall's inhabitants and employees, the mass of fragmentary first-person testimony must be worked together in a series of cumulative or collective portraits. These will gain in focus and depth from chapter to chapter, for much of the evidence yields multiple insights, and issues discussed early on gain in documentation and comprehensibility from later incidental appearance, just as dramatic characters reveal themselves not only in soliloquies but also in dialogue with others.

A consequence of this method is that small stories must be accorded a certain life of their own, though I have labored to keep them succinct and readable. It is, unfortunately, difficult to convey the charm of the German language employed by the many writers, few of them equipped with much education, who penned the Stavenow documents. It is an idiom of considerable bluntness, but also of conviction, fervor, shrewdness, and humor, and a challenge to translate into English. For interested readers, the German text of the most significant and interesting translated passages appears in this text's manuscript version, copies of which are accessible at the Geheimes Staatsarchiv Preußischer Kulturbesitz in Berlin and the library of the University of California, Davis.

The discipline of history's strength lies in multidimensionality, multi-causality, and non-reductionism, or avoidance of treating events of one order as reflections of another. Here I approach the spheres of social relationships, culture, economics, and politics as autonomous, though not hermetically sealed off from each other. I aim to interpret them both singly and in their interrelationships. In his memorable book, *Metahistory: The Historical Imagination in Nineteenth-Century Europe*, Hayden White forcefully argued for historical works as literary and ethico-ideological-philosophical creations. White did, indeed, wonder whether "the archival report" might not be exempt from his strictures. But raw documentation in no way speaks coherently for itself. There is no way that historians can, literally, "reconstruct" a historical past that stands outside themselves in unchanging, self-generated objectivity awaiting, as Peter Novick put it, the self-styled scientific historian's "immaculate perception."[26]

---

[26] Hayden White, *Metahistory. The Historical Imagination in Nineteenth-Century Europe* (Baltimore, 1973), ix. Peter Novick, *That Noble Dream: The "Objectivity Question" and the American Historical Profession* (Cambridge, 1988), 38. Cf. Allan Megill, *Prophets of Extremity. Nietzsche, Heidegger, Foucault, Derrida* (Berkeley, 1987); Gavin Kendall and Gary Wickham, *Using Foucault's Methods* (London, 1999); Victoria Bonnell and Lynn Hunt, eds., *Beyond the Cultural Turn. New Directions in the Study of Society and Culture* (Berkeley, 1999). On the complexity of the culture concept, see Adam Kuper, *Culture: The Anthropologists' Account* (Cambridge, MA, 1999).

History is an intellectual construction, driven by manifold existential concerns, but nonetheless (if it is to be more than authorial musings and pronouncements) based on posing answerable questions and marshaling evidence in fashioning explanations satisfying logic's rules and knowledgeable specialists' doubts. It is not necessarily – though some think otherwise – less rigorous than natural science, whose findings are likewise theoretically framed, provisional, and subject to revision. But it confronts problems of interpreting human motives and subjectivity, and issues of moral judgment and meaning, that scientists do not always face.

These pages address the questions that guided my reading of the Stavenow documents. Other questions might be raised, but I believe the problems posed here have been resolved in a manner that the evidence strongly and often conclusively supports. I have framed the argument with the controversial issues in Prussian–German history in mind that this introduction has discussed, including noble authority and coercion, village subordination and insubordination, the quality of everyday public and private life in both high and low social settings, the relation of rural society to the state, and the early nineteenth-century dissolution of the centuries-long bond between manor and dependent villages. Other issues are imaginable, but these are important ones.

The question might arise of the constructed nature of the first-person testimony preserved in the documents. Undoubtedly, the common people's voices are heard not literally but as they were recorded by judges, pastors, estate managers, state officials, and others commanding literacy's techniques and occupying positions of authority. It would be preferable to escape these mediators, and the suspicion that they censored their interlocutors, putting words in or taking them out of their mouths. But it is the historian's job to deal with this problem, rather than wish it away. Though nuances of spoken language may be lost, transcribers of the common people's words usually had no interest in distorting their substantive content and intent but, instead, sought to formulate them as accurately as possible, whether for the sake of witnesses, court, or third parties. First-person testimony is the historian's most valuable source, whose systematic discrediting would be an act of epistemological nihilism. Let the reader judge whether, in the following pages, there are instances, unremarked upon by myself, that raise doubt about such words' authenticity.[27]

---

[27] For interesting reflections on these problems, deriving from the use of documents similar to many of those employed here, see Ulrike Gleixner, *"Das Mensch" und "der Kerl". Die Konstruktion von Geschlecht in Unzuchtsverfahren der frühen Neuzeit (1700–1760)* (Frankfurt/Main, 1994), part I and passim.

Finally, the reader will perhaps notice the absence of certain terms that might seem wedded to this book's theme – for example, "peasant." This word does not describe a social reality immediately familiar to anyone living in the English-speaking world. In common parlance it pejoratively conjures up miserable, pitiable, or contemptible small cultivators, while in the scholarly literature it usually identifies village farmers living by "traditional" cultural codes within "authoritarian hierarchies" in "pre-modern polities." It does not well translate the word *Bauer*, which I render as "farmer" or "village farmer." As a term for rural common people in general, "villagers" justly eclipses "peasants."

Another word missing here is "serf" and, in its collective form, "serfdom." In English it denotes villagers tied to the soil under a feudal landlord's jurisdiction and defenselessly exposed, through his command of their hereditarily bound physical persons, to his exploitation of their labor and other resources. The villagers who figure in these pages were "subjects" (*Untertanen*) rather than serfs. Forms of personal serfdom (*Leibeigenschaft*) did exist in German east Elbia, including some eastern parts of Prussia, but not at Stavenow and its Brandenburg environs. Subject status had disadvantages, but much is lost, and nothing gained, by imposing feudal serfdom's vocabulary on the society these pages portray.

Early modern German historians probe the mysteries of *Herrschaft*, but here it translates cleanly as "lordship," especially when applied to noble authority and jurisdiction, though subjective and moral-psychological meanings pose important problems. As for "modernization," it is a questionable concept, especially in its old-fashioned sociological sense, also common among historians, of an axial break between "traditional" and "modern" society occurring in the age of the Enlightenment, French Revolution, and industrialization. "Modernity," too, often figures as a teleological concept pointing more or less subtly to present-day liberal-democratic capitalist society. While any society is, literally, "modern" in relation to its own past, the idea of modernity is nonetheless useful if understood, not as an end-station known in advance, but in its historicity and multiple forms.[28] Yet it is not self-evident that these pages' actors were "pre-modern people." Their identities must be empirically grasped, rather than inferred. Though profound differences will emerge, I believe the reader will be struck by the many ways in which the Stavenowers are immediately comprehensible – more brother, one might say, than Other.

---

[28] A persuasive, historically concrete theorization of the western world's protean modernities: Peter Wagner, *A Sociology of Modernity: Liberty and Discipline* (London, 1994).

After the deluge: a noble lordship's sixteenth-century ascent and seventeenth-century crisis

In December 1649, the Baron von Blumenthal's bailiff Johann Lindt signed his "Account of the Ancient Castle and House Stavenow, from the Year 1433 to 1649." As an epigraph to this chronicle, filled with quarrels over ownership and money, Lindt invoked the Christian sentiment that "the Lord's blessing brings wealth without worry and labor." Arriving at Stavenow in 1647, after his rich employer, a powerful courtier, had acquired it in bankruptcy proceedings, the lordship's "totally ruined condition" after the Thirty Years War might well have seemed a lesson in the need for divine grace.[1]

The oldest memories of Stavenow linked it to war and plunder. Lindt cited a chronicler's account of how in 1433, during the robber knights' era, the Duke of Mecklenburg captured through betrayal the Stavenow castle, only to spare the warriors occupying it, provided they serve him on request in the future. They agreed with a handshake and a promise, "which counted for more among the nobility of those days than an oath." Whether or not this gallant story was true, Lindt – a sober burgher – "let it pass."[2]

In 1405, the Quitzow lineage, renowned for warlordism and brigandage, acquired Stavenow. In the late fifteenth century, the Quitzows, beating their swords into plowshares, turned to market production on their broad seigneurial lands. Under the forceful entrepreneur Lütke von Quitzow, Stavenow's master in the years 1515–56, the property flourished, acquiring a structure and extent that survived into the nineteenth century (and, shorn of lordship over its villages, into the twentieth). Lütke's litigious son Albrecht presided for another forty years. In 1601 an inventory displayed the lordship in robust condition, its estates

---

[1] Geheimes Staatsarchiv Preußischer Kulturbesitz (GStAPK), Berlin: Provinz Brandenburg, Rep. 37: Gutsherrschaft Stavenow, No. 43, fos 1, 11. Further citations from the Stavenow estate archive will bear folder number and folio page(s) alone.

[2] No. 43, fos. 12–13.

and perquisites paying a handsome income, its villages rendering extensive unpaid labor services and other rents in cash and kind. In 1614,
Cuno, one of Albrecht's five sons, inherited Stavenow, borrowing heavily to pay his three brothers their 20 percent shares of the 1601 appraisal value of 50,367 silver Reichstalers.[3]

Of Cuno, upon whom the storm of the Thirty Years War broke,
Lindt wrote:

from the start he could not honor interest payments owed his creditors, so
that one of them after the other sequestered the property's various incomes
and appurtenances. Thus the Stavenow estates' buildings and other assets
were so far ruined, before and during the continuous warfare, that Cuno
von Quitzow suffered before his death from want and poverty, and died in
misery.[4]

After 1626, the Catholic Emperors' and Protestant territorial princes'
warring armies, having invaded and occupied the Brandenburg electorate, contested its control. In the early 1630s Cuno and his family met
their end, perhaps from the plague or other disease, perhaps at swordpoint. The warring troops camped at Stavenow, murderously plundering until the late 1640s.

As the local fighting waxed and waned, the ravaged lordship's
creditors – thirteen burghers and five nobles – pressed for auction. In
1647 Stavenow fell to Joachim Friedrich von Blumenthal, owner of
neighboring Pröttlin lordship. He was a diplomat and courtier in the
service of Brandenburg's Hohenzollern ruler Frederick William, the
"Great Elector" (r. 1640–88). Blumenthal bid 26,360 Reichstalers, half
the 1601 value, overtrumping brothers Dietrich and Achatz von Quitzow,
the landlords at nearby Eldenburg and their lineage's only surviving
members with a Stavenow claim. Yet the Brandenburg nobility's feudal
right to succeed a fiefholder enjoyed by all the deceased's brothers and
their male descendants limited Blumenthal's title to forty-five years.

---

[3] Hagen, "How Mighty," passim, and Sack, *Stavenow*, pp. 77–88. 1601 appraisal: No. 255. It was
valued at 67,156 Brandenburg silver gulden (*märkische Gulden*), equivalent to Rhenish gulden, one
of the two principal monies of account in early modern Germany, the other being the taler (or
Reichstaler). Both were silver-based currencies. 1 Rhenish gulden (fl.) = 24 Lübeck schilling (ß);
1 schilling = 12 pfennig (pf.). 1 taler = 24 groschen (= 32 Lübeck schilling); 1 groschen = 12
pfennig. On pre-1618 monetary questions: Karl Heinrich Schäfer, "Märkischer Geldkurs, Preise
und Löhne in früheren Jahrhunderten," *Wichmann-Jahrbuch* 1 (1930): 74–7; Wilhelm Jesse, *Der
wendische Münzverein* (Braunschweig, 1967), 208–19; Emil Bahrfeldt, *Das Münzwesen der Mark
Brandenburg*, 3 vols. (Berlin, 1889–1913), vol. II, 528–33. On German monetary and metrological
history generally: Aubin and Zorn, *Handbuch der deutschen Wirtschafts- und Sozialgeschichte*, vol. I,
658–75; vol. II, 934–58.

[4] No. 43, fos. 22, 37.

The Quitzows might then reacquire Stavenow for the 1647 sale price plus such capital improvements as Blumenthal made. They would have another, final chance twenty-five years later, in 1717.[5]

Having recounted these unsentimental arrangements, Lindt congratulated Blumenthal on Stavenow's acquisition "by good title" (*bonotitulo*), wishing him "happy success, rich blessings, peaceful and friendly neighbors, good health, long life, and thereafter eternal joy and blessedness, Amen, Lord Jesus, Amen."[6] Similar hopes doubtless resounded at the 1647 banquet celebrating Blumenthal's proprietorship. Bürgermeister Georg Krusemarck, lawyer and town councilor in the nearby textile and market town of Perleberg, organized this event, seating numerous guests at nine tables in the long-uninhabited Stavenow manor-hall. To Blumenthal he wrote of the troubles it cost him "to clear out and clean up the house," employing the labor of "unwilling subjects and farmers."

Yet the banquet featured many delicacies: sixty crabs, a fresh salmon, a pike and four eels, salt cod and 100 herring, two rabbits, venison, a wild boar's head and hindquarters, ox-tongue in aspic, chickens and 240 eggs, dried beef, 30 pounds of bacon and two hams, a calf and 61 pounds of other meat, six large casks of beer and twenty small casks of imported wine, including Rhenish Mosel. Much rye bread was eaten, along with 66 pounds of butter and 20 pounds of wheat flour. There was dried fruit and Holland as well as sheep's cheese. Tobacco was smoked, while the Perleberg apothecary supplied spices and other rarities: sugar, saffron, nutmeg, capers, cardamom, raisins, ginger, pepper, almonds, and fresh lemons. The cook earned a fat 8 talers, though "the women who scrubbed and washed day and night in the kitchen for five days" together received but one-sixteenth as much.[7]

Stavenow in these years is accessible to the mind's eye, thanks to Lindt's account and a 1647 inventory. In 1675, upon the expiration of Blumenthal's tenant-farmer's lease, notary Johannes Lindt, bailiff Lindt's son, made a similar survey. These accounts, paired with prewar records, exhibit the lordship as it emerged from the sixteenth into the seventeenth century, and as it was to remain, after numerous improvements, into the early nineteenth century.[8]

[5] Ibid., fo. 6. Fritz Martiny, *Die Adelsfrage in Preussen vor 1806 als politisches und soziales Problem* (Stuttgart, 1938).
[6] Ibid., fo. 12.   [7] No. 278, fos. 1–15.   [8] No. 32, fos. 1–40; no. 67, fos. 1–33.

THE SEIGNEURIAL HEADQUARTERS

Stavenow lay along the eastern bank of the southward-flowing Löcknitz stream (see map 3). The seigneurial headquarters comprised buildings essential to the manorial economy and the lordship's dwelling places and chapel, fortified and surrounded by a moat. On an adjacent road stood laborers' quarters, an inn, and a smithy. Intersecting it was another road crossing the Löcknitz. The Imperial and Swedish armies, Lindt wrote, had "occupied this area as a pass." But the "dangerous times of war" now over, the bridges were rebuilt and tolls once again charged: 6 groschen for loaded wagons (a sizable fee), 1 groschen for empty.[9]

To reach the seigneurial house, the traveler passed over one drawbridge and across the terrain of the manorial outbuildings to another. This surmounted a renovated moat and issued through a gate-house onto the manor-hall's rectangular courtyard, centered on a well. In typical seigneurial style, the gate-house was built of brick and timber, with a tiled roof. Flanking its heavy doors were various work-rooms and a plank-floored and glass-windowed dwelling and office with a fireplace for manorial officials.[10] Adjacent stood an ancient, "four-cornered high tower with very strong walls," covered in 1667 with "good oak wood." It housed vaulted chambers, one atop the other. First was the subterranean dungeon, possessing in 1675 "an iron-bolted door [and] prisoners' block with four pairs of handcuffs clamped to it, made from the previous body-irons." The skyward chambers were sitting rooms with fireplaces and chimneys or tiled stoves, or both. The wall of one of them displayed Cuno von Quitzow's likeness, with Quitzow arms opposite and two painted bedsteads, "but without canopies." In others there were "two wicker sitting chairs" and a sleeping-bench. All had windows, some of twelve panes. At the tower's top were eight gables, their windows in 1675 still shattered.[11]

The tower led into the manor-house, some 112 feet long, facing the courtyard. Blumenthal acquired it with a badly damaged roof and walls, rotted timbers, and "not a single window-pane." Costly repairs ensued. The basement housed two vaulted storage chambers, one leading underground to the tower's dungeon. A courtyard entrance led into a kitchen with a "large and tall" cooking-hearth and a "bread cabinet

---

[9] No. 43, fo. 37.
[10] On architectural measurements: No. 668, fos. 1–6. The *Gebind* (*Verbind*) – or space between upright timbers by which buildings were measured – approximated 7 feet.
[11] No. 67, fos. 2, 5.

with barred doors." Above the hearth, foods were smoked. Adjacent was a room with iron-barred windows "where the blessed Frau von Quitzow is said to have lived while lying in." Nearby were a toilet (*Secret*) and a small vaulted chamber with a heavy iron, broken-locked door. Here the notaries found "three large chests containing all sorts of letters and loose papers," plus a smashed filing cabinet. The remaining documents they sealed and saved (to the present day).[12]

The second story housed a long, oaken-floored room called the "dance-hall," with fireplaces at both ends, a dining table, and benches under the nine courtyard windows. Here were a locked liquor cabinet and a large painted chest, both displaying Quitzow arms. Stairs led into a room with a stove, a table with benches, and an "old easy chair." Further steps led to a small tower with a fireplace overlooking the gardens. An adjacent chamber held a "good canopied bed, a foot-stool, two windows, and a toilet with a door." The third story contained three bedrooms, with fireplaces and toilets. Above these rooms were decorative gables.[13]

Flanking the manorial hall stretched the three-storied "second house." A strong entry-door led into a decoratively painted living room with a brick floor. Down a spiral staircase was a large kitchen, communicating with a "kitchen attic" containing – doubtless for cook or servant – a bedstead and toilet. On the second floor were a food storage room, an armory with gun racks, and a room with a tiled stove and four windows "where they say the school was held." On the third story was "the guest room," with a floor of green and yellow tiles, a heating oven, and a table with four benches. Adjacent were a bed-chamber, "with two painted bedsteads, one with canopy," and a sitting room with a fireplace and toilet.[14] The courtyard also housed a stall for sixteen horses and a church. The chapel boasted two gold-leafed chalices (one bearing Quitzow arms) and two plates for the Host which sub-bailiff Jürgen Gerloff "delivered for security's sake to Bürgermeister Joachim Hasse, of blessed memory, after Perleberg's plundering in 1639." The church's ceiling was wooden, its floor painted boards. The pews were missing. There was an altar cemented into the wall, and a canopied pulpit flanked by "effigies of Dr. Martin Luther" (*D.M.L.*). Adorning the walls were Cuno von Quitzow's likeness and wood-panel paintings of "old Lütke von Quitzow and his blessed wife" (*Hausfrau*). In the church cellar was a "long kitchen table."[15]

---

[12] No. 43, fos. 23–4. No. 32, fo. 11.   [13] No. 32, fos. 8–9. No. 67, fo. 6. No. 709, fos. 168–71.
[14] No. 32, fos. 12–13. No. 67, fos. 7–8.   [15] No. 67, fos. 9–10, 29. No. 32, fos. 15–16.

Departing these headquarters, the traveler returning to the north–south road passed the seigneurial baking and brewing house, slaughterhouse with smoke-oven, swine-pen, and grain-storage barn, very large, with four entrances. A big livestock barn stood alongside a ruined house with a 28-foot living room and two windows. The soldiers plundered and burned many outbuildings but, starting with the brewery, Blumenthal promptly rebuilt them (in brick and timber, with thatched roofs). Ditches and fishponds, now choked with weeds, surrounded them. Behind the manor-hall, toward the Löcknitz, there had been vegetable and hop gardens, flax land, and horse and ox pastures. One of Blumenthal's first concerns, Lindt wrote, was "to have measured out and planted with special delicacies fine gardens for pleasure and kitchen."[16]

Across the road stood the inn, some 112 feet long, with gables front and back, masonry vestibule, and thatched roof. But "the soldiery [*Soldatesca*], who often camped nearby, tore down the inn and completely ruined it." In 1571, the innkeeper held seigneurial land for sowing 5 bushels of winter rye and 7 bushels of summer barley and oats. We shall see what food value such measures possessed. He received pasturage for three head of cattle and forage for fourteen pigs. He kept two horses "so that he could, if needed, make trips at the lordship's expense." The inn purveyed Stavenow's beer, paying a yearly lease of 4 gulden (or 3 talers) and, the customary charge upon tavernkeepers, a pound of pepper. Nearby stood the lordship's head plowmen's and livestock herders' houses, each with a vegetable garden and cowshed, but they too the soldiers destroyed. To replace them construction was underway in 1649 on a four-family house some 90 feet long.[17]

In 1675, after a quarter-century of poor markets and harsh taxation during which the Blumenthals leased Stavenow to tenant-farmers, the lordship's condition was partly worse than in 1647. Leaseholder Holle, who with his wife departed the property that year, had – like his predecessors – undertaken at seigneurial instruction some improvements. There was a new orchard and a new gardener. In 1664 the inn was rebuilt, with an eighteen-windowed lower room joined by a carpeted staircase to two upstairs bed-chambers, each with two small windows. The downstairs floor was of alder planks "glued together." An entry-gate with heavy doors led to the courtyard and stables. A tall hedge

---

[16] Ibid., fos. 16–20; no. 43, fo. 25.   [17] Ibid., fo. 40; no. 131, pt. I; no. 705, fo. 128.

enclosed rear gardens and bake-oven. The nearby tile-roofed smithy, 28 feet wide, housed anvil and bellows set on alderwood floor.[18]

In 1675 many buildings were "very damaged" and "decrepit." The former school-room "has completely broken away" while the church had been "removed." The swineherd and dairy-mistress inhabited the house attached to the livestock barn. Its second story could bear no traffic, the chimney was collapsing, one ceiling beam was broken and propped up, and in the front the timbers had sunk into the ground, requiring a stoop to enter the living room.[19]

THE RISE OF EAST-ELBIAN COMMERCIALIZED MANORIALISM

An east-Elbian lordship's income flowed, first, from its own directly managed demesne land – arable cropland, pastures, meadows, and forest – and, second, from its village-dwelling subject farmers' labor services and other dues. Further incomes, such as rents paid by millers and artisans under seigneurial authority, varied accordingly. The domanial fields' breadth determined the yearly rye harvests, sown in the fall and reaped the following summer, and of spring-planted oats and barley, cut after the rye. Until superseded in the eighteenth century, this cereal cultivation system left one-third of arable fallow each year, its fertility to be renewed by grazing (and by sparse plantings of nitrogen-fixing peas, a common food and fodder). Sometimes, too, small flax crops – for linen cloth fiber – dotted the fallow. The other two fields, once harvested, served as pasture before plowing resumed. Meadows, often found along stream-beds, yielded hay which, with cereal straw, kept the manorial horses, cattle, and sheep alive through the wintry days when grazing was impossible.[20]

Though always exposed to weather risks, grain harvests were improvable by repeated plowings to aerate and weed the land, grazing's fertilizing effect, and applications of animal manure and mulches. The goal was to maximize seed sown and germinated: the better the soil was tended, the heavier the sowings. Arable land's customary measure was not spatial extent, but yearly quantity of sowable seed, in bushels (*Scheffel*) and tons (*Wispel* [24 bushels]). In the late eighteenth century,

---

[18] No. 67, fos. 14–15.   [19] Ibid., fos. 8–10.
[20] Hans-Heinrich Müller, *Märkische Landwirtschaft vor den Agrarreformen von 1807. Entwicklungstendenzen des Ackerbaues in der zweiten Hälfte des 18. Jahrhunderts* (Potsdam, 1967); Abel, *Geschichte der deutschen Landwirtschaft*; Achilles, *Landwirtschaft in der frühen Neuzeit*.

following the adoption of fallow-free rotations, seigneurial seed-yield ratios of rye, barley, and oats at Stavenow averaged 1:4–6. Earlier, harvests of "the third kernel" were satisfactory, while "the fourth kernel" was good. To produce sizable marketable surpluses, seigneurial farms needed to be large. This was true, on a smaller scale, of a lordship's farmers' holdings on the village fields, if they were to support numerous households and pay taxes and seigneurial rents.[21] The broader the pasturage and the richer the meadows, the more numerous the cattle and sheep a noble estate could maintain – valuable both for indispensable manures and butter, cheese, wool, meat, and hides. Forests fattened livestock, especially the multitudinous pigs grazed on autumnal beech nuts and acorns and also fed on the manorial brewery's by-products, the remnants of tons of barley. Forests were still more essential for the lumber and firewood massively consumed at the manor and profitably sold in the villages and local towns.

The seigneurial arable and pastures demanded many hands and ample horsepower. To secure these on satisfactory terms was noble lordship's essential economic function (in contrast to its military and judicial purposes). The landlords' claims on their villagers' labor and incomes bore the stamp of feudal power and ancient privilege, not free-market calculations. They reached back to the twelfth and thirteenth centuries, when German warlords and frontiersmen conquered or infiltrated the east-Elbian lands of Holstein, Brandenburg, Mecklenburg, Silesia, and Pomerania (all then Slav-settled lands), as well as Balt-inhabited Prussia farther east. Settling colonists and restructuring preexisting villages, they founded an agrarian regime that underwent gradual Germanization, lasting, with many twists and turns, into the twentieth century.

Medieval German society in the east-Elbian lands encompassed villages possessing communally held fields, parceled out in hereditary leasehold tenure to their members' households, mainly as largeholdings designed to support a cultivator with family and servants while leaving a surplus to pay rent and tithes. In such villages, part of the communal land – typically, two to four times a village farmer's acreage – supported a nearby manor. This belonged to the entrepreneur or nobleman who

---

[21] The Brandenburg *Scheffel* or bushel approximated 1.5 modern Anglo-American bushels and varied in weight by grain type and in volume (slightly) by region. Eighteenth-century weights of the Berlin bushel (similar or identical to that in use at Stavenow) were: rye – 40 kg (88 lbs); barley – 32.5 kg (72 lbs); oats – 24 kg (53 lbs). Abel, *Agrarkrisen und Agrarkonjunktur*, 294. Cf. Müller, *Landwirtschaft*, 203; Otto Behre, *Geschichte der Statistik in Brandenburg-Preußen* (Berlin, 1905), 277 (rye – 45 kg; barley – 38 kg; oats – 25.5 kg). On grain yields: Müller, *Landwirtschaft*, 102ff.

settled the village, or increasingly (as time passed) to an enfeoffed vassal of a higher lordship dominating the locality – whether a magnate nobleman, the church, or a territorial ruler, such as the Brandenburg margraves (bearers, after 1356, of the title of Elector within the Holy Roman Empire). The typical village also possessed lands supporting the parish priest and an enlarged mayor's holding. Serving manorial lords' and village notables' labor needs, a few smallholders were settled, tenurially bound to work as required, without pay or at regulated wages. Largeholding farmers owed the local seigneur but a few days' annual work with teams and plows, and help in the manorial harvests.[22]

Fourteenth- and fifteenth-century plague revealed the deadly imbalances that had accumulated between village populations, food supply, and feudal rents. In disease's train, in Brandenburg as elsewhere in Europe, came civil war and noble brigandage and gangsterism. Around 1475, the Brandenburg countryside offered a desolate spectacle. Depopulation by disease and strife had left many villages completely abandoned, others only half-settled. The villages' manorial lords had mostly long since lost their functions and incomes as feudal warriors. Before or during the late medieval crisis, the Brandenburg margraves auctioned off many fief-distributing powers for irregular tax grants from corporate nobility and upper clergy.[23]

The strongest surviving manorial lords grew land-rich. To their demesnes they joined, legally or by usurpation, unoccupied subject farms or even whole deserted villages. This expanded lordship over land (*Grundherrschaft*) they paired with strengthened judicial lordship (*Gerichtsherrschaft*), gained by margravial jurisdictional grants and exercised through manorial courts overshadowing the villagers' assemblies. But landlords' wallets and strongboxes were mostly empty. From the late fourteenth century, prices fell with population. Village farmers, if they did not desert their holdings, bid down seigneurial rents. Landlords often pawned to local burghers for ready cash the grain rents their villagers owed them.[24]

---

[22] On medieval German colonization and settlement: Carsten, *The Origins of Prussia*; Hans K. Shulze, "Die Besiedlung der Mark Brandenburg im hohen und späten Mittelalter," *JbGMOD* 28 (1979): 42–178; Herbert Helbig, *Gesellschaft und Wirtschaft in der Mark Brandenburg im Mittelalter* (Berlin, 1973); Materna and Ribbe, *Brandenburgische Geschichte*, 85ff; Enders, *Uckermark*, ch. I; literature cited in Hagen, "How Mighty the Junkers?", 83ff, and "Village Life in East-Elbian Germany and Poland, 1400–1800."

[23] Evamarie Engel and Benedykt Zientara, *Feudalstruktur, Lehnbürgertum und Fernhandel im spätmittelalterlichen Brandenburg* (Weimar, 1967); Enders, *Uckermark*, ch. II.

[24] Cf. Hagen, "How Mighty," 89–94. On the nobility's legal powers: Friedrich Grossmann, *Über die gutsherrlich-bäuerlichen Rechtsverhältnisse in der Mark Brandenburg vom 16. bis 18. Jahrhundert* (Leipzig, 1890).

In the late fifteenth century, there began a pacification of society under resolidified princely power and a population recovery which, accompanied by rising agricultural prices, continued into the early seventeenth century. In this long secular trend's favorable setting, many Brandenburg noblemen – Stavenow's Lütke and Albrecht von Quitzow typified them – prospered impressively as enterprising and improving landlords. Like their counterparts throughout east Elbia, they confronted their villages with demands for novel and oppressive labor services. Only so could they avoid paying heavy wages to freely contracted workers for bringing their now-extensive domanial lands under cultivation. The landlords imposed the new labor services as feudal rent, owed the manor for the villagers' possession of their farms, hereditary though their tenures were. The seigneurial court claimed such labor, legalistically, as a public service, akin to road maintenance, underpinning the lordship's exercise of local government.

Although earlier the margraves admonished the nobility against oppressing their subjects with harsh labor, in the sixteenth century the Brandenburg rulers complacently tolerated the landlords' imposition on village cultivators of two or three days of weekly toil on seigneurial land. The Electors more readily relented since they too were great but impecunious landlords, possessing numerous and far-flung princely estates whose managers were proceeding no differently from the landed nobility in recruiting villagers' unpaid labor.[25]

These aggressive seigneurial initiatives figure in the historical literature as "the enserfment of the east-Elbian German free peasantry," an episode in the larger development often referred to as the "second serfdom" in central and eastern Europe. This terminology is misleading, since, with few exceptions, there existed in German east Elbia no "first serfdom" such as that of the early medieval west. Still, the valid and momentous point remains that, while the late medieval villagers of the Mediterranean and western European lands cast off the bonds of serfdom to attain legal equality with burghers and other commoners, in

---

[25] On the landed nobility's relationship to the princely state and their economic activities, see, in addition to the literature on individual noble lordships and crown estates cited in the bibliography: Peter-Michael Hahn, *Struktur und Funktion des brandenburgischen Adels im 16. Jahrhundert* (Berlin, 1979); Peter-Michael Hahn, "Adel und Landesherrschaft in der Mark Brandenburg im späten Mittelalter und der frühen Neuzeit," *JbfBLG* 38 (1987): 43–57; Hartmut Harnisch, *Die Herrschaft Boitzenburg* (Weimar, 1968); Hartmut Harnisch, "Die Gutsherrschaft in Brandenburg. Ergebnisse und Probleme," *JBfWG* 4 (1969): 117–47; Hartmut Harnisch, "Zur Herausbildung und Funktionsweise von Gutswirtschaft und Gutsherrschaft," *JbfRG* 4 (1972): 178–99; Hartmut Harnisch, *Bauern – Feudaladel – Städtebürgertum* (Weimar, 1980); Enders, *Uckermark*, ch. III; Jan Peters, "Inszenierung von Gutsherrschaft im 16. Jahrhundert: Matthias v. Saldern auf Plattenburg-Wilsnack (Prignitz)," in Peters, *Konflikt und Kontrolle*, 248–86.

east-Elbian Europe in the late fifteenth and sixteenth centuries an opposing tendency prevailed. The landed nobility, eager to bring their estates into production for favorable domestic and export markets, pressured local ruling princes, such as the Brandenburg Electors, into issuing new statutes binding the personally free villagers to the soil, so that they could not legally combat demands for more burdensome feudal rents with threats to depart to the towns or other lordships.[26]

In Brandenburg, as elsewhere in east Elbia, the nobility also sought to restrict village communes' access to princely lawcourts, where they might remonstrate against new seigneurial burdens. The Berlin Electors repeatedly endorsed landlordly complaints about their subjects' "frivolous lawsuits" against them. Yet the princely regime, jealous of its jurisdictional sovereignty, never surrendered its right to hear villagers' appeals against seigneurial oppression, expensive though such cases were. It was virtually impossible for individual villagers to bring landlords to justice for wrongs committed against them alone. But the Brandenburg farmer could rightfully quit his holding and move away from his lordship's jurisdiction, on condition – not necessarily easily fulfillable – that he secure a substitute farmer acceptable to the manorhouse. Other sixteenth-century pro-landlord legislation obliged subject farmers' children whose labor was not essential to parental holdings to offer themselves to their lordship as farm servants for a period of several years (or even until they married). In such compulsory service (*Gesindezwangsdienst*) they earned room, board, and miserly wages. After the Thirty Years War, statutes expressing the government's and nobility's interest in repopulating the war-torn countryside decreed that subject farmers' sons could not refuse inheritance of parental farms or landlords' demands that they rebuild and occupy devastated holdings.[27]

Except in Brandenburg's Uckermark and Neumark Districts (see map 3), village farmers' legal subjection did not restrict the right to hold and transmit property, contract marriages, or take action in courts of law so as to qualify them as serfs (*Leibeigene*) and their legal status as serfdom (*Leibeigenschaft*). These terms, familiar from medieval German legal usage and baldly expressing dominion over subjects' physical bodies, had acquired ominous and shameful connotations. They seldom, if

---

[26] On the "second serfdom" in central and eastern Europe: Kaak, *Gutsherrschaft*; Michael North, "Die Entstehung der Gutswirtschaft im südlichen Ostseeraum," *ZHF* 26 (1999): 43–59; Jerome Blum, "The Rise of Serfdom in Eastern Europe," *AHR* 62 (1957): 807–35; Hagen, "Capitalism."

[27] Ernst Lennhoff, *Das ländliche Gesindewesen in der Kurmark Brandenburg vom 16. bis 19. Jahrhundert* (Breslau, 1906); Hagen, "Working," and "Crisis."

ever, appeared in sixteenth- and seventeenth-century Brandenburg statutes. Nor were they interchangeable with the usual legal term for dependent villagers – *Untertanen* ("subjects") – or for their personal juridical status – *Untertänigkeit* ("subjection"). The dependency these terms described was not a personal attribute but a consequence of occupying a farm from which unpaid labor services and compulsorily recruited servants could be claimed. In an authoritative formulation of 1790: "subjection clings to the farm" (*Untertänigkeit klebt dem Hofe an*).[28]

Non-farmholding villagers and their children were exempt from compulsory farm-servant recruitment, though they might agree to work at the manor for prevailing statutory wages. They could quit their native jurisdictions for other villages or for the towns, provided they purchased a release certificate (*Losschein*) from the seigneurial court. Subject villagers were free to marry as they saw fit, so long as they could, whether as laborers or farmers, support to seigneurial satisfaction a household. In reality, exploitative and tyrannical landlords must have been common, though their numbers are unknown. The individual villager, faced with intolerable circumstances, might abscond, but the landed householders sought defense in communal resistance and legal action.

During the new agrarian regime's first phase, from the late fifteenth century to the outbreak of the Thirty Years War, the Brandenburg villagers' anti-landlord litigation, like the impact of heightened seigneurial domination on their personal and familial lives, largely remains to be investigated at the grass-roots level.[29] For the following period, from the Thirty Years War to the early nineteenth century, the pages below will measure the compulsion and lack of freedom they suffered, and seigneurialism's other effects on their lives and well-being. Sixteenth-century east-Elbian agrarian laws aimed to neutralize landlordly competition for still scarce farmers and manorial workers and to prevent villagers from bidding down rents and pushing up wages. How far they succeeded in the pre-1618 era emerges from the movement of village dues and manorial services, the value of manorial workers' real wages, the manor's production costs (supplementing the villagers' unpaid services), and from seigneurial net profits.

The landlords' successful burdening of largeholding farmers with weekly manorial service (*Hofdienst*) of two or three days' labor with a team of horses, and the smallholders with corresponding manual work,

---

[28] No. 353, fos. 12–13 (language of the government-mediated Urbarium [see ch. 9]).
[29] But see the above-cited works of Grossmann, Enders, Harnisch, and Peters.

was the chief prize of their rent offensive. The farmers' contemporary testimony, and the record then and subsequently of manor–village strife, show that these were well-hated burdens. But, though the historical literature largely holds otherwise, the villagers were not wholly defenseless against the manorial onslaught. A regional investigation with a good claim to representativeness shows that village farm rents, by the late fifteenth century, had fallen (in constant monetary values) well below levels recorded a century earlier in the 1375 Brandenburg cadastre.[30] This consequence, favorable to villagers' interests, of the late medieval agrarian depression was unlikely to persist once the downward trend of population, rent, and prices reversed into the long European growth cycle of ca. 1475–1618. The terms of trade, both domestic and international, between foodstuffs and manufactures shifted in the sixteenth century in agriculture's favor. In Brandenburg, tax levies on the villages remained intermittent and tithes commonly vanished following the Protestant Reformation. Farm incomes rose, including those of such villagers as the Stavenow Quitzows' farmers. The execrated new seigneurial labor services were the landlords' cut of their subjects' holdings' expanding value, which might instead have been taken in money or product rents.

Sometimes the villages shouldered the new labor services on condition that previous rents in bushels of grain or ringing coin be held at or reduced below late fifteenth-century levels. The crucial matter was the share of the villagers' surplus, beyond what was essential to household reproduction, that seigneurial rent consumed. We will see that this proved sizable but not confiscatory. For the landlord, the question was whether his villagers' weekly exertions at the seigneurial demesne farms and their children's compulsory service as seigneurial farmhands satisfied his labor needs, sparing him wage bills and production costs he would otherwise confront.

The fine Renaissance houses of the large landowners among the Brandenburg nobility, the late-humanist culture they embraced, and their political strength witnessed their sixteenth-century enrichment. Their rural subjects' unpaid or ill-paid labors earned the landed nobility comfortable or opulent livings, and it is easy to imagine that many Brandenburg villagers shared the utopian anti-aristocratic egalitarianism of the rebels who launched and fought the Peasants' War of 1525 in west and south Germany. For reasons still not fully clear, this great

[30] Hagen, "How Mighty," 88ff.

uprising failed to spill over into the northeastern German lands (except for parts of Baltic Prussia).[31] Historians assume that the east-Elbian nobility's grip on their villages was too iron-clad to be challenged. Yet in comparatively underpopulated Brandenburg, where bowing to seigneurial labor services yielded family farms better than merely self-sufficient, incentives to rebel were weaker than in the more densely set-tled, land-poor, and heavily taxed German heartlands. In 1572, the humanist Wolfgang Jobsten wrote that "everyone knows the many fine resources that are to be found in the Mark Brandenburg, though they were more available 30–40 years ago than now. Many foreign [German] peoples such as Franconians, Meisseners, Silesians, and Rhinelanders settled there to live." Other early modern writers referred as well to sixteenth-century immigration into Brandenburg, swelled perhaps by flight from the Peasants' War.[32] Such contemporary sources as have come to light do not suggest that sixteenth-century commer-cialized manorialism deterred widespread reoccupation of deserted vil-lages or broke settled villagers' will to stay on their lands.

STAVENOW'S SEIGNEURIAL ECONOMY AT THE SIXTEENTH CENTURY'S END

Pre-1618 landlords did not succeed in shifting all production costs onto villagers' shoulders. Most noble estates needed to employ their own expensive teams of oxen and horses, with voluntarily recruited drivers to lead the way in plowing, harrowing, and hauling. The permanently engaged manorial servants' wages in cash and kind, especially food and drink, were considerable. Converted into money values, they amounted at Stavenow, at the sixteenth century's close, to about 470 gulden annually – a figure that, capitalized at 4 percent, exceeded (at 11,750 gulden) the capitalized value of 8,454 gulden the Quitzow brothers assigned the farmers' weekly labor services in the 1601 estate appraisal (see table 1.1).[33]

The Quitzows also leased to "foreign subjects" – nearby farmers not under their jurisdiction – valuable grazing rights in exchange for plow-ing and other fieldwork which they evidently did not count on their sixty-three subject farmers to finish promptly. Such freely contracted

[31] Heide Wunder, "Zur Mentalität aufständischer Bauern," in Hans-Ulrich Wehler, ed., *Der deutsche Bauernkrieg 1524–1526* (Göttingen, 1975), 9–37; cf. Franz, *Geschichte des deutschen Bauernstandes*, 131ff; Blickle, *Revolution of 1525*.
[32] Quoted in Grossmann, *Rechtsverhältnisse*, 17–18, n. 4.
[33] See table 1.1, below, and Hagen, "Working."

work was reliably carried out, while compulsory labor services were notorious for shoddiness and absenteeism: the appraised value of one day's voluntary fieldwork with a horse-team was six times higher than an obligatory day's efforts. The Quitzows were not unaware of their villagers' labor's defects. They agreed that "even though nowadays [1601] fullholders' services, especially when they are not given food and drink, are rated at 200 gulden, since this is an appraisal among natural brothers, and because it is not uncustomary hereabouts, we reckon the fullholder's service at only 100 talers [133 gulden], and the smallholder's at 50 talers [66 gulden]."[34]

Still, the Quitzows could take satisfaction in their Stavenow income (see table 1.1).

Though the Thirty Years War ravaged these incomes, in 1647 bailiff Lindt planned to restock the Stavenow seigneurial home-farm with twelve plow oxen and 118 cattle, including 68 new milk cows.[35] The 1601 inventory credited every ten head annually with one barrel (*Tonne* [113 liters]) of butter, worth 16 gulden, and one of cheese, worth 4 gulden: "profits from annual sale of barren animals help the lordship's proprietor cover labor and other costs; this is also why prices of butter and cheese are set so low."[36] Many swine could be kept at Stavenow. "So too," Lindt fulsomely wrote, "have the poultry, such as ducks and geese, the finest and most useful accommodations that could be found on a landed estate."[37] About seigneurial gardens, a 1584 inventory reported that large hop plantings were customary, while "of cabbage, carrots, onions, apples, pears, and cherries much can be sold beyond what is needed for consumption."[38]

Along the Löcknitz stream stretched seven seigneurial meadows, apart from another leased to village farmers "who could get no hay."[39] They yielded, in mowings that began in May at Whitsuntide, 457 large wagonloads (*Fuder* [ca. one English ton]) of hay, all internally consumed as fodder. Across the stream stood most of the lordship's woodland, precisely surveyed following earlier quarrels with neighboring lordships over forest rights. Altogether, they encompassed 740 *Morgen* (420 hectares [1,050 acres]) in hardwood (oak and beech) and softwood

---

[34] No. 255, pt. IV.
[35] Cf. no. 705, fos. 22–7, 34.
[36] No. 255, pt. IX. Cf. no. 43, fo. 24. 1 *Tonne* = 100 *Quart* = 114.5 liters (Müller, *Landwirtschaft*, 203).
[37] No. 43, fo. 24.
[38] No. 705, fos. 128–9. This inventory (no. 704, fos. 134–6; no. 705, fos. 127–9), though undated, is doubtless Lindt's "old register" of 1584 (cf. no. 43, fo. 46).
[39] No. 131, pt. I.

Table 1.1   *Composition of the Stavenow lordship's market value, 1601*
(capitalized at 4 percent)[a]

	Value (gulden)	%
Manor-house and demesne farm buildings[b]	5,813	8.6
Forest income	15,552	23.2
Income from demesne production		
Grain sales	12,104	18.0
Livestock	10,917	16.3
Fisheries and gardens	3,615	5.4
Rent of seigneurial mills	4,400	6.5
Income from seigneurial courts and jurisdictional fees	1,649	2.5
Income from subject villagers' rents		
Fixed rents of Stavenow's subject farmers		
Labor services	8,454	12.6
Rents in grain	1,375	2.0
Rents in cash	864	1.3
Short-term services of "foreign subjects"		
Labor services	1,609	2.4
Rents in grain	804	1.2
Total	67,156	100.0

[a] No. 255, part VI: "Although it is customary in these parts to capitalize properties at 3 percent" – to arrive at high market values – "because this is an appraisal among brothers" and not among "wild strangers," the Quitzows agreed upon a rate of 4 percent (= annual income × 25).
[b] No. 255, part I: "Although originally such buildings cost much more to build."
Source: no. 255, fos. 1–32. This appraisal set the Brandenburg (märkisch) gulden (reckoned at 24 Lübeck schillings) on a par with the Rhenish gulden (= 0.75 Reichstaler).

(alder and birch).[40] Good years yielded acorns and beechnuts to fatten 800 pigs. Some of these woods covered the long-deserted villages of Dargardt and Gosedahl, seemingly abandoned because of inferior plowland, patches of which the lordship leased for grain or money rents to neighboring villagers.

Here Stavenow held hunting rights, though a neighboring, land-poor gentry family had earlier feuded over them with the Quitzows. The 1584 inventory remarked of the Stavenow hunt, here and elsewhere,

[40] 1 *Fuder* = ca. 20 *preussische Zentner*; 1 *Zentner* = 110 *Pfund* = 51.5 kg. The Brandenburg (*kurmärkischer*) *Morgen* (400 square rods [*Ruten*] or 0.5674 hectares) was the standard areal measure until displaced in the late eighteenth century by the Magdeburg *Morgen* (180 square rods or 0.2553 hectares). Müller, *Landwirtschaft*, 203.

that "one can sometimes have big game, such as stags, pigs, and deer." Still, in 1601 the Quitzows forbore from capitalizing hunting as an asset, saying that it "costs more than it brings in."[41] Farther away stood more seigneurial woods, enclosing a "beautiful large pond" with "handsome fish" of various types that "stocked it by themselves from the Löcknitz stream."[42] The 1584 inventory wrote of the seigneurial fisherman that "he must daily deliver from the Löcknitz to the manor four table fish, if it is a fish day and, if it is a meat day, two table fish, as well as a fish for baking, if one is wanted."[43]

Near the manor-house were fenced enclosures, one for horses, one for young calves and plow oxen, "so that the plowmen may rotate teams, unharnessing and returning oxen they drive in the morning and bringing out the others, without need for any special herder."[44] The adjacent domanial arable stretched southeastward. All trace had disappeared of the Stavenow village with which the manor had originally shared this land. Laid out – untypically – in four fields, it was large enough for annual sowings of 11 tons of rye, 10 tons of either "rough" or "white" oats, and 5.5 tons of barley. A ton of buckwheat was also sown, some of it – along with peas and broad beans – in sections of the fallow field ("after which the land bears a very good rye crop"). The fallow also bore small flax plantings.[45] Lindt thought the Stavenow manor-farm, "because it is sandy soil, can be worked at low cost, so that by keeping three plowmen and twelve oxen – allowing for changing of teams once or twice daily – and three farmhands [*Knechte*], everything can be well cultivated without the need for other plows." The lordship did not depend – except for pre-sowing harrowing – on villagers' labor services to farm these broad seigneurial acres (which in 1810 comprised 608 hectares, though by then the lordship's arable had considerably expanded).[46] Adjacent was a sheep-farm, plundered during the war. Earlier it kept 500 head, grazing them as seasons and plantings allowed. This herd, following the 1601 reckoning, had a capitalized value of 1,333 gulden. Enclosing the plowland on three sides was "a beautiful, pleasant forest" of 480 hectares, with hardwood providing forage for 500 pigs. Lindt recommended rebuilding the nearby brick-kiln, ruined by the Quitzows' "bad housekeeping" and "impecuniousness."[47]

Eastward lay Semlin manor-farm, with arable unshared with other cultivators and new dairy and sheep farms. In 1810 its cropland

[41] No. 259, pt. XIV; no. 705, fo. 128.   [42] No. 43, fo. 77.   [43] No. 705, fo. 128.
[44] No. 43, fo. 38.   [45] Ibid., fo. 40.   [46] Ibid.; no. 258, fos. 7–10; cf. table 10.3, below.
[47] No. 43, fos. 42, 77.

spanned 322 hectares. Here was an outbuilding, inhabited by a shepherd and his wife, alongside a large but ruined house and a tile-roofed, two-storied "summer building," seemingly for workers tending the 90 cattle and 1,500 sheep earlier kept here. Nearby was one of the lordship's numerous fishponds, capitalized at 150 gulden because of its pike, carp, and humbler species.[48] The arable, "good and loamy," could bear annual sowings of 32 tons of rye, barley, and oats, together with fallow-planted buckwheat and peas. But after the war sowings fell by half. Of labor services Lindt wrote that "earlier, because of the many subject farmers, only one [manorial] horse-team for hauling manure and harrowing needed to be kept." Here too was forage for 240 pigs, at a seasonal charge per head to Stavenow subjects of 18 groschen, and to "outsiders" of 1 taler.[49]

Stavenow's third demesne farm was a small "knightly manor" (*Rittersitz*) in nearby Premslin village. One of the Quitzows had always lived here, including most recently Cuno, "until the end of his days." The house, surrounded by a drawbridged moat, had been of stone and wood, with a tile roof, but now lay burnt and ruined. Its dairy-farm, with good pasturage and meadows, had kept 100 head. Still standing was "the building where the dairy-mistress lived with maids and other servants," though tiled stove and windows were missing.[50] The seigneurial arable (1810: 166 hectares), though not intermixed with Premslin villagers' lands, followed the same three-field rotations and usages governing them. Fallowing "fattened" the land so that it could bear summer peas before fall rye sowing.[51] Manorial grain plantings, once 23 tons, were now, on the overgrown fields, "tiny." Lindt observed that "the estate has its labor nearby in the village . . . namely nineteen fullholders and one smallholder, who easily carried out the cultivation here." There were five usable manorial fishponds. As for grazing seigneurial sheep on village land, "the villagers did not want to allow a herd here, but now that most of the farms are deserted, they cannot stop the lordship."[52]

Such were Stavenow's principal directly owned assets. There was also, until Blumenthal sold it, a town house in nearby Perleberg that Lütke von Quitzow bought in 1556. Still in fair condition, it was wooden, with a slate roof and in the garden a "fine walled tower," three stories high, which Lütke called "*Balchfriede*" (roughly: "retreat from life's turmoil"). Though a nobleman, Lütke acquired with this residence all the

[48] No. 32, fo. 34; no. 131.   [49] No. 43, fo. 45; no. 131; no. 705, fo. 22.   [50] No. 32, fo. 28.
[51] No. 131.   [52] No. 705, fo. 22. No. 43, fos. 55, 60.

usual burgher's rights, including freedom to pursue a trade and brew beer. Probably, like his Quitzow and Blumenthal successors, he rented hunting rights on the town's broad farmland and heath.[53] The Junkers' rise usually figures as the burghers' loss, but these small details suggest a coexistence of east-Elbian landed gentry and townspeople that, in English history, was entirely normal.

The long sixteenth century brought an agriculturally led economic growth to Brandenburg and its neighbors that benefited successful and fortunate burghers (and village farmers) alongside Junkers. This point vanishes in a literature stressing Malthusian demographic imbalances of population and food-supply in sixteenth-century Europe and spiraling indebtedness among high-spending nobility and rulers. Yet the Quitzows' fashioning of the Stavenow estates into a valuable and productive large-scale enterprise shows that the Junkers' rise represented vigorous economic growth: 83 and more tons of annual sowings were a mini-mountain. Based on long-understood technology and much uncooperative labor, commercialized manorialism represented extensive rather than efficiency-gaining intensive growth. Yet at the macrolevel it was a multiplier of domestic wealth. But what price did the village farmers and laborers pay who made such Junkers as the Quitzows rich?[54]

STAVENOW'S SUBJECT VILLAGES

The 1601 appraisal assigned nearly one-third of the lordship's value to levies on villagers. But their economic value stood even higher, for without their unpaid (or ill-paid) labor, the seigneurial arable could only have been farmed at a heavy cost in wages and fixed capital. Sustaining the subject farmers in their service to the manor-hall were their own old-established farms. As elsewhere in east-Elbian Germany, the Stavenow villagers' holdings were measured in *Hufen*, a concept recalling the old English "hide of land." During medieval colonization, village settlements were laid out, or arose anew on earlier Slavic foundations, endowed with extensive fields of arable and pasturable land (*Feldmarken*), along with meadows and woods. The *Hufe* encompassed

---

[53] No. 43, fo. 82; no. 131.
[54] Cf. Eric L. Jones, *Growth Recurring. Economic Change in World History* (Oxford, 1988); Hagen, "Crisis," "Capitalism," "*Sonderweg*," and "Village Life"; reappraisals by east European historians of commercialized manorialism in east-central and Balkan Europe in Daniel Chirot, ed., *The Origins of Economic Backwardness in Eastern Europe. Economics and Politics from the Middle Ages until the Early Twentieth Century* (Berkeley, 1989).

shares of these communal lands large enough to support a household, including elders and a servant or two. The farmstead's buildings, gardens, and orchards sat alongside its neighbors, near its hereditary plots in the open fields. Such fields were, usually, three in number, although often villages possessed additional, infertile lands, sown only every few years, and otherwise used as pasturage.

For reasons obscure – perhaps related to colonists' origins in the fertile Low Countries and western Germany – the *Hufe* proved too small, on the often sandy eastern soils, to support a family farm. Nearly everywhere, village holdings came to encompass larger areas: two *Hufen*, as at Stavenow, or more. Such fullholdings (*Vollbauern-* or *Hüfnerhöfe*) were typical, though villages also counted some smallholdings (*Kossätenhöfe*). Though named after cottagers, these usually comprised arable land, sometimes equal to half a fullholding, in separate sections of the communal fields. In the sixteenth century, and after 1648, some fragmentation of village land occurred, especially division of fullholdings into halfholdings. At the village margin, dwarf cottage holdings appeared, with a house and garden and, at most, patches of arable. But while farm shrinkage was pervasive in early modern western and southern Europe, and in Poland, Bohemia, Saxony and Silesia, it was rarer in Brandenburg-Prussia, perhaps because population was thinner. Preservation of the larger farms, able to render labor services with horses, also reflected the interest both of gentry and government, with its numerous princely manor-farms.[55]

As on seigneurial land, the measure of village farmers' arable was the quantity of sowable seed. Because areal surveying only triumphed after 1700, the *Hufe*'s precise surface equivalents in earlier times are usually unknown. In eighteenth-century Brandenburg, it comprised 30 "large" or "Prussian" *Morgen* (as opposed to the smaller "Magdeburg *Morgen*" predominant in the nineteenth century). This term ("morning") originally referred to the land a plowman could cover in half a day. Two "large" *Hufen* encompassed 85.5 English acres (34 hectares), one-third of which lay fallow (leaving 57 acres [23 hectares] for yearly planting). A fullholder also possessed shares of the village's woods and meadows. Custom said that, on average land, 1 bushel was sowable on 1 *Morgen* (and hence 40 bushels annually on 2 standard *Hufen*). An eighteenth-century Stavenow fullholding sowed 48 bushels: 24 of rye and 12 each of barley and oats.[56]

---

[55] On European trends: Scott, *Peasantries*.   [56] Müller, *Landwirtschaft*, 16ff, 102ff, 142ff, 203.

After the Thirty Years War, Stavenow's creditors and prospective buyers keenly surveyed the villages. Their devastation and desertion crucially influenced property value, but it was also essential to determine farmers' prewar obligations. In the 1630s, landlordly controls on Brandenburg villages broke down amid war's incursions. To the seventeenth century's end, seigneurial and state officials faced the challenge of compelling surviving farmers to reshoulder prewar rent and tax burdens while resettling abandoned farmsteads. Amid long-enduring postwar labor shortages, both old-established and new farmers resisted a return to prewar rules, especially since in the 1650s Elector Frederick William's regime launched a revolutionary program of new taxation to raise a standing army, the foundation (alongside the fiscal bureaucracy) of nascent Brandenburg-Prussian absolutism.

Historians long held that, in a 1653 compromise with the government, the Brandenburg corporate nobility traded consent to heavy new taxation of their subjects for freedom to exploit more ruthlessly their villagers' land and labor – above all through the imposition of heavier labor services and enclosure of deserted village land into seigneurial demesne. Certainly some of the nobility's political representatives advocated such exchange. But in practice the villagers, though paying (if at swordpoint) the state's new taxes, resisted oppressive landlordly demands. In the seventeenth century's second half, this contentious play of forces between state, landlords, and village farmers dominated Brandenburg's countryside.[57]

In 1649 the Stavenow authorities investigated villagers' obligations. Their sworn informant was Stefan Strasse, "a farmer sixty years old who served House Stavenow for thirty years as forest bailiff and field foreman." They entitled his testimony "Approximate Account of the Stavenow Subjects' Peacetime Service and Rents." Paired with bailiff Lindt's records, it opens to the mind's eye the following picture of the lordship's villages at the war's end.[58]

Karstädt village

This lay some three kilometers northeast of the manorial seat. According to the 1686 Prignitz District cadastre – a tax register – it was home to eight fullholders and seven lesser cultivators. Six large and four small

---

[57] On the historiography of early Brandenburg-Prussian absolutism, and for a full exposition of the argument advanced here: Hagen, " Crisis," passim.
[58] No. 131, fos. 1–14; cf. no. 705, fos. 22–7, 34.

farms stood under Stavenow, the other five under one or other of three other lordships – illustrating the widespread fragmentation of power over individual villages that centuries of noble land sales and inheritance and marriage settlements wrought. Here Stavenow exercised jurisdiction "high and low," also nominating the pastor. Only over their own subjects did the other lordships sit in judgment.[59]

Stavenow's Karstädt fullholders were obliged, old Strasse said, to "come to the manor at six in the morning on Mondays, Wednesdays, and Fridays with a horse-team, or if horses are not needed, with another person on foot, and stay until they are told they can come in from the fields with the cowherder." Smallholders served the same hours, but sent only one manual laborer for work "with the head."[60] If asked to deliver seigneurial letters, a burden their class bore, they won one day's service remission for every day of walking. Lindt recorded that, apart from weekly labor, fullholders each year worked two days in the manorial vegetable gardens ("in the cabbage" and "pulling rootcrops"), two days at sheep-shearing, and one day at breaking ("swinging") flax, though Strasse thought this hard task earned remission.

Before the war, the village's eleven bigger farmers, for grazing rights on seigneurial land, rendered the Quitzows six plowing and three harvest days, while at Christmas the five "foreign subjects" among them cut two wagonloads of firewood, delivering them to the manorial kitchen. The largeholders drove with their own teams the lordship's grain and other products to urban markets, and fetched goods essential to seigneurial production (even millstones), within eight or nine German (40–5 English) miles. For this they earned remissions. Landlordly demands for heavy haulage stirred resistance. In the 1601 inventory, the Quitzows agreed that "grain transports which the people must perform each year in addition to their manorial service are . . . for compelling reasons assigned no appraised value." This meant almost certainly that the farmers, if not refusing such trips, were receiving some significant seigneurial reward for them.[61]

In the late July and August harvests, when rye, oats, and barley were successively brought in, the farmers each sent a mower and a stacker for one week's work, starting at 7:00 A.M. Each pair's daily quota was one wagonload of grain wheeled into the seigneurial barn. Strasse's

---

[59] Werner Vogel, ed., *Prignitz-Kataster, 1686–1697* (Cologne/Vienna, 1985), 116–17.
[60] Sixteenth- and seventeenth-century smallholders performed services with the "hand," "head," "neck," or "foot." Eighteenth-century Stavenow knew only "hand services."
[61] No. 255, "Dienste."

testimony implies they received manorial food and drink, though rations may not have exceeded the "piece of cheese and bread" which the 1584 register granted an unpaid laborer. In the August hay harvest, fullholders sent wagons with two workers for loading and driving. After reaping the rye, the lordship donated casks of beer, each holding three barrels, to the harvest feast. Strasse thought three casks were shared among the five main service villages. Lindt denied the Karstädters food and drink, but allowed them a cask of beer to themselves: "with that they must be satisfied for the whole harvest."[62]

The Karstädters possessed communal oak woods for grazing pigs and (with seigneurial permission) for cutting lumber. Landed households held softwood parcels for firewood. The lordship decreed that when acorns were plentiful, Premslin village's pastor could fatten two pigs; "otherwise he may send [the swineherd] only one." The village possessed a "fine church" (1675).[63] In 1686, the mayor and two other farmers swore before the taxmen that fullholders' lands were sowable yearly with but 28 bushels, at minimal yields of 1:3 for rye and 1:2 for barley. Their meadows were fair, but pastures and livestock-raising were "bad." They had woodland forage for but one household pig, and no fishery. Despite these unimpressive attributes – whose mediocrity the villagers lamented – all farms except one had been rebuilt and resettled since the war. The cadastral commissioners rated Karstädt in the second of three tax categories.

In 1647, Stavenow's four Karstädt smallholdings and three fullholdings were occupied, though General Wittenberg's soldiers had earlier plundered and burned the village. In resettling devastated and deserted farms, Stavenow officials sought the whereabouts of the families that had last possessed them. But the notaries could find "no heirs" for two of three abandoned fullholdings. Of the third they learned there was "a maidservant still alive who belongs to the farm, who is said to be staying in the Altmark but with no intention of returning here."[64] But of the same farm Lindt wrote two years later that there were "heirs present . . . who are of a mind to occupy" it. Lindt also reported that he had settled a new village mayor, Joachim Nagel, "born in Lower Saxony" or, as Strasse more precisely said, in Holstein. Nagel was one of many immigrant fortune-seekers from relatively unscathed regions into heavily ravaged Brandenburg, where large farms – including mayoral holdings – were easily had.

[62] No. 131, "Dorf Karstedt"; no. 704, fo. 135; no. 43, fos. 50, 73.
[63] No. 131, fo. 4; no. 67, fo. 22.   [64] No. 32, "Carstedte."

Lindt conceded the Karstädters' strong tenurial rights, noting that mayor Nagel, who married one of the farm's heirs, received a "purchase deed" (*Kauff Brieff*) after "old people" appraised the farm buildings and other assets he was acquiring.[65] His only privilege as mayor – Strasse called him "hereditary mayor" – was to gather free of charge seigneurial windfall wood. In return, he led the mowers in the seigneurial harvest, and drove, or had his team driven, first in line in weekly manorial service, during which, Lindt wrote, "he receives nothing, neither food nor drink." About his and the other mayors' village authority the sources, before the next century, are silent. Of Nagel's land, Strasse said he held 2 *Hufen*, each sowable with 18 bushels, "for which he gives House Stavenow 12 bushels of rye yearly, half at Michaelmas [29 September] and half at St. Martin's [11 November]." The lordship further charged his farm with yearly delivery of 6 bushels of rye to the Premslin pastor.

Nagel's fullholding neighbors owed the same heavy burden of 18 bushel grain rents, variously deliverable in 12 bushel payments to the manor and 6 bushel lots to the local clergy, or altogether to Perleberg burghers to whom the Quitzows once mortgaged them for ready cash. The arable-poor smallholders owed labor rents only, except that they, like all other landed householders large and small, rendered the manorhall payments of medieval provenance signifying feudal and jurisdictional subjection: ten eggs at Easter; a fowl at harvest-time; four times yearly a "hunter's bread," "which must be large enough to feed four dogs"; and 1–2 pounds of rough flaxen yarn which the subject households' women spun.[66]

Such were the lordship's fulsome claims on the Karstädters, whose grain rents were heaviest among all those delivered by Stavenow villagers. At the Thirty Years War's end, the farmers here were no more well equipped with horsepower and other livestock than their neighbors elsewhere. Among sixteen fullholders in various villages whose cattle and draft animals Strasse enumerated, each possessed, on average, 2 oxen, 2.33 cows, and 0.67 horses – meager by eighteenth-century standards. Yet a 1650 report pictures the Karstädt farmers rendering services and rents as recorded in Lindt's 1649 *Hausbuch*. If so, this reflected – despite their self-deprecating 1686 testimony – the good quality of

---

[65] No. 43, fo. 46.
[66] No.131, "Dorf Karstedt"; no. 704, fos. 135–6. The 1601 appraisal (no. 255) assigned the tributary payments low Lübeck schilling values: hens – 1.5; breads – 0.5; eggs – 10 per schilling; 1 pound yarn – 1.

their arable and meadows, which in the eighteenth and nineteenth centuries made them the lordship's most prosperous farmers.[67]

Blüthen village

Three kilometers east of Karstädt lay Blüthen, a large village under
Stavenow's jurisdiction and church patronage. Here the 1686 cadastre
registered farms of seventeen fullholders, nine halfholders, and four
smallholders. The arable was good, yielding "the fourth kernel," but
mediocrity of meadow, pasture, and woodland consigned Blüthen to
the second tax category.[68] The village had a pond but, Strasse said, "a
few years ago the Imperial soldiers" – probably hunting for fish and
booty – "drained it."[69] Stavenow's farms numbered seven full- and two
halfholdings, all but one deserted in 1649. Seven other landlords shared
command over the remaining twenty-one. As in all Stavenow's villages,
the large farmers rendered three days of weekly labor with horse-
teams, "but when they are required to serve at Stavenow manor they
may, since this village lies farthest away, arrive one hour later and be
dismissed one hour earlier than the others." For grazing rights on
seigneurial land Blüthen village plowed two extra days annually.[70]

Among Stavenow's subjects, conflict simmered because households
paid grain rents in very unequal measure, ranging from 6 to 24 bushels,
though the fullholder's norm was 12. The 1650 managerial report
observed that "no one can rightly say what the holdings' rents and labor
services are."[71] All owed cash rents on seigneurial meadowland. The
three Stavenow farms entitled to engage in tavernkeeping, one distinguished by Strasse as "the most respectable," each paid an annual
license fee of 1 pound of pepper. As in other Stavenow villages, the
Blütheners, Lindt claimed, owed the lordship annual grain-haulage to
the Elbe, or wherever else it was sold; when the manor needed salt, they
could be sent (laden with grain) to fetch it from Lüneburg, across the
Elbe and beyond Brandenburg's borders, at their own cost in fodder,
food, and drink.

Before the war, the Blüthen pastor had been Hermannus Hoffmann
(or, to Strasse, Magnus Havemann), subsequently promoted to an
Altmark town. The Blüthen living was "very meager," magnifying its
occupant's conflict with a Perleberg church over meadow rights. The
Quitzows, acting from *"guter Affection,"* granted Hoffman three 6-bushel

[67] No. 705, fo. 25.   [68] Vogel, ed., *Prignitz-Kataster*, 123–5.   [69] No. 32, fo. 31.
[70] No. 131, "Dorf Blüthen."   [71] No. 705, fo. 25.

pieces of seigneurial land, asking him to preach on Fridays at Stavenow, when "he was fed." The church, with its gold-plated silver chalice and bell, survived the war. Of seigneurial patronage rights, the 1601 appraisal said that, "since they bring in no payments, and are more of a burden, especially because much effort and care go into the appointment of true and able preachers, [they] are assigned no value."[72] At Stavenow and elsewhere in Brandenburg, the tithe on villagers' land officially vanished with the Roman rite, though in places it persisted as a secularized seigneurial rent. After the Reformation it was the noble landlords' job, working as church patrons with the prince-appointed Lutheran Consistory, to secure – partly still at villagers' cost – the parish clergy's livelihoods.

Glövzin village

This village, 4–5 kilometers east of Stavenow, belonged primarily to Baron Blumenthal, who drew rents from fourteen of seventeen full-holders and four of ten smallholders. The 1686 tax assessors thought "the arable near the village is good, but in the outlying field it is worse." Altogether it yielded the "third kernel," fitting the second tax category. The Glövziners' pasturage and grazing were good, but "they are much burdened by two sheep flocks" Stavenow and another lordship had introduced on deserted farmland, even though in 1649 Lindt recorded an agreement protecting, as he thought, villagers' interests.[73] In 1649, eleven of Stavenow's twenty-one farms stood devastated. Mayor Jacob Schröder was still alive, "but his farm was burnt down a few years ago," forcing him to flee to a nearby lordship. Lindt recruited one new farmer from the Altmark. A ruined household's son agreed to rebuild the family holding. Of a deserted farm with a "good house," Lindt reported, "the sons are living in Hamburg and although they have been summoned several times, they have not presented themselves." Strasse remembered one abandoned holding as "a nice farm."[74]

The Glövzin fullholders' money and grain rents, like the Blütheners', bore traces of old, obscure inequalities. The smallholders – whose land, Strasse said, was good – yearly rendered the manor, apart from usual minor feudal dues, 4 bushels of barley, their class's tribute grain, as well as 7–11 tribute hens. The village housed both a smith and a tailor, who inhabited a cottage the lordship endowed with land sowable with 6 bushels. The

---

[72] No. 255, "Stavenow," pt. XI.   [73] Vogel, ed., *Prignitz-Kataster*, 115–16.   [74] No. 43, fo. 72.

tailor performed one day's harvest work and "at the manor made old and new clothes for the lordship and all the servants, receiving meals when he did so. For new clothes he was paid. For mending the old ones he held a Löcknitz meadow yielding two wagonloads of hay." His feudal dues were five eggs and two loaves.[75] Glövzin's church retained its "good-sounding bells," while its altar, pulpit, and pews were still intact.[76]

In Glövzin lived Stefan Strasse himself, farming one hide. "He reports that, so long as he held the field foreman's office, the Quitzows freed him from rent, but that when he retired, he should serve one day weekly with the neck. In the rye harvest, however, when the free (*freye*) and the unfree (*unfreye*) mowed, he should help one day with mowing."[77] This passage contains the Stavenow archive's only generalized reference to lack of freedom among the villagers. Whether or not its author – probably the estate manager's sub-bailiff and clerk (*Schreiber*) – quoted Strasse accurately cannot be known. His text might seem to say, harshly, that villagers liable to ordinary manorial service were unfree persons. But since such legally free individuals under seigneurial jurisdiction as millers, blacksmiths, brewers, and shepherds never needed to work in manorial harvests, freedom here must refer to exemption, whether purchased or freely conferred, from weekly service, though not from the lordship's harvest.

Premslin village

Adjacent to Glövzin, across a water-course widening into a millpond, lay Premslin, another settlement under Stavenow's jurisdiction. Here lived twenty-four fullholders (nineteen serving Stavenow) and three smallholders (two serving the pastor, one serving Stavenow). The 1686 cadastral commissioners found its arable good, in the second tax category. Observing fine distinctions of agrarian measurement, they reckoned that from each rye-bushel sown the Premsliners harvested threescore sheaves (*3 Steige*), and from each barley-bushel forty-eight sheaves (3 *Mandeln*). From each score of rye-sheaves they threshed out 1 bushel of grain and, from each *Mandel* of barley, 0.75 bushel. In average yields, "this amounts for rye to the third kernel." The village had "bad meadows," the fullholders harvesting two to three farmer's wagonloads (smaller than seigneurial wagonloads) of hay and the few

---

[75] No. 131, "Dorf Glovetzin."   [76] No. 67, fo. 22.   [77] No. 131, "Dorf Glovetzin."

smallholders none at all. "Pasturage, grazing, and livestock-raising are good . . . No forage for pigs or fishery. Necessary firewood."[78]

Before the war, Strasse recalled, fullholders served "with teams three days weekly throughout the year, plowing, manuring, and hauling wood, grain, and whatever else was needed, and receiving neither food nor drink."[79] The villagers labored heavily cultivating Stavenow's Premslin manor-farm, accounting, seemingly, for low rents here in cash and kind. But, in 1647, only seven of the lordship's farms were settled. The smithy had been raided and plundered for firewood. "The same wanton ruin," Lindt wrote, "occurred to all other farmsteads."[80] Some farmers or heirs were living in still-intact rooms or barns, but others had died, vanished, or moved away, like the Völsch family, to "a foreign land, but no one knows where."[81]

There was here a fullholding ("Kopman's deserted farm") that had lain uncultivated since before the war. Strasse reported that, "after the lordship for many years received nothing from this holding, it brought a piece of arable under the plow, sowable with 2 bushels, called '*das Weitlandt.*'" This is a rare reference to seigneurial enclosure of village farmland, whose legality sixteenth-century edicts limited. Lindt described this as conversion into "lordship's land." Except for Lütke von Quitzow's rounding out of his Premslin manor-farm by purchasing additional land, Stavenow emerged from the fifteenth century with land enough, from preexisting seigneurial reserves and the entirely deserted villages it appropriated, to spare it the temptation later to seize village land for enclosure. This harmonizes with recent judgments downplaying enclosures in the sixteenth-century emergence of commercialized manorialism.[82]

Lütke von Quitzow acquired, through negotiations with the government, *jus patronatis* over Premslin's church, previously exercised by Stepenitz monastery, which was disbanded at the Reformation. His contentious son Albrecht repulsed claims to co-patronage of the von Karstedt family at nearby Kaltenhof lordship, who also commanded some Premslin farmers. The Stavenow Quitzows were buried in this church, where a stone tablet commemorated them on a separate family altar. The family's servants lay buried in Glövzin cemetery. In 1550 Lütke spent 100 gulden to raise the Premslin church tower and install three bells. Although the war damaged the church's interior, its "beautiful"

---

[78] Vogel, ed., *Prignitz-Kataster*, 114.   [79] No. 43, fo. 66.   [80] Ibid., fo. 70.   [81] No. 32, fo. 29.
[82] No. 131, "Dorf Premslin." Cf. no. 43, fo. 68. On pre-Thirty Years War enclosures: Hagen, "How Mighty," 108, 113; Hagen, "Crisis," 311; Enders, *Uckermark*, 171ff.

building and bells survived, as did a carved and painted wooden baptismal font.[83]

The Premslin pastor, whom the well-educated Lindt called the preacher and the unlettered Strasse the priest, was born in nearby Perleberg. The year 1649 was his forty-fifth in office. Attached to his parsonage were 2 hides, whose tillage before the Reformation the priest had undertaken with his own horses. Thereafter Lütke von Quitzow assigned two "parish smallholders" to cultivate them with their teams during once-weekly service.[84] Lütke also reduced Glövzin's and Karstädt's churches to Premslin filials, assigning for all three ministries' support over 100 bushels of yearly grain rents, along with lesser dues, payable by various villagers to the Premslin parsonage.

In the three villages, the Premslin pastor "enjoyed all clerical incomes, such as those from congregational offerings, baptisms, weddings, burials, sausages [and] eggs." In return he was obliged on Sundays to preach an early Karstädt sermon, followed by another at the eight o'clock Premslin service. He also preached four times yearly at Glövzin, and each Wednesday at Stavenow manor-hall, though in a gesture of "good-will" the lordship forbore from summoning him during sowing and harvesting seasons, when he needed to manage his own household economy. The lordship gave him yearly provisions of eggs, two sausages, a wagonload of hay, 12 bushels of rye (and another half-bushel for his sexton), a sheep, and "a dry tree for firewood."[85] Because he "complained greatly of walking" from one chapel to the other, the lordship granted him, as horse fodder, a further yearly wagonload of hay and 6 bushels of oats. Assisting him was the sexton, who lived from 6 bushels of sowings on Glövzin churchland, and from rye-tribute of one-half bushel each from Premslin fullholders and one-quarter bushel from smallholders. Among other duties, the sexton read and sang at religious services, acted as schoolmaster, and – during seigneurial hunts – joined the village smith "to help clear the ground and stretch out the nets."[86]

Near the pastor's and the sexton's houses stood a cottage built and occupied long before the war by the seigneurial court bailiff and jailor (*Vogt*) Otto Strasse. Later the lordship assigned it for life to the Premslin pastor's widow (the parsonage going to a new pastor's family). It was later rebuilt and occupied by another Stavenow sub-bailiff, Philipp Strasse, "whom his lordships the Junkers honored by granting it, along

---

[83] No. 32, fo. 28; no. 43, fo. 57.   [84] No. 131, "Dorf Premslin."
[85] No. 43, fo. 59; no. 131, "Rittersitz Premslin."   [86] No. 131, "Dorf Premslin."

with garden and meadow, in hereditary possession, because of his long and true service." Philipp's widow then wed Jürgen Gerloff, who until 1647 served – at the same time as Stefan Strasse – as a manorial official, renting the cottage from the lordship. Now Gerloff wanted release from Stavenow's jurisdiction to settle under the Eldenburg Quitzows, where-upon the lordship "not unjustly" took back the cottage, reserving it for a "much needed" new blacksmith.[87]

Local springs fed the pond dammed by the Premslin grist-mill, one of Stavenow's more profitable appurtenances. As was customary in Brandenburg, it was leased hereditarily to professional millers for a sub-stantial cash deposit and annual rents. Lindt wrote that the Premslin mill exercised monopoly rights within a radius of two German (ten English) miles. All Premslin, Glövzin, and Karstädt villagers were obliged to patronize it, or suffer fines and the confiscation of grain milled elsewhere. In 1648 Blumenthal financed the repair of war dam-age to the mill and the miller's house, which the proprietor and his pre-decessor's widow now occupied. There was, nearby, a windmill, which Lütke erected in 1542 with princely consent. Although millstones and ironworks survived, the need never arose after 1648 to refurbish it.

Before the war, the miller's yearly payments to Stavenow were 10 tons of rye, with a substantial capitalized value of 1,800 gulden. But in 1650 the mill's grain rent had fallen to 5 tons. Previously the miller also fat-tened four seigneurial pigs, and delivered the lordship quantities of eggs, geese, and chickens, although "because of the fish in the pond he may keep no ducks whatever." The 1584 inventory observed of him and his counterpart in Mesekow village that "they must repair the bridges, gate, and doors [at Stavenow manor-hall], for which they receive no pay apart from food and drink."[88]

His lease granted the Premslin miller seigneurial land for 8 bushels' sowings, meadow and pasture for four cows, and the right to drive twelve pigs into the woods, two of them, "for the mill grease," free of charge. The previous miller's widow's demand that the lordship pay her 20 talers for a millstone her husband had bought shows that the manor was responsible for the mill's good condition. The 1601 appraisal remarked that "every year a considerable sum goes for stone cutting and iron." Millers lived mostly from fees they charged their captive customers.[89]

---

[87] No. 32, fo. 30.   [88] No. 705, fo. 129; no. 131, "Rittersitz Premslin"; no. 67, fo. 18.
[89] No. 32, fo. 27; no. 43, fo. 63; no. 705, fo. 22; no. 259, "Stavenow," pt. V. Werner Peschke, *Das Mühlenwesen der Mark Brandenburg. Von den Anfängen der Mark bis um 1600* (Berlin, 1937).

The 1686 cadastral commissioners added these notes on Premslin, which reveal both the princely regime's interest in the unresettled, tax-liable farms and the uses to which they were put:

One lodger, Jochim Gühle, living on the deserted smallholder's farmstead. A deserted smithy . . . No tavern . . . A cowherd, who also herds sheep. A swineherd. Among deserted fullholders' farms, Herr von Blumenthal uses Oden's, Tuhrmann's and Kaufmann's for the dairy farm he runs in this village. Teves's, Thom's, Meyer's, Sandberg's and Backuhl's farms are rented out to village farmers. The preacher Johann Wilhelm uses Hans Hecht's farm, half in place of incidental income and for the other half he pays Stavenow cash. Widow von Winterfeldt uses Hermann's farm to provision her knightly estate at Kaltenhof.[90]

Such official scrutiny reduced the likelihood that Stavenow or Kaltenhof lordship would permanently appropriate abandoned taxable farms, though historians long supposed such noble enclosure common after 1648.

Mesekow village

This settlement lay three kilometers south of Stavenow, on the Löcknitz stream. Unlike the lordship's other villages, it housed only smallholders, each farming – according to the 1686 cadastre – somewhat less than 1 hide of sandy arable. Pasturage they rented from neighbors. Their communal woodland sufficed for fuel, but not for swine forage. They could each harvest five cartloads of hay from their meadowland, and had "some fishing in the Löcknitz." These meager resources placed them in the third tax category.

Lindt noted that prewar tax rolls listed Mesekowers as "*Fischer Cossaten*," suggesting origins as early medieval fishermen. In "good times of peace," Strasse complacently reported, "they had to serve with the hand as often as they were told." By this account, they stood alone among Stavenow's subjects in liability to unlimited labor demands. Lindt wrote that their manorial service "was only used in gardening, digging . . . baking, brewing, flax-work and similar women's work [*Weiberarbeit*]," although men mowed in the seigneurial rye and hay harvests.[91] Still, the 1601 appraisal rated their labors higher than usual, saying that "although they only serve with the neck, they must work more than other smallholders."[92] In 1647 only two farms were cultivated by

[90] Vogel, *Prignitz-Kataster*, 114.   [91] No. 131, "Dorf Mesekow"; no. 43, fo. 79.
[92] No. 255, "Stavenow," pt. IV.

proprietors, although four other cultivators' widows were on hand. The mayor was, "thank God, in tolerable condition," although "he will not admit to owing any grain rent," despite prewar 6-bushel levies from each farm. Already by 1649, probably because such smallholdings required fewer draft animals than larger farms, all eight households were resettled, one by a wheelwright from distant Holstein.[93]

Mesekow also housed a Löcknitz-driven grist-mill. Though ruined in the war, its value, capitalized in 1601 at 2,600 gulden, occasioned a rapid reconstruction, even if postwar grain rent stood, at 5 tons, well below the prewar 14 tons. Although the lordship gave the Mesekow miller a small piece of arable, his "entire income and provisions" derived from "the fifth bushel" which Lindt thought he was authorized to charge his customers – lordship excepted – though in the eighteenth century the miller's fee was but every sixteenth measure, or cash equivalent.[94] Mesekow's pastor preached on Sundays at Stavenow "and also performs his office there in both sacraments." The parsonage possessed some arable and meadow, but the lordship supplemented its income with a ton of rye from the local mill and 5 percent interest on 200 gulden that Lütke donated in his 1564 testament. The pastor claimed rents from Eldenburg's Quitzows, but collecting them "had been hard for him" and "even in good times he had many complaints." The church had a "little bell" and, still in Perleberg safekeeping, a gold-plated silver chalice.[95]

Garlin and Sargleben villages

Karstädt, Blüthen, Glövzin, Premslin, and Mesekow were Stavenow's most valuable service villages, but in two others it commanded some additional farmers. These were Sargleben and Garlin, neighboring settlements lying 5–6 kilometers northwest of the manorial headquarters on the Löcknitz's far side. Garlin was a complex and resource-favored settlement, encompassing in 1686 the holdings, subject variously to five lordships, of eleven fullholders, seven halfholders, six smallholders with arable, and twelve cottagers without. Its soil and other attributes placed it in the highest tax category. Its arable yielded the fourth kernel, its meadows produced eight hay cartloads for each of two mayors and five each for other farmers. Pasturage was good, and woodland forage fattened three pigs for each landed household. Two fullholdings formerly

---

[93] No. 32, fo. 25; no. 705, fo. 27.   [94] No. 43, fo. 76; no. 131, "Dorf Mesekow"; no. 705, fo. 27.
[95] No. 43, fos. 74–5; no. 67, fo. 16.

kept taverns, but they gave up, "because it doesn't pay." Instead, the villagers bought beer in the distant town of Putlitz, a settlement lacking urban liberties under the lordship of the prestigious lineage of the Gans Edlen Herren zu Putlitz.[96]

In 1686 there was a knightly manor in Garlin, given by the family von Mundt to their son-in-law von Karstedt, with land in the village and on a nearby deserted village's fields, "which is," the cadastral officials skeptically wrote, "supposedly tax-free land." The "priest" cultivated 2 hides, while the church possessed a 2-bushel plot whose proceeds accrued to the village commune. In 1686 a villager cultivated one of seven deserted largeholdings, but the remaining unoccupied farms local nobleman von Karstedt had mostly appropriated. He appears to have made the one attempt near Stavenow to enlarge – or create anew – a noble estate by the enclosure of deserted village land. Karstedt maintained here a dairy-farm, "about which it is not known whether it is [non-taxable] fief land or [taxable] village land." He also cultivated a deserted halfholding, "half of which the [Karstedt] overlordship is thought to have engrossed long ago." The manor also incorporated a fullholding and eight cottagers' farms. On one farm Karstedt "had a house with two dwellings built for his threshers," on another he had a sheep-farm, and yet another he rented out for 7 talers yearly.

The Stavenow manor drew Garlin rents from the blacksmith, two fullholders, a landless cottager, and the only "free mayor" (*Frey Schultze*) it could boast of. Also known as "enfeoffed" or "court-holding mayors," these were privileged commoners occupying big farms – in Garlin, up to 3.5 hides – originally laid out as the properties of non-noble entrepreneurs who directed medieval colonization at local level (*Lokatoren*), and who settled in the new communities as judicial and administrative chiefs. Since the late middle ages the Brandenburg nobility had, in a still ill-researched process, engrossed into their demesne land many free mayors' farms. Apart from hankering after mayoral land, landlords doubtless sought to undermine these village courts, which were originally independent of knightly manors. Even where free mayors did not disappear, the trend was towards their judicial eclipse by seigneurial courts and, in police and administrative affairs, by ordinary farmers the manor appointed as mayors to maintain village order, both by enforcing seigneurial directives and upholding customary law. Remaining free mayors survived as a small number

---

[96] Vogel, *Prignitz-Kataster*, 308.

of juridically unconstrained yeoman farmers, buying and selling their farms under noble supervision.

In Garlin, there were, oddly, two free mayors, subject to different lordships. In 1649 Stavenow's was a certain Joachim Kratz, whose rights to adjudicate village affairs "in case something happens there" it championed, though with doubtful effect, against the ordinary mayor appointed by a rival manor. Of Kratz's duties, Lindt wrote that "according to old people's reports, [he] was obliged to keep a horse year in and year out for use as required by House Stavenow. But it supposedly frequently happened that Stavenow servants wore the horse out or even rode it to death, so that [Kratz's] father complained." Old Kratz's proposal prevailed that, instead of keeping the horse, he would perform short and long hauls, with two or four horses. When he or his servants were away, "on the first night he must himself provide the food and fodder, but thereafter they must be given to him."[97] Lindt reported of Stavenow's two other Garlin farmers that "because the Löcknitz often runs fast and high," they frequently missed service. So the lordship transferred to them seigneurial transports previously weighing on Blüthen's three tavernkeepers, while these shouldered the Garliners' fieldwork. "But in this matter the overlordship is free at any time to alter its disposition."[98]

Nearby Sargleben was a poor village, with two arable fields, one for largeholders and one for halfholders. The landed cottagers cultivated a long-deserted village's fields. Sargleben possessed middling forage for one or two pigs per farm. "They have a great deal of overgrown land, which is sandy and no good." Some deserted holdings yielded 8 talers' yearly rent, roughly the annual direct tax owing from 1 hide. The taxmen assigned Sargleben to the third category. While five lordships shared command over twenty-seven farms (including seventeen cottage-holdings), none held demesne land there. Stavenow's subjects were six mini-smallholders, with no arable "but only meadows and gardens behind their houses." Before the war they served three days "with the hand." It was, probably, to gain such labors that Stavenow gave them cereal and pasture land on deserted Dargardt village's fields. For this they paid grain rent, as was customary, equal to the amount – here, 6 bushels – of annual sowings. In 1649, these holdings were mostly devastated and abandoned. Joachim Könne, who was in "bad shape," occupied one. He served one day and "admitted to no rents in cash or

[97] No. 43, fos. 32–3.   [98] No. 43, fo. 34; no. 32, fo. 37.

kind." Hans Schulze, speaking of Blumenthal and his estate managers, "claims that because he was His Most Worthy Grace's carriage-driver, they did him the favor of putting him on labor-service commutation payments [*Dienstgeld*] for the rest of his life" so that, instead of actually working, he paid 5 talers yearly.[99]

Such village portraits conjure up this rural society's diversity, as well as the heavy blows the great war rained on it. Though governed by noble lordships and princely officials, the villages' usages, including rents, were not arbitrarily changeable. While some villages and individual farms were ill-endowed, others were capable of good yields by local standards and worth defending against overweening demands.

LANDLESS VILLAGERS AND MANORIAL WORKERS

The pauperization that sixteenth-century population growth and social inequality inflicted on the lower orders in western and southern Europe and adjoining German lands is only faintly discernible in Brandenburg. This is perhaps because of patchy sources and lack of research. Still, two of the strongest demographic accelerators at work west of the Elbe operated only feebly farther east. These were, first, partible tenures within a system of commercialized agriculture and, second, robust urbanization, resulting from burgeoning industry and trade, and from bureaucratization and militarization accompanying early modern state-building.

In Brandenburg and elsewhere in east-Elbian Europe, a symbiosis emerged in the sixteenth century between large landed estates – whether owned by nobility, territorial princes or, in Catholic and Orthodox lands, the church – and villagers' farms. The estates' very existence limited available land, while fullholders' farms, if they were to yield human and animal muscle for unpaid labor services, needed to remain, by western standards, comparatively large, and so also impartible among heirs. The margin within the village for new families' settlement was narrower than it would have been had no obstacles to farm fragmentation existed. Although commercialized manorialism could coexist with different forms of aristocratic and princely power, ranging from Polish gentry republicanism to Brandenburg-Prussian noble-princely co-sovereignty, to Muscovite autocracy, it neither released enough surplus labor to the towns, nor built up sufficient purchasing

---

[99] Vogel, *Prignitz-Kataster*, 305; no. 43, fos. 35–6; no. 705, fo. 24.

Table 1.2   *Census of the Brandenburg Middle Mark's village*
householders, 1624

Category	Number	%	Average number per village[a]
Fullholders (*Bauern*)	7,563	44.8	10.3
Smallholders (*Kossäten*)[b]	5,347	31.7	7.3
Cottagers (*Hausleute*)[c]	787	4.7	1.1
Shepherds, other livestock herders, housed farmhands	1,917	11.4	2.6
Millers, smiths, fishermen[d]	1,269	7.4	1.7
Total	16,883	100.0	23.0

[a] Among 734 villages: 689 farming villages, 35 fishing villages.
[b] 5,259 "full smallholders" (*ganze Kossäten*), 88 "half smallholders" (*halbe Kossäten*).
[c] The entries entitled "*Paar Hausleute*" and "*Einzelne Hausmänner*" lack definition, but must refer to taxable independent householders without arable land, such as Stavenow's various cottagers. Cf. Hagen, "Seventeenth-Century Crisis in Brandenburg," 312.
[d] 171 millers, 477 smiths, 612 fishermen (also 9 linen-weavers and tailors).
Source: Friedrich Grossmann, *Über die gutsherrlich-bäuerlichen Rechtsverhältnisse in der Mark Brandenburg vom 16. bis 18. Jahrhundert* (Leipzig, 1890), 138.

power in the villages, to stimulate urban development on a western European scale. Towns grew on the strength of local industry and trade, and as governmental centers, but only modestly. In Brandenburg, the capital, then called Berlin-Cölln, numbered but some 10,000 in 1618.[100]

A picture of prewar rural Brandenburg emerges from the 1624 tax census of Middle Mark villages, encompassing most of the electorate (see table 1.2). Since it counted only independent householders, the many servants, rent-paying lodgers living on farmsteads, and itinerant poor are indiscernible. Though its exactitude is doubtful, the numbers of large and small farmers are probably fairly accurate, since the main direct taxes fell on their lands.

The smallholders' high numbers show that, after sixteenth-century population growth brought back into cultivation (after late-medieval village desertions) nearly all available land reserved for fullholders, expansion followed of smallholdings toward the limits of village size and soil fertility. But most smallholdings, like Stavenow's, still possessed fair amounts of land. The cottagers' sparse numbers suggest that

[100] Wolfgang Ribbe, ed., *Geschichte Berlins*, 2 vols. (Munich, 1987), vol. I, 344; Duplessis, *Transitions*; Hagen, "Capitalism."

seigneurial authorities were not yielding to pressure to settle their farmers' non-inheriting children, or other landless people, on mini-properties. Doubtless many farmers' non-inheriting offspring married into full-holdings or among the smallholders.[101]

Apart from inheriting or marrying into a farm, or arduously resettling a deserted one, there were few other paths, following villagers' early years of servant status, to married householder's rank. Most insecure among the landless were lodgers, renting quarters from landed households and living by day labor. Whether married, single, or widowed, many were impecunious, especially the elderly and those with children. Whatever useful purposes they fulfilled, seigneurial authorities did not like them. The system of labor rents aimed to minimize need for wage labor, while lodgers' presence within landlords' jurisdictions threatened poor-relief expenditures. In their 1601 settlement the Quitzows harshly declared "the fellows who live in the farmers' outbuildings are assigned no value, but instead ways should be sought to clear them out of the villages."[102] This was, seemingly, wishful thinking, for in 1649 Strasse testified that "the lodgers have been obliged since olden times to work one day weekly at the manor and in the rye harvest to do daily raking, for which they are given food and drink."[103]

While lodgers lived hand to mouth, farm servants – if they were personally free agents – worked on yearly contracts. They labored at manor-farms (married or unmarried, depending on age and position), or as resident unmarried farmhands for landed villagers. Landlords could recruit fullholders' sons and daughters as compulsory servants for several years at least – the obligatory eighteenth-century term was three – after which they might remain as freely engaged workers. Before the seventeenth century's end Stavenow records are silent on servants and laborers, except for a wage-register included in the 1584 inventory, one of the earliest such accounts surviving from Brandenburg lands. It describes a scene unlikely to have changed much before war engulfed the Electorate, unless a few more workers were recruited.[104]

The 1584 wage-roll listed twenty-seven positions, excluding lettered officials such as estate managers and sub-bailiffs and the Quitzows' domestic servants. Of jobs registered, sixteen were men's, eleven

---

[101] The 1624 cataster registered only thirty-six fullholders' farms, and forty smallholdings, as unoccupied or abandoned. Another 7 percent of all taxable village farmland had been enclosed into seigneurial estates, mostly since about 1575.
[102] No. 255, "Stavenow," pt. IV.   [103] No. 131, "Einliggere."
[104] Inventory of 1584 (note 38 above).

women's. At Stavenow manor lived the seigneurial fisherman, with the highest yearly pay (18 gulden, boots worth 1 taler, shoes worth 20 schillings). Next were two field foremen and a wood bailiff, each receiving 14.3 gulden and fisherman's footwear. These men, the Strasses' and Gerloffs' precursors, were probably all married. Then came two head plowmen-mechanics and another bearing this title also serving as gate-keeper. Each earned 5 gulden yearly and two pair of shoes, worth 12 schillings, the value also of other lesser workers' shoes. The cowherd and swineherd both worked with "lads" (*Jungen*), though the "goose and calf herder" worked alone. They earned 3 gulden and two pairs of shoes, but the boys earned shoes and nothing more.[105] Among women, there were cook and dairy-mistress, both earning 3 gulden, though only the latter received footwear (three pairs of shoes). They supervised three female farm servants, each earning 2.66 gulden and two pairs of shoes. The dairy-mistress received a quarter-bushel's harvest of seigneurial flaxseed, but was responsible for her own bedding. The other women each received cloth rations of 40 ells of various linens.

At Premslin and Semlin manor-farms were two dairy-mistresses and four female workers, paid like their Stavenow counterparts, and two cowherds, whose wages were, at 5 gulden, higher than at Stavenow (and who also received linen cloth for two shirts each). The two shepherds earned no money wages but instead exercised the right, customary in their calling, of maintaining together with the seigneurial flock their own sheep and lambs. Apart from the shepherds, these manorial employees (*Hoffvolck*) each received yearly bread rations amounting to 9 bushels of rye, or about 1 kilogram daily. As we shall see, this corresponded roughly to the daily adult consumption that eighteenth-century government officials and economic writers recommended.[106]

The rye flour was delivered, along with other food, to the two demesne farms, where the dairy-mistresses managed baking and cooking. Apart from rye, each farm received 8 bushels of oats "for groats"; 1 bushel each of barley, buckwheat, and peas; three-eighths of a barrel of butter; 480 cheeses; 240 herring; 16 pounds of dried fish; two fattened pigs; one slaughtered cow; two sheep and two lambs; and "also at each farm a small quarter-barrel of beer given the dairy-mistress every four weeks." Each manor-farm had milk-cows and vegetable and fruit gardens. The shepherds, who often lived in encampments, received separate cereal rations and salt for cheese-making.

[105] Ulrich Bentzien, "Der Häker," *DJV* 11 (1965): 16–34.
[106] On nutritional standards Hagen: "Working," 148, and ch. 4, below.

At Stavenow headquarters, a more old-fashioned system prevailed. The cowherd and swineherd, and one or more of the plowmen, possessed separate provisions and the right to graze their own animals for meat and dairy products. The 1584 register offers no details on the fisherman's and field foremen's households. In 1649, Strasse reported that, when forest forage was good, the estate manager – with subordinates to feed – could fatten eight pigs, the head foreman four, the sub-foreman two and the wood bailiff one. The 1584 register said only, of "the Stavenow workers," that "they are given weekly fare, namely for each person weekly four loaves, one pound of butter and one of bacon, and seven cheeses." Other food "they fetch from the manor-house." The dairy-mistress also received a monthly beer ration. In place of this apparently cumbersome system "it is thought better to issue rations as at the other demesne farms."

Though money wages were low, manorial servants' food provisions do not look inadequate. Though it is unclear how many of them were compulsorily recruited, these probably included the unmarried female servants and young men, while the adult majority with developed skills worked voluntarily, even if on the lordship's terms (buttressed by princely statutes limiting wages to landlordly advantage). Their cash earnings were correspondingly low or derisory, but they received other necessities – including some clothing – in natural income or allocations.

Their diet, though heavy in cereals and starches, contained meat and fish in more than negligible quantities. This was true also of such laborers as those employed by waterworks contractor Phillipus Hase, who in 1560 built moats and ditches at Stavenow. For this he received 310 gulden (233 talers) in cash, and provisions for himself and his men of "one barrel of butter, one and a half barrels of cheese, 36 bushels of rye, 1 bushel of salt, twenty barrels of beer, 4 bushels of peas, four sheep, 3 bushels of buckwheat, 1 bushel of wheat, two fattened pigs, eight sides of bacon, one old cow, his thin beer, [and] 12 bushels of carrots and turnips." It struck Lindt in 1649 that "this contract was much higher" than the one he had negotiated to rebuild the Stavenow bridges and moats: 280 talers (370 gulden), 2 tons of rye and one each of peas and barley.[107]

Seigneurial workers' well-being cannot be reduced to diet or other recompense. Not before the eighteenth century do Stavenow records

[107] No. 43, fos. 22–3.

open windows into their individual and familial lives. Yet it is evident that, before the Thirty Years War, the Quitzows invested considerably, however grudgingly, in a paternalist labor regime that did not skimp on food.

CONCLUSION

In fundamental ways, Stavenow lordship was a microcosm of rural Brandenburg and east Elbia. Although there were noble jurisdictions before 1618 that imposed heavier or lighter seigneurial dues and services, the three-day norm of weekly labor rendered by full- and halfholdings such as Stavenow's probably reflected a pattern more prevalent than others.[108] If the Quitzows' boundaries were farther flung than many lesser squires', and their incomes richer, there were also grander lineages and properties.[109] Similarly, both in its economic ascent under propitious sixteenth-century skies and its decline amid seventeenth-century storms, Stavenow's manors and villages shared the larger society's fortunes. The Thirty Years War cut the lordship's market value in half. The number of its farmers declined about equally, while survivors' holdings in fixed capital and livestock were much inferior to their peacetime predecessors'. Such losses were probably characteristic, on average, of the whole land.

Despite sixteenth-century statutes tightening village farmers' subjection to manorial authority, noble landlordism at Stavenow, as in most other parts of Brandenburg, possessed features in common with aristocratic seigneurialism in western and Mediterranean Europe. Although, compared to his English and French counterparts, the Brandenburg village farmer's personal liberty was restricted, his landholding's size and the hereditary tenure he normally possessed placed him above many a smaller and more precariously situated western and southern European farmer.

[108] Cf. bibliography, section on local and regional studies. On the Brandenburg Electors' princely demesne farms (crown estates) and subject villagers: Kurt Breysig, *Geschichte der brandenburgischen Finanzen in der Zeit von 1640 bis 1697: Darstellung und Akten: Erster Band* (Leipzig, 1895). Cf. Friedrich Mager, *Geschichte des Bauerntums und der Bodenkultur im Lande Mecklenburg* (Berlin, 1955); Gustav Aubin, *Zur Geschichte des gutsherrlich-bäuerlichen Verhältnisses in Ostpreussen von der Gründung des Ordenstaates bis zur Steinschen Reform* (Leipzig, 1910).

[109] On magnatial holdings: Harnisch, *Herrschaft Boitzenburg*; Peter-Michael Hahn, *Fürstliche Territorialhoheit und lokale Adelsgewalt: Die herrschaftliche Durchdringung des ländlichen Raumes zwischen Elbe und Aller (1300–1700)*, (Berlin, 1989); Werner von Kiekebusch, "*Geschichte des Klosters Heiligengrabe seit der Reformation*" (unpub. ms., 1949, in GStAPK, Provinz Brandenburg, Rep. 16, no. 16).

Much reflection has centered on the gulf that opened between western Europe, on one side, and central and eastern Europe, on the other, as a result of commercialized manorialism's post-medieval emergence in the east-Elbian lands. Like many other Brandenburg landlords, the Stavenow Quitzows shipped their grain westward, on ships plying the nearby Elbe, when prewar harvests were good enough to persuade the princely regime to open the land to exports. Such noble enterprise heavily exploited villagers' labor and material resources. But everywhere in Europe the burden of seigneurial rent bent villagers' backs. Precisely how the common people fared under differing political and legal conditions is a question awaiting comparative research on costs and returns of village farming under noble landlordship in eastern, central, and western Europe.[110]

For the Quitzows to establish themselves as profit-making, if not profit-maximizing, masters of large-scale, commercialized production, it sufficed to modify inherited medieval structures. Above all, seigneurial rent needed to be renegotiated to assure the manor-hall the unpaid labor it sought without provoking communal revolts or the massive flight of individual householders. The evidence does not suggest that legislative restrictions on villagers' freedom of movement played a crucial part. From this vantage-point, the distance separating the Brandenburg Junker from the English landlord is perhaps not more remarkable than their proximity. In the sixteenth century, both turned their old-established seigneurial powers to the purposes of commercialized agriculture. But if the advantages they reaped are clear, the costs their divergent methods imposed upon dependent villagers are harder to assess.[111]

Still-influential views hold that the Junkers degraded their subjects into mute and miserable servility. Before rejecting this judgment, it must be conceded that the Stavenow papers from the sixteenth and seventeenth centuries offer no coherent alternative to a seigneurial perspective. Undoubtedly this view screens out those coercive strategies, whether ideological or physical, upon which social and political domination in part depends. The maintenance of inequality entails, variously, violence both

---

[110] On pre-1618 agricultural exports: Hagen, "Crisis," 307–11. Cf. Walter Naudé, *Die Getreidehandelspolitik und Kriegsmagazinverwaltung Brandenburg-Preußens bis 1740, Acta Borussica, Getreidehandelspolitik*, vol. II (Berlin, 1901); Hugo Rachel, *Die Handels-, Zoll- und Akzisepolitik Brandenburg-Preussens bis 1713, Acta Borussica, Handels-, Zoll- und Akzisepolitik*, vol. I (Berlin, 1911). Cf. Scott, *Peasantries*; Antoni Mączak et al., *East-Central Europe in Transition: From the Fourteenth to the Seventeenth Century* (London, 1985); Chirot, ed., *The Origins of Backwardness in Eastern Europe*; and North, "Entstehung der Gutswirtschaft."

[111] Dewald, *The European Nobility*, passim.

gentle and harsh. But except in extreme cases of individual or collective protest and ensuing repression, the coercion on which noble land-lordism rested, in Brandenburg as elsewhere in Europe, was unlikely to leave many traces in seigneurial records, if only because its everyday applications seemed self-evidently right and necessary.

Such considerations are important, because Stavenow documents offer only the thinnest of evidence, before the eighteenth century, of seri-ous manor–village friction, and then only temporarily or sporadically – and without mention of violence – under Lütke von Quitzow's regime in the 1530s and 1540s.[112] In 1594 Dietrich von Quitzow at nearby Kletzke estate, preparing a lawsuit claiming his uncle Lütke at Stavenow had wrongly inherited more than his brothers, including Dietrich's father, wrote of an agreement of 1515 apportioning labor services among themselves:

The old people report that the farmers who served at the Stavenow manor in those days usually paired up, two to a team. That is why Lütke got so many more farmers and labor services. The same old people know very well whether the services were left as they had been. They say they had to work the whole week through at the manor, and deliver letters and make transports on Sunday.

Whether, as Dietrich believed, Stavenow labor services were lighter in 1515 than at other Quitzow manors is unverifiable. But if the old-timers' words Dietrich reported were true, Lütke confronted his new subjects with the demand for unlimited labor, for which the phrase "six days at the manor, letters on Sunday" was embittered code.[113]

After the mid-sixteenth century the three-day labor service regime prevailed. No other Stavenow documents suggest rising manor–village tension before the Thirty Years War. Nor do the numerous and voluble 1647–50 records support the widespread view that seigneurial authorities, in the war's aftermath, sought to reassemble their village workforces by coercive force. This does not show that manor–village relations were suffused, as conservatives once imagined, with feudal patriarchalism or defined, as economic historians are tempted to suppose, by a contrac-tualism as advantageous to both parties as the balance of scarce resources permitted. Presumably Stavenow's masters acted the role of their subjects' benevolent patrons as often as self-interest allowed. The villagers doubtless sought ways to minimize manorial burdens. Neither tactic blocked the intrusion of seigneurial violence onto the scene. Its occurrence may have gone unrecorded.

---

[112] Hagen, "How Mighty," 101ff.   [113] No. 707, fo. 14.

Still, invocation of physical coercion in any severe measure (despite its occurrence in some known cases) is unnecessary to account for the form the landlord–village relationship assumed by the Thirty Years War's eve. Unpaid weekly labor services were, however deeply hated, a sixteenth-century rent increase in the villages rather than their enslavement. The challenge is to measure the weight of this heavy, though not necessarily ruinous, burden. Not surprisingly, there is much evidence from lordships other than Stavenow of east-Elbian farmers' uncooperative and insubordinate, if seldom openly rebellious, attitude toward their overlords, both before, during, and after the war.[114] In the mid-seventeenth century, as the age of absolutism descended upon Brandenburg-Prussia, seigneurial despotism and village defenselessness menaced the countryside, but they did not rule it.

---

[114] In sixteenth-century Brandenburg, village protest bordered on insurrection under the von Bredow jurisdiction. See *Geschichte des Geschlechts von Bredow: Herausgegeben im Auftrage der Geschlechtsgenossen*, 3 vols. (Halle, 1872–90), vol. I, 2, 174–268. Beyond relevant works already cited, see Helga Schultz, "Bäuerliche Klassenkämpfe zwischen frühbürgerlicher Revolution und Dreissigjährigem Krieg," *ZfGW* 2 (1972): 156–73; Günter Vogler, "Probleme des bäuerlichen Klassenkampfes in der Mark Brandenburg im Spätfeudalismus", *Acta Universitatis Carolinae: Studia Historica* (Prague) 11 (1974): 75–94; Harnisch, "Klassenkämpfe der Bauern in der Mark Brandenburg"; Grossmann, *Rechtsverhältnisse*, chs. 2–3.

The Prussianization of the countryside?
Noble lordship under early absolutism, 1648–1728

In the century after 1648, the military-bureaucratic Prussian monarchy, born of war's miseries and Elector Frederick William's ambition, grew to robust maturity. Its governors imagined their "Sparta of the North" as a phalanx of provinces in which, behind the standing army's shield and under centralized officialdom's restless eye, the estates of the realm industriously rendered tribute to the new order. The nobility would surrender sons to the army and, as landlords, suffer their villagers' heavy taxation to fill the royal coffers. The burghers would ply the peaceful arts, free from conscription but paying stiff imposts on manufactures and luxuries. The literati, mostly bourgeois-born, would preach, teach, and work for the new regime, subordinate to the Junkers but rewarded with tax-exempt government posts and ennoblement prospects. The villagers would serve as soldiers, billet troops as bad luck decreed, and each month pay, in hard-earned coin, their communities' debts to the fisc.

Careerism and corruption in government, and subjects' class egoism and duty-shirking, dimmed this vision of absolutist state-building. Yet the bloodletting of the Thirty Years War, the heavy fiscal exactions and human costs of Frederick William's wars in the 1650s and 1670s, and the long-lasting European economic depression of the seventeenth century's second half, worsened by consumption-throttling effects of absolutist taxation, left Brandenburg-Prussian society ill-positioned to resist the steely new regime. A sea-change had occurred, catching all in its currents.

After 1648 the Stavenow lordship's inhabitants confronted postwar reconstruction under the dual constellation of nascent absolutism and economic troubles, especially severe, as plunging grain prices signaled, in arable farming. This plight faced all those many Prussian subjects living as villagers under noble landlords. Yet, while the top-down history of Hohenzollern state-building is familiar, the experience amid this process of the rural population and their local governors, understood not as chronicle but as microhistory of society and political order, remains a sparely inscribed page.[1]

There is symbolism in the Stavenow lordship's ownership. The Barons von Blumenthal, after purchasing Stavenow, drifted out of the courtly favor they originally enjoyed, settling into a life of provincial aristocracy. After some hesitation, they invested heavily in Stavenow, aiming to bind it to their Prignitz property network. The Quitzows' heirs, epigones of pre-absolutist Brandenburg, lacked the coin to recover their ancestral property. Instead, in 1717, as Blumenthal fortunes faded, a paragon of the new order, Lieutenant-Colonel Andreas Joachim von Kleist, foreign to the Prignitz District, bought Stavenow with the help of gifts bestowed on him by Frederick William I, "the soldier king" who raised Prussia to the threshold of a great power.

Stavenow's example might seem to support the reigning view on the Brandenburg-Prussian nobility's relation to the new state: the "compromise theory" that, in exchange for the Junkers' assent to a military-bureaucratic monarchy independent of corporate aristocratic control, the regime reinforced their landlordly powers while offering them preferred positions in the army officer corps, the high bureaucracy, and at court. Lieutenant-Colonel von Kleist, who repaid his sovereign's favor with loyalty unto death, embodies this interpretation. Yet Stavenow might validate another view, highlighting noble paternalism's survival, though overshadowed by royal absolutism. Did not landlords join villagers to ward off absolutist intrusions? Did not noble patriarchy rule out reckless exploitation? Did not ambitious monarchy, bent on militarist power politics, roughly interpose tax collectors and army recruiters between rustic lord and villager, subordinating both to tradition-smashing Berlin bureaucrats?

This perspective easily shades into aristocratic apology.[2] But there is empirical warrant to argue that the landed nobility, if not their office-seeking brethren, resisted the armed monarchy's rise. They sought to shield their rents and uphold their fulsome sixteenth-century powers of constitutional co-sovereignty.[3] At Stavenow, before the seventeenth

---

[1] On Altmark nobility: Hahn, *Fürstliche Territorialhoheit.*

[2] Hahn skirts this danger, evident in Gerd Heinrich, *Der Adel in Brandenburg-Preussen* (Darmstadt, 1965). Influential depictions of symbiotic manor–village relations opposed to centralized state power are Otto Brunner, *Land and Lordship. Structures of Governance in Medieval Austria*, Howard Kaminsky and James Melton, eds. (Philadelphia, 1984 [German: 1939]), xii–xli; Otto Brunner, *Adeliges Landleben und europäischer Geist* (Salzburg, 1949).

[3] For this argument in full, based on the corporate nobility's political records: Hagen, "Crisis."

century's end, nothing suggests landlords availed themselves of new exploitative powers gained from the absolutist regime. But neither is benevolence much in evidence. The Blumenthals coolly sought their own advantage, yet their interest in resettling war-torn villages elicited concessions lightening villagers' burdens.

At the eighteenth century's dawn, population recovery and economic upswing inspired landlords to cancel such concessions and restore pre-1618 rents. In the Prignitz District, this triggered impassioned anti-seigneurial protests, also engulfing Stavenow's villages. When imperious Lieutenant-Colonel Kleist arrived, he found his subjects' discipline and zeal for his welfare much deficient. His proprietorship's first decade witnessed severe crises and confrontations. These inspired Kleist to undertake major reorganizations, including significant concessions to win village cooperation in ambitious plans to raise his estates' production and profits. Like many other eighteenth-century Brandenburg-Prussian estateowners, Kleist became – in the English phrase – an improving landlord.

THE MANORIAL ECONOMY IN THE POSTWAR RECONSTRUCTION ERA

The Blumenthals inhabited Stavenow only fitfully, entrusting it to salaried managers or leaseholding tenant-farmers. In the 1680s Caspar Friedrich von Blumenthal, Stavenow's purchaser's son, rebuilt Stavenow, mindful that in 1692 the Quitzows might reclaim it at its 1647 price. His counter-strategy was to invest so heavily in improvements – *meliorationes* – as to drive the recovery cost beyond Quitzow means. But in the 1650s and 1660s, little incentive arose to spend large sums. Grain prices were low and farmer-resettlers scarce who did not require seigneurial outfitting in livestock, equipment, and lumber. Princely policy, acknowledging war survivors' strong labor-market position, guaranteed new colonists six "free years," unburdened by royal taxes and seigneurial dues, to complete their arduous work, including clearing the overgrown fields for plowing and sowing. It was an era of government bounties for killing the wolves and bears that had reappeared, and of edicts against unscrupulous colonists' disappearance at their free years' end to begin another round under other landlords who, satisfied to find new tenants, asked no questions.[4]

[4] Ibid.

The war subverted social hierarchy. In Blüthen village nobleman Hans von Viereggen and his wife, while rebuilding their knightly manor, lived on an abandoned farmstead alongside their own subjects. In 1657 Thomas von der Knesebeck, commissioner of Brandenburg's highest tribunal, the Berlin Chamber Court (*Kammergericht*), settled various Blüthen disputes, including villagers' and Stavenow administrator Martin Zacken's demand that Viereggen conform to "neighborly law" and pay support to the church and its pastor. The bourgeois Zacken also demanded that the Junker Viereggen pay "hunter's bread" owed to Stavenow by the subject household he was occupying. Viereggen refused, but the court dissented, instructing him to contribute voluntarily "out of good-will and the impulse of Christian devotion," until he had "sold" his present abode. Viereggen denied that he or his wife "insulted or threatened" bailiff Zacken. The court agreed villagers could lease pasturage to "foreign sheep," provided that Viereggen enjoyed his present farm's grazing rights (in return for paying the village shepherd). Stavenow's herds could likewise graze the abandoned farmsteads until resettled. As this case shows, the princely regime did not abandon the postwar Junkers to their own devices and desires.[5]

In 1694 Stavenow manager Heinrich Zicker recalled that bailiff "Zuschlag" – a sobriquet meaning "surcharge" – managed the lordship from 1658 to 1666, and "for his bad administration was arrested and taken to Spandau fortress."[6] The Blumenthals then engaged tenant-farmer Wolfgang Holle, who until 1675 paid 1,100 talers yearly for all usages, excluding timber rights and swine foraging, which the Blumenthals kept. The 1675 inventory registered in Holle's Stavenow living room a "red chest" the baron had given his leaseholder's wife.[7] Holle's lease paid only 4 percent on Blumenthal's 1647 investment. After 1649, Stavenow lost eight farmers to death or desertion, leaving its villages in 1675 nearly as thinly settled as in 1647 when, measured against 1614, the occupancy rate had fallen by half. An epidemic killed Holle's sheep. For lack of labor services he kept, apart from horses, four "large plowing oxen," sowing altogether 25 tons of rye, barley, and oats, a third of 1614 production. The cattle and pigs were similarly diminished, though Holle's wife kept some turkeys ("Calcutta hens"). He had, as good farming required, plowed all fields three times before sowing.

The lordship owned "a set of handcuffs, leg-irons with a lock, and hand-irons with a chain." These could be clamped on insubordinate

---

[5] No. 709, fos. 135, 139.   [6] No. 282, fo. 16.   [7] No. 67, fo. 8.

subjects alongside criminals. But a 1683 register of the lordship's lawsuits mentioned no village conflicts, and the dungeon appeared then as
"a jail without a door."[8] This was a detail from bailiff Zicker's 1682
Stavenow inventory. The estate manager's house was "completely new,"
with brick and fieldstone floor and plank ceilings. The living room displayed a bible and a Latin devotional work. Zicker had a study, kitchen,
and "sleeping room" with canopy bed. There were 40 pounds of linen
yarn and two spinning wheels, awaiting the hands of the bailiff's wife,
daughter, or servant. Apart from Zicker's own, the appraisers found
that "the bedding is all very bad and has always been used for the servants."[9]

From 1680 to 1691 the Blumenthals invested 32,000 talers at
Stavenow, including 9,000 talers in the manor-hall: ten times their earlier spending. Though improved prospects for estate agriculture were
indiscernible, the Blumenthals prevented Cuno Hartwig von Quitzow
from recovering "his ancestral seat." So Quitzow's lawyer Stappenbeck
described it, appealing to the crown for a loan enabling his youthful and
impecunious client to buy out, with the help of his prospective wife's
dowry, the Blumenthals at Stavenow. Stappenbeck also followed common practice in obtaining an opinion from a university law faculty,
Brandenburg's "widely renowned University of Frankfurt on the
Oder," supporting young Quitzow by concluding from evidence
Stappenbeck supplied that the Blumenthals were wrong not to obtain
Quitzow permission before cutting and selling "8, 9 or indeed 12,000
oak trees" from Stavenow's forests to finance their investments. Such
"forest devastation," Stappenbeck claimed, violated the Blumenthals'
limited usufructuary rights, although he saw no reason why, after recovering Stavenow, young Quitzow should not sell off 2,000 oaks – at
4 talers each – to repay his debts.[10]

Quitzow's exertions were typical of innumerable landownership
struggles before the government's 1717 abolition of feudal title encumbrances on noble properties, including the recovery right Quitzow
sought to enforce. After 1717, noble estate sales were final. This, the government correctly predicted, would strengthen landlords' investment
incentive and improve agriculture. In his legal duel with Quitzow,

---

[8] Ibid., fos. 25–6; no. 709, fos. 4–11; no. 709, fos. 165–7 (court register, 1666–83).

[9] No. 709, fos. 4–11. In 1687 Stavenow's manager (*Amtmann*) was Gustav Hero, while in 1694 the
Blüthen pastor was J. F. Hero. Such kinship ties among rural notables were common. In 1682
Zicker, later *Amtmann*, was "*Amptschreiber*," or sub-bailiff and scribe (also called *Kornschreiber*).

[10] No. 271; no. 333; no. 709, fos. 175, 191, 197–8, 218–25.

Blumenthal prevailed. In 1683 he obtained sworn affidavits from a Berlin land surveyor and three building artisans that Stavenow manor-hall was in immediate need of repairs, "to make it a proper and comfortable dwelling." The surveyor wrote his name, while the workmen signed with crosses.[11]

Zicker's assistant Gustav Hero kept a scrupulous record of the 1688–91 improvements. Carpenters, cabinetmakers, and bricklayers supplied artisan labor, daily earning 8 groschen plus food and drink. From this comparatively good wage they perhaps paid subordinate hands. Other manual laborers earned 4 groschen daily. The farmer-resettlers who had exhausted their free years could not evade unpaid construction services, though seemingly, like paid workers, they received seigneurial "beer, bread, and victuals." The fullholders with horse-teams hauled, doubtless resentfully, lumber and other building materials to and from the Elbe river, as well as on manorial terrain. Smallholders put their hands to such tasks as collecting fieldstones, while all farmers framed buildings, plastered walls, and cleared land of overgrowth.

The Blumenthals, maximizing *meliorationes*, rated dependent villagers' exertions equal to free laborers (4 groschen daily) or freely contracted haulers (1 taler daily for driver and team). Quitzow's lawyer, minimizing them, treated the work as normal manorial service, and therefore per smallholder worth 9 pfennigs (0.75 groschen) daily and per fullholder – because of his horsepower – 1.5 groschen. These were proportional values, on a thrice-weekly work schedule, of yearly labor service commutation fees of 9 talers (largeholders) and 4.5 talers (smallholders). Slowly and grudgingly performed, villagers' unpaid labors, whether in agriculture or building, might only have justified these very low sums. But the Blumenthals, like most commanders of compulsory labor in central and eastern Europe, preferred to see them as valuable assets.[12]

Stavenow's reconstruction allowed some subjects to supplement farm incomes with wage labor. Chim Lentzen, a Blüthen fullholder, worked in 1689 as a woodcutter and sawyer, earning a respectable 80 talers (though he probably had workers to pay). A carpenter with fifteen

---

[11] No. 709, fos. 168–71.
[12] Ibid., fo. 3: Zicker's accounts covered "beer, bread, and victuals" given out during construction work. On central and east European estateowners' economic mentality: Witold Kula, *An Economic Theory of the Feudal System. Towards a Model of the Polish Economy 1500–1800* (London, 1976 [Polish: 1962]); cf. related literature in Hagen, "Village Life," 160.

laborers built cottagers' houses for 45 talers each, including oak and pinewood worth 16 talers. The lordship valued fullholders' new houses and outbuildings at 200 talers, smallholders' at 100 talers. Villagers rebuilding farmsteads themselves received seigneurial lumber, including oak timbers.[13]

In 1694 administrator Zicker departed, submitting to the Blumenthals' Berlin lawyers an appraisal of Stavenow for leasing purposes.[14] The manorial seat and demesne farms were now rebuilt, four-fifths of subject farms resettled. Thanks to long-term rising livestock prices and recovery from the postwar grain-price slump, the lordship was once again a profitable enterprise. Measured against the 1624–33 average, Berlin rye prices fell from 1660 to 1690 by 30 percent. Taking account of the Reichstaler's permanent devaluation in 1667 throughout the Holy Roman Empire by 14 percent, the price drop was steeper still.[15] Stavenow administrators reacted by limiting arable farming to two-thirds of 1614 sowings, and concentrating on livestock, whose value rose over the century. Beer brewing and distilling of grain spirits (schnapps or "brandy") consumed much grain. Stavenow's tavern sold these drinks, purveying in 1691 40 barrels (4,240 German quarts) of manorial schnapps.[16]

Many pigs – Zicker thought 240 – could be fed on brewing and distilling by-products. The Stavenow forests fattened an additional thousand belonging to the lordship's villagers and employees, each earning 6 groschen forage fees. By limiting sowings, more pasturage was gained. The manorial sheep flock at 1,400 head was far larger than before, and the cattle herd, though smaller, was more profitable. Zicker proposed expanding the herd to 200–300. Because pasturage was rich, every eight cows would produce favorable yields of one barrel of butter (220 pounds) and two of cheese. Zicker counseled clearing a wood to widen the arable and fuel a new glassworks alongside the seigneurial brickworks (earning 50 talers yearly from 90,000 bricks). This would help pay for the many draft-animals the lordship maintained, numbering 36–40 plow oxen and 8–12 horses for harrowing, altogether four times the 1614 numbers. But, Zicker wrote, "since the villages are pretty well settled and the subject farmers are doing better, now that the hard times

---

[13] No. 709, fos. 8ff, 25, 29–33.   [14] No. 282, fos. 1–16.
[15] Table 1, Hagen, "Crisis," 321. Apart from the 1690s and 1710s, when sporadic harvest failures raised prices steeply, the post-Thirty Years War decennial average Berlin rye price hovered slightly below the 1624–33 level through the 1720s. Prices in Naudé, *Getreidehandelspolitik*, vol. II, 568–9; Behre, *Statistik*, 277.
[16] No. 709, fos. 236–41.

of rebuilding are over," more could be asked of them, "so that in future such a large number of teams will not have to be kept and the livestock can be distributed differently."[17]

About the farmers' labor services and other rents, Zicker remarked that, where once fullholders exceeded fifty and smallholders twenty-five, "now hardly half the services with horses are on hand, although" – he benignly added – "if the people are given help, more will soon be available."[18] More severely, he reported that "these seigneurial services, whether with teams or by hand, must be performed three full days each week," during which the workers "receive not the least bit of bread or the like."[19] Among subjects with rebuilt farms and expired free years, prewar rents had not been restored. Zicker's account, paired with another from 1699–1700, shows that where, earlier, three service days were claimed, now on average the fullholders worked 2.5 days, and not always with teams. Where, earlier, on average each fullholding paid 7 bushels of grain rent, now just 3.6 were collected.[20]

In Blüthen or Sargleben, where farmers still enjoyed free years, Zicker was unsure of their rents. As for villagers' lesser seigneurial obligations, such as spinning, hauling millstones, or manning nets during hunts, "in my time they haven't done these things, and whether or not they ought to, I don't know. In my time they had enough to do with construction work." As for money dues or rents, "I can't say I know what they are, but most of the farmers wouldn't pay them."[21] These laconic remarks breathe the realism that led Zicker to lower rent demands on farmers – still a scarce asset – to rebuild the lordship and resettle its villages.

Similarly, Zicker did not skimp on wages paid manorial servants and other indispensable employees, even though 1694's seigneurial outlays for seventeen employees were not much lower, as a proportion of land-lordly income, than for twenty-seven workers a century before. Despite 1667 monetary devaluation, manorial workers' cash wages had risen considerably, reflecting long-enduring postwar labor shortage. Their allotments in kind approximated 1580s' levels, signaling perhaps their adequacy in provisioning workers' households. The head plowman-mechanic now earned 10 talers, against 3.75 talers in 1584, but his

---

[17] No. 282, fo. 6.   [18] No. 282, Teil 9.
[19] Ibid.: following each seigneurial field's harvest the lordship gave them a barrel of beer, worth about 1.5 talers apiece (no. 640).
[20] See tables and data in Hagen, "Crisis," 329ff, based on Stavenow records nos. 282 and 356.
[21] No. 282, fos. 8–9.

21 bushels of cereals and peas were roughly the same as senior manorial workers' in 1584. Best paid in 1694 was the field foreman–court bailiff, with 19 talers and 27 bushels, and the forester-hunter, with 18 talers, various food grains, and oats for his horse. The brickmaker earned 22 talers "each time he fires his oven," plus 5 talers for digging his own clay, "since no one will dig the earth for free." He received 8 bushels of cereals, one barrel of beer or 2 bushels of malt (for his own brewing), ninety cheeses and 3 pounds of bacon or 2 pounds of butter. The fisherman once earned 12 talers and 21 bushels. "But in my time," Zicker wrote, "there has been no fisherman, so I can't say how high he can bring his wages. I did the fishing with the foreman and the servants."[22]

A cowherd and young pig-herding helper also lived at Stavenow. Together they received 5 talers and 32 bushels, plus shoes, doubtless the senior partner's. In return, the cowherd "must be the first and the last to feed the animals." They lived with the plowman in a lodgings building that also had rooms, still unoccupied, for rent-paying day laborers. Here also was a male farmhand, earning 9 talers, two shirts, and two pairs of shoes. The women included the combined dairy-mistress and female overseer, receiving 4–5 talers, a woolen skirt, two pairs of shoes, and 20 ells of linen. The cook's wages were lower, the dairy-mistress's female helper's and housemaid's lower still. All female workers received linen yardage and low wages, with shoes and clothing only for the senior. At Semlin and Premslin – which Zicker (who spelled Perleberg as "Berdelberg") called "Sembslin" and "Brembslin" – both manor-farms employed plowmen and dairy-mistresses living as married couples. These pairs each earned 13 talers, 25 bushels, two pairs of women's shoes, and half-bushels of sown flax. Both farms employed cowherds, one married and the other single. In place of shoes they received, among other wages, 16 groschen – equal to a freely contracted laborer's four days' pay. The shepherds remained contracted entrepreneurs, not wage-earners.

Zicker said nothing of compulsorily enlisted servants, but doubtless the least well paid among Stavenow's seventeen employees – youthful herders, maids, male farmhands – bore this status. In numbers and cost, they were a minor presence. Obligatory service, whose value to landlords historians stress, could not greatly lower labor costs. To freely recruited, mature workers the lordship gave separate dwellings and firewood and, to the married and perhaps others, gardens, cow pasturage,

---

[22] No. 282, "Deputanten."

and forage for a pig or two at the usual fee. For early modern landless workers these conditions were not bad, for which they could thank labor scarcity and customary norms of diet and income.

Such was Stavenow's condition, seen through Zicker's eyes, in 1694. Instead of cleaving to unalterable tradition, his management strategy responded to market conditions. He estimated Stavenow's current annual net income at 1768 talers, plus 582 talers for the farmers' unpaid manorial services, a marketable asset since any leaseholder could be charged this sum to acquire them. The Blumenthals' lawyers, anticipating higher commodity prices and additional villagers, raised Zicker's numbers to 2,552 talers, including 630 talers for labor services. Considering the taler's 1667 devaluation, Zicker's forecast matched Stavenow's appraised return in 1601/14 of 2,014 talers. A note of 1694 recorded that "former Eldenburg sub-bailiff Hoyer has declared himself ready to pay 2,000 talers for a lease on the Stavenow estates." Hoyer's offer, excluding his own projected profit, stood almost twice as high as tenant-farmer Holle's 1660s and 1670s leases. With postwar reconstruction and resettlement largely finished and agricultural prices rising, Stavenow had surmounted the seventeenth-century crisis.

Historians have long assumed that subject farmers' post-1648 plight was doubly grim, burdened by absolutist taxation (the benignly named *Kontribution*) and heightened seigneurial exploitation to recover lost incomes by squeezing more rent from fewer villagers. But a closer look shows that the farmers, once their "free years" ended, passed on to the landlords some of the military-bureaucratic regime's costs by declining to fully render prewar dues and services. The Junkers were unwillingly complicitous, bidding against each other for settlers, offering – or tolerating – lower rents, and granting servants incomes above the statutory minimum. Following village resettlement, signifying Brandenburg-Prussia's gradual demographic recovery from seventeenth-century bloodletting, farmers' bargaining position weakened and the threat arose that landlords would reimpose prewar rents. Though the post-1648 setting did not rule out seigneurial coercion and brutality, this cannot be taken as the prevailing norm, but must be documented case by case.[23]

The 1686 Prignitz cadastre showed that village resettlement was far from complete. In a sample of 50 of 267 villages, the occupancy rate among landholding farmers was 73 percent. In the neighboring Ruppin

---

[23] For this argument at macro-level: Hagen, "Crisis," 318–35.

District the corresponding figure, at 87 percent, was considerably higher, but in the seven villages housing Stavenow subjects, it was, at 66 percent, lower still.[24] The danger lurked, in government and village eyes, that the nobility would engross unsettled holdings into their demesne, shrinking the tax base and village arable, but the evidence marshaled here counsels caution in judgments on illegal enclosures. Settled farmers, looking for broader pastures, often paid seigneurial rent for unoccupied holdings in their midst, even if this raised their taxes.

A SCENE FROM LATE SEVENTEENTH-CENTURY VILLAGE LIFE: THE 1679 GLÖVZIN FIRE

At the eighteenth century's dawn, Blumenthal officials began pressuring Stavenowers to render seigneurial rents as Lindt recorded them in 1649. An era was beginning of manor–village conflict, which surfaced in 1700–2 regional protests and led to the Kleists' 1720s reforms. A preliminary glimpse of the village stage on which these events unfolded emerges from a July 1679 document, recording several Glövziners' testimony on the "great conflagration" which wreaked havoc in their community.[25] Blumenthal sub-bailiff Andreas Reinecke called on Stavenow seigneurial judge, Perleberg Bürgermeister Johannes Henricus Tanckenius – whose latinized name framed his dignity as "Imperial Notary Public" – to investigate. Tanckenius first administered "the pure physical oath" to the witnesses. This was a judicially important procedure whose solemn and awe-inspiring nature remained intact in the following century. It was "physical" because it required raising the arm, properly displaying the fingers, and verbally repeating the text read by a court official. One version of the oath, intended for Stavenow use, was recorded between 1649 and 1690. It offers the only surviving statement of Christian belief as seigneurial authorities formulated it for villagers:

Warning to all who would swear falsely, what raising the fingers signifies. First, raising the three fingers signifies, by the thumb, God the Father, by the second finger, God the Son, and by the third, God the Holy Ghost. Of the other two fingers, folded down into the hand, the fourth signifies the precious soul, which is hidden among mankind, while the fifth signifies the body, which is a smaller

---

[24] Calculations based on Vogel, *Prignitz-Kataster*, 111–17, 122–5, 304–9, and passim. Ruppin data from Günther Franz, *Der Dreissigjährige Krieg und das deutsche Volk*, fourth edn (Stuttgart, 1979), 20–1. Among Stavenow halfholdings and smallholdings, 74 percent had been resettled, but among fullholdings, more expensive to equip and paying heavier taxes, only 57 percent.

[25] No. 327, fos. 1–5.

thing than the soul. The whole hand signifies one God, one Creator, who has made all creatures on earth.

Whoever secretively and wrongly, or falsely and untruly swears an oath, is saying the same thing as the following: if today I swear falsely, so I ask of God the Father, God the Son, God the Holy Ghost, the Holy Trinity, that I be excluded and expelled from the community of God and his Saints, and that a curse be laid on my body and my life and my soul.

Secondly, if I swear falsely, so I ask of God the Father, God the Son, and God the Holy Ghost that the inexhaustible mercy of our Lord Jesus Christ, His fear, His troubles, His bitter suffering and dying, His stern hard death and innocent martyrdom, be withdrawn from me, poor sinner, and lost.

Thirdly, if I swear falsely, so shall God the Father, God the Son, God the Holy Ghost, and the infinite mercy of our dear Lord and Savior Jesus Christ not come to me in consolation and help at the final moment, in that hour when body and soul do and must part.

Fourthly, if I swear falsely, so shall my soul, represented by the fourth finger, and my body, represented by the fifth, together be damned at the Last Judgment, because I, perjurious person, shall and must stand godless before the Tribunal. Also shall I be parted from the community of God, from His word and from all the Elect, and shall I be deprived of gazing on the presence of God Our Dear Lord Jesus Christ.

Let every pious Christian be strictly warned hereby against false and untrue oaths, so that he may not be given over for punishment to the Devil and his company, to whom by falsely swearing he subjects himself, and so that God His only Creator and Savior does not withdraw from him his precious soul. May God Almighty graciously guard against this, through Christ Our Lord. Amen.[26]

The fire broke out in thirty-two-year-old smallholder Steffen Schultze's house. Schultze said he was then in the field, inspecting damage the cowherd had done his oats. When he left home, his wife was there alone with his "smallest son," aged two. Later she sent their five-year-old boy to fetch fire embers from the neighbors. Seeing the smoke, Schultze ran home "and saw all his rooms engulfed in fire." Asked if his negligence or his family's caused the fire, he said evasively: "God would know." Other people told him his five-year-old started the fire in his livestock stall, "which the boy admitted to his grandfather Boltzer Henning, who promised him a new smock if he would tell." Schultze "left it to God whether this was true or not."[27]

Schultze's wife, Lucia Hennings, twenty-eight, said that "she was standing in front of [linen-weaver] Daniel Tieden's house and, when [Tieden] called to her that her stall was burning and then started shouting, she fell to the ground in fright." Because there were only a few live

---

[26] No. 28, fo. 66.   [27] This and the following from no. 327, fos. 1–4.

coals in her hearth, where a pot of cheese was hanging, her son fetched new fire at Jürgen Ebel's house, after an old woman there secured it with a cover. At home he delivered it to his mother personally. She said of her son that, "when the people promised to give him something, he said that he and Jürgen Zeggel's son had brought the fire into the stall and blown it into flames. But when he was threatened with hard punishment and told to tell the truth he cried out 'no, he didn't do it.'"

Smallholder Jürgen Ebel, thirty-eight, was home when the fire started. "He had eaten some bread and butter, because it was almost six o'clock and dinner time." His visiting aunt was driving in his calves when she saw the blaze. He summoned his wife and children and, foreseeing their fate, "threw a cooking pot and some flour outside, by which time his house was completely aflame." He agreed the fire might not have occurred had Schultze's wife been home. Ebel's farm servant Christoph Becker, aged twenty, "was in his master Jürgen Ebel's house, sitting on a chair." After seeing the fire outside, he ran back in, but could save "only his wooden trunk." Later he met Schultze's five-year-old and said, "you rascal, what have you done?" but the boy replied, "*ach*, I didn't do it."

Fullholder Jürgen Zeggel, thirty, was standing at his farmstead's entrance when "the old woman cried out fire. He looked around and saw nothing but smoke and flame." Seeing there was "no rescue," he went into his house "and threw outside what he could." Smallholder Jochen Hecht, thirty, said he had been in Perleberg, fetching beer for a christening. "From Perleberg bridge he could see very well there was fire in their village." Finally Judge Tanckenius interrogated court bailiff Lorentz Köhne. He had been visiting linen-weaver Tieden, and ran to Schultze's house "and tried to help save things but the fire quickly got out of hand." Tanckenius wrote that Köhne "questioned the two children in every way, but because they say both yes and no, and because the talk of five-year-old children is childlike and inconsistent, one cannot conclude anything from it, so there is no reason to record it." As for the adults, however terrifying the penalty of damnation for perjury, the sworn witnesses spoke with everyday concerns in mind, and without conceding incriminating points.

THE PRIGNITZ VILLAGERS' 1700–1702 MOBILIZATION AGAINST LANDLORDLY PRESSURE

A 1700 document illustrates Stavenow lordship's businesslike manner for recruiting new tenants. Hans Wilcke reported "he would like to rebuild the former Chim Heinrich's deserted holding, and if [the lordship] wanted to accept him as an hereditary subject [*Erb-Unterthan*], he was willing." He would render labor services and other rents, "whatever they are." The court recorded that "for this, his mother Anna Marwitzen and his brother Ludwig Wilcke vouched," adding that "if he would be a loyal subject, he is hereby accepted and granted the usual six free years, together with some oak timber," with instructions "to build a good farmer's house and barn."[28]

In 1699–1700 the lordship compared villagers' current dues and services with Lindt's 1649 "housebook." They discovered many displeasing discrepancies in an almost fully resettled village population of seventy farmers, including only seven still enjoying free years. Four holdings remained unrebuilt, while another's proprietor had absconded. Of Karstädt and Blüthen fullholders, with 1649 deliveries of 6–18 bushels, officials now observed that "these subjects, as can be seen in the housebook, are supposed to deliver grain rents, but have never given anything and have always claimed it is impossible." Sargleben's smallholders said that, rather than paying grain rents, "they would prefer to quit their holdings." The Glövziners likewise paid nothing, nor did the Mesekowers, of whose labor services it was aggressively remarked that "they are only working three days weekly now." Stavenow's Garlin fullholders "serve only one day and refuse the other." One produced an occupancy deed from former tenant-farmer Holle, stipulating but one day weekly.[29]

Although many other villagers in the Prignitz and elsewhere had similarly succeeded in unshouldering pre-1618 rents, by the eighteenth century's dawn landlords were bridling. In the year 1700 a regional protest movement flared up, engulfing 130 villages. This dramatic event, formerly locked in the archives, deserves full-dress staging, but these pages confine themselves to its manifestations near Stavenow. Already in 1656, during Elector Frederick William's war with Sweden and Poland, Prignitz villagers protested new taxes and old rents. They also showed a readiness for self-defense already manifested during the Thirty Years War by their formation of irregular armed bands. The Elector issued a glowering edict against 1656's turmoil, which included money-raising to pay lawyers and village leaders' delegations to Berlin.[30] The Prignitz sheriff was to post the edict in the villages, and pastors were to read it in church. The movement threatened to spill over into the neighboring

---

[28] No. 200, fo. 3.   [29] No. 356, fos. 1–8.   [30] Details in Hagen, "Crisis," 317–18.

Altmark District, inspiring the "deputies of the lord prelates, nobility, and towns" there to petition their district governor:

A number of Prignitz villagers have assembled and bound themselves, arms in hand, to free themselves from the *Kontribution* [tax] and other current burdens, while they also do not want to render their overlords labor services and rents. Now we must indeed recognize that the burdens incessantly imposed on the land, ruinous to all livelihoods, are almost impossible for the poor people to bear, and may well give cause for some impatience. This moves us, the [Altmark] estates, to implore higher authority for moderation and the alleviation of such pressures.

Yet the "evil of rebellion" was inexcusable and must be stifled in the cradle, particularly since the Prignitzers had begun "to hold conventicles and infect [the Altmarkers] with the same poison." The Altmark estates called therefore for "exemplary punishment" of Prignitz "ringleaders."[31]

Other protests visited Brandenburg in the seventeenth century's second half, some inspired by the urban excise tax's introduction (which common people supported to break the propertied classes' tax privileges), others by statutes attempting to ratchet down wages driven skyward by labor shortage.[32] These were precedents for the Prignitzers' new actions, which the local corporate nobility sputteringly denounced in a 1701 letter to Frederick I, newly crowned "king in Prussia":

The common peasantry joined together most punishably in the year 1700 to free themselves from dues and services, and accordingly collected money from house to house in all [Prignitz] villages. When we learned of this audacious and insolent uprising, the District Commissioners denounced the plot to Your Royal Majesty, and received the order issued to Crown Agent Marece [Marees] to investigate the conspiracy on the spot, which he has begun to do.

So that these defiant and foolhardy people might revenge themselves on us, they have newly assembled a large fund of money, going from house to house, and submitted a supplication filled with many false charges, obtaining a [government] mandate that the aforementioned Crown Agent should study and report on their complaints.

Though the nobility acknowledged the government had graciously heard their "considerable distress," they were dismayed that it conveyed villagers' complaints to Berlin's Chamber Court. They were confident the "insubordinate people" could not prove their charges. Nor was the whole nobility culpable "if one or another overlord may have

---

[31] GStAPK, I. Hauptabteilung, Rep. 22, Nr. 72a, Fasz. 11: Bauernunruhen in der Prignitz: edicts of 19.V.1656 and 5.VII.1656.
[32] Carsten, *Origins*, ch. 13; Hagen, "Crisis," 327–8.

committed some infringements." Meanwhile "these arrogant people have shown themselves very disobedient and have committed great excesses."[33]

The nobility complained some villages had already initiated lawsuits before the Chamber Court. Against the government's intended "fiscal investigation to our great disadvantage" – seemingly a general inquiry into Prignitz taxes and rents – the nobility vehemently protested. They asked the king instead to punish ringleaders, who had allegedly collected more than 1,000 talers, while directing aggrieved villages to the "regular courts." The government denied wishing to submit the Prignitz nobility to dreaded "fiscal investigation," wanting only to supply necessary information to "our Chamber Court as the supplicants' *forum ordinarium*."[34]

Following royal investigator's Marees' dispatch, the "mayors and communes of all Prignitz villages" petitioned him "most humbly" to convey their grievances to the king. They requested

that where possible our grain rents be converted to money, because some of the overlords sell much grain in other places, and also ship it from the land, by which our beloved grain is often made very expensive. But if we villagers had the grain, we could sell it in our region and so give the poor a helping hand, while our overlords only practice usury with it. And our meager draft-animals are so burdened by [the nobility's] grain-haulage, and otherwise transporting them on journeys, that often they are left dead on the road. Also the villages complain about the [lordships'] enlargement of the bushel measure for grain rents, since formerly the rent bushel contained only three quarter-measures, as can be proven, but now they are using their own large bushel measure.[35]

Here grain market recovery is evident, particularly in the nobility's zeal to resume their once profit-rich exports. The villagers' petition-writing lawyers invoked the government's old-established export controls holding domestic prices down for common consumers' (and taxpayers') good. The landlords' introduction of larger bushel measures for tribute grain, if true, aimed seemingly to reverse the post-1648 downward rent slide.[36]

The nobility's view, expressed by estateowners von Platen and Winterfeld, the locally resident, royally appointed Prignitz District

---

[33] GStAPK, I. Hauptabteilung, Rep. 22, Nr. 72a, Fasz. 15: Klagen der Ritterschaft in der Priegnitz gegen aufgewiegelte Untertanen, 1701–03 (unpaginated). Berlin. 31.X.1701.

[34] Ibid., 1.XI.1701.

[35] GStAPK, I. Hauptabteilung, Rep. 22, Nr. 72a, Fasz. 14, Beschwerde von Dörfern über Dienste und Abgaben, 1700–01: fo. 235.

[36] On metrological strife between landlords and villagers: Witold Kula, *Measures and Men* (Princeton, 1986 [Polish: 1970]). On Brandenburg-Prussian grain export trends: Naudé, *Getreidehandelspolitik*, vol.II, passim.

Commissioners (*Landräte*), was that "the subject farmers are rising up against their overlords." The villagers had allegedly sought a royal ruling declaring them "free of grain rents, and that they should pay their overlords not more than 1.5 groschen yearly per hide." This was a wild exaggeration of mayors' and communes' demands, but perhaps reflecting the utopian hopes the rent protest's outbreak inspired. The commissioners exhorted the government to scorn the "enraged rabble's demands." They reported that Erdmann Wille, a protest leader and farmer, was arrested while collecting money and investigated by a seigneurial court. Forwarding Wille's interrogation transcript, they urged "exemplary punishment" in Berlin or at Lenzen crown estate. Possibly this was a call for Wille's execution, since otherwise they would presumably have advocated transportation to Spandau fortress. Warning that crown farmers were joining the insubordination, the commissioners invoked the nobility's and government's common landlordly interests.

One hundred and thirty Prignitz villages drew up grievance petitions, whose study collectively would repay effort. Five such documents survive from Stavenow villages. They show that the Blumenthals, who through the 1690s tolerated shrunken rents, were now turning the screws. From Glövzin village an unidentified "street-corner scrivener" (*Winkelschreiber*) wrote that "the fullholders must make as many hauls to Berlin as His Lordship demands and moreover pay [internal] tolls on his grain, which takes them seven days and six nights," but yielded only four days' remission. Herr "von Blumdahl" grazed four summer sheep flocks on the villagers' fields, endangering crops and pasturage, "so that we can hardly keep any livestock at all." Finally, "the Herr Count has built a jail, called the 'sink-hole,' where head and hands are locked up and [the prisoner] has to stand so long it almost breaks his back in two."[37]

Karstädt village's farmers denounced the von Wartenbergs for excessive labor demands and oppressive haulage "which our ancestors did not do." Stavenow's six fullholders lamented they were asked for 18 tribute rye-bushels "although we can only sow 18 bushels." Haulage was longer, tribute yarn and bread weightier.[38] The Blumenthals' eight Mesekow smallholders, including two women, doubtless widows running farms with grown children or servants, raised bitter complaints. The food and drink their forebears received during service had vanished. They were

---

[37] These and preceding grievances: GStAPK, I. Hauptabteilung, Rep. 22, No. 72a, Fasz. 14.
[38] Ibid., fo. 237.

now "supposed to give 6 bushels of grain rent, which for long years were not demanded of us." When they balked, the bailiff "sent threshers into our barns and seized the 6 bushels with force." They protested that "we poor people don't wish to refuse the 6 bushels, if we were only given food and drink as of old. But that we should do the service and each give 6 bushels yearly is unfair and we cannot bear it."

Mesekow's old mayor said they were always entitled to forage swine in their woods.

But when the village was devastated, and only two of us remained, I, Jürgen Behse, exerted myself to get some additional people. Estate manager Jüstis Zuschlag took away our forage rights, but departed overlord Herr von Blumenthal of blessed Christian memory showed mercy. We paid 10 talers yearly, forage or no forage. But now this right has been canceled and our fields and borderlands are overrun with 700 [seigneurial] pigs, not sparing sowings on our narrow field. And it has been threatened that, if our own pigs are found there, they will be shot dead. If this isn't changed, the village will be ruined.

A nearby noble house reclaimed a meadow from them while Stavenow doubled its meadow rent. Eight years previously Bailiff Hero imposed six days of yearly hand labor "which our ancestors didn't perform."[39] Garliners lamented still other abuses. Farmer Andreas Panckow said "necessity forces me to charge" that the Winterfeld lordship, after commissioning him four years earlier to rebuild a holding his father once inhabited, reversed its decision. Although "I hauled the pinewood lumber, which is still lying there, the Winterfelds don't want to give me [the holding], but instead have enclosed it [into their demesne] for their estate manager, whereby I, a poor man, am much injured and obstructed."[40] Garliners also denounced the von Winterfelds' and Karstedts' enclosure of six abandoned farms, "which we must now cultivate in manorial service," though there were people "who would gladly have [a farm] but cannot get one." The lordships grazed flocks on enclosed land, "so that our poor animals must starve, yet we must use them in service on land that once belonged to villagers."

One of Garlin's free mayors denounced the Blumenthals for demanding long trips with four horses, to Berlin or Magdeburg, whenever they wanted, and for raising his annual labor commutation fee from 10 to 25 talers, "which is impossible for me." Stavenow free mayor Schloh found rent rises the more embittering for his having negotiated agreeable terms with previous Blumenthals.[41] The numerous Garlin smallholders fulminated, not against landlords, but against full- and

---

[39] Ibid., fos. 29–30.   [40] Ibid., fo. 12.   [41] Ibid., fos. 13–15.

halfholders. "We must bear half the troop billeting and other public charges." But the bigger farmers kept more land than was right, and concealed its proper distribution, "so that almost no one knows, nor wants to say, and they keep it hidden and we poor people can get no bread." Declaring the pastor also guilty of wrongful enclosure, they begged investigator Marees "to reap beloved God's reward" and succor them.[42]

Marees instead pursued "instigators and ringleaders," but villagers "unanimously" refused, he reported, to name them. Their "great need and grievances" alone moved them. A 1699 edict proclaiming a "new livestock tithe" provoked them to collect money to send deputies with supplications to Berlin. A royal "declaration" having, seemingly, rescinded this impost, the villagers resolved to seek "some remission of dues and services, because they were overburdened."

> This news [Marees wrote] one village heard from the other, and so they joined together, believing that, since most were so poor and badly off, they could accomplish nothing alone but should act together. All deny wishing to initiate lawsuits against their overlords. Instead, they wanted to see whether through most humble pleas they could gain some alleviation from Your Royal Majesty.

Marees' inquiries eventually identified, as "principal agitators," village mayor Peter Rogge and Perleberg burgher and master baker Michel Burow. Accomplices were the aforementioned Wille (Wilcke) and three fellow farmers. Mayor Rogge arranged meetings in baker Burow's house. In the town of Kyritz, meetings also occurred, organized by farmer Hans Milatz – possibly the same Stavenow subject who later led religious and other protests in his village. The baker authored the movement's proclamation supporting farmer Wilcke's village money-raising. At their meetings, Rogge "asked the assembled subject farmers whether they had any charges against their overlordships and, if so, to bring them to him" so that he might present them in Berlin. Rogge's "aim was to try to get access to the old Land Book, according to which the [villagers'] dues and services would have to once again be fixed." Of this plan Wilcke said: "if it succeeded it wouldn't be a year before things would be put back on the old footing."[43]

Did such a "land book" exist? Neither the 1686 cadastre nor the 1624 Middlemark census surveyed rents. The 1375 Brandenburg Land Book and related tax-registers of 1450 and 1480 recorded tribute grain, but could they have survived in village memory? Labor services were

[42] Ibid., fos. 22–3.
[43] GStAPK, I. Hauptabteilung, Rep. 22, Nr. 72a, Fasz. 15, Eberhardt Marees's report, 7.III.1702.

private-law arrangements varying from lordship to lordship and never officially recorded. Perhaps "the old Land Book" was wishful thinking, expressing the idea that, at commercialized manorialism's outset, tolerable dues and services had been fixed. If consulted, it would unmask new rent demands as unjust.

Doubtless Rogge, Burow, and Wilcke were sternly interrogated, perhaps tortured, to force confessions and the revelation of accomplices. The baker forswore any right to represent the villagers or receive their money, nor was Rogge mandated to speak for the Prignitzers. The aforementioned mayors' memorial, allegedly composed by Rogge and requesting grain rent conversion into cash, "only the fewest villages knew of, or approved." Clinching their guilt, Marees remarked that, even if villages had "great complaints, still no subjects in the land had the right, by law or custom, GOD BE PRAISED," to engage in collective action. Villages could only plead injustices individually before the courts. Marees said no one would admit to contributing more than "three or at most four groschen." The leaders disclaimed recording the money collected, "under the pretext they cannot read, and so couldn't write it down." Baker Burow possessed a money account totaling 40 talers, but Marees suspected they gathered much more. "Some of the nobility believe" their farmers each invested "up to 16 groschen in this cause."

Marees summarized the 130 villages' grievances, citing first the "high grain rents they must give their overlordships, sometimes even exceeding their rye sowings." Second was the bushel measure's enlargement, occurring "almost every year." While "their forebears paid according to the then-usual small tribute bushel," the "ordinary bushel" now cost the villagers much more.

In preceding years of harvest failure [in the 1690s], the overlordships demanded tribute grain from them with the greatest rigor, sending threshers into their barns who willfully threshed out the grain. And because they received not the least remission, and instead their bread-grain was taken from them, they had later to buy it dearly, falling in debt that ruined some of them completely.

The lordships demanded novel field labors, abusing farmers' servants so "atrociously" that new hands were unhireable. Junkers seized villagers' pasture, meadow, and woods, refusing their share of taxes and billeting on abandoned holdings, even when their bailiffs cultivated them. Though devastated farms were still "numerous," landlords avoided resettling them, using them as seigneurial sheep-runs and dairy-farms, and impounding village livestock grazed on them. Finally, long-distance haulage was oppressive. "These and other causes have moved the farmers as a whole to most humbly seek Your Royal Majesty's most merciful alleviation, because there are many poor subjects for whom gaining their rights from their overlordships is impossible." The lordships had not told their story "because they have reservations about submitting to an inquiry instigated by their subjects." Though he advocated the five ringleaders' punishment, Marees thought some villages' complaints were justifiable. Others admitted their rents were no greater than their predecessors', but still were unmanageable. Marees proposed a "general commission" that would "investigate everything thoroughly, interrogate both overlords and subjects," binding all parties to its decisions.[44]

Meanwhile the District Commissioners and their Junker colleagues wrote the crown denouncing the villagers' "harmful and shameful uprising," which threatened "to thoroughly disgrace the whole region." They would tolerate the Chamber Court's hearing individual villages' "imagined grievances" but clamored for retribution against ringleaders, claiming they illegally raised over 600 talers. The government complied, transporting the five defendants to Spandau fortress for indeterminate terms of hard labor. Villages not individually seeking judicial redress were condemned to *perpetuum silentium*. The protesters' treasury would be confiscated to cover debts owed the government.[45]

As the condemned leaders were led off to prison, tumults arose among their followers, trying to halt their departure from Perleberg. Crown investigator Voswinckel concluded that Paul Hagen incited these events, after having earlier helped steer the movement. Voswinckel arrested Hagen and interrogated him at Berlin's royal police headquarters (*Königliche Haus Vogtey*). A portrait emerges of an educated estate administrator who abetted a village upheaval. Hagen, fifty-three, was a Mecklenburg country pastor's son. Describing his career, he said:

he was a servant first for Lübeck cathedral canon von Döhnen, then 3½ years for Wismar syndic Dr. Schwarzkopff. Then he was bookkeeper-bailiff on a certain von Bernewitz's estates. Thereafter he worked on his own brother's estate. Then he was with Herr von Bredow in Wagenitz [outside Berlin] for years. From there he went to Perleberg, where he married a widow, whom he found to have many debts. Because he couldn't pay them he had to sell the house and move away, to Mecklenburg, where he leased a farm, which after 15 months burned down. For three years he leased a small estate from Captain von

[44] Ibid.   [45] Ibid., documents dated 7.III.1702; 22. III.1702; 14.II.1703.

Didden, where he likewise had much bad luck with livestock epidemics, so he took a manager's job with the Captain. Fifteen months later he moved as bailiff to Schilde near Perleberg. After 3½ years this estate was leased and he spent a year without employment [convalescing] in Suckow near Perleberg, until at this year's Whitsuntide he went to work for Frau von Besewich in the Altmark, where he was arrested.[46]

He was now, another report said, "a noble widow's estate administrator."[47]

Traveling an upward path toward life as entrepreneurial tenant-farmer or independent burgher, Hagen's chariot broke its wheels on various misfortunes. Asked about Burow's agitation, Hagen, who was the baker's brother-in-law, conceded "he was always going in and out at Burow's, and every day saw farmers there." He knew nothing of money-raising until he overheard Marees' scribe say, "Burow, Burow, the receipts are going to deal you a great blow. You and the Spiegelhagen mayor wrote your names on them." Asked if he composed farmers' petitions for Burow's use, Hagen said "he wrote a supplication for them, which they took with them." But Herr Gause, seemingly Burow's lawyer, "gave it back, saying it was no help."

After the ringleaders' removal to Spandau, Hagen did nothing further, "except to pen for the baker's wife an account of about 6 talers which the farmers gathered for the prisoners." He was unaware this was punishable. Asked about writing other farmers' supplications and sending them to Burow's wife, "he didn't know, he thought perhaps he wrote one more, but whether it arrived here [in Berlin] he didn't know." He admitted helping the baker's wife, because her apprentice did not write legibly, but denied accepting the villagers' money. Hagen allegedly "voiced the subject farmers' grievances" when their leaders were taken to Spandau. He said "the farmers didn't want to let the prisoners leave, but they all wanted instead to climb on the wagons so they couldn't move. So he told them they shouldn't do that, there was a royal command and they mustn't act against it." Asked whether he had not actually said, "when the king returns, the farmers should bring their complaints to him again," Hagen said "he couldn't remember." Had he not also said of the king, "if he doesn't help you he should be driven out of the land?" This Hagen swore, "with many protestations," he had not done.[48]

[46] Ibid., Protocollum, 11.X.1702.
[47] GStAPK, I. Hauptabteilung. Rep. 22, Nr. 72a, Fasz. 15: 17.VIII.1702 ("Lit. G.").
[48] Ibid.: Protocollum, 11.X.1702.

Voswinckel uncovered Hagen's letters. In 1701 he wrote to his brother-in-law, expressing thanks for baker Burow's "love and charity." "If my back pain did not so discomfit me, I would have come and expressed my opinion in words." Instead, he wrote about the best strategy for getting the villagers' supplications to the king. This was vital, he thought, since investigator Marees' affections lay with Count Blumenthal and Baron Putlitz, whose villagers "are raising the gravest charges." Putlitz's bailiff said the baron read his subjects' complaints and "cancelled and crossed out those he didn't find proper." To avoid the king's displeasure when handing over villagers' charges, Hagen recommended a simultaneous plea for royal mercy. "Now the dice are in play," he added portentously, "and it would be good if all villagers earnestly represented their cause in prayer to Almighty God. For God has the hearts of kings in his power, and He can lead and guide them like the waters in the brooks." Hagen invoked God's aid both for his brother-in-law's sake and "for us all."[49]

With this letter Hagen sent another to the defendants' lawyer showing that the two village mayors were to hand the Prignitzers' supplications to the king, though Marees intercepted these men and sent them home. Of the writings they hoped to present at court, Marees wanted to know "who the author of this rebelliousness was," and how much money had been collected. Meanwhile the government-mandated recording of individual villages' grievances occurred, "according to which," Hagen wrote, "some of Herr Baron von Putlitz's villages suffered under pharaonic plagues." Fearing that Marees, in his bias toward Putlitz and Blumenthal, would not report their villagers' full complaints, Hagen proposed they be communicated verbally to the king. He also wrote a statement he hoped to give the king "through a good patron." Hagen beseeched lawyerly protection and "Mighty God's gracious help" against Marees' "hard threats against this legal action's authors."[50]

Hagen addressed another letter to his sister-in-law, baker Burow's wife, after her husband's arrest. He wrote that "the nobles" had received a royal mandate to "sharply" interrogate their subjects about money contributed to the protest. "The nobles told the king the subjects gathered a great sum, and that 4,000 talers were still in a mayor's possession, and the king wishes to know about this, and punish hard the villagers' presumption and wickedness." Until this question was clarified,

[49] Ibid., "Lit. A": 18.IX.1701.   [50] Ibid., "Lit. B": n.d.

Hagen opined, Burow and comrades were not likely to gain release. Of
their Berlin lawyer Hagen said "I do not trust him, for he was not true
to our cause." He asked Burow's wife to engage a new advocate.
"Otherwise the nobles will, as usual, keep chattering to the king about
the villagers, and the prisoners will pay the price."

Now the dice are on the table, and he who knows how to defend himself will
reach the goal. God stands by the just, He champions the cause of the poor,
and secures the suffering their rights. (On the threats facing me I remain
silent, and pay them little mind.) Under His protection I have launched my
venture, and am therefore undaunted.

"After reading this," he asked, "please consign it to the flames."[51]
     Hagen also wrote a letter for Burow's wife, Ursula Stargardts, to her
"dear husband" in Spandau fortress. Her salutation invoked "Jesus in
greeting and consolation." The imprisoned baker had written her of
their plight, "and indeed," as she wrote, "that you along with the others
are perishing and consuming your money." As in other early modern
prisons, Spandau inmates could not easily survive on official provisions,
but needed money to buy food and otherwise endure incarceration's rigors. She mentioned a "good friend's" efforts to persuade the government
to release them, but nothing could be decided before the king's return.
"No money is coming in from the farmers, and what was recently collected the aforementioned [good friend] took to Berlin." She promised
to send cash, but "it's impossible for me to come to you."
     She complained of their apprentice, who wanted to "play the master"
and beat her "black and blue with a broom handle" before absconding
to his father. "I wish you could soon return home to help me with the
business. I often think of you, and it pains me that in your present circumstances you can't get provisions. Our livelihood has been very poor
for some time, so I can't send you much money." As his "faithful wife"
(*getreue Frau*), she invoked "God's protection" and sent him, "along with
all his good friends, friendly greetings, also for your comrades." Hagen –
speaking as "this writer" – added wishes for Burow's "immediate home-
coming."[52] Later, Hagen wrote his "heartily beloved [*hertzliebe*] Frau
sister-in-law," saying ominously "the affair" – her husband's release –
"stands in great danger, and therefore must be begun and advanced with
much thought and particular wisdom."[53]
     Hagen recorded contributions from thirty-six Prignitz village mayors
and individual villagers given his sister-in-law to defend and support the

[51] Ibid., "Lit. C."   [52] Ibid., "Lit. D."   [53] Ibid., "Lit. E."

prisoners. The sums, varying from a few groschen to 1 taler, totaled about 25 talers. Three Stavenow villages figured among the ringleaders' supporters. Another account showed over 30 talers spent, including 9½ talers in cash and provisions sent to Spandau.[54] The gravest charge facing Hagen personally was having publicly incited the Perleberg crowd against the Prussian king. Voswinckel produced the testimony of Hans Adam von Saldern, a resident at Plattenburg castle. The Salderns ranked among the richest Brandenburg nobility. He claimed he heard, in a church official's presence, from Perleberg Bürgermeister Tancken[ius], Stavenow seigneurial judge, that Tancken witnessed Hagen's talk of driving the king from the land.[55] But Tancken later respectfully wrote Voswinckel, saying he only knew of Hagen's statement at third hand, from two Perlebergers who heard it from a certain Bergholtz. Yet Bergholtz denied having witnessed Hagen's words, hearing of the incident from an unremembered source. Voswinckel believed Hagen's letters showed unequivocally that he was guilty of aiding and abetting the imprisoned leaders in "inciting the subject farmers." But since no one would admit hearing from Hagen's own mouth the "slanderous and highly punishable speech" against the king, Voswinckel ordered the city council to put Bergholtz to an oath which, maintaining his story, he duly withstood.[56]

The government forbore from finding Hagen guilty of treasonous talk against the king without first-hand evidence. The punishment his other rebellious acts provoked remains, like the prisoners' further fortunes, for deeper study to uncover. Yet several points are clear. When, at the seventeenth century's close, noble landlords turned the screws on village rents, broad-based protest arose, aiming through appeal to the crown to return to earlier rents thought more tolerable. Facing deadly sanctions against sedition, the movement presented itself as a law-abiding appeal for royal succor. Probably its leaders shared Hagen's fervently expressed hope for divine protection. Though aided by such burghers and administrators as Burow and Hagen, the villagers acted independently, led by mayors and farmers. The crown's agents accepted that seigneurial abuses should be investigated and regulated, though the government, intolerant of concerted village action and swayed by the Prignitz nobility's protestations of innocence, harshly punished village leaders while requiring their followers to choose between costly litigation and "perpetual silence." It is hard to judge whether governmental impulses to shield

---

[54] Ibid., "Lit. F."   [55] Ibid., "Lit. G."   [56] Ibid., "Lit.H/I," 1.XI.1702.

villagers from seigneurial excess (*Bauernschutz*) grew stronger under the impression of protest movements such as this one, and whether individual landlords drew in their horns in its aftermath.[57] Here, at least, the authorities rescinded an edict imposing a new "livestock tithe" on some or all villages.

The Blumenthals forced most of their Stavenow villagers to shoulder their pre-Thirty Years War obligations in place of the laxer regime still prevailing, according to 1699–1700 records, on the 1700–2 protests' eve. When in 1711 the Blumenthals leased Stavenow to tenant-farmer Neumann, the villagers were again performing services as Lindt and Strasse described them in 1649, except that fullholders now paid commutation money to escape one or more weekly workdays. But while, in the 1680s, the lordship collected 3 talers yearly for each commuted day, the fee was now 6.6 talers, or 20 talers for all weekly labors. To evade just one day a farmer needed to sell 9–10 bushels of rye – no trivial quantity, especially in face of the lordship's effort to reimpose old-established grain rents.[58]

The 1711 survey said of the Sargleben smallholders that "bailiff Wolff reports that Count von Blumenthal reduced weekly services from three days to two, asking only that they should do something in return for the lordship." The Sarglebeners "admit to three days, but can't serve them, which is why His Grace the Lordship released them." Tribute grain deliveries were lowered to 4 bushels.[59] The Blütheners still refused all grain rents, swearing these had been given for seigneurial lands now lost. Stavenow's two Garliners were put on 12-taler commutation, which "the Herr Imperial Count of blessed memory" further reduced for three years.

The 1700–2 protests erupted when a landlordly rent offensive, inspired by population recovery and brightening markets, coincided with northern European misery following harsh winters and resultant crop failures in the 1690s. Berlin rye prices stood at crisis heights in 1699, as they did at Stavenow, where local prices also signal harvest debacles in 1693 (when death-to-birth ratios soared) and in 1697. If, as Marees said, the villages were "poor and badly off," these events were partly responsible,

---

[57] On *Bauernschutz*: Georg Knapp, *Die Bauernfreiung und der Ursprung der Landarbeiter in den älteren Theilen Preussens*, 2 vols. (Leipzip, 1887); Rudolph Stadelmann, ed., *Preussens Könige in ihrer Thätigkeit für die Landwirtschaft*. 3 vols. (Leipzig, 1878–7). Knapp's and Stadelmann's documentation of official debates on policy toward subject farmers, though important for revealing occasional strong advocacy of pro-village positions (some put into eighteenth-century practice), sheds little light on rural protest movements.
[58] Stavenow, no. 355, fos. 1–14.   [59] Ibid., fo. 7.

and doubtless helped trigger subsequent protests. Seigneurial rapacity at such moments must have especially goaded the villagers. Their forebears' 1650s agitation stood in historical memory for emulation – and not for the last time, though the 1700–2 action neither staved off landlordly rent hikes nor its leaders' incarceration.

CHANGING THE LORDSHIP: FROM BLUMENTHALS TO KLEISTS

Stavenow's 1717 sale brings to light the logic animating seigneurial production, especially under the management of the non-noble tenant-farmers to whom the nobility often leased their properties. Historians have neglected this subject, whether because it seemed an unpromising realm of hidebound tradition reinforced by technological rigidity, or because it seemed seigneurial profits flowed as reliably as harvest vagaries allowed, assuming villagers' unpaid labor was satisfactorily exploited. Such perspectives, though not wholly skewed, overlook commercialized manorialism's market dependency. The temptation facing landlords and their lessees to squeeze the villagers arose from the challenges they faced in earning acceptable returns on capital.[60]

In 1717 Lieutenant-Colonel Andreas Joachim von Kleist acquired Stavenow for 44,000 talers paid the Blumenthals, who were bereft of an adult male family head. Kleist rewarded the Quitzow heirs with 10,000 talers for abandoning their final claim to recover their lineage's 1647 loss. Royal arbiters estimated the Blumenthals' *meliorationes* at 21,432 talers. Kleist also paid a surcharge of one-sixth on the 1647 price as a premium (*Agio*) reflecting rising property values. Accepting the 44,000 talers, the Blumenthals tacitly settled for but 13,000 talers in improvements.[61] The arbiters reckoned that, since 1647, seigneurial rye plantings had, through brush-clearing and "soil-cleansing," increased 90 percent. Other improvements included seventeen meadows cleansed, an orchard of 410 apple, cherry, pear, and plum trees planted, and fishponds restocked with carp. These were worth 4,000 talers. Repairing the Stavenow residence and rebuilding its manor-farms cost 11,000 talers. A sinister item at seigneurial headquarters, worth 1 taler and mentioned with the dungeon, was the "pillory with neck-irons," for

---

[60] Kula, *Theory*; Müller, *Landwirtschaft*, 108–42; James L. Roth, "*The East Prussian Domaenenpaechter in the Eighteenth Century: A Study of Collective Social Mobility*," (Ph.D. dissertation, University of California, Berkeley, 1979).
[61] No. 220; no. 30, fos. 1–7.

punishing lawbreakers and miscreants and exposing them to public censure.

The lordship's resettlement of thirty-six fully devastated and ten partially destroyed village farms cost 5,921 talers. Monetizing fullholders' labor services at 20-taler yearly commutation fees, adding 6 groschen for feudal tribute payments' cash value, and capitalizing the 20.6.- total at 6 percent yielded 338 talers, half credited to seigneurial investment, half deriving, seemingly, from settlers' labors. A 1718 survey mustered the villages for their new owner's inspection. Farmers' sowings were much heavier than the 1686 cadastre reported. Fullholders planted 24 rye-bushels and 12 of both barley and oats, along with quarter- or half-bushels of fallow-sown peas and flaxseed. Village harvest increases are evident in the water-mills' seigneurial rents, which rose from 12 tons in 1694 to 22 tons in 1718.

The appraisers found the houses and farm buildings of but six farmers, including four smallholders, in bad rather than acceptable or good condition. Virtually all possessed standard stocks of draft-animals, equipment, and seed, apart from a few whose horses were sick. Farmers owed full measures of services and dues. The fullholder not paying commutation fees "serves three days weekly with four horses and two servants" (one of whom might – but need not – be himself). "He must help mow and gather the rye at all three manor farms" (whose barley and oats the lordship reaped with its own teams and manual laborers). He and the other farmers "must together shear the lordship's sheep" and one day yearly "break the flax" and one day "swing" or clean it. Their households each owed 4 pounds of spun flax. "Formerly they hauled 24 bushels of rye to the nearest Elbe town, but now they carry only 18 bushels." In one ailing fullholder's case, 16 groschen bought release from haulage. A few villagers owed commutation arrears, but indebtedness to the manor was mostly negligible.[62]

A new burden on Stavenow's Garlin free mayor was the duty, probably onerous, to give the lordship or its people food and fodder, and bread for their dogs, when hunting in his neighborhood. He received food and drink for overseeing the Garliners' annual plowing in return for their Stavenow grazing rights. If the lordship sent its court bailiff to Garlin, the mayor owed him meals. He owed 25 talers cash rent, a charge denounced in 1701 as "impossible." A few landless cottagers had settled in Stavenow's villages. One rented for 8 talers yearly a house,

[62] No. 260.

garden, meadow, and land for 5 bushels' sowing. He worked one day in the seigneurial rye harvest with the scythe and in the barley harvest one day "with the hook" (or sickle).

The villagers' early eighteenth-century resistance to resumption of full dues and services left few traces in 1718. In Garlin and Sargleben, the lordship gained compliance by renting scarce meadowland. Rising grain prices helped the farmers pay commutation fees, sparing their teams damage in manorial service. Unfortunately, the next few years visited harvest failures on Stavenow and other Brandenburg regions. Grain shortages followed, bringing Kleist disappointing returns on his recently invested capital. For his tenant-farmers, the consequences were ruinous.

THE PERILS OF ARISTOCRATIC ESTATE-LEASING

The Blumenthals' last leaseholder was Georg Neumann, who arrived in 1711. His 1719 accounts displayed him sowing 10 percent more grain than bailiff Zicker in the 1690s. But where Zicker kept many seigneurial draft-animals (36–40 oxen, 8–12 horses), Neumann relied on villagers' obligatory traction, keeping only five horses and six oxen. Thus he could expand the cattle herd from Zicker's 106 to 163. Epidemic-prone sheep-raising had again proven risky. Neumann received goats from his predecessor instead of sheep, and left behind 418 sheep where Zicker kept 1,400. Neumann stocked the carp ponds with 4,600 fish. Seigneurial distilling equipment was worth a solid 200 talers. Among other equipment there were "two flax twisters on wheels, each with five irons." More evidence of heightened judicial coercion emerges in the first appearance of the "Spanish overcoat [*spanischer Mantel*] with iron fittings." This was a heavy barrel-like device, associated with the armies of the Thirty Years War. It was fastened, as a muscle-pulling and back-bending torment, on lawbreakers' heads and shoulders for periods of several hours, while they stood on public display. The lordship also possessed two flintlock rifles, two flintlock pistols, and two swords, valued modestly at 5 talers altogether.[63]

To replace Neumann, Kleist engaged Ludwig Meyer. Meyer submitted the customary leaseholder's estimate of manorial assets. Reckoning these at 4,563 talers, and deducting 20 percent to reward his own labor and entrepreneurship, he offered Kleist 3,800 talers yearly, nearly twice

[63] No. 240, Inventar 1719.

Table 2.1 *Appraisals of the Stavenow estates' assets acquired by lease, 1694 and 1719*

	1694				1719			
	Quantity	Appraisal value[a]	Total value	%	Quantity	Appraisal value	Total value	%
1. Grain sowings[b]								
Rye	24	12t			24	16t		
Barley	18	10t			10	14t		
Oats	6	4t			17	10t		
Total	48		504t	21.4	51		702t	15.4
2. Livestock								
Milk cows	106	4t	424t		210	4t	840t	
Sheep	1,400	10t	140t		1,900	6t	304t	
Swine/forage			255t				531t	
Total			819t	34.8			1,675t	36.7
3. Subject farmers' labor services								
Fullholders	38	12t			48	20t		
Smallholders	21	6t			23	10t		
Total			582t	24.7			1,112t	24.4
4. Grain rents (rye)								
Mills	12	12t	144t		22	12t	264t	
Subject farmers	2	12t	30t		6	12t	72t	
Total	14		174t	7.4	28		336t	7.4
5. Other incomes[c]			272t	11.5			738t	16.1
Total 1–5			2,351t	100.0			4,563t	100.0

[a] In talers per unit (or per 100 sheep).
[b] In tons (*Wispel*), to even number.
[c] 1694: cash rents (47t), wood sales (100t), brickyard (50t), hunting fees (50t), and court fees (25t). 1719: alcohol sales (150t), fishery (179t), buckwheat and flax sowings (37t), brickyard (100t), court fees (40t), incomes from gardens (60t), poultry sales (44t), house and meadow rents (58t), tribute hens and eggs (11t), millers' rents in cash (24t), barren cattle (35t).
Sources: no. 282 (1694); no. 240 (1719).

the 2,000 talers proposed in 1694. Kleist could be happy with this sum, but for Meyer it was risky. And, as usual with such leasings, it menaced the villagers. Table 2.1 shows that Meyer expected to ride a rising wave of grain prices (elevating cereal crops' appraisal value), while much expanding livestock production. But the lease's high cost also reflected the 75 percent rise since 1694 in fullholders' labor services, viewed as

Table 2.2   *Marketable assets of the Stavenow estates acquired by lease,
1694 and 1719*

	Appraised marketable or cash values	
	1694	1719
Grain sales	504t	702t
Livestock production	819t	1675t
Grain rents	174t	336t
Other incomes	272t	738t
Total 1–4	1,769t	3,451t
Leasehold fee	2,000t	3,800t
Deficit	−231t	−349t

Source: As in table 2.1.

marketable assets. Leasing them was essential to estate production and to acquire villagers' grain rents.

The Stavenow leaseholders paid well for villagers' labor services: 466 talers yearly in 1694 and 890 talers in 1719.[64] Reckoning them as labor costs, the seemingly wide margin, favoring leaseholders, between the estate's appraised value and leasehold fee proves illusory, as table 2.2's display of projected cash incomes shows.

To cover this deficit and profit 5 percent from his investment, leaseholder Meyer needed 539 more talers than his own appraisal forecast. His 1694 predecessor similarly needed 431 talers. Commutation fees, if collected, only offset heightened costs of seigneurial traction and wages. It helped that statutory appraisal techniques presupposed low cereal and livestock prices, giving tenant-farmers extra income from short-term price rises. Yet, in this setting, leaseholders' interests recommended squeezing all possible uncompensated labor and horsepower from the villagers and collecting every conceivable fee. Their interest also counseled maximal employment of compulsorily recruited servants. The villagers rightly feared these consequences when the lordships leased their estates.

From artisans' and laborers' house rents and other humble sources Stavenow reaped 120 talers yearly in coin, which Kleist left in Meyer's hands. They agreed that:

[64] These figures represent appraised labor-service values of 582 talers and 1,112 talers discounted by 20 percent. This was – as Meyer's offer illustrates – the customary method, applied to the total appraised value, of determining net leasehold payment.

in improving and reinforcing the moat, laying out the garden, or when construction work needs to be done at the manor farms, [Meyer] will not neglect to avail himself of the farmers' compulsory haulage or manual labor. But if any construction jobs need to be done with great dispatch, so that the leaseholder has to hire workers, Herr Lieutenant-Colonel agrees to pay them [from this fund].

Heavy frosts blighting 1719–20 harvests decimated Meyer's and Kleist's expectations, revealing that the profits they pursued depended precariously on villagers' strength. In 1721 Kleist, "for weighty reasons," abruptly canceled Meyer's lease.[65] Kleist's brother and future Stavenow co-manager, Bernd von Kleist, captain in the "highly esteemed Prince Heinrich Regiment," and Kleist's influential lawyer, Simon Hünicke, arrived from Berlin to settle Meyer's accounts and engage for a six-year lease Carl Conrad Schmidt, hitherto a crown estate lessee.[66] Before the unwillingly dismissed Meyer received any refunds, an inventory was necessary, executed by lawyer Hünicke. Aiding him were three Stavenow-appointed village mayors, serving as appraisers, especially of livestock. Meyer claimed his own *taxatores*, "which one cannot deny him," Hünicke wrote, "especially considering they will swear a separate oath." Meyer chose "three honorable mayors from other jurisdictions," who were warned "to guard themselves against the injurious sin of perjury."[67] The appraisers formed pairs, one for Kleist, one for Meyer. Final values comprised averages of the three pairs' estimates.

Thus, entrusting seigneurial interests to "honorable mayors," it emerged that in 1721 Meyer left behind grain sowings, livestock, and equipment worth slightly more than the 1719 inventory.[68] Meyer's first two harvests were poor. The villagers fell deep in debt. Meyer now claimed 636 talers from them. The farmers' distress struck the millers, who for lack of clients could not pay Meyer his 8.5 tons of tribute grain, worth 238 talers. Meyer could not collect nearly 900 talers in anticipated income, after agreeing to pay Kleist a leasehold fee that the harvest failures made impossibly high.

Captain Kleist and lawyer Hünicke mustered the debt-laden villagers. Forty-three farmers owed altogether 599 talers, or on average

[65] No. 240, 29.VI.1721.

[66] Ibid; no. 174, fo. 2.

[67] No. 240, 30.VI.1721.

[68] The method of appraising the crops' value in the ground was to combine market price per bushel, fixed officially for appraisal purposes, with a sum representing the "cultivator's pay." For rye, the formula was 18 gr. per bushel + 8 gr. cultivator's pay per bushel = 26 gr. total; for barley, which required more plowing, it was 15 gr. + 12 gr.; for the less labor-intensive oats and buckwheat, 6 and 15 gr., respectively, + 4 gr.

14 talers in a 1–43-taler range. These were mostly labor service commutation fee arrears. Only a few had thought themselves prosperous enough to commute all three weekly service days. But, despite present difficulties, only seven returned to full service, as did Daniel Mentz. He "acknowledges his [19-taler] debt and promises to pay it between now and St. Martin's Day [November 11]. He declares he will fulfill his manorial service *in natura* and for that purpose will keep two competent servants." Peter Schütte would pay by St. Martin's "or expect that another competent farmer will be settled on the holding." Blüthen mayor Jacob Meyer complained he received his heavily indebted farm "in very bad condition," but was ordered to settle at St. Martin's or be replaced by "another and better farmer." Ernst Niemann had but four weeks to clear his 41-taler account "or his grain harvest will be confiscated," while two others were threatened with seizure of their assets by the court bailiff. Writing's utility in the farmers' lives emerges in a ruling concerning Erdmann Mentz, charged with 4 bushels arrears, who "will not acknowledge them, but produces a receipt for 2 bushels, which were then credited to him."[69]

The villagers' debts mostly arose in 1719–20, but already in 1718 trouble had arisen, prompting Kleist to ask his neighbor von Karstedt to lend his subjects grain. Now Karstedt demanded repayment of 43 bushels of rye. He reckoned his 1718 loans at 21 groschen per bushel. In 1719 his charge rose to 26 groschen and in 1720 to 36 groschen. Leaseholder Meyer advanced rye at 32 groschen. These rates were high, but lower than the Berlin peaks of 40 groschen in 1719 and 46 groschen in 1720 – the highest between 1700 and 1740.

Meyer departed Stavenow without rancor but defeated, victim both of villagers' weaknesses and Kleist's impatience. Two years later Schmidt found himself unceremoniously turned out, his lease – as he thought – highhandedly canceled six weeks before its second year's expiration. He, like Meyer, bid 3,800 talers yearly rent. The first years he paid, but then faltered. "I asked Lieutenant-Colonel von Kleist most politely and obediently," Schmidt wrote in his self-exculpatory defense, "to let things continue, so that these troubles might have been avoided and I would not have suffered such great and dreadful losses." But instead Kleist sent lawyer Hünicke, "without timely notification and without my knowledge or presence," to transfer management to Kleist's brother.[70] This was a crushing blow:

---

[69] No. 240, 2.VII.1721.   [70] No. 174, fo. 2.

I survived two very miserable leasehold years, when I had not only a very bad grain price, but also earned little from swine-foraging fees and suffered from the sheep dying and from flooding. Consequently, as I can prove, I lost 2,000 talers during these two years. But now I have been removed from the leasehold, and cannot hope to benefit from the trouble, work, and money I invested in improving the soil, while Lieutenant-Colonel von Kleist can expect the best from swine forage and arable too.[71]

Deducting various improvements, Schmidt diminished his debt to 462 talers, though Kleist rejected some claims. Schmidt was proud of the well-fertilized condition in which he left the cropland. When Meyer left, he claimed, the manure was still piled up, so "there was hardly a place on the courtyard for a table to write down the *taxatores'* estimates, and because of the manure and filth one could barely enter the garden." Schmidt countered the reproach of selling hay (rather than using it as fertilizer-yielding fodder). But he sold little, all from "wet and swampy places, so I couldn't use it, nor could I safely feed it to the livestock." Besides, "I had rich straw harvests, so I could make more manure than my *Antecessor.*"

Schmidt penned the only surviving eighteenth-century discussion of Stavenow fertilizing. While manorial cattle were meant also to yield dairy foods and meat their production of manure was vital, since in pre-industrial agriculture throughout Europe adequate fertilization was a great challenge. Schmidt claimed 1 taler's credit for each bushel he sowed on fully fertilized land, and on half-fertilized land a half-taler, for a considerable 439 talers altogether. Schmidt's account indicates he sowed only one-third of his rye on fertilized land. But he planted all his peas, and much more barley than Meyer had sown, on manured fields. Oats were seldom fertilized, and Schmidt minimized their cultivation in more valuable though more cost-intensive barley's favor. "I acquired," Schmidt wrote, "my own team of horses and a yoke of oxen for manuring," that is, to haul manure to the fields, a task he could not impose wholly on the villagers, who resented the strain heavy pulling exerted on their teams. By his reckoning, which doubtless applied elsewhere in Europe, the fertilization cost more than seed sown. Lacking sufficient fertilizer, Schmidt – like his predecessors – used the villagers' labor services in two or three rounds of manorial plowing before sowing.[72]

---

[71] Ibid., fo. 7. Further citations below: ibid., fos. 3–11.
[72] Mark Overton, *Agricultural Revolution in England. The Transformation of the Agrarian Economy 1500–1800* (Cambridge, 1996). Cf. Duplessis, *Transitions*; Dewald, *Nobility*; Achilles, *Landwirtschaft*; Hagen, "Capitalism."

Schmidt protested Kleist's brother's and lawyer Hünicke's method of livestock appraisal:

I put it to Your Excellency's consideration, whether I must accept an appraisal carried out by Stavenow's own subjects and officials. Between tenant-farmer Meyer and myself the Stavenow subjects might properly perform an appraisal. But there is a great difference between me and Lieutenant-Colonel von Kleist, since [he] is manorial lord and the *taxatores* are his subjects and beholden to him.

He bought 40 calves at 1.16.- each, yet the appraisers reckoned them at 1.3.-. This loss was "very hard." A Frisian bullock that Kleist, evidently intent on improving his herds, commanded Schmidt to buy was overlooked in the inventory, despite its high value of 9 talers.

Schmidt demanded credit for winter stall-feeding Kleist's two-year-old riding mare, and pasturing it for two months. Kleist's brother should pay him 2 talers weekly for using Schmidt's two work-horses: a measure, seemingly inflated, of traction's high value. As for the manorial gardens, on Schmidt's arrival, "as I can prove with witnesses, they did not even suffice for keeping house." Now "everything is fully and abundantly planted, both in the hop garden and in the kitchen garden." This he accomplished with villagers' labor services worth 30 talers, which he claimed as credit, together with 7 talers he paid a laborer to clear out an overgrown meadow. As for milk cattle, the dairy leaseholders at the two outlying manor-farms had paid him their yearly fees. But at Stavenow he managed the dairy himself, and claimed 27 talers lost income.

Because Captain Kleist's takeover deprived Schmidt of six weeks' lease benefit, he demanded compensation. From the villagers' labor services, he claimed, pro-rating annual commutations, 80 talers. Fullholders were redeeming one weekly service day. Schmidt claimed only part of what he "paid in cash" for services.

Had I been able to actually employ the services, I could demonstrably have benefited more for, first, I would have had my grain hauled to Havelberg and Sandau and profited 6 talers per ton, because there the rye-bushel sells for 20 groschen [instead of 14 groschen at Stavenow]. More, I could have used the services to plow the fallow for 24 tons of sowings, for which I could have been paid 4 talers per ton [since he started with no plowed fallow].[73]

The high profitability of long hauls to market is evident. Havelberg and Sandau lay both on the Elbe export route and close to the populous markets of Berlin, Potsdam, Magdeburg, and Saxony. Schmidt did not

[73] No. 712, fos. 17–18.

ponder whether villagers would comply. Either he reckoned on bend-
ing them to his will, or on winning them with concessions.

Kleist quibbled, claiming the fallow had been plowed before Schmidt
arrived. He charged Schmidt 100 talers for the loss of ninety pear
saplings, building repairs, manorial swine's damage to fields and meadows, and taking fish eggs from the ponds. Finally, Schmidt owed 17 talers
to nine manorial servants in wage installments and cash substitution for
their shoes and linen. But three workers drawing natural provisions
received "too much," borrowing from the manorial cash-box and food
stores. The cowherd Christian Schumann owed Schmidt 1.5 talers cash,
plus 4.5 talers for cereals, a "kitchen sheep" (costing 14 groschen), and a
pig (3 talers). Other workers also owed Schmidt for mutton, pork, peas,
fodder oats, and salt.[74]

Schmidt's self-justificatory report throws everyday light on the
tenant-farmer system. Historians regard such non-nobles as Meyer and
Schmidt as exemplars of advanced farming, though the crown estate
leaseholders oftener earn the accolades. These usually enjoyed more
secure leases, of nine years or more, than did the landed nobility's tenants. Yet Meyer and Schmidt were also profit-maximizing entrepreneurs. They aimed to sell on the best accessible markets. They sought
productivity gains. They intended to squeeze every advantage from the
villagers' compulsory labors, which, as Schmidt said, he had "paid for
with cash." But with a landlord such as Kleist, who faced no unyielding
creditors of his own, the tenant-farmers' horizons of calculability and
profit-taking opportunities shrank drastically.

Noble proprietorship may, as historians assume, have hobbled early
capitalist agriculture. Yet in England, where aristocratic landlords
leased their arable to market-oriented farmers of commoner origins,
innovation and efficiency slowly marched forward. In Brandenburg-
Prussia, the absolutist regime, whose crown estates in 1740 encompassed a third of the realm's farmland and forest, promoted through its
domanial leaseholders a kind of "agricultural revolution" whose advantages eventually found emulation in such private lordships as
Stavenow.[75] But such noblemen as Lieutenant-Colonel Kleist were not
disposed to extend their tenants' deadlines. If, following post-1648 agricultural reconstruction, the seigneurial economy was to properly profit
landlord and leaseholder alike, the villagers needed to fulfill their duty.

---

[74] No. 712, fos. 62–3.
[75] Treue, *Wirtschaftsgeschichte*, 29. Cf. Overton, *Agricultural Revolution*; Duplessis, *Transitions*; Dewald,
   Nobility; Hagen, "Capitalism"; Achilles, *Landwirtschaft*.

THE "EQUALIZATION" OF BLÜTHEN VILLAGE

In 1723 Lieutenant-Colonel Kleist petitioned the government to "equalize" the Blütheners' farms. He asserted that 30 hectares they had long been cultivating was Stavenow's seigneurial land. Thus he triggered a struggle pitting himself – militarized nobleman, royal protégé, and newcomer among local landlords – against the old-settled gentry and their bureaucratic allies. Kleist claimed his subjects suffered discrimination at the hands of the six other Blüthen lordships' farmers, but his aggressive pursuit of self-interest was transparent. The story illuminates Kleist's new regime, the villagers' condition, and the nobility's relations among themselves and with the government.

Kleist appealed to the Brandenburg War and Domains Board (*Kriegs- und Domänenkammer*), directed, conveniently, by his attorney Hünicke. This was a mighty agency, handling military administration, tax collection, and crown estates' leasing and supervision. "Because of the arable's unequal distribution," Kleist wrote, "Blüthen village is in a very bad way." Echoing Kleist was Prignitz District Commissioner von Platen, the senior among three estate-owners serving both as royal officials and spokesmen of a gentry whose intermittent provincial assemblies presented lists from which the government appointed the commissioners. In 1724 the War and Domains Board compliantly instructed its agent Stoltz, cooperating with Commissioner Platen and the Blüthen lordships, to "accurately survey the lands and assign each subject an equivalent and equally accessible portion."[76]

Among twenty-five full- and half-holders, Kleist's nine farmers bore the heaviest burden of labor services or commutation equivalents, but delivered the lowest grain rents. Village taxes were uniform: for the fullholder, 16 groschen monthly in *Kontribution*, plus 10 groschen "*Reitergeld*" in lieu of troop-quartering. These levies totaled 13 talers annually, while Stavenow fullholders' seigneurial rents were worth 22 talers.[77] Surveyor Stoltz discovered that "repartition" would cost the crown's farmers, subjects of Eldenburg state domain, "quite a lot." It emerged also that the Blütheners altogether possessed only 43 hides of land, though they needed 44 if each fullholder was to be fairly taxed. The War and Domains Board ordered Kleist to supply the missing 29 *Morgen* of land from the 53 *Morgen* he claimed.[78]

---

[76] No. 712, fo. 86.   [77] Ibid., fo. 129.   [78] Ibid., fos. 123, 131–2: no. 596, fos. 62–3.

Table 2.3 *Blüthen landholdings following 1726 "equalization"*[a]

	Full-holder	Half-holder	Small-holder	Church/pastor	Cottager	Village commons
Number of holdings[b]	18	5	3	1	2	
Category of land						
Arable						
Open fields[c]						
First-class	26.4M	14.0M	4.0M	3.0M	–	
Second-class	17.0M	7.5M	2.3M	9.0M	–	
Third-class	17.1M	9.5M	5.0M	3.0M	–	
Side-field	–	–	3.7M	–	–	
No. of strips	36	22	11	18	–	
Total *Morgen*	60.5M	31.0M	15.0M	15.0M	–	
Farmstead and adjacent gardens	1.4M	1.0M	1.7M	3.7M	2.3M	
Commons						
Village green						13.0M
Pastures and vegetable gardens						97.0M
Livestock enclosures and roadways						18.0M
Pond						0.8M

All land	Arable	Smallholders' arable	Farmsteads/gardens	Commons	Total
In *Morgen*	1,378	13	46	128	1,565
In hectares	785	7	26	73	892

[a] In large Brandenburg *Morgen*, each of 400 square rods. 1 *Morgen* = 0.57 hectare = 1.425 English acres.
[b] Fullholder: *Zweihüfner*; halfholder: *Einhüfner*; smallholder: *Cossat*; cottager: *Brinksitzer*. Two three-quarters holders each held 45 *Morgen*.
[c] Rated by soil fertility.
Source: no. 605, fos. 6, 19 (n.d. [mid-1726]).

Stoltz found villagers' rents unequal, those with "bad land" paying more than those with good; some holding 2.5 hides, others less. Two Kleist subjects only maintained full holdings by farming what Stoltz concluded was seigneurial land, long ago given them. His redistribution plan accorded each fullholder 60.5 *Morgen* or two "large hides," distributed equally among three fields. Smaller farmers had proportionally less. Stolz's plan, eventually realized in practice, precisely displays village land use (see table 2.3).

The arable bore fixed names: "winter field," "summer field," and "fallow field." Each farmer cultivated numerous plots: the average fullholder held thirty-six strips, 1.5–2 *Morgen* (ca. 2–3 acres) apiece. Such fragmentation distributed land equally by fertility and insured each farmer against total loss, since some strips could be hoped to yield normally even if others disappointed. The smallholders held some open-field land and the rest in their own separate field, where in other villages all smallholders' land lay. The pastor cultivated a smallholder's share. The villagers' house gardens were large, and unbound by communal rules. Of Stavenow's Jochen Ohlert, one of two cottagers, it was noted that "because he previously had no open-field land, he doesn't enter into redistribution, but only keeps his garden, which without farmstead amounts to 2 *Morgen*, 92 square rods or 4 bushels of sown grain." Thus house gardens could, if necessary, bear cereal crops.[79] Blütheners also cultivated sizable "cabbage gardens on the commons."

The government's award to Kleist of 24 *Morgen* of long-cultivated village land stirred outrage, even if he surrendered the other 29 *Morgen* he claimed. In 1725 Bernd Kleist, managing Stavenow for his brother, who was on active duty and living with his family in Potsdam, wrote Major General von der Goltz, Perleberg garrison commander, requesting the billeting of thirty soldiers in Blüthen to halt resistance to Stoltz's survey among "some of the farmers."[80] Two weeks later a letter reached the District Commissioners from "the entire Blüthen commune, except the two fullholders Jacob Meyer and Johann Kiecks belonging to Stavenow." Its author, a nameless petition-writer or lawyer, said that "we poor hard-pressed people" protested Kleist's seizure of land which "from time immemorial" had been in the village's "*continua et non contradicta possessione.*" To compensate Stavenow's farmers for Kleist's acquisition, they would have to convert pasture to arable. Grazing and livestock would shrink. The soldiers Kleist loosed on the village had seized five geese and sixteen chickens, and committed "all sorts of excesses." The petitioners lamented, exaggeratedly, that they were losing one and a half hides: "we fullholders are being made into three-quarters holders and the halfholders are suffering corresponding losses."[81]

This petition arrived in Berlin bearing a cover letter from Prignitz District Commissioners Platen, Graevenitz, and Bülow. Platen had switched sides against Kleist, taking his colleagues' stand that Stavenow was depriving Blüthen of 4 tons of taxable sowings, the crown farmers needed more land because they paid heavier grain rents, and none of the villagers wanted the equalization.[82] Overruling the commissioners, the government ordered an assembly held to distribute and demarcate

---

[79] No. 605, fo. 32.   [80] No. 597, fo. 10.   [81] No. 596, fos. 77–9.   [82] Ibid., fos. 80–1.

the newly surveyed holdings, adding that "an army commando of thirty men with an officer will be present to hold the people there in obedi-ence." Such precautions were prudent, since "the previous *possessores*" attacked Stavenow's Martin Zander as he worked the land Stoltz assigned him. They were crown farmers, who "ganged up together and drove away the army commando" – a junior officer and two soldiers – who were protecting Zander.[83]

At the assembly, Lieutenant-Colonel Kleist requested the new boundary between manorial and village land be marked by "mounds" to forestall new disputes. Government emissaries Hünicke and Ganse agreed, "again warning the subjects to desist from previous insubordi-nation," though in vain.[84] Kleist was soon writing to Blüthen's five other lordships, addressing them as "much esteemed neighborly friends." Condemning the violence, he complained that "some farmers are following their evil custom of needlessly stirring up trouble at truth's expense."[85] But his neighbors stiffly replied that their subjects' "contin-ual laments" prevented them from honoring Kleist's proposed meeting. They condemned the new boundaries, "against which" – they menac-ingly wrote – "indeed we could take steps," but rested content to second the Prignitz commissioners.[86]

Kleist wrote the War and Domains Boards refuting Platen's "blind report." Platen was unfit to judge, since "his nearest relatives and their subjects" were interested parties. Platen's "blind affection for his kin" led him into distortions. That farmers paying heavier seigneurial rents should have more land than others was false, since all bore the same tax burden. "The dues [*praestationes*] payable the lordships derive solely from agreements [*pacta*] concluded with the subjects when they take their holdings and do not change taxable land's status." The farmers now protesting losses would hold, even after equalization, "in reality five times more taxable sowings than they swore they had in the inaccurate [1686] Prignitz cadastre." Seigneurial land Stavenow long ago rented its Blütheners entailed "separate payments and rents," like other noble land given Stavenow's Karstädters and Blüthen's pastor. Blütheners might complain that Kleist's recovery of his land diminished their grazing, but "because of laziness they don't clear off the useless bush covering half their arable and instead plant useful and good meadows where they should, so they have mainly themselves to blame for shortages."[87]

---

[83] Ibid., fos. 37, 45–6.   [84] No. 712, fos. III–12.   [85] No. 596, fo. 88.   [86] Ibid., fos. 45–6.
[87] No. 482, fos. 1–6.

If soldiers seized poultry this was a "slight penalty for such outrageous disobedience." The insubordinate farmers flouted the royal equalization order, and "though it was often read to them they did not mend their behavior." The entire conflict was "nothing more than agitation stirred up among the farmers by contrary-minded spirits." Should unlawful resistance continue, Kleist urged that some of the "disobedient farmers, as an example to the rest, be sent for a few months as prisoners to Spandau." He even suggested threatening the insubordinate villagers' lordships – his "esteemed neighborly friends" – with like punishment.

The War and Domains Board sent a new investigator to hear Kleist's foes' testimony. They opposed equalization without retention of the land Kleist claimed, which, as the 1686 cadastre allegedly showed, belonged to Blüthen. Though the Blumenthals sought the land in 1705, the Chamber Court ruled otherwise. Anti-Kleist farmers said Surveyor Stoltz was wrong to divide the land in August when, before rye sowing, "every industrious husbandman has already fallowed, plowed, and in good measure manured his land . . . He cannot give such well-cultivated land to a careless slacker." The Stavenowers' antagonists said that "because of their three days' weekly manorial service, Stavenow subjects' teams are frequently outside [the village] and so their land is only sparsely manured." And when the Stavenowers are put on 20-taler commutation payments, "they have to sell livestock and so then they make less manure." Kleist wrongly accused villagers of laziness. They had not sacrificed arable to pasture, but to gain additional fodder they cultivated part of their fallow. They praised their own repeated "fruitful plowings."

Kleist's rival landlords, piously taking responsibility for "their subjects' conservation," denounced his brother's "animosity and *machinationibus*." Bernd Kleist, unable to cow the local gentry, "cools his temper at their poor subjects' expense," summoning troops without consulting the "*superpossessiones*," that is, themselves. Captain Kleist "terrified the poor people with the thirty soldiers, cursing them as scoundrels and threatening to wipe them out." He and his military friends ordered the villagers not to cultivate their former plots, on pain of being taken by soldiers to Perleberg "and stretched out on the sweating bench." Five tons of rye seed therefore went unsown. Of Lieutenant-Colonel Kleist his antagonists generously concluded that "no exception could be taken to his *integrité* and neighborly deportment, if he were able more often to visit his estates and look into their condition and administration himself." But they demanded that his brother, whose objectives "aimed solely at oppressing the farmers," be denounced to the king.[88]

After this hearing Platen and his fellow District Commissioners submitted a self-defense against Kleist's charges of "partisanship and untruth." Platen, without explaining his initial support of Kleist's claims, now said they were hollow. As for Kleist's insinuations about tax evasion, "we do not dispute that, in many villages, heavier sowings take place than the cadastre reported." But if Blüthen's taxes were raised, the burden "would fully ruin" it, because "their present quota is high enough." The village was divided. At the last hearing, "as we arrived and the bell was sounded for convocation, the Stavenow farmers, who were in their houses, did not appear."[89]

Kleist wrote worriedly from Potsdam to Lenzen Bürgermeister Johann Erdmann Hasse, the Stavenow manorial judge and family attorney he appointed in 1723 after leaseholder Schmidt's departure. Two of Kleist's Blüthen farmers were under pressure, since they depended on land Kleist was appropriating while the other fullholders refused them compensation. Now one of them, mayor Jacob Meyer, "has absconded with sack and pack, and if the poor people don't get help soon, I'll lose the other as well." Kleist instructed Hasse to tell the authorities forcefully that, "if the resurveying isn't soon brought to conclusion, I'll certainly lose the other farmer, since it's impossible for the people to manage amid the prevailing confusion." A bailiff's letter informed Kleist that Meyer took "his entire inventory – livestock, tools, and everything." To search for him was pointless, since he had certainly fled to safety in nearby Mecklenburg.[90]

Kleist seemingly gained the regal ear, for an order from Frederick William I's inner circle to the District Commissioners upheld his wish that the present harvest and the next sowings should follow the new boundaries. Kleist's subjects must be protected from harassment, which had led one of them "to abscond and several others to make known they might follow his example." As for the survey, "our von Kleist" had challenged Platen and fellow commissioners to pay 1,000 talers into the "recruitment fund," which Frederick William I drew upon, among other purposes, to expand his regiment of specially tall soldiers, as a wager that Kleist's claims were hollow. Kleist would hazard the same handsome money against them.[91]

[88] Ibid., fos. 6–7.   [89] No. 624, fos. 1–3.   [90] No. 712, fos. 169–72.   [91] No. 596, fos. 58–9.

The government asked Kleist to respond to the commissioners' charges. He and Judge Hasse wrote from Potsdam, harshly recapitulating Kleist's criticisms and pugnaciously defending his brother against "the disgraceful defamations and untrue calumnies." Brother Bernd only called for troops to provide Stoltz's surveyors with "the most pressingly needed cover against farmers' violence," which District Commissioners and their "friends and in-laws" had encouraged.[92] Kleist's intransigence triumphed. The anti-Kleist party capitulated, counseling against prolonging the conflict, since farmers could not prepare the fallow field for fall sowing without knowing what land was theirs. Kleist's two subjects would therefore gain admittance "into the common fields."[93] The five crown farmers dissented. They were the chief losers, since their pre-equalization holdings were biggest. They petitioned the king to save their lands, without which "we will be completely and totally ruined." They asked protection from Kleist, emphasizing his responsibility for the previous year's "military execution," in which their cooking pots were impounded and "our women were grievously thrashed from one corner to the next." They threatened resigning their holding, "out of fear."[94]

Judge Hasse assembled the Blütheners "to bring the land conflict to an end." The newly surveyed plots were redistributed by lot and the two Stavenow fullholdings integrated into the open-field system. Hasse called the crown farmers before the village mayoral court and asked whether they would "permanently abide" by the new order. They said they were "well content and better off now," a sentiment, seemingly forced, likewise elicited from the other farmers.[95] After-tremors followed. The government ordered Major-General Goltz to investigate charges against Captain Kleist and punish libels against him. Instructed by Berlin to supply copies of his documentation, District Commissioner Platen replied that "by a strange coincidence some of the reports were no longer on hand."[96]

Judge Hasse later summoned two crown farmers and warned them to leave their Stavenow colleagues to harvest the lands assigned them in peace. They were to return the grain they had "already secretly taken" from these fields or face asset impoundment.[97] Later the Blütheners decided to parcel out the disputed 29 *Morgen* saved from Kleist's grasp, cultivated provisionally as "cabbage gardens," into open-field strips.

---

[92] Ibid., fos. 101–2; no. 632, fos. 2–3.   [93] No. 596, fos. 60–1.   [94] No. 712, fos. 159–60.

[95] No. 407, fo. 33.   [96] No. 596, fos. 22, 85–6.   [97] Ibid., fo. 57.

Some villagers aimed to partition this land into private holdings. Hasse and Captain Kleist thought it necessary to bind them solemnly, on pain of 1-taler fines, to observe only "communally" fixed usages.[98]

So ended Blüthen equalization, "an altogether convoluted" affair, as Hasse said.[99] Kleist sought to engross land he thought his own, though given the villagers before the Thirty Years War. The government's interest in protecting its tax base limited Kleist's ambitions, leading to the disputed land's partition to ensure that fullholders would actually cultivate the 2 hides on which their taxes were levied. Although the entire village surrendered land, the crown farmers, having expanded cultivation beyond the other fullholdings' range, lost most. Here seigneurial and government regulation halted the strong tendency of villages to produce a largeholder oligarchy.

The equalization shows that the seigneurial enclosure of land worked or owned by villagers was no easy matter. Government intervention alone did not prevent Kleist from working his will unhindered. The other noble landlords, allied with the District Commissioners, raised barriers, as did insubordinate and violence-ready villagers, to high-handed action on Kleist's part. No doubt Joachim von Kleist, as one of Frederick William I's senior army officers, enjoyed royal favor, enabling him to overcome an unfavorable 1705 Chamber Court ruling and recover some of the land. As for Goltz's soldiers, the damage they inflicted, assuming the women suffered no serious injury, was less than ruinous. The absolutist regime triangulated the interests of noble landlords, fisc, and land-poorer villagers.

THE KLEISTS' REFORM OF SEIGNEURIAL PRODUCTION

Blüthen equalization was but one of the Kleists' resolute steps following leaseholder Schmidt's peremptory dismissal. Contemplating manorial economy and villagers' obligations, they found order and discipline sorely lacking. After many investigations and decrees, they crowned their work with a compendious 1727 estate manual or *Hausbuch*. In it, its author Judge Hasse recalled that, despite Blumenthal *meliorationes*, when Kleist arrived in 1719,

everything was still in very bad shape. In particular, the buildings were very dilapidated, the fields were either overgrown with brush or covered with stones, or they were not properly cultivated and fertilized. The meadows were

[98] No. 407, fo. 42.   [99] No. 30, fos. 26–7.

swampy . . . and in general everything was so ill-kept that . . . Lieutenant-Colonel von Kleist in his first five years could not even enjoy a 5 percent return on his invested capital. Numerous debts obliged the first two leaseholders to withdraw before their years were up. But now, by the Lieutenant-Colonel's efforts, and especially by his brother Captain Berend von Kleist's four-year presence here, the lordship has been quite remarkably improved, as is evident in the estate inventory [the present *Hausbuch*] which the Captain instructed the court to make.[100]

The compliant Bürgermeister could expect these words to please his seigneurial patron. Still, the *Hausbuch* displays the lordship in a condition, unrivaled since before the Thirty Years War, on which the two brothers might well have congratulated themselves.

The manorial seat had grown more populous through settlement of workers providing new muscle for seigneurial production. The lordship's residence appears in eighteenth-century dress, as a "noble hall with two wings, two floors, and eight good rooms." The stable housed twenty-two riding horses, with two grooms' lodgings. The court bailiff had his own house. A large brewery included living quarters for brewer and helpers, an arched-ceiling cellar with masonry "hop kettle," malt dryer, brandy distiller, and fourteen-barrel copper brewing vat. "Beer is brewed every fourteen days or oftener, depending on whether there are few or many workmen here."

A large new brick-and-masonry dairy building displayed a "double-layered tile roof." Here were "parlor and bedroom" for the estate manager, "who supervises fieldwork and the Stavenow home-farm in general," and lodgings for the field bailiff/clerk assisting him. The Kleists had built a dovecote and "grouse-house." Various manorial employees and servants occupied two four-tenanted residences, each with baking oven. A large "cottagers' house" comprised "five apartments and as many chimneys, built of timber and masonry and tile-roofed." A similar house with four cottagers' dwellings was, like the smithy and smith's house, new. The tavern contained two public rooms and "requisite lodgings." The new "bee garden" housed beehive and honeymaking house. The church tower was new since 1726. None of Stavenow's eighteen buildings was thatch-roofed, though some at the nearby sheep-farm still were.[101]

The *Hausbuch* registered eleven gardens, including an "ornamental garden with all sorts of French fruit trees, newly planted in 1720."

---

[100] Ibid., fos. 6–7. [101] Ibid., Th. I.

Behind the manor-hall toward Löcknitz stream lay a meadow, "mowed for the horses in the summer." Seven other kitchen and fruit gardens supplied seigneurial household and servants. Tavernkeeper, smith, and shepherd possessed separate gardens, "and the cottagers and married servants, of whom there are fourteen, have cabbage gardens by the cottages half-free, and for the other half they work at certain tasks in the summer harvest."[102]

The Stavenow arable now encompassed three fields, the old four-field system having caused "a great deal of disorder and damage." Measured in sowings, the land encompassed 53 tons of cereals, two-thirds planted annually.

The arable here is good rye land, and now that it has been cleansed of stones and brush it can comfortably yield the third kernel year in and year out, and indeed the fourth kernel if it is steadily kept in good cultivation and manuring, and if to this end it is diligently mulched to increase fertilization.[103]

The Stavenow hay yield of 394 manorial-sized cartloads was good, as was pasturage, "so there can well be wintered over 100 milk cows, 150 other cattle, eight foals and a stud-horse, to draw young horses from." No other horses were needed, because "the farmers provide enough services."[104] The *Hausbuch*'s expectations for sheep, swine, and poultry were robust (see table 2.4). To Stavenow's deciduous forest of oak, beech, ash, birch, and alder were added in 1725 two plantations of the pines that, because of their toleration for sandy soil, began to proliferate in the eighteenth century. Hasse reckoned 500 talers' earnings from annual wood sales, "without forest damage or diminution." Oak and beech forage could fatten 330 pigs. Carp swam again in the castle moat and other ponds held pike and five other table fish.[105]

The *Hausbuch* left unmarried manorial servants unmentioned, but recorded names and settlement terms of freely contracted, married cottagers. Among them were seven laborers, four bearing Stavenow farmers' names. Each received, apart from lodgings, two cabbage gardens, meadow for keeping one cow and heifer or calf, and forage for two pigs gratis. They each paid 16 talers rent and worked without pay nineteen days in summer grain or hay harvest. Likewise contracted were a carpenter, a linen-weaver, and a manorial fisherman. The field foreman, nightwatchman, cowherd, and swineherd, working full-time for Kleist, enjoyed the same usages, but paid nothing or little in cash or labor. The smith could keep, for 17 talers yearly, three head of cattle

---

[102] Ibid., Th. II.   [103] Ibid., Th. IV.   [104] Ibid., Th. V.   [105] Ibid., Th. VI–VII.

Table 2.4   *Projected seigneurial production and incomes, 1727,*
compared with earlier real or anticipated output.

	1727	1719	1694	1601/14
Plantings (tons)				
Rye	35.0	24.0	24.0	32.3
Barley	14.5	10.5	18.0	11.5
Oats	19.5	17.0	6.0	33.0
Total	69.0	51.5	48.0	76.8
Livestock				
Milk cows	240	210	106	154
Sheep	2,200	1,900	1,400	1,000
Pigs	1,120	[531t]	1,020	?
Hay[a]	744	?	?	627
Grain rents[b]				
From mills	22.0	22.0	12.0	22.0
From villages	10.0	5.8	2.5	10.2
Total	32.0	27.8	14.5	32.2
Subjects				
Full/halfholders[c]	52	51	38	50
Smallholders[d]	25	23	21	27
Landless cottagers-laborers[e]	19	2	0	0

[a] In seigneurial wagonloads.
[b] Payable to lordship alone (excluding ecclesiastical grain rents).
[c] Performing labor service with horse-teams.
[d] Performing manual labor service.
[e] Wage laborers and part-time craftsmen, as distinct from contracted manorial servants.
Source: 1727: no. 30 (projection); 1719: no. 240 (Meyer's appraisal [projection]); 1694: no. 282 (Ziecker's reported output); 1601/14: no. 255 (appraisal for sale [reported output]).

and forage freely 3–4 pigs. The tavernkeeper, employing various ser-vants, paid 22 talers for cropland and to graze four cows and fatten six pigs.

The *Hausbuch* sketched the anciently deserted Dargardt village, whose ruined farmhouses and church were still discernible. Stavenow held three-eighths and Eldenburg crown estate the remainder of its fields, which Stavenow leased to its Sargleben smallholders and Garlin farmers for grain rents. The same villages leased meadows for 69 talers yearly. The Garliners rendered forty-two days of unpaid plowing for Dargardt grazing and forage. Semlin manor-farm now possessed a managerial dwelling with two wings, each with two parlors and two bedrooms. The lordship leased some of its inalienable "knightly land" to its four Karstädt smallholders. The clay soil was good, and better plowing for drainage would produce higher yields. One horse-team harrowed and hauled manure, while "the farmers do the other field-work." Yet among the cattle were twelve draft-oxen, witnessing a continuing need to reinforce villagers' traction with the lordship's own. At Premslin manor-farm, a manager's house was under construction. The land was good, cultivable entirely by the villagers without need for seigneurial teams. The woodlands had been replanted in oak trees.[106] A leaseholding dairyman lived here, paying 5 talers per head for Stavenow's sixty milk cows. A seigneurial foreman supervised fieldwork, earning lodgings and fuel, 12 talers cash, free fodder for a cow and calf, 19 bushels of grain and peas, a half-bushel of salt, and yearly a pig and sheep.

The *Hausbuch* said the Kleists equalized all village hides, each fullholder now holding land for annual plantings of 24 rye-bushels and 12 each of barley and oats. In Premslin, Kleist equalized grain rents and paid off cash sums owed to urban creditors that had long been petty burdens on many villagers. Low uniform grain rents of 3 rye-bushels from each fullholding replaced the former "great differences" in rents "which had immoderately weakened some farms." The fullholders' Elbe grain-hauls had fallen from 24 to 18 bushels, but the *Hausbuch* emphasized their duty to work in the seigneurial rye harvest "outside manorial service" (beyond the usual three weekly service days). The farmers' other unpaid sheep-shearing, garden, and flax-work now figured as the "seven extra days," absolvable with six actual days' manual labor.[107]

Glövziners' and Karstädters' rents and services mirrored Premsliners', except that Glövzin fullholders now all delivered 6 rye-bushels instead of an earlier 8 maximum. Blütheners gave 12 bushels, as of old, but now rendered two rather than three weekly service days. Sarglebeners, for extra seigneurial land, now delivered 4 bushels and served two days weekly. Mesekow smallholders retained 6-bushel rents, but had seigneurial pasturage and forest mulch for three days' extra manual labor yearly. Karstädters had long owed – perhaps in return for seigneurial pasture or meadowland – heavy 18-bushel rents, partly payable to Premslin's pastor. Now seigneurial deliveries fell to 12 bushels, while pastoral payments ceased, as Kleist liquidated the

---

[106] Ibid., Semlin.   [107] Ibid., Premslin.

Quitzows' ancient debts, long serviced by village grain deliveries to the church. The Kleists equalized at modest levels villagers' tribute grain deliverable to local pastors, remitting – as for the Karstädters – old-established burdensome excesses while pocketing remaining, previously pawned rents.

Kleist resettled one of Stavenow's few remaining abandoned farms. His smallholder Johann Krumm proposed to rebuild for his married son's habitation "Kopmann's deserted farm," a three-quarter holding previously leased to local farmers. Krumm pledged "all his worldly possessions." Kleist agreed "to invest the son with hereditary possession," granting necessary lumber along with six years rent-free and promising also to arrange tax exemption, but leaving the Krumms to buy horses and other stock. At the swearing in, the lordship promised Krumm's son succession for his heir.[108] Kleist unquestioningly accepted villagers' hereditary tenure. A settled farmer's rents and services were sufficiently valuable.

The *Hausbuch* forecast seigneurial harvests and other production considerably beyond ill-fated leaseholder Meyer's 1719 projections. The Kleists even aimed to surpass early seventeenth-century peaks, as table 2.4 shows.

To reach these ambitious goals the Kleists settled many new workers. They were prepared to pay heavier wage-bills to secure an adequate labor supply. The grain rent reductions they conceded sought to fit their subjects for more diligent toil. But they did not forget to think also of coercion.

THE KLEISTS' NEW DISCIPLINE

In 1723, Judge Hasse recorded, probably at Kleist's dictation, instructions doubtless meant for villagers' ears.

Herr Administrator [leaseholder Schmidt] is leaving and Herr Colonel himself is taking over his estates' management. Every subject performing manorial services shall therefore come and do diligent and competent work, especially at planting time.

All subjects shall render good manorial services, arrive at the manor at proper time, and work just as well, by hand or with horses, as they do on their own land, and also use the same kind of wagon.

[The villagers shall not, on pain of double penalties, ignore court summonses.] Much less should they absent themselves from manorial service when called to it, or they will work two days instead of one, or spend a day in jail.

---

[108] No. 200, fos. 223–4.

The proclamation also menacingly promised enforcement of royal orders concerning the residual manorial service obligations of retired farmers.[109]

Hasse and Captain Kleist later assembled Stavenow's housed laborers and cottagers. They were all "to take good care of their lodgings," paying quarterly rents. Accepting rent-paying lodgers required seigneurial approval. Such sub-tenants rendered one day's unpaid weekly manual labor, if claiming manorial food rations, or one day biweekly, if they fed themselves. The burden of laborers' meals, and the lordship's continuing readiness to supply them, are evident. If cottagers grazed more than the two head of cattle allowed them gratis, they would pay standard fees. They could freely collect fallen forest wood, but whoever stole timber or fencing "shall pay 2 talers more than the wood's value or, depending on whether man or woman, wear the Spanish overcoat or the fiddle" – the latter a neck-encompassing, pain-inducing device, lighter than the overcoat – "for a whole day."[110]

In 1726, the Kleists and Hasse summoned Stavenow farmers from Blüthen, Glövzin, and Premslin. They said they wished "the farmers to shoulder their burdens equally and have the same farmland and meadows." Each village's grain rents were made uniform, although – a sign of the Kleists' initial aggressiveness – the payments announced here were twice those the *Hausbuch* later recorded from Glövzin and Premslin. These terms "shall in the future be strictly and firmly observed, and those farmers who oppose this order and system will have to leave their farms." Yet the lordship soon reduced its rent claims.[111] Because these fullholders were already cultivating equal arable, this rent standardization provoked less conflict than Blüthen equalization. But the four Glövzin smallholders resisted repartition, leading the court to order the mayor and aldermen to perform the job, threatening recalcitrants with "eight days' lying here [in Stavenow dungeon] in chains."[112]

Accompanying its rent reforms, and to gain future cooperation, the lordship leased its Blüthen, Glövzin, and Premslin farmers parcels of Löcknitz meadowland to increase their meager communal hay supplies. Kleist had already regulated Premslin pasturage. Observing that "great disorder with the livestock has taken root" there, he issued a new grazing schedule (see table 2.5).

Farmers' lodgers had no grazing rights, nor could they share their landlords' allocations, but needed to pay the village to include animals

---

[109] No. 704, fo. 32. [110] No. 200, fo. 22. [111] Ibid., fos. 48–9. [112] Ibid., fos. 61–2.

Table 2.5   *Livestock grazing rights in Premslin village, 1724*

Allowable number of animals	Draft-animals (horses or oxen)	Cattle	Sheep	Geese[a]
Category of farmer				
Fullholder	8	4	16	25
Halfholder	6	4	12	19
Smallholder	4	2	8	13
Cottager	–	2	4	–

[a] For the fullholder: four geese, one gander, and twenty young geese.
Source: No. 200, fos. 23–4.

in communal herds. Villagers could only exceed their allocations at the cost of similar payments. Cattle could substitute for horses or oxen. Some trouble attended these usages' demarcation. Two Premsliners, von Karstedt subjects, complained the commune was infringing their grazing rights, but Karstedt, Hasse wrote, "concedes that, after he took away some cropland from these farmers, they should only rank as halfholders, not fullholders." Not just the Kleists were reclaiming land from their villagers.[113]

The Premslin farmers' communal pasturage was not unfavorable, though whether they possessed enough hay and straw adequately to winter over their animals is questionable. Hence the new Löcknitz meadows' importance. Hasse recorded that, although a wagonload of hay was worth at least 1 taler, the lordship rented these meadows, yielding several loads, to Blütheners for 8 groschen and one day's plowing, to Glövziners for 16 groschen, and to Premsliners for 12 groschen. The Kleists strained to extract the last penny from these dealings, though without full success, for the *Hausbuch* later recorded meadow rents of 8 groschen from Blütheners and 12 groschen from the others, whose allotments were larger. The Mesekow smallholders earlier enjoyed access to seigneurial meadows, but in January 1727 the court informed them that "because of the Löcknitz's improvement and the very expensive clearing of its meadows," they would have to pay for their usages with two days of yearly "pasture service." They agreed, provided the lordship gave them a stand of soft wood near the mill pond, which it did.[114] Disadvantaged in the meadow-leasing were the comparatively prosperous Karstädters, who lost land they had rented for 20 talers

[113] Ibid., fos. 23–5.   [114] Ibid., fos. 61–2.

yearly. Possibly they found other meadows, though the Blütheners asked to be "protected from the Karstädters."

These streamside meadows were a valuable acquisition. The Kleists rented them cheaply, partly to forestall farmers' excuses about their draft-animals' weakness when heavy exertions were demanded. As some said who thought their allotments too small, "they won't even have two cartloads apiece, and with that it will be impossible to bring their animals through the winter and perform manorial services." The judge agreed to investigate. Soon thereafter the lordship leased the Premsliners additional meadowland, at another 12 groschen per farm.[115]

In 1727 Kleist supplied the recently rebuilt Stavenow church tower with three bells, Berlin-cast and weighing 1,260 pounds. They bore Kleist's arms, and cost 278 talers. Among their purposes was doubtless a more scrupulous accounting of time.[116] Yet neither bells nor Kleist's concessions made the farmers overnight into model subjects. In 1728 Hasse summoned them before the Stavenow court to hear the following announcement:

Many disorders have been observed in the performance of manorial services, since some people bring such poor horse-teams they can't finish the job, while others work so unconscientiously and disobediently that nothing gets done. His Excellency Colonel von Kleist has ordered this state of affairs corrected, if only by having those who cannot bring a serviceable team do their work manually. Those who do possess teams with a good wagon and other equipment will serve from Easter until three weeks after Michaelmas [29 September] from six o'clock in the morning until returning home at six o'clock in the evening, with a rest at midday of two or three hours after unharnessing and feeding the horses. From three weeks after Michaelmas to Easter they will report for service at eight o'clock in the morning and leave again at four o'clock, stopping at midday for one to one and a half hours. They must demonstrate the greatest possible diligence in their work or, if they do not, expect to be removed from their holdings and replaced by better farmers. Manual labor services must be performed by farmers themselves, or they must send able people in their place, or otherwise expect the same punishment. They must also report for service at sunrise and leave only at sunset, and not rest at midday longer than one hour. In the harvest, there can be no fixed hours for service with horse-teams, which must be regulated according to the work that needs doing.

Judge Hasse's audience was somewhat indifferent. He recorded in his transcript book that, "as the preceding resolution was to be publicized to the subjects," seven Glövziners "had already left, and for this disobedience they shall each pay 6 groschen or stand two hours in the

[115] Ibid., fos. 68–9. [116] No. 712, fo. 205.

Spanish overcoat." Three of the seven then turned up "and excused themselves, saying they had not gone away but were down among the farm servants," having left the meeting section where the landed house-holders sat. Hasse decided "their punishment will be overlooked." But the Glövziners were slow to improve. Later that year, Hasse recorded that "Glövzin commune was advised to show more good faith in mano-rial service or face hard corporal punishment."[117]

In 1728 Bernd Kleist moved to his own Pomeranian estate. Replacing him was tenant-farmer Johann Friedrich Hartz, to whom Colonel Kleist leased Stavenow until 1740. Judge Hasse's 1728 work rules coin-cided with the inauguration of Hartz's – as it transpired – sometimes brutal regime. Captain Kleist's final act at Stavenow was to assist in a drastic revision of the farmers' retirement and inheritance practices. Though never implemented, it illuminates the Kleists' efforts to bend their subjects to their will. Speaking for Joachim von Kleist, captain and judge recorded in the *Hausbuch* that they had seen all too well

how the farms here must necessarily fall into inescapable debts and ruin because of premature, long and tedious retirements, since elders select for themselves the best cropland and meadows while heaping on children receiv-ing the farm all burdens but withholding from them the best enjoyment of the above-mentioned lands. So it is hereby once and for all permanently decreed that in future the present retirees, so long as they live peaceably on the farm-stead and help with its work, may remain there. But in future no more fixed retirement provisions are to be allowed. Instead the proprietor shall remain the household's master so that the son or the daughter who has a mind to take over the farm one day will assist the farmer all the more industriously or, in the opposite case, shall have no hope to gain the farm.[118]

This decree, though couched in Hasse's righteous rhetoric, reveals a seigneurial effort to concentrate the villagers' resources in the hands of the tax- and rent-paying proprietors. By denying household heads com-fortable and lengthy retirements, the lordship aimed to prevent the dispersion of farm assets on which it based rent claims. And by strengthening working farmers' – and through them the lordship's own – authority over prospective heirs, the Kleists aimed to improve discipline constraining young adults. Village youth's late marriages and dependency on parents, employers, and seigneurial and military authorities produced pent-up frustrations that sometimes exploded in insubordination or violence, including in manorial service, to which farmers often sent sons in their own stead.

---

[117] No. 200, fos. 97–8.   [118] No. 30, fos. 48–9.

CONCLUSION

Eighty years after 1648, neither lordship nor farmers could suppose all was well in the countryside. If in the seventeenth century's second half the villagers took advantage of their scarce numbers to ratchet down seigneurial rents, they still carried, in a period of low prices, the new burden of absolutist taxation. After the eighteenth century's turn, despite the 1700–2 anti-rent movement, Prignitz landlords restored earlier exactions' full measure, if not exceeding them. Kleist reimposed the pre-1618 Stavenow labor regime in exchange for lowering previously claimed, though not necessarily actually received, grain levies, and for villagers' access to seigneurial meadowland. Would the future reward Kleist's efforts to secure his subjects' industriousness?

Stavenow's history from the sixteenth to the early eighteenth century makes a fundamental point about east-Elbian rural society, of which it was one among many microcosms: there was no fixed and stabilized manor–village relationship, but rather continual struggle for freedom of movement and material advantage on both sides, within an ideological setting of mutual obligation and solicitude. The noble landlords wielded government-backed disciplinary and police powers, but whether these could be effectively and profitably applied depended on a constantly tested and renegotiated manor–village power balance. It was not a society in which those invested with lordship could rely on deferential obedience. Neither was it a patriarchal society in which villagers could count on their master's good will. Nor was it a society so dominated by landlordly and absolutist coercion that common people could not defend themselves and gain advantages under propitious circumstances. The Blumenthal–Kleist transition shows also that new lordships, however determined to tighten the screws, confronted deep-rooted local practices and precedents impossible to banish with imperious flourishes.

It was a semi-marketized society, but capitalist development did not uniquely power its trajectory. The absolutist state-builders steered it both toward more intensive commercialization and toward bureaucratization and militarization, even if historians have exaggerated the centralizing and commandeering Prussian state's achievements. Among nobility and villagers alike, family and property played dominant roles, yet it was not an immobile, tradition-bound, or merely self-reproducing society, but one caught in historical flux requiring its members' constant adaptations. At stake were not just the loss of familial and individual reputation and income, but also the chances of worldly gain. In this, though it was a society far removed from the present, it was not a wholly foreign land.

3

Village identities in social practice and law

This chapter and the next enter village farmers' households and mental worlds, in search of their conceptual repertory and social and economic practices. The method is both analytical and descriptive, illustrating discursive and social patterns with the many pictures preserved, snapshot-like, in the records. These are synchronic chapters, encompassing the eighteenth and early nineteenth centuries, rather than linear narratives. They offer an ethnography casting unaccustomed light on ordinary people's lives in Brandenburg-Prussia. They also set the stage for the impassioned and sporadically violent lordship–village struggle stretching from the mid-eighteenth to the early nineteenth century. But understanding is first needed of the values and aspirations stiffening villagers' resolve, the material culture they protected or sought to improve, and the limits of their powers, solidarity, and courage.

This chapter considers personal identity's prime settings in household, marriage, and kinship. It addresses villagers' subordination to seigneurial authority, both in their legal persons and property and marriage rights. It examines social-cultural marriage practices and family and household life's quotidian dynamics. Among its focal points is family's or kinship's power to mold individual identity, or the balance between communally and subjectively ordered behavior. The reigning view is that village solidarities coerced individuals into conformity with norms and practices ensuring community survival and reproduction in face of manifold material and political threats. Family and kinship interests dictated marriages. Modern individuality, emotionality, and sexuality were only rudimentarily present. Gender-ordered age groups' successive rites of passage dominated life experience. Women bowed to men, while village elders governed the younger and deferred to landlords and state officials, seeking their backing.[1]

[1] Influential (or relevant) formulations: editors' introduction to William I. Thomas and Florian Znaniecki, eds., *The Polish Peasant in Europe and America*, 2 vols. (New York, 1956 [original: 1918–1920]);

123

Stavenow evidence supports these views, but not unequivocally. Reality was more complex, revealing greater degrees of individuality and subjectivity, among both women and men, than standard thinking foretells and greater fragility and tension in social structures whose village-ordering efficacy is often exaggerated. Death, despite religion's consolations, was a great disrupter. Facing elemental uncertainties, and with little help from lordship or state, villagers relied on kin-ordered and communal devices. When these failed, or when the authorities narrowed survival margins, reactions were often explosive.

HOUSEHOLD, MARITAL, AND PARENTAL TIES

Farmers large and small, at Stavenow and elsewhere in Germany where impartible land inheritance prevailed, lived in stem-families. These embraced parents managing the farm and paying rents and taxes, such children as had not yet found work outside the household, and grandparents or other elders inhabiting the holding as retirees, usually in separate quarters. Even if children had reached working age, servants to help in farming and performing manorial service were often present. In their absence or the elders', space was rented to lodgers, often day laborers. At the parent farmers' death or retirement, son or daughter married and inherited the holding, while remaining siblings, when grown, looked elsewhere for livelihoods.

German scholars long fixed their interest on the large-scale household community *("das ganze Haus")*. In its village form, this institution,

Eric Wolf, *Peasants* (Englewood Cliffs, NJ, 1966); Daniel Thorner, ed., *A. V. Chayanov on the Theory of Peasant Economy* (Madison, WI, 1986); Teodor Shanin, *Peasants and Peasant Societies: Selected Readings* (Oxford, 1987); Steven L. Hoch, *Serfdom and Social Control in Russia: Petrovskoe, a Village in Tambov* (Chicago, 1986); Michael Mitterauer and Reinhard Sieder, *The European Family* (Chicago, 1982 [German: 1977]); Richard Wall et al., *Family Forms in Historic Europe* (Cambridge, 1983); Hans Medick and David Sabean, eds., *Interest and Emotion: Essays on the Study of Family and Kinship* (Cambridge, 1984); Michael Flinn, *The European Demographic System, 1500–1800* (Baltimore, 1981); Beatrice Gottlieb, *The Family in the Western World from the Black Death to the Industrial Age* (Oxford, 1993); Hugh Cunningham, *Children and Childhood in Western Society since 1500* (London, 1995); Pieter Spierenburg, *The Broken Spell. A Cultural and Anthropological History of Preindustrial Europe* (New Brunswick, NJ, 1991); Wehler, *Gesellschaftsgeschichte*, vol. I; van Dülmen, *Kultur und Alltag*; Ogilvie and Scribner, *Germany: A New Social and Economic History*, vol. II; editors' introductions to Peters, Enders, and Harnisch, *Bauerntagebücher*, especially Harnisch's on demography, family, and household, as well as Harnisch's article, "Bevölkerung und Wirtschaft. Über die Zusammenhänge zwischen sozialökonomischer und demographischer Entwicklung im Spätfeudalismus", *JbfWG* 10 (1975): 57–87. Emphasizing, as these pages do, a wider range of village voices and individuation are Sabean, *Power*; Sabean, *Property*; Schlumbohm, *Lebensläufe*; Medick, *Weben*; Gleixner, *"Der Kerl"*; Wunder, *"Er ist die Sonn."* Cf. Heinz-Dieter Kittsteiner, *Die Entstehung des modernen Gewissens* (Frankfurt/M, 1991); Charles Taylor, *Sources of the Self: The Making of the Modern Identity* (Cambridge, MA, 1989).

presumably of medieval or older provenance, was thought by its nineteenth-century social-conservative admirers to have gathered stem-family members, servants, and lodgers under patriarchal farmer-managers' authority. When the "whole house" gave way to the modern, privatized nuclear family, the unhappy result was that servants and laboring poor formed their own disorderly and insubordinate households independent of the middle and upper classes' benevolent control.[2]

At Stavenow, the stem-family prevailed, but its members did not, seemingly, conceive it as a family. Consciousness, and its cultural manifestations in various mentalities, pose analytical challenges. The Stavenowers' thoughts and feelings are not unmediatedly accessible, but only in documents, especially the seigneurial court's. Yet from 1721 to 1771 there are dense records both of managing farmers' or their widows' remarriages and intergenerational farm transfers, including retirement settlements. The court then drew up precise farm inventories and contracts governing new proprietors' succession. Disputes often arose later, generating more records. Hundreds of transcripts survive concerning myriad other civil and criminal court cases, many with supporting documents, some written by the villagers or literate agents on their behalf. In these records the villagers speak with still audible tongues, indirectly, in the testimony the seigneurial judges put to paper, but also directly, in words quoted in the transcripts or set in writing.

Such sources highlight the distinction between historical evidence and interpretive or theoretical concepts. Stavenow kinship terminology is bereft of a name for the group to which the terms "family" (or "stem-family") or "whole house" refer. The word "family" (*Familie*) was not unknown, but its appearance in village discourse only once proves its marginality, especially considering the context. In an angry exchange between farmer David Zeggel and widowed Frau Berkholtz, Premslin manor-farm leaseholder, Zeggel impugned her honor, exclaiming before witnesses that she came "from families that long ago would have deserved the gallows if only they had been caught."[3] The families Zeggel meant were broad transgenerational lineages, not parent-centered households.

In seigneurial eyes, what counted were the farms or holdings their subjects cultivated, and the managing farmer's competence and

---

[2] See, on Brunner and his critics, Kaminsky and Melton's editor's introduction to Brunner, *Land and Lordship*; Mitterauer and Sieder, *European Family*. Superseding Brunner on medieval conditions is Werner Rösener, *Peasants in the Middle Ages* (Urbana, IL, 1992 [German: 1985]).

[3] No. 326, fos. 216, 220.

obedience.[4] Still, villagers might be expected to have had a name for their household groupings, yet the records are silent. Whether the agreeable concept of "house community" or "house companionship" prevailed elsewhere in Germany, just once did Judge Hasse hint at the possibility, writing, of a mentally stricken retiree's drowning death, that "the wife and other house companions and neighbors would be able to provide more information."[5] The court and villagers themselves routinely spoke of everyday farm management: "household" (*Haushaltung*) and "economy" (*Wirtschaft*). The first term meant both keeping house and running a farm. Thus leaseholder Hartz "officially consented" to eighteen-year-old Joachim Bahlcke's succession to the parental *Haushaltung* following his father's premature death.[6] Hasse ruled that retiring parents on a marginal smallholding "will not be permitted to maintain a separate household, but instead are to be provided for [by the managing farmer] in a single household only."[7] The verb *haushalten* meant no more than heading the farm. Hans Schultze said that, after twenty years, "he no longer wants, nor is he able, to run the household with the mother" (his wife) and so proposed retiring in his stepson's favor.[8] Recently widowed Anne Marie Bucken testified she "is no longer able to run the household because she is three score years old."[9] Rarely, outgoing parents and succeeding couples agreed during their transition to manage the household "communally" or "in common."[10]

Wirtschaft meant house and farm as domestic economy, with related phrases for managing it. Thus village mayor Caspar Kettelhöhn suffered his step-daughter's charge, seconded by "her mother's sister's husband," that, since marrying onto the farm, the debt-plagued defendant had "not run it well," diminishing its resources to her disadvantage.[11] A smallholder said of his deceased wife Catherina Grunewald that, while he was admittedly not her sole heir, "since he had had her constantly ill, so that she could not head the household," and because he alone paid for her burial, he might rightly claim her whole inheritance.[12] Speaking of *Hauswirtschaft*, or management of household as opposed to farm, Mary Jacobs testified she worked a half-year caring for her dying aunt Frau Grunewald, doing "all the housework." For this she claimed,

---

[4] *Höfe*. The colorless word *Wirt* was the most common recorded term for a subject farmer, employed five or ten times more often than "subject" (*Untertan*) or "farmer" (*Bauer*).
[5] *Hausgemeinschaft, Hausgenossenschaft*. No. 591, fos. 68–9.
[6] No. 591, fos. 45–6.   [7] No. 200, fos. 175–6.   [8] No. 715, fos. 42–4.   [9] Ibid., fos. 35–9.
[10] No. 664, fos. 1–6; cf. no. 200, fos. 207–8; no. 200, fos. 9–10; no. 326, fos. 194–8; no. 324, fos. 17–18; no. 591, fos. 12–13; no. 326, fos. 111–12, 139–43.
[11] No. 200, fo. 35.   [12] No. 356, fos. 5–6.

with other heirs' backing, 2 groschen daily payment.[13] Characteristic too was Erdmann Mentz's wish to remarry "because now as a widower he could neither run his farm nor even less also raise his children, some of them still minors."[14]

Mentz's statement, distinguishing between farm management and childcare, shows that "household" and "economy" were not synonyms for "family," but practical, work-oriented terms. Though parents, children, and grandparents – and sometimes other relatives – cooperated in house and farm work, these concepts did not signify parentally centered kin groups, still less charge them emotionally or normatively. Yet this discursive vacuum does not prove that psychological-emotional bonds between parents and children were weak. If villagers did not speak explicitly of family, a possible explanation lies in the instability and transience in husband–wife relations wrought by the high mortality stalking this society: a theme that reappears below. Individuals' socially and kinship-bound names are also instructive.

Men's dominant roles were interrelated: farmer, household head, father. To inherit, acquire, or maintain a farm, marriage or remarriage was essential. From this, in a society uninterested or unversed in contraception, followed numerous children.[15] Thus, a man might stand before the court as *Bauer* or *"Baursmann"* (farmer), *Wirt* (manager, proprietor) or, if he married onto a holding for a fixed term, prior to maturation and marriage of the farm's heir, as an "interim proprietor."[16] His status as householder emerged in the term *Hauswirt* or "householder and cultivator" (*Haus und Ackermann*).[17] Hasse described David Hecht as "houseman and tavernkeeper": a fullholder with liquor license.[18] The term *Hausmann*, which faded from judicial use, could highlight the housed farmers' class status, as in a dowry including "bedding with linen and clothing customary among housemen," or one with textiles "befitting a houseman."[19]

In a wife's eyes, the farmer was a husband (*Mann*). In wartime 1742, after the village mayor brutally beat Hans Ebel, accusing him of tax evasion, Ebel's wife confronted his antagonist with the words, "Lord God, Jochen, why did you thrash my husband so?" The mayor dismounted and imperiously whipped her on the arm and head "so that she was

---

[13] No. 358, fos. 78–84.
[14] No. 200, fos. 175–7; cf. no. 326, fos. 141–3; no. 326, fos. 19–20; no. 200, fos. 207–8; no. 323, fo. 8; no. 326, fos. 103–4.
[15] On high fertility and lack of contraception among Brandenburg villagers, see Peters, Enders, and Harnisch, *Bauerntagebücher*, and Harnisch, "Bevölkerung und Wirtschaft."
[16] No. 712, fos. 8–10; no. 200, fo. 40. [17] No. 200, fos. 164–5; no. 712, fos. 46–9; no. 591, fo. 28.
[18] No. 200, fos. 228–9. [19] Ibid., fos. 200–1, 197–9.

completely black and blue."[20] To his children, the farmer could be, not just father, but "corporeal [physical] father," as was Lorentz Benecke, who married Hans Röhr's widow. If Benecke "raised little Joachim Röhr as befits a corporeal father," any children the widow bore him would receive "inheritance shares and appropriate marriage settlements from the holding," though seven-year-old Joachim would have the farm.[21] Farmers were also frequently step-fathers and, of adopted children, "foster-fathers."[22] The respectable and propertied among them would also be other people's children's godfathers.[23]

Farmers' daughters perhaps dreamed of higher things, but they were fortunate to maintain birth status by inheriting the parental farm or marrying onto another. In court these women usually figured as wife (*Frau*), mother, or widow. *Frau* also signified female household head, as when retired women referred to "the present *Frau*" on the holding.[24] In farm wives' conflicts with female servants, *Hausfrau* or *Wirtin* came into play, underscoring house mistresses' authority as proprietors. In 1729, a maidservant, having spread tales of malevolent magic, sat two days in jail for "babbling against her own mistress."[25] Farm wives often figured as step-mothers, sometimes abusing their step-children and sometimes abused by them. The court often mediated, as in ordering a newly succeeding young farmer "to give his [widowed] step-mother full retirement" – provisions for two adults – "for twenty years, so she may raise the two small children" – the new proprietor's half-siblings. "After twenty years she shall enjoy half-retirement for life."[26] Step-mothers, like step-fathers, were linguistically assimilable to real parentage. Anna Maassen, marrying onto a farm, was instructed to raise her step-child as a "corporeal mother." Even if her husband predeceased her, she would then be protected on the holding "and not driven away."[27] Another ruling guaranteed a widower's new wife life tenure "if she is a fitting mother, industriously devotes herself to improving the farm, raises her step-children in the fear of God and otherwise in a praiseworthy Christian manner," and treated any future children she might bear equally with "those already present."[28]

As wife, the female householder appeared as *Ehefrau* or even *Eheweib* ("married woman").[29] But *Weib* alone could convey contempt. When

---

[20] No. 326, fos. 80, 93–4; no. 715, fo. 47.   [21] *Leiblicher Vater*. No. 200, fos. 187–9.
[22] *Stiefvater, Pflegevater*. No. 326, fo. 143; no. 326, fo. 221; no. 324, fos. 24–5.
[23] *Gevatter*. No. 326, fos. 194–8: no. 324, fos. 17–18.
[24] No. 715, fo. 47.   [25] No. 200, fos. 125–6.   [26] No. 324, fos. 2–3; no. 326, fos. 63–6.
[27] No. 200, fos. 197–9.   [28] Ibid., fos. 230–1.   [29] No. 324, fos. 20–3.

Grete Heydemanns, enraged at insults to her children and herself, took revenge on her neighbors' son, the victim's father testified that "people came around and said the woman must have been drunk to beat the boy that way."[30] The seigneurial impounder (*Pfänder*) Hans Röhr, whose contentious job it was to prevent villagers from grazing livestock on or otherwise violating lordly land, charged farmer Peter Babekuhl with resisting his horses' impoundment. Babekuhl allegedly punched Röhr in the neck, knocking off his hat. Röhr woundedly testified that "a gang of women" drove him away, so that he lost his hat. He successfully claimed 4 groschen in restitution, plus fines. Babekuhl fruitlessly minimized the incident, adding that Röhr injured his arm. He spoke more circumspectly of the presence of "ten female persons."[31] Far worse were such terms of abuse as *Hurenweiber* ("whores").[32]

Widowhood among healthy younger women with material resources was but a pause between marriages. Among older women, the term "mother" or "old mother" was widespread, eclipsing their widowed condition. Hasse recorded of housewife Anna Ladewichs, whose husband had recently died, that "the widow has driven the old mother" – Frau Ladewichs's widowed mother-in-law – "from the holding."[33] On another occasion Hasse referred to "old mother Marie Blohmen, Ebel's widow."[34] The term "mother-in-law" appeared, though – doubtless accidentally – its male counterpart escaped recording. But a woman's husband's mother might also expect her daughter-in-law to address her as mother. The widow Hoffmeister testified that her deceased son's wife "had never treated her old mother [the complainant] as befits a child and in future will also never do so."[35] But new farmer Johann Kiecks promised his own "old mother" – she was fifty-nine – "lifelong food and all necessary care, including clothing, and altogether to treat her as befits a son."[36] Sons-in-law assumed similar responsibilities.[37]

Such filial obligations, incumbent on adults, were learned in childhood. No court vocabulary signified infancy, apart from "little child" (*kleines Kind*), applicable also to seven-year-olds. In the early eighteenth century, Blüthen pastor Hero employed in the parish burial register the terms "little son" (*Söhnlein*) and "little daughter" (*Töchterlein*), and even the double diminutive for step-daughter (*kleines Stieftöchterlein*). But later the register spoke only of sons and daughters, infants or older.[38]

[30] No. 589, fos. 9–10.   [31] *Hauffen Weiber Volck; Frauensleute.* No. 200, fo. 137.
[32] No. 591, fos. 73–4; cf. ch. 9.   [33] No. 715, fos. 26–7.   [34] No. 714, fos. 179; no. 715, fos. 15–16.
[35] No. 200, fos. 94–6.   [36] No. 358, fos. 107–10.   [37] No. 712, fos. 6–7.
[38] Blüthen Parish Burial Register, Pfarramt Blüthen, West-Prignitz.

Children lived with parents until their early teens. Among a deceased farmer's ten children, a daughter of fourteen was "still at home." Following their retired mother's wish, the new proprietor would "keep the littlest son [aged twelve] on the farm until he has taken communion."[39] After religious confirmation children often began work as servants and apprentices. Taken together, children were siblings (*Geschwister*). The concept of biological sibling appeared, as when the court mentioned a deceased woman's "corporeal brother," though vanished.[40] The terms "half-brother" and "half-sister" prevailed, and parents spoke of "step-children." A farmer tried to escape a twenty-year-old debt, saying "this year he has already given a lot of money to his step-children."[41] A step-father retiring in his step-son's favor acknowledged that farm repairs had depleted his "cash reserves," to his step-daughter's disadvantage. They agreed that, following an elderly widow lodger's death, the step-daughter should have her "living-room for life-long occupancy, especially since she is only in frail health."[42]

Yet multiple marriages might dissolve kinship ties. Following the death of the man she distantly described as "her husband's step-son" and his widow's remarriage, an elderly female retiree lost all direct links to the proprietors of the farm she once managed and from which she now felt obliged to flee.[43] Such misfortune was not the common lot of numerous grandparents and step-grandparents living in retirement, many for long years. A "grandmother" died after having "enjoyed thirty years' retirement," longevity requiring her own retired successors to make the best of living together with the managing farmer and his wife until the grandmother "departed this temporal realm."[44] But untimely deaths sometimes compelled grandparents to take co-responsibility for the farm or risk losing retirement benefits. After young Christoffel Wilcke, having lost both parents to illness, inherited a smallholding, the court ordered the lodger on the premises to help farm it, noting that a grandmother was present and working.[45]

Grandfathers often served as guardians of their deceased children's offspring, who appear, not as grandchildren (*Enkel*), but as their "daughter's – or son's – child or children." Hasse ordered retiree Havemann, embittered at his daughter's death and his son-in-law's remarriage on Havemann's former holding, "to conserve his daughter's child's estate" – her maternal inheritance – "and not secretly give any

[39] No. 591, fos. 51–2.   [40] No. 358, fos. 78–84.   [41] No. 326, fo. 132.   [42] No. 513, fos. 51–4.
[43] No. 715, fo. 47.   [44] No. 200, fos. 44–5.   [45] No. 326, fo. 216.

of it to his nieces and nephews."[46] A farmer could become an unwilling grandfather if, as happened to Stoffel Seyer, his daughter bore an extramarital child. The child's father, Heinrich Fischer, was "not yet free from the soldiers" and could not obtain his commanding officer's permission to marry the mother. Hasse ordered Fischer to pay, meagerly, "the grandfather" 2 talers in yearly child support and the mother 1 taler.[47]

Kinship language did not far extend beyond the parental hierarchy. Here the commonest judicial term was "brother-in-law," though again, accidentally, its feminine counterpart escaped detection. Brothers-in-law were often farm proprietors tied together by marriage to the sister of one of them, and by her dowry, much of which the bride's brother – instead of her retired father – was bound to deliver. Sometimes he failed, leading to disputes. Brothers-in-law lent each other money, and were often drawn into their married sisters' household quarrels. They backed widowed sisters-in-law in legal matters, especially farm inheritances. Thus newly widowed Liese Muchorn needed permission from her deceased husband Jürgen Neumann's brother – the court called him her "brother" – to accept a remarriage offer tendered by a prospective interim farmer. Her brother-in-law agreed on condition the farm's inheritance be reserved for her children by his departed brother.[48]

Aunts and uncles were "mothers' – or fathers' – sisters and brothers" or their spouses (*Vaterschwestermann*), while cousins were these relatives' daughters and sons (*Mutterschwestersohn*). *Vetter*, also meaning cousin, rarely appeared. The modern, French-derived vocabulary of aunt (*Tante*), uncle (*Onkel*), and cousin (*Cousine*) found no echo among Stavenow villagers.[49] Nephews and nieces figured as "brothers' – or sisters' – sons and daughters" (*Schwestertochter*). A nephew might rescue his elderly aunt from neglect by sheltering her on his farm, or an uncle might suffer punishment on his nephew's behalf, as in a quarrel during manorial service between farm servant Hecht and field foreman Wirtung. Wirtung complained that Hecht "rammed him in the chest with a log." Hecht said "he was very sorry. He did it because the foreman beat his sister's son, which he only wanted to prevent." For this Hecht stood for a half-hour before the church door in the Spanish overcoat.[50]

---

[46] *Tochterkind; Bruderkinder*. No. 200, fo. 44.   [47] No. 664, fo. 3.   [48] No. 326, fos. 111–12.
[49] No. 554, fos. 1–7; no. 200, fo. 35; no. 326, fos. 139–40; no. 343, fos. 112–13; no. 714, fo. 41.
[50] No. 591, fos. 14–15; no. 715, fo. 47.

Concerning a step-niece, the elderly, dying widow Ebels instructed Pastor Carsted to write the following awkward words in her last will and testament:

And since her half-sister's daughter Catharina Röhlen was taken in by her, the *defuncta* [widow Ebels], almost in place of a child of her own, or at least as a little child; and since she rendered [her step-aunt] during her illness the truest services and care, and never expressed any irritation about doing so; so it is her will that the aforementioned Catharina Röhlen should, following her death, inherit the bed upon which she rested, as a token of her recognition.[51]

GUARDIANSHIP

Death's frequency among parents raised the role of minor children's court-appointed guardians (*Vormünder*) to high importance. Where godparents are only distantly discernible, giving small gifts of money to godchildren, guardians often served over long years of legal minority. The court appointed them from among nearest relatives, preferably the deceased's, since often surviving marriage partners remarried and produced additional children whose interests might conflict with preexisting step-siblings'. Village mayor Heinrich Besen's widow, testifying at her remarriage that none of her deceased husband's relatives were alive, proposed two unrelated farmers as her children's guardians. The court concurred.[52] Guardians' numbers varied, from one for four children to two for one. Grandfathers often served, grandmothers only rarely. Guardians most often were sworn in "by handshake, in place of a corporeal oath." Among landholders, guardianship was not status-segregated but kinship-oriented: a smallholder or lodger or tailor might look after a fullholder's children's interests.[53]

The guardians held their charges' inheritances until they married or made themselves independent, and defended them against unfair or abusive treatment. At Hans Dreger's death, it took "much talking" to his widow by his brother, guardian of the deceased's daughter by a previous marriage, to win her consent to reserve some of the farm's depleted assets for her step-daughter's future benefit. Simultaneously, her guardian took into safekeeping items the girl's paternal grandfather, dead a year already, bequeathed her: iron cooking pot, ax, trunk with

[51] No. 324, fo. 10.   [52] No. 715, fos. 8, 13–15.
[53] No. 591, fos. 30–2; no. 326, fos. 149–50; no. 326, fos. 154–6; no. 715, fo. 10; no. 715, fos. 70–1; no. 326, fo. 200; no. 324, fo. 19; no. 513, fos. 31–5.

lock, bed, coat.[54] At smallholder's wife Marie Bahlckens' death, her
three-week-old daughter gained two guardians to ensure the child's
future maternal inheritance: 17 talers, 14 talers of which the widower
had already given one guardian (the deceased's brother), plus an oak
cupboard and trunk holding the infant's mother's copious wardrobe
and bedding. The guardians received the trunk key, agreeing to yearly
"air out the contents in the sun."[55]

Guardians might defend inheritances against their claimants, as
when an unremarried widower mayor died, leaving five minor sons.
Their maternal grandfather guardian found they had partly spent their
inheritances – 19 of 54 talers – before the court could assign them
equally.[56] Where numerous children figured, younger sons' guardians
might indignantly find their charges' marriage portions smaller than
elder non-inheriting sons'. Guardians also bore responsibility for aiding
their charges' households in hardship. After the lordship won a farmer's
son's release from active military duty, enabling him to relieve his widowed mother as the paternal farm's head, the twenty-two-year-old
householder assumed, among other debts, a claim for 14 talers which
his guardian lent their mother.[57]

Guardians sometimes initiated suits to defend their charges against
physical assault, as when Johann Krumm's complaint led the court to
find that Jürgen Ebel "has been very unjustifiably beating his wife as
well as his children." Hasse ordered Ebel to hire a new "boy" to replace
his step-son, Krumm's charge, as Ebel's farm servant, so the ill-used
youth could serve elsewhere, and "because the housewife is growing old
and feeble."[58] Guardians' wards sometimes died, burdening them with
burial costs. David Hecht financed one such burial. It took him twelve
years to gain some recompense when Judge Hasse assigned him a collection of saws, axes, and timber-chain (though he earlier willfully took
a bible from his charge's household).[59]

OTHER KINSHIP CONCEPTS – INCLUDING "FRIENDS"

Stavenowers may not have spoken of parentally ordered families, but
they were conscious of the larger kinship groups encompassing them.
In this sense the word "family" once surfaced. Another uncommon and
perhaps ritualized term was "people" (*Leute*). In 1729, a quarrel between

---

[54] No. 200, fo. 246.   [55] No. 326, fo. 200; no. 324, fo. 19.   [56] No. 713, fos. 117–20.
[57] No. 358, fos. 85–8.   [58] No. 326, fo. 214.   [59] No. 200, fos. 209–11.

two households over accusations of magic and witchcraft found court resolution, one housewife declaring of opposing farmer and maid-servant that "she knew nothing of Milatz's and Niemann's people except honor and goodness."[60] But "people" oftener applied to servants or workers or a particular place's inhabitants, as when smallholder Schütte, accused of colluding with his lodger in the theft and sale of seigneurial firewood, protested innocence, saying indignantly of such lawless renters that "they [the Karstädt farmers] didn't want to suffer these people any longer in the village."[61]

The term "close relatives" occasionally appears in wills and testa-ments, meaning kin whether paternal or maternal. Halfholder Hans Müller, retiring with his wife, decreed that such cash, clothing, and bed-ding as they might bequeath should go to their "nearest relatives, pro-vided no quarrels or conflict arise."[62] Spousal kin could be distin-guished from one's own "side," as when new farmer Michael Glissmann and his wife agreed that, should she predecease him without children, he would inherit her estate to her "side relatives'" exclusion.[63] A blunt terminology appeared at farmer Jochen Seyer's and his wife Trine Muchows' retirement in new proprietor Friedrich Schütte's favor. Muchows reported she "is satisfied Schütte should take her farm, if he marries her sister's daughter, so that in old age she might have someone of her own [*von den ihrigen*] who will treat her well." But Schütte had already found a fiancée. A compromise led Seyer and his wife to declare themselves "satisfied that Friedrich Schütte should also take a stranger onto the farm." This cost Schütte 30 talers and a promise to provide them – "the parents" – with retirement portions "such as the father" – the previous proprietor – "had with the mother."[64]

It may surprise that the Stavenow papers' commonest term for rela-tives in general was the agreeable "friends" (*Freunde*), though too much amity should not be assumed.[65] The word could signal a kin-free con-nection, as when a farmer "disgustingly cursed" mayor Hans Nagel, only later to testify that he and Nagel "were neighbors and good friends."[66] A woman marrying onto a farm gained life tenure there "if she lives in peace and friendship with the parents."[67] But when David Zeggel cursed Frau Berkholtz "and her friends" (*Freundschaft*), he meant

---

[60] Ibid., fos. 125–6.   [61] No. 326, fos. 129–30.

[62] *Nehesten Verwandten*. No. 712, fos. 46–9; no. 358, fos. 104–6.

[63] *Seitenverwandten*. No. 513, fos. 40–5.   [64] *Frembde Person*. No. 591, fos. 52, 56, 58.

[65] The literature cited in note 1 on family and kinship offers no instances of this meaning of friends and friendship.

[66] No. 591, fos. 25, 30.   [67] No. 326, fos. 191–4.

relatives in no friendly sense.[68] In inheritance settlements, "friends" usually meant "relatives," as when a retired father, "to avoid all suspicion," agreed "upon the friends' wish" to swear he had not furtively taken his deceased son's money-bag.[69] Other "misunderstandings among the friends" might arise, or spouses' or retirees' "friends'" claims might be excluded, to the farm's current proprietor's benefit.[70] Dying widow Ebels, who bequeathed her bed to her step-niece, noted bitterly in her will that "her Karstädt friends would hardly concern themselves with her burial," so they "had not the least claim or right to her meager possessions."[71]

"Friends" often figured in decisions concerning minors, as when they approved twenty-year-old Christoph Buck's marriage and inheritance of his parental cottage following his widowed mother's death.[72] Or "the friends and guardians" might intervene to find their minor charges' widowed mother a husband and "competent farmer in the absence of a farmhand" – testimony in 1757 to labor shortage during the Seven Years War (and to many remarriages' unsentimental nature).[73] "Nearest friends" could signal "nearest relatives." Karstädt mayor Hans Nagel agreed to be guardian of widowed Glövzin mayor Jürgen Nagel's four children, saying he was Jürgen's "closest friend." A grandmother and uncle appointed guardians were "the children's closest friends."[74] Likewise, "side relatives" was matched by "friends on both sides."[75]

Whether kinship and marriage entailed love is a question discussions below of household life and illicit sexuality will illuminate. But of love the court rarely spoke. Nor, when it did, did the feelings of the individuals in question necessarily correspond to expectations, as when Hasse instructed newly appointed interim farmer Joachim Nagel, whom widow Zanders "has decided to marry on her holding," to "love the widow and raise and provide for the children."[76] Hasse once noted that Christian Wilcke, left by his wife's death with a three-week-old daughter, himself paid 1.5.- talers for inventorying the deceased's estate "out of love for the child."[77] Two less didactic instances are suggestive. Among the reasons for Jürgen Ebel's "very unjustifiable beating" of his wife and children were his wife's "shameless talk and inopportune love for her children from her previous marriage."[78] And, when deceased Marie Schulten's estate was inventoried for her four children's benefit,

---

[68] Ibid., fos. 216, 220.   [69] Ibid., fos. 194–8; no. 324, fos. 17–18.
[70] No. 200, fos. 20, 209–11; no. 713, fos. 117–20.   [71] No. 324, fo. 10.   [72] No. 323, fo. 8.
[73] No. 326, fo. 240.   [74] No. 715, fo. 10; no. 326, fos. 154–6.   [75] No. 200, fos. 164–5.
[76] No. 326, fos. 239–40.   [77] Ibid., fo. 200; no. 324, fo. 19.   [78] No. 326, fo. 214.

Hasse wrote of the dowry she brought into marriage with Joachim Hintze that "the two geese which she gave him out of love shall not be reckoned to it."[79]

STAVENOW FARMERS' PROPERTY RIGHTS AND STATUS AS SEIGNEURIAL SUBJECTS

In contrast to individual life's biological fragility, village farms displayed imposing longevity. The great majority derived from medieval colonization and, despite such disparities as Colonel Kleist high-handedly equalized, most had existed for centuries. Their occupants' property rights, and the seigneurial powers overshadowing, limiting, or annulling them, bore weightily on social identity. Village farmers' status as "hereditary subjects" stemmed from cultivating a holding rendering seigneurial rents and services. Unlike serfdom, subjection attached to farm, not person. But once a villager took the subject's oath, he and his family could only escape its obligations by recruiting a substitute farmer acceptable to the lordship. When a managing farmer retired, the lordship could demand of one of his sons that he step into his father's boots. Should other farms stand unoccupied, the lordship could require the new farmer's brothers to cultivate them.[80]

Did east-Elbian villagers look on farm tenancy as a blessing or a curse? Did they see the farms as their patrimony, or were they burdensome service holdings the Junkers saddled on them? Despite the rise of commercialized manorialism with its heavy labor demands, the subject farmers normally retained inheritance and other property rights (though these excluded division and sale of their land apart from the farmstead). But after the Thirty Years War, a widespread weakening of village tenures occurred. The lordships took control of many devastated and deserted farms. Though obliged to resettle them, they assigned the new cultivators hereditary usufructuary rights only. Where real serfdom had emerged before 1618, as in Brandenburg's Uckermark and Neumark Districts, Pomerania and Mecklenburg, the postwar era witnessed the conversion of many previously hereditary holdings, often now deserted, to short-term, non-hereditary tenures,

---

[79] No. 715, fo. 10.
[80] Fundamental: Lieselott Enders, "Das bäuerliche Besitzrecht in der Mark Brandenburg, untersucht am Beispiel der Prignitz vom 13. bis 18. Jahrhundert," in Jan Peters, ed., *Gutsherrschaftsgesellschaften im europäischen Vergleich* (Berlin, 1997), 399–427. Grossmann, *Rechtsverhältnisse*; relevant statutes cited in Hagen, "Crisis."

resettled with cultivators who might be transferred against their will from one farm to another.[81] The first, less onerous development prevailed at Stavenow, as in most of Brandenburg. In practice, Stavenowers' inheritance rights were strong and jealously embraced. Across the generations, into the twentieth century, they perpetuated a kin-ordered, if not exactly family-centered, farm ownership shielding a modest property accumulation that also benefited non-inheriting children.

At the farmer's swearing in, the court issued his "occupancy certificate" (*Hofbrief*). In 1726 Judge Hasse negotiated a farm's passage from Joachim Schultze, whom Hasse described as the holding's "possessor," to his son Hans Jürgen. Untypically, the "property transfer" had occurred three years previously, but now the lordship "formally accepted" the son "as a [seigneurial] subject on his paternal farm," as was confirmed by "this certificate of inheritance and occupancy."[82] The courts, and pastors, routinely described village farmers, whether large- or smallholders, as "owners," "proprietors," or "possessors."[83] Intergenerational farm transfers frequently qualified as "hereditary and proprietary." In 1745 fullholder Stoffel Seyer, "because of age and advancing weakness," proposed to retire. He and his wife agreed, "with the lordship's consent," to a "hereditary and proprietary transfer" to Dietrich Maass, who was "of good mind to marry and who had made fitting proposal" to Dorothea, the Seyers' nineteen-year-old daughter.[84] Other transfers were either "hereditary" or "proprietary," as when Joachim Seyer gave his son Caspar "his farm and appurtenances in proprietary [possession]," or when Heinrich Fischer, disabled by "great [physical] weakness," ceded his holding "hereditarily" to his married daughter.[85]

Hereditary tenure stood beyond dispute. When Stefan Bahlcke died prematurely, saddling his wife and seven children with a debt-burdened fullholding, Hasse thought it "questionable whether the farm should be left with the widow and her children." But seventeen-year-old Joachim, flanked by his guardians, appealed to his father's will and testament "and to his inheritance right," adding that Kleist had promised him the

---

[81] Cf. Grossmann, *Rechtsverhältnisse*; Harnisch, *Boitzenburg*; Enders, *Uckermark*; Kaak, *Gutsherrschaft*; Mager, *Geschichte des Bauerntums*.

[82] No. 200, fos. 200–1.

[83] *Besitzer*: no. 712, fos. 6–7, 30–1; no. 200, fos. 24–5, 148–9, 216–19; no. 324, fo. 10; no. 714, fos. 73–4.

[84] *Erb- und eigentümlich*: no. 664, fos. 1–6; no. 200 (1726), fo. 203; no. 200, fos. 204–7, 212–15.

[85] No. 714, fos. 73–4; no. 713, fos. 18–20; no. 200, fos. 216–19; no. 358, fos. 5–6.

farm. A year later, having found a properly dowered wife, he was sworn in.[86] Grete Häwecke, for whom Peter Ebel had been – as Hasse bluntly wrote – "found as a bridegroom," inherited her paternal fullholding, but only after a review of her two older brothers' claims. One, Johann, was a tailor in "London in England" (*Engelland*) while Peter, the other, "has also gone away and has no desire to take the farm, as attested in a certificate he gave the sister." Since the farm would bear the cost of supporting and, one day, burying the retired parents, Hasse annulled the absent brothers' otherwise legitimate inheritance claims.[87] The lordship also agreed that devastated or deserted farms' new tenants should possess strong tenures, as when it entertained bids to take the misfortune-plagued Blüthen mayor's farm, recently "furtively abandoned" by its tenant. Smallholder Peter Mattheis's proposal prevailed, opening the slippery path of social ascent to him. In turn, miller Richter took Mattheis's smallholding, obligating himself to its rents. Both transfers were hereditary.[88]

Farmers thought it their right to designate successors, though this they often shared with wives, especially after acquiring farms through marriage. Sometimes, when stricken down before retirement, they issued deathbed decrees, as did Stefan Bahlcke. Pastor Willebrand put to paper, heeding Bahlcke's wife's wish, her husband's last will: "Stefan Bahlcke, after having long withstood his sickness, senses his end draws nigh … He would like to see his widow and children protected on the farm until the children are raised, because his son [Joachim] is still too young to head the household and would willingly wait another twelve years." Bahlcke urged Willebrand to intercede with the lordship. Young Joachim did not have to wait, but soon, with a wife, gained the farm.[89]

A smallholder died "on the first day of Easter," leaving his wife and year-old daughter. The court scribe recorded that "on his sickbed the late Johann Griese requested of Herr Bürgermeister [Judge Hasse] that he should be so good and see that the farm is reserved for his only surviving child."[90] Posthumous circumstances might overturn such testaments, as when the court filed farmer-tavernkeeper David Hecht's "last will and opinion," with stipulations concerning inheritance by his first-marriage son and provisioning on the farm of his second wife and two young children she bore him. Yet, the same day, Hecht's widow agreed to marry her step-son's new wife's father and move with her children to his farm. For Hecht's son, this transformed his step-mother into his mother-in-law.[91]

Painful quarrels could arise over elderly farmers' conferral of succession on one son rather than another. Eldest son Joachim Fischer junior appeared in court, charging that father Joachim senior refused him the farm he once promised, favoring instead his younger half-brother Christian. Old Joachim gruffly said:

the farm is his, and he can give to whoever he wants. The plaintiff left him and could give him nothing, and instead earned something for himself. But the other son Christian held out with him, and gave him what he needed, while the eldest son didn't concern himself about him, and so he shall not have the farm. He is now nearly seventy years old and can't properly work the farm, so he wants to give it to his youngest son.

Eldest son Joachim junior said, "in his own justification," that:

he in no way abandoned his father. First he served here at Stavenow manor for five years, and then returned home to the father. But then he was enlisted among the soldiers [for five years] before getting his discharge. Since then he has served the lordship for some seven years, and the father hasn't asked him for money, otherwise he wouldn't have failed to help him. His brother [Christian] hasn't put anything into the farm except what he got from it, and he took something with him when he went to his regiment.

Questioned about this, favored son Christian, twenty-five, said he spent 8.10.- talers in fees (bribes) to get the permission to marry justifying his active-duty discharge, but claimed it was his own money. Though his older brother disputed this point, he also offered Christian livestock if he yielded succession. Joachim junior would even work at home for farmhand's wages if his father wanted a few more years as household head. Old Joachim stubbornly insisted that, if his younger son did not succeed him, he would "continue running [the farm], so as not to have to live" – this was doubtless a stock phrase – "at the children's mercy, because if he didn't have what he needed, he would have to go away," meaning, seemingly, he would have to go begging. The eldest son offered immediately to give his father 20 talers, promising "he wouldn't have to go away." Hasse ruled that since the old father now wanted to remain household head, the eldest son should help him run the farm. In time, the lordship would select as successor the son "who comports himself best and most peacefully." Here, family dispute weakened the would-be autocratic (yet fearful) father's authority, leaving

---

[91] No. 324, fos. 2–3; no. 326, fos. 63–5.

Kleist to decide the issue. This unhappy story's conclusion is undiscernible, but thirteen years later the younger son Christian occupied the paternal farm.[92]

Other fathers excluded sons they found objectionable. Christian Nagel charged his younger brother, Glövzin mayor Jürgen, with failing to pay him his full inheritance from the parental farm. Jürgen replied that "he himself didn't want the farm. The father forced it on him. The father didn't want his brother to have it, because he was a hell-raiser." Aggrieved, Christian recalled Jürgen's engagement party when, in their father's presence, his brother promised him 15 talers. Jürgen protested, saying their father only instructed him to give his brother what he could, adding that he alone paid for his parents' subsequent burials. Compromising, Hasse ordered Jürgen "without fail" to give Christian a "two- or three-year-old heifer in the spring."[93]

In eligible sons' absence, daughters inherited parental farms, provided their husbands were acceptable to parents and lordship. Fullholder Stefan Ebel, retiring "because of age and because this past year he completely fell apart, so he can't run his farm any longer, wishes to hand it over to his eldest daughter Ilse Ebels."[94] Daughters' claims could be as scrupulously enforced as sons'. A woman in her thirtieth year married and took her father's onetime farm, although by her eighth year she had lost both parents, subsequently living with a step-father, three successive step-mothers, and four half-siblings.[95]

Women marrying onto non-parental farms were promised life tenure for their dowries invested in the farm and for raising such children or step-children as fell to their lot. Sometimes, women received assurances that, should their husbands die, they might – whether they had children or not – head the farms themselves, provided they paid rent and taxes. This was especially feasible on smallholdings, with manual labor services a woman could herself perform.[96] But normally widows were expected to remarry or retire in a new proprietor's favor. Their deceased husbands' relatives might meddle in their choice of a new partner, as when a widow's brother-in-law claimed the right, as eldest of his deceased brother's siblings (though not his sister-in-law's children's guardian), to approve the parental farm's disposition, as amicably occurred.[97]

Interim farmers appointed during the minority of children whose fathers had died acquired strong tenurial rights. Johann Wilhelm

---

[92] *Der Kinder Gnade leben.* No. 326, fos. 141–3.   [93] *Juchheier.* No. 591, fo. 80.
[94] No. 712, fos. 44–5.   [95] No. 326, fos. 188–9.   [96] No. 712, fos. 30–1.   [97] No. 326, fos. 111–12.

Pankow, a journeyman carpenter who "with lordship's permission" married onto a halfholding, received assurance, for agreeing to raise two small step-children "until they can earn their bread," that he could "dispose of the farm as his own for twenty years."[98] The court approved Joachim Nagel as a twelve-year interim farmer responsible for two newly acquired step-sons; "if the eldest son doesn't prove suitable," Nagel could carry on until the younger son succeeded him.[99]

Farm inheritance descended from parents to children, excluding collateral relatives or "friends." When farms passed through inheriting daughters' marriages to the lineages of sons-in-law, Stavenowers sometimes sought to restore the farms to the parents' progeny through arranged marriages. We may recall the retiring farm wife who wished the successor farmer to marry her niece, "so that in old age she might have someone of her own who will treat her well." Strong tenurial rights promised the elderly security and welfare, if not well-being.

SEIGNEURIAL AUTHORITY OVER FARM INHERITANCE

Despite the Kleists' blustering threat, recorded in their 1727 housebook, to abolish farmers' retirement provisions and revise inheritance customs, in practice they accepted hereditary succession. Yet the lordship could intervene when suitable or consensual heirs were lacking, or economic crisis struck. In 1770 the lordship arranged twenty-two-year-old Friedrich Nagel's army discharge, appointing him farm heir over his older brother, also a soldier. Their father had died in 1765 at age fifty-one, but his widow had not remarried, perhaps because of the post-Seven Years War manpower shortage. In 1770 she was running the farm with two female servants, a sickly daughter, and a young son. Sizable debts had accumulated, including 31 talers' arrears in labor-service commutation and 24 bushels of grain rent, plus servants' wages, blacksmiths' bills, and 24 talers borrowed from neighbors. "But of these debts" wrote Hasse's successor Judge Betich, Kleist "wants to cancel all but 6 rye-bushels at 15 groschen each and tribute hen and ten eggs, to help the young farmer and in hope he will acknowledge this with thanks." The widow gained customary retirement provisions.[100]

Here the lordship, though locked then in bitter conflict with its villages, displayed patriarchal benevolence, erasing 42 talers' debt.

[98] Ibid., fos. 194–8; no. 324, fos. 17–18.   [99] No. 326, fos. 239–40.   [100] No. 358, fos. 85–8.

Whether young Nagel showed proper gratitude is unknown, but that Kleist rescued his farm is clear. Similarly, in 1724 the lordship invested landless lodger Johann Kiecks with a Blüthen fullholding abandoned in ruination by its runaway tenants. Kleist supplied Kiecks with new livestock, equipment, lumber, and a year free of rents and labor service, "which he accepts with thanks." Seigneurial self-interest is transparent, and probably upwardly mobile Kiecks' gratitude was genuine.[101]

When other lordships' villagers married into Stavenow's jurisdiction, as Eldenburg crown estate subject Hans Glissmann did, they needed a "release certificate" (*Losschein*) verifying legal departure from home jurisdictions. Whatever arrangements they might privately have made, the Stavenow lordship alone could invest them with a farm. Glissmann's betrothed's parents were hesitating to give him their farm, but Hasse ruled that, following the public announcement of Glissmann's marriage to their daughter, the wedding must occur. Glissmann would take the farm the following year, as duly occurred. Stavenow wanted Glissmann as farmer, just as Trine Vey Mattheisen, despite her stepfather's doubts, wanted him as husband.[102]

The lordship could dictate interim farmers' terms, as when in 1788 Eldenburg subject Christian Guhl married onto a Blüthen farm for twenty years. Major Kleist reserved the right to "assign him a few more years."[103] The lordship also appointed new cultivators when adult male heirs or female heirs' husbands were lacking. Colonel Kleist procured Joachim Seyer's army discharge, on condition he marry the widow of an accidentally killed seigneurial employee. Seyer was to farm the smallholding the deceased would have inherited. This arrangement inflamed the deceased's elderly mother's opposition. She pleaded unsuccessfully for her and her unmarried daughter's and son's right to retain the holding. Unfortunately for them, Kleist was satisfied the deceased's father had promised his doomed son and daughter-in-law the farm, justifying the colonel in conferring it upon the widowed daughter-in-law's new husband. Here, too, seigneurial dramatics were evident in Kleist's patronage of a loyal servant's widow. Hasse warned that, if peace were not maintained, the new proprietor and his wife would lose "their right [*Recht*] to the farm." The intransigent old widow vainly demanded retirement allotments from her unwanted son-in-law. She was, Hasse ruled, to have a back room in the house and "the same food and drink as her son-in-law puts on his own table." If the deceased seigneurial

---

[101] No. 200, fos. 9–10.   [102] No. 591, fo. 107.   [103] No. 513, fos. 55–9.

employee's young son survived and "behaved properly toward the lordship," he would inherit the farm.[104]

This was forceful seigneurial intervention, yet acknowledging villagers' property rights. In most farm transfers, the lordship could only seek to influence choices among available male heirs and inheriting daughters' husbands. These usually appear as decisions taken in the village households. Doubtless villagers wished to freely select their successors, but the lordship insisted formulaically on its confirmation right. After fullholder Joachim Ulrich's wife died, leaving two young sons and an infant daughter, he expressed the wish at his remarriage that his eldest son should inherit the farm. But Hasse voiced the lordship's will that it should fall to the first-marriage son "who is best suited."[105] Widowed Joachim Ohlert anticipated the court's response, stipulating upon remarriage that, if he died prematurely, his new wife should run the farm for eighteen years until his six-year-old son Heinrich inherited it at age twenty-four, "if he is well suited."[106] A similar wish was expressed, "if the overlordship does not think better."[107]

But the lordship sometimes overrode such pronouncements. When fullholder Joachim Maass remarried, Hasse ruled that whichever child from his first or impending marriage proved "most competent, most obedient to the parents, and the truest and hardest worker for the lordship will have the most hope" of inheriting the farm.[108] After farmer Jürgen Kratz's death, farmhand Joachim Thomss married the widow with five children and succeeded as interim farmer for twelve or fifteen years, depending on whether the eldest, who was then sixteen years old, "marries out or is not found competent by the lordship, so that the farm falls to the second son."[109] Yet the lordship only very rarely imposed successors against parents' and siblings' wishes. Occasionally it even accepted new farmers who had earlier disappointed seigneurial expectations. Such was Joachim Hecht, whose army discharge the lordship obtained so he might take the fullholding upon which his father had died six years earlier, leaving a widow and ten children. The court installed young Hecht "on condition he behaves himself better than he formerly did," and that he support his mother and pay his siblings' marriage portions from farm resources.[110]

Villagers' preference for male primogeniture yielded before the higher necessity, in other family members' interests, of having a competent

---

[104] No. 200, fos. 216–19.   [105] No. 326, fos. 73–4.   [106] Ibid., fos. 154–6.
[107] No. 200, fos. 212–15.   [108] Ibid., fos. 230–1, 228–9, 204–7; no. 323, fos. 5–6.
[109] No. 554, fos. 1–7.   [110] No. 591, fos. 51–2.

household head who could find a marriage partner with a good dowry or marriage portion. Seigneurial interest pointed in the same direction. It speaks for the efficacy of the more or less laconic negotiations between lordship and villagers preceding farm transfers that, in the well-documented years 1721–71, only three court-ordered farmers' evictions are recorded, all because of unmanageable debt.

Nor did farmers shake off subject status by recruiting "competent husbandmen" as substitutes, as was their legal right. Instead, villagers' sons, if so inclined, evaded farm inheritance altogether, while weary farmers sought early retirement on their holdings. When, rarely, the technical term for substitute farmer appeared, it served a different purpose. The parents of Catharina Zeggel, a newly installed full-holder's wife, obtained court assent that, should she be widowed, she would not be "expelled from the farm," provided that, if her children could not yet inherit, she remarried with a "capable householder" (*Gewehrsmann*).[111] Jürgen Zeggel took over a cottager's holding assured that, if he paid off its 25-taler debt, his daughter would inherit, if she too married a "capable householder."[112] Leaseholder Schmidt colloquially described one incoming farmer as "the new *Gewehrsohn*" and another as "the new *Gewehrsahm*," equivalents for "possessor." These farmers were not, despite their titles, serving to enable others to escape subject status.[113]

In the early nineteenth century, during negotiations accompanying seigneurialism's abolition, disputes arose over ownership of village farmers' "iron stock" of livestock and equipment, that is, of the working capital essential to a farm's operation and inalienable from it. The noble lordships often claimed that, since their forebears had furnished materials for rebuilding devastated farms after the Thirty Years War, and often also supplied farm animals and tools, villagers who after 1811 gained their farms in freehold should retroactively pay compensation. In good condition, the iron stock or *Hofwehr* was fairly valuable, as emerges from Judge Betich's 1767 account of a standard fullholder's iron stock. Of livestock it comprised the four best horses, two milk cows, two sheep, a breeding sow and pig for slaughtering, two geese and a gander, and a rooster and two hens. The equipment included two wagons, two plows, five harrows, timber-chain, bushel measure, farmhand's bed and bedding, one pair of sheep-shears, a milk churn, full and half beer barrels, three iron pots and "the largest brass pot." To this Betich

[111] No. 523, fos. 1–16.   [112] No. 200, fo. 16.   [113] No. 712, fos. 44–5, 46–9.

added all the grain in the barn and fields, except what belonged to retiring householders.[114]

After 1763, Major Kleist's conflicts with his villages inspired the broadest possible iron-stock definition, deducting such assets from a farm's inheritable property. Thus the lordship penalized its subjects for insubordination. In the 1727 Stavenow housebook, Judge Hasse and Captain Kleist had contented themselves with iron stock encompassing "four horses, two cows, one sow, one broad and one narrow wagon with necessary gear, one complete plow with a pair of iron plowshares, four harrows," plus seed-grain.[115] Yet neither the 1727 housebook, the voluminous 1759 Stavenow estate appraisal, nor other eighteenth-century documents staked seigneurial claim to farmers' iron stock's ownership. The point in defining it was to distinguish working capital which new farmers needed from the residual "estate" (*Vermögen*), distributable as legacies among non-inheriting children. The lordship limited its rare claims to iron-stock ownership to individual cases, as when leaseholder Schmidt noted of two recently resettled farms that the "requisite seed-grain and equipment" belonged to Kleist. But when Michael Glissmann took over his farm in 1726, Hasse recorded that he and his wife held "the farm, the iron stock, and the inventory in full hereditary proprietorship." In 1728, when Kleist handed over a deserted holding for resettlement, he left its new proprietor to assemble the iron stock.[116]

The villagers' investment with their holdings and corresponding subject status entailed various practicalities and theatrics. This proceeding – the "acceptance" – occurred in court in the presence of the seigneurial lord or one of his relatives, his leaseholder or estate manager. For occupancy certificates new farmers paid a fee and swore the "subject's oath." Signatories to this rather elaborate document were the judge and the farmer – in writing or with a mark – and often also, at remarriages, the children's guardians. The new proprietor kept the original, of which a copy, sometimes also signed by him, reposed in the court's protocol book.

The certificate did not confer ownership free and clear, but guaranteed, against dues and services owed the lordship, the new farmer's life tenure and right to bequeath the farm to heirs. The certificate's physical

---

[114] No. 358, fos. 32–4.
[115] No. 30, Th. IV. The Kleists' definition was little different than the first on record (no. 355, fo. 1 [1711]): "the winter and summer grain of all kinds," four horses, two cows, one sow, one wagon, and one plow.
[116] No. 712, fos. 6–7, 46–9; no. 200, fos. 204–7, 223–4.

possession was important. In 1727, Heinrich Kniepenberg, taking the Blüthen mayor's holding abandoned by runaways, requested a certificate's issuance "to insure the farm [in his possession] so that he can rebuild it."[117] Hans Zeggel ill-conceivedly brandished his certificate to prove that his daughter and her husband were demanding a larger dowry payment than it warranted. The defendants had raided his farm, seizing animals as their own. As Hasse studied the certificate, Zeggel's case weakened, whereupon he claimed he supplied his daughter's wedding not with the promised half-barrel of beer, but a barrel and a half instead. Hasse nevertheless enforced the defendants' claims.[118]

Occupancy certificates recorded all farm debts, including dowries and marriage portions payable in future. Thus Jürgen Gewert, having recently married a farmer's widow, faced his sister-in-law's claim on her departed brother's holding. Because the charge was unlisted in Gewert's certificate, Hasse overruled her, but Gewert peaceably agreed to surrender a calf.[119] The certificate also registered retirement provisions the new householder owed his precursor and wife. Failure to deliver might lead to severe conflict, resolved in court by punishments and the original agreement's enforcement. Often certificates specified rents and labor services, though the lordship had a Machiavellian interest in their ambiguity. An early eighteenth-century farmer produced a certificate issued him many years earlier stipulating but one day's weekly labor service, a provision the lordship could only alter at a new proprietor's succession.

The certificate might also define the farm's landholdings. In 1751 a newly installed fullholder claimed from smallholder Krumm land which, he claimed, Krumm had wrongfully taken "by force." This occurred, as the plaintiff's step-father Hans Schultze averred, "on the day before Lieutenant-Colonel von Kleist traveled to [East] Prussia, " where he died on army duty. Schultze had therefore been unable, as he complained, to appeal to Kleist against this loss. Fortunately for Krumm, his 1728 certificate confirmed his possession of the disputed land long before Kleist left for Prussia. This incident illustrates the decades-long reverberations of Kleist's "equalizations," and villagers' invocation of an idealized seigneurial authority.[120]

The certificate's issuance cost the new farmer about a taler. He also paid "acceptance money" (*Annahmegeld*), 1 taler for Stavenowers and 2 talers for outsiders new to the jurisdiction. Once the lordship postponed

---

[117] No. 200, fo. 64; no. 713, fo. 260.   [118] No. 326, fo. 201.
[119] No. 715, fos. 16–17; no. 523, fos. 1–16.   [120] No. 715, fo. 42.

these fees' payment for six years. In 1788 Major Kleist asked of a new outsider farmer "only 1 taler and made a gift to him of the rest, since he is taking the farm in bad circumstances." The fees were neither trivial nor crushing.[121] The formalities usually ended with the new farmer's "corporeal oath." In 1787 one, after hearing a warning against perjury, promised with upraised hand to be an "obedient and peaceable subject."[122] In 1724 – amid the equalizations – Johann Kiecks promised, "with raised fingers," to render the dues payable from "my farm." He swore further "to enter into no council against [the lordship] but, should I learn of one, to report it faithfully. So help me God through Jesus Christ his son!"[123] It was exceptional that in 1722 a farmer taking a newly rebuilt farm, whose iron stock the lordship claimed as its own, promised "neither to sell nor to alienate nor remove anything against the lordship's knowledge or will."[124] Occasionally, the oath was waived, as when Judge Betich recorded that Christoph Marwitz "promises the lordship, with a handshake in place of the oath, all due obedience, loyalty, and subjection."[125]

Farm transfers and the marital, guardianship, and retirement agreements accompanying them usually engaged numerous interested parties. After one such negotiation round, Hasse noted that all persons present "agree this compact shall be upheld firmly and unswervingly," whereupon the new householder was "formally" swore in and the certificate signed, including by Hasse and leaseholder Hartz.[126] In 1726, after Joachim Maass swore "by hand and mouth," Hasse wrote with Latinate flourish that the transfer was now "ratified" (*ratihabiret*).[127]

Table 3.1 illustrates hereditary tenure's strength and the property-holding continuity prevalent in the eighteenth century.

Despite the lordship's occasional reservations against male primogeniture, in over 40 percent of these cases the eldest son or step-son inherited the farm. In 20 percent, the eldest daughter or step-daughter and her husband succeeded. Another 22 percent comprised the proprietor's younger children or step-children, so that 83 percent of farm transfers occurred between parents and children. In 14 percent, the farm passed to entirely unrelated persons. In six of these nine cases, the lordship designated the retiring farmer's successor; in the others the proprietor and his wife found acceptable new cultivators.

---

[121] Ibid., fos. 26–7; no. 513, fos. 55–9; no. 200, fos. 28–9, 187–9; no. 714, fos. 73–4.
[122] No. 513, fos. 40–5. [123] No. 200, fos. 9–10. [124] No. 712, fos. 46–9.
[125] No. 358, fos. 5–6; no. 513, fos. 31–5. [126] No. 713, fos. 18–20. [127] No. 200, fos. 207–8.

Table 3.1   *Farm transfers among full and halfholders in Stavenow villages, 1721–71.*

Transfer of proprietorship	Number	Percentage of cases
From father to eldest son	22	34.4
From step-father to eldest step-son	4	6.2
From father to eldest daughter	6	9.4
From step-father to eldest step-daughter	7	10.9
From father or step-father to younger children or step-children	14	21.9
From proprietor to collateral relative or relative by marriage	2	3.1
From proprietor to kin-unrelated successor	9	14.1
Total	64	100.0

Source: Stavenow court farm transfer records.

Social mobility into landholding farmers' ranks was limited. In ninety-seven known instances from 1721 to 1771, turnovers from fathers to sons or daughters with spouses from families of equal landholding status accounted for seven of ten farm transfers. In the remaining cases, a new proprietor or his wife rose up from a lower status (if not income) group, although when such farms were economically weak (as about half were) the heir was actually marrying below his or – more frequently – her station.

PARENTAL AND SEIGNEURIAL POWERS OVER VILLAGERS' MARRIAGES

First marriage inaugurated adulthood's dignity and autonomy. In now vanished language, to marry was "to come to honor." An unmarried but pregnant woman's impending child's father could promise – assuming, he cautiously added, the baby arrived when expected – that "he will bring her again to honor" through marriage. Across the eighteenth century, marriage partners' wedding costumes were "dresses/suits of honor."[128]

Around age fourteen, children entered servant status, whether bound to parents at home or in another household. Though their circumstances might not be intolerable, they anticipated the moment when, in

---

[128] Ibid., fos. 200–1, 246–9; no. 591, fo. 102.

the judicial phrase, they would marry or "become their own masters" (*ihr eigen werden*).[129] For most young people, even upon reaching maturity in their twenties there was no alternative to marriage but further service under another's authority. Marriage alone could confer some degree of independence. A common term for marrying was the verb *freien*, as when poverty-hounded smallholder Christian Jetschurki reported "he had married off [*gefreyet*] one sister but three were still unmarried [*unbefreyet*]." Although etymologically distinct from the word "free" (*frei*), it yet may have reinforced marriage's connection with autonomy.[130] A colloquialism for women's marriage, employed by sexton Sauber, was the verb *verfrauen*, meaning to "become a wife." Sauber equated it with ecclesiastical *copulieren*, or church marriage.[131]

Though weighty in the bride's and bridegroom's lives, marriage was also an important social and economic event to the uniting kin groups, and even the lordship. Among landholding farmers, first marriages coincided with previous proprietors' and wives' retirement. Marriage portions were fixed which a new cultivator would pay his or his bride's unmarried siblings from farm resources. Incoming brides' dowries loomed large because they helped offset these impending losses. For the lordship, marriages replaced one village farmer, perhaps a reliable and valued one, with another whose capacity to render dues loyally was untested. These aspects of marriage might seem to have smothered the couple's personal wishes under a thick blanket of parental and seigneurial interest calculation. But the bridal pair were anything but disinterested parties. It was essential that a man marry an "able helpmate" (*tüchtige Gehülffin*), as was also true of women.[132] To oppose "pre-modern" strategies of advantage to "modern" romanticism is misleading. The challenge is to understand, not only elders' rationales for sons' and daughters' unions, but the combination of "interest and emotion" driving marriage partners' choices.[133]

Occasionally parents tried to predetermine children's future spouses. They might seek to secure farm transmission in their own lineage, as did elderly smallholder Hans Ebel, who retired after his one son and only child married into a fullholding. Ebel, "with his son's approval," gave his farm to local day laborer's son Christoph Marwitz. Marwitz, now marrying – in the hard post-Seven Years War years – a fullholder's

---

[129] No. 200, fos. 175–6.
[130] No. 715, fo. 42; no. 554, fos. 1–7; no. 591, fos. 56, 58; no. 326, fos. 100–1; no. 200, fos. 197–9.
[131] No. 591, fos. 12–13.   [132] No. 200, fos. 148–9.
[133] Medick and Sabean, *Interest*, and note 1, above.

meagerly dowered non-inheriting daughter, promised Ebel and his ailing wife the customary fruits of retirement. They agreed that, in future, one of Marwitz's children should marry one of Ebel's son's children, so as to put the old father's holding in possession of both families' descendants. Otherwise, Marwitz would pay Ebel's son 50 talers for the farm, should it be his children "who reject the marriage," or 35 talers, should it be Ebel's son's children.[134]

Such conditional arrangements better illustrate veiled property sales than parentally dictated marriages. Similar was an understanding between a still-childless retiring smallholder and his non-kin successor that, should the retiree and his wife "perhaps still produce a child, it should be married to one of the new proprietor's future children, whereupon [the retirees'] estate will remain [after their deaths] with the farm." Here the new proprietor had an incentive to steer inheritance toward his precursor's lineage.[135] More ticklish was a settlement at a fullholder's widow's remarriage. Her children's guardians and "the relatives" agreed the widow and her new husband would farm twelve years, whereupon her daughter, now ten, would marry a son of her dead husband's predecessor. Though both departed farmers bore the same name, Hasse saw no danger of illicit kinship. The deal illustrates the complexities that accumulation through premature death of successive inheritance claims could produce (although here the projected union never occurred).[136]

The one record of a parentally dictated marriage accompanied fullholder Daniel Mentz's death. Mentz left his wife Dorothea Zeggels "with a poor estate and considerable debt." Since the widow could not run the farm, "she decided to transfer it to her daughter," twenty-year-old Marie Mentzen, "and to marry her to Peter Hecht from Postlin." A twenty-two-year-old son lost his succession right, though not without modest compensation. Imperious as this display of maternal sovereignty was, the marriage survived. Having avoided court charges of any kind during their farm tenure, the partners retired twenty-two years later in a married daughter's favor.[137]

It was on economically troubled farms at times of the proprietor's retirement or unanticipated death that parents, especially young women's, were most likely, as was frankly said in 1751, "to be of good mind to restore the holding to proper condition by marriage."[138] Yet, as in this instance, debt frightened off prospective suitors, making arranged

---

[134] No. 358, fos. 5–6.   [135] Ibid., fos. 70–1.   [136] No. 326, fos. 139–40.   [137] Ibid., fos. 122–3.
[138] No. 715, fos. 30–1.

marriages easier to contemplate than conclude. Stable or strong farms did not lack for candidates among landholding farmers' non-inheriting children with decent marriage portions. Evidence of parentally dictated unions is sparse, even though parents' engagement in strategizing and negotiating their children's marriages was probably energetic. Nor did the lordship impose partners on unwilling children. In 1752, halfholder Schulze retired, after twenty-six years, in favor of one of his two daughters and her husband. But then "many great conflicts" arose because old Schulze wanted his new son-in-law's brother to marry his other daughter Lena, though she had fallen ill, perhaps irredeemably. Hasse ruled "this was not to be forced on the children against their will, but must be left to Divine Providence." Schulze was persuaded "to abjure all quarreling and conflict," whereupon "all discord was overcome and all forgave each other from the heart."[139]

Apart from judicial mediation, the lordship might accept or reject prospective new farmers. The absence here of controversy doubtless reflected the prudence with which marriage plans were formulated. But various considerations, including the need for sturdy subjects, might induce the lordship to accept as a married farmer a man whose earlier behavior, as instanced above, had been disrespectful. The lordship possessed still other powers impinging on village marriages. A subject wishing to marry and settle under another jurisdiction needed the Stavenow court's "release certificate" (*Losschein*), accompanied by – or functioning as – a "marriage certificate" (*Trauschein*), verifying its holder's legal departure. Subjects exiting with dowries or marriage portions paid seigneurial tax of one-sixteenth the goods' value. The certificate's issuance at reasonable cost could not lawfully be denied, though the lordship could claim its statutory right to hire farmers' children who were not departing expressly to marry, unless they had already served the manor.

The lordship could assist or impede its subjects' efforts during their years of active and inactive military duty to obtain discharges and marriage certificates authorizing them to take a farm they or their intended wives were inheriting. Frederick II, not wishing farmers' sons to associate army service with blockage of inheritance and marriage rights, wanted such discharges routinely issued. But much could depend on soldiers' lordships' readiness to advocate release and also on soldiers' ability to pay for the certificate. In 1741–2 Hasse sought discharges for

[139] Ibid., fos. 45–6.

two soldiers who confessed to fathering extramarital children with young women under Stavenow's jurisdiction, and now, perhaps to escape Frederick II's deadly wars, declared themselves ready to return home and marry the mothers. Here the lordship pursued its interest – successfully in one soldier's case – in minimizing poor-relief and disorder in its bailiwick.[140]

Villagers moved in and out of the Stavenow jurisdiction with disputes over certificates of release or marriage rarely arising. Agnese Zeggels "requested through her father" – young women could not act alone in such matters – permission to marry a non-Stavenow farmer. Her father reported her dowry as one horse, two cows, and a heifer, apart from wedding provisions, clothing and bedding. The court appraised the livestock at 20 talers, taxable at 1.8.- taler, upon which payment the marriage certificate would be issued.[141] Hasse released another farmer's daughter "if she pays 8 groschen on her inheritance" – a cow and a calf – "and 6 groschen for the certificate."[142] The nearby lordships, including Eldenburg crown estate, matched Stavenow's obligingness. Captain Karstedt at Kaltenhof penned a release ("*Losgebung*") for Joachim Müller to quit his Kaltenhof smallholding to take from retiring childless relatives a Stavenow halfholding, saying he did this "unwillingly, in view of [Müller's] loyalty and industriousness." But he was content to see Müller and his wife "seek their fortune," asking only that Stavenow return the favor.[143]

Villagers sometimes accused neighboring lordships of abusing their powers over marriage and residence changes. When Erdmann Mentz took his brother's farm, he said he was well over forty years old, and thus beyond army service. He had worked long years for von Platen at Kuhwinkel, "who told him many times that he held [Mentz's] discharge papers, but would not give them to him until he married." Since Mentz failed to marry, he remained – resentfully – on active duty, with its yearly maneuvers between spring plantings and summer harvests and, in wartime, exposure to battle.[144]

In 1731, farmer Hans Schultze found himself appealing a second time for seigneurial protection. "The Colonel had gotten him released from the soldiers," he said, so he might marry and settle under Stavenow lordship. He now asked Kleist's help in receiving a modest

[140] Büsch, *Military System*, and dissenting literature cited in the introduction. No. 326, fos. 73, 79, 141–3; no. 358, fos. 32–4, 98–103; no. 513, fos. 55–9.
[141] No. 591, fo. 35. [142] No. 200, fo. 132. [143] No. 712, fos. 46–50; no. 719, fo. 20.
[144] No. 513, fos. 45–51.

inheritance from his parental farm in another jurisdiction. Though he earlier obtained residency release there, "the bailiff [now] told him they couldn't let him go." Hasse agreed to intercede. Whether or not Schulze gained his legacy, he stayed at Stavenow. In his depiction, a grasping bailiff tried both to tie him down and thwart his inheritance rights, throwing him on Kleist's mercy.[145]

THE CULTURAL PRACTICES OF MARRIAGE

The Stavenowers followed no unusual marriage rites. The documentation attributes courtship initative to men, as when Dietrich Maass was "of a good mind to marry" nineteen-year-old fullholder's daughter Dorothea Seyers. He "therefore made proper proposal for her hand." Her parents "had no objections," agreeing to give him their farm "in hereditary possession." Maass offered "all his possessions" and, as down-payment, paid the bride's father's 9-taler seigneurial debt and 6 of 28 talers he owed his eldest daughter's day-laborer husband. Here a farmer gained debt relief from his son-in-law.[146] It was also said that a man made "seemly proposal" or "had brought suit" or, when candidates were scarce, that someone "appeared as a bridegroom."[147] Proposals were usually addressed to brides' fathers, but widowed mothers also approved or rejected them.[148] On courted women's responses records are laconic, noting at most (though crucially) that one was "willing."[149]

Formal betrothal or engagement was solemn and even legally binding, entailing gift-giving, including sometimes money or goods from marriage portions or dowries. Following arguments about a bride's parents' farm handover and retirement, Hasse lectured the obdurate father that "while marriage consummation requires parents' consent, the engagement has already occurred," sealing the farm transfer. "The marriage was to proceed promptly."[150] Engagements were cancelable, though at risk of painful scenes and material losses. The middle-aged widow Trine Zeggels agreed to marry Hans Schütte, but Schütte "has been for six weeks bed-ridden without hope of recovery. The engagement is hereby revoked and the sick man leaves the widow free to marry someone else, since she cannot run the farm by herself." The stricken Schütte returned to his erstwhile fiancée the "cloth she bestowed on

---

[145] No. 591, fo. 28.　　[146] No. 664, fo. 5.
[147] No. 200, fos. 204–7; no. 715, fos. 8, 13–15; no. 200, fos. 220–2; no. 591, fo. 107.
[148] No. 326, fo. 211.　　[149] No. 200, fos. 246–9.　　[150] No. 591, fo. 107.

him as a gift, demanding she return the hard taler he gave her." But she claimed the money had gone for the engagement celebration. Schütte's father argued these could not have exceeded 1 groschen per person (a modest festivity). The widow, relaxing her tight fist, returned the money.[151]

Broken engagements were legally actionable. Marie Schütte summoned Joachim Niemann six days after his marriage into a smallholding's proprietorship. Four years earlier, she said, when both worked at Stavenow manor, Niemann promised her marriage, giving her "a Frisian dress" as pledge and making suit to her parents. She imagined "she was dealing with a decent fellow." Niemann weakly claimed "what he said wasn't meant seriously." Hasse ruled that "for her waiting and trouble and for his impertinence he will pay plaintiff 6 talers" – a large sum – "once and for all," whereupon all parties shook hands.[152]

Another case displayed farmer Joachim Brüning speaking for his wife's niece, Liene Völschen, "who had wanted to marry the defendant," her erstwhile suitor who had meanwhile married another farm-inheriting woman. "She brought a coat to him and lent his foster-father 2 talers." The defendant also collected from her father's farm 4 rye-bushels, seemingly as wedding festivity contributions. The defendant's foster-father denied receiving money, claiming instead to have "foddered a cow and seven sheep for her during the cold winter," though the spurned Liene said she worked the whole summer for her intended father-in-law for the fodder. The defendant claimed he sowed flaxseed for her and gave her stockings. Hasse ordered the fickle suitor to return the coat and grain to Liene, saying other gifts and obligations balanced out. This complicated reckoning shows how engagement initiated the economic exchanges so central to marriage.[153] Similarly, a farmer's son who had fathered an extramarital child but now, in 1745, was a wartime soldier unable to marry the mother, offered, the better "to ensure his promise of marriage," to give two steers to his future father-in-law, who would graze them for his daughter.[154]

Engagement and marriage festivities are barely discernible. On one occasion, the engagement party occurred in the bride's parental dwelling. It witnessed the earlier-mentioned dispute in which a non-inheriting son claimed he had not received his proper marriage portion from his bridegroom brother, though at the party and in their father's presence he was promised 15 talers. Possibly similar pledges often occurred, even if not

[151] No. 326, fo. 222.   [152] No. 591, fo. 24.   [153] No. 326, fo. 143.   [154] No. 664, fos. 1–6.

formally proclaimed to assembled guests.[155] But the binding events governing property transfers were farm inventory, in which mayors and aldermen appraised livestock, and issuance of the newly married proprietor's occupancy certificate, recording marriage portions owed the new couple's siblings and their own "goods brought in."

The night before church weddings, celebrations would take place, confined perhaps to bridegrooms' and male friends' revelry. A serious fight once flared up at a wedding between farmers' sons on wartime soldierly duty. Witnesses said the combatants had a long-standing quarrel, but composed it at the pre-wedding celebration "before the wedding guests departed." The following day, passage to the church was accompanied by still unmarried young men's pranks. A soldier among them halted the ceremony "by throwing grenades," until the pastor had him chased away. Later the wedding party convened at the groom's parental house. Considerable eating and drinking took place in the living room, with music and dancing on the adjoining barn's threshing floor.[156] Joint celebrations of siblings' double marriages occurred, as when a fullholder's son married a fullholder's daughter upon inheriting his father's farm, while his younger sister married a non-inheriting fullholder's son embarking on a cottager's and day-laborer's life.[157]

Food and drink for first-marriage celebrations were an inheritance right. The parental farm owed children a wedding or, if they died prematurely or unmarried, burial. The first such provision, unchanged into the nineteenth century, was called simply "the wedding" or, because both partners' households contributed, "half-wedding." In a 1767 court definition, marriage payment "according to village custom" comprised, both for small- and largeholders and from bride's and bridegroom's family farms, "3 bushels of rye, one barrel of beer, and an edible pig."[158] Another formulation, expressing fullholders' daughters' claims, was "one barrel of beer, a sack of rye, and a yearling pig" or, "if she marries out to another place," and didn't take payment *in natura*, a solid 6 talers instead.[159] A farmer promised his siblings "a small lean pig at 2 talers that he will fatten for them."[160] A women might only be assured "a wedding appropriate to her station."[161]

When a new farmer anticipated supporting young siblings or stepchildren for long years, or otherwise bore heavy burdens, wedding provisions might be thinned. Hasse recorded of "two girls" that, "because

[155] No. 591, fo. 80.   [156] No. 326, fos. 144–6.   [157] No. 663, fos. 1–3, 7.   [158] No. 358, fos. 31–2.
[159] No. 326, fos. 100–1.   [160] No. 714, fos. 73–4.   [161] No. 554, fos. 1–7.

they are still young and will be fed and maintained on the farm into their twelfth year," each would only receive "for the wedding 3 rye-bushels and a barrel of beer."[162] Another farmer promised only beer and 2 bushels "and whatever else he can give out of good-will."[163] Some wedding contributions modified customary measures, adding a sheep alongside the pig or substituting for the pig a steer, an ox, an "old cow" (or two), or another head of cattle. The village mayors sometimes grandly contributed (from one side only) three pigs or even three pigs and a steer.[164] But over time the burden of inheritance claims and farm debt tended to diminish slightly wedding provisions recorded in occupancy certificates. From 1721 to 1771, the average mandated contribution, in thirty-four instances, was 2.5 bushels of rye, one barrel of beer, and half a pig, worth altogether about 5 talers. But each wedding normally consumed double portions, plus various additions, suggesting that Stavenow farmers' marriages did not usually lack for bread, drink, and meat.

Women customarily received from parents the bridal costume or "dress of honor," embodying the dignity both of marriage and person married.[165] Descriptions are missing, but bridal dresses must have exhibited a certain finery, since their value was fairly high. Farm transfers typically mandated the new proprietor to give his sisters dresses of honor or 5 talers instead.[166] A young woman once received, instead of the dress, "the farm's second-best horse [apart from the iron stock] and 5 talers," while another took 8 talers in cash.[167] An unwed mother was promised 11 talers for her dress when – or if – her fiancé returned from Frederick's wars, although this good sum was partial compensation for surrendering the farm inheritance to her younger sister.[168]

Marriage dresses figured in young women's dowries given them by parents, as when a retiring mayor and his wife said of their unmarried daughters that "they want to give them their dresses of honor."[169] Female heirs also sometimes inherited such dresses. But young women might have to forgo claiming them. Three mature daughters of deceased parents, Hasse wrote, had not labored on the familial smallholding, "but found their own work and so earned their own dresses of honor,"

[162] No. 712, fos. 44–5.   [163] No. 713, fos. 18–20.
[164] No. 200, fos. 212–15, 246–9; no. 591, fos. 51–2, 54, 56, 58; no. 326, fos. 76–8; no. 715, fos. 35–9; no. 324, fos. 33–4, 47.
[165] No. 358, fos. 32–4.
[166] No. 715, fos. 45–6; no. 324, fos. 33–4, 47. Elderly women's and widows' dresses of honor: "black serge dress, waistcoat, apron, scarf" (no. 358, fos. 81–4).
[167] No. 358, fos. 34–6; no. 554, fos. 1–7.   [168] No. 664, fos. 1–6.   [169] No. 326, fos. 191–4.

which therefore they could not demand of their step-parents.[170] This shows that marriage dresses were a reward for unpaid toil on the parental farm. As for young men, one future bridegroom's parents promised him 5 talers for his "suit of honor." Another would receive from his fiancée's family farm "a calf for the suit of honor in place of bride's coat [*Braut Rock*]," an item newly engaged women also gave their fiancés.[171]

Yet another matrimonial exchange, of high symbolical and practical value, was the marital or "bridal" bed.[172] Invariably a female contribution, it sometimes possessed considerable value, unsurprising in a cool climate where beds were the finest furniture. A 1764 "marriage bed" comprised a wooden frame and canopy (10 talers); two heavy covers (7 talers); and four pillows, three linen sheets, two "of 18 ells." Altogether it was worth 23 talers, equal to a strong horse or several grown cattle.[173]

DOWRIES, MARRIAGE PORTIONS, AND "GOODS BROUGHT IN"

Everyday language proclaimed marriages unions of goods as well as hearts and souls. Asked to specify his new bride's dowry, widowed halfholder Dreger "recalled that with his present wife Anna Dorothea Maaßen he was gaining through marriage [*erheurathet*] two cows and a heifer," plus textiles "such as befitted farmer and householder," and a promised 20 talers and foal from her father's farm. Dreger assigned his first-marriage daughter "the livestock and other goods his departed wife had married upon him [*an ihn zugefreyet*]." An incoming farmer acquired his inventory "through his future wife."[174]

Cash, livestock, and other goods that marriage partners brought into their new household had various names. Non-inheriting mature children received "settlements" (*Abfindungen*).[175] These, combined with recipients' cash savings and other acquired or homemade items, formed marriage portions, called among women "marriage goods" (*Eheguth*), "bride's trove" (*Brautschatz*), or dowry (*Aussteuer, Austattung*).[176] Gender-neutral terms were marriage gift or dowry (*Mitgift*) and, commonly, "goods brought in" (*Eingebrachtes*), as when a farm wife, in a sexton-penned account, referred dryly to "my things or goods brought in."[177]

---

[170] No. 200, fos. 212–15.   [171] No. 664, fos. 1–6; no. 326, fos. 122–3.
[172] No. 713, fos. 18–20.   [173] No. 717, fos. 138–40; no. 712, fos. 30–1; no. 513, fos. 45–51.
[174] No. 200, fos. 197–9; no. 664, fos. 1–6.   [175] No. 200, fo. 206; no. 591, fos. 2–4; no. 200, fos. 187–9.
[176] No. 200, fos. 230–1; no. 358, fos. 7–11; no. 714, fos. 73–4; no. 591, fos. 56, 58.
[177] No. 591, fos. 12–13; no. 200, fos. 187–9; no. 200, fos. 157–62: no. 326, fo. 136.

Marriage portions comprised most of the non-landed villagers' inheritances, though retirees' personal property eventually also fell to the heirs. But such legacies were usually pittances, while marriage contributions – in court language the "marriage settlement and paternal inheritance" – were often fairly considerable.[178]

Apart from wedding provisions and personal effects, incoming husbands usually brought a combination of cash and livestock, both inherited and saved from bachelor earnings. Young Lorentz Benecke, marrying a smallholder's widow, promised "goods brought in" from his parental farm of 30 talers, a horse, a cow and a heifer, and "for himself from wages he has earned another 20 talers."[179] Michael Glissmann, also marrying a widow, received only wedding provisions from his father, but had himself accumulated 30 talers, a cow and a heifer, and five sheep.[180] Outsiders might bring cash only, as when Stoffel Möller enriched with 100 talers his bid for a widow's hand.[181]

A strong marriage portion was Johann Schröder's, who in 1767 entered a fullholding with "two cows, two heifers, one horse, 120 talers cash, and his other property."[182] The largest recorded Stavenow marriage contribution was Joachim Nagel's, marrying in 1760 into a Karstädt fullholding. Nagel's money-bag held 200 talers of his own cash. His father, also a Karstädt farmer, approved the marriage, promising his son "a horse, cattle and sheep," and more livestock in future. He declared that, if his son died, he would demand nothing of the widow. These propositions "the widow accepts with thanks." The elder Nagel apologized that "he cannot divest himself entirely of his worldly goods."[183]

"Goods brought in" were essential to offset farm resource loss to non-inheriting children. Their value could loom large, particularly if the donor should die prematurely. At Peter Schröder's marriage to full-holder's widow Anna Köhnen, a routine formula established that, if he predeceased her, his solid marriage contribution – a horse, four cattle, six sheep, and 80 talers cash – would stay in her hands.[184] The aforementioned Joachim Nagel's father had no business surrendering claims on his son's marriage portion. It disclosed, if not his own miserliness, an awareness of such costly investments' riskiness in a world of sudden and unforeseeable death. But married women's property rights were strong enough that when a widow left her deceased husband's farm to marry

---

[178] No. 591, fo. 28.   [179] No. 200, fos. 187–9.   [180] Ibid., fos. 204–7.   [181] No. 326, fos. 111–12.
[182] No. 358, fos. 34–6.   [183] No. 326, fos. 239–40.   [184] No. 591, fos. 56, 58.

onto another holding, she could recover her dowry, except for iron-stock livestock.[185]

Men's "goods brought in" were often valuable, both because bachelors' earnings were higher than single women's, and because in marrying farm heiresses men acquired property – if seigneurially encumbered – for themselves and their progeny. Yet, in this society favoring male primogeniture, it was far commoner for women to marry onto spouses' parental farms, so that women's dowries were oftener bestowed on husbands than men's marriage portions on wives. Although brides added money and other accumulated goods, the dowry's richness or poorness witnessed their fathers' or step-fathers' fortunes. In 1765, farmer Hans Ebel inventoried in his own hand the "bridal trove" of farm wife Johanna Fischer, who died after three years' marriage, leaving a widower now remarrying. Johanna's dowry had been exceptionally good for a halfholder's daughter: "two milking cows, four fertile ewes, one yearling foal," plus "two chests, one oak and one pine, both painted brown," and a linen-weaving loom. "Along with this she got 25 Reichstalers cash in good old money and 65 talers in not bad half-taler pieces *de anno* 1758" – devalued coinage of the Seven Years War – "which now amount in Brandenburg currency to 46 talers 2 groschen and 1 pfennig." Her linen, bedding, and clothes were also voluminous. Her successor as farm mistress – also named Fischer – possessed a good dowry, beyond textiles, of two cows, six sheep, a bed and loom, and "60 current Reichstalers in silver and gold coin."[186]

Households marrying off numerous children calculated marriage portions accordingly. When Hans Nagel succeeded his father as Karstädt mayor, two of four sisters' shares remained to be paid. The two married daughters each received, their parents reported, "20 talers, a horse, two cows and a heifer, dress of honor, beds, linen, sheets, loom, oaken chest, and spinning wheel and stool." The unmarried daughters, ages twenty-one and twenty-three, would have 20 talers, plus "one horse or 12 talers; two cows in the sixth and eighth year, respectively, if such are on hand; and a heifer of one or two years." Each already held from the farm's flock ten sheep and six lambs, whose wool they were doubtless making into clothing or selling. They would also receive the same household goods as their older sisters, plus wedding provisions. Fortunately for the young new proprietor, his bride had already given him 30 talers and promised 30 more, plus six head of livestock, the

[185] No. 358, fos. 3–4.   [186] No. 664, fos. 1–6.

usual household goods, bedding and such linen as "he will be satisfied
with," two stools and two metal cooking pots with a hearth pothook. In
customary words the partners agreed each would inherit the other's
estate (*"letzt Leib, letzt Gut"*).[187]

Karstädt mayor Nagel had ten years previously pledged one daughter "immediately for her dowry" a horse, two cows and a calf, "and also
promised to help her with sheep and pigs." Though he gave her 20
talers instead of additional livestock, he kept his word, for farmers,
whether brides' parents or siblings, were legally bound to deliver court-
registered dowries.[188] Nagel's new daughter-in-law received explicit
permission to remarry on the farm, should her husband predecease her.
This varied the commoner assurance given dowered first wives that, if
widowed, they might remain on the farm, if only as retirees. Doubtless
better-off farmers aimed to rise to the social challenge of giving children generous endowments. In 1770 a young fullholder's bride's father
gave her a horse and cow and nine sheep, "and otherwise wants as far
as possible to help the proprietor get started."[189] Twenty years earlier,
the same farm changed hands in straitened circumstances. The inheriting son was allowed to reduce his settlement obligations to his unmarried brothers below what their older brothers had received. But "if the
new proprietor is blessed on the farm with good fortune [*Glück und
Segen*]," he would give them an additional calf, and raise a cow for
another brother, still a little boy, "if he lives."[190]

By marrying proprietors' daughters, men might find themselves
obliged by preexisting parental decrees to pay marriage portions to
non-inheriting siblings-in-law. Incoming smallholder Joachim Niemann
agreed to give his wife's two sisters each 10 talers and two cattle, while
her brother, who had already gotten a foal, would have the same cash
and a horse and cow. Niemann would also contribute wedding provisions.[191] As we saw, smallholders' portions might be better, but often
parental gifts among lesser farmers consisted only of some livestock, the
usual textiles, and a modest wedding contribution. A 1765 dowry counted
only two cows and a horse, "double bed, linen, and respectable clothing." Cows would be added "when opportunity arises."[192]

As "dresses of honor" showed, clothing possessed great symbolic and
material significance. It was women's most valuable and proudest personal possession. Unmarried women acquired their own clothes and

[187] No. 326, fos. 191–4.   [188] No. 714, fos. 73–4.   [189] No. 358, fos. 85–8, 97.
[190] No. 715, fos. 23–5.   [191] No. 713, fos. 18–20.   [192] No. 200, fos. 200–1; No. 358, fos. 5–6.

linen, but mothers also provisioned them with textile goods, so their respective shares are not easily discernible. A widowed father promised his daughter dowry livestock, leaving her to assemble "bedding, clothes, and chests and drawers [*Kisten und Kastengeräthe*]."[193] A farm-inheriting bride reported she had "already received" necessary textiles from her parents. Hasse recorded of a mayor's daughter marrying on her parental farm that she was satisfied with the bedding given her. "The mother also does not want her to go short-handed in linen."[194]

Whatever the provenance, first brides needed textile goods in quantities and quality reflecting "their proper needs" (*anständige Nottdurfft*), or that were "appropriate to their estate" (*nach ihrem Stand*).[195] What exactly these were must be surmised from post-mortem accounts of young wives' possessions, since textiles were not inventoried at marriage. Goods acquired in early post-marriage years were probably mainly textile yardage and workday clothing. An idea of the contents of young brides' trunks and chests emerges from the textiles left behind after three years of marriage by ill-starred smallholder's wife Johanna Fischer, whose 1765 estate, as we saw, Hans Ebel surveyed. First came eight tablecloths, four in the "goose-eye" style and four of "damask." There were seven hand-towels "of the same type." Bedding included "two fine-woven linen bedsheets" and two others with homespun borders; "a white linen bedcover with two pillow cases," plus the same in checkered blue and white; and a bed with mattresses. Johanna's linen comprised three pieces of fine material, each 15 ells long and 1 ell wide; four pieces of coarse linen in the same dimensions; and five pieces of the humbler type of homespun linen (*Hede*).

The "blessed woman's" clothing included twelve good "undershirts" and 20 good linen "outer shirts." There were five good women's caps, one of black velvet, and three pairs of gloves, including one in black plush and "one pair of Danish brown-leather fingered gloves." There was a good "woman's black muff" of roughly tanned fur. Of bodices or camisoles with matching dresses, made of "crêpe des dames," one was black and one violet. Among other camisoles, two were of flowered woolen damask, and two were "brightly striped and homemade." Such inventories customarily identified homemade clothing, revealing by contrast the considerable extent to which villagers' dress was bought from merchants or was tailor-made.

---

[193] No. 200, fos. 175–6.   [194] Ibid., fos. 220–2; no. 324, fos. 4–5.
[195] No. 326, fos. 154–6; no. 715, fo. 10; no. 591, fo. 54.

The unfortunate Johanna also owned four sashes, including one of black woolen damask and two in blue. She counted four homemade striped women's dresses, and seven other homemade "ordinary daily" dresses, including one red Frisian dress. She had eight variously colored aprons, seven of fine linen and one of muslin. There were eight scarves, one "double-silk," "one plain silk," and one "half-silk," three muslin, one printed cotton, and one white linen. She had also eight bonnets, four with lace and four "mourning bonnets." These clothes and textiles she doubtless delivered in her brown oak and pine chests. She also owned a loom. This smallholder's dowry was strikingly better than that of fullholder's wife Trine Zeggels, who likewise died after three years' marriage. Her textiles encompassed but five dresses, several of printed cotton, and four bodices, plus shirts, caps, apron, and two "French scarves" (*walsche Halstücher*). Her linen was minimal, though including two long and two square tablecloths. Her oak chest had lock and handles. She brought in an oak bed frame and spinning wheel (*Spinnwercker*) with chair.[196]

Looms and spinning wheels appear erratically in inventories, though linen and wool production's pervasive importance required most households to possess them. In the best dowries both were present.[197] A 1727 halfholder's new wife arrived with "a loom and five combs," while a new 1805 fullholder pledged to fashion "the oak wood on hand" into looms for three sisters and trunks for two brothers.[198] Dowries often also included furniture, such as a new bride's oak table with two benches and a sideboard. The same housewife arrived with a child's cradle, three metal cooking pots, and wooden and ceramic kitchenware. A smallholder's bride brought "two chests, two cooking pots, ten bowls, three ceramic pots, one cupboard, and fire-iron." Metal cookware could be valuable: in the 1720s a fullholder's wife's kettle was worth 6 talers (and her cow 4). New housewives' poultry possessed some value too, such as 8-groschen geese and 3-groschen hens.[199]

The court might record a bridegroom's – and his father's – approval of the betrothed's proposed dowry, suggesting the offer of acceptable "goods brought in" was a legal precondition of marriage.[200] Yet the dowry remained a married woman's property. A childless widow might depart her deceased husband's farm with it, in part or whole. The dowry also figured in a deceased mother's "maternal estate" (*Muttergut*),

---

[196] No. 200, fos. 230–1. [197] No. 326, fos. 191–4. [198] No. 200, fos. 212–15; no. 513, fos. 31–5.
[199] No. 200, fos. 197–9; no. 358, fos. 61–3; no. 591, fos. 30–2; no. 718, fos. 48–9.
[200] No. 358, fos. 64–9.

inheritable by her children upon their maturity, though entrusted meanwhile to her widowed husband's possession. A young bride's 16-taler dowry money might repose in her step-father's "safekeeping." Whether or not the money was earning interest, her ownership was undisputed.[201] Dowries owed non-inheriting daughters from parental farms were a personal property right. Catharina Hechts, a farm-inheriting woman, would have a 30-taler cash dowry, plus natural payments. If she remained unmarried after age twenty-five, she would receive five yearly 6-taler installments. This shows that, at maturity, unmarried women could claim their dowries' cash component, possibly as compensation for parental farm labor.[202] Judging from the compendious court record, it happened but rarely that dowries promised were not fully delivered, requiring brides and their husbands to summon negligent kinsmen to court.[203]

WIDOWHOOD AND REMARRIAGE

Dowries were capital investments securing women life tenure on husbands' farms. When Marie Sabine Niemanns entered her first marriage, the court recorded her dowry, "in exchange for which" she would eventually receive customary retirement provisions.[204] New proprietors' brides might remain on the farm as widows and, if fortune smiled, take a new farmer as husband. The question was tension-fraught: if the widow did not soon remarry, peril would envelop the farm, and the deceased farmer's siblings might seek to reclaim it.[205]

As we saw, a prematurely widowed wife's farm tenure might be conditioned on raising step-children properly, or on living "in peace and friendship with the parents" (retired parents-in-law).[206] A young widow might also wish to recover her dowry to remarry elsewhere. This was delicate, since it drained farm capital. Probably few such women regained their full investment. In 1742 a farmer quarreled with his widowed step-mother over the issue. Finally they agreed, "in Christian manner," that the step-son "did not forbid her to marry, but would settle over dowry and retirement rights by giving back her cows and 8 talers cash."[207]

Conventionally, remarriage was duty, increasingly businesslike with advancing age. But the consequence of spousal death, barring remarriage,

---

[201] No. 715, fo. 10.   [202] No. 358, fos. 34–6.   [203] No. 326, fo. 200; no. 324, fo. 19.
[204] No. 358, fos. 72–4; no. 200, fo. 44.   [205] No. 714, fos. 73–4.
[206] No. 200, fos. 197–9; no. 326, fos. 191–4.   [207] No. 326, fo. 95.

was retreat into retirement. Christian practice, like heartfelt emotion, counseled pausing between marriages, but the lordship sometimes countenanced deviations. It obtained a "most gracious royal concession" allowing farmer-tavernkeeper Hecht to remarry "before the customary year of mourning's expiration."[208] Sometimes justified by appeal to "divine providence," remarriages were facts of life.[209] Eva Richters, left at her husband's death with five children, found herself "forced by need once again to marry."[210] The court might instruct a husband to "love the widow and raise and provide for the children," but it could also brusquely note of another second husband that "he will assume proprietorship and take the widow with the inventory."[211] Widows' remarriages required the approval of children's guardians – often their deceased husband's parents or relatives. But social logic made a new proprietor's marriage to a widow with children preferable to shunting them into retirement, where they would compete for resources with existing retirees.

Widowed farmers with young children might well feel themselves "urgently required" ("*höchst gemüssiget*") to find new wives, and nothing suggests, in a world where widowers remarried oftener than widows, that tolerable partners were lacking.[212] Marriages of convenience like that of farmer Joachim Mentz, aged about sixty, with a propertyless lodger's daughter, aged forty-two, six months after the death of Mentz's wife of twenty-four years, were unexceptional.[213] Even retired farmers took new wives. Jürgen Nagel married childless widow Anne Jahncke after losing his wife of long years. Nagel, Hasse wrote, "finds himself obliged, because of advancing weakness in old age and to have necessary care and cleanliness, to remarry with a respectable woman."[214]

MARITAL CONFLICT

Documents speak but faintly of gratifications Stavenow farmers and their wives found in each other's company. But neither does evidence abound of marital strife – partly because village and seigneurial authorities turned a blind eye to its tolerated forms. Fullholder Peter Hecht dowered one sister, married to smallholder Krumm, but not another, who married tailor Schulze. Following Hecht's death, his widow "gave 10 talers to the old father" – that is, her deceased husband's father, who

[208] No. 200, fos. 228–9.   [209] Ibid., fos. 164–5.   [210] No. 554, fos. 1–7; no. 715, fos. 8, 13–15.
[211] No. 326, fos. 239–40; no. 591, fos. 56, 58.   [212] No. 715, fo. 10; no. 200, fos. 175–6.
[213] No. 718, fos. 48–9.   [214] No. 716, fos. 305–6.

wanted to give it to son-in-law tailor Schultze. "The father wept, saying that the tailor … had beaten his wife because her sister received all her dowry on one day," whereas the unhappy tailor's wife was still awaiting hers. Perhaps the old father's tearful intervention spared his daughter further blows, but the tailor did not suffer for beating her.[215]

A rare intervention against domestic violence occurred in 1756. Maidservant Anna Marie Möllers begged release from her contract with fullholder Hans Brunst. Möllers testified that Brunst's wife "scolded her as a marriage-wrecking whore and beat her." "She couldn't stand it any longer." On court day, farmer Brunst was unheroically "not at home," but his combative spouse blamed Anna Möllers, "since she not only wouldn't obey her as *Hausfrau*, but also was always stirring up quarrels and fights between her and her husband through false boasting, such as that he pays more attention to [Möllers] than to herself." Brunst's wife was incensed at her servant's gossip that she "peddled bread and other things in the village and got herself drunk on brandy." Frau Brunst complained that the maidservant "besmirched" her husband, saying he was "hostile" to his wife, "couldn't stand [their] children, and begrudged them their bit of bread, and even that on New Year's Eve he had got into such a row and fight with her that, if their neighbor Christian Nagel hadn't come at midnight and rescued her, he would have killed her."

Neighbor Nagel said Brunst's was "a pretty godforsaken household, and that the children had fetched him on various occasions, including recently on New Year's Eve, and begged him to save them, because otherwise their father would kill their mother." Nagel calmed the situation. In his manly view, "if the wife would only keep quiet, the husband wouldn't be driven to such rage." Nagel said "he couldn't always be there to hinder the misfortune that further quarreling and fighting would likely bring." He thought "since the maidservant caused the conflict," Brunst ought to replace her with a man.

Stavenow administrator Lützow reported that "there couldn't be much good about the maidservant." She worked previously for seigneurial dairyman Bulhorn, where "there was also much conflict among the servants, and with the mistress." Hasse calculated what Brunst owed Möllers in pay, linen yardage, and flaxseed sown, and for the six days' manorial service she had performed with him since New Year's. The sum in cash was 4 talers. Möllers declared herself ready, "if

[215] No. 200, fos. 209–11.

she got this money, to quit the farm this very instant," asking only the court bailiff to accompany her "so she could fetch her trunk and belongings in peace and order." Hasse agreed, ordering Brunst to pay and his wife "to control her loose mouth and not to excite her husband to rage through unfounded suspicion and unbridled scolding and cursing, thereby bringing his blows down on her."[216]

These unhappy scenes occurred in a first marriage's fourteenth year. When Brunst succeeded his father, the farm was sound, but later he had difficulty paying his two siblings' inheritances and the farm servant's wages his brother-in-law claimed. His wife came, untypically, not from a landed family, but was the head plowman and workers' foreman's daughter under Karstedt lordship. Yet no other record of strife involves her. In 1769 Hans Brunst retired on his run-down and heavily indebted farm, though whether his wife was still his first bride is unknown. Rivalry and jealousy divided this story's women. Whatever Brunst's attitude toward his maidservant, Hasse absolved him of all improprieties, including brutally beating his wife and terrorizing his children, whom perhaps he scorned. The maidservant's charges, if she aired them publicly, probably accorded with common conceptions of village misbehavior and dishonor, even if Brunst's wife was innocent. Christian Nagel's judgment seems right that this was a "godforsaken household."

On one other occasion alone did the court warn against domestic violence between husband and wife. This was the case in which a wife's "shameless talk and untimely love of her children from the previous marriage" led her husband, with whom she "constantly quarreled and exchanged blows," to "beat her very unjustifiably." Hasse curtly ordered "the wife to keep still, the children to be obedient, [the husband] to refrain from all beating and cursing about she-cats [*Weiberkatzen*], and the youngest son to hire himself out at Michaelmas," to be replaced by "a new boy, because the wife is gradually growing old and afflicted."[217] Here, fifteen years into a woman's second marriage, marital strife flared, partly from her husband's and his nineteen-year-old step-son's conflict. But in her previous marriage stormy scenes also arose, implicating her retired father and unmarried sister. Hasse commanded her and her first husband on pain of corporal punishment to cease fighting and cursing, threatening the whole household, if they did not "refrain completely from outrages and strife," with "full-scale investigation."[218]

[216] No. 326, fos. 203–4.   [217] Ibid., fo. 214.   [218] No. 591, fos. 98, 107–9.

These incidents show that, even when gross marital violence went unpunished, it ran the risk, after a certain point, of exposure and censure before court and public. Such outcomes' rarity argues for the deterrent's efficacy. But other household strife's frequency suggests that low-intensity marital conflict was not uncommon, especially when economic tensions tightened. Still, farmers' wives had defenses. They were the household's and farm's indispensable co-managers, and even, through their dowries, co-owners of some assets. They were also, in seven of ten cases, farmers' daughters whose parental lineages might intervene on their behalf, as guardians sometimes did. Married women signaled association with their natal household by regularly keeping parental surnames rather than adopting their husbands'. They employed the possessive singular case: Anna Marie Möllers, or "Möller's Anna Marie." Among farm brides and remarrying farm widows from known home villages, only 12 percent hailed from non-Stavenow settlements, mostly from nearby villages. The others married in or near their birthplaces, and so were not far distant from kindred "friends."[219]

Divorce or separation were virtually unknown among eighteenth-century villagers. One case arose, settled in 1800 between Mesekow mayor Beese and his former wife. Beese, Stavenow's judge told Major Kleist, compromised "because the matter was already so damaging," though the emotional stakes are indiscernible. Beese refunded his wife's dowry and paid her one-sixth his net worth. This cost 212 talers, a big sum he needed to borrow, for which Kleist's approval was sought and given. Beese had also to return his ex-wife's sheep and clothing. He would pay her 9 talers yearly in child-support (*Alimentation*) until his younger son's tenth birthday. At Michaelmas, Beese's second son would join his household, probably to help work the farm.[220]

PARENTS AND CHILDREN

The court commanded a routinized rhetoric of conjugal and parental love, as when Hasse instructed a widower to pay for recording his infant daughter's maternal estate "out of love for the child."[221] The villagers themselves affirmed parental duties with mixed expressions of enthusiasm and stoicism. New brides prepared for their futures, for cradles

---

[219] Likewise, most husbands were nearby farmers' sons: only 18 percent married into the Stavenow jurisdiction from outside (sixty-seven female and eighty-three male cases.)
[220] No. 604, fos. 1–2.   [221] No. 326, fo. 200; no. 324, fo. 19.

often accompanied their dowry beds, ready to receive the infants they would soon "beget" or "bear into the world."[222]

Mothers faced public censure for the neglect of infants. In 1728, a young widow's right of remarriage following her husband's accidental death encountered the deceased's mother's and sister's bitter opposition. This many-faceted case figured earlier as an instance of seigneurial intervention in disputed farm successions. Kleist arranged the discharge of his subject, soldier Joachim Seyer, who agreed to marry young widow Hoffmeister and take the smallholding her husband had been about to inherit when he died. But the old widow claimed her son had never been formally installed as proprietor. Having slept with (*beschlaffen*) and impregnated Anne Liese Eberts, he was obliged to marry prematurely, before his now deceased father's retirement. His infant son was not born on their farm, where the child's mother later moved only because "her brother gave her no peace on her own family's farm." The old woman said her son's widow cursed her as "an old cat" and "showed her no filial respect [*kindlich nicht begegnet*] and never would in the future. They would instead live together in constant conflict."

The old widow pleaded for a month's delay so as to petition Kleist for her daughter Grete's or surviving son Ludwig's right to inherit the farm. If he assented, she and her children would, if necessary, "live on bread and water." Daughter Grete, saying she had invested all her earnings in the farm, offered to raise her departed brother's son as her own: "she always had the child with her, since its mother didn't trouble herself with it." Defensively, the young widow denied cursing her mother-in-law and neglecting her son. It was only "because it's cold in the room where she sleeps, and the child is used to sleeping in the cradle, [that] the grandmother keeps it with her in the night." She protested that, although the elder Hoffmeister had not transferred the farm to his son, he promised it, and she and her husband invested their labor in it.

Failing to reach an acceptable compromise, Hasse said Kleist's decision would be binding. Joachim Seyer, who as prospective new household head might reasonably have shrunk from cohabiting with such in-laws, declared that "rather than living in squabbling and conflict, he'd be content if the Colonel allowed him to marry the widow without the farm and give him his work here [at Stavenow], provided that the

---

[222] No. 326, fo. 222; no. 326, fo. 73; no. 324, fos. 29–32.

woman and child got a proper settlement from the farm." He wanted to live in peace and hold his wife to the same course. But he had been told that "the [old] mother said she'd rather be broken ten times on the wheel than have him on the farm."[223]

Here the plaintiffs, brandishing all rhetorical weapons, had – vainly – alleged several filial and parental failings to justify their succession claim. Records of more positive parental behavior toward children are scarce, but a 1772 case offers insight into prevailing attitudes. Fifty-year-old smallholder Panckow, arrested for risking village conflagration by illegally smoking his pipe outdoors on his farmstead, said he had been sitting smoking in his living room when a child fetched him to help the thatcher repair his roof. Panckow was then caught working, pipe in teeth. He excused himself, saying "if he hadn't been such a dumb fellow and if he'd had his senses about him, he would never have made such a mistake. But at the time he was completely beside himself, because a child of his lay so ill with the pox that it died three days later." Berlin's Chamber Court draconically sentenced Panckow to two months' hard labor at Spandau fortress. But it added: "his condition at the time, as his child lay dying, diminishes the penalty" (by one month), since presumption of *"pietas paterna"* (paternal affection) ruled out "indifference." Whatever Panckow's feelings, he could plausibly invoke his distress, which the judges duly weighed in their scale.[224]

Parents were free to punish children, and no cases alleged this power's abuse. But laying hands on children other than one's own risked trouble. Smallholder Koltzer and wife charged fullholder Zeggel with failing to punish his children for calling Koltzer's children "pig-mouths" (*Schweine Fresser*). Defendant Zeggel compounded the affront, denouncing Frau Koltzer as "drunken whore and cheese thief" (*Sauff Hure und Käse Dieb*), whereupon "the whole village came running." Zeggel, denying cursing her, said "when [Koltzer's wife] assaulted his son and pulled his hair, the people gathered around and said" – in an above-cited phrase – "the woman must be drunk to be beating the boy." Yet these offenses balanced out, and the parties made peace.[225] Conversely, parents had little recourse against blows their older children suffered as servants of harsh employers. Such a youth's father publicly cursed mayor Nagel, excusing himself by saying "it enraged him that [Nagel] thrashed his boy so badly he had a fever for days."

[223] No. 200, fos. 94–6.   [224] No. 510, fos. 4–5, 8–9.   [225] No. 589, fos. 9–10.

Yet Hasse fined the father 1 taler, chiding him for causing trouble during fieldwork, "where it is least fitting."[226]

Though the court rarely investigated violence against children, it sometimes pronounced harsh sentences on youthful offenders. In 1730 Hasse found a mayor's son and his companion guilty of stealing, as "often happened," carp and other fish from seigneurial waters. He fined their fathers and ordered the boys, "to deter others, to be shackled for two days" – in late November – "to neck-irons that will be erected at the pond." In 1729, a neighboring lordship jailed four Stavenow farmers' sons, but they escaped with their parents' help. Hasse thereupon (lightly) fined the parents and sentenced the boys, guilty – according to Captain Wartenburg – of smoking tobacco, slinging rocks, and evading arrest by the field bailiff (whose whip they tried to seize), to "one more night in the cellar."[227]

Yet evidence of violence against children is limited, while many records show that parents, step-parents, foster-parents, and guardians were expected to offer children under their authority security and support. Doubtless unmarried youths yearned to escape servant status and "go out on their own" or "start something of their own." But life in the parental household offered some gratifications. Fathers could endure seigneurial wrath in their families' name, as when Stoffel Zeggel ignored a 1732 summons to the lordship's barley harvest. Kleist's bailiff reported him "so impertinent as to say he had to bring in his own harvest first, since if he and his children had no bread, the bailiff would give him none." For this and related offenses – Hasse called them "crimes" – Zeggel paid a fine and suffered two hours in the "Spanish overcoat."[228]

Widows managed farms with their more or less grown children's help, until one married and took over. Some instances project pictures of family solidarity, as on a fullholding that in 1726 passed to Jochen Maass and his new bride Trine Zeggels. Jochen's father died in 1717, and the following nine years "the widow [Anna Sieben] and her children kept house in common, while son Jochen had already been obliged, because of his father's sickly condition when alive, to head the farm six years." By 1726 the widow and her eldest son had co-managed for fifteen years. Anna Sieben entered retirement, taking "for this year" a pig for fattening, a cow, and a goose. Among new proprietor Jochen's six siblings, Dorothea had married a Stavenow fullholder, Peter was a

---

[226] No. 591, fos. 25, 30.   [227] No. 200, fos. 147–8.   [228] No. 591, fos. 52–3.

farm servant in a non-Stavenow village, "Hans doesn't have his full understanding," Johann was a mustered-out soldier, Liese served at Stavenow manor, and Friedrich "lives on the holding with the manager."

Jochen promised brother Peter a marriage portion of "a sack of rye, a cow, and a barrel of beer," while "feeble-minded Hans shall be fed on the farm and buried at its expense." Ex-soldier Johann had received cash instead of a cow, and would have wedding provisions when he married. Liese would receive three cattle with wedding provisions, while her mother would give her such bedding and linen as she had not yet received. Married Dorothea had gotten a larger dowry, "because with her mother she helped bring up [*gross führen*] the other children." Friedrich, who stayed to work the farm, would have a horse, steer, and wedding provisions. With these pledges "all the children declare themselves satisfied."[229]

In another case, widow Vey Ebels, mother of ten, ran a Premslin full-holding six years, until her son Jochen Hecht obtained army discharge and with his new wife took the farm. Jochen was the second eldest son, following Hans, who was "unhealthy." Also living at home were elder daughter Trine Sophie, fourteen-year-old Anne Margarete, and twelve-year-old Andreas. Another daughter was a maidservant at Premslin manor-farm; a son was a married lodger in a local village; a furloughed soldier, twenty-four, and another unmarried son, twenty-two, worked nearby as farm servants; and a daughter, twenty, was in urban service in Perleberg. The non-inheriting children's inheritances would be modest: wedding provisions and one head of livestock. Unhealthy Hans was promised a horse and the youngest boy a foal.

Widowed mother Ebels wished to care in retirement for the two younger children. The three unmarried children still at home could, she said, either stay or leave, but the new proprietor "should keep the youngest son at home until he has taken communion." With rare generosity, the court pronounced the farm "in praiseworthy condition." It possessed sound buildings, six good horses, ten cattle, six large pigs, twenty sheep (individually owned by family members), and twenty-two fowl. Of liabilities, the mother said "because son Jochen always protected her from want [*ihre Noth immer vorgekehrt*] and indeed had invested 50 talers in the farm, she had no other debts." This was the aforementioned Jochen whose army discharge the lordship secured and who now took the farm on condition he cared for his mother, paid his

---

[229] No. 200, fos. 207–8.

siblings' marriage portions, and "behave[d] himself better than he formerly did."[230]

Finally, there was Anne Marie Bucken, widow of farmer Stoffel Zeggel who "passed away" (*verblichen*) in 1735. In 1751, she declared herself "no longer able to manage the farm because she was already threescore years old." For sixteen years she headed the household, assisted by a maidservant and – so far as possible – by her seven sons, one of whom, discharged from the army, now took the farm. Three others were lodgers and laborers on nearby farms. One died in the Austrian war, while the two youngest were under arms. The farm was sound, with minor debts and retirement quarters – living room, two other rooms, and stalls – "still new." "The mother has laid in her own grain, fruit, and victuals."[231]

SIBLING RELATIONSHIPS

Solidarity and cooperation between siblings, as between parents and children, doubtless strengthened material and psychological life. At intergenerational farm transfers, new proprietors promised burdensome inheritance payments to brothers and sisters, and sometimes life-long support to the ill or disabled. But often a sibling stayed home as a laborer or to help raise orphaned children or tend sickly parents (*Handreichung tun*).[232] A retiring father "decreed" the new proprietor's lame brother, twenty-eight, would remain on the farm and work as much as he could, for which he would be "fed until his death" (*zu Tode gefühdet*). Their sister Vey struck a note of discord. She "presumed to claim" the estate of their grandmother, dead after thirty years' retirement. Vey tended the old woman, and felt entitled to inherit not just her personal goods (worth 12 talers), but her cooking pots and rye allotment in the fields. These latter claims Hasse denied, since they concerned appurtenances of the retirement quarters, now occupied by Vey's father. But the new proprietor agreed to pay 9 talers for Vey's past services.[233]

The youngest Stavenow farmer on record was seventeen-year-old Joachim Bahlcke who, having hastily married a wife the same age, succeeded his deceased father. His step-mother moved with four small children, aged two to ten, into retirement and "will help the young people

---

[230] No. 591, fos. 51–2. [231] No. 715, fos. 35–9. [232] No. 326, fos. 191–4.
[233] No. 200, fos. 200–1; no. 326, fos. 200–5; no. 513, fos. 51–4.

so far as possible." Joachim "wanted to keep sister Trine [twelve] with him and will pay wages to half-sister Marie [twenty-two]."[234] But, contrasting with such solidarity, sibling conflict sometimes flared, particularly when marriage portions went unpaid. The aforementioned instance, in which a retired father tearfully pleaded with his successor-son's widow to pay his daughter's overdue inheritance, displays unedifying strife among brothers and sisters and other relatives. No inventory occurred when the son died, so that "misunderstandings arose among the kinfolk." The dowryless sister's aggrieved husband took the deceased farmer's saws, axes, and timber-chain; the "old father" and his wife commandeered "kettles, tubs, chairs and table"; the deceased son's guardian, who paid for the burial, seized the household bible.[235]

Other sibling quarrels expressed resentment at real or imagined inequalities. Smallholder's widow Liese Besen sullied the memory of her sister, also a smallholder's wife, calling her, among other names, "the madame." Widow Besen testified that the deceased sister's husband and daughter had "frightfully beaten her and torn out much of her hair." Her brother-in-law said widow Besen insulted them and his departed wife in his house and "spread rumors [against them] for a whole week." He admitted beating her, "but with hands, not cane." The wife of the farmer with whom Liese Besen lodged refuted this testimony, saying the defendants "badly beat [widow Besen] with a stick and pulled out her hair." Hasse found both plaintiff and defendants guilty. He commanded them to reconcile "as befits Christians," sentencing Liese Besen to be (painfully) chained in the dungeon for one hour and her assailants two.[236]

RETIRED ELDERS AND THEIR SUCCESSORS ON THE FARMSTEAD

Law and custom bound retired farmers to the new cultivator and his wife, of whom one or the other was usually the elders' child or step-child. But, with dowries or marriage portions paid, parents' and non-farm-inheriting children's relations might weaken, partly because retirees could not offer much further support. A farmer, having married off a daughter, might be obliged to assist her in economic difficulty, but such transactions are rarely documented. A three-quarter holder lent

---

[234] No. 591, fos. 30–2, 54, 119–21; no. 326, fos. 116–17.   [235] No. 200, fos. 209–11.
[236] Ibid., fos. 119–24.

his son-in-law, the freeholding Garlin mayor, 64 talers, only to see the ne'er-do-well abscond, deserting his wife and child. At the new proprietor's accession, the creditor-father said, "because he feels compassion for his daughter," he would claim only 40 talers, so as to ease the debt burden on the newcomer, responsible for supporting his ruined (and, as it happened, shortlived) daughter in retirement. It was a measured compassion.[237]

The principle governing intergenerational relations was that all household members should work on the familial holding so far as necessary and possible. Inheritance rights varied accordingly. The aforementioned seventy-year-old Joachim Fischer excluded his eldest son from farm succession for having left to support himself as a seigneurial worker, while his younger son "stuck with him and gave him what he needed, while the elder hadn't worried about him."[238] A young farmer refused his brother's inheritance claims, arguing he alone for four years had "fed" their recently deceased mother, though Hasse imposed a compromise.[239] Fullholder's wife Trine Neubauers charged her brother-in-law Heinrich Hewecke with seizing her deceased mother-in-law's "estate," although Trine's husband Peter Hewecke gave his mother "to her ninetieth year her retirement-portion food provisions," while she "merely received living quarters" at the defendant's farm. Trine demanded her brother-in-law pay the pastor's burial fee (1.10.-). Here, two brothers shared their old mother's support. Heinrich countered that the "estate" fell to his sister Marie's children, "who are completely dispersed." Hasse pronounced the legacy unrecoverable, since the recipients "have gone their separate ways," and ordered the brothers to share the pastor's fee. Here non-inheriting youth disappeared, cutting ties with relatives left behind.[240]

Retirement contracts bound outgoing couples to "lend the new proprietor in every way a helping hand," while he pledged to "tend their land just as well as his own."[241] Succeeding his deceased father, a fullholder formulaically promised "to provide his old mother lifelong with food and all necessary care, including clothing, and in every way to treat her as befits a child."[242] Retirees' economic rights were legally enforceable, limiting abuse they might otherwise have suffered. Yet household conflicts involving retirees, though not multitudinous, often

---

[237] Ibid., fos. 157–62.   On modern old age: Christoph Conrad, *Vom Greis zum Renter. Der Strukturwandel des Alters in Deutschland zwischen 1830 und 1930* (Göttingen, 1994).
[238] No. 326, fos. 141–3.   [239] No. 591, fo. 80.   [240] No. 589, fos. 3–4.   [241] No. 714, fos. 73–4.
[242] No. 358, fos. 107–10.

appear. Sometimes proprietors refused the full measure of retirees' benefits, as was charged against Joachim Hintze by his retired mother and, speaking on her behalf, his brother. The defendant allegedly diminished her pasturage and orchard rights, and did not properly sow her flaxseed. He denounced her claims as excessive, but Hasse upheld the decade-old contract, warning that if the dispute were not resolved, the mayor would investigate and inform the court.[243]

Sometimes retirees fought among themselves, as when Hedwig Seyers fled the retirement quarters she shared with her husband Hans Schultze to take refuge with the new proprietor Reimar Guhl, her previous-marriage son. Schultze denounced wife and step-son to Hasse, who ordered Guhl "to tell his mother she must return immediately to her husband." Schulze's abusive ways emerge from Hasse's ruling that he "must supply her with her wifely fare [*Frauen Brodt*]." Hasse ordered the family to "behave themselves peacefully" or face eight days' jail on bread and water. The twenty-six-year-old Guhl and his younger brother committed physical violence against their step-father, but Hasse's threatened investigation never occurred.[244] Sixteen years later, their mother died, after thirty-seven years with Schultze. He amicably settled his wife's estate with Reimar Guhl and his sister Anna, giving them jointly the maternal cow. Anna took the deceased's clothing and linen, Reimar a cooking pot. Schultze kept the rest, which with his own possessions his new wife Trine Gedickens would inherit. Step-father and step-children signed with crosses. After stormy beginnings, realism triumphed among these warring and impecunious parties.[245]

Kinship ties' attenuation or rupture by death's vagaries might yield discord and neglect of the elderly. Smallholder Havemann retired in his daughter's and her new husband's favor, but she soon died, and her husband quit the holding rather than remarrying on it. Another daughter took the farm, but died five years later. Her widowed husband took a new wife, leaving old Havemann retired in a household bereft of kin. Resentful, he seized his second daughter's valuables, intended for her surviving child, rather than leaving them to her widower and his wife, who were raising the child. He took his daughter's dress (probably her dress of honor) and – rare item – an amber necklace, aiming to give them to his brother's children. Hasse, enforcing orthodox inheritance practices, ordered Havemann to return the purloined goods to his son-in-law, "or suffer his retirement income's reduction." Havemann was to

---

[243] No. 591, fo. 127.   [244] No. 715, fo. 47.   [245] No. 358, fos. 46–7.

"conserve the estate" of his grandchild and forbidden to "furtively make gifts" to his nephews. Probably because the small farm was weak, the court revoked his right to separate retirement provisions, ordering him to move into the proprietor's house, work as much as possible on the farm, and "be satisfied [along with his son-in-law] with the holding's resources." Doubtless this was not the retirement Havemann expected seven years earlier.[246]

Some retirees suffered by outliving younger kin. Anna Kiecksen, "three and a half score years old," took refuge on nephew Johann Kiecks' fullholding. She was Hans Kahlcke's widow, who had been a comparatively well-off farmer under Perleberg's town magistracy, rather than nobility or crown. With Kahlcke she spent sixteen years farming and fifteen years in retirement. On his death the farm passed to her step-son, whose widow then took a new husband, bearing him eight children. Although Anna said a Perleberg lawyer reckoned her claim from her husband's estate at 150 talers (his two brothers having each gotten 100 talers), she received only 90 talers. With no one willing to care for her, "she couldn't hide herself away in the retirement cottage any longer." Before her successors let her leave "they forced her to share everything [she possessed] with them." She asked Hasse to help her "as a poor widow to gain what was hers" but, failing that, she assigned her claims on her former farm to her nephew, "because he agreed to take her."[247]

The court sought to protect the elderly, if only to limit indigence. In 1740 a married woman from another jurisdiction, Anne Ebels, appeared (with a male kinsman) before Judge Hasse on her aged grandmother's behalf. Ebels, a landless man's wife, advanced an unusual inheritance claim – after twenty-nine years – to her paternal holding, a mayor's farm. It passed in 1711 to her brother, who with several other brothers died in that epidemic-plagued year. The then-proprietor's widow's brother, Joachim Hecht, took the farm. Ebels charged Hecht with failing to support her or her grandmother, whom Ebels lodged with her own daughter in a nearby village. "But since then she has had to be removed from there. She can't live any longer in the cottage, because it's collapsing and unrepaired."

Ebels proposed to tend the grandmother on the reclaimed mayor's holding, since the old woman "couldn't go begging." Hasse proposed Ebels and her husband take the mayoral retirement quarters for five

[246] No. 200, fo. 44.   [247] No. 715, fo. 47.

years, helping Hecht improve the holding before changing places with him. Hecht refused, saying he bore the mayoral burden by himself "through such long years," undisturbed by Ebels in his title. Hasse ruled that "since the mother" – that is, the grandmother – "has received nothing for four years and cannot beg, and has a right to maintenance from the farm," Hecht must annually give her 1 bushel of rye and one of barley groats. Though Hecht's 1711 title was legitimate, Hasse dismissed him in 1742 from the mayoral office for brutally beating a farmer neighbor. His successor was one of plaintiff Ebels' kinsmen, not her husband. Yet court intervention had partially relieved an old woman's misery.[248]

Villagers sometimes hesitated to retire on farms which, for lack of heirs, passed to kin-unrelated proprietors. The aforementioned Liese Muchows wanted her husband's successor to marry her niece, "so that she would have one of her own people to treat her well in old age." But since incoming farmer Schütte was engaged to another woman, Muchows and her husband Jochen Seyer had to accept a "stranger." Unfortunately, their premonitions were justified. Eight years later the court ordered Schütte to deliver their past-due grain and firewood. Hasse had earlier commanded them all to cease quarreling and shake hands, while retiree Seyer had paid 6 talers for breaking the arm of a certain Marie Schütte, probably his successor's kinswoman. After Seyer's death, his widow only received her provisions amid Schütte's insults. Three years later she lamented that "she gave [Schütte] their farm and had been good to him, but he was very unthankful and cursed her as a whore and a cat, and hit her too with his fist." She demanded protection and that Schütte should haul her compost and otherwise help her. Hasse observed that Schütte "makes himself out as very innocent," claiming she cursed him. Schütte would help her, if she would "do some raking." She said she would pardon him if he "improved himself." The court threatened "serious inquiry" should such incidents recur. Here, evidently, some acceptance of coexistence survived, or emerged, among battle-weary cohabitants.[249]

In one unusual case, a farm passed to a new proprietor against the previous cultivator's widow's wishes. Though she was entitled to retirement, bad blood between her and her successor eventually led her to new quarters in a non-Stavenow village. The new farmer claimed she left without cause, and Hasse rejected most of her arrears demands.

---

[248] No. 591, fo. 96.   [249] Ibid., fos. 81, 98; no. 326, fos. 65, 117.

Although in non-controversial cases retirement support might be granted a claimant not living on the farm supplying it, local observance strongly favored resident retirees. Unscrupulous or malevolent proprietors might try to "drive [someone] from the holding" to recover retirement provisions for themselves. The court acted to protect elders from such a fate, which at Stavenow rarely struck them.[250]

Younger widows living with small children in retirement might also, like elderly and solitary women, face abuse or neglect. Three years after Trine Brunsten's step-son Joachim Sötebier succeeded his deceased smallholder father, she complained that "many difficulties" had arisen over their agreement that she and her two young children should take their meals with Sötebier. She said "for her there was nothing on the table." Hasse assigned her separate retirement provisions. She would help on the farm and "treat the children right and not spoil them." If quarreling and fighting resumed, she would return to Sötebier's table. Judging by her loom, wool, lambs, and retiree's flax allotment, she would fulfill with spinning and weaving her pledge to earn some money.[251]

Most insecure were women who married widowers in retirement. Such was Marie Seyers' situation, whom retired farmer Stefan Ebel wed, bringing her onto his son-in-law Andreas Hecht's farm. When old Ebel died, Marie declared her husband's "dying wish" was that she should have half the crops growing on retirement land. Instead Hecht confiscated them, along with the retirees' fruit and livestock. Yet "she had carried her husband about and nursed and fed him like a child." Hecht resented her for "marrying into the retirement quarters," and for not helping with fieldwork or bearing the costs of her husband's sickness – for soap and medicine – and burial. He conceded she could keep her dowry, but all other retirement assets were his and the deceased's surviving children's, two still unmarried. "She had," Hecht rudely said, "no right to the farm and could go back where she came from." She was obliged to depart, but Hasse let her take half the retirees' rye, plus barley and oats, fruit and livestock "for her necessary living support." Hecht would also have to haul three wagonloads of manure, which she and her deceased husband had gathered and mixed with compost, "wherever she wants."[252]

Occasionally tensions between retirees and successors erupted in violence. Together with his wife, Daniel Mentz faced charges of physically

[250] No. 591, fos. 97–8.   [251] No. 200, fos. 148, 212–15.   [252] No. 591, fos. 93–4.

attacking his mother. Two years later Hasse threatened mother and daughter-in-law, if they did not cease exchanging blows, with Stavenow dungeon, "and to stand half a day in public in the fiddle."[253] The worst conflict arose on Johann Höpfner's farm, six months after he succeeded his father Samuel. Johann petitioned for "protection," complaining his father had beaten him on his farmstead during the harvest. His father – probably about sixty – said his son had fought with a brother-in-law "because of godless talk" and "smashed his face in." To stop the mayhem, he hit his son over the head with a harrow beam. He added, damagingly for his own innocence, that his son refused him the generous retirees' grain provisions of the transfer agreement. Young proprietor Johann's wife, Anna Catharina Ladewichs, said her father-in-law "cursed her as a whore, and if she wasn't to have any peace, she was in a bad way." The pummeled brother-in-law blamed Johann for provoking the fight with insults and curses, but noted that this occurred "in the street, and not on [Höpfner's] farmstead." To initiate violence at another's house, no matter the cause, was punishable. Though the men deserved 2-taler fines "or to be chained crooked in the dungeon for two days," Hasse dismissed them, since they were "parents and children," admonishing adherence to the transfer agreement.[254]

Three years later, old Samuel was dead. His widow stood in court, saying her son Johann had cursed her "as a witch and a French whore." He also hit her on the head four times. "She couldn't work enough to satisfy him," and wanted "what was hers, so she could move away." Johann protested, claiming with implausible filial piety that his mother, though she had borne her husband five children in a long marriage, had cursed "his blessed father" despite Johann's warnings. She replied "she couldn't work so hard anymore in the winter." The hearing ended in reconciliation. But two years later, after Johann Höpfner's death and his wife's remarriage to a new proprietor, Hasse noted "the widow has driven the old mother from the farm."[255]

The Höpfners' quarrels exemplify in extreme form the dangers accompanying intergenerational transitions. It was a time when retired farmers had not yet accustomed themselves to loss of command. In 1726, halfholder Müller handed over his farm to Hans Wolgast, "because of age and the onset of weakness." But Müller wished to have, "so long as he lives, command [*das Befehlen*] over it," with retirement provisions like his parents'. Wolgast, surprisingly, "gladly agreed."

---

[253] No. 200, fos. 17, 47.   [254] No. 591, fos. 127–8.   [255] No. 326, fo. 150.

Young Judge Hasse also assented, though the court normally recognized farm proprietors' managerial authority.[256] The incident stands alone, but old Müller's reluctance to drop the reins was doubtless not unique.

As elders retired, their sons or sons-in-law faced their most difficult years. Responsibility for rents and taxes weighed on them personally for the first time. Children were being raised but were not yet old enough to work, so that farm servants needed to be hired even as full, or overly full, retirement shares of the farm surplus were relinquished. In these circumstances, toleration of low-grade strife evidently limited court intervention to cases threatening dangerous violence.

DEATH AMONG ADULTS AND THE ELDERLY

Stavenowers did what they thought possible to hold death at bay, but resignedly accepted its incursions. The seemingly pious Hasse early employed a poetical rhetoric. In 1725 he wrote that a villager, "after enduring a nine months' illness, has exchanged temporality for eternity [*Zeit mit der Ewigkeit verwechselt*]." He recalled a "grandmother" who, after having for thirty years "enjoyed retirement," "departed this temporal life" (*Zeitligkeit verlassen*). Leaseholder Schmidt spoke laconically of "passing on" (*vorbey komt*), language Hasse later echoed.[257]

Severe or fatal illness could be economically ruinous. A deceased farmer's inventory registered no cash "because he has been very sick for six years and in [nine months] has hardly risen from bed."[258] A retiring farmer "for a long time suffered apoplexy seizures," producing a "great debt burden."[259] An inventory noted that "there are no textile yardage reserves because during the [now deceased] husband's illness everything was sold except for everyday necessities."[260] A farm wife made thirty-eight purchases of whale-oil (*Thran*) as medicine for her fatally stricken middle-aged husband. This cost a considerable 20 talers, leaving her stripped of cash at her hastily arranged remarriage.[261]

The villagers usually died at home, but – with one striking exception – there is little record of the theater of death in which they expired. Pastors were often present to receive confessions. They, or Hasse, might record dying wishes concerning inheritances and survivors' provisions. We

---

[256] No. 200, fo. 203.
[257] Ibid., fos. 187–9, 44–5; no. 323, fo. 8; no. 712, fos. 6–7; no. 715, fos. 35–9.
[258] No. 200, fos. 28–9, 187–9.   [259] Ibid., fos. 220–2.   [260] No. 326, fos. 111–12.
[261] Ibid., fos. 194–8; no. 324, fos. 17–18.

saw how pastor Willebrand wrote of Stefan Bahlcke that "after a long-withstood illness [he] senses his approaching end," and how dying widow Ebels called pastor Carsted. He wrote that Ebels, "born Elisabeth Seyers, with undisturbed comprehension said to me, her father confessor, on her sickbed that she owed no debts except to her sister's daughter Catharine Marie Hechts," who should have one of the deceased's cows. The other cow, along with her other goods, she willed to the farm's "present possessor," Hans Joachim Hecht, "since her relatives in Kahrstedt would trouble themselves but little over her burial, while he has promised her a funeral as is here customary and will faithfully fulfill his promise." Her animadversions on indifferent kinfolk led the pastor to the humble disclaimer: "I leave judgment to the lordship's court, tendering only witness to what I have heard."[262]

Respectable burial was vital to villagers' sense of dignity and mortal worth. New proprietors promised not only to supply food and drink at non-inheriting siblings' weddings, but alternatively, should siblings die without marrying, to pay for their funerals, as when a farm transfer provided that "the fourth [child] Anna Marie will be fed on the holding until her death and buried at its expense."[263] Among retirees, surviving partners sometimes paid for their deceased spouses' funeral charges, but seemingly more customary was their successors' obligation to bury them both. A 1767 agreement said "the old people will be honorably laid to earth by the farm, since they will help with work according to their abilities."[264] In another case, the elders' possessions were to be divided between two non-inheriting children, except that the third child, who took the farm, would receive two sheep and his parents' large cooking pot, on condition "he has them honorably laid to earth."[265]

A respectable funeral featured a sermon devoted to the deceased's memory, preached before the corpse laid out in its coffin. The pastor's fee between the 1720s and 1740s was 1 taler, while burials earned sextons 3 groschen. The 1744 costs of burying Marie Rungen, a fullholder's unmarried sister-in-law, conjure up some of the cultural practices involved. The "coffin boards" cost 1 taler, while 6 groschen went to build the coffin and a half-groschen to paint it. "To make the [funeral] wreath together with the materials" was, at 6 groschen, comparatively expensive. A half-groschen went for "brandy for the women who

---

[262] No. 324, fo. 10; no. 358, fos. 78–84; no. 326, fo. 221; no. 324, fos. 24–5.
[263] No. 326, fos. 201–5.   [264] No. 358, fos. 34–6; no. 326, fos. 191–4.   [265] No. 358, fos. 32–4.

dressed the corpse," while "to make the stockings for the deceased" cost a groschen. Farmer Jürgen Ebel supplied the wake with a barrel of beer, a half-bushel of dried peas, along with herring, bread and butter, another wreath, and candles, for a total of 2.19.- talers. Including pastor's and sexton's fees, the funeral cost altogether 5.12.- talers. If nothing more was contributed, it was a restrained, though not utterly spartan, occasion. Marie Rungen departed in peace, unsurprisingly, for there is no court record of funeral strife.[266]

The sacral aura enveloping dying appears in the death in 1726 of the aforementioned Martin Hoffmeister, seigneurial employee who fathered an extramarital child but wed its mother. He and his wife were contentiously taking possession of his paternal farm when disaster struck. Hasse wrote:

Today sub-bailiff Halentz reported that head plowman [Hoffmeister] at Semlin had the misfortune of falling from a tree where he wanted to cut out a dry branch. And because he fell on his ax, which cut through the bone in his leg, his friends took him first to Quitzow village to the farmer there famous for his cures. Because of the nature of the illness, the farmer did not want to accept him, and directed them to the surgeon in Perleberg. But in being transporting there he lost all his marrow, and the army field doctor as well as the other surgeons pronounced him lost. So, wrapping him in a cold bandage, they sent him back. He had himself placed in a coffin and carried home in this manner. And finally he died when they drew up to his house. He received Holy Communion in Perleberg and prepared himself very well for death.[267]

CONCLUSION

These pages' scenes from household and private life show that family and kinship relations might explode in verbal or physical violence. But the need to maintain the farm as a productive enterprise, the inescapability of its members' frequent interaction, and their dependence upon one another for material well-being forced restraint on warring impulses, or at least compelled them – on pain of judicial punishment – to compose differences "as befits Christians." Across the entire eighteenth century, there is no sign in the Stavenow court transcripts or Blüthen-Mesekow-Stavenow parish register of murder or manslaughter among villagers. Infliction of grave bodily injury was a rare event, though not ordinary, often painful, assault and battery.

[266] No. 324, fo. 8; no. 324, fos. 34–7; no. 200, fos. 44–5, 135; no. 358, fos. 107–10.
[267] No. 200, fo. 40.

If evidence of extreme conflict at home and among close relatives is sparse, the documentation of positive emotion does not reveal much more than widespread marital and kin-ordered solidarity and mutual support. No doubt stronger passions, both destructive and positive, sometimes moved these villagers, as discussions below of lawbreaking will show. But perhaps the human interactions displayed in these pages – pragmatic, self-serving, benevolent, and altruistic by turns – typified the experience of daily life among family and kin.

Viewed against the broad horizon of western European and North American experience, the Stavenow villagers' weak idea of the family but strong sense of household and kinship ties set them at odds with the religious and social thought of the day, which steered toward the emotionalization and privatization of nuclear family life. But the Stavenow pattern is not untypical of a much wider reality, stamped by frequent family reconstitution through remarriage. The villagers' and seigneurial court's meticulous attention to property and inheritance rights, including the orphaned child's, fitted into a largely low-wage western world in which even the most meager assets helped advance their owner toward release from unmarried servitude.

It may seem surprising that, in east-Elbian Europe with its muscular noble lordships and subject farmers, property and tenurial rights were so robust and scrupulously enforced through communal oversight and judicial practice. But the disabilities of subject status in its common German east-Elbian forms, though real (if pervasively misunderstood), left the villagers' legal personalities and judicial access intact. Stavenow's masters accepted prevailing law and custom, exerting strong discretionary and patronly powers to advance their interests within their often ambiguous limits. The pages below will reinforce this picture of Stavenow lordship, and by extension noble lordship elsewhere in Brandenburg-Prussia, not as untrammeled seigneurial domination but, in comparison with west Germany and western Europe, a powerful form of landlordism over subjects themselves possessing generally recognized legal and property rights. In this perspective, east-Elbian German villagers living under conditions similar to those at Stavenow – a majority of all such country people – appear as community-bound and kinship-enmeshed family farmers more comparable than has been thought to their western European counterparts, even if the rents their landlords exacted differed considerably.

4

Daily bread: village farm incomes, living standards, and lifespans

Brandenburg, like all east-Elbian Germany, was a land of noble lordships housed on large estates. Yet, Junker-obsessed, historians often forgot that this society's primary cell was the village farm. The villagers' inner circle were the team-driving largeholders, exercising first claim on the communal open fields' plowland and pasturage, meadows and woods. Subordinate and fewer were smallholders, often with separate lands and even villages. The nobility's and crown's demesne farms depended on horse-drawn labor services. Without landholding households, the villages would have been cottagers' and estate-laborers' colonies. Though lying in the large estates' shadow, east-Elbian villages were, like much of the countryside in west and south Germany and western and eastern Europe, a world of middling family farmers, self-sufficient producers and, except in bad years, surplus-sellers on nearby markets.

Historians long assumed, on little evidence, that landlordly exactions and military-bureaucratic extractions reduced Brandenburg-Prussian farmers to threadbare subsistence at best, exhausted penury at worst. Recent research has uncovered comfort and capital among crownland colonists (a kind of state yeomanry), and among short-term leaseholders working the Uckermark nobility's lands (a kind of homespun entrepreneurial tenantry).[1] These were small, legally exceptional groups. It remains to illuminate, with first-hand evidence, the material condition of old-regime Prussia's prototypical country dwellers – subject farmers such as Stavenow's.

The smoldering manor–village conflicts which, at Stavenow and elsewhere, caught fire in the half-century after 1763 cannot be rightly read without knowing farmers' material conditions. Of broad interest too are

---

[1] Peters et al., *Bauerntagebücher*; Hartmut Harnisch, "Bäuerliche Ökonomie und Mentalität unter den Bedingungen der ostelbischen Gutsherrschaft in den letzten Jahrzehnten vor Beginn der Agrarreformen," *JbfWG* 3 (1989): 87–108.

eighteenth-century living standards. These were, among ordinary people, doubtless inferior to today's, though milk and honey still flow
unevenly. But old-regime European common people's material well-
being and want need closer scrutiny. Pessimistic judgments strongly color
prevailing views on early modern life.[2]

The subject sprawls. Here we look – both with eyes on quantitative
data and ears attuned to the lordship's and villagers' own words – at the
village farm's resources and productivity, market and other cash transactions, savings, surpluses, and debts. Vital to well-being were housing,
diet, and clothing, which have figured already in preceding discussions
of marriage portions and inheritances. Villagers' laborious lives culmi-
nated in retirement, and elders' incomes illuminate social expectations
and rewards. These are ill-explored themes. So too are sickness, mortality, longevity, and the east-Elbian demographic regime generally,
about which these pages offer perhaps surprising conclusions. A realistic understanding of this rural society, like others in the early modern
world, requires discrimination between the varying paths of fate and
fortune.

THE NOBILITY'S VIEW OF THE VILLAGE FARM

The voluminous documentation says little of villagers' actual sowings or
reapings, or of how they divided their harvests between seed-grain, household consumption, seigneurial rent, and sale. But in the mid-eighteenth
century farmers' output and consumption came under discussion among
Stavenow managers and business associates. Their views model the village
farm as they thought it should function.

Frederick II's zeal for settling immigrant colonists led his officials in
1751 to contact Maria Elisabeth von Kleist, *née* von Hacke. This was the
wife of Colonel Kleist, who in 1739 died on duty in East Prussia.
Widowed with ten sons and five daughters, she commanded the lordship, aided by officials and servants, until her death in 1758. The government now informed her that anciently deserted Dargardt village,
whose lands Stavenow shared with Eldenburg crown estate, was to be
resettled by village farmers, who would supply labor services to work a
new manor-farm Eldenburg would establish. Separation of the two
lordships' respective Dargardt shares was necessary. Should Stavenow

[2] Exemplary views: Abel, especially *Massenarmut*; Jerome Blum, ed., *Our Forgotten Past Seven Centuries of Life on the Land* (London, 1982); Ogilvie and Scribner, *New Social and Economic History*. On Prussia specifically: Treue, *Wirtschaftsgeschichte*.

patriotically follow the crown's example in settling its Dargardt lands, it would receive valuable government aid and concessions.

Frau Kleist soon received a letter from Privy Councilor von Thiele in Berlin. Despite his official title and noble surname, Thiele was a land speculator. Since the government had decided, he sententiously wrote, "to have all the deserted village fields settled by ENTREPRENEURS . . . I would rather have the PROFIT of such ENTERPRISE myself than leave it to another ENTREPRENEUR." He had offered to manage the settlement of Eldenburg's Dargardt share. The new colonists, as Frederick II insisted, would be personally free perpetual leaseholders on fixed rents (*Erbzinsbauern*). The new demesne farm would pay the crown a solid leaseholder's fee. The confident Thiele now offered to sell his Dargardt development rights, when officially confirmed, to Frau Kleist for a handsome 6,000 talers. He recommended she merge her Dargardt lands in his scheme, to reap, by "ENTREPRENEURING for herself," both his anticipated profits and her own. Though possessing professional knowledge of estate agriculture, he perhaps proposed this "advantageous [*avantageusen*] commerce" to burden Frau Kleist with the risks while pocketing an easy profit. Yet he said "it would be even more agreeable to me" if she sold him her Dargardt share, for which he offered 3,500 talers. Alternatively, he would pay 200 talers perpetual yearly lease on her Dargardt lands, easily remittable from the annual 1,500-taler profit he forecast on the whole venture.[3]

Thiele underestimated Frau Kleist. Her Berlin lawyer, Herr Wackenroder, recommended overtrumping him by proposing to the crown that Stavenow alone settle all Dargardt. Wackenroder suggested she pointedly ask the government for time "to weigh the matter with the six of my sons who already stand in Your Royal Majesty's war service." In 1752 she successfully played this powerful card, obtaining the full Dargardt title, including extensive forests, on condition of settling twenty-three "foreign families" and paying the government a modest annual fee.[4]

Thiele revealed to Frau Kleist his concept of the prospective farmer-colonists' properties, inventories, dues, and services. He supposed the fullholder with 2 hides would annually sow 20 bushels both of winter and summer grain. His arable would yield "the fifth kernel." He should have 5 hectares of pasture, yearly yielding five wagonloads of winter hay fodder. His iron stock should count four oxen, three horses, "some

---

[3] No. 715, fos. 84–5.   [4] Ibid., fos. 86–9, 143, 109–10.

geese and pigs." Each colonist would build his farmstead with free lumber and receive 150 talers to buy iron stock. He would have three years tax- and rent-free, but only one year free of labor services. Thiele aggressively expected each fullholder to deliver heavy yearly grain rents of 24 rye-bushels and 12 each of barley and oats. He would pay 5 talers money rent, a tithe on newborn livestock, render natural payments of two geese, six hens, and sixty eggs, and have his womenfolk spin six balls of yarn, "for which he will receive the flax." His weekly labor services would be one day with a team and one day's manual labor, though in the summer harvest-quarter this schedule would be doubled. He would make strenuous seigneurial hauls, in several trips, of 48 bushels (about 2 tons) up to forty-five miles distant. Of villagers' liabilities Thiele breezily wrote that "labor services need not be reckoned among them, since after all the farmer must keep teams and servants to cultivate his own fields."[5]

Thiele reckoned the new farmers' rye sowings would yield "$4\frac{1}{2}$ kernels." After deducting next year's seed, half the surplus would cover home consumption and, through sale, production costs. The other half went "for rent." Barley and oats would yield the fifth kernel, of which good shares could be sold "for the lease." Likewise, while the household needed two cows, the produce of the other two could be monetized at 8 talers annually. Altogether, Thiele valued the farm surplus at 55 talers. Subtracting 33 talers for seigneurial rent left the colonist with 22 talers net profit, though from this sum all cash purchases, and eventually taxes too, would have to flow.

Frau Kleist gave Thiele's blueprints to her son Friedrich Conrad who, following military service, rose to Privy Councilor in the noble-dominated Brandenburg estates' public administration (*Landschaft*), oriented to landlordly interests. Friedrich Conrad, conservatively reckoning lower colonists' yields, thought a farm family could not pay Thiele's rents and survive on the remaining surplus. The new settler would have a wife and children, male and female farm servants, and a "boy to tend the horses." On the crown estates, annual bread-grain estimates for one person were 8 bushels "or even 10 bushels for every grown-up fellow [*Kerl*]." Yet Thiele's householders would retain only 26 bushels. Once they paid full taxes, their annual cash surplus would be 15–19 groschen with which the colonist would have, Friedrich Conrad wrote, to "equip himself with indispensable tools and ironwork, pay servants, buy

[5] No. 704, fos. 96–7.

firewood, and meet his most pressing needs as a human being (*Mensch*). Under these conditions, which are not just difficult but impossible, no one will take a farm here."[6]

The Kleists set lower Dargardt rent targets. Hasse figured the full-holders would have, apart from arable, meadows yielding 10–12 hayloads, house gardens, hop plantation shares, logged-off trees for firewood, and communal alderwood shares for fencing and fuel. Each fullholder would annually harvest 50 full-size *Morgen*, whose sowings "are reckoned at only 24 bushels of rye and 12 bushels each of barley and oats."[7] Following Dargardt acquisition, the Kleists' good standing with Frederick's regime rewarded them with the adjoining long-abandoned Gosedahl village lands. Here, on 10 hides, four fullholders and two smallholders would settle. For lack of communal meadows and pastures, one-fifth of each farm's arable would have to be spared tillage. Assuming the soil to be good, Hasse forecast sowings of 2 bushels per *Morgen*, instead of the 1-bushel calculation applied to Dargardt and the manorial economy. "Reckoning only on [harvesting] the third kernel," grain rents would tally 16 rye-bushels and 16 together of barley and oats. "But," the judge benevolently added, "so that the tenant-farmers settled here will have better subsistence only 12 rye-bushels and 6 each of barley and oats will be demanded."[8]

Here Hasse, who knew villagers' circumstances intimately, played the Kleists' profit-maximizer. Gosedahl was never colonized, but because of sandy soil left partly under forest cover and partly leased, as of old, to non-Stavenow farmers for modest rents. Such heavy grain rents as Hasse imagined could be levied there were never extracted from Dargardt's colonists, whose stubborn bargaining reduced natural payments from each fullholding to 12 rye-bushels. Their remaining dues approximated other local fullholders': two days' weekly team-driven labor, the third day commuted to cash; four extra days harvesting rye at the new Dargardt manor farm ("Kleistenhof"); one annual 18-bushel grain-haul to the nearby Elbe; and the symbolical tribute hen. They evaded the harsher terms both Thiele and Hasse thought fastenable upon free colonists.

The Dargardters' occupancy of fullholdings against three-day weekly labor service and 12-bushel tribute grain defined, in legally free settlers' eyes, an acceptable Brandenburg family farm. They were better situated than old-established Stavenowers not by virtue of rents, taxes,

---

[6] Ibid., fos. 119–20.   [7] No. 715, fo. 238.   [8] No. 704, fos. 115–16.

or likely production surpluses but as hereditary perpetual leaseholders empowered, eventually, to sell their farms (though not the land itself) for cash, and exempt, as "foreign" colonists fearful of the Prussian army, from conscription and wartime haulage.

THE VILLAGERS' GRAIN HARVESTS AND OTHER FIELD CROPS

Inventorying a farm in spring 1742 Hasse observed that "bread-grain is on hand," while of maturing winter and completed summer sowings he exclaimed "praise God!"[9] Cut sheaves were farming's greatest prize, but Thiele's and Stavenow's conflicting reckonings showed their grain yields were debatable. Yet some evidence of village harvests survives in church accounts. Mesekow village record-keeping, after having ceased "within human memory," began again in 1684, when farmer and church elder (*Gotteshausmann*) Jacob Blume delivered 11 talers to bailiff Zicker for safekeeping. With other savings this raised parish capital to 19 talers, from which villagers borrowed small sums at the yearly cost of 1 groschen per taler (4.16 percent). Loan interest and parish harvest earnings swelled the fund.

The "holy land" (*Heil Land*), which variously the miller leased, the sexton rented, or the commune cultivated, could bear 8 bushels' sowing. The 1686 cadaster credited Mesekow arable with "the third kernel." Between 1697 and 1732, eleven threshed-out communal rye harvests multiplied sowings by 3.4. In four cases the range was 1.5–2.5, in two it was 3.0, in four it rose to 4–5. If yields of three or more were good, for every bad year there were two better ones. One oats harvest yielded 1:6, one of buckwheat 1:7. The villagers' reward for cultivating the "holy land" was a half-barrel's harvest beer.[10]

Fuller evidence survives from Rossow village, in Brandenburg's comparatively fertile Uckermark District. In 1651–96 the Rossowers regularly cultivated the parsonage's land, yearly sowing on average 8 bushels both of rye and barley. Productivity was higher than at Mesekow. On average, thirty-six rye harvests yielded 1:4.4, thirty-nine barley harvests 1:4.1. Rye – but not barley – yields below the third kernel were rare.[11] As at Stavenow, the harvesters stacked scythe-cut grain in the fields in

[9] No. 326, fos. 76–8. [10] No. 640.
[11] GStAPK, Provinz Brandenburg, Rep. 16, no. 95; Amt Brüssow-Löcknitz: Kirchenregister von Rossow, 1651–1696. Fourteen rye harvests produced yields below 1:4.4, including four below 1:3; fifteen barley harvests fell below 1:4.1, including nine below 1:3.

sheaves, twenty for rye (a "*Stiege*"), fifteen for barley (a "*Mandel*").[12] The real test was not the number of sheaves, but bushels threshed from them. The Rossow accounts record threshers' payment, taken in shares, averaging every eleventh rye-bushel and every twelfth of barley, thinning the parsonage's net gain to the fourth rye kernel and 3.8 for barley.

The sparse Mesekow data – and 1686 cadastral estimates – gain plausibility in Rossow's well-documented perspective. The villages' churchland harvests, discounting Rossow's better soil, found a rough match in Stavenow's domanial yields, which in 1760 Hasse computed on eleven-year averages as 3.5 for rye and oats, 4 for barley, 3 for peas.[13] Of the Blüthen mayor's farm Hasse wrote in 1730 "the land is well conditioned and need only be plowed for sowing." A year later a nearby estate official leasing it said "I've cultivated the soil as well as I could, the same as my own."[14] Yet this comparatively good farm won but 2.5 kernels from its 1730 rye harvest. The 1686 cadastre estimated the Stavenow villages' yields at (or below) threefold or fourfold at best. Though the farmers doubtless exerted themselves more purposefully working their own land than the parish's or lordship's, it seems prudent in judging their handiwork, at a certain risk of underestimation, to credit them with manorial and churchland yields for rye (3.5), and 1760 manorial averages for barley (4.0) and oats (3.5).

As for villagers' sowings, customary practice approximated seigneurially prescribed measures: for fullholders – 24 rye-bushels, 12 each of barley and oats, plus – on best fallow – half-bushels both of flaxseed and peas. Farmers might slightly vary their sowing mix. One inventory found the usual seed in the ground, except that more barley diminished flax, peas, and broad beans.[15] A mayor's farm planted winter rye, but small quantities of spring wheat (a local rarity) and buckwheat, plus barley, oats, and peas (but no flax). Because war had pushed up fodder prices, another farm planned 1756 sowings of 18 bushels of oats and 6 of barley, plus peas and flax.[16]

After 1750, farmers appear leasing small land parcels to other cultivators or the landless. Hasse found that, while a farmer had planted 20 rye-bushels, he also permitted five others to sow 1 or 2 bushels on his land, levying the customary charge equaling seed sown. Some farmers needed to boost output, while others settled for minimal returns. Probably

---

[12] Unlike scythes for grain harvesting, sickles rarely appear in farm inventories. No. 200, fos. 207–8.
[13] No. 259, pt. III.   [14] No. 200, fos. 234–5; no. 591, fos. 19–20.   [15] No. 200, fos. 28–9.
[16] No. 324, fos. 20–3, 34–7.

renters, when farmers themselves, acted under the pressure of large household numbers; when married cottagers, they were likewise expanding food supplies, but when unmarried laborers, they were perhaps honing – or parading – their skills as cultivators.[17]

Sometimes impecunious farmers rented land against cash advances. The court investigated a fullholder who leased 6 bushels' land to five villagers, including a sexton, at a low 12 groschen per bushel. Condemning this practice as abusive, Hasse ordered its cessation, on pain to the lessor of corporal punishment and to the lessees of crop confiscation.[18] Another fullholder in the crisis year 1771 leased land to a married cowherd from outside the jurisdiction. The court, discovering no other "foreign grain," let it stand, noting that the farmer, who was being evicted for incompetence, had sown his other land only incompletely and badly.[19] Farmers might lease land to others, while cooperating in its cultivation. An absconded shepherd had sown 2 rye-bushels, "providing his own manure," though the lessor-farmer hauled it and helped in the shepherd's harvest.[20] Even if such transactions were commoner than sparse evidence suggests, they remained occasional and marginal dealings. Non-farmers had little access to rentable land, though parish property sometimes qualified. In Klockow village there was some infertile churchland, "which deceased smith Kunst, with no knowledge of plowland, leased for 2.5 talers, thinking to draw a greater advantage from it." Later he acknowledged his mistake, but paid the sum, "to keep his word."[21]

The picture so far drawn finds refinement – and corroboration – in early nineteenth-century emancipation records. Surveyors measured farms eligible for freehold conversion, dividing arable into seven fertility classes. First came "barley land, first and second class"; analogous oats land; then "rye land," sowable every third, sixth, or ninth year.[22] The better the land, the heavier its sowings and harvests. Barley II was sowable with 1 rye-bushel per Magdeburg *Morgen* and would yield 4.5 kernels. If sown in barley, this category allowed 12.5 percent heavier sowings, at the same yield rate. On abundant "three-year rye land," rye sowings fell to 0.625 bushels with yields of 1:3, with sowings of the lower-priced "rough oats" a bit heavier but with equal harvests.

Government surveyors, with no bias for or against the villagers, rated their land on a scale which, excluding rare first-class barley land, ran from

---

[17] Ibid., fo. 36.   [18] No. 326, fo. 214; no. 715, fos. 26–7.   [19] No. 358, fo. 115–20.
[20] No. 601, fos. 15–16.   [21] No. 720, fos. 73–5.
[22] This system reduced all cultivable land to barley I, e.g., barley II:barley I = 7:9; this ratio for oats I was 5:3, for rye I – 7:2, and rye III – 14:1. No. 441, fos. 13–46.

Table 4.1 *Pre-emancipation landholdings in Stavenow villages (in hectares)*

	Components of individual farms (Average size per holding)					Communal lands[a] (Total size)		
	Arable land	Meadow (leased)	Meadows (owned)	Pasture	Woods	Meadows	Pasture	Woods
Village farm type								
Blüthen								
Fullholder	29.0	0.9	–	2.5	2.5	4.5	24	24
Glövzin								
Full	24.5	0.9	–	------7------		–	?	25
Half	14.4	0.9	–	-----5.6-----				
Small	11.0	0.8	–	-----1.7-----				
Cottager	4.6	----------------0.6---------------						
Mesekow								
Half	10.5	1.7	–	-----7.3-----		–	–	42
Premslin								
Full	26.3	0.6	1.9	-----5.9-----		–	13	–

[a] Individual access in proportion to farm size and number of village holdings.
Sources: Blüthen: no. 405, fos. 22–68 (1814–17); no. 406, fos. 14–26 (1824); Glövzin: no. 426 (ca. 1816); no. 513, fos. 34–5 (1815); no. 427, fos. 1–10 (1814–17); Mesekow: no. 198, fos. 8–10 (1842); Premslin: no. 441, fos. 10–15 (1818).

1:4.5 for the three bread-grains to 1:3 (or less).[23] Surveyors' measurements show also that seigneurially prescribed sowings closely reflected productive potential (see table 4.1). The average Stavenow fullholder cultivated 104 Magdeburg *Morgen* of arable land (26 hectares/65 acres), planting two-thirds yearly. Sowing 48 bushels produced a density per *Morgen* of about 0.75 bushel, consistent with the surveyors' cautious judgment of soil fertility.

Reckoning sowings at seigneurial norms and yields at seigneurial levels, the Stavenow fullholder's yearly surplus – after setting aside next year's seed – averaged 60 bushels (ca. 2.6 tons) of rye, 36 of barley, and 30 of oats. We look below at the bite household consumption took from these stores. But how often did harvest failure rob farmers of full measure? This question evades a precise answer. Taking exceptionally high

[23] No. 433, fos. 14–22. Yields and sowing on first-class barley land are not recorded here. On oats land class I, rye was sowable at 0.875 bushels with fourth-kernel yields; of oats, a full bushel yielded 4.5 kernels. The Magdeburg *Morgen* (of 180 square rods [*Ruthen*]) measured 0.25 hectare, while the "large" Brandenburg or Prussian *Morgen* of the eighteenth century (400 square rods) equalled 0.57 hectare. Sowings and yields on six-year and nine-year rye land were so low that such soils were usually grown over in pasture-grass and wood.

annual minimum Berlin prices as a guide, in the period 1690–1740 Brandenburg rye harvests were – or appear to have been – bad in or preceding 1699, 1709, 1712–14, 1718–20, 1726–7, 1736, and 1740. In the 1740s and 1750s, high prices prevailed in 1745–6 and 1756. They recurred in 1761–3; the long period November 1770 to March 1773; in 1795 and 1799–1806, especially 1804–6. Some of these were war years, when transport difficulties and army demand elevated prices independent of harvest failures. Heavy grain exports to England during the French Revolutionary wars also boosted prices.[24]

At Stavenow exceptionally high prices prevailed in 1693, 1697, 1699, 1717–20, and 1724 ("such a bad year," a debt-ridden farmer said).[25] In spring 1735 Stavenow leaseholder Hartz wrote the Prignitz District Commissioner of serious village harvest deficits, preventing full current winter and summer plantings. Because the *Kontribution* tax was based on sowings, harvest failures could justify tax remissions. The fields, said Hartz, "are mostly only badly planted, and in some villages grain shortage has left many tons of seed unsown" – 13.5 tons in the four principal fullholders' villages. "Nor has anything been sown by the lodgers" – including the elders – "so that therefore, and because not even half the rye has come up, it would not be improper to help the poor subjects with some measure of remission."[26] And, like almost everywhere else in east-Elbian Germany, the years 1770–2 tormented Stavenow's villages with the eighteenth century's worst subsistence crisis: three successive rye harvests fell disastrously short, along with two summer plantings. Judge Betich wrote in 1772 of the "previous year's harvest failure," while the Blüthen parish register displays these years' chilling mortality.[27]

Brandenburg birth-to-death ratios from 1688–1730 and 1747–1805 include (in peacetime) three negative years, when deaths outnumbered births: 1719 and 1772–3. This supports other evidence of severe harvest failures immediately preceding these years. Times of sharply fallen or low though still positive ratios were 1693, three years in 1716–21, 1729, 1749–51 (postwar years), 1767, 1771, 1775–6, 1781, 1785–6, 1789–90, and 1800–1.[28] In Blüthen parish decennial birth-to-death ratios in the period 1694–1819 are negative for the 1770s alone. But, while harvest failures

[24] Prices in Naudé, *Getreidehandelspolitik*, vol. II, 568–72; vol. III, 624–31; vol. IV, 647–63; Behre, *Statistik*, 277; Abel, *Agrarkrisen*, appendix, table II. Rye scarcities could drive up barley and oats prices, but summer grain prices might soar independently. Rye prices peaked oftener than barley or oats.
[25] No. 200, fo. 23.   [26] No. 713, fo. 110.   [27] No. 718, fos. 12–13.
[28] Behre, *Statistik*, 447 (data for 1730–47 mostly missing).

raised mortality, epidemics could have the same effect even with sufficient food.[29] Evidence is imperfect, but full-scale subsistence crises were rarities, while years of local or regional shortages and high prices were commoner, tending to occur erratically in clusters. Grain shortages led Stavenowers to borrow grain for food and planting from the lordship or its neighbors. They paid the locally prevalent high price, but the Kleists showed patience in awaiting repayment, charging (as law required) no interest. In July 1721, with a normal harvest assured, the lordship called in its villagers' debts from 1718–20.

Individual arrears mostly comprised unpaid money dues and tribute grain. Farmers absorbed bad harvests' shock by suspending seigneurial rent in favor of household consumption (and unremitted tax bills). In the few cases where payment for borrowed grain was still delinquent in 1721, quantities lent were not great (6–16 bushels). Altogether, individual 1721 debt was manageable (5–20 talers), except for three embattled households owing 28–44 talers. All debtors agreed, on pain of harvest confiscation, to pay fully the coming fall.[30] An arrears survey from 1744–8, compiled at the Silesian wars' end, included borrowed grain but twice. Other debt was unpaid rent. The burden, borne by a village minority, was not crushing: the heaviest obligation comprised 7 talers and 8 rye-bushels.[31]

The Stavenow lordship's very precise accounts of rye and other grain sales, from nine years between 1746 and 1759, record numerous purchases by non-landed villagers, but only a few small sales to the landed. In two cases only did buyers pay in money borrowed from local parish funds. In three others the transactions were seigneurial loans. Otherwise, buyers paid cash at prices slightly below local town prices.[32] As for tribute-grain arrears in these years, delinquents numbered 4–8 yearly, owing on average 5–8 bushels. In 1751–2, eight farmers liquidated their mostly minor arrears.[33] Thus villagers did not frequently seek grain advances for consumption or seed. Their harvests were, seemingly, usually adequate, though sometimes not to fully cover rent. The average annual grain surpluses proposed above probably approached

---

[29] Pfarramt Blüthen. Pastor Karl Gross's unpublished tables. The 1694–1819 decennial live-birth average was 166, from which the largest negative deviations occurred in the 1690s, 1710s, and 1720s.

[30] No. 240: 2.VII.1721.

[31] No. 714, fos. 184–5. The 1746–7 seigneurial grain ledger shows that, among fifty-one deliveries due, six were delinquent (three from the five main service villages). No. 274.

[32] Cash accounts from 1746–59: nos. 265, 207, 208, 229, 270, 233, 262, 261, 237.

[33] Grain ledgers from 1748–53: nos. 228, 211, 232, 281, 236.

village reality in all but the worst years. They overlook the occasional bountiful harvest, when savings might accumulate to cushion future hardships.

Because grain yields were low, farms needed to be large, requiring long days of fieldwork. Before plantings several plowings occurred, partly to suppress weeds and partly because fallow grazing fertilized the land but thinly. The villagers plowed their own stall-manure and compost into rye and barley land, though in unknown quantities. The average largeholding's five cows would, during winter stall-feeding, eat about 5 tons of hay and straw. Whether resulting manure sufficed is doubtful. Yet in 1731 a bidder on the Blüthen mayor's holding asked for one year rent-free, "since the land is not properly manured."[34] Villagers' small fallow plantings of peas and broad beans had nitrogen-fixing effects, though they valued these crops for other reasons. They thickened their compost heaps with communal or seigneurial leaves and pine needles. The authorities once discovered them, in their zeal for collecting soil amendments, illegally carting off Eldenburg crown forest's turf, destroying seedling trees.[35]

In large home gardens, farmers grew vegetables (especially cole and root crops), hops, fruit, and nuts. In 1747, four Premslin farmers complained their neighbors had carved out from the arable small plots which they added to their gardens, thus reducing communal grazing. The defendants appealed to "His Royal Majesty, who wants such gardens extended and improved, not reduced," adding that "most people in their commune agreed." So too did the court. Although grain-sowing losses were minor, the Premsliners had a choice and preferred to expand garden land.[36] The Blüthen villagers agreed in 1761 that each farm would continue to cultivate, apart from its own garden, two communal "cabbage beds," an "old" one and a "new" one "on the pasture." Here, too, the commune had carved additional gardens out of grazing or wooded land.[37]

Potatoes (*Kartoffeln*), whose spread in eighteenth-century Europe as fodder and food was portentous, first appear at Stavenow in 1727 as "*Tartüffeln.*" They long remained a garden rather than field crop. At mid-century they figured in food pantries as *Ertoffeln* or *Gatoffeln*.[38] After

[34] No. 591, fos. 19–20.   [35] No. 714, fo. 14; no. 513, fos. 37–9; no. 326, fo. 65.
[36] No. 326, fos. 134–5. Emancipation officials described these lands as "field ends" near the farmsteads, "cultivated every year." No. 448, fo. 43.
[37] No. 557, fos. 1–3, 9; no. 717, fos. 212–13.
[38] No. 200, fos. 73–5; no. 358, fos. 61–3; no. 324, fos. 20–3; no. 358, fos. 129–34; no. 324, fos. 34–7.

1800 high-yielding potatoes overshadowed bread-grains in cottagers' and laborers' diets, inaugurating the proliferation of mini-holdings dependent on potato plantations. But in eighteenth-century Stavenow villages no revolutionary effects of this food are evident (though it slowly replaced older root crops), nor did the lordship cultivate it widely. Across Electoral Brandenburg, potato sowings 1765–1801 rose tenfold, to 27,000 English tons, with weight yields doubling from 1:3.5 to 1:6. Most plantings occurred in sandy districts, while the relatively more fertile Altmark, Prignitz, and Uckermark followed distantly.[39]

Villagers thought communally regulated open-field grain cultivation workable. But in the mid-eighteenth century, seigneurial manor-farms, at Stavenow and throughout Prussia (especially on the crown estates), adopted fallow-free rotations of cereals and fodder crops on enclosed fields. The villagers showed only a glimmer of readiness, offset by the fear of unmanageable costs, to abandon the three-field system. In 1773, in Garlin village, the five local lordships withdrew and enclosed ("separated") their arable from the open fields. The smallholders, willingly or not, followed suit, leaving the fullholders alone within the old communal system. In 1791 Carl Ludwig Sieghorst, a yeoman-like free mayor, petitioned the government for separation of his three hides. "I wish to be released," he said, "from vexatious community [*lästigen Gemeinschaft*] with full- and halfholders and have my possessions in a single tract, to use and cultivate them better." An inquest would determine whether such action was "possible and useful."

The farmers, speaking at the free mayor's house, accepted Sieghorst's enclosure right, claiming it also for "each and every one of us." If it was feasible for him, but not them, why should he alone benefit? The royal commissioners questioned the farmers' seriousness, suspecting they sought to block Sieghorst's exit. The officials thought non-fullholders would lose too much land through drawing individualized farms' new boundaries, and that each farmer would have to keep his own livestock herder, at unbearable expense. The commissioners' counter-proposal, not manifestly superior, was that fullholders form their own unseparated tract, and lesser farmers another. "But the farmers would not vote for this." Finally, the farmers conceded "they are not individually inclined of their own free will to separation, but were forced into it by Sieghorst's proposal." As "people of no means" (*unbemittelte Leute*) they could not pay separation costs, and asked to be spared them.

---

[39] Behre, *Statistik*, 237.

"Without giving any particular reasons," they refused to sign the day's protocol.

In 1792 the commissioners ruled that Sieghorst could withdraw, since "he displayed good knowledge of agricultural economy," while improvements were impossible within the three-field system because decisions there required so many people's assent. For the farmers, separation would not be advantageous, because the common meadows, pastures, and woods could not be divided into individualized parcels. Yet after 1811 freehold-conversion surveyors formed the farmers' lands into individualized holdings. Seemingly the commissioners' 1791–2 views were excessively cautious. Though enclosure's costs alarmed the villagers, they agreed to consider it, if shown they would benefit.[40]

Reluctance to abandon a centuries-old agrarian regime did not mean indifference to gain within it. The distinction between good and bad work and good and bad luck was clear. In November 1752 Hasse wrote of remarrying fullholder Michael Glissmann's farm that "winter grain has been fully and praiseworthily planted. Grain for rent and spring sowing, along with what the household will need until next harvest, is in the barn."[41] These were signs of a competent and successful farmer. And when, at summer's end, the villagers staged their harvest celebrations, they could well judge their labor's rewards.[42]

THE VILLAGE FARMERS' LIVESTOCK AND EQUIPMENT

Open fields, household, and livestock coexisted symbiotically. Horses and oxen supplied traction; cattle, sheep, pigs, and poultry supplied food and fertilizers. Farms, though sizable, were barren without livestock. A household's wealth was evident in its animals. Yet finite grazing on fallowed arable, post-harvest stubble, village pastures, and in the communal woods limited livestock holdings. The animals a farm could winter over, instead of selling or slaughtering in the fall, depended on its oats and straw, and the hay cut on its communal meadow parcel which, like its open-fields cereal land, was a fixed and individualized allotment but, unlike its arable plots, enclosed by fences.[43]

The Kleists granted, as we saw, low-cost Löcknitz meadow leases to farmers whose village hay harvests were insufficient. The lordship also sold them hay, an expensive commodity, for 2 talers a wagonload, four

[40] No. 720, fos. 32–43. [41] No. 326, fos. 187–8. [42] No. 200, fo. 135. [43] No. 591, fo. 126.

times a wagon of firewood's cost and twice a male worker's weekly wages. Straw too was costly: a day's wages in 1760 bought three bales.[44] Official post-1811 surveys assigned Löcknitz meadows middle-range productivity: twice mowable, yielding annually 14 hundredweight of hay per *Morgen*, on a scale descending from 18 hundredweight to single cuts yielding but 4 hundredweight. To winter over a cow required 10 hundredweights of hay and 225 bundles of winter and summer straw, reducible by formula to 19 hundredweights of hay. This meant, the surveyors calculated, that in Blüthen village, which produced 870.5 hundredweights, the eight fullholders could among them keep 45 head, or 5–6 each. For grazing purposes, horses were equivalent to mature cattle and oxen, though they also ate oats, if skimpily.[45]

Stavenow villagers' grazing rights, tied to unchanging numbers of landed households, remained stable. After Kleist's equalization in Premslin village, each fullholder could freely graze eight communally herded horses or plow-oxen, four cattle, sixteen sheep, and five breeding geese. Cattle could substitute for draft-animals. Some excess capacity was evident in the rule that whoever grazed additional animals "will help," beyond usual charges, "the commune pay the *Kontribution* and in other ways." Grazing rights and accompanying pasturage and meadowland were valuable enough to eclipse a farm's annual sowings as the basis, within the communes if not in law, for direct tax assessments.[46] For grazing infractions, Premsliners whose animals, when not under the communal herders' care, damaged planted fields or off-limits pasturage owed the commune the price of a quarter-barrel of beer and for subsequent offenses a half-barrel, the money to be spent for communal welfare (and not, as earlier, drunk by the guilt-free farmers).[47]

In 1818 freehold-conversion officials found these rules still valid. The Premsliners depended, for lack of good communal pastures, on open-field grazing and leased meadows. But this, the officials pedantically calculated, still supported 365 (plus "2,471/4,092"[!]) head of large animals (convertible at 10:1 ratio into sheep and 6:1 into breeding geese). The twenty-four fullholders held 90 percent of all grazing, but three smallholders, one cottager, and the parsonage and church between them grazed thirty-one large animals.[48]

---

[44] No. 704, fo. 112; no. 324, fos. 50–2; no. 591, fo. 58.
[45] Hundredweight (*Zenter*): 51 kilos (112 pounds): no. 405, fos. 9–21, 65–8. Emancipation officials' *"Grossvieheinheiten"* expressed rough equivalency in grazing and foddering between cattle, oxen, and horses (no. 441, fo. 20).
[46] No. 713, fos. 260–1; no. 326, fos. 80, 93–4.   [47] No. 200, fos. 23–4.
[48] No. 441, fos. 13–46: *Kossäten* – 7–8 large animals each; cottager – 2.4; parsonage and church – 7.

For subject farms' purposes, these were not unfavorable allotments. In Glövzin, identical shares prevailed.[49] The Blütheners agreed in 1761 that fullholders could graze fourteen draft-animals and cattle; any more would mean "complete ruin." This "amicable" court settlement on grazing and other village "benefits" forced retreat on halfholders and smallholders who exceeded their limits, whether in grazing, woodcutting, or communal gardening. Catalyzing the ruling was the wartime obligation burdening all farmers to join in distant hauls of military provisions to Kolberg, on the Pomeranian coast. The fullholders complained that lesser cultivators, enjoying communal usages beyond what their status allowed, evaded their haulage.

The court now ruled that Blüthen's halfholders could graze but half and landed smallholders one-third the largeholders' number of horses and cattle, with proportional haulage duties. Fullholders not exhausting their grazing rights might lease them to lesser neighbors, "but no one may take advantage of this arrangement to graze animals from outside the village." A mini-smallholder, with 4 bushels' sowable land (off the open fields), lost his free grazing of a cow and three sheep. Retired farm couples could send two cows and two sheep to pasture; single elders could keep but one cow. The court, in three of the village's six seigneurs' presence, surveyed the twenty-six Blüthen farmers' livestock holdings. On average, the eighteen fullholders had, with four horses, eight cattle, fourteen sheep, and two oxen, reached their grazing limits. Lesser farmers held, proportionally, fewer draft-animals and more cattle and sheep. "The mayor, on account of his many troubles and trips," freely grazed an additional riding horse and four sheep, while "the aldermen, for their considerable efforts and sacrifices," could each keep two additional sheep.[50]

Although historians have emphasized manor–village conflict over open-fields grazing rights, Stavenow evidence for this is sparse. But on the Löcknitz meadows, even after their leasing, seigneurial grazing access – in the winter after the hay cuttings – disadvantaged the villagers. At Mesekow, the miller's grazing rights on communal land aggravated the smallholders there, who paid considerably during freehold conversion to buy him out.[51] Responsibility in Blüthen for the communal bull circulated among fullholders, "but the boar will be passed around and fed" among all cultivators. The main constraint on villagers' swine-holdings was the forage fee for autumn access to seigneurial oak

---

[49] No. 427, fos. 11–18.   [50] No. 557, fos. 2–3; no. 717, fos. 212–13.   [51] No. 408, fos. 74–5.

and beech woods. At other times, big farmers might entrust the village swineherd with as many pigs as they wished, or face limits of five or six.[52]

Fullholders' grazing rights reflected both the village commune's character as, principally, an association of landholding farmers, and seigneurial interest in large farms. The 1761 Blüthen survey shows that fullholders' livestock was numerous, especially for wartime, but it counted young animals with mature, and was silent about quality or value. From the 1721–71 years there survive 105 household inventories from among fifty-seven full- and halfholders. The livestock they registered present the picture shown in table 4.2, both for three roughly equal periods with about the same number of inventories, and for the whole half-century.

Horse holdings were stable across this half-century. The small decline in cattle and pigs, if statistically significant, perhaps resulted from the rigors of Frederick II's wars (1740–2, 1745–8, 1756–63). Many inventories, unaccountably, included no sheep, drawing averages down. Farms with sheep typically kept 12.5, with a falling tendency after 1755. Oxen were rare – only twenty appeared in fifty years. Their value approximated horses'. Goats were not communally grazed, presumably because of their destructive habits. Though known in the nineteenth century as the poor man's cow, only one was inventoried (though landless families may have kept them). Poultry included chickens, geese, ducks, and turkeys, averaging nineteen per farm.[53] Summing mature horses and cattle and new-bred offspring, the average farmer drove 12–14 head into communal pasturage. Fullholders held more horses – 5.3 per farm over the half-century – compared with 4.3 for halfholders. This fitted their heavier labor-service duties, though all farms with one or more hides needed to keep four work-horses.

Grazing and food-supply constraints worked against large horse holdings, yet in 1754 seven Glövziners each kept 6–9 horses. Probably some were raising horses for sale on local markets.[54] Farmers' horses' appraised value nearly tripled in this half-century, propelled by population growth, rising grain prices, and army demand. Old and marginal animals, worn-out in manorial service, depressed averages well below the best teams' value. A smallholder's four horses, two "very old," were "small and bad."[55] A deceased halfholder's four horses, worth but 17

[52] No. 557, fos. 1–3, 9; no. 717, fos. 212–13.
[53] Poultry values, 1720–71 (groschen): hens: 1–3; geese: 3–10; ducks: 2.
[54] No. 630, fos. 1–2.   [55] No. 200, fos. 187–9.

Table 4.2   Mature livestock holdings of Stavenow farmers, 1721–1771[a]

	1721–39	1740–54	1755–71	1721–71 Avr.	1721–71 % change
Number of mature livestock per farm					
Horses	5.0	5.0	5.0	5.0	–
Cattle	5.25	5.0	4.5	4.9	−14
Pigs	4.0	3.5	3.5	3.8	−13
Sheep	6.75	1.5	6.5	8.7	− 4
Livestock prices at Stavenow (current talers)[b]					
Horses	4.2	8.4	11.2	7.9t	+171
Cattle	4.1	6.7	7.0	5.9	+69
Pigs	1.4	2.2	2.4	2.0	+71
Sheep	0.6	0.7	0.9	0. 7	+50
Value of livestock per farm (current prices / appraisals)					
Measure I[c]		51.5	90.0	98.0	80.0	+ 90
Measure II[d]	1720–59 = 66.5t	1760–89 = 92.5t		1760–1810 = 105.5t	
	[1721–1810 = +59% = avr. 88t]				

Rye prices at Berlin[e]

Decade:	1701–10	1711–20	1721–30	1731–40	1741–50	1751–60
	35.8	51.2	40.1	46.3	48.3	47.9
	1761–70	1771–80	1781–90	1791–1800	1801–10	1811–20
	50.2	57.2	55.6	63.6	102.5	79.0

Population (Electoral Brandenburg)[f]

Absolute	1750	1763	1770	1780	1790	1800 (n = 546,000)
Relative	100	95.0	115.0	121	128	141

[a] Excluding foals, calves, piglets, and lambs.
[b] Prices incorporate without modification the devaluation in 1750 of the Prussian taler, but not the temporary currency inflation of the Seven Years War, which was followed by restoration of 1750's taler value. The Brandenburg "current taler" (*Courant Taler*) was a money of account consisting of real coinage minted from one "Imperial Mark" of silver (234 grams) according to these proportions: pre-1667: 9 talers per Mark; 1667–90: 10.5 talers; 1690–1750: 12 talers; 1750–1821 and thereafter: 14 talers. Naudé, *Getreidehandelspolitik*, vol. II, 506. To 1738 the Imperial German Reichstaler numbered 10.5 talers to the silver Mark and after 1764 12 talers. From this money of account the coinages of the various German states more or less diverged. See Aubin and Zorn, *Handbuch der deutschen Wirtschafts- und Sozialgeschichte*, vol. I, 666–70; Rachel, *Handels-, Zoll- und Akzisepolitik*, vol. II, 865.
[c] Average farm stocks at current prices.
[d] Mean of appraised values of all farm stock or all livestock in iron stock (including data from nine inventories from the years 1772–1810).
[e] Abel, *Agrarkrisen*, appendix, table 2, prices converted by Abel to constant values (grams/silver).
[f] Excludes Brandenburg districts east of Oder river (Neumark). Behre, *Statistik*, 458.
Sources: Stavenow farm inventories, 1721–71.

talers in 1788, counted two 7–8-year-old geldings ("Wallachians") and two 4–9-year-old mares, one blind.[56]

Horses fit for fieldwork and hauling were typically 2–15 years old. One horse, the appraisers said, was "old but can still do its work."[57] A farm in 1808 kept four good horses aged 7–15 years, each worth on average 27 talers.[58] In 1724, Kleist gave a new farmer 20 talers cash for two work-horses, plus 8 talers for a wagon, 1.5 talers for a plow, and 2 talers for harnesses.[59] If in 1724 10 talers bought a work-horse acceptable in seigneurial eyes, in 1764 a foursome averaging 15 talers each was "in good condition according to village standards."[60] A fullholder's three 24-taler horses (1747), and another's four averaging 31 talers (1760), show that Stavenowers sometimes possessed valuable animals.[61] Two village mayors with 10–13 horses were probably breeders and traders.[62]

Good cattle, too, possessed above-average value. In 1721 Stavenow's Garlin free mayor's farm, though bankrupt, counted eleven head: two five-year-old "yellow cows" worth 7 talers each, plus an 8-taler "red spotted cow," two lesser-valued ten-year-old cows, two five-year-old "red steers" worth 7 talers each, three calves together worth 5 talers, and a 1.5-taler yearling bullock.[63] A smallholder kept four milk cows, three heifers, and three calves, together worth 86 talers (1767).[64] Milk cows ranged in age and value from four years and 16 talers (1808) to fourteen years and 4 talers. As for oxen, a Dargardt smallholder colonist's "black and brown" pair were worth 22 talers.[65]

While boars were communal property, each farm kept its own breeding sow, which might with seven piglets be worth 4 talers (1767) or itself alone 8 talers (1808). Growing fast, young pigs quickly gained value, especially after forest foraging, which could raise their worth fivefold. A fattened pig could fetch 3 talers, but not much more. Occasionally a farm's swine numbered 13–16, but usually fewer, since fattened pigs were slaughtered each winter for home consumption and sale.[66] Mature sheep, whose value lay mainly in wool, rated 1 taler in the mideighteenth century. Unmentioned in communal grazing regulations, they were entrusted to village shepherds. Customarily each household raised a few sheep for wool, but some kept 24–5.

---

[56] No. 513, fos. 55–9.   [57] No. 326, fos. 141–3; no. 591, fos. 2–4; no. 713, fos. 117–20.
[58] No. 513, fos. 45–51.   [59] No. 200, fos. 9–10.   [60] No. 717, fos. 138–40.
[61] No. 554, fos. 1–7; no. 324, fos. 50–2; no. 358, fos. 7–11; no. 358, fos. 36–51.
[62] No. 200, fos. 157–62; no. 326, fos. 191–4.   [63] No. 200, fos. 157–62.
[64] No. 358, fos. 36–41.   [65] No. 324, fos. 20–3.
[66] No. 717, fos. 138–40; no. 715, fos. 35–9; no. 323, fos. 5–6.

Sheep succumbed to murderous epidemics. In 1745 Hasse wrote of a farm's ten sheep that, "because of the present dying of sheep almost everywhere, these are already in bad shape and doubtful."[67] But epidemics left documentary traces only in the 1740s. In 1742 disease beset both horses, cattle, and sheep. Horses suffered again in 1744 and cattle in 1749.[68] Such visitations occasioned many-sided debits, including – to the state – losses in tax remittances and – to the lordship – losses of labor services or the cost of replacing, for impecunious subjects, iron-stock horses. In 1744 Stavenow's bailiff wrote Perleberg War Commissioner Richter that a farmer in two years lost eleven horses and so could perform neither manorial service nor army haulage.[69]

As we shall see, farm wives occasionally risked court punishment for protecting livestock from disease by magical means, such as hanging amulets on animals. Farmers themselves sometimes took desperate action to spare themselves threatened losses. In 1749 town authorities accused village mayor Peter Ebel of having through a middleman (retired soldier and village lodger) sold a Perleberg clothier "a cow infected with the presently raging pestilence." They charged four other farmers with selling eight diseased cows, which caused burghers' own livestock to die while other town animals had to be killed. These acts of "enormous maliciousness," the Perlebergers said, deserved punishment by fortress imprisonment. Stavenow's court, reluctant to surrender jurisdiction over its farmers, agreed to investigate. The outcome is unknown, but Peter Ebel remained mayor. Perhaps the burghers denounced the wrong men, but that sick animals were sometimes fraudulently sold must have been generally accepted.[70] In 1765 cattle plague again descended. When Perleberg garrison troops arrived to shoot infected animals, Peter Hecht illegally removed his five cows, exposing other villages to danger, for which the District Commissioner instructed Stavenow's judge to punish him.[71]

Since farmland and buildings were not marketable, and farmstead inhabitants' sometimes valuable personal possessions, notably clothing, were not monetized, livestock nearly always accounted for most of a farm's inventoried worth. Converting Stavenow farmers' average livestock holdings to money values at current average local prices yields a nearly 80 percent rise between 1721–39 and 1740–54, and a 90 percent increase during the half-century ending in 1771. Averaging cash values assigned in the almost century-long period 1721–1810 (although data are thinner after 1771) produces a 59 percent rise between 1721–59 and

[67] No. 664, fos. 1–6. [68] No. 200, fos. 209–11. [69] No. 326, fo. 109.
[70] No. 598, fos. 13–14. [71] No. 600, fos. 12–13.

1760–1810. By either measure Stavenow farmers' livestock rose from 50 talers or more in the early eighteenth century to around 100 talers later in the century. These were not large sums, but neither were they measures of misery. They correspond to medium-sized farms geared to the subsistence of a stem-family with one or two servants. They do not substitute for income, but show that farm resources in traction, meat, dairy food, and marriage-portion livestock gifts typically accorded with both seigneurial and village expectations.

Livestock was the most valuable iron stock, but farm equipment was less negligible than the historical literature's emphasis on costly nineteenth-century mechanization suggests. In 1767, equipment listed as inalienable stock included three kettles and "the largest brass pot," two types of wagon ("wide" for harvests and "narrow" for heavy hauling), two plows, five harrows (valuable if iron-toothed), one butter churn, two beer barrels, timber-chain, bushel measure (Berlin standard), farm servant's bed and bedding, and sheep-shears.[72] Other commonly inventoried items were scythes for cutting grain and hay, threshing flails, rakes, shovels, mattocks, hay and manure forks, fodder choppers with knives, saws, axes and cleavers, hammers, awls, handheld scales, iron lamps, shoulder baskets, wooden snow sledges, cabbage barrels, looms, and spinning wheels. One smallholder possessed wheelwright's tools, but otherwise farmers' equipment served cultivation and household purposes.

A plow with a chain and a pair of iron shares might rate 3 talers, harnesses 4 talers, a servant's bed (rarely) 6.5 talers, and wagons with various attachments 14 talers. Copper and brass kettles, apart from cooking, served for brewing. Because of their indispensability and metal value, court bailiffs targeted them for impoundment in punishment of unpaid fines. A fullholder displayed a good set (1760): two large half-barrel copper kettles weighing 16 pounds each (8 talers); two brass kettles weighing 8 pounds, and three smaller ones.[73]

VILLAGE FARMERS' OPERATING COSTS, TAXES, INCOME, AND NET EARNINGS

Labor costs

In 1731 fullholder's widow Trina Fahrenkrug dictated to sexton Sauber an "Account of What I Have Spent Here of My Dowry," enumerating

---

[72] No. 358, fos. 32–4, 36–41. [73] Ibid., fos. 36–41; no. 513, fos. 45–51; no. 324, fos. 50–2.

expenses during six months when she managed the farm herself. Apart from buying step-children's clothing and food, she paid 8.5 talers in direct taxes and owed her brother Erdmann – her senior farm-hand – monthly wages of 1 taler. She paid 3.3 talers commutation money, reducing labor services to two days weekly, performed by broth-er Erdmann and a helper. The senior maidservant earned half-yearly wages of 2 talers plus 14 groschen shoe money, the junior maid 16 groschen, while the "little boy" earned but a hat worth 3 groschen. Temporary harvest labor cost 1 taler, communal swineherd 4 groschen, and miller's annual fee 15 groschen. Legal charges consumed 3 talers: 18 groschen livestock impoundment fines, and 2.6.- talers to Hasse for "two letters." Wagon repairs cost 1 taler, a bedroom door-lock 7 groschen. Income went untallied, except for 5 talers the tailor paid for Trina's departed husband's and mother's clothes.[74]

Trina's example shows that Stavenowers' prime cash obligation was the *Kontribution* tax, requiring monthly installments paid the mayor for official delivery. Wages came next, paid directly to farm servants or, indirectly, in commutation fees. The fullholder needed at least one strong worker – preferably two – to supplement his own muscle, plus a boy tending livestock. Rarely did he buy himself free of more than one weekday's seigneurial labor, so that unless he himself performed the work with a household member, he needed to send two servants with a horse-team twice weekly.[75] Nor could he cultivate his own land without a sturdy laborer, while his wife needed a female helper. Though often grown children performed this work, it was also common – perhaps because of attendant submission and discipline – for farmers to hire more distant and helpless kin, such as orphaned or semi-orphaned nephews and nieces, or unrelated workers, while their children entered service elsewhere. Either way, workers cost money in room, board, clothing, shoes, and wages.[76]

Labor-cost burdens on farms without considerable family engage-ment are evident in Christoffel Schenck's expenditures during four months in 1730 when he ran the vacated Blüthen mayor's farm. Schenck, an estate official, worked with hired labor while awaiting – vainly – his son's release from service elsewhere. He kept a young farmhand, paying 1.5 talers cash wages, 12 groschen for shoes and 2.5 groschen for pants-linen. A maidservant earned 4 derisory groschen monthly. Schenck hired manual laborers at 1.5–2.0 groschen daily, plus

[74] No. 591, fos. 12–13.   [75] *Dienstgeld*: no. 240; no. 30, pt. VIII; no. 259, pt. XIV.
[76] No. 324, fo. 52.

food and drink. He received some wheat – "very unclean" – when he took the farm, but "with threshers and many day laborers" he consumed it all (showing that workers sometimes ate wheat bread). Altogether he spent 17 talers in four months on taxes and wages.[77]

The highest recorded annual male farmworker's cash wages were Trina Fahrenkrug's brother Erdmann's 12 talers. Like him, sibling-servants were often their employers' creditors. In 1730 Erdmann's precursor Friedrich Maass was serving his fourth year on his now-deceased brother's (Trina's husband's) farm. Friedrich lent his brother 5 talers for two cows slaughtered at his first wedding and, later, 3.5 talers to bury the wife his brother then wed. At his brother's death, Friedrich lent Trina 6.5 talers for the burial. Now he claimed 7 talers back-pay from the farm, which he did not inherit but passed instead to Trina's new husband, while Erdmann took Friedrich's place. Here a cash-laden farmhand helped finance his sibling-employer's impecunious household.[78] In 1747 a farm liquidated its 35-taler debt to a hired hand, spent mostly on taxes and commutation fees, through the worker-creditor's marriage to the widowed farm wife, lifting him (exceptionally) into proprietor status. He brought into the household, respectably enough, two horses, eight sheep, and his tools, and paid 4-taler legal fees.[79]

In the absence of kinship ties, fullholders' adult servants (*Knechte*) might earn 9 talers "plus shoes" in their first two years, and 10 talers thereafter. When tavernkeeper-farmer David Hecht claimed, against his departing servant's demand for 10 talers back-wages, to have duly paid, Hasse demanded proof or compliance.[80] In wage disputes initiated by aggrieved servants, Hasse enforced contracts (if conforming with royal wage tariffs) or otherwise imposed statutory rates. In 1741 farmhand Koltzer claimed unpaid wages from former employer Andreas Appel's widow. She said he had not served his term and, though not entitled to shoes, had still received them. Koltzer produced an unusual written statement, penned by a literate villager:

I hereby inform you that farmer Andreas Appel has hired farm servant Johan Koltzer[.] He started work three weeks before Easter and promised to stay until Michaelmas [29 September]. Therefore he [Appel] has promised him 2 talers 12 groschen and one pair of shoes, one shirt, one pair of trousers, one pound of wool, to which I, Adam Barnhöfft at Bresch, attest.

---

[77] No. 591, fos. 19–20.
[78] No. 200, fos. 246–9. An eighteen-year-old son, working at home, would earn 4 talers yearly: no. 326, fos. 139–40. Another (younger) son would receive only meals: no. 591, fos. 38–9.
[79] No. 554, fos. 1–7.   [80] No. 200, fos. 75–6.

Ignoring clothing provisions, Hasse found Koltzer legally entitled to but 2 talers, which he ordered the widow to pay.[81] Koltzer's precaution in having his agreement with Appel recorded signals apprehension about unfaithful employers, but did him no good. On workers who quit prematurely without providing acceptable replacements, the court imposed wage loss or heavy fines.[82]

Young manservants earned 4–8 talers cash yearly. All servants received small bonuses – "God's money" – when hired or rehired for a year. A farmer might sow and harvest a bushel of oats as a worker's hiring fee and for one month of work, an obligation the court rated at 16 groschen, while warning the claimant against seizing the grain on pain of 6 talers fine.[83] These small sowings, opposed by government and landlords, helped bachelor workers raise animals to bring into future marriages. The court noted one farmhand in possession of two horses. Another accepted back-pay on the hoof.[84]

Women farmhands' yearly wages were 3–5 talers, plus shoes – monetizable at 12–24 groschen – and linen. Hasse approved a woman's pay at an annual rate of 4 talers, 20 ells of rough and 8 ells of fine linen, together worth 2 talers, and some harvested flax. She demanded 1 groschen daily for seigneurial harvest work performed with her employer.[85] An urban tailor's village-born wife claimed – when her family inherited money – 5 talers yearly for her sixteen years' work on the home-farm.[86] Though underpaid, women were strong and valuable workers. A fullholder's widow for several years operated her farm, though with difficulty, with two adult maidservants, a teenage son (until conscripted) and an eleven-year-old son.[87]

Apart from shoes, women might claim, in place of linen, "half a dress" (12 groschen), men might receive three shirts and a pair (or more) of pants. Young workers might resemble the "poor boy who serves only for his clothing," who faced charges of allowing his dog to kill a local nobleman's goat, which he and his comrades allegedly furtively cooked and ate. His master doubted the accusation, saying the boy's dog was "a little thing, smaller than a cat."[88] Another boy, owed a 1-taler yearly wage by a debt-ridden farm, was known in court only by his first name.[89] A young man's good, though undelivered, 1770 clothing allotment included two pairs of pants, two shirts, a jacket (30 groschen) and

[81] No. 591, fo. 158.   [82] Ibid., fo. 114.   [83] No. 200, fos. 220–2.
[84] No. 326, fos. 36–7; no. 715, fo. 31.   [85] No. 326, fos. 203–4.
[86] Her husband settled for 30 talers plus costs. No. 718, fo. 39.
[87] No. 358, fos. 85–8.   [88] No. 326, fo. 100.   [89] No. 200, fos. 220–2.

a *Brusttuch* or neckerchief (15 groschen), totaling 3 talers.[90] Other boys earned 2 talers and "linen and shoes."

Taxes

A typical farm's wage bill is hard to estimate, since costs varied with employment of unpaid family workers and hired hands' ages, while much pay was in food and clothing. Probably, when employing both a male and female worker and a boy, money wages and shoes alone consumed 15 talers yearly or more. As for taxes, the *Kontribution* reflected villagers' cadastrally registered sowings: farmers' monthly payments in groschen equaled the (nominal) number of rye-bushels they planted each fall. Though the cadastre underestimated actual sowings, this tax, together with old pre-absolutist levies, was a heavy burden which, as the 1711 Stavenow appraisal showed, farmers tried to minimize by obfuscating their arable's extent, customarily measured in hides.[91] Of Karstädt fullholders it reported that "the subjects say they have no hides, only pieces of land, on which they pay 15 groschen [monthly] *Kontribution*." In Premslin "they know nothing of hides, but give according to sowings, and thus 17 groschen, and smallholders 6 groschen." The Mesekow smallholders likewise "give 9 groschen monthly and thus 3 talers every eight months." The seigneurial judge believed Glövzin fullholders each held two hides, but they balked. Neither villagers' "[tax] receipts" nor occupancy deeds, the appraisers concluded, conveyed "correct information." Blütheners admitted they held their land in hides, for which fullholders paid 18 groschen monthly *Kontribution*, plus 50 percent surcharge for "forage and boarding fees" instead of billeting troops. The old-established head and hearth taxes claimed 1–2 groschen monthly. Altogether, a 1711 fullholder paid taxes of 25–30 groschen monthly, or 12–15 talers yearly.[92]

Despite small modifications in 1733–45, direct taxes remained substantially unchanged until 1820.[93] Table 4.3 illustrates the Stavenowers' eighteenth-century tax burden.

---

[90] No. 358, fos. 115–20.
[91] Paul Gottlieb Wöhner, *Steuerverfassung des platten Landes der Kurmark Brandenburg*, 3 vols. (Berlin, 1805), vol. I, 40ff.
[92] No. 355, fos. 1, 3–5.
[93] In 1733 the government formally substituted a higher *Kontribution* for the previous hated, if sporadic, obligation to quarter and feed cavalry troops. But Stavenowers were already paying the surcharge in 1711.

Table 4.3   *Village farmers' annual direct taxes, 1745–1820
(in talers, groschen, and pfennigs)*

Village and farm type	Land tax[a]	Troop quarter[b]	Hearth tax[c]	Hearth surcharge	Total
Glövzin					
Fullholder	9.4.6	3.1.0	0.21.0	0.6.1	13.8.7
Halfholder	5.3.5	2.12.2	0.12.0	0.3.6	8.7.1
Landed cottager	1.12.9	1.10.4	0.12.0	0.1.0	3.12.1
Mesekow					
Halfholder	4.18.4	2.8.8	0.12.0	0.5.10[d]	7.20.10
Premslin					
Fullholder	9.4.6	3.15.0	0.18.9	0.6.2	13.20.5
Halfholder	6.3.0	2.18.0	0.18.9	0.4.1	9.19.10
Blüthen					
Fullholder	9.2.2	3.14.4	1.6.0	0.6.1	14.4.7
Karstädt					
Fullholder (1719 land tax/troop quarter rate)		14.0.0			

[a] *Kontribution.*
[b] *Fourage- und Speisegeld (Cavallerie-Geld).*
[c] *Hufen- und Giebelschoß.*
[d] Includes 1812 war surcharge.
Sources: no. 451, fos. 79–80; no. 408, fos. 42–4; no. 449, fos. 52–5; no. 474, fos. 1–8;
Lieselott Enders, ed., *Historisches Ortslexikon für Brandenburg, I: Prignitz* (Weimar, 1962), 172.

A 1756–7 document shows the Stavenowers paying 3 groschen per winter per child for compulsory schooling. A "poor tax" (*Armengeld*), levied on halfholders at 10–12 groschen yearly, appears after 1800, but only sporadically.[94]

In 1731 we glimpse a farmer sending his manservant with a load of grain for sale in Lenzen on the Elbe.[95] Since farmers paid taxes largely with such earnings, crop price trends were crucial. Table 4.4 displays these in current (nominal) form, uncorrected for monetary fluctuations.[96] A 14-taler direct tax bill translated, at average pre-1753 Berlin prices, into 15 rye-bushels, sinking in the forty post-1766 years to under 10.[97] Probably, to pay all taxes, fullholders needed before mid-century to sell, at provincial prices, about 16 rye-bushels and, after 1763,

[94] No. 324, fos. 20–3; no. 427, fos. 36–9; no. 433, fos. 14–22.
[95] No. 591, fos. 2–4.
[96] Unlike table 4.2's price series, which was reduced to constant silver values.
[97] In the mid-eighteenth century, Stavenow grain sold at local prices slightly lower than Berlin averages. Cf. Naudé, *Getreidehandelspolitik*, vol. III, 624–33; no. 427, fos. 36–9.

Table 4.4   *Average annual grain prices in Berlin, 1703–1806*
(to nearest groschen)

Decade	Rye	Barley	Oats
1703–12	19	18	12
1713–22	24	21	15
1723–32	20	18	13
1733–42	24	19	14
1743–52	23	19	14
Decennial average, 1703–52	**22**	**19**	**14**
1766–75	33	23	18
1776–85	27	20	16
1786–95	32	26	20
1796–1805	47	38	28
Decennial average, 1766–1805	**35**	**27**	**21**

Source: Behre, *Statistik*, 277.

about 12.[98] They must have varied sales between the three main cereals according to current prices and household and farmstead needs for food and fodder.

Of tribute grain the average fullholder owed the lordship some 7 bushels.[99] The measure was the "Berlin bushel," rather than the sporadically employed local "small measure," standing to its Berlin counterpart in a ratio of 12:11. Witold Kula interestingly explored manor–village conflicts, and various forms of veiled exploitation, resulting from disputed or differential measures. At Stavenow there is little evidence, except during the 1700–2 regional protests, that metrology provoked strife.[100] The 1746–7 seigneurial grain ledger lists

[98] Assuming their marketed grain met merchants' quality and cleanliness standards. Inferior products required sale in larger quantities. No. 324, fos. 20–3.

[99] In bushels: Premslin – 3; Glövzin and Mesekow – 6; Blüthen and Karstädt – 12. The Karstädters had, since before 1717, also rendered 6-bushel payments to the Premslin pastor. Interpretation of the Karstädters' condition is made difficult by their cash settlement with the lordship during post-1811 freehold conversion, obviating documentation on landholdings and other resources surviving from other villages. Possibly the 6-bushel church payments were rent for meadows or other assets. The Karstädters did not press the Stavenow lordship for meadowland when this was parceled out in the 1720s.

[100] Kula, *Measures and Men*. The Berlin bushel retained virtually constant size in the years 1682–1868. After the metric system's 1868 adoption, the previously prevailing Berlin bushel yielded to the "new bushel" with a volume of 50 liters or 0.5 hectoliters; the earlier bushel had held 55 liters. Naudé, *Getreidehandelspolitik*, vol. II, 529–30. In 1727 the Karstädt fullholders were registered as owing 12 bushels of tribute grain, in 1760 only 11. This suggests the lordship earlier accepted tribute grain delivery in the smaller, provincial bushel measure. The 1790 Urbarium specified such payment in Berlin bushels without eliciting protest.

twenty-nine payments arriving *in natura* and sixteen in cash, at lordship's prices.[101]

In money rents, including labor-service commutations, 1748–55 manorial accounts show farmers collectively paying 534–79 talers yearly. Arrears varied from 1747's 118 talers, mostly repaid in 1748, to 7–14 talers thereafter. In 1754–5, all fullholders bought themselves free of one day (6.16.-), while ten commuted two days or more.

We can conclude that royal and seigneurial exactions cost the typical eighteenth-century fullholder about 27 bushels of rye yearly. Household consumption amounted, as we shall see, to 6 bushels of rye and 6 of barley per adult, and half these rations for elders and children. Reckoning average households at four adults (including servants), one retiree, and two children over six years (leaving younger children aside), rye consumption would have totaled 33 bushels, and barley 19 bushels.[102]

Farm production, income, and assets

Table 4.5 offers a balance sheet of the Stavenow farmer's grain economy.

Livestock foddering removed much of a farmer's oats and some other grain from the marketable surplus. Home brewing of weak beer consumed some barley. And, since harvests fluctuated and local prices lagged behind Berlin's, while home consumption varied by household membership, table 4.5 offers but an approximation. Doubtless there were years when rent and taxes consumed or exceeded a farmer's earnings from grain sales. Still, the long-term price trend favored him. As a share of his grain surplus's value, taxes and rents declined in the eighteenth century by one-third. He was left in good years with a marketable grain surplus of some value (though less than table 4.5 projects).

Stavenow farmers also profited from (ill-documented) livestock sales. Buyers were local town slaughterers, such as one in Perleberg who accused David Busse of breaking an agreement to sell his mutton-sheep

---

[101] No. 274.

[102] An 1826 court appraisal followed the old rule, reckoning half the open-field cereal harvest, after deduction of seed, to household consumption as food or fodder, leaving the remainder for sale. No. 433, fos. 14–22. By this measure, average Stavenow fullholdings would have possessed for their own consumption 30 bushels of rye, 18 of barley, and 15 of oats – more than the text above assumes. Yet given oats' seemingly small part in the human diet, the text's estimates are preferable. Accepting that oats might replace rye as a food, the two approaches yield similar results.

Table 4.5 *Estimated average fullholder's grain production, consumption, and marketable surplus*

	Rye	Barley	Oats	Total	%
Average yields (per seed sown)	3.5	4.0	3.5		
Sowings (bu.)	24	12	12		
Surplus (bu.) minus seed set aside	60	36	30		
Surplus minus home consumption	27	17	30		
Value of surplus (Berlin prices)					
1703–52	25t	13t	18t	56t	
1766–1805	39t	19t	26t	84t	
Cash value of tribute grain					
1703–52				7t	
1766–1805				10t	
Labor-service commutation fee (one day)				7t	
Net value of grain surplus (after deduction of grain-rent, taxes, and commutation fee)					
1703–52				28t	
1766–1805				53t	
Cash value of tribute grain, taxes, and commutation fee as a share of market value of grain surplus					
1703–52					50%
1766–1805					36%

Sources: as in text above.

(though Busse claimed the butcher never fetched the animals).[103] In 1761 a farmer sold a brewer three steers for 25 talers plus 8 groschen urban excise tax.[104] In 1744, a farmer sold a noblewomen a horse for 22 talers, but Hasse ruled he charged too much – it was a year of equine disease – and ordered a 7-taler refund.[105] Farmers sold spare horses at local markets, sometimes provoking charges of cheating, as when a townsman reproached a Stavenow farmer, righteously complaining that "one oughtn't to swindle a Christian" (though Hasse dismissed the suit).[106]

[103] No. 200, fo. 127.   [104] No. 326, fo. 241.   [105] No. 326, fo. 111.   [106] Ibid., fos. 67–8.

Villagers also sold livestock among themselves. In 1760 a farmer paid a farm-managing widow the good sum of 22 talers for two oxen. She also sold firewood for 3 talers and straw for 2 talers, while a trader bought a pig for 3 talers.[107]

Occasionally farmers sold livestock to the lordship. The 1746–55 cash accounts record a few purchases of village pigs and cattle. Two farmers, including a widow, sold the lordship pregnant cows at 11 talers each. The estate manager bought two good cows for 28 talers from a village mayor and four heifers, for 28 talers, from another fullholder. The lordship sometimes sold the villagers young cattle, and once a communal bull. Never did farmers sell the manor their grain, though they sometimes bought small quantities there, while the lordship once bought straw from them for 38 talers. The avenues of manor–village trade appear little traveled.

An 1826 appraisal reckoned a smallholder's annual profit on a milk cow at 5 talers, young cattle at 1 taler, and sheep (during a sheep-raising boom) at 3–4 per taler. Pigs and poultry, as objects mainly of home consumption, had little market value. Such formulaic accounting assumed that dairy foods, livestock, and wool beyond household need would regularly be sold, comprising 40 percent of this (arable-poor) farm's annual earnings. Bigger farms' grain profits loomed larger, but they too made such livestock sales.[108]

Village tavernkeepers, who were also farm proprietors large or small, bought neighbors' pigs and grain in small quantities.[109] Tavernkeeper David Hecht traded in wood, contracting in 1721 with a Perleberg merchant to deliver cut pieces worth a sizable 450 talers. The buyer charged that Hecht's wares were 68 talers short. Hecht produced an account "which he, however, as a man unversed in reading," could not decipher. The court rejected the buyer's complaint, saying a written contract against Hecht was invalid without its prior approval by Stavenow administrators – an instance of the lordship protecting its unlettered subjects against urban antagonists. Hecht was probably a middleman for neighboring farmers, who sometimes sold wood from their farms' communal woodland shares to urban buyers, and for whom hauling wood and other goods to town yielded occasional cash. Tavernkeeper Hecht paid them 1 taler per load to distant Havelberg, plus 4 groschen in "herring and beer money." Hecht paid a farmer 16–19 groschen for shorter hauls, while selling him a cow and harvest

---

[107] No. 324, fos. 50–2. [108] No. 433, fos. 14–22. [109] No. 200, fo. 135.

beer on credit and lending him a taler for taxes.[110] A farmer sought compensation for a village's impoundment of a draft-horse, asking – in vain – 8 groschen per day, as if that were its income-earning value.[111]

Late eighteenth-century government reports emphasized the importance of Prignitz village trade in hops and fresh and dried fruit. Though nothing suggests that Stavenowers possessed any more important income source than grain sales, all farms possessed fruit gardens. On one farmstead "the garden is full of trees," while a free mayor's farm counted seventy-four plum, twenty-three apple, and eighteen pear trees.[112] Still, in their villagers' income estimates, neither entrepreneur Thiele nor Conrad von Kleist foresaw major earnings from livestock and gardens, which earned perhaps 10–15 talers annually. Such income helped offset farmers' myriad costs, including – to lengthen an already long list – blacksmiths' fees, ranging from 4 groschen to replace a plowshare iron to cumulative bills of 5 talers or more. Wheelwrights made wagon repairs and others roofed and renovated farm buildings, at 3–4 groschen daily plus food and drink.[113] Natural payments occurred, as when a farmer paid the sexton and another worker in fruit for harvest labor, or a roofer received sown flaxseed, or one farmer paid another 4 groschen, 1 barley-bushel, and two bread loaves.[114]

How well did Stavenow farmers steward assets and liabilities? One measure of competent management was endurance as household heads. From 1721 to the mid-1770s, three farmers suffered eviction (*Exmittierung*) for unmanageable debt, two as victims of 1770–2 harvest failures. In the 1720s several debt-plagued farmers absconded. Commoner than eviction or flight was a farm's deterioration in a failing or sickly proprietor's hands, leaving his successor to restore its strength and, through court-ordered debt liquidation, depriving heirs of anticipated portions. Contemplating twenty-six farms whose 1721–71 fortunes were recorded in two or more intergenerational transfers, relative decline is evident, though not precisely quantifiable, in half the cases. Premature death, debt, and inability to honor

---

[110] No. 589, fos. 1–3; no. 200, fo. 135; no. 591, fos. 57–8; no. 715, fos. 35–9.
[111] No. 597, fos. 130–1.
[112] No. 200, fos. 234–5; no. 200, fos. 157–62. See the annual economic reports, which would repay further study, submitted by the Prignitz *Kreis-Direktorium* to the Berlin government in 1786–94: Brandenburgisches Landesarchiv, Potsdam, Provinz Brandenburg, Rep. 2, D. 42. See also Harnisch, *Agrarreform*, 32ff.
[113] No. 200, fos. 216–19; no. 358, fos. 115–20.
[114] No. 591, fos. 30–2; no. 326, fo. 132; no. 715, fo. 17.

non-inheriting children's or retirees' claims were such misfortune's prime causes (working alone or together), resulting in two cases in bankruptcy and eviction. On the happier thirteen farms, the strongest trend was recovery from weakness to relative soundness, measured by farm capital, low debt, and satisfaction of family members' expectations, though in five cases strong conditions persisted from generation to generation.

Thus, perhaps, did farmers' fates ebb and flow. Communal limits on arable productivity and livestock capacity hedged prosperity in. To reap like one's neighbors; to keep as many prime animals as possible; to eat and dress befitting one's rank; to properly celebrate festivals of season and life-cycle; to marry off one's children respectably; to retire with customary benefits: these were, in this rural society, life's purposes for all those who did not, for better or worse, drift away from it.

A farmer fulfilling these ideals, if self-centeredly, was Joachim Ditten, Premslin fullholder and village mayor. In September 1789 (as the French Revolution was overturning seigneurialism and feudal rents) Ditten and his wife retired, handing their farm after thirty years' work to one of their six children. They were well provisioned for old age, and the farm was properly stocked, though burdened by 67 talers in debt, mainly unpaid commutation fees. Although Ditten and his son squabbled over it, this debt also derived from the partial rent strike accompanying the embittered conflict then prevailing between villages and lordship. The seigneurial judge ruled vindictively that the debt threatened the younger children's marriage portions. After deduction of iron stock and goods Ditten took into retirement, his estate tallied a mere 12 talers, embodied in an extra wagon and plow. He had, Ditten said, "no other assets except for this year's harvest, which will pay seigneurial and royal charges and provide sustenance for the proprietor and his people."[115]

This was a lapidary description of the subsistence holding, yielding little more than enough to maintain and reproduce the household and pay taxes and rent. It fits the experience of retired halfholder Schmidt, who in 1753 resumed heading his farm following the untimely death of a son who succeeded him ten years earlier. Next year old Schmidt's daughter-in-law found a new husband, journeyman carpenter Pankow, who arrived with 100 talers. Relinquishing the farm to Pankow, Schmidt – good at accounting – reported that in his eight months'

[115] No. 523, fos. 1–16.

management, he earned 56 talers from the farm and paid out 55 talers, and now owed the widow 20 groschen.[116]

In the sixteen cases among the 110 inventories of 1721–71 in which the court fully balanced farm assets against debts to assess net worth, the resulting 109-taler average shows that some farmers accumulated more capital than Ditten (who took valuable possessions into retirement). But many inventories did not monetize all assets. Otherwise, more cases would have exhibited positive net worth, though many would have reflected Ditten's circumstances, and others a deficitary, if still viable, condition. It was sometimes difficult to distinguish between farm assets and household members' possessions (such as clothing or savings). Yet, the 109-taler average in farm property may have applied fairly widely: it equals an average eighteenth-century farm's livestock values (in table 4.2), plus 20–30 talers representing other farm capital.

MATERIAL CULTURE AND VILLAGE FARMERS'
STANDARD OF LIVING

Housing and fuel

The 1727 *Hausbuch*, like court inventories of individual holdings, appraised the condition of farmers' dwelling-houses and outbuildings. Money values were absent, since the farms had mostly been rebuilt after the Thirty Years War with the lordship's lumber, and in law now belonged to it (leaving occupants only usufructuary rights). But even when buildings were farmers' hereditary property, they, like indivisible iron stock, were excluded from the monetized household estate shared among inheriting children.

Although farmsteads varied with proprietors' status, all fullholdings possessed dwelling-houses centered on a relatively large, hearth-heated living and dining room (*Stube*). Adjacent were bed-chambers, sometimes under lock and key.[117] The entry and hallway (*Hausflur/Diele*) often included a kitchen whose cooking-hearth communicated with the living-room fireplace. Sometimes the farm servants' bedrooms, and the stalls for the horses and cattle they tended, were attached to the dwelling's back. Otherwise such spaces appeared in the farmstead's gate-house

---

[116] No. 326, fos. 194–8; no. 324, fos. 17–18. For similarly situated Wustrau farmers, see Takashi Iida, "Hof, Vermögen, Familie 1700–1820: Die brandenburgischen Dörfer Manker und Wustrau (Kreis Ruppin) im Vergleich," *JbfbL* 50 (1999): 142–82.

[117] No. 200, fos. 216–19.

(*Torhaus*) or separate stall buildings. Barns, like wells and baking-ovens, stood at a distance from dwelling-houses. Gate-houses usually faced the street, with entry and wagon storerooms. Sometimes they housed retirees' lodgings, though often these stood elsewhere on the farmstead, miniature versions of the main house. Halfholders and lesser smallholders possessed fewer separate buildings. Sometimes their barns were built onto dwelling-houses, or retirees had no separate house, but lived in rooms or a room in the proprietor's house with their own heating ovens.[118]

Buildings were constructed in half-timbered style. They stood on raised foundations, with planked floors, except near the hearth (and in other work spaces), where a "hard floor" – of clay or plaster – lay.[119] Between upright and cross timbers ran clay-plastered walls of sticks. Timber rafters held up the roof, which was covered with heavy straw and reeds. Hearths with canopies and chimneys were of brick or stone. Houses sometimes possessed "windbreaks" or enclosed vestibules outside entry doors. Shutters covered glass windows. Fences enclosed the farmsteads.

The court appraiser usually found fault with farms' condition. Of mayor Nagel's better than average buildings Hasse wrote that in the dwelling-house, 56 feet long, "the living room and side chambers are newly rebuilt." The rest of the farmstead was in fair shape, though the roof needed improvement "when he has the chance" and the hearth canopy needed enlargement. Also "no more fire should be made in the hallway." The barn was 49 feet long and in fair condition. "The gate-house, apart from the through-way and wagon storage, has two [newly roofed] stalls above which straw and fodder are stored." The baking-house, 21 feet long, was "somewhat old." There was a second "baking-oven in a planked shed near the retirement house." The retirees' cottage faced the street and was "new with living room and bed-chamber, also stalls, but the hearth canopy is no good and must be built lower down."[120]

Of another fullholder's house Hasse wrote that "it has a living room with two side chambers and two other rooms off the hallway." The roof was "bad" but timbers and plaster were adequate. "Behind the baking house oven there is a loft with a staircase, and there are also flour bins

---

[118] No. 591, fos. 119–21; no. 326, fos. 116–17; no. 324, fos. 4–5. See plate 14 for an illustration of the 1750s' floor plans of Dargardt settlers' new houses.
[119] No. 591, fo. 4. Hahn, *Territorialhoheit*, 412.
[120] No. 326, fos. 191–4.

and a large kneading trough." The retirees' house was "very old and dilapidated."[121] On another farmstead, the retirees' house was "good" while the main dwelling and barn were "very dilapidated." A house might be "still habitable" despite a windstorm-damaged roof. Hedges and wells could be "broken down," doors, thresholds, and fences bad. The 1727 *Hausbuch* said guardedly that a farm's "dwelling-house and retirees' house are old but can still stand."[122]

A thirty-year-old barn might still be "good," but eventually time took its toll, while impecuniousness sometimes delayed repairs. In 1730 Hans Dreger's halfholding displayed patched-over walls and an old roof needing replacement, while its "upright timbers, rafters, and joints, which are of pinewood, have been completely eaten away by worms." The "fruit garden is filled with trees," but the farmstead "needs fencing and a gateway, because it has none."[123] Harsher judgments on buildings occurred: "totally dilapidated," "completely broken down," "very damaged," "worthless." Yet these were extremes. The 1727 survey, with no reason to exaggerate, found among seventy-one large and small farmers' houses 70 percent to be "good" or "new"; 13 percent "fair" or "average"; while the rest – 17 percent – were either "bad," "very bad," or "old."

Seventy other appraisals, scattered across the years 1721–71, found 37 percent of dwelling-houses good, 29 percent average, 16 percent poor, and 18 percent bad. Thus, while in 1727, after some four decades of intensive resettlement, 84 percent of farmers' houses were in good or normal condition, in the course of the half-century ending in 1771 just 66 percent fell in this range. The good – because relatively new – housing stock of 1727 deteriorated noticeably, although most farmers' dwellings throughout the period appeared unobjectionable. Only once did Judge Hasse pronounce a farmstead's buildings "in praise-worthy condition." Another's were "in good condition according to local standards."[124]

In 1786 the Brandenburg Fire Society began insuring Stavenow farms at an annual rate which, in 1816, amounted to 20 groschen per 100 talers of value. The appraisal measured farmhouses, all insured for 50 talers, at 35–65 feet by 32–40 feet. Barns (50 talers) were as large or larger than houses, livestock stalls (25 talers) were long and narrow, while retirees' houses (25 talers) measured 25 by 20 feet or larger.

---

[121] No. 554, fos. 1–7.   [122] No. 30: Premslin.   [123] No. 200, fos. 244–6.
[124] No. 591, fos. 51–2; no. 449, fos. 63ff.

Altogether such farmsteads were insured for 150 talers. Smallholders, who might only have small houses and barns, held coverage for 50–150 talers, the landless cottagers (like the three schoolhouses) for 50 talers. The Garlin free mayor's farmstead, with bigger and better buildings, rated 300 talers.

The pastors' and millers' buildings were considerably more valuable than the village farmers'. Blüthen's parsonage rated 300 talers, barn and gate-house 200 talers, stall 100 talers and – setting a godly example of cleanliness – laundry-house 50 talers, totaling 650 talers. Premslin's parsonage was insured for 475 talers. The Mesekow miller's conjoined house and mill rated 400 talers, plus outbuildings at 200 talers, while Premslin's miller, with both water- and windmill and 300-taler barn, carried 1,400 talers' coverage. Seigneurial firefighting equipment – hoses and hooks – appeared in 1760, and in 1809 rated 200 talers. Similar gear was only installed in three Stavenow villages in 1799, though each farmstead was supposed to have water and buckets. Considering that costs probably held insured values low, villagers' buildings possessed modest but not negligible worth. Half-timbered buildings insured at Stavenow for the seigneurial tavernkeeper, gardener, blacksmith, schoolmaster, and estate laborers bore similar insurance. But non-subject households, such as free mayors or millers, and dwellings of such notables as pastors and higher estate officials, stood high in quality and value above village farms.[125]

Crucial to farmhouse comfort was cooking and heating fuel. Post-1811 emancipation officials determined that Premslin village, without any communal woodland, lacked sufficient fuel, although fullholders possessed large though doubtless over-harvested wood stands on their own land (table 4.1). The lordship reported that "at best" Glövzin village could meet its fuel needs. Forest inspectors found in the woods here "alders 5–30 years old, young oaks and birches, 80–200-year-old oaks." On heavily grazed communal pastureland there was "a small oak plantation" and scattered oaks young and old, but mainly "alder and birch brush, in very bad condition." Mature oaks needed preservation for acorn foraging. The Glövziners said their woods were once larger, but "recently" they had sold timber "out of necessity."[126]

Blüthen fullholders' wood parcels were sizable, as was communal woodland. A 1765 ruling confirmed Mesekow halfholders' rights to

---

[125] No. 294, fos. 1–2, 10–15; no. 353, fos. 78–9; no. 51, fo. 22; no. 433, fos. 14–22.
[126] No. 427, fos. 22–5.

graze animals and cut alders and birches in three woodlands where the lordship owned more valuable wood. Mesekowers were making "pine plantations" which the lordship acknowledged as the commune's "real and true property now and in the future."[127] Villagers obliged to purchase firewood faced heavy costs. The above-mentioned 1826 smallholding budget reckoned "wood to be bought" at 9 talers annually, more than all taxes. But some households, particularly fullholders', possessed firewood in sufficiency. In 1751 one had accumulated reserves of 12.5 wagonloads.[128]

Wood theft, as elsewhere in old-regime rural Europe, was common. Villagers pilfered landlords', pastors' and, occasionally, each others' woods.[129] Yet at Stavenow, between 1723 and 1756, the court heard such cases on average only about once yearly, imposing – often on multiple defendants – heavy fines and sometimes physical punishments. Nineteen cases involving landholding villagers show that two-thirds of offenders were farmers from Glövzin and Premslin, large villages with little wood. Other villages contributed but few cases. Two-thirds of all guilty verdicts fell in 1743–5 and 1747, amid hardships of livestock epidemics and war. Seigneurial zeal for forest-law enforcement perhaps fluctuated, but fuel shortages did not, seemingly, drive villagers into continual clashes with the manor.

In post-1811 negotiations, village woods were exempt from seigneurial compensation if judged essential to communal fuel needs. The rural moral economy held that adequate firewood was a landholder's, if not every villager's, natural right.[130] Most thefts expressed villagers' claim on household fuel, as when smallholder Jetschurki was arrested for cutting a wagonload of seigneurial "beech branches." For this he paid the forester 6 groschen plus 9 pfennigs impoundment fee. "Punishment of two hours in jail-irons," Hasse wrote, "was duly carried out, because [previously] he promised future improvement."[131] A landless man's wife defended her husband's cutting of forty village alders, telling her accusers – the commune – "they had to steal their wood, otherwise they couldn't get any."[132]

Such poor villagers saw no choice but theft, but others claimed to act by right. Four farmers instructed their servants to harvest a

---

[127] No. 408, fos. 1–8.   [128] No. 715, fos. 35–9.   [129] No. 630, fos. 1–2.
[130] Renate Blickle, "*Hausnotdurft*. Ein Fundamentalrecht in der altständischen Ordnung Bayerns," in Günter Birtsch, ed., *Grund- und Freiheitsrechte von der ständischen zur spätbürgerlichen Gesellschaft* (Göttingen, 1987), 42–64.
[131] No. 712, fo. 108.   [132] No. 326, fo. 114.

seigneurial oak that had caught fire, believing they had salvage rights. They denied the Stavenow hunter-forester's charge of setting fire to the tree, but admitted cutting the wood, which cost them 12 groschen fines per wagonload, plus the forester's fee. They also drew lots to determine who among them would suffer the "Spanish overcoat" for one hour, although one them – a repeat offender – separately endured the same punishment.[133] A prosperous miller and his blacksmith son-in-law illegally cut seigneurial beechwood when only entitled to harvest alder fuel. Hasse dismissed their appeal to traditional right, based on their trades' needs, charging them for the wood and imposing fines.[134]

Jürgen Kratz, the miller's kinsman and a well-stocked farm proprietor, protested a sentence of one day in jail-irons, plus fine, for cutting "many young alders," saying "he had already received so many blows for this [from forester Prittwitz] that he didn't want to cut any more brush for the rest of his life."[135] A miller's wife (acting through a servant) and two village mayors were condemned for "wood fraud," suggesting again that pilferage might stem from concepts of right based on tradition, momentary need, or belief in seigneurial usurpation rather than poverty.[136] But illicit trade in wood and fuel also generated numerous punishments. A nobleman accused three farmers of buying two oaks his subject had plundered from his forest. Though they knew the wood was stolen, "they hauled it away secretly, by moonlight." The pilferer had also wielded his ax in Stavenow woods. Accomplice Frau Hennens admitted selling Stavenow farmers a 5-taler stolen oak, because of her "great need." The buyers claimed ignorance, but Hasse ordered them to pay the wood's value plus stiff fines, totaling a heavy 12 talers. Here two lordships jointly took a hard line.[137]

Every autumn an urban wood market was held. A Stavenower claimed he bought there what Hasse, fining him 3 talers, judged stolen beechwood. In 1723, a Wittenberge merchant was apprehended with 480 pieces of stavewood stolen from Stavenow. Such thefts of cut wood, stacked in the forests for transport, especially infuriated the nobility. The court determined the merchant bought the wood from debt-plagued Stavenow farmer Lent, who used a false name. Lent's village enemies accused him of trying to recruit them as accomplices. He endured three days in jail-irons, and soon thereafter absconded.[138]

---

[133] Ibid., fos. 104ff. [134] No. 591, fos. 99–100. [135] No. 326, fo. 131.
[136] No. 591, fo. 115; no. 326, fos. 104–5, 109–11.
[137] No. 200, fos. 120–3. [138] No. 593, fos. 1–7.

Some tried bribing foresters to avert their eyes from wood thefts. Neighboring estate administrator Stein accused Peter Ebel of pilferage and offering Stein's wood bailiff a bushel of oats "so he wouldn't report him."[139] Dargardt farmer-colonist Peters stole Stavenow birchwood for Mecklenburg sale. After his denunciation by the seigneurial field bailiff, the forester arrested him. Peters later murderously assaulted the bailiff.[140] Two lodgers stole seigneurial wood which their farmer-hosts hauled to Perleberg for sale, earning 12 groschen for transport. The lodgers disappeared, leaving the farmers to pay the fines and disingenuously bewail the lodger-class's treachery. A furloughed soldier, a smallholder's step-son, colluded with a subsequently absconded farmworker in stealing wood worth 1.5 talers. The step-father, responsible for the fines, said "the two wanted to make some beer money."[141]

Evidence is sparse of wood theft pitting villagers against one another. Village impounders reported it for hearings and fines, independent of the seigneurial court, to mayors and aldermen. Two farmers stealing brush from their neighbors' woodlands suffered fines plus 12-groschen beer money to the commune.[142] The Premslin impounder once brutally beat a Quitzow village linen-weaver for pilfering communal woodland. He excused his violence, saying the Quitzowers often stole Premslin wood, requiring him to employ two villagers to patrol day and night. His mayor corroborated this, complaining that the Quitzowers' lordship did not punish them for their depredations.[143]

Furniture and other household goods

Earlier discussions of dowries and farmsteads' iron stock highlighted some of the villagers' essential houseware and personal belongings. Apart from best clothing, their greatest valuables were familial beds and metal cookware. The most impressive farmer's bed on record rated, with bedding, 24 talers, while the same holding's "servants' beds are still in good condition."[144] Marriage beds were "beds for two persons," contrasting with servants' "single beds."[145] Householders' beds comprised wooden frames with linen-covered and straw-filled mattresses, pillows, and feather-stuffed covers. These might consist "half of purchased bedcover yardage and half of homemade blue-striped linen," with pillowcases of "various Münster cloth." In one house, one double bed reposed in the living room and another in a bed-chamber; there was

---

[139] No. 591, fos. 57–8.   [140] No. 577, fo. 3.   [141.] No. 326, fos. 129–32.   [142] No. 591, fo. 126.
[143] No. 326, fos. 110–11.   [144] No. 717, fos. 138–40; no. 324, fos. 13–14.   [145] No. 200, fos. 232–5.

also a "manservant's bed for the children." For infants there were cradles.[146] A fullholder's marital bed might be "in bad condition" and yet
worth 8 talers. Lower values occurred only among smallholders, and
for workers' beds. The manservant's bed often occupied a barn room,
the maidservant's the back dwelling-house.[147] A farmhand's bed
might comprise "a mattress, two thin bolsters, a pillow, a cover with
casing, and a rough linen bedsheet."[148] At 3 talers it could be rated
"good" but there was also "an old farmhand's bed hardly worth a
half-taler."[149]

A solid farm's other furniture might include – apart from beer, butter,
cheese, and other food-storage barrels, butter churns, and wash
tubs – "a food cupboard, an oak milk cupboard, an ashwood dining
table, two stools, a pine and an oak chest," along with "[oil] lamp, candlestick, [and] very small mirror."[150] Another farm displayed "a birchwood table and two benches [20 groschen], ten wooden spoons and
twelve wooden plates [4 groschen], fourteen plates and bowls and other
earthenware [5.5 groschen], a flour bin [1 taler], a large kneading trough
[2 talers], a good chest [1.5 talers], two pepper mills [1 groschen]."[151]

The Karstädt mayor's 1754 furniture counted an easy chair along with
double-doored oak milk and food cupboards. Such cupboards, accompanied by clothes closet, "living room chest," and ubiquitous trunk-like
locked chests, might each rate several talers or more.[152] Typically, the
whole household, apart from separately housed retirees, ate at the
benched dining table, though in unknown order. One farm exhibited "a
table and four chairs," together with a "large easy chair." Another counted "two women's chairs" and yet another displayed a "braided [wicker]
chair."[153] Dishes and bowls were inexpensive pottery. Tin-lidded mugs,
glass bottles and wire candlesticks appear.[154] Inventoried table utensils
were wooden spoons only.

Cookware included iron-stock copper and brass kettles. Some households possessed 5–7 of these, the largest (of copper) weighing 17–29
pounds. One half-barrel kettle, "brand-new," was in 1776 worth 9
talers.[155] Among other metalwares, a mayor's farm counted "a small
copper fish-kettle" and "tin fish bucket . . . four tin-lidded mugs, two
iron [frying] pans, tin grater, broken sieve, roasting spit." Oil-burning
lanterns and cheap candles, plus hearth, served for lighting. Farmhouses

---

[146] Ibid., fos. 197–9.   [147] No. 715, fos. 35–9; no. 324, fos. 29–32.   [148] No. 554, fos. 1–7.
[149] No. 714, fo. 179; no. 715, fos. 15–16.   [150] No. 324, fos. 13–14; no. 717, fos. 138–40.
[151] No. 554, fos. 1–7; no. 200, fos. 246–9.   [152] No. 326, fo. 200; no. 324, fo. 19.
[153] No. 200, fos. 187–9; no. 358, fos. 64–9.   [154] No. 718, fos. 48–9.   [155] Ibid.

might count "two tin candlesticks [and] tin wall-candle reflector." The hearth's iron kettle-hook might rate a taler, an iron frying pan 5 groschen.[156]

Although very many Stavenowers could not sign their names, ability to read, if laboriously, was more widespread, and farmsteads sometimes possessed religious books. Of one "hand-bible" it was noted that it belonged to the farm, while in two cases there were seigneurially bestowed New Testaments, likewise reckoned among non-distributable assets. The largest library comprised "two Crüger's songbooks, one *House Postil*, a New Testament donated by the lordship, one prayerbook *sub titul. Spring of Spiritual Water*."[157] Another inventory found "one old catechism, one big songbook, a Frankfurt catechism, a New Testament," though "the deceased sold the bible."[158] One farm's bible rated 16 groschen, its two songbooks 12 groschen, but mostly books were old and worn. Upon a farmer's death, Hasse wrote of the deceased's bible and soldier's songbook that "they will be put aside for the little boy."[159] Inventories invariably registered livestock and debts, but other household and personal possessions more inconsistently. Though books appear in only sixteen cases, seemingly every farm was – or should have been – equipped with a New Testament and songbook. Yet it testifies to low engagement in religious study (if not religious thinking) that so few households possessed other books.

Textile yardage's and clothing's extent and importance appeared in women's dowries and "goods brought in" to newlyweds' households. Villagers regularly harvested flax, laboriously "swinging" and "breaking" it for spinning and linen-weaving, important spheres of women's work. Most households possessed spinning stools and distaffs, but looms with combs and shuttles, reaching 5 talers' value, appear only twelve times. Seemingly, many women delivered thread to neighbors or village linen-weavers for working into cloth.[160] Yet the above-cited evidence suggests that looms may increasingly have accompanied women's dowries.

Homespun linen clothed both family and servants. Widow Zanders, ably managing her farm between marriages, possessed "80 ells of linen produced this winter and on hand for servants' use."[161] At 1–2 groschen per ell, her supply rated 3–6 talers. Other yardage for family use carried a higher value, such as "four 16-ell linen pieces at 40 groschen each."[162] Another widow wished to weave her 38 pounds of fine and

[156] No. 200, fos. 232–5.   [157] No. 324, fos. 13–14.   [158] No. 554, fos. 1–7.
[159] No. 200, fos. 187–9.   [160] No. 324, fos. 13–14.   [161] Ibid., fos. 50–2.
[162] No. 717, fos. 138–40.

rough flaxen yarn "without charge" into linen for her children.[163] On another farm, "32 pounds of flax haven't yet been combed out."[164] Linen apart from clothes might reach 11 talers in value.[165] One supply included "two bedsheets of fine linen, two of coarse linen, three heavy tablecloths, one homemade, and two heavy towels." Such textiles might display the "goose-eye" pattern. Another household counted eight long tablecloths (2 talers), four "four-cornered tablecloths" (1.5 talers), and two double hand-towels (2.25 talers).[166]

The prime item in men's closets was the overcoat, whether "Sunday" or "daily," of woolen or mixed woolen cloth. Gray was the commonest color, alongside green. They were modestly valued, upon the owner's death, at 16–24 groschen or more. They also appeared with matching pants. When well worn on one side, they were "turned." Next came jackets, often of blue or red, worn over shirts with neckerchiefs. One farmer owned "ten good shirts, the others old." Another had eight shirts worth 6 groschen each. Workday pants were often leather. One farmer owned two pairs: "one calfskin and one sheepskin." A farm widow's bridegroom purchased for 9 talers his predecessor's two coats and jacket, two pairs of leather pants, sixteen shirts, and leather gloves. There were, finally, stockings and hats. Farmers' marriage costumes go unmentioned, perhaps because they were worn out or given to children. Of deceased farmer Kratz's clothing his three sons took overcoats and waistcoats, leather pants, shirts, stockings, hats and caps. This was doubtless the usual disposition of expired farmers' clothes, unless hard-pressed widows sold them.[167]

Deceased farm wives' clothing was also given to – or set aside for – daughters. As above-discussed exemplary dowries showed, young women's clothes could include many pieces and attain considerable value, though advancing age and misfortune diminished quantity and quality. Catherine Bohnen, who died in her first marriage's eighth year, bequeathed, apart from lesser items, but three waistcoats or jerkins, seven dresses, and two scarves "of good purchased white linen, one with lace."[168] Yet married women's closets were often fuller. A halfholder's widow with a young son owned "eight Sunday dresses, four jackets, three waistcoats, three bodices and [her] daily clothing." Two dresses were of purchased material, including black serge, while

---

[163] No. 358, fos. 85–8. [164] No. 200, fos. 187–9. [165] No. 324, fos. 29–32.
[166] Ibid., fos. 13–14; no. 200, fos. 187–9.
[167] No. 200, fos. 187–9, 44–6, 212–15, 209–11; no. 717, fos. 138–40; no. 554, fos. 1–7.
[168] No. 326, fos. 154–6.

the others were of "cotton or homemade material." The jackets were "all of serge or purchased material." Other workday clothing "was of no value."[169] A recently married halfholder colonist's wife bequeathed at her death nine caps "all very good," seventeen bonnets with lace, "three bad," twenty-nine outer shirts and eighteen undershirts, eight camisoles and bodices, and various aprons. Dresses were missing, perhaps having been sold during her illness.[170]

The richest villager's wardrobe belonged to Catherine Schultzen, Blüthen tavernkeeper-halfholder Ohlert's wife. A well-dowered Lenzen artisan master's daughter, she died lucklessly in 1758 after some ten years of marriage. Her husband inventoried her possessions, excluding "daily things, to be used for the children." Pride of place (apart from 92 talers capital, mostly deposited at interest with an urban kinsman), went to a "black dress of English flannel," followed by a "colored [or printed] half-silk dress," and "colored dress in crêpe des dames." She also owned a "red and white striped cotton dress" and a "striped flannel dress." In thinner cotton she had three variously striped dresses. There were eight jerkins or camisoles, of brown poplin, reddish silk, half-silk, "flowered calamanco," striped cotton and "crêpe des dames." Her aprons counted one bright-striped and one muslin, from which also two pairs of sleeves with borders were made. She had seven scarves (four homemade linen), eight laced bonnets (plus four "bad" ones), and five caps, one of "double brocade," one "blue damask," and one "double material with red and green flowers." Of gloves there were three pairs in white and one in plush, along with a "black bearmuff." Apart from various items of bedding and household linen, there were seven multicolored pillow-cases, a mirror, and an "Altmark songbook."[171]

The Blüthen tavernkeeper's wife may have been the best-dressed village woman, but there were rivals. Her neighbor Marie Wolgastin's 1764 clothing rated 52 talers, including eleven dresses, sixteen camisoles and bodices, twelve each of chemises (*Unterhemde*) and outer shirts (*Überhemde*), twenty-seven caps and bonnets, plus a 12-groschen muslin scarf.[172] A Karstädt fullholder's deceased wife's oak chest counted nine dresses, three red and four blue; four camisoles, two reddish serge; three bodices – black, blue, and gray; five aprons; four scarves; and nine undershirts and twelve outer shirts. "The remaining everyday things have been given to the children."[173]

[169] No. 200, fos. 187–9, 28–9.   [170] No. 326, fo. 200; no. 324, fo. 19.
[171] No. 324, fos. 38–9, 48–9.   [172] No. 717, fos. 138–40.   [173] No. 324, fos. 13–14.

A deceased Mesekow farm wife's 1759 wardrobe displayed a "bright green dress at 4 talers," "a blue woolen camisole at 2 talers," and a "French linen apron in violet . . . at 20 groschen."[174] In 1726 a Blüthen halfholder's wife owned, apart from brown, gray, blue, and black serge and cotton dresses, "a red kersey-cloth dress," blue serge and calamanco bodices, a bright blue silk scarf, a serge apron, and nine caps, two canvas, one red damask, one yellow with red and green flowers, and one brown with red and blue flowers.[175] On the same farm, fifty-three-year-old Anna Dregers left at her 1776 death linen yardage and other textile materials worth 83 talers, plus 42 talers' worth of clothes. Considering her twelve large linen pieces were worth 42 talers, she may have been a seamstress. Among her clothes were twenty-four women's chemises and outer shirts, ten dresses, twelve camisoles and bodices, plus two new pairs of gloves.[176]

These wardrobes depict the upper range of villagers' ornamental clothing. They show that considerable money might be spent on manufactured textiles, including cottons and other imports. Not every household could muster such finery, but its value was not so high as to place it – in lesser quantities – beyond the reach of farm families unplagued by misfortune. When sewing their own clothing, women's only cash outlay was for manufactured textiles. But sometimes, perhaps often, farm households engaged local tailors' services. In 1726 Jochen Maass's fullholding owed tailor Schulz 4.5 talers. By Maass's 1730 death the debt had risen to 6 talers, which his widow reduced by giving Schulz her husband's best clothes. This farm in 1749 owed 1.9.- for yardage for "children's clothing" bought in Perleberg.[177]

Shoes and boots are largely invisible, except as regular components of farmworkers' wages. In "shoe money" young servants received 12–14 groschen yearly, older workers 1 taler. Fullholder David Busse's debts afford a glimpse into farmers' expenditures on themselves and their families. In 1742 Perleberg shoemaker Peters "implored" Hasse to compel perpetually debt-ridden Busse to pay his overdue bills. In 1735, Peters cobbled Busse one pair of men's shoes (20 groschen), one pair for his son (17 groschen), and one for his daughter (12 groschen). The next year he made five pairs for Busse's wife and daughters (12 groschen each), pushing the debt toward 5 talers. Seemingly, Busse and family bought new shoes biennially at best, but his household was hard-pressed. Possibly other villagers wore better shoes. Still, their absence

[174] Ibid., fos. 29–32. [175] No. 200, fos. 197–9. [176] No. 718, fos. 48–9.
[177] No. 591, fos. 42–3; no. 326, fos. 139–40.

from inventories argues against high value, though they may have served their purposes. A household fight, during which one antagonist hit the other over the head "with a boot," confirms this item's presence.[178]

Food

No iron law governed villagers' grain consumption. We saw that Conrad Kleist, contesting speculator Thiele's assumptions, invoked government estimates that adult workers consumed 8 bushels of bread-grain annually or even, if men, 10 bushels. To regulate exports and manage state granaries, Prussian officials tracked provincial grain production and consumption. Their results (and possibly their measures) varied considerably. A 1772 East Prussian judgment allocated 10 rye- and 2 barley-bushels to adults, and half that to children aged 6–14. Another (perhaps over-theoretical) estimate found rye consumption varying with soil heaviness (and, correspondingly, effort expended in fieldwork). Townspeople seemed to consume less bread-grain than toiling villagers, from 5–6 bushels per adult to as little as 3 (in courtly Potsdam). Under Frederick William I, Prussian soldiers received 2 pounds of rye bread daily, the flour equivalent of about 7 bushels annually. Another of the "soldier king's" officials set average annual per capita rye consumption, for both adults and children, at 6 bushels (ca. 240 kilograms/528 pounds).[179]

A late eighteenth-century bureaucratic survey of adult diets in fertile (wheat-growing) Magdeburg province, based on crown-estate and seigneurial evidence, found the common man eating wheaten foods on four annual holidays. "But since in farmers' households wheat flour is baked, apart from holidays, [also] at baptisms etc., one should reckon on 5/16 of a bushel per person." If, as was uncommon, wheat was eaten coarsely milled as soup groats, or finely ground for dumplings, rations would rise accordingly. About rye, Magdeburg officials said:

Customarily [bread] is milled half as rye and half as barley. But men's and women's needs are not equal, and one reckons, including bread for evening supper and feeding the dogs, 8 bushels for the man and 5 for the female [*Frauenzimmer*]. By this measure a man needs 4 [rye-] bushels and a woman [*Weibesperson*] 2.5. When only rye flour is used [unmixed with barley], it is

---

[178] No. 591, fos. 12–13; no. 321, fos. 30–1; no. 326, fo. 113.
[179] Behre, *Statistik*, 226. The Berlin/Brandenburg pound (*Pfund*) equalled in weight the English/US pound. Müller, *Landwirtschaft*, 203.

ground more finely than commissary [coarsely ground soldiers'] bread. Hence one estimates that 7 bushels are needed for the man and 4.5 for the woman [*Frau*].

In these reckonings, adult men consumed 4–7 rye-bushels. Barley might be an important bread component, consumed in large measures. Finely ground barley flour was essential to soups which, by this account, Magdeburg countryfolk ate every day except Sundays and the four holidays. Thus 2.5 bushels were needed, but now, "in view of potato cultivation, only 1.25." On thirty-nine Sundays of the year, "if garden foods are unavailable," barley groats would be cooked, requiring $\frac{3}{8}$ bushel of unmilled barley. Dumplings were usually made from barley, and served 107 times yearly (twice weekly and on holidays). Without barley in their bread, adult women and men still consumed 4 barley-bushels annually, but with mixed rye-barley bread, 2.5 to 4 bushels more. Oats were absent from the Magdeburg diet.[180]

Assuming that Stavenow villagers' bread was largely rye, and that they otherwise consumed barley at Magdeburg levels, adult men needed 7 bushels of unmilled rye and 4 of barley, adult women 4.5 and 2.5 bushels, respectively. The average adult, male or female, would thus have eaten 6 bushels of rye and 3 of barley, an estimate of total bread-grain consumption consistent with other eighteenth-century projections, including Conrad Kleist's. In 1805, a fullholder's farm granted a widow retiring with three small children arable land with average annual net yields of 7 bushels of rye and 8 of barley, or about 4 bushels per capita.[181]

Above-reckoned estimates of Stavenow farmers' household consumption and marketable grain surpluses set adult shares (somewhat higher than most other reckonings) at 6 bushels of rye and 4 of barley, with half these amounts for retirees and children aged 6–14. But did households regularly possess such provisions? Apart from seasons of scarcity, when deprivation or want stalked all villagers, some farmers suffered from ill-luck or improvidence. In mid-October 1726, when harvests ought to have been finished, a farm whose proprietor had recently died possessed "but little rye" and no barley or oats.[182] In October 1731, on another similarly stricken farm, of food there was "nothing on hand," although winter seed was mostly sown and there was "some dried fruit in the barn."[183] Yet many inventories found adequate or good grain supplies. In November 1725 a halfholder held grain enough

[180] Ibid., 226–7. [181] No. 513, fos. 31–5. [182] No. 200, fos. 204–7. [183] No. 591, fos. 30–2.

for plantings and household needs. A 1739 farmer-tavernkeeper had 14 rye-bushels and his next rye crop in the ground. Thirteen years later Hasse wrote in November of the same farm that "seed has been fully planted in praiseworthy manner; grain necessary for rent and summer seed is in the barn, together with what will be needed until next harvest." Another farm, at winter 1742's end, possessed bread-grain sufficient until next harvest. On another farm in November 1750, "the grain and fodder harvest is completely in the barn," although bad crops the previous year had obliged the (now retiring) proprietor to buy seed-grain.[184]

Except for wheat eaten on ceremonial occasions, bread was always rye. Villagers baked it in large loaves in farmstead ovens. The 1727 house-book assigned villagers' tribute breads, of ancient feudal origin, 16 pounds in weight and 4 groschen in value. A man claimed unpaid laborer's wages from a neighbor, amounting to 4 groschen cash, a bushel of barley (20 groschen) and two 3-groschen breads (making them, at manorial valuation, 12-pound loaves).[185] Apart from bread-grains, farms commonly kept supplies of barley, buckwheat, and oats milled as groats for porridges and soups. Despite their absence in official estimates, oats played their part, as emerges from a solid farm's 3 bushels of better-quality "white oats" among its "victuals on hand." One record of millet groats also survives. A 1768 farm possessed "a reserve of 8 bushels of rye for bread" plus "groats enough to last to the harvest." Potatoes begin to appear after mid-century. Peas were important for soups.[186]

Village farmers were free during plowing, sowing, and harvesting seasons, against minor tax payment, to brew beer for household consumption, using their largest copper vessels, sometimes called "brew-kettles." The product was a staple, low-alcohol drink. For celebrations villagers bought beer from local taverns, provisioned by seigneurial brewers, or in nearby towns. Home brewing consumed part of the farmers' harvest as malted barley, often inventoried. A halfholder's supplies during fall planting included 6 bushels of malt, worth 4 talers. Farmers grew necessary hops in home gardens or bought them. One possessed 8 bushels of malted barley and "enough hops as are needed."[187]

[184] No. 200, fos. 187–9; no. 591, fo. 23; no. 326, fos. 187–8, 76–8; no. 715, fos. 25–6, 8, 13–15.
[185] No. 715, fo. 17.
[186] No. 358, fos. 36–41; no. 718, fos. 48–9; no. 591, fos. 19–20, 12–13; no. 358, fos. 54–8; no. 326, fos. 194–8; no. 324, fos. 17–18, 20–3.
[187] No. 358, fos. 36–41, 54–8.

The corporate nobility collected the brewing tax through its agent, the *Ziesemeister*. Home brewing was forbidden to cottagers and small-holders, but violations occurred. *Ziesemeister* Schmidt found smallholder Mentz in possession of illegal malt, and fined him 12 groschen. The turbulent Mentz twice ignored pay summonses, whereupon Schmidt seized Mentz's kettles and auctioned them on the Perleberg town square for 3 talers. After deducting fine and court costs, Schmidt gave 1.2.- to Mentz who, though protesting his innocence, said he would rather have paid "than let himself be put to such hardship." Hasse mistrusted Mentz, but found the kettle seizure and fines excessive, and resolved to consult with Schmidt and Kleist. This incident displays tax officials' considerable harassment power, and the intermittent tensions between manorial authorities and revenue collectors.[188]

Apart from beer (and schnapps), villagers apparently drank only dairy and fruit concoctions. A 1756 smallholding possessed "a small barrel of drinks."[189] Coffee only appears, after mid-century, in such comfortable households as the manorial dairyman's, with no sign the villagers drank it. Honey probably substituted for sugar. The farmers' kitchen gardens – often called "cabbage beds or bean fields" – yielded onions, carrots, beets, and turnips alongside cole crops and beans. Householders harvested leaves from cabbage plants, as emerges from an agreement granting retirees "permission now and then to pluck a dish of cabbage for cooking"[190] In six months a farm widow expended dowry money for "cabbage seed (6 groschen)," "4 bushels of field-turnips (1 taler)," "cooking fat for cabbage (16 groschen)," and small quantities of peas and broad beans.[191] Green beans, sometimes cooked with bacon, bore high value (40 groschen per bushel in 1776). Present too were sauerkraut in barrels, white cabbage, turnips, and horseradish. Potatoes' importance as food was still modest. Not until the late eighteenth century did easily cookable varieties, instead of gnarled fodder roots, become widespread.[192]

Apart from 12 pounds of valuable butter (2 talers), dairy foods left little record. Yet for consumption and sale they were important, as such equipment as "cheese baskets," butter churns, milk cupboards and barrels, and tin butter containers suggests.[193] A staple of manorial workers' and doubtless also farmers' diets were small, dry, herb-seasoned cheeses.

[188] No. 200, fo. 140. On the tax (ca. 2–3 groschen per bushel of malt brewed): Wöhner, *Steuerverfassung*, vol. II, 89ff.
[189] No. 324, fos. 20–3.   [190] No. 326, fos. 232ff.   [191] No. 591, fos. 12–13.
[192] No. 718, fos. 48–9; no. 358, fos. 61–3; Abel, *Landwirtschaft*, 288ff.   [193] No. 718, fos. 48–9.

Eggs were valued, not cheaply, at ten to the groschen. Fruit – apples, pears, plums – was essential for soups and drinks. Green apples appear, but oven-dried fruit, often worth a taler per bushel, was commoner.

Protein derived not only from certain vegetables, but also from fish. Pickled herring, stored in "fish barrels," cost 30 groschen per one-eighth-barrel.[194] Salt cod was also eaten, along with fresh fish, as household "fish kettles" (and theft from seigneurial ponds) testify.[195] Goose fat was valued. One farmer possessed "a tub with the meat of eight geese," while another had "four halves of fat goose," probably smoked, at 4 groschen each, and "two whole pieces of [beef] suet, at 1 taler."[196] But the staple meat, and chief fat source, was pork. Though inventories listed it as "sides of bacon," at weddings fattened pigs were slaughtered, as on a mayor's farm, where three pigs and a steer fed the guests. The retiring mayor later left his son-in-law and successor "bacon from one pig" and "barley for [fattening] the piglets."[197]

Salt for curing bacon, heavily taxed and expensive, appears in the 1760s at 1 taler and in 1776 at 1.8.- per bushel. Bacon sides varied by weight, but were appraised between the 1720s and 1770s at around 2 talers. In 1776 two sides weighed 36 pounds – a sign of the villagers' pigs' small size – making each pound worth 2.3 groschen, not a trivial sum. The maximum number of inventoried sides was three (ca. 54 pounds). For sizable households this did not portend much per week, though food supplies were probably low when inventoried, depleted by illness, weddings, funerals, and removal into retirement quarters. As for sausage, only perishable mettwurst appears by name (4-6 groschen each), but doubtless slaughtered pigs yielded others, along with slender hams and hocks.[198]

This evidence does not clearly illuminate village food consumption, but it establishes the centrality of bread-grains and vegetables. Manorial accounts of 1809–10 confirm this point, though they suggest that farmers' meat consumption may have been higher than inventories indicate. Monthly records of the four demesne farms, employing altogether twenty-four unmarried laborers, most in the compulsory ranks, yield the following annual consumption – excluding vegetables, eggs, and fruit – per worker: 10 rye-bushels and 5 of other cereals; 10 bushels of potatoes; a quarter-bushel of peas; 175 cheeses; 225 quarts of milk; 44 pounds of butter; three-quarters of a fattened pig; one sheep or calf;

---

[194] No. 591, fos. 19–20.   [195] No. 200, fos. 147–8.
[196] No. 324, fos. 20–3; no. 358, fos. 36–41.
[197] No. 591, fos. 56–8; no. 324, fos. 4–5.   [198] No. 718, fos. 48–9.

and one-quarter of a slaughtered cow. Daily individual consumption of weak and strong beer averaged 1.5–2 liters. After 1760 schnapps entered the worker's diet, amounting in 1809–10 to about 1 liter monthly.[199]

This diet seems better than manorial workers' provisions in 1584 (see chapter 1). It offers 3.5 bushels more of cereals and 10 bushels of potatoes, an entirely new food, though certainly some of these potatoes, and bread-grains too, fattened domanial livestock. The rise of robustly yielding potato culture reduced other vegetables' consumption, though by 1809–10 it had not yet diminished workers' bread, as happened later.[200] Doubtless demesne-farm managers, some of whom were married, ate more meat than their workers. Yet, recognizing unequal consumption, manorial laborers seem to have eaten as much meat in 1809–10 as in 1584, if not more. Perhaps because of the Napoleonic wars' trade disruptions, fish are largely absent from the later menu, though in the mid-eighteenth century the lordship seasonally fed workers herring and salt cod, which remained through the nineteenth century ordinary people's food. While it is not certain workers' diet improved between 1584 and 1809–10, it appears not to have worsened.[201] An explanation points to a village farmers' diet not inferior to what the lordship offered their sons and daughters. Food at the manor comparable to that received at home may have been the price of compulsory workers' acceptance of three-year service terms. If this is true, some measure of the fresh meat (beef and mutton) eaten at demesne farms should be added to farmers' pork consumption.

Still, maintaining adequate and secure food supplies was material life's greatest challenge facing the villagers. Leaving aside wrathful fate's crop- and livestock-destroying visitations, poverty and improvidence could reduce families to hunger resulting in sickness and death. To eat without contributing to household income was asking for abuse. Halfholder's widow Trine Brunsten, with two children aged five and eight, shared meals with her son and his wife, the new proprietors. Trine lamented that for her and her children "there was nothing on the table." She wanted to earn some money, "so she would not always have to hear [the proprietors'] reproach that she did nothing but eat their bread with bacon fat [*Grede Brodt*]," a synonym for farmhouse luxury.

[199] Nos. 62, 191, 202.
[200] Hagen, "Working"; Hainer Plaul, *Landarbeiterleben im 19. Jahrhundert* (Berlin, 1979), 259–69; Theodor von der Goltz, *Die Lage der ländlichen Arbeiter im Deutschen Reich* (Berlin, 1875), 435ff.
[201] As Abel and Braudel hold, following Schmoller's thesis of early modern "depecoration" (decline in pig-farming). Cf. Hagen, "Working."

Hasse ruled that her son should supply Trine and her children yearly with 8 bushels of bread-grain and winter a cow for them. He would sow flaxseed for her, give her 3 pounds of wool and some lambs, some dried and "green fruit, when God blesses them with it," thirty eggs, "half a pig, which she will receive from him salted down," plus a pig to fatten for the future and a vegetable garden. Seemingly Trine, who owned a loom, would occupy herself with textiles. Hasse warned her to avoid "quarreling and fighting," help with farmwork, and not spoil the children, or she would be sent back to her son's table.[202]

If dependence on others for food was punishment to be feared, the charge that one's table was bare could be a potent insult. Contentious farmer Hans Zeggel and Dietrich Busse quarreled with Christian Grambeck, charging him with cursing them as "carrion eaters" ("*Aassfroter*") and Busse's wife as a whore. Grambeck admitted saying, as he paid Busse a court-ordered 2-taler fine, that Busse "ought to have left the carrion alone," unleashing a fight in which Busse pummeled Grambeck on the head with his boot, while Zeggel seized him by the hair. Hasse, though faulting Grambeck "with his talk of carrion," fined them each 1 taler.[203]

Debts

Court-registered debts were liens, secured by farm assets, inscribed in incoming cultivators' occupancy deeds. They included borrowed money, seigneurial rent arrears, marriage portions owed to siblings, and unpaid wages and craftsmen's bills. Other debts, in case of non-payment, required adjudication, and might be invalidated. Table 4.6 shows that court-approved farm debt rose from a moderate household average of 18 talers in 1721–54 to twice that amount between the Seven Years War and the 1770–2 central European subsistence crisis. Yet, as a proportion of average livestock value – apart from grain crops, farms' principal asset – debt held steady (ca. 36 percent) between the first and last subperiod.

Fullholders' debts ran higher than halfholders', presumably because of higher labor costs and larger marriage portions. Mesekow halfholders were exceptions and, while relatively strong Karstädt farms could perhaps support higher debt, Blütheners' low debts seem accidental (see table 4.6).

[202] No. 200, fo. 148.   [203] No. 326, fo. 113.

Table 4.6   *Average village farmers' inventoried debt, 1721–71*[a]

	1721–39	1740–54	1755–71	1721–71
All farmers				
Fullholders	22t	18t	41t	25t
Halfholders	12t	19t	24t	18t
Average	18t	19t	36t	24t
	(*n* = 25)	(*n* = 25)	(*n* = 24)	(*n* = 74)
All farmers in principal service villages				
Blüthen (*n* = 17)				15t
Glövzin (*n* = 13)				20t
Karstädt (*n* = 12)				35t
Mesekow (*n* = 10)				23t
Premslin (*n* = 17)				26t

[a] Data from seventy-four cases, evenly distributed among the three sub-periods, drawn from the principal service villages listed, together with five cases from other villages.
Source: Stavenow farm inventories, 1721–71.

Apart from occasional artisans' bills, townspeople's claims were rare, though in 1747 Hasse ordered repayment of 22 talers that an elderly Perleberg woman loaned to three "thankless farmers" during recent "long and hard winters."[204] Rarer still were tax arrears. Villages' communal responsibility worked powerfully against individual non-compliance, leading farmers to acquiesce first to tax-collectors' – and mayors' – menacing demands.

The largest single credit source were parish funds, administered by the pastor and aldermen under noble church patrons' oversight. Among thirty-three loans, mainly from the five Stavenow churches, sums (in a 2–45 taler range) averaged 12 talers – a good cow's value. Hardship might temporarily reduce the customary one-twenty-fourth annual interest, as when Hasse allowed a new farmer on a debt-burdened holding to service a 31-taler church loan at 1 taler yearly.[205] Sometimes parish funds financed building renovation, but villagers also turned to private lenders, as when in the credit-poor 1760s a farmer borrowed 33 talers at 5 percent for a barn. In 1805 soldier Kiecks' paternal farm owed 34 talers in building loans, one from Kiecks' day-laborer uncle, who had entrusted his kinfolk with 20 talers, and 14 talers from the new farmer's unmarried older sister.[206] Church funds also provided emergency relief,

occasionally accumulating to dangerous levels. Johann Schenck inherited
a farm burdened with 45 talers' church debt, plus 36 talers owed to such
individuals as a miller, a day laborer, and a townsman. A fullholder died
after long tenure, leaving his widow, as Hasse noted, "with poor assets
and considerable debt," including three months' tax arrears, plus 15 talers
commutation fees and 33 talers owed four churches. Church loans might
also benefit cottagers, such as the impecunious and ill-housed Buck family, whose 1771 mini-farm owed the church 13 talers and interest arrears,
plus 14 talers in other debts.[207]

Local pastors – prosperous rural notables – benevolently granted
church-fund loans, but otherwise evidence is sparse of their material
aid to needy villagers. Among retiring farmer Stefan Bahlcke's 1768
debt of 71 talers were, apart from Stavenow church's 25 talers, 2 talers
owed the "Frau Pastor" for 2 bushels of rye. Here, in Major Kleist's
presence, the court ruled that, because of heavy debt, non-inheriting
children should receive nothing beyond wedding provisions. Yet buildings were judged good, livestock and iron stock were intact, and old
Bahlcke gained normal retirement provisions. His debts mainly hurt the
younger children.[208] Perhaps pastors offered last-minute help to desperate households more often than inventories indicate, as when in 1771
a farmer, sinking under unprecedentedly high debts and soon to be
evicted in disgrace, borrowed 6 talers from widowed Frau Pastor
Carsted.[209]

The lordship confined its entanglement in villagers' financial embar-
rassments to (infrequent) loans of seed and bread-grain, rent delays
and, in extremity, pleas for government tax waivers because of bad harvests or animal epidemics. Seigneurial firewood sold for cash only. A
farmer once paid rent arrears with woodcutting. Occasionally the lordship acknowledged arrears payments with written receipts, but such
documentation seems exceptional. A villager claimed paying twelve
years earlier still-contested debts of 25 talers in commutation fees and
servants' wages, though, as Hasse noted, "with no proof." Still, he dismissed the plaintiff.[210] Labor scarcity could induce the lordship to cancel arrears. We saw how in 1770 Major Kleist abandoned a 42-taler
claim, "to help out the young proprietor and in the hope that he will
acknowledge this aid with thanks." In 1771, after luckless Johann Prill's
eviction, Kleist freed his successor of rent arrears of 32 talers and
37 tribute-grain bushels, though reserving the right to recover it from

Prill, should he ever be able to pay.[211] But the force of seigneurial eviction threats is evident in a case involving the Glövzin tavernkeeping farm. Christian Diercks testified in 1726 that the previous farmer "Neumann ruined the holding," and now was lodging in the retirement quarters, paying Diercks 2 talers yearly, of which Diercks passed 1 taler on to "the mother" (Neumann's), also inhabiting the farm. Hasse, weighing Diercks's 8-taler church debt, ordered him to pay in two years or depart. Diercks hastened to comply.[212]

The court often regulated farmers' debts to relatives and other villagers which, with church loans, comprised most obligations. Some long remained unpaid, such as 4.5 talers a farmer owed a kinsman, an "old [debt] from the time of the [unspecified] year of high prices."[213] Debt payment schedules regularly accompanied farm transfers, but poor or irresponsible farmers often reneged, and non-payment might persist for years, until (often after bare-fisted altercations) the court again intervened. Many debts were settled in kind: one farmer settled for a 1-taler pig, another redeemed a seigneurial loan with hops.[214]

Debts to craftsmen, especially blacksmiths and occasionally millers (though they normally took fees in kind), could be burdensome, but rarely exceeded 6–8 talers. Unpaid wages, on sound holdings, were seldom high, though Hasse once ordered an ox sold to pay maidservants' arrears.[215] But, for farmhands who had departed the Stavenow jurisdiction, collecting even small sums from impecunious former masters might be arduous. Occasional laborers, such as the two who – at a daily 3 groschen each – spent a week rebuilding a farm's retirement cottage, might wait for their pay.[216] New farmers' obligation to supply siblings' marriage portions translated, when unfulfilled, into psychologically explosive household debt, though with luck such charges fell due at manageable intervals. A 1755 fullholding owed nearly 100 talers, mostly in unpaid inheritances and inter-familial loans, but the incoming new proprietor's 70 cash talers promised relief.[217]

Most farmers sporadically labored under considerable debt, little of it productive or capital-renewing. Many farm transfers occurred when, especially through sickness in the proprietor's family, deficits swelled. A marriage bringing in a bride's or bridegroom's resources then helped sanitize finances. Otherwise, illness-stricken households might dissolve in poverty, as could also befall a healthy proprietor

[211] No. 358, fos. 85–8; no. 358, fos. 115–20.　　[212] No. 200, fos. 45–6.
[213] No. 714, fo. 179; no. 715, fos. 15–16.　　[214] No. 664, fos. 1–6.　　[215] No. 715, fos. 23–5.
[216] No. 324, fos. 50–2.　　[217] No. 326, fos. 210–12, 205.

hammered by harvest failure or livestock epidemics. In 1730 a Blüthen farm wife testified that:

because her husband Heinrich Kniepenberg had suffered such bad luck since taking the mayor's holding, and for some time now has been afflicted with serious illness, they were no longer able to render their rents and labor services. So that the farm doesn't fall out of good order, she wants, in her husband's name, to give it up and hand it over.

The same day Hasse visited Kniepenberg, "since he can't leave his house," to hear the stricken man's own words. Kniepenberg's seigneurial debts were "many," and other creditors loomed. His farm, though reduced to minimal livestock, displayed "well-conditioned land" and good buildings, though floor repairs were needed. Hasse wrote that:

Kniepenberg was then asked how he thought he might pay his debts. He reckons that through his long-enduring illness he has been completely impoverished, and knows of no way except to rely on God on high and the gracious lordship. He asks that, until the end of the matter [i.e., until his impending death], he be given the necessary daily bread.

A week later Hasse recorded that "the lordship has cancelled [Kniepenberg's] debts."[218]

In 1771 Major Kleist evicted the aforementioned Prill, crushed by debts of 150 talers plus 37 tribute-grain bushels: the heaviest debt reported of any Stavenow farmer. Two years previously Prill succeeded retiring Hans Brunst, heir-bereft farmer whose wife-beating had earlier landed him in court. Prill laconically conceded failure: "he had no more cattle and no fodder or bread-grain on hand." The lordship would have to save his two meager horses from starvation. Prill, who (like Kniepenberg) bore a name foreign to local farmers' ranks, took the farm already debt-burdened. He twice left annual seigneurial rents unpaid. He owed neighbors 4 talers they lent for taxes, plus four years of church interest. He paid neither blacksmith's nor wheelwright's bills, nor, for two years, farmhands' wages, including one Anna Brunst's. Prill had, the court wrote, "wrecked the farm."

Kleist faced great difficulty replacing Prill, as "royal law" required. Lodger Caspar Grotke showed interest until learning of the holding's debts, whereupon he withdrew, though Kleist offered to cancel arrears and supply summer seed. Finally, Peter Schmidt, like Grotke an outsider, took the farm, after Kleist gave him seed and a horse. Prill "handed over the holding in extraordinarily bad condition," including "completely

---

[218] No. 200, fos. 232–5.

ruined" retirement quarters. Accordingly, he and his wife and three children (left with but clothing and linen) had no claim on retirement provisions, though Schmidt was obliged to grant them to still-present old Brunst and wife. The strength of the farmers' claims on retirement portions from their farms is here evident, though Brunst was hardly living in milk and honey.[219]

The last recorded Stavenow farmer's eviction occurred in 1775, when the court compelled Jürgen Höpfner with his wife and children to quit their Karstädt fullholding. In 1771 Höpfner, twenty-six, succeeded his step-father, H. H. Brüning, who had successfully weathered twenty-one years as interim proprietor. Höpfner then accumulated 50 talers' commutation and tribute-grain arrears. He owed other creditors 20 talers, his horses were dead or sold, summer seed was lacking. Eight years later, living as a Blüthen lodger and probably subsisting from day labor, Höpfner died of dropsy, having recently lost two children to childhood diseases (apart from another dead in 1773).

Possibly Höpfner suffered harvest failures in the crisis year 1772, though his post-harvest 1771 marriage was well provisioned and festively paired with a young step-sister's marriage to a farmer's son embarking on a cottager's life. In 1779 the bridegroom-cottager was dead, while previous fullholder Brüning and his wife, who had appeared to be entering well-stocked retirement, disappear from the records (as do the two 1771 brides). This comprehensive misfortune's other victims were Brüning's children by his first and second wives. The daughter marrying the cottager received a cow and three steers, but Höpfner seems not to have given his other three half-siblings their promised two winter-fed steers and 5 talers.[220]

These were the few recorded debt-induced household dissolutions, as distinct from crisis-ridden intergenerational transfers driven by sickness and debt. The court normally only evicted farmers with unmanageable seigneurial debt. Unpaid servants' wages or siblings' inheritances, even when sizable, did not usually menace farmers' tenure, though they could expect the court to enforce payment. Yet there was Peter Häwecke who, Hasse wrote, "for a long time now has been suffering from a stroke," which produced "a great debt burden" (37 talers). Colonel Kleist ordered Häwecke's 1727 retirement in favor of a son-in-law "found as bridegroom" for Häwecke's daughter. The ailing farmer had depended on hired hands and short-term workers, including a nameless boy.[221]

[219] No. 358, fos. 115–20.   [220] No. 663, fos. 1–7; no. 663, fos. 4–6.   [221] No. 200, fos. 220–2.

Debt could serve strategic functions. Farmhand Joachim Thomß lent his terminally ill employer 26 talers, plus advancing 9 talers for taxes and commutation fees. Thomß then made the rare move of marrying the farm widow, waiving his debt claims. He agreed to pay off 60 talers in other farm debt, including 25 talers owed urban lenders and 10 talers to his predecessor's son, a Leipzig tailor.[222] But another farmer refused his worker's wage claims because "the farmhand pocketed some of the proceeds from grain he hauled to Lenzen and sold, and he willfully ruined the horses, so he will first have to make amends before his demands are met."[223]

Despite occasional peaks, ruinous to some, the average household burden, as table 4.6 showed, suggests that debt was not Stavenow farmers' prime nemesis. Ill health, bad luck, and – considering the apparent outsiders to landed villagers' ranks whose farms failed – lack of reinsurance within the community seem the greater menaces (leaving aside the ill-documented question of farming competence). Low debt might imply credit seekers' lack of collateral and scarcity of lenders, both signs of economic weakness. But judgment of Stavenow farmers must rest on this chapter's whole array of factors. The lordship and court were also effective brakes on reckless indebtedness. This point may be appreciated by contemplating the sorry fate of Christoffer Schlohe, Garlin free mayor, who enjoyed greater independence of seigneurial power than subject farmers. Such local notables might rise higher than ordinary villagers, but also fall more steeply.

In 1721 Kleist evicted Schlohe, who "because of his bad conduct" could no longer manage his farm or pay its charges. His successor Christoph Erhardt, though "a total outsider," made an impressive and profitable career within the Stavenow jurisdiction. Schlohe had long been free mayor but, as Erhardt later testified (1751), "the profligate way of life of the preceding owner [Schlohe], completely given over to drink, and his refusal to let himself any longer be compelled [to pay his debts] by the civil courts, caused him to join the *Soldatesque.*" Schlohe became a soldier, presumably outside Brandenburg-Prussia, deserting wife and children to escape his creditors and, doubtless, to persist in his dissolute ways. Referring to himself, Erhardt said "the farm was heavily indebted and devastated when he took it, so that no one wanted it, and he paid all debts and largely fed and raised the children their father abandoned." After

---

[222] No. 554, fos. 1–7.   [223] No. 591, fos. 2–4.

their mother's death in retirement on Erhardt's farm, "he gave the children their maternal inheritance."

Though Schlohe left behind nine mature horses and eleven head of cattle, his farmhouse was "completely dilapidated" and so appraised (since free mayoral farms could, unlike subject farmers', be sold) at a derisory 12 talers. He owed the lordship three years' rent (94 talers). There were another 215 talers' debt, including 64 talers borrowed from his father-in-law, 22 talers from his cavalryman brother, and 22 talers owed Sargleben village's mayor in "monthly money" for taxes. For a half-year's farmhand's work he owed a wife's relative 6.5 talers (a weekly scale of 6 groschen cash). A married woman worked four days sheaving in the rye harvest, claiming 2 groschen daily. Apart from other unpaid wages, Schlohe borrowed money from Garlin church and twelve other individuals. Stavenow leaseholder Meyer absorbed as his own losses, or paid out to Schlohe's creditors, 140 talers, reclaiming these from Kleist in 1721.[224]

Schlohe's 309-taler debt – a sum possibly 40 talers too low – dwarfed ordinary farmers' liabilities. But his farm was larger and more valuable than theirs, and he and his wife came from rural notable lineages – including free mayors and millers – who bequeathed them richer marriage portions and better intra-familial credit than lesser farmers commanded. Yet nothing prevented a farmer with Schlohe's advantages from drinking them away. In the 110 inventories of 1721–71, among many cases of debt, illness, and other misfortune, there is none in which pursuit of drink, gambling or other such recklessness figured plainly in a subject farmer's retirement or dispossession. Farm proprietorship was, seemingly, a status valued well enough to prevent such outcomes, while seigneurial power to intervene judicially in household affairs worked to discipline ordinary farmers and distance them from Christoffer Schlohe's fate.

Money

Money meant coins, easy both to conceal and lose to unscrupulous hands. But hoarding one's savings was unnecessary. Sizable sums such as inheritances or marriage-portion cash components were, if not immediately spent, safely investable. Hasse once decreed, after a husband's and wife's successive deaths, leaving their firstborn child doubly

---

[224] No. 200, fos. 157–62; no. 715, fo. 44.

orphaned, that the deceased mother's estate should be converted to silver and "securely lent out against landed property," to assure the girl her future maternal inheritance. Properly registered in occupancy deeds, such investments were inescapable obligations on which current farm proprietors, whether original borrowers or not, paid 4 percent annual interest. Such arrangements were equivalents among villagers of interest-bearing, land-backed promissory notes circulating among the nobility.[225]

Money was also depositable at interest in parish funds. Jochen Mentz entrusted 10 talers to Frau Kleist, who placed them in the Premslin "church account," assuring Mentz of 10 groschen yearly interest.[226] Yet this transaction stands alone, suggesting that villagers – though farmers readily borrowed parish funds – rarely entrusted their own money to them, perhaps unwilling so to reveal their resources to seigneurial eyes. The myriad small loans the villagers contracted among themselves, especially those secured by farm occupancy, comprised an informal deposit-banking system alongside parish funds.

Villagers could also turn to semi-professional moneylenders. One was Mesekow halfholder Johann Schmidt, who in 1744 retired after successfully farming twenty-six years or more. He died in 1761, whereupon his widow produced a notebook recording money he had lent or otherwise was owed him. From the Prignitz District's politically powerful von Platen family he claimed 43.5 talers for horses – showing that retirees might engage in horse-trading. To five people in and outside Stavenow's jurisdiction, one an estate administrator's widow, he lent 92.5 talers, raising his loans altogether to 136 talers. To allay other heirs' suspicions, Schmidt's widow judicially swore that no cash was on hand when he died. She sold linen for 10 talers and two pigs for 8 talers to pay burial and related expenses, and this was "true as may God through His son Jesus Christ help me to blessedness." Schmidt, whose household displayed considerable competence and well-being, was one of the few elderly retirees whom the documents show dying in village-style prosperity.[227]

If, when a farmer or retiree died, family discord or desperation prevailed, charges of concealment of the deceased's money might arise, or raiding of the deceased's goods might occur. In 1754 Schmidt himself swore, "to avoid all suspicion, and at the relatives' wish," that he received or took no cash from his dying son, who inherited the farm from him, and whose shoes old Schmidt later filled for six months, until

---

[225] No. 326, fos. 194–8; no. 324, fos. 17–18.   [226] No. 326, fo. 211.   [227] Ibid., fos. 241–2.

his son's young widow remarried. At the remarriage hearing, Schmidt's grandchildren's guardians said there was "general talk" that the son's widow had "a lot of money" when her husband died. She agreed to swear an oath, saying "she received no cash after the death except for 12 talers that were still in the money-bag at the time the father [that is, old Schmidt] counted them, and which were immediately spent on servants' wages and the household." There was also, she testified, "one hard taler" – a 1-taler coin – "and 1 gulden [an 18-groschen piece], which was godfather's money," to be saved for its child recipient. In this household, in which good sums circulated, and where both proprietor and farm wife succumbed successively to untimely deaths, oaths worked, effectively, to allay tensions and suspicions.[228]

On another Mesekow farm, riven by strife among brothers competing for its 1748 inheritance, the warring men charged that their sister Trine Fischers, when their mother died, stole over 2 talers (including one silver taler) from the maternal wooden chest. Martin Huth testified that, when he visited the Fischers' house – sleeping there, along with Trine and her brother, in the living room – she stole, in the night, 1 ducat (equaling 2 talers) and two 2-groschen coins from a money-bag in his trousers. Trine proclaimed innocence, offering to swear on it. Hasse dismissed the allegations, saying better evidence was needed, and vetoed the oath, not wishing to cheapen courtroom vows' still-potent effects.[229]

Married women might possess good money, especially if dowry cash was not immediately spent, but invested at interest or left in their own hands. When Catherina Grunewald, retired farmer Ebel's wife, died, her two nieces and heirs challenged Ebel's claim that, apart from clothing and furniture worth 14 talers, she left no cash. The nieces said their aunt had a "corporeal brother," whereabouts unknown, for whom Judge Betich punctiliously appointed a local farmer as "curator." The widower claimed his wife's dowry included 9 talers for two cows, but this money never reached his hands. He admitted the wooden chest held 4 talers, but he claimed earning them himself. He did not pretend to be sole heir, probably because he married his wife late in life. But he thought that, "because he had had her constantly ill, so that she couldn't head the household herself," and because he paid for her burial, her meager estate was his.

"To avoid conflict" Ebel proposed to share with the nieces his wife's worldly goods "as she specified them on her deathbed." The nieces, one

---

[228] Ibid., fos. 194–8; no. 324, fos. 17–18.   [229] No. 326, fos. 147–8.

having tended the deceased and kept house for six months, rejected this argument, denying the deceased had been always sick, and "moreover the widower was obliged to support his wife." They demanded Ebel swear he seized no cash. If he did, they would leave him his wife's bedding and "dress of honor," which, befitting a remarried widow, consisted of black serge coat with matching camisole and apron. The court read the oath, whereupon Ebel "recalled there was another bag of money containing not quite 30 talers." He could not bring himself to risk eternal damnation for a handful of coins. Betich inventoried the deceased's possessions, now including "money in cash which the widower testified he found in the deceased's bed-straw." Unsealing the bag, Betich counted 25.5 talers, to which Ebel added 4.5 talers his wife gave him. He swore to "God the All-Knowing" he had delivered the money correctly, whereupon Betich decreed the estate's division among Ebel and nieces, to which all assented, signing with crosses.[230]

Although villagers did not always have cash in pocket, locked chest, or bed-straw, it regularly passed through their hands, sometimes in good quantities and coin denominations. Before Christmas 1741, farmer Dietrich Hecht brought a "half pistolette," a 2.5-taler coin, to Perleberg moneychanger Catherine Klosse, who subsequently appeared at Stavenow, with a kinsman-bookbinder, claiming Hecht swindled her. She offered to convert his money – he needed smaller coins – but only into "small change," while Hecht wanted "Brandenburg coinage," probably multi-groschen pieces. Klosse said they compromised, but then Hecht left without handing over the pistolette. This Hecht denied, appealing to his reputation for trustworthiness. Hecht's wife persuaded him to pay Klosse 1 taler, provided that if the missing coin materialized, she would reimburse him. Here, possibly, a moneychanger fell victim to a villager's trick.[231]

Doubtless there was a money-value hierarchy, according to coins' varying prestige and acceptability. Dowry cash was most impressive if delivered in gold coins, as were a farmer-tavernkeeper's wife's 20 talers.[232] Dowry money might arrive "in cash and gold," as just-mentioned Hans Ebel wrote of "60 Reichstalers in currency" when inventorying a new farm wife's 1765 "bride's treasure." Her deceased predecessor's dowry counted "25 Reichstalers in good old [pre-1756] money and 65 talers in ½-pieces [half-taler coins] de anno 1758, which in Brandenburg currency amount to 46.2.1 talers." Ebel knew precisely the relation of the Seven Years War's devalued money, often called "Saxon money" because it was

[230] No. 358, fos. 78–84.   [231] No. 591, fo. 101.   [232] No. 326, fos. 73–4.

coined by Frederick II's agents in occupied Dresden, to standard German money of account, as measured in Reichstalers and Brandenburg equivalents. Another 1765 dowry's values were given in "old [prewar] money."[233]

The Stavenow court did not invariably report whether, at farm transfers, cash was on hand, though this was a standard rubric. Among the 110 1721–71 inventories, only fourteen cash entries appeared. In eight cases, none was reported, and in six cases sums ranged from 40 to 92 talers, including new dowry money. Doubtless there were always cash-bare households, especially – owing to proprietors' sickness or death – during intergenerational transfers. Yet probably cash and other precious metal were, by family agreement, concealed from uncontested inventories, or informally divided among heirs before appraisals, to avoid drawing attention to them. A deceased farm wife was presumably not unique in leaving behind – under the "silver" heading – "a small, gilded locket [*Schaustück*], worth about 8 groschen, hanging from a thin silver chain about a finger long." Yet this modest piece, along with an earlier-mentioned amber necklace, was the only jewelry recorded among farming families in fifty years.[234]

Nor was the court usually interested in money the villagers had, as individuals, lent out to their neighbors. Still, it is clear the Stavenowers' assets reposed more in livestock and wardrobes than money-bags. They worked in a monetized economy, and many patiently saved, especially as youths, to accumulate marriage portions. Once settled on farms, they invested money remaining after rents and taxes in livestock and consumer goods. When need arose, they called in loans, if they had made any, or "silverized" their livestock.

THE CONDITION OF NON-INHERITING SIBLINGS

We saw that most farm transfers occurred between fathers or step-fathers and eldest sons or step-sons (40 percent) or eldest daughters or step-daughters (20 percent). In only one-fifth of cases did a younger child or step-child inherit the family farm. What was the fate of their landless siblings? Evidence is confined to seventy-two notations of occupation or status of landed families' mature children at their parental holding's transfer (see table 4.7).

[233] No. 358, fos. 7–11. In 1770: 8 talers Saxon = 3.5 current talers = 100:44 (no. 358, fos. 85–8). Ebel's ratio: 100:32. No. 358, fos. 3–4.
[234] No. 324, fos. 13–14.

Table 4.7   *Status of non-inheriting children of landed households at their family farms' intergenerational transfer, 1721–1771[a]*

	Women		Men	
Status	No.	%	No.	%
Married as co-proprietor of non-parental full/halfholding				
Civilians	12		1	
Former soldiers	0		7	
Total	12	32%	8	22%
Married as co-head of non-landed household	9	25%	1	3%
Unmarried farm servants				
At home	5		5	
On other farmers' holdings	6		8	
At manor	2		0	
Employer unspecified	3		0	
Total	16	43%	13	36%
Active-duty soldiers			10	28%
Urban artisans			3	8%
Whereabouts unknown			1	3%
Total	37	100%	36	100%

[a] Working age: 12–14+ years.
Source: Stavenow farm inventories, 1721–71

Over three-fifths of these women were married, either to farmers, housed laborers, or (once) a sexton. Most women still in service would also eventually marry, just as the married had, typically, worked as maidservants at home or elsewhere nearby (including the manor). A few examples illuminate farm daughters' fates. A halfholder's children from two marriages numbered in 1747 two sons (one a soldier, fighting with the other for farm succession) and seven daughters. One daughter was a Mecklenburg cutlery-sharpener's wife, one a lodger's and another a halfholder's wife, one was in service with local nobility, two with farmers in a nearby non-Stavenow village, and one, aged eighteen, worked at home.[235] Among women in a 1732 household counting ten children, one served her brother on the parental farm, one worked in Perleberg and another for Premslin manor-farm's leaseholder, and one, fourteen, was "still at home." A halfholder who, judging from his prosperity in retirement, had enjoyed

[235] No. 326, fos. 141–3.

good fortune as a farmer married one daughter to a Perleberg master blacksmith and another to a farmer-tavernkeeper in a nearby village.[236]

Among table 4.7's men, nearly all were or had been soldiers. Following basic training, active conscripts were on peacetime furlough most of the year and obliged by necessity to work, so that most should be reckoned among farm servants. One in four men had advanced, by marrying a farmer's daughter, from soldier to landed proprietor, and other active soldiers would follow this example. Others would marry and establish laborers' households (although here but one had done so). Only three farmers' sons became urban artisans, all tailors (in London, Leipzig, and Altmark's Stendal). The peripheral role of employment at the manor, whether compulsory or free, is evident, though doubtless several older persons in this group served three-year obligatory terms before attaining their current positions.

A 1726 household counting five sons and two daughters was young Joachim Maass's fullholding. One of Joachim's sisters had married a local halfholder, the other worked at Stavenow manor. His brothers were a soldier-laborer, furloughed from the von Dönhoff Regiment; a nearby farmhand; and Hans, "not in his right mind," at home with a younger brother.[237] In an above-mentioned family with ten children, one man succeeded to the farm's proprietorship, one was at home in ill health, one was a married lodger, two (one a soldier, aged twenty-four) were local farm servants, and one, aged twelve, was "still at home."

Thus some farmers' non-inheriting daughters eventually married into landed households, but others, if they escaped servant status, at best married landless workers of some sort. Farmers' able-bodied sons were soldiers before marrying into farms or settling into landless laborers' lives, single or married. As for landless households' children moving into landed status, these data show only three women and three men so rising, plus a journeyman carpenter.

Six of the ten servants working on parental farms were physically or mentally disabled. Among six children of retiring halfholder Joachim Schulze (who could give them "little or nothing by way of inheritance") there were in 1726, apart from the son succeeding him, the lame Joachim, twenty-eight, who (as his father "decreed") would work as much as possible and "be fed and cared for until death."[238] When in 1752 this farm's new proprietor of 1726 retired in a son-in-law's favor, it

---

[236] No. 591, fos. 51–2. Mesekow: Johann Schmidt's farm, document of 3.XI.1750, reference misplaced.
[237] No. 200, fos. 207–8.   [238] Ibid., fos. 200–1.

was agreed about one of the four non-inheriting daughters, that "Lena probably will not marry because she has until now been sickly; she will help by working for her brother" – her new brother-in-law – "for fair wages, and after her parents' death she will have a free room in the house." The new proprietor would pay marriage portions (including "5 talers for the dress of honor") for the other three daughters, aged twenty-five, twenty, and fifteen or, "if they should die," provide their burial.[239] Of the sister, aged nineteen, of a twenty-two-year old farm-inheritor it was agreed that "Eva Nagels is somewhat frail." If this prevented her from "earning her keep through service and labor, the new proprietor wants to and must grant her maintenance on the holding."[240] A farm couple retired in favor of their son Johann Wilhelm, whose brother Fritz, "not in command of his full understanding," was "in pitiful condition." Fritz's mother wanted to "provide him lifelong with shirts, stockings, and linen." Fritz would work as he could on the farm and receive his livelihood from his brother. "The proprietor wants to take good care of him."[241]

Such provisions, along with other disbursements from the parental farm, show that, in this rural society, impartible land inheritance did not so much cast younger children aside in the eldest-born's favor as saddle new proprietors with often heavy transfer payments or other support obligations.

Retirement benefits

On their arduous lives' horizon, Stavenow farm couples foresaw surrendering their holding to heirs and living out their days as beneficiaries of the retirement provisions – *das Altenteil* – which their proprietary years, filled with responsibilities and pressures, had earned them. But historical hindsight overlooks retirement benefits' crucial importance in structuring villagers' lives and relationships to seigneurial authority. Doubtless able and strong-willed farmers derived rewards from proprietorship, not least an active voice in communal affairs, including struggles with the manor. They commanded their households, as independently of others' will as possible. These were attributes of farmers' authority – subordinate though it was to higher powers – which wives, within their sphere, shared. Apart from aversion to earthly life's twilight, farmers had good reasons to cling to their proprietary rights,

---

[239] No. 715, fos. 45–6.   [240] No. 358, fos. 85–8.   [241] Ibid., fos. 61–3.

Table 4.8 *Age at death among men and women thirty-nine years and older: villages of Blüthen, Dargardt, and Mesekow, and Stavenow manor settlement, 1694–1799 (both sexes)*

Age	40–9	50–9	60–9	70–9	80–9	90+	Total
Number/%	108 17.5%	119 19.3%	177 28.6%	144 23.3%	53 8.6%	17 2.7%	618 100%

Source: Blüthen Pfarramt: Begräbnis-Register. Computations from Pastor Karl Gross's statistical tables.

persevering until retirement at a propitious and dignified moment, when the farm's resources would secure them good provisions.

From 144 late seventeenth- to early nineteenth-century notations, it emerges that the average farmer's tenure as household head was twenty-one years. Premature mortality cut many down, but among these careers eight extended to 40–7 years, sixteen to 30–9, and thirty-one to 25–9. Altogether, 38 percent of these farmers headed their households twenty-five years or more. They needed to persevere until competent sons could succeed them, or until daughters' marriages recruited able successors. Data on newly installed farmers' ages are sparse (fifteen cases), yielding an average of twenty-eight years, though in a 17–42 range the median was twenty-six. Yet twenty-eight probably closely approximates the age when most eighteenth- and nineteenth-century farmers took their holdings.

Although average tenure lasted but twenty-one years, among those who survived middle age retirement normally arrived later than the sum of marriage-age and farm-tenure (forty-nine years) suggests. Let us consider eighteenth-century longevity, as reflected in Blüthen's parish register, among men and women who lived past age thirty-nine (see table 4.8). Because they encompass many members of non-farm households, these data are only suggestive of farmers' and their wives' longevity. They show that roughly one-fifth of villagers living to age forty died in their forties and another one-fifth in their fifties. Nearly 30 percent died in their sixties, and the remaining one-third at seventy or beyond. By age 63.5, half who lived past age thirty-nine had died. That is, age 63.5 was this group's median age of death. It follows that for farmers who lived to hand the reins to their successors around or before age sixty – when sons or sons-in-law stood ready to succeed them – retirement for many would reach well beyond age 63.5.

Retirement might last, for whoever reached it, as long – or longer – than childhood and youth. Considering retirees' advancing physical weakness and dependency, security of their material provisions – such as harvests of arable plots, and pasture, garden, and firewood allotments – was crucial. Yet, from the new farm proprietor's angle, with his own family to raise, siblings or in-laws to provide with marriage portions, and farm servants to hire until his children could replace them, retirement benefits, if overly generous, would drain away vital resources. This perspective the lordship shared, and state authorities too, who inclined to think that farmers strove unjustifiably to retire into early comfort and leisure, escaping taxpayer and subject-farmer status.

We saw how, in the 1727 *Hausbuch*, Colonel Kleist tried to ban court-enforceable retirement and instead impose a common family regime on elders and youth alike. But his edict remained a dead letter. As the future showed, the lordship could regulate but not abolish farmers' claim (in local rhetoric) to "fair" retirement benefits "equal to their ancestors'" or "as [his or her] parents had them" or as were "customary" or "usual in the village." Judge Hasse approved retirements in these terms in 1731–2, not long after Kleist's salvo against them.[242] Earlier Hasse had indeed restricted retirement benefits, invoking in 1724 not Kleist's but the royal will. Erdmann Mentz, a widower with five children on a weak smallholding, found a second wife in Marie Lawerentzen, whose dowry included livestock but no money. Hasse recorded that she would receive, should Mentz predecease her, "maintenance and clearly specified retirement benefits." But he added that:

after the royal decree established once and for all that land shall no longer be included in retirement portions, nor shall separate households be granted to retired parents, but instead they will simply be cared for on the farm in a single household, so must Marie Lawerentzen content and satisfy herself with being taken onto this farm as a mother.[243]

Such an edict does not figure in the literature on Frederick William I's agrarian policies, but it is imaginable that this choleric ruler would have tried to abolish fixed and separate retirement benefits customary at Stavenow and elsewhere in Brandenburg-Prussia where hereditary tenures prevailed.[244] In 1726 Hasse ruled laconically that a retiring halfholder and his wife would receive "maintenance" if they worked together with their successors, even while appending an inventory of

---

[242] No. 324, fos. 33–4, 47; no. 591, fos. 51–2, 38–9; no. 326, fos. 210–12, 205; no. 358, fos. 32–4, 5–6; no. 715, fos. 45–6; no. 712, fos. 30–1; no. 358, fos. 34–6.
[243] No. 200, fos. 175–6.   [244] Stadelmann, *Preussens Könige*, vol. I, passim.

the meager estate of a recently deceased "grandmother" who "had enjoyed [this farm's] retirement portion for thirty years."[245]

In a 1728 case of a mother-in-law's claims on a smallholding whose inheritance by an unwelcome new son-in-law she bitterly resented, Hasse let her keep the food supply she had independently assembled and occupy "the room outside [the proprietary couple's] living quarters next to the threshing-floor." But she could not ask more than "to eat and drink with the son-in-law as well as he can manage in his own house." She asked to be given "fixed shares of grain harvest, trees, and vegetable gardens." Hasse said the proprietor was free to make such arrangements, but she had no right to them, though he was bound to sow and harvest flaxseed for her.[246] In 1730, Hasse decreed, concerning another smallholder's widow who was retiring in her still unmarried eldest son's favor, that she should live in the retirement quarters. "But as for separate food provisions, they are by Herr Colonel's express command not to be granted, but she must be satisfied, until he rules otherwise, with eating at the proprietor's table." Meanwhile, "the son will look around for a capable helper" (wife).[247] Hasse ruled similarly about halfholder retirees, adding that in return for their labor "the farm will bury them in customary fashion."[248]

Yet, in the next generation (1751–2) the lordship approved full-scale retirement portions on the last-mentioned two farms. These retirement-benefit restrictions all concerned hard-pressed small- or halfholdings, while in the years 1726–32 Hasse ratified customary benefits on several fullholdings and a stable halfholding. The court confined its curtailment efforts to weaker and smaller farms, though imperiled larger farms were never exempt. After 1731 the court ceased enforcing seigneurial and government threats to abolish retirement portions, but economic difficulties sometimes eliminated them. When in 1771 the aforementioned Prill was evicted, he – predictably – lost retirement benefit claims, though his precursor's remained in force.[249] In 1761 the court denied retirement benefits on a halfholding because of its poverty, though noting that the new proprietor would give the sixty-six-year-old retiree and his fifty-year-old wife garden land and try to get them a cow.[250] Yet when in 1768 a fullholder retired after thirty-seven years in his son's favor, leaving behind 71 talers' debt, he and his wife received court approval, with Major Kleist present, of normal retirement provisions.[251]

[245] No. 200, fos. 200–1, 44–5.   [246] Ibid., fos. 216–19.   [247] Ibid., fos. 148–9.
[248] No. 713, fos. 18–20.   [249] No. 358, fos. 115–20.   [250] No. 326, fo. 242.
[251] No. 358, fos. 64–9.

As we saw, the dowry or marriage portion of someone marrying onto a farm, if satisfactorily large, established a retirement benefits claim, even if the newcomer's spouse (and farm owner) might die prematurely. When in 1747 a farm widow remarried, she relinquished her dowry's ownership (thus surrendering withdrawal rights to marry onto another holding) in return for retirement benefits on her deceased husband's farm. Her new husband, who invested 60-taler assets, heard that retirement benefits would be "bestowed" on him after 12–15 years, but only if the holding hadn't "worsened" under his stewardship. Here, to enable a remarrying mother to serve a full proprietorship term with a second husband, Hasse proposed setting aside the eldest son's inheritance claims (encouraging him to "marry out") in favor of the younger son's. Should the widow predecease the new farmer, he would work out his term and then retire.[252] In another case, though a man marrying a farm widow contributed 67 talers, Hasse ruled only that, should his wife predecease him, he would, "if circumstances justified it, be protected on the holding." This provision's uncertainty seemingly reflected the children's guardians' and court's pressure on him to raise his step-children properly.[253]

Marie Jägers, marrying a farmer-widower, gained retirement provisions through her dowry, but should she claim it on her husband's death, she would be entitled to withdraw only 10 talers and a cow (half the dowry's value), apart from personal possessions.[254] Journeyman artisan Pankow, who invested 100 talers in a halfholding, was promised retirement benefits (provided he properly cared for his new wife and step-children). His deceased predecessor's father, the aforementioned, well-heeled retiree Johann Schmidt, was occupying the retirement quarters. But since Schmidt's wife, a customs agent's widow whom he married in retirement, "brought nothing into the farm and does not work on it," the elders received half-provisions only.[255]

Sixty-five surviving retirement agreements of 1721–71 display the court instructing most new farmers to give retiring elders the customary benefits. This held without trend changes in forty-five (69 percent) of these cases. In nine cases (14 percent) retirement benefits, because they entailed larger grain sowings or livestock holdings, were better than average; in the remaining eleven cases (17 percent) they were, for opposite reasons, worse. Judging by these figures, retirees on four of

---

[252] No. 554, fos. 1–7.   [253] No. 323, fos. 5–6.
[254] No. 326, fos. 149–50, 187–8; no. 358, fos. 54–8.
[255] No. 326, fos. 194–8; no. 324, fos. 17–18.

every five Stavenow farms could expect to claim in full the old-age provisions for which they labored.

Exemplary of fullholders' highest expectations were benefits conferred on Karstädt mayor Hans Nagel and his wife, retiring in 1754 after thirty-six years or more. They would occupy the farmstead's free-standing retirement house, with the use of designated barn spaces. They would have "their cows," plus access to farmstead pasturage and two wagonloads of hay; cereal land in each of the holding's three fields, which the new proprietor, as was customary, would cultivate for the retirees; a "broad garden" near their lodgings; eleven trees – seven apple, three pear, and one nut; a vegetable garden on communal land; four firewood stands; and use, when necessary, of horses handed over to Nagel's son. Upon one retiree's death, benefits would be halved. The survivor would pay burial costs and otherwise "not give anything out," that is, would alone inherit the deceased's goods. The heirs would bury the surviving retiree, sharing the inheritance among themselves, "unless a still unmarried daughter stays with [the parents] and tends them, in which case she will have double portion."[256]

Among halfholders, Lorentz Behn's benefits, after a seventeen-year proprietorship, were exemplary: "free lodging" and barn space; arable land sowable in 5 bushels; meadowland, plus three gardens; six fruit trees; two cows, three sheep, one sow with two piglets; and "for firewood, whatever there is among the alders bordering the fields." Upon one retiree's death, grain plantings would decline to 3.5 bushels, but gardenland would remain undiminished. Behn's neighbor and fellow halfholder Joachim Janentz received similar provisions. Hasse added that "Janentz is leaving a chair and stool in the living room for himself and the same for his wife."

Halfholder Hans Schulze, retiring at forty-eight after twenty-six years, received provisions "as his predecessors had them": land sowable in 5.25 bushels; in a fourth, occasionally sown field also a plot; a firewood stand, two meadows, a garden with fruit trees, "and also a garden on the field." His retirement livestock included a cow and calf, four pigs for slaughter, a "suckling foal," and four geese. He kept five metal cooking pots.[257] Evidence is thin on provisions for landed cottagers and smallholders, which may only have been granted, if at all, from case to case. When poor smallholder Joachim Seyer retired after twenty-eight years, he and his wife received no cereal allotments, but kept a living

---

[256] No. 326, fos. 191–4; no. 664, fos. 1–6; no. 513, fos. 37–9.
[257] No. 323, fo. 7; no. 326, fos. 124–6.

room and bed-chamber in the house, a garden, four trees' fruit, and one of Seyer's four horses (expendable since such farms rendered manual labor services).[258]

The most valuable provision was arable land, located on "the retirees' field," or "where the other retired people have their land" (in open-field sections reserved for elders).[259] Eighteenth-century norms, widely observed, were – for fullholders – land sowable in 4.5 bushels per adult and – for halfholders – 3 bushels. Allowing for annual fallowing and pasturage of one of the three fields, these figures translated into actual sowings of 1.5 bushels each of winter rye and summer barley per adult fullholder, and 1 bushel correspondingly per halfholder. At average yields, these sowings supplied each retired fullholder, after setting aside next year's seed-grain, with 8.25 bushels of bread-grains, while each halfholder's net harvest was 5.5 bushels. These were acceptable rations for retirees free of heavy labor, perhaps leaving fullholders with small surpluses for sale or fodder. Except rarely, fullholder couples claimed no more than land sowable in 9 bushels.

Improbably, the highest allotment went to a woman, Anne Bucken, who headed a fullholding for sixteen years following her husband's death, working the farm with her six sons' help. In 1751 she retired in a married son's favor, saying "she could no longer head the household because she was now threescore years old." Among other provisions, she kept a horse and land sowable in 10 bushels. "As for grain, fruit and other victuals, the mother has laid in her own supplies." Considering that three non-inheriting sons worked on local farms, while the other two – a third had died in recent wars – were active-duty soldiers, there was seemingly no kin to share her comparatively ample bread.[260]

Custom and necessity allowed retirees to keep a milk-cow, paired in one widow's case with a she-goat. The new proprietors were obliged to give these cattle winter fodder, and help overwinter such pigs, sheep, and poultry as elders kept. The profits and status deriving from livestock ownership often tempted retirees to burden their successors with heavier claims. Peter Schröder, having in ten years' interim proprietorship reinvigorated a mayoral farm, won approval to take into retirement two cows, "the crooked-horned and brown-uddered ones," plus a calf; two slaughtering pigs plus piglet; seven sheep and six lambs; and half the farm's geese. He also tried, unsuccessfully, to keep a horse or two. Still, his competence as farmer-mayor paid these dividends on the

---

[258] No. 326, fos. 199–200.   [259] No. 358, fos. 32–4; no. 591, fos. 56, 58.
[260] No. 715, fos. 35–9.

hoof, plus good cereal rations and two retirement rooms in the main farmhouse ("the living room and bed-chamber next to the kitchen").[261]

Some farmers, reluctant after long years to surrender command, struck hard bargains, even when leaving farms weak or run-down. Jürgen Nagel, after farming thirty-six years, accepted his son's succession, but then tried to renege because of "anger and hostility" between them. Hasse reported that Frau Kleist could not approve old Nagel's proposal to keep house for a few more years, since "he has run the holding into poverty and desolation." Yet he trekked into retirement with two cows, seven sheep and lambs, fifteen geese and chickens, and an ox – plus, among many other things, "necessary hops" for brewing harvest beer.[262] More typical were such livestock as the cow, four sheep, and pig granted in 1727, despite numerous debts the elders left the new proprietors to pay.[263] Or, if retirees received additional animals, they pledged reciprocity, as when the proprietor agreed to fodder and graze a mare for his retired uncle, on condition he could use it when necessary, though its foals would belong to the uncle, doubtless for eventual sale. Another retiree took a cow and two cattle, promising them as future wedding gifts to an unmarried daughter and son.[264]

Elders' temptation to carry off more assets than the farm could bear may have clashed with new proprietors' inclination to exploit elders' labor for their own purposes. Yet, judging from court records, neither tendency, inherent in village structure, won out. Elders were expected to offer helping hands but not, except at harvests, to join in heavy field labor. Mostly elders busied themselves with their own sustenance, working their gardens, tending their animals and fruit trees, and processing – among women – their flax. The court occasionally registered successors' agreement to give them manure, composting leaves, or pine needles for gardens, beyond their arable plots' obligatory fertilization. Working garden land ("to sow cabbage seed") substituted for the earlier preoccupation with arable. When a retiring farmer failed to agree with his successor step-son over 1771 land allotments, including potato gardens, two "friends" on each side negotiated a compromise. In a 1789 agreement, potato land was separately allocated alongside customary gardens (while recently introduced pinewood supplied elders' fuel).[265]

The stem-family retirement system could not fail to generate many intra-familial conflicts, as drastic quarrels recounted above show. Elders'

---

[261] No. 324, fos. 34–7; no. 324, fos. 4–5.   [262] No. 715, fos. 23–5.   [263] No. 200, fos. 220–2.
[264] No. 712, fos. 46–9; no. 326, fos. 100–1. Cf. no. 591, fos. 119–21; no. 326, fos. 100–1.
[265] No. 712, fos. 46–9; no. 358, fos. 129, 133–4; no. 523, fos. 1–10.

difficulties arose when kinfolk supporting them in retirement predeceased them, leaving them to strangers' mercies, but also when too many retirees pressed claims on single holdings. When a mayor's widow found it "highly necessary" (because of three young children) to remarry, Hasse warned her new husband that, so long as the present retirees lived, he would have to run the farm, because it could not support two sets of elders. Yet at least once, double retirements on the same farm became unavoidable. Illness forced a farmer of twenty years' standing to transfer his indebted though otherwise sound halfholding to his daughter and son-in-law (whose recruitment the farm's troubles had made difficult). Since a previous owner and his wife inhabited the retirement quarters, it was decided that, if the ailing farmer survived the winter, he and his wife "will stay in the house at the proprietor's table until the [previous] retirees die. Also, they will occupy the living room until the proprietor can modify the bed-chamber into a living room for them."[266] Alternatively, new farm couples faced the unattractive prospect, should they not persevere until both retirees died, of sharing half-benefits with a surviving elder.[267] Or, if retirement dwellings were uninhabitable, elders might be billeted on new proprietors, as when an incoming son-in-law learned that his widowed mother-in-law would be sharing his table. If he did not want to "have her in the living room," he would need to renovate the retirement quarters. Otherwise, "she will in the future, if she lives, have half-provisions and the living room's use, plus a bed-chamber."[268]

Retired widows risked neglect, but their claims on provisions were strong and enforceable. When women married into farms, their benefits, should their spouses predecease them, were often written into occupancy deeds.[269] But more often these were specified at retirement.[270] Filial piety favored them, as when a son succeeding his deceased father (1771) promised "to supply his old mother lifelong with food and give her all necessary care, including clothing, and in every way treat her as a child should." She could, if she wanted, move into retirement quarters, where she would have a cow, a cooking pot, and 6 talers (paid in installments). In that case, her son would "fix up a room for her" and give her the usual cereal allotments and gardens.[271] A half-century earlier, widowed Anna Hannen retired after successfully managing a halfholding for several years following her husband's death. Her son pledged to "give her free housing in the outbuilding, which he would

---

[266] No. 715, fos. 8, 13–15, 30–1.   [267] No. 326, fos. 111–12.   [268] Ibid., fos. 122–3.
[269] No. 716, fos. 305–6.   [270] No. 358, fos. 85–8.   [271] Ibid., fos. 107–10.

put in order for her," and supply her with such provisions "as are customary in the village." Though she would cook for herself, "when she
joins in her son's work he will give her food and drink." On the same
farm in 1768, a farm wife took a mirror into the retirement quarters.[272]

Retirement of widows with young children weighed heavily on farm
resources. A new proprietor agreed to deliver 8 bushels of annual sowings to his mother and three young siblings, though after six years
rations would fall to 5 bushels' yield.[273] Before a widowed farm wife
(luckily) married out into a widowed farmer's household, her step-son
agreed, on taking his father's holding, to build a new retirement house
and "give his step-mother full provisions for twenty years, so she may
raise the two little children." Thereafter she would have half-benefits,
including nut and pear tree, "as long as she lives."[274] At halfholder
Pankow's third marriage, the court approved his request that, if he died
first, his new wife would have full retirement benefits, instead of the
widow's half, so she might raise Pankow's three young children from
earlier marriages.[275] Even on an endemically poor cottager's holding, a
widow, who ran the household alone for nine years but then retired in
favor of a (hopefully) soon to be married daughter, was granted 6 bushels'
sowings to raise three or four children.[276]

Most court conflicts over retirement benefits concerned the mal-
treatment of weak or socially isolated elders, though sometimes retired
parents tyrannized their offspring. Mothers overstepped bounds as well
as fathers. After nineteen years of proprietorship, smallholder's widow
Sophie Follstedten had, as her successor step-son-in-law complained,
"highhandedly taken cattle and sheep into retirement," plus "long
straw needed for roof repair," while also sowing grain on rented land
and taking various farm tools and furniture. Hasse ordered everything
returned for proper inventory, on pain of losing retirement provisions
altogether. Ten years later Sophie moved away. Her younger son
claimed inheritance from the farm, but the court conceded him only
his mother's assets when she died, noting that "in 175[7] she took a lot
of things into retirement" and that smallholdings could not generally
pay cash to non-inheriting children, "as local observance against such
practices shows." Her son would therefore have only wedding provisions from the farm. Here a willful widow won several rounds, if not
the final one.[277]

[272] No. 712, fos. 30–1; no. 358, fos. 62–3.   [273] No. 513, fos. 31–5.
[274] No. 324, fos. 2–3; no. 326, fos. 63–5.   [275] No. 358, fos. 36–41.   [276] Ibid., fos. 111–12.
[277] No. 326, fo. 211; no. 358, fos. 31–2.

Women marrying widowed retirees could not claim benefits once their husbands died, and seem mostly to have moved away, accompanied sometimes by acrimony. Though evidence is thin, village mayors seemingly mediated retirement disputes, perhaps stopping them short of court hearings and unwelcome publicity. Hasse heard a retired fullholder's widow's complaint that her son skimped on her pasturage, pear tree, and flax-sowing rights. The son said his mother demanded too much. Hasse ordered an earlier retirement contract to be honored, charging the mayor to investigate and report to him, which closed the case.[278]

If custom and court worked to ensure that most retirees enjoyed provisions locally considered adequate or good, while some elders prospered in retirement, most left meager estates at death, though these might nonetheless spark quarrels. A fullholder's wife complained that, after her husband "gave his mother food provisions into her ninetieth year," her brother-in-law, who only housed the old woman, seized the deceased's possessions and refused to pay the 2-taler burial charge. The defendant countered that the goods were given to his sister's children. Hasse ruled that "since the children have gone away from one another, the two brothers must pay the preacher."[279] In 1726 Hasse inventoried an elderly "grandmother's" estate tallying 12.5 talers, including a heifer and three sheep, 2 bushels of harvested barley, one of oats, 1.5 bushels of rye in the ground, and straw. She also left a loom, spinning wheel, linen yardage and "very old bedding." She had a storage chest (16 groschen), a trunk of "torn-up linen," an old chair, two cooking pots with hearth-hook, and "two dresses and a jacket worth nothing." Her burial cost 27 groschen, plus a half-barrel of beer (20 groschen).[280]

In 1729 J. J. Havemann died on his former halfholding after ten years' retirement. His estate, which he bequeathed to his ward, a six-year-old granddaughter, included cooking pot, trunk with lock, ax, bed, and coat. His cow (4.5 talers) the farm proprietor sold to pay his church-fund debt.[281] Not all retired halfholders left such exiguous estates. The above-mentioned Hans Ebel tried to conceal from co-heirs his deceased wife's 30 cash talers. Among her other possessions, worth 21.5 talers, were her dress of honor, bible, songbook, New Testament, and a 2-taler easy chair.[282]

One retired fullholder's possessions were those of Adam Koch, who remarried on his son's farm the young Dorothea Huthen, day laborer Mayer's widow. She arrived with a five-year-old son and "goods

[278] No. 591, fo. 127.   [279] No. 589, fos. 3–4.   [280] No. 200, fos. 44–5.   [281] No. 200, fo. 24.
[282] No. 358, fos. 78–84, 81–4.

brought in" worth 37 talers, including a 6-taler bed, cow and two sheep, clothing, furniture, and tools. She promised to depart at Koch's death, nor would they inherit from each other, but rather bequeathed their estates to their children – in Koch's case, to his younger son who did not inherit the farm. His goods were worth 26 talers, counting cow and three sheep, furniture and tools. Here a laborer's widow, not destitute but needing a home, joined an older man, retired already eleven years, in a marriage of mutual advantage.[283]

SUBJECT FARMERS' AND OTHER COMMON PEOPLE'S MATERIAL FORTUNES BRIEFLY COMPARED

Retired farmers' possessions at death were mostly meager. They surrendered their greatest assets to their successors, though in retirement allotments they possessed surrogate mini-farms. By contrast, a tailor in the Altmark town of Salzwedel who died in 1776 left an estate, mostly in cash, of 353 talers. He was Johann Hewecke, a Stavenow farm family's non-inheriting son who migrated to town, entering a trade requiring little initial investment, proverbial for its poverty, but marrying (though his wife died in 1762) and getting ahead. Contrasting his material condition with subject farmers' is instructive.

Judging from his nineteen volumes of religious literature, mainly of Herrnhuter provenance, the frugal widower Hewecke was a Lutheran Pietist. Among inventoried possessions was an "annuity policy from the Herrnhuters for 500 talers for the deceased Johann Havecke," dated 1762. Since in 1776 its appraised value was nil, it was, seemingly, a policy covering the lives of himself and his deceased wife, payable to the survivor. If so, this was the source of his 353 talers' cash holdings. Tailor Hewecke left 50 talers to his serge-maker landlord and wife. His burial cost 30 talers (far more than most village burials). Otherwise, most of his estate went to a sixteen-year-old niece and twelve-year-old nephew, children of his deceased sister, a Glövzin farm wife.[284]

Johann Koch was these children's guardian, having married onto their mother's farm after her death. Koch, to whom Hewecke bequeathed 20 talers, faced a demand from a certain master tailor

[283] Ibid., fos. 130–2.
[284] No. 718, fos. 39, 50–66, 93. Salzwedel's Bürgermeister sent Hewecke's legacy to judge Betich "in a sealed linen bag," listing coin number and type, including 266 talers in "Brandenburg, Braunschweig, and French Pistolen à 5 Reichsthaler," 3-taler ducats, "fine species talers" (worth 1.5 talers), and everyday coinage.

Mertens, husband of another of departed tailor Hewecke's sisters, for 80 talers, representing sixteen years of unpaid wages Mertens' wife claimed for her work as an unmarried woman on the family farm. Koch acknowledged this debt, but said his wards' mother died, together with her husband, "in great poverty" on their farm, leaving Koch the orphaned children's caretaker, responsible for retiring many debts, including 14 still unpaid talers. The children having inherited nothing, Koch refused Mertens more than 30 talers, plus travel and lawyer's costs of 6.5 talers. Mertens offered to take the orphans into his own household, teaching the boy tailoring "and placing the daughters in a good family's service," but finally accepted Koch's terms. Thus Hewecke's young heirs would receive at maturity payments of about 100 talers each, minus what their guardian justifiably spent on their upbringing but plus accrued interest.[285]

The differences between tailor Hewecke's circumstances and the Stavenow farmers' in whose midst he was born illuminate their positions in the larger society. Hewecke possessed silver buttons, shoe-buckles, two spoons worth 6 talers, and a pewter wineflask and teapot – all items conspicuously absent from farmers' inventories (though many possessed, as he did, a brandy flask and glasses). His clothing, linen, and bedding did not much differ in description or value from the better sort in the villages, except for a "blue and white linen caftan" and "two old wigs" (1 taler). His furniture and tools were simple and inexpensive – seemingly appurtenances of life in rented rooms. His books, though worth only 3 talers, included "Hübner's *Lexicon of Government and the Press*" and "Hübner's *Geography*," works signaling political interests found in no Stavenow households, plus two volumes of "public speeches." The founder and leader of the Herrnhuter or Moravian Brethren, Count von Zinzendorff, authored eleven of Hewecke's books, and the Pietist founder August Hermann Francke another. There were also the *Pennsylvania Speeches*. Stavenowers, by contrast, possessed only basic religious texts and songbooks, plus a few inspirational readers.[286]

Apart from considerable cultural differences evidenced by Hewecke's modest library, his economic life varied from his village relatives' in its monetized character, while their assets were largely fixed, or invested in livestock and textile goods. Considering that skilled urban workers often earned but a taler or two per week, it must have cost Hewecke considerable effort to buy the family annuity which, seemingly, had yielded his

---

[285] Ibid., fo. 62.　　[286] Ibid., fos. 51ff.

weighty cash-box. His frugality underscores the importance of savings, especially when the rural stem-family retirement system's old-age cushion was missing (though the Herrnhuter annuity shows that urban equivalents existed).

Another useful contrast with Stavenow farmers' condition emerges from a look at Hans Bahlcke's and Anna Schultzen's cottager existence. They possessed a house and garden "on the road" in Garlin village, renting plowland for 7 bushels' cereals sowings plus meadow. In 1744 Bahlcke, who until then had been the previous owner's lodger, bought it in freehold. He paid 70 talers cash, plus owing the Stavenow manor for its overlordship 2 talers annually and nine days of unpaid manual labor. Bahlcke perhaps rented other land, but lived also from wage labor. After his death, his widow sold the holding to Johann Eschike for 60 talers, who "gives her lifelong free lodging." In 1771 four of her husband's relatives protested exclusion from his estate. They said Bahlcke announced, shortly before dying, that he would leave behind 400 talers.

Anna Schultzen said "he never had 400 talers at one time, and hardly 100 talers of their goods brought in were still on hand, since the portions were no longer full." She listed her dowry as 200 talers cash, plus a good horse, seven head of cattle, sheep, and pig, tallying 127 talers. The whole dowry, excluding clothing and textiles, was worth – perhaps she was pridefully exaggerating – 330 talers. Of her husband's estate she had spent 8 talers burying him, leaving 100 talers cash plus 5 talers in small coins, 7 talers' worth of household goods, and 30 talers from the cottage's sale (the relative-plaintiffs having received the other 30 talers). She said she needed to keep what she had for her maintenance, because she could earn nothing more. Since Bahlcke died, she had spent only what was necessary – about 10 talers yearly.

After further wrangling, the plaintiffs took 25 talers, leaving widow Bahlcke to live out her days with 110 talers and free housing. As in tailor Hewecke's case, the cash component among Bahlcke's and his wife's assets was relatively large compared with typical village farmers', but cottagers lacked the security of a lifelong place on a normally self-sufficient farm. Widow Bahlcke's meager yearly money outlays also show, incidentally, that frugality and money-saving limited cash-based consumption among the common people.[287]

---

[287] No. 326, fo. 114; no. 358, fos. 52–3, 104–6. Farmers subject to Perleberg's town magistrates' jurisdiction and paying rent to them may have held assets in the 300–350 taler range, more than Stavenowers usually bequeathed. No. 715, fo. 47. More prosperous, too, were hereditary leaseholders in Manker village (Ruppin). Cf. Iida, "Hof, Vermögen, Familie."

MORTALITY AMONG STAVENOW VILLAGERS

Death is material fortune's final arbiter. A discussion of its timing and causes offers a concluding perspective on life in village households. Fuller demographic analysis must be left to other hands. These pages concentrate – as standard demographic history literature (interested in fertility and population growth) seldom does – on longevity and mortality, sorted out along sex and social-class lines. The evidence weighed here derives from unpublished statistics compiled during and after World War II by Pastor Karl Gross, who from the 1920s until his death in the mid-1980s indefatigably shepherded the Blüthen parish. For centuries this encompassed its namesake village, the seigneurial and laborers' settlement at Stavenow, the post-1750 colonists' village of Dargardt, a non-Stavenow smallholders' village (Groß Linde) and, sporadically, the halfholders' village of Mesekow. Its parish register of marriages, baptisms, and burials runs virtually unbroken from 1694. Pastor Gross abstracted valuable data from it, constructing statistical tables drawn on already in preceding pages. To them I add an analysis of mortality in the period 1765–1800 (see table 4.9).[288]

We begin by considering average age at death of those 324 Blüthen parishioners, excluding twelve stillborn babies, buried in the years 1765–1800.[289]

Among all farmers, men who lived past sixty died on average at seventy-three, and woman at seventy-two. Among retired farmers, men's average death-age fell to sixty-nine.[290] Since only two men over sixty were active farmers, it follows that retirement among farmers not stricken by earlier deaths occurred around or before sixty, and lasted 9–13 years or more. Among other post-sixty groups, male cottagers' and laborers' longevity outstripped the farmers', mainly because a quarter of this group lived to the 80–97 range, while only one ninety-year-old farmer did so. It is questionable whether the results concerning rural

---

[288] On old-regime rural German demography, apart from Harnisch's above-cited works: Schlumbohm, *Lebensläufe*; Medick, *Weben*; Ernest Benz, "Population Change and the Economy," in Ogilvie and Scribner, *Germany*, vol. II, 39–62; John Knodel, *Demographic Behavior in the Past: A Study of Fourteen German Village Populations in the Eighteenth and Nineteenth Centuries* (Cambridge, 1988). Cf. Flinn, *European Demographic System*; E. A. Wrigley and R. S. Schofield, *The Population History of England, 1541–1871* (Cambridge, MA, 1981).

[289] The number of burials closely followed the number of deaths. Stillborn babies and deceased infants received unceremonious but theologically correct burials (as the pastors noted, "in quiet"). No motive for ignoring such deaths is evident. Illegitimacy rates were low, and extra-marital births duly registered.

[290] Three among these nineteen farmers retired before age sixty.

Table 4.9   *Average age at death in Blüthen, Stavenow, Mesekow, and Groß Linde, 1765–1800*

Age group	Under 1 (in weeks) M F T	1–14 yrs (in years) M F T	15–39 yrs M F T	40–59 yrs M F T	60+ yrs M F T
All burials (n = 336)	15 16 16	3.6 3.7 3.6	31 27 29	51 50 50	73 72 72
Among these:					
a. Farmers[a] (n = 174)	14 14 14	3.6 3.3 3.5	30 27 29	50 49 50	71 73 72
b. Cottagers/laborers[b] (n = 114)	15 22 20	3.3 3.6 3.5	32 25 30	54 50 52	76 72 73
c. "Notables"[c] (n = 28)	28 7 17	3.5 3.3 3.4	-no cases-	47 44 45	75 68 70
d. Retired farmers[d] (=subset of category a) (n = 46)					69 72 71

[a] Full and halfholders and their families, including adult children in household.
[b] Smallholders (*Kleinkossäten*), cottagers (*Kätner, Büdner*), farm servants (*Knechte, Mägde*), less skilled artisans and lower-placed seigneurial workers and employees (none living primarily or exclusively as farmers).
[c] Skilled artisans, seigneurial employees in supervisory positions, educated and propertied elites.
[d] *Altenteiler, Altsitzer*, including widows identified as *Altenteilsfrauen, Altsitzerinnen.*
Source: Begräbnisregister, Pfarramt Blüthen, 1765–1800. Total cases included twenty persons of unspecified social status.

"notables," given such small numbers, are significant. Altogether, post-fifty-nine longevity was not unfavorable, but how many villagers reached this age (see table 4.10)?

Infant and childhood mortality struck cruelly, as everywhere in the eighteenth century, mowing down about 45 percent of all those born alive. Table 4.9 showed that infant death occurred on average at 3.5–5.0 months, and among children of 1–14 at 3.5 years. Mortality then fell to much less lethal levels from fifteen to fifty-nine, though about one in four died in this period, on average at age twenty-nine among those under forty and thereafter at age fifty. The result was that, among both men and women, only a quarter of the whole population survived beyond sixty into old age. It was these elders alone who lived on average to age seventy-two.

It was men's fate to die in childhood, youth, and early adulthood in much larger numbers than women. In the eighteenth century's last

Table 4.10   *Mortality by age group (in percentages), Blüthen Parish*[a]

Age group (years):	under 1	1–14	15–39	40–59	60+	Total
Male and female						
1765–1800 (*n* = 336)	20.2	25.9	12.2	15.2	26.5	100%
1694–1799 (*n* = 1,444)	17.2	26.5	13.5	15.7	27.1	100%
Male 1765–1800	22.2	30.1	13.9	15.1	18.7	100%
Female 1765–1800	18.2	21.8	10.6	15.3	34.1	100%

[a] Excluding stillborn babies, numbering thirty-two in the period 1694–1799.

third, 52 percent of males died before age fifteen, in contrast to 40 percent of young females. In young adulthood (15–39) 131 males died for every 100 females. Only in their forties and fifties did men and women die in equal proportions. After sixty, the surviving one-third of all females died, while because of earlier mortality only 19 percent of the males remained to pass away. Beyond age sixty, village women were twice as numerous as men.

Average life expectancy was low for all people born into this rural world, especially for men. Among males born into subject farmers' households it was particularly short (see table 4.11).

Average life expectancy reached 32.6 years among all persons but, because of women's lower mortality in their early decades, their lives stretched eight years longer than men's.[291] Nor did women's prospects vary greatly between social groups. But among men – destined in general for shorter lives – the forecast among farming households' sons was, at twenty-five years, ominously low, both compared with their female social counterparts' average lifespan of thirty-seven years and, even more, with the male cottager's and laborers' thirty-eight years.

We may begin to explain this state of affairs, so unfavorable to farmers' sons, by considering reported causes of death in the 1765–1800 period. Table 4.12 displays these data for the whole death cohort of 336 persons (including stillborn).

It is highly doubtful that Blüthen's pastors correctly identified diseases delivering their parishioners to heaven's gate. The uncertain fit between eighteenth-century illnesses' common names and modern medical language worsens the problem. Still, table 4.12 shows clearly enough that respiratory or pulmonary diseases and sicknesses displaying one or

[291] Similarly, Pastor Gross's eighteenth-century data yield a median death age among live-born of thirty years.

Table 4.11   *Life expectancy (excluding stillborn), Blüthen parish, 1765–1800*

	Male n Age	Female n Age	All n Age
All groups[a]	162 28.4	166 36.7	328 32.6
Farmers	93 24.8	81 37.3	174 30.6
Cottagers/laborers	49 38.1	65 35.0	114 36.3
"Notables"	13 27.1	15 38.4	28 33.2

[a] Includes eleven persons of unspecified status.

another type of pox were the great killers, as late eighteenth-century data on mortality throughout the Prussian kingdom in the year 1777 confirm.[292]

In Blüthen parish, the single most lethal malady was, seemingly, *pneumonia typhosa* and the related illness, commonly known as "hot chest fever" (*hitziges Brustfieber*) or simply "chest fever."[293] It ravaged all age groups beyond infancy, accounting for 55 percent of deaths among people over sixty. The distinction between it and tuberculosis or consumption (*Schwindsucht, Auszehrung, Dörrsucht*) was uncertain, as pastors' frequent pairing of one or the other with "chest fever" shows. Also respiratory in nature were coughs (possibly diphtheria) and "colds" ("*Steckhusten,*" "*Herbst*"). Altogether, four of ten villagers died of these afflictions. Poxes, killing one in seven villagers, were a scourge almost exclusively of children beyond the age of one year. Smallpox was commonest but measles appeared as well, often linked with diarrhea and dysentery or with "miliary disease" ("*Friesel*"), a catch-all term that may have covered scarlet fever among other illnesses.[294] These were all epidemic diseases striking in waves (1772, 1779, 1790, 1795–6), as was also true of "hot chest fever" (1772–3, 1796), though its incidence was regularly high.

The great menace to infants was "epilepsy," sometimes paired with "teething cramps." This affliction undoubtedly differed from modern epilepsy. Its equivalence with the term "misery" (*Jammer*) betrays eighteenth-century contemporaries' helplessness in face of infant pathologies. Death in childbirth was largely infants' stillbirth, with remarkably – perhaps implausibly – few adult women dying

---

[292] Behre, *Statistik*, 150.
[293] I follow the translation of common names into modern terminology in Max Höfler, *Deutsches Krankheitsnamen-Buch* (Hildesheim, 1970 [original: 1899]). Pneumonia: p. 139.
[294] Ibid., 169–70. On miliary disease: *Black's Medical Dictionary*, ed. Gordon Macpherson, 37th edn (London, 1992), 378.

Table 4.12   *Assigned cause of death among all groups, Blüthen parish, 1765–1800 (absolute numbers)*

Age group (years):	Under 1 M	F	T	1–14 M	F	T	15–39 M	F	T	40–59 M	F	T	60+ M	F	T	Total T	%
Respiratory diseases																	
(a) Tuberculosis	1	0	1	3	2	5	6	1	7	0	1	1	5	3	8	22	6.5
(b) Pneumonia/fevers	3	1	4	7	4	11	10	4	14	13	18	31	14	26	40	100	29.9
(c) Coughs/colds	4	2	6	1	5	6	0	1	1	1	0	1	1	0	1	15	3.8
(a–c) Subtotal	8	3	11	11	11	22	16	6	22	14	19	33	20	29	49	137	40.2
Pox and measles																	
(a) Pox	0	2	2	11	8	19	0	0	0	0	0	0	0	0	0	21	6.3
(b) Measles	1	0	1	7	5	12	0	1	1	0	0	0	0	0	0	14	4.4
(c) "Miliary"	0	0	0	8	3	11	0	2	2	0	1	1	0	1	1	15	4.2
(a–c) Subtotal	1	2	3	26	16	42	0	3	3	0	1	1	1	0	1	50	14.9
"Epilepsy"	17	18	35	4	2	6	0	1	1	0	0	0	0	0	0	42	12.6
Childbirth	9	7	16	0	0	0	0	2	2	0	1	1	0	0	0	19	5.7
Tumors/cancer	0	0	0	0	1	1	1	5	6	2	1	3	4	4	8	18	5.5
"Old age/weakness"	0	0	0	0	0	0	0	0	0	0	0	0	1	13	14	14	4.2
"Strokes"	2	1	3	0	0	0	2	0	2	1	1	2	1	4	5	12	3.5
Diarrhea and dysentery	0	0	0	5	1	6	1	0	1	2	0	2	1	0	1	10	3.0
Dropsy	0	0	0	0	0	0	1	1	2	2	0	2	1	3	4	8	2.5
Accidents	0	0	0	1	3	4	1	0	1	2	0	2	0	1	1	8	2.5
Gout	0	0	0	0	0	0	0	0	0	0	0	0	1	2	3	3	0.9
Other/unspecified	0	0	0	3	3	6	1	0	1	2	3	5	1	2	3	15	4.5
Total	**37**	**31**	**68**	**50**	**37**	**87**	**23**	**18**	**41**	**25**	**26**	**51**	**31**	**58**	**89**	**336**	**100.0**

from ill-fated deliveries. Among the elderly, death from tumors ("*Geschwör*," *Geschwulst*) and cancer ("*krebsartige Krankheit*") overshadowed death caused by "age and weakness." Dropsy struck some elders and a few of the younger, as also did "strokes" (*Schlagfluss, Blutsturz*), often accompanied by effusions of fluids or blood. Gout was uncommon. Three cases appear of "hot prostration fever" (*hitziges Faulfieber*), which was, possibly, typhus. Among children, fatal accidents occurred, often around boiling water or hot food, as they did also among adult men at the workplace, especially in forestry and construction.[295]

---

[295] Behre's data (*Statistik*, 150) on 117,715 deaths throughout the kingdom in 1777: from "epilepsy and teething cramps" 16 percent; smallpox 14 percent; tuberculosis or consumption 10 percent; "hot chest fever" 9 percent; old age and weakness 6 percent; "dropsy and tumors" 6 percent; "diarrhea and colics" 5 percent; convulsive coughing 4 percent; measles 4 percent; strokes 4 percent; "worms and growths" 4 percent; premature and still births 3 percent; and gout 1 percent. Deaths of women in pregnancy and childbirth accounted for 1.5 percent. There were only 358 recognized cancer cases (0.3 percent) and 91 suicides (0.08 percent).

Table 4.13   Chief assigned causes of death in households of farmers, cottagers/laborers, and "notables" (Blüthen parish, 1765–1800, by sex).

	Farmers					Cottagers/laborers					"Notables"				
	M	F	T	%	(%M)	M	F	T	%	(%M)	M	F	T	%	(%M)
Respiratory diseases															
(a) Tuberculosis	7	3	10	6	(70%)	6	3	9	9	(67%)	1	1	2	8	(50%)
(b) Pneumonia fevers	25	24	49	30	(50%)	13	24	37	37	(35%)	5	4	9	36	(55%)
(c) Coughs colds	5	5	10	6	(50%)	0	3	3	3	(-0-)	1	0	1	4	(100%)
(a–c) Subtotal	37	32	69	42	(54%)	19	30	49	49	(39%)	7	5	12	48	(58%)
Pox and measles															
(a) Pox	7	4	11	7	(64%)	2	5	7	7	(29%)	1	1	2	8	(50%)
(b) Measles	5	3	8	5	(63%)	4	1	5	5	(80%)	0	1	1	4	(-0-)
(c) Miliary	7	5	12	7	(58%)	1	0	1	1	(100)	1	1	2	8	(50%)
(a–c) Subtotal	19	12	31	19	(61%)	7	6	13	13	(54%)	2	3	5	20	(40%)
"Epilepsy"	10	10	20	12	(50%)	5	9	14	15	(36%)	2	2	4	16	(50%)
Childbirth (incl. stillborn)	6	7	13	8	(46%)	2	1	3	3	(67%)	0	0	0		
Tumors/cancer	5	5	10	6	(50%)	2	5	7	7	(29%)	0	1	1	4	(-0-)
"Old age/weakness"	1	8	9	5	(11%)	1	4	5	5	(20%)	0	0	0		
"Strokes"	3	2	5	3	(60%)	2	3	5	5	(40%)	0	3	3	12	(-0-)
Diarrhea/dysentery	7	1	8	5	(88%)	3	0	3	3	(100%)	0	0	0		

Total	Farmers					Cottagers/laborers					"Notables"				
	M	F	T	%	(%M)	M	F	T	%	(%M)	M	F	T	%	(%M)
	88	77	165	100	(53%)	41	58	99	100	(41%)	11	14	25	100	(44%)

While eighteenth-century Blüthen parish death rates peaked in the 1770s, doubtless owing to the 1770–2 subsistence crisis, they were not much lower throughout the century's second half. This suggests – though the issue is complex and, for lack of sufficient evidence, irresolvable here – that high mortality was primarily a function of endemic or epidemic illnesses rather than of periodic malnutrition, though when food grew short, mortality levels rose decisively.

By looking at principal assigned death causes, ranged by sex and social group, another step can be taken toward explaining men's greater susceptibility to early death, especially among the farming class.

Tables 4.13 and 4.14 show that, among landholding villagers, male farmers and same-sex kin died more often than females from pox diseases and the diarrhea/dysentery often accompanying them, and from tuberculosis. Among male farmers, susceptibility to respiratory diseases, poxes and diarrhea/dysentery, and "strokes" was higher both than among men in general and among male cottagers/laborers.

Table 4.14 *Sex-specific assigned cause of death among all social groups,*
Blüthen parish, 1765–1800

	M	F	T	(%M)
Respiratory diseases				
(a) Tuberculosis	14	7	21	(67%)
(b) Pneumonia and fevers	43	52	95	(45%)
(c) Coughs and colds	6	8	14	(43%)
(a–c) Subtotal	63	67	130	(48%)
Pox and measles				
(a) Pox	10	10	20	(50%)
(b) Measles	9	5	14	(64%)
(c) Miliary	9	6	15	(60%)
(a–c) Subtotal	28	21	49	(57%)
"Epilepsy"	17	21	38	(45%)
Childbirth (incl. stillborn)	8	8	16	(50%)
Tumors and cancer	7	11	18	(39%)
"Old age and weakness"	2	12	14	(14%)
"Strokes"	5	8	13	(38%)
Diarrhea and dysentery	10	1	11	(91%)
Total	**140**	**149**	**289**	**(48%)**

Probably high male mortality in farm families, concentrated in infant and childhood years, resulted from farming households' relatively large size. Earlier marriages among farmers yielded more children, while the presence on the farmsteads of hired servants, lodgers, and retirees further swelled households. This magnified the risk, compared with smaller households of cottagers/laborers and "notables," of infectious disease. The parish register often records successive multiple deaths in villagers' households. In 1772 Stavenow's innkeeper lost an eight-month and a three-year-old daughter to measles before his wife died three years later, misfortunes which seemingly forced him to surrender his post to a linen-weaver. More happily, his wife's father, a former Stavenow bailiff, had five years earlier "died at age seventy-five at the inn among his children." In thirteen August 1779 days lodger David Häcker and his wife lost children of three, seven, and one year to "measles and dysentery." Probably they were – as lodgers – inhabiting a fullholder's farmstead and exposing its co-residents to danger.

In February 1781 a fullholder died of "hot chest fever" at age sixty-one, followed two days later by his fifty-one-year-old wife. In late winter 1788 a halfholder and his wife lost a son of three weeks to "epilepsy" and convulsive coughing or diphtheria. In the next two months a son and daughter, five and two years old, succumbed to the same cough. Nine years later they lost another young child, before the husband died at sixty in 1799. In April 1794 a fullholder lost a young daughter; then in November, following a stillborn son's birth, his twenty-eight-year-old wife died of "untimely labor and dropsy." In March 1796 a forty-six-year-old fullholder's wife died of "hot chest fever," leaving "three minor children," among whom a ten-year-old boy died three weeks later. In 1797 a fullholder's young son and old mother, dead in quick succession, were buried on the same day, the boy "with his grandmother."

Seemingly, young males died oftener than young females owing to greater susceptibility to childhood epidemics. Among early-adult men (ages 15–39) higher death rates followed from liability, especially among farmers, to respiratory diseases. Probably this resulted from the pressures of the first and hardest phase of new proprietors' careers: payment of taxes and rendering of labor services, raising of their own new families, and provisioning retired elders. Overwork imposed by such burdens may have struck the men, in their fieldwork more exposed than women to harsh weather, with extra force and lowered defenses against rarely dormant infectious diseases in their vicinity. Probably, too, the farmer's life was psychologically harder than the housed and permanently contracted laborer's or craftsman's, even if, as often happened, these men were poorer than farmers.

Low social standing, and often attendant poverty, did not prevent many villagers from living into their later years. In 1764 Hans Birwieck, "a poor blind man," died at fifty-four of chest fever. "He was," the pastor wrote, "maintained by the commune as one of the housed poor [*Hausarmer*] and buried by it." In 1790 an unmarried female lodger, a cowherd's daughter, died of chest fever at sixty-four. "She was," the pastor unforgivingly remembered, "a deflowered virgin" (*Deflorata*). In 1796 the cottager Joachim Schlohe, the absconded and inebriated free mayor's descendant, expired at sixty. "He had the gout for thirty-eight years, so that he had twisted hands and feet and mostly had to sit or be carried around, and yet through much patience and trust in God he nourished himself by means of spinning."

At Stavenow manor, a lodger's (probably a retired estate laborer's) old widow died at ninety-five, a former manorial foreman at eighty, and a thresher's widow at sixty-eight. Two former workers – thresher and stable hand – died at ninety-three and ninety-seven respectively, while former estate manager Böhmer died blind and deaf in 1800 at the age of eighty-two, all three having long received "the bread of mercy" (*Gnadenbrot*) from the lordship. Also recipient of charitable rations from the manor, where probably she had worked, was Trine Besen, "85$\frac{3}{4}$ years old, unmarried lodger and mother of a child out of wedlock, born in Mesekow, and supported by Major von Kleist's grace."

The village farmer was both a relatively autonomous proprietor and the lordship's and state's subject (as well as parents' son, if they were still living on his farm). Among parish register entries from 1765 to 1800 none hint at alcoholism or other social pathologies as contributing death causes, nor does other evidence suggest that such factors aggravated men's mortality, despite fulsome drinking on ceremonial occasions and occasional brawls. Nor does many young men's removal from the community through military service explain the picture the parish data paint, since men and women are evenly balanced among the buried dead, while inclusion of victims of war and other military death would only heighten the sexes' mortality imbalance. Numerous furloughed soldiers died and were buried in their native villages.

The conclusion follows that greater exposure on farmsteads to infectious disease and farm proprietors' early career pressures largely account for higher mortality and lower life expectancy among males in farmers' families and households. Among men who weathered childhood's and young adulthood's dangers to become established proprietors, village commune members, and housefathers, there perhaps flourished a certain veterans' pride in surviving battles that mowed down many of their peers.

POPULATION GROWTH AND DEMOGRAPHIC TRANSITION
AMONG STAVENOW VILLAGERS

Blüthen parish's mortality regime blends into the variegated picture this chapter paints of villagers' material lives, pervaded both by shadow and light. Death's toll was heavy, but it remains to consider births and ask whether the broad European dynamic since the eighteenth century – the demographic transition – is evident here. This began with rising marital fertility, due to falling marriage ages. Major population growth followed, despite continuing high mortality, until medical improvements lowered infant and childhood death, inspiring parents – increasingly confident of children's survival – to limit family size. The twentieth-century outcome was a low-mortality regime of slow – or no – growth in a vastly larger

Table 4.15   *Age at marriage, Blüthen parish, 1800–1946*

	Average age		Median age		Largest marriage cohort	
	Men	Women	M	W	M	W
1800–49						
Blüthen	31	27	27.5	24.5	23	24
Stavenow	32	28	29.5	28	28	28
Gr. Linde	32	26	27.5	23	25	23
Average	31.5	27	28	25	25	25
1850–99						
Blüthen	28	26	28.5	25	26	26
Stavenow	35	28	26.5	26	26	25
Gr. Linde	31	26	28	24.5	27	23
Average	31.5	26.5	27.5	25	26.5	24.5
1900–46						
Blüthen	29	25	27.5	23	28	22
Stavenow	28	25	25	23	24	21.5
Gr. Linde	28	25	28	24.5	27	23
Average	28.5	25	26.5	23.5	26.5	22
1800–46						
Average	30.5	26	27.5	24.5	26	24

population than the eighteenth century's. Within Stavenow boundaries, demographic history awaits definitive treatment, but Pastor Gross's data open some windows.

Nineteenth- and twentieth-century patterns suggest that eighteenth-century marriage ages were relatively high (see table 4.15). Blüthen was dominated by fullholders, Groß Linde by smallholders, while Stavenow was a laborers', craftsmen's, and manorial employees' settlement. Table 4.15 shows that, while farm ownership facilitated earlier marriages, landlessness entailed later marriages. Yet, in the nineteenth century's first half, average marriage ages were quite high in all three settlements, as doubtless was true earlier. On average in the three villages, median ages, which lessen second marriages' statistical effect, were still – at twenty-eight years for men and twenty-five for women – high, although the numerically largest cohorts show that many in the farmers' villages married at age 23–5.

In the nineteenth century's second half, with mortality peaks in the 1840s, 1850s, and 1880s and the "long depression" of 1873–96 compli-cating adjustment to the market economy, marriage ages in farming vil-lages stayed high or rose, while falling slowly among the landless. Only after 1900 did marriage ages fall more rapidly, especially among the

Table 4.16 Age at death (Blüthen, Stavenow, Groß Linde, Mesekow), 1694–1946

Age (years)	0ᵃ–1	1–4	5–9	10–14	15–19	20–9	30–9	40–9	50–9	60–9	70–9	80–9	90+	Total
1694–1799: n	32 248	248	97	38	34	72	89	108	119	177	144	53	17	1,476
1694–1799: %ᵇ	2 17	17	7	3	2	5	6	7	8	12	10	4	1	
	└─36%─┘		└─10%─┘			└─13%─┘		└─15%─┘				└─27%─┘		

Median age of death (including stillborn): 25
Median age of death (excluding stillborn): 30

Age (years)	0ᵃ–1	1–4	5–9	10–14	15–19	20–9	30–9	40–9	50–9	60–9	70–9	80–9	90+	Total
1800–99: n	106 422	269	80	35	56	94	77	142	198	260	228	74	8	2,049
1800–99: %	5 21	13	4	2	3	5	4	7	10	13	11	3	0.5	
	└─39%─┘		└─6%─┘			└─12%─┘		└─17%─┘				└─27%─┘		

Median age of death (including stillborn): 26
Median age of death (excluding stillborn): 38.5

Age (years)	0ᵃ–1	1–4	5–9	10–14	15–19	20–9	30–9	40–9	50–9	60–9	70–9	80–9	90+	Total
1900–46: n	8 104	38	16	5	11	58	44	26	48	97	130	68	4	657
1900–46: %	1 16	6	2	1	2	9	7	4	7	15	20	10	0.5	
	└─23%─┘		└─3%─┘			└─18%─┘		└─11%─┘				└─45%─┘		

Median age of death (including stillborn): 53
Median age of death (excluding stillborn): 55

ᵃ Stillborn.
ᵇ Percentages here and elsewhere in this table are to the nearest whole number, and may not equal 100.

landless and farming-village women. Yet from 1800 to 1946, variation in average age rates among the three half-centuries was only ±1–2 years.

Pastor Gross also sorted marriages by wedding month. In the eighteenth century, half or more of all marriages in the farmers' villages occurred in October and November, immediately after the harvest. This custom weakened in the following centuries, but then, too, about 40 percent of Blüthen and Groß Linde marriages were celebrated post-harvest. Across the centuries, from 1694 to 1946, 71–7 percent of marriages occurred between October and April. In the more variegated Stavenow settlement, this pattern was weaker, but still predominant. Thus, before the mid-nineteenth century (including, by extension, the eighteenth century), marriage ages were high, while weddings followed harvests which, if very weak, doubtless caused postponements. This pattern limited the number of children surviving even from marriages in which mothers lived through full fertility terms. Under such conditions, rapid population growth was possible only if mortality plummeted.

In the nineteenth century, the median death age (excluding stillborn) rose – because of greater post-childhood longevity – from thirty to thirty-nine (see table 4.16). Yet infant and child mortality (to age fourteen) also climbed, from 45 to 47.4 percent. The explanation probably lies in proliferating families among the landless, and the rigors among landowning farmers of survival under post-emancipation conditions. Only after 1900 did infant and child mortality fall decisively, to 26 percent, high though that still was. The proportion of villagers who died after age sixty after 1900 jumped by two-thirds, while the median death age neared fifty-four years. Improvements in health practices and medicine bent the mortality curve permanently down, while marriage ages continued slowly to decline.

With such stable marriage and mortality patterns prevailing throughout the nineteenth century, population growth was far from turbulent (see table 4.17). Low nineteenth-century annual growth accelerated after 1895, though not greatly. As for the eighteenth century, extrapolation backwards from 1800 populations might be possible, although the Stavenow lordship's post-1648 repopulation depended on farmers' resettlement, incomplete until about 1720. Population movements subsequently reflected generational turnover among settlers, Frederick II's wars, and the 1770–2 subsistence crisis.

Table 4.17   *Population of the Stavenow villages, 1800–1939*

Village	Pop. 1800	Hearths No.	Avr. size	Pop. 1895	Increase since 1800	Yearly increase 1800–95	Pop. 1939	Increase since 1895	Yearly increase 1895–1930
Blüthen	277	39	7.1	340			413		
Dargardt	197	24	8.2	240			272		
Garlin	325	65	5.0	348			364		
Glövzin	223	49	4.6	280			258		
Karstädt	164	33	5.0	396			1,426		
Mesekow	87	19	4.6	123			122		
Premslin	295	47	6.3	317			448		
Sargleben	206	42	4.9	279			209		
Stavenow	123	19	6.5	261			66		
Total	**1,897**	**290**	**5.5**	**2,584**	**+36.2%**	**+0.38%**	**3578**	**+38.5%**	**+0.88%**

Source: Lieselott Enders, ed., *Historisches Ortslexikon für Brandenburg, I: Prignitz* (Weimar, 1962).

Excess of births over deaths in these three villages amounted, during the entire eighteenth century, to but 484 (see table 4.18), or a net addition (ignoring out-migration) of five persons yearly. Proportional variations between decades show marriages rising (at a declining rate) to the 1750s, plunging in the 1760s, seemingly because of war casualties among men, and again in the 1770s, doubtless because of harvest failures and attendant mortality. Marriages then proliferated to 1840, except during the 1810–19 war decade. Eighteenth-century births followed marriage trends with a decade's lag.

Deaths were high in the eighteenth century's first years, when murderous epidemics raged, including, for the last time, plague in some Prussian provinces, notably East Prussia, though seemingly not in Brandenburg. Death's frequency rose in the 1730s, perhaps because of generational turnover (though possibly bad harvests figured), and again in the mid-century war decades, rising still higher in the 1770s before falling to the 1840s (except for a 1800–9 rise, owing perhaps to war and generational change). Only the 1770s witnessed an absolute excess of deaths over births, though this relationship was also unfavorable in the 1740s, 1750s, and 1780s. Premarital or extramarital births were infrequent, but not rare. They numbered eighty-seven or 4.8 percent of all eighteenth-century births in these settlements – commonest in largeholders' Blüthen, rarest among Groß Linde smallholders.

Table 4.18 *Marriages, births, and deaths in Blüthen, Stavenow, and Groß Linde, 1694–1799*

	1694–9	1700–9	1710–19	1720–9	1730–9	1740–9	1750–9	1760–9	1770–9	1780–9	1790–9	1700–99: Total
Marriages												
n	24	45	40	35	49	54	58	48	35	48	45	481
%[a]		187	89	88	140	110	107	89	73	137	94	
Births												
n	79	180	149	151	159	157	158	214	163	162	182	1,754
%		227	83	101	105	99	100	135	77	98	112	
Deaths												
n	41	78	86	75	111	137	146	146	166	140	144	1,270
%		190	110	87	148	123	107	100	114	84	103	
Excess of births over deaths												
n	38	102	63	76	48	20	12	68	–3	22	38	+484
Birth/death ratio	1.9	2.3	1.7	2.0	1.4	1.1	1.1	1.5	.98	1.2	1.3	1.4
Birth/marriage ratio	3.3	4.0	3.7	4.3	3.2	2.9	2.7	4.5	4.7	3.4	4.0	3.6

[a] Percentage in relation to preceding decade.

Source: Pastor Gross's tabulations from the Blüthen parish registers. Absolute numbers include Gross's interpolations for the periods 1700–29 and 1740–9 of forty-four births and (for the 1740s) twenty-six deaths to compensate for some data loss.

Table 4.19 *Marriages, births, and deaths in Blüthen, Stavenow, and Groß Linde, 1800–1909*

	1800–9	1810–19	1820–9	1830–9	1840–49	1850–59	1860–69	1870–79	1880–89	1890–99	1900–9	Total
Marriages												
n	62	45	59	70	60	58	67	70	55	53	47	646
%[a]	137	73	131	119	86	97	116	104	79	96	89	
Births												
n	181	213	212	199	269	233	216	205	210	168	141	2,246
%	99	118	100	94	135	87	93	95	102	80	84	
Deaths												
n	152	120	113	149	154	164	143	151	158	118	91	1,513
%	105	79	94	132	103	106	87	106	105	75	77	
Excess of births over deaths												
n	29	93	99	50	115	69	73	54	52	50	50	734
Birth/death ratio	1.2	1.8	1.9	1.3	1.7	1.4	1.5	1.4	1.3	1.4	1.5	1.5
Birth/marriage ratio	2.9	4.7	3.6	2.8	4.5	4.0	3.2	2.9	3.8	3.2	3.0	3.5

[a] Percentage in relation to preceding decade.

Table 4.20   *Marriages, births, and deaths in Blüthen, Stavenow, and Groß Linde, 1910–1939*[a]

	1910–19	1920–9	1930–9	Total
Marriages				
n	33	56	46	135
%[b]	70	170	82	
Births				
n	104	132	116	352
%	74	127	88	
Deaths				
n	117	78	73	268
%	129	66	93	
Excess of births over deaths	−13	54	43	84
Birth/death ratio	0.8	1.7	1.6	1.3
Birth/marriage ratio	3.2	2.4	2.5	2.6

[a] Data for Groß Linde to 1929 only.
[b] Percentage in relation to preceding decade.

These oscillations find reflection in decennial birth/death ratios, whose eighteenth-century average was 1.4, with peaks indicating higher birth rates in the century's early decades, when village resettlement was still occurring. The birth/marriage ratio seems instructive primarily as a crude substitute for number of children per household: the century's average was 3.6 births per marriage. This was, coincidentally, the average number of children present in inventoried households in the 1721–71 years. In 1800, the number of persons per hearth averaged, as table 4.17 shows, 5.5, again suggesting the typical household harbored some three children.

Finally, to put eighteenth-century demography in perspective, tables 4.19 and 4.20 present 1800–1939 data analogous to Table 4.18's.

Between 1800 and 1909, the excess of births over deaths tallied 734, or only seven persons per year. The 1840s and 1850s witnessed few marriages and numerous deaths, doubtless effects of harvest crises and disease, a pattern replicated in the hard-pressed 1880s. Falling marriage, death, and birth numbers after 1880 reflect out-migration to cities and overseas, and early manifestations perhaps of lower twentieth-century mortality and fertility. Nineteenth-century birth/death and marriage/birth ratios are nearly identical to the previous century's.

This shows, revealingly, that the demographic regime during most of the nineteenth century represented a prolongation rather than break with the eighteenth-century system, even though premarital or extra-marital births rose to 11.2 percent of all births between 1800 and 1909. This unhappy statistic soared especially in Stavenow village, a manifestation, probably, of new behavior among post-emancipation wage laborers. Table 4.20's 1909–39 data convey World War I's impact, and otherwise display falling tendencies, especially in mortality, but also in annual growth (averaging three persons) and premarital births (10.5 percent) The next demographic upheavals derived from World War II casualties and the post-1945 arrival of refugee settlers from east of the Oder–Neisse line.

In the eighteenth century, the Stavenow demographic regime displayed structural stability, despite oscillations triggered periodically by epidemics, bad harvests, war, and generational turnover. It could perhaps be called a high-mortality equilibrium system, though not of the harshest kind. In it, among all persons surviving birth, two of every three lived past the age of four, while fewer than one in ten perished between five and fourteen. One in eight died between fifteen and thirty-nine, one in six between forty and fifty-nine, and one in four after sixty.[296] This system's survival deep into the nineteenth century, with some improvements but also with some worsening, shows that the exactions of eighteenth-century noble lordship did not alone determine the villagers' demographic condition. Slow population growth, reinforced by shrinkage of the land available for new village settlements, kept the value – if not the price – of human labor high. This circumstance figured silently in the lordship's and villages' uneasy truces and periodic clashes.

CONCLUSION

These last two chapters have painted a picture of an eighteenth-century village world at odds with persistent popular and scholarly images of "pre-modern peasant society" and "east-Elbian serfdom." Instead, we see medium- and largeholding farm families on hereditary tenures leading lives filled with arduous work and exposed to deadly biological hazards, but bereft neither of material security and assets nor

---

[296] Cf. Schlumbohm on high and low mortality regimes in pre-industrial Germany in *Lebensläufe*, ch. 3. Mortality in the Stavenow villages was lower than among the farmer/weavers of Württemberg. Medick, *Weben*, ch. 4. Cf. Arthur E. Imhof, *Die verlorenen Welten* (Munich, 1984).

psychological and existential rewards. Modern ideas of progress, free-dom, and work make it difficult to grasp the meaningful and satisfying aspects of the Stavenowers' lives. But it is worth attempting, for their condition was in many ways characteristic of the largely agrarian west-ern world of the eighteenth and nineteenth centuries. And if we are to understand the Stavenow villagers' stiff-necked contention with their lordship, which also was not untypical of east-Elbian Europe, their strengths must be known along with their weaknesses.

5

*The Kleists' good fortune: family strategies and estate
management in an eighteenth-century noble lineage*

The Brandenburg-Prussian Kleists were a prolific clan whose genealogical history fills three nineteenth-century tomes. Their name famously survives in the works of tormented and rebellious Romantic playwright Heinrich von Kleist (1777–1811). In *The Prince of Homburg* he dramatized the sensitive issue of the absolutist monarchy's claims to its noble subjects' loyalty. In the previous generation, his distant relative Ewald von Kleist, truer to his kinsmen's political devotions, composed patriotic encomiums to Frederick II's Prussia. Yet the great king's favor was fickle, and while several Stavenow Kleists figured gloriously in Prussian military annals, another suffered momentary disgrace and imprisonment, prefiguring, as family tradition reports, Major von Tellheim, hero of German *philosophe* Gottfried Ephraim Lessing's popular comedy, *Minna von Barnhelm.*

Kleist tenure at Stavenow (1719–1809) shadowed Prussian absolutism, which matured under Frederick William I and expired in 1806, following Napoleon's crushing defeat of departed Frederick II's celebrated army. Stavenow's two principal owner-managers, Andreas Joachim von Kleist (d. 1738) and son Joachim Friedrich (d. 1803), were both army officers, as were eight of Joachim Friedrich's nine brothers. The Stavenow Kleists thus perfectly embodied eighteenth-century Prussia's militarized nobility. By contrast, the Quitzows symbolized, in their robber baronage and defiance of feudal overlords, the anti-absolutist late medieval and early Renaissance nobility. The Blumenthals, wealthy courtiers both of Brandenburg-Prussia's Great Elector and Habsburg Austria, epitomized the transitional Baroque age, from crepuscular Holy Roman Empire to steely absolutism's dawn. Metaphorical too was the Kleists' supersession at Stavenow by Baron and State Minister Otto von Voss, eminent among the high bureaucratic nobility which after Frederick II's death rose to new pinnacles of state power.

This chapter highlights the interplay between noble careers (and requisite incomes) and the management of a large-estate economy such as Stavenow's. There are two angles of interpretation. One approaches the east-Elbian nobility as tradition-bound, paternalistic landlords, bereft of strategies to improve incomes except through their seigneurial economies' *extensive* growth via areal expansion, accepting existing agricultural techniques and labor organization. Joint subordination with their villagers to the absolutist fiscal-military regime left landlords little room for innovation, against which, besides, conservative temperament and exiguous education biased them.[1] Commoner is the view that many noble landlords squeezed their subjects to maximize feudal rent, including labor services, while sapping village strength through the enclosure of subject farmers' land into manor-farms. This was extensive growth through hyper-exploitation of repressively organized labor. The Hohenzollerns' post-1713 protection of village farmers for military and fiscal reasons – *"Bauernschutz"* – set limits. Yet these policies' promise presumed the ability of provincial administrators – many themselves noble estateowners – to withstand gentry self-interest and combat landlordly abuses.

Either way, the seigneurial economy remained structurally static, though villagers might suffer long-term degradation under it. Innovation allowing *intensive* growth – gains in labor's or capital's productivity – was magic workable only at royal command. On the myriad crown estates, government policy pressured bourgeois tenant-lessees to separate their land from villagers' and adopt fallow-free rotations on the resultant enclosures; to plant high-yielding fodder crops (clover, turnips, potatoes); to replace farmers' compulsory service with wage labor paid from commutation fees; and – haltingly, at century's end – to liquidate village subjection itself, so once-dependent farmers might become hereditary crown tenants, paying money rents but otherwise disposing freely of their property. Such state-launched changes' effect stirred some Junkers to emulation, though most balked at easing their villagers' lot.[2]

---

[1] Hahn, *Territorialhoheit*; Martiny, *Adelsfrage*. Cf. Kaak, *Gutsherrschaft*; Hagen, *"Sonderweg"*; Jones, *Growth Recurring*.

[2] Emphasis on Junker exploitation stamps left-liberal and Marxist literature. Emphasis on Hohenzollern protection of subject villagers derives from the statist liberalism of Stadelmann, *Preussens Könige* and Knapp, *Bauernfreiung*. Johannes Ziekursch exposed its limits in *Hundert Jahre schlesischer Agrargeschichte* (Breslau, 1927). For a measured defense of state policy, see Otto Hintze, *Die Hohenzollern*, and "Preussische Reformbestrebungen vor 1806," in O. Hintze, *Regierung und Verwaltung* (Göttingen, 1967). Cf. Koselleck, *Preussen*, 78–142. On domain lessees: Müller, *Landwirtschaft*,

Thus the self-aggrandizing power-state, acting through such middle-class agents as university-trained cameralist (mercantilist) bureaucrats and crown estate lessees, partly succeeded in dragging the noble-dominated agrarian private sector into early semi-capitalist modernity. Alongside this view these pages range another argument: that costs of family reproduction at stable or, preferably, rising levels of prosperity and status, generation after generation, pressured noble landlords to adopt productivity-raising techniques (if not pioneer them) whenever feasible. The pressure was not irresistible. How heavily it weighed against the nobility's strong, almost instinctive impulse to squeeze their subject farmers varied by individual, and with resistance encountered. At Stavenow, villagers' obduracy steered the lordship, bent on profit-elevating improvement, toward greater reliance on freely recruited wage labor. Such east-Elbian noble lordships as Stavenow were sophisticated and complex enterprises, market-oriented and open to eighteenth-century innovation.

ANDREAS JOACHIM VON KLEIST'S PATH TO PROSPERITY

At Stavenow, the Quitzows profitably pioneered sixteenth-century commercialized manorialism. When post-1648 commodity and labor markets improved, the Blumenthals undertook significant capital investments, while enforcing village rent hikes. After Colonel Kleist's 1719 arrival, energetic village "equalization," along with the sacking of two lease-holding tenants, aimed to multiply the fruits of his new property.

Royal patronage delivered Stavenow into Kleist's hands. He was one of four brothers born on a small Pomeranian estate. Orphaned at seven, he lived with a grandmother until her death. In 1694, at fifteen, he "found himself obliged," presumably by impecuniousness, to volunteer for "war service." After paging four years for Count Alexander von Dohna, he advanced to sub-officer status in Dohna's regiment. Fighting in the War of the Spanish Succession raised him in 1702 to sub-lieutenant. The next year, the crown prince, the future Frederick William I, having received Kleist at court, appointed him lieutenant in his own regiment. After many combat exploits, Kleist gained a captaincy and, in 1710, his own

and James Roth, "The East Prussian *Domänenpächter* in the Eighteenth Century: A Study of Collective Social Mobility" (Ph.D. dissertation, University of California, Berkeley, 1979). See also Gustavo Corni, *Stato assoluto e società agraria in Prussia nell'età di Frederico II* (Bologna, 1982), with a German summary, and Gustavo Corni, "Absolutistische Agrarpolitik und Agrargesellschaft in Preussen," *ZHF* 13 (1986): 285–313. Dewald, *Nobility*, highlights Junker backwardness and repression, as does Treue, *Wirtschaftsgeschichte Preussens*.

company in the crown prince's regiment. In 1715 he rose to lieutenant-colonel, and in 1724, at forty-six, attained colonel's rank with command powers in the king's bodyguard regiment. In 1736, at fifty-four, Kleist mounted the pinnacle of soldierly success, acquiring independent command over a vacated regiment, known under his leadership, by royal order, as the "young Kleist" regiment.

Unfortunately, Kleist could not bask in this achievement, dying two years later on duty with his troops in East Prussia. His regimental colleague, Captain Fabian Wilhelm Hohndorff, not a nobleman, confined his eulogy of Kleist's character to military virtues. "It is noticeable," Hohndorff concluded,

as something special about him, that throughout his life Providence kept a particularly gracious eye on him. For although whirring and clattering weapons were his youth's sport and the shield his arm's cover, the protection of the Almighty preserved him in the greatest of dangers from any wounds or injuries.

Whether Kleist was more than conventionally religious is unknown, though a nineteenth-century clergyman-genealogist extolled him as "a doughty warrior for Jesus Christ." His brother Bernd Christian (1680–1749), after retiring to the Pomeranian parental estate, chronicled the local church, piously averring, "I have since my youth experienced in special measure the goodness of my God."[3]

In 1716, Andreas Joachim von Kleist, aged thirty-eight, married sixteen-year-old Maria Elisabeth von Hacke, daughter of prosperous Brandenburg gentry. In his 1729 will, Kleist gallantly credited her with enriching him with a handsome 75,000-taler dowry. But these funds did not purchase Stavenow. His genealogist thought Frederick William I rewarded him with this fief, slipping from Quitzow fingers, as a gift. Yet Judge Hasse plainly wrote, as the 1719 sale contract confirms, that Stavenow cost Kleist 44,000 talers of his own money paid to the Blumenthals and 10,000 talers to the Quitzow lineage.

Rising in the officers' ranks and the king's favor, Kleist received valuable royal grants: an income as nominal manager of two crown estates and a prebend as deacon of Pomeranian cathedral chapter Cammin, which alone yielded annual interest on 8,000 talers. In 1714 he inherited a quarter-share of the modest Pomeranian parental estate, purchasing another fraternal portion, both of which he later sold to his brother

---

[3] Gustav Kratz, *Geschichte des Geschlechts von Kleist*, 3 vols. (Berlin, 1862–85), Th. III, Abt. III, 329–32. Stavenow Kleists' family tree: no. 166, fos. 34–5 (n.d.).

Bernd, who retired to Pomerania in 1724. Above all, on Christmas Eve 1715 Frederick William I conferred upon Kleist and influential minister of state Friedrich von Grumbkow various landed properties near Berlin of District Commissioner Cuno von Wilmersdorf, who had, seemingly, died heirless.[4] Doubtless Kleist sold his share and invested in Stavenow. In this sense the lordship was indeed a royal gift. Soon after buying out the Quitzows, Kleist sold to Philip Jänicke, a Havelberg wood wholesaler, and Jänicke's brother Peter (conveniently, a "Royal Building Commissioner") Stavenow timber worth 20,050 talers, to pay off the Blumenthals. This large-scale culling harvested 720 oak trees, worth 6–10 talers each, beech firewood (3,600 talers), and various cut oak (10,000 talers). This extensive logging's authorization was, presumably, also a royal gift.[5]

These details converge on an important point about aristocratic fortunes, for at his death Kleist owned the rich Stavenow lordship debt-free, plus a Potsdam house where, between 1718 and 1735, all but one of his fifteen surviving children were born. Moreover – and here his wife's dowry and inheritance went to work – he possessed investments (*"Capitalien"*), held in interest-bearing, land-secured loans (*"Wechsel"*), richly tallying 119,825 talers.[6] The nobility needed to accumulate such liquid capital. Annual net agricultural income varying uncertainly, two obligations in life were difficult to meet relying on current estate revenues alone. Foremost was the accumulation of marriage portions and early-career stipends payable to noble children. Second was the possession of capital for lending to friends and associates and building a network of clients and reciprocal benefactors.

Although private bankers in Berlin and elsewhere paid deposit interest, real-estate-secured loans were entered in the "Prignitz *Landbuch*" as mortgages repayable from land rents and so undefaultable, if not always easily collectable. For example, Kleist lent 10,000 talers at the customary 5 percent interest to Christian Friedrich von Ribbeck, whose (perhaps formulaic) motive was "my landed estates' improvement." The money Kleist lent, "in cash and laid out on a board," was recorded by coinage – various taler and two-thirds taler pieces. If currency values changed, he would be repaid, at either party's request with a year's advance notice, in equivalent coin.[7]

In 1722–38, his most prosperous years, Kleist engaged in many such transactions. He transferred his Pomeranian prebend at interest to a

[4] No. 711, fos. 5–8, 43.   [5] Ibid., fos. 101–2; no. 704, fo. 47.   [6] No. 716, fo. 235.
[7] No. 89, fos. 4–6.

cousin. He lent a fellow officer 1,000 talers in order, as the borrower said, "to take over my company," perhaps referring to payment into the king's famous "recruiting fund" as his promotion's price. In 1737 Kleist lent "married couple" Baron Friedrich von Bülow and Baroness *née* von Arnim 5,300 talers interest-free for one year, probably a politically strategic transaction. He lent money to other Bülows, and to Dohnas, Jagows, and Rochows – all prominent names among Brandenburg-Prussia's nobility.[8]

Kleist's wife's dowry and inheritance perhaps funded these loans, as was likely of two large 1733 transactions. Kleist lent 32,000 talers to a von Kannenberg, about whom nothing is known. Interest payments arrived punctually until the loan was called in at Frau Kleist's 1758 death. The other loan doubtless witnessed Kleist's efforts to cement ties with Prignitz notables. He lent 32,122 talers to District Commissioner von Grävenitz, guardian for minor grandchildren in place of their departed father, a debt-burdened landowner illustriously named Leopold Friedrich Gans Edler Herr zu Putlitz. This liability proved nerve-wracking to the Kleists. As for bourgeois borrowers, the Kleists entrusted 14,000 talers to Herr Wenckstern in Lenzen on the Elbe, Judge Hasse's residence. Possibly Wenckstern was a merchant. Kleist also lent tax-collector Stappenbeck 500 talers.

In his 1729 will, Colonel Kleist saluted his "heartily beloved marital partner [who] at our marriage's consummation and thereafter brought to me some 75,000 talers of her own, with which all I have and possess was purchased and acquired, and so stems from her."

After my eventual and – God grant! – blessed death, she shall, therefore, so long as she lives and remains in constant widowhood, alone possess my material estate and other wealth . . . and draw and enjoy their full usufruct. She shall not be obliged or compelled to answer to anyone, much less to render accounts, whether to our children or anyone else.

The children would remain in financial dependency on their widowed mother. Nor did Kleist wish to prescribe a guardian, whether "from the family" (his larger kin group) or "imposed by the authorities," for minor children present at his death. He was "completely confident of the upright and tender love, devotion, and care which my beloved marital partner will bestow on our children" and so wanted them to remain "under their Frau Mother's natural guardianship alone." He wished her, though, to accept "Herr Privy-Councilor von Marschall's" services

---

[8] Ibid.

as legal assistant and counselor (*Beystand*). Of Marschall, who co-signed
the will, Kleist wrote that their "upright friendship" would lead him to
accept this office's "exertions."

Should Kleist's widow remarry, "she shall be compensated once and
for all from my estate with a child's portion," leaving the rest for their
children according to the law. Here, plainly, Kleist discouraged his
wife, not yet thirty, from taking a new husband. He expressed his
"undoubted confidence" that his children would respect his will and
their mother's wishes after his death. Should they, breaking the Fourth
Commandment, prove "disobedient or refractory," or demand more
money than their mother wished to give them, their paternal inheritances would be shrunk to the legal minimum. As for last rites, Kleist
asked that "my people [*die Meinigen*] bring my corpse for permanent
burial to the Stavenow church, which I built expressly for that
purpose."[9]

In 1737, his children approaching maturity, Kleist decreed by letter
from East Prussia his five daughters' inheritances, which his widow subsequently faithfully disbursed. Each daughter would receive trousseau
and other wedding gifts worth 2,000 talers plus 10,000 talers cash
dowry. In 1750, newly married Charlotte Maria von Pannewitz *née*
Kleist acknowledged receipt of these handsome payments from her
"gracious Frau Mama," abjuring further paternal or maternal inheritance.[10] As for Kleist's ten sons, after 1739 they became eligible to
receive generous annual family allowances of 500 talers, to finance
careers as junior officers or officials. Most began drawing this income
at age 17–18, after leaving home to enter military service, though several
received smaller payments earlier, including Friedrich Conrad at age
thirteen, perhaps because he alone attended boarding school. Frau
Kleist's will declared these stipends payable from family capital investments to 6,000-taler limits. The ten sons' 60,000 talers equaled the five
daughters' combined inheritances and dowries.

Each son would also inherit a one-tenth ownership share in Stavenow,
which the brothers were, Frau Kleist stipulated, to hold "in common and
undivided." Before Frau Kleist's death, payments to her non-resident
sons changed. They would now have, until (after their mother's death)
gaining their full legacies, unlimited 500-taler yearly stipends from the
family capital fund as inheritance advances, the military officers among
them also receiving one-time 1,000-taler payments for "*Equipage.*"[11]

---

[9] No. 712, fos. 262–3.   [10] No. 715, fo. 5.   [11] No. 58, fos. 36–7.

TWO STAVENOW MISTRESSES' LAST WILLS

Frau Kleist's 1748 "testamentary ordinance and disposition" survives only in draft. "First," she piously began, "I commend my soul into my Savior's hands." She proudly acknowledged her departed husband's references to her dowry and inheritance. She named her children as sole heirs, warning against upsetting family unity with excessive monetary claims or other disobedience. Should a daughter die before marrying, her sisters would share her 12,000-taler allotment. The brothers would proceed correspondingly, except that, if surviving brothers' inheritances from family capital investments reached 30,000 talers apiece, any further vacated shares (apart from Stavenow estate ownership) would be distributed among their sisters. Should a surplus beyond children's shares remain in the capital fund, it was at their mother's death to be divided equally among all. If family capital investments ran low, daughters' claims would precede sons'. Although brothers inherited more than sisters, partly because they would need – when married – to buy land, Frau Kleist clearly favored as much as possible her daughters, whose inheritances helped all conclude advantageous marriages: one to a regimental commander, two to other army officers, one to a Hannoverian estateowner and official, and one to a well-propertied Brandenburg nobleman.[12]

Frau Kleist's will was a laconic and business-like document, as comparison shows with the 1692 testament of Baroness Louise Hedwig ("Loyse Hedewig") von Blumenthal, born Freyin von Schwerin. She was the widow of Baron Privy Councilor Caspar Christoph von Blumenthal, his lineage's second and last to possess Stavenow as an adult. Louise Hedwig's preamble declared her wish to provide for her "beloved children" and forestall controversy, "for love and harmony preserve families." She piously emphasized that her burial should be "without ceremonies and useless splendor."[13] Her debts would be minor, "since I am accustomed never to buy anything that I cannot immediately pay for." Unlike the Kleists, she instructed her sons to remember "the poor" with a 100-taler gift, while her servants and final attendants should be properly paid and rewarded. Since Stavenow alone, of her three houses, was not fully furnished, the son who took it would have a Turkish rug, yellow damask bedding, and "the large tapestries I inherited from my father." All three sons would acquire,

[12] No. 5, fos. 18–20; no. 58.   [13] No. 709, fos. 271–6.

"through God's grace and their blessed father's industrious provision, well-built and beautiful estates and houses."

Louise Hedwig wished her "beloved and obedient daughter," who "until now has treated me with respect and obedience befitting a child," to live according to her station. "Since a lady is not allowed, nor is it respectable, to seek her own fortune," the daughter would receive her mother's Berlin town-house, with furnishings Louise Hedwig inherited from her father. This provision, she admitted, overrode instructions of her departed "marital master" (*Eheherr*) that the house be bequeathed to a son. But since she and her husband never reached final agreement, while she herself inherited the house from a certain count and kept it up, it was, she argued, part of her dowry or "goods brought in" of which she was entitled to dispose.

The daughter would also receive all cash in her mother's possession at death, and all promissory notes payable specifically to Louise Hedwig alone. She would have various silverware, including gifts her mother received from godparents. "And because I have during my lifetime, out of motherly affection and as occasion warranted, gradually given her my jewelry," so her daughter should keep it, though the remaining estate – silver, capital, and other goods – was to be divided equally. To her condemnation of any heir who should attack or dispute her will she added an invocation of "misfortune and God's punishment," so the offender would learn that "on God's grace alone everything depends." If her daughter died unmarried, the Berlin residence should go to the brother who "loved her most fraternally," so that it would "not fall into outside hands or be sold beyond the family."

Louise Hedwig lived long beyond this will's date. Illness may have occasioned its composition, but it displays pride in her own inheritance, while witnessing disagreement between herself and her departed husband over its distribution after her death. Possibly Louise Hedwig believed a mother's property should accrue largely to her daughters. In any case, the transition from pious Baroque to cooler Enlightenment sensibilities is discernible in the Blumenthal and Kleist testaments.

PRIVATE MONEYLENDING'S PERILS

Colonel and Frau Kleist's marriage was rich in children: ten sons and five daughters lived into adulthood, and an eleventh son died in youth. Such numerous progeny challenged parental resources, especially liquid capital to fund living allowances and marriage portions.

Unsurprisingly, Kleist tempers flared when debtors' payments wavered. Two instances are instructive, while illuminating other important issues. In 1725 Kleist lent 500 talers at 5 percent interest to Perleberg tax-collector Wilhelm Stappenbeck and his wife Melosina. Soon Stappenbeck fell into arrears, whereupon the impatient colonel withdrew 500 talers in cash from "my churches in Mescho, Blüthen, and Gross Linde, also Premslin, Glövzin, and Karstedt," giving them in return the Stappenbeck debt. Hasse drafted this transaction, which the colonel signed as "Jochim von Kleist." He recovered his capital, but at his villagers' expense, who might otherwise have borrowed the church funds he raided. By 1729 Stappenbeck was dead. Forced into bankruptcy, his widow repaid the 500 talers from the sale of her house for 450 talers (though insured for 971 talers), and the adjoining (urban) farmland and outbuilding for 440 talers. Her first-marriage son claimed 234 talers in unpaid maternal inheritance, but he settled for 100 talers cash and unsold household inventory.[14]

By 1735 widow Stappenbeck was also dead, leaving 107 talers in unpaid interest on Kleist's 1725 loan. From Potsdam Kleist wrote Hasse: "Pay attention seriously that this is properly paid. I will gladly, so far as I can, help the poor children," by which he meant the Stappenbeck orphans, now under guardianship in an Altmark town. "But I don't want to lose the money I lent in cash. I have children enough of my own." Two years later, Kleist wrote the orphans' guardians: "While I have true compassion for the poor children, you will understand that I cannot impose on the church loss of its capital or revenues." Offering his "services" to the guardians "or their charges," he demanded (and appears to have soon gotten) payment. Here a wealthy noble landlord hounded misfortune-stricken burghers and their orphaned children for debts which, by Kleist's standards, were minor, though not insignificant.[15]

The second case arose from Kleist's 1733 loan of 33,122 talers to District Commissioner Hans von Grävenitz, guardian of his Putlitz family grandchildren. In 1737 Susanna Sidonia, Baroness von Putlitz *née* Wöldecken wrote Judge Hasse, complaining that Grävenitz was two years delinquent in paying her yearly widow's stipend (*Alimentation*) from her deceased husband's estate. Without this money she could "no longer manage." She wanted a court order forcing Grävenitz to comply, though without intent to injure the Kleists.[16] At *Trinitatis* 1737 (the end of June) Grävenitz failed to pay the colonel's 1,656 talers annual interest. Kleist complained to the Berlin authorities, spurring Grävenitz

[14] No. 712, fos. 117–20, 264. [15] No. 713, fo. 98; no. 715, fo. 73. [16] No. 597, fos. 91–2.

to a self-exculpatory letter blaming the widow: she imperiously demanded her annual 300 talers take precedence before other rightful claims, including Kleist's and Grävenitz's grandchildren's (seemingly her stepchildren). This unjust arrangement, Grävenitz charged, prevented his paying Kleist from the Putlitz heirs' principal income source: annual rent their Nettelbeck estate leaseholder paid Grävenitz.

Kleist's view was that the non-payment problem arose from conflict dividing Grävenitz from Thomas Heinrich von den Knesebeck, the Nettelbeck tenant (and bearer of a respected noble name). This, wrote Grävenitz, was putting it "far too mildly, [for] it appears that [Kleist] is acting in league with the Nettelbeck tenant to snatch the estate out of the poor minors' hands." But "to sell [Knesebeck] the estate, as has sometimes been asked of me, is beyond my power." Grävenitz proposed instead to pay the Putlitz debts by selling Nettelbeck timber. There were 9–10,000 trees left, "if only the lessee hasn't ruined them."[17] Soon Kleist wrote Hasse expressing gratification that Knesebeck had paid his arrears to Grävenitz, but wondering why Grävenitz had not delivered Kleist's share. He urged Hasse to turn the screws. "I am indifferent to whether the estate is transferred to me, the whole capital is returned, or interest is paid as before," provided payments were prompt. Perhaps Kleist indeed had designs on Nettelbeck. But he insisted Hasse find a solution, "especially since it was on Your Well-Born's advice that I put out this capital." Here Hasse was directing Kleist's local Stavenow affairs – and also serving as his scapegoat.[18]

Following Kleist's 1739 death, tenant-farmer Knesebeck wrote to Frau Kleist and Hasse complaining that the Kleists' Berlin lawyer Wackenroder had filed charges for interest arrears, not against Grävenitz, but against himself. Knesebeck charged Grävenitz with unlawfully selling Nettelbeck wood and withholding widow Putlitz's *Alimentation*. Moreover, "two years ago [Grävenitz] had me buy for him two oxen in Lübeck. He gobbled them up, and I haven't received a schilling since."[19] Grävenitz fired back a list of Knesebeck's sins and omissions which offers a good picture both of conflicts between noble landlords and tenant-farmers and prevailing estate agriculture strategies. Knesebeck was adopting the newly fashionable fallow-free rotational system. "He makes great enclosures to his own intended profit, and uses for fencing many hundreds of cartloads of bush and some thousands of oak and beech posts." If Knesebeck wanted enclosures,

---

[17] No. 713, fos. 151–2.   [18] No. 597, fos. 63–4.   [19] Ibid., fos. 53–5.

he should pay their cost himself, rather than plundering Nettelbeck timber. Knesebeck also diverted forester's and wood bailiff's services to his own purposes, leaving woods exposed to villagers' pilferage, which had already claimed "100 and more oak trees."[20]

Grävenitz charged Knesebeck with bringing Mecklenburg grain for sale into Brandenburg, though this was officially prohibited, and that he "wants to force the villagers to cart the grain to Perleberg," which Grävenitz as District Commissioner "must inhibit." For this he had reported Knesebeck to the Berlin authorities. Knesebeck injured Grävenitz's honor, publicly proclaiming he cheated his minor wards by pocketing minor feudal rents and paying his own expenses from their incomes. And while Knesebeck protested wood sales, Grävenitz wrote that his guardian's contract permitted them "and the tenant-farmer must suffer them." Concerning the compulsory service of subject farmers' offspring, about which Stavenow documents say almost nothing, Grävenitz claimed Knesebeck "makes bold to use force to compel the subjects' children to work for him as servants, whether their parents can spare them or not." Instead of such transgressions, "he should hire his own servants and treat them so that he can get them of their own free will." Knesebeck's lease did not allow compulsory recruitment, "so he must abandon this claim, for I will not let the subjects be ruined on his account." Here a District Commissioner recognized tenant-farmers' abuse of compulsory servants as a danger to be avoided in negotiating leases.

Knesebeck also tormented his subjects, Grävenitz charged, with illegal grazing. Having converted much manorial arable to enclosures where only cattle grazed, he loosed his sheep on remaining open-field land shared with villagers. "He doesn't even spare the people until the sheaves are out of the fields, but grazes his sheep among the sheaves, daily provoking the villagers and causing me the greatest annoyance." If this did not stop, "I need only give the villagers the signal and they will quickly drive the [manor's] shepherds from their fields, and then the lessee will see what he can get away with and whether he can make enclosures and not let village shepherds graze on his fields, as previously had to be allowed." Knesebeck was claiming Grävenitz abused his authority by compelling Nettelbeck villagers to act as his servants, but Grävenitz had proven this false with four witnesses. If Knesebeck did not yield, Grävenitz would reveal "what spirit rules this man." He summoned Knesebeck's annual accounts, offering to publicize the feudal rents he himself rightfully collected from Putlitz

[20] No. 713, fos. 233–6.

villagers. Knesebeck would have to treat Grävenitz, "an honorable man," with "more respect or the row will start up again afresh."

These charges and counter-charges display the zeal with which landlords (Grävenitz) and noble entrepreneurs (Knesebeck) competed for the profits flowing from villagers' labor and rents. They show too that technological innovation might well proceed at villagers' cost. Both men denied overstepping their authority in demanding villagers' compulsory service. Seemingly they wished to avoid the appearance, in Berlin's and perhaps also the local gentry's eyes, of abusive landlordism.

Knesebeck defended himself in a plaintive 1739 letter taking Hasse to task "for not keeping a better eye on [Grävenitz] in Herr Colonel's interests, and for not bravely going after Grävenitz as soon as I reported all the confusion to you." Though Knesebeck had fallen into arrears, he faulted widow Putlitz for self-absorption and Grävenitz for not finding other sources from which to pay Kleist's interest, "for one can borrow money everywhere at 4 percent."

How the man [Grävenitz] harasses me, and in so doing injures his poor charges, no one can believe . . . He even forbids the subject farmers, in defiance of Royal Wage Statutes, to deliver their children to me as servants . . .

God will help me to finally have done with this wicked man, but my family's sighs and tears, wrung from them by the heavy rent I pay, will rest, in God's own words, on his soul like glowing coals. I commend myself to you and remain with much consideration, etc. etc. your most faithful servant.[21]

Frau Kleist received a similar letter. She sent it to Hasse with a note, dated at "Staffno," in which she pointed out "what a pile of rubbish Herr von Knesebeck has once again sent, but no money." She was especially exercised by Knesebeck's arrears from the previous year.

Please don't forget about the 220 talers in interest. I can assure you I need them, and owing to my present many expenses have suffered considerable injury because they have been so long held up . . . [The money] is being demanded of me, and I'm suffering too great a loss. I can tell you that I've already once had to borrow money because of it and [if it isn't soon paid] I'll have to do so again . . . And if every year there's going to be such a row about interest payments, I'd rather not lend any money . . . I am very worried about it, and see nothing in it but annoyance. But, for the rest, I remain, with a compliment to the Frau Bürgermeister etc. your devoted servant.[22]

In September 1739 Berlin's Chamber Court ordered the Prignitz sheriff to proceed to execution against Knesebeck as Frau Kleist had

---

[21] Ibid., fos. 178–9. [22] Ibid., fos. 188–9.

requested, to compel payment of 1,276 talers' outstanding interest. On Christmas Eve, Knesebeck was still defiant, demanding his complaints' satisfaction. Eventually Knesebeck delivered the annual leasehold fee (2,200 talers) and Frau Kleist received her money. But in 1741 she again sought government enforcement against Knesebeck and Grävenitz, strategically invoking her need to support "my three children serving in the army."[23] Probably these years' widespread bad harvests compounded Knesebeck's difficulties, for Frau Kleist drew Putlitz interest with no apparent further strife until her death. The conflicts of 1737–41 show that, rich though they were, the Kleists could fall into undignified money squabbles, sometimes for lack of ready cash.

FRAU VON KLEIST'S STAVENOW REGIME

Under Frau Kleist's administration (1738–58) two salaried administrators, Christoff Erhardt and Martin Böhmer, successively managed Stavenow. In 1754 she agreed with her ten sons to entrust managerial supervision to the well-educated fifth eldest, Friedrich Conrad, sole civil official among them. She ruled her household, drawing very large natural provisions from the domanial economy and receiving its net profits in cash. She engaged herself with her children's educations, marriages, and careers. She stewarded family investments, accepted money on deposit from various Stavenowers, and lent small sums to them.

The indefatigable Judge Hasse drew up the 1758 inventory. Frau Kleist died suddenly, he recorded, of "dysentery and a stroke" and "during these dangerous times" – with Brandenburg exposed during the Seven Years War to enemy occupation – he inventoried her valuables two days later and then the larger household.[24] To Mademoiselle Elisabeth Charreton, Frau Kleist's longstanding companion, familial accountant, and domestic chief of staff (of likely Huguenot refugee descent), Hasse entrusted 100 talers, though with other extraordinary expenses she eventually disbursed a sizable 378 talers for the burial and wake.[25]

In ready cash, Hasse found 1,441 talers, including 300 talers in high-value gold coins ("Friddors," "Louisdors"), but also 625 talers in 4-groschen Brandenburg, Mecklenburg, and Lüneberg coins and 130

---

[23] No. 714, fos. 36–9; no. 713, fos. 153, 193.
[24] No. 10, fos. 1–44. Cf. Lieselott Enders, "Die Vermögensverhältnisse des Prignitzer Adels im 18. Jahrhundert." *JbfbLG* 47 (1996): 76–93.
[25] No. 716, fo. 280. Frau Kleist's medicine (4.5 talers): no. 53, fo. 5.

talers in 1-groschen and 2-groschen coins of similar provenance. Altogether she held 6,250 small-denomination coins. There was also a chest containing, "in bad [devalued wartime] money" the equivalent of 820 good talers paid Frau Kleist on obligatory deposit by the Premslin miller. Here too were 15 talers in church-fund interest on money the Kleists themselves had borrowed. As for gold, pride of place among numerous display objects went to a medallion exhibiting the seventeenth-century Polish king Sigismund III Vasa, weighing "91 ducats at 2.18.-talers per ducat," worth 250 talers. The Kleists' thoughts contemplating this piece would be interesting to know. A smaller medallion of Great Elector Frederick William was, like a weighty "Portuguese" gold Hamburg coin, worth 26 talers. Altogether, cash, good and bad, plus gold tallied 2,841 talers.

Among Frau Kleist's papers were promissory notes signed by various debtors, including elder sons, and an interest-bearing note for 8,000 talers deposited with the corporate nobility's credit agency, the Kurmärkische Landschaft. There were receipts for 1,200 talers, show-ing the Kleists had regularly paid Stavenow's modest annual land tax of 30 talers, and a 400-taler bond, doubtless war-occasioned, promising 5 percent interest. Frau Kleist had lent a neighbor, Frau Generalin von Winterfeldt, 2,000 talers at 5 percent. Interest on various personal loans was in arrears. Receipts from her four eldest daughters and their hus-bands showed all dowries had been fully paid. Here was her husband's 1729 will, and correspondence with her Berlin banker Christian Friedrich Schultze and the powerful Berlin arms manufacturers, omnibus entrepreneurs, and financiers Splittgerber und Daum. All these items fell under the rubric, "Credit Affairs of the Family [*Famille*]."[26]

Hasse reckoned all obligations owed Frau Kleist, including advances beyond her sons' 6,000-taler cash inheritances, at 91,890 talers. Her debts, with no interest arrears, totaled 12,692 talers. She had accepted deposits bearing 5 percent interest from various employees and acquaintances. She held 800 talers from Mlle Charreton, 200 talers from Premslin manor-farm leaseholder widow Bergholtz, and 500 talers from Stavenow innkeeper Haussmann. The Premslin miller's orphaned children's guardians deposited 950 talers with Frau Kleist, while a married manorial laborer entrusted her with 100 talers. Her carriage-driver and his assistant both gave her their savings (130 talers

---

[26] Schultze, Conrad Kleist's trusted associate, was, apart from his banking and accounting activi-ties, a tax-receiver for the Kurmärkische Landschaft. No. 53; no. 716, fo. 269.

and 20 talers). So too had her fisherman deposited 70 talers, in 4- and 2-groschen coins, along with a brother's 20 talers. A Perleberg postmaster placed 500 talers with her and a Lenzen apothecary 700 talers. To Blüthen pastor Bertram and his spinster sister Frau Kleist paid interest on 1,000 talers. She held money from farther afield, such as 1,500 talers received from Hoffräulein von Bredow and Berliner Herr Frantz's 1,050 talers. No subject farmers or humble villagers entrusted her with savings. In church funds she held 1,530 talers, doubtless believing they originated with Stavenow's possessors. The pastors and aldermen made loans from church-fund interest, rather than capital. Frau Kleist does not appear to have determined their recipients, nor did she transact such business. Evident, again, is distance between lordship and villagers.[27]

Hasse met with Stavenow servants and employees to settle their pay, following Frau Kleist's "wage-books." Among household servants, whose income was not high compared to what skilled village laborers could earn, cook Braun earned 5 talers monthly, and had accumulated 186 talers' back pay. Though Frau Kleist perhaps paid interest on his unpaid wages, this is undocumented. Chief house servant Friedrich Henning at Michaelmas (29 September) received yearly pay of 21 talers and shoes. The principal female servant, "housekeeper [*Haushälterin*] Freudenbergen," collected 18 talers in February, while nine other housemaids claimed their yearly pay – from 2 to 16 talers – at Michaelmas. Her two drivers would pocket 47 talers between them. Hasse did not forget his own yearly salary of 40 talers, payable on Trinity Sunday (end of June).

If Frau Kleist possessed rich jewelry, she had dispossessed herself of it. Hasse found a "small gold ring with a health-stone," which Frau Kleist willed to Mlle Charreton. There was much silverware, inventoried by weight. Among brasswares were coffee and tea-making equipment – the first references at Stavenow to these now fashionable drinks. Porcelain too was modish, and the household exhibited eighty-four pieces, along with nine mirrors. At managerial headquarters, where permanently employed unmarried laborers took their meals, Hasse found forty-four earthenware bowls and sixteen serving pots, along with nine stoneware butter dishes.

The manor-hall counted fifty beds, not including manorial laborers'. The servants' room housed six fully equipped beds. Hasse counted

---

[27] The churches also placed 300 talers with the Brandenburg Cathedral Chapter and 120 talers with a Grabow burgher. On Frau Kleist's transactions: no. 716, fos. 207–8, 232–3, 239, 283, 285, 288. In 1753, she held 1,200 talers from lessee Bergholtz and 1,000 talers from Stavenow manager Erhardt.

forty-two tables, twenty-seven chairs, and thirty-three wooden closets. The kitchen displayed 24 pounds of coffee, 3 pounds of tea, plus a sugar-loaf ("hat"). Other food included smoked bacon, "a piece of smoked Hamburg meat," "a sausage with some butter," buckwheat groats, flour (including wheat), baked goods and "some bread for lordship and servants," dried and fresh fruits, ample Rhine wine plus some Mosel and French wine (*"Frantzwein"*), six bottles of "spoiled Hungarian wine," and three bottles of "Provence oil," probably olive. At managerial headquarters were a half-barrel of beer and 1,386 quarts of brandy.

The library shelved fourteen books, ten religious. These included an octavo Halle Bible (1719), a prayer and songbook (1735), a deluxe edition of Kreutzberg's *Reflections on Each Day in the Year*, Stohchen's *Edifying Sermons*, Noll's *The Saints' Joy in Jehovah*, Tilemann's *16 Steps to Jesus Christ's Throne of Grace*, Rambach's *Reflections on Jesus Christ's Sufferings*, and the anonymous *Joyous Heavenly Feast of God's Children*. Among the authors none appear to signal a Pietistic orientation. There were two home medicine handbooks, a 1758 calendar, and funeral orations. More revealing were the pictures Hasse inventoried. There were "seventeen family portraits," quite likely of the fifteen children and parents, and a painting of "the Stavenow castle and estate," plus maps of the lordship. Portraits hung of Brandenburg-Prussian rulers and wives, beginning with Great Elector Frederick William and ending with "the presently ruling Royal Majesty of Prussia," Frederick II, whom Hasse, perhaps oddly, did not specifically name. Present also were three small round portraits of the "royal family," referring also, presumably, to Frederick II and his (unhappy) queen. These pictures focused the Kleists' secular loyalties: their own nuclear family, landed estate, and Prussian monarchy.

Hasse inventoried domanial livestock and equipment. Four Stavenow carriage horses pulled a four-seater, a three-seater, a "large hunting sled," and a calèche or lightweight carriage with metal-bound wheels. The fowl included a swan, 135 turkeys, 135 hens, 44 ducks and 22 ducklings. Hasse noted, seemingly reproachfully, that "the top farmhand ate the other ducklings." The dovecote was "poor." Of hunting gear there were fox and otter traps, fishing nets and weirs. Apart from the huntsman's own dogs, there were three whippets, two bird dogs, and a dachshund. In the newly built orangerie sat twenty-two lemon, orange, grapefruit, fig, laurel and myrtle trees, all tubbed. The vegetable garden counted thirteen glass cold frames and eleven glass cloches.

The 1758 inventory pictures a gentry matriarch living in provincial comfort rather than aristocratic splendor. Eighteenth-century modernity touched the household's material culture but not, seemingly, its intellectual life. Yet Frau Kleist had presided over the successful marriages of her daughters and several sons, all of whom were dispersed across the kingdom, some in highly prestigious positions. The Stavenow lordship typifies one matrix from which the successful Prussian nobility sprang. Doubtless character traits acquired in such a household, under such considerable figures' tutelage as Colonel and Frau Kleist, were indispensable to their children's achievements. But these fifteen noble careers could only be launched with money, flowing copiously from commercialized manorialism into interest-bearing capital funds or directly into seigneurial pockets.

THE KLEIST DAUGHTERS' MARRIAGES AND SONS' CAREERS

Colonel Kleist fixed his children's inheritances before his eldest daughter Sophia Dorothea's 1737 marriage. She had been named, diplomatically, after the reigning Prussian queen, the colonel's beneficent royal patron's consort. At nineteen, she married Major-General Samuel von Polenz, aged thirty-seven and a Berlin regimental commander. Her father evidently relished the match, for beyond his daughter's dowry he gave the couple his Potsdam house. He could afford this gesture, since he was obliged now to reside with his regiment in East Prussia. His wife removed herself, seemingly, to Stavenow, where he spent his leaves. She traveled to East Prussia, where she bore their last child in 1736. By 1749 four of their five daughters had found husbands, the elder preceding the younger. The fifth and youngest daughter's wedding occurred only in postwar 1763. The 1749 marriage contract alone survives, but seems typical. It displays Prussian noblewomen's impressive property rights in marriage and widowhood.

In August 1749 Charlotte Marie von Kleist, aged twenty, was engaged at her bridegroom's Tranitz home property to Anton von Pannewitz, "hereditary lord of eight estates" southeast of Berlin. There they lived without children until Pannewitz's death in 1782, his widow dying in 1805, leaving a nephew as heir. The 1749 contract, which the Pannewitzes signed at Tranitz and the Kleists on the wedding eve at Stavenow, proclaimed that after the impending October marriage the couple "will, in constant love and loyalty, treat one another as befits persons of the married estate and as will inspire in the gracious Frau mothers" – the wedding partners' fathers were dead – "happiness and satisfaction."[28] As for money, "the Fräulein bride will bring to her bridegroom, immediately at his request, a capital of 10,000 talers, which is, in conformity with both parents' disposition, her paternal and maternal inheritance. This sum the Herr bridegroom, who will properly acknowledge receipt, will employ to his estates' benefit." The bride also promised "jewels, silver, clothing, linen, bedding and other housewares, of which a specification will be composed," worth 2,000 talers, on which Pannewitz would receive 5 percent interest until paid in full.

Pannewitz designated 4,000 talers of his fiancée's gift "as the dowry" (*Ehegeld*), leaving 6,000 talers as a residuum, discussed further below. He promised to give Charlotte Marie "as counter-bequest" 4,000 talers of his own, a gift on the morning after the wedding (*Morgengabe*) of 800 talers, and – intriguingly but obscurely – 1,000 talers "in consideration of female rights" (or "privileges"). If he died before his "much beloved" wife, she would receive not only "mourning befitting her station but also the best carriage, together with the horse-team used to draw it." She would reside at her husband's Tranitz or Catlow estates – she died at Tranitz – or receive 100 talers' annual housing allowance. At her chosen estate, she would have house and garden, greenhouse, stalls for her horses and her guests' mounts, and necessary firewood. She would also receive, "instead of customary payments *in natura*, which lead to many conflicts, 200 talers' yearly alimentation money." Moreover, "by here-prevalent law on noble property, she will [if widowed] be paid 10 percent interest on the bridegroom's 4,000-taler counter-bequest, and 5 percent interest on the 6,000-taler residuum as well as on the 800 talers and 1,000 talers given her as morning-gift and in consideration of female privileges." Thus, apart from housing and alimentation stipend, she would receive 790 talers yearly widow's annuity.

Should she die or remarry, these provisions would lapse, and her husband's 4,000-taler "counter-bequest" would revert to his heirs. As a widow, she would be entitled to receive in cash – on six months' notice – her 10,000-taler inheritance and her husband's 1,800-taler marriage gifts and "what she otherwise brought into the marriage," or draw interest on these sums. If she died without remarrying, these same assets would fall to her own heirs. "Moreover, whatever the Fräulein

[28] No. 15, fos. 1–4.

bride acquires during marriage through gift or inheritance or otherwise will remain in her free disposition."[29]

If Charlotte Marie, having borne children, predeceased her husband, he could claim half the 4,000 talers of her inheritance designated as dowry, the rest of her wealth brought into the marriage being reserved for their children as maternal inheritance. In children's absence he would acquire the entire dowry, while her other assets would fall to her Kleist lineage heirs. As guarantee of these arrangements' fulfillment, Pannewitz pledged "all his wealth," in the form of a mortgage on his property granting his widow or her heirs, in case of default, "right of retention" of five of his estates. To the entire contract the bridegroom assented with sealed signature, alongside co-signatures of his widowed mother *née* Arnim, a male relative who added that he "consents to this marriage," two noble witnesses and a notary. On the Kleists' side, the bride's signature was preceded her mother's, "M. E. widow von Kleist born von Hacke," and followed by her four eldest brothers'. In 1750 Charlotte Marie signed a declaration that she and "my beloved husband" (*mein geliebter Gemahl*) had received from "gracious Frau Mama" the 10,000 talers' "marriage and settlement money" and the 2,000 talers for trousseau and "goods brought in," to which Pannewitz and his witnesses attested.[30]

Compared with nineteenth-century upper-class women, the Kleist sisters' marital property rights, particularly as heiresses and widows, were very strong.[31] But even among the nobility life was precarious, with death interrupting marriages and raining down inheritances. A 1760 letter, written in French to Conrad Kleist by an unidentified married sister illustrates this point. She and her husband were preparing to leave on a trip.

That very night My Husband succumbed to such a violent colic that we were obliged to summon the doctor at midnight. Heavy vomiting and diarrhea continued for five days. Sleepless nights accompanied by misery. It was the most dangerous kind of colic, one calls it Colique Colora. I assure you [*vous*] that My Husband was very close to death. It was thanks to the Lord's grace that he escaped.[32]

[29] Ibid., fo. 3. Seemingly the widow could request payment in cash, upon her husband's death, of his "counter–bequest" of 4,000 talers, though a previous clause required that it revert to his heirs after her death. It follows that she was entitled to interest earned on this sum, but not to dissipate the capital itself.

[30] No. 715, fo. 37.

[31] Frevert, *Women*, pt II; Wunder, "*Er ist die Sonn*," ch. XI and passim.

[32] No. 717, fo. 47. A quite early reference to cholera. Cf. Richard Evans, *Death in Hamburg. Society and Politics in the Cholera Years, 1830–1910* (London, 1987), 226ff.

Moreover, as the 1749 contract's reference to feudal law shows, property still figured partly as familial appurtenance. A marriage portion ought not, should a bride die childless, be entirely lost to her lineage. Nor, should her husband die prematurely, ought a bride to lose her inheritance, for she would need assets for a second marriage. Similarly, the husband's "counter-bequest" to his wife, though not other gifts, was for her – if no children were present – a usufructuary asset during her lifetime rather than absolute property, since on her death it reverted to his heirs. The contract embodies but one instance of a larger, lineage-oriented conception of feudal property within a noble class with strongly egalitarian inheritance practices.[33]

About Charlotte Marie's husband nothing is known except that he belonged to the Order of the Knights of St. John. The Hohenzollern, who founded the order, rewarded its noble members' civil or military virtues with lifetime prebends from incomes of church land secularized in the Protestant Reformation. Certainly Charlotte Marie's marriage gained her wealth, station, stability, and longevity. About the other three Kleist daughters still less is known. Friedericke Wilhelmine – female version of her father's royal patron's name – married Captain Hans Christoph von Podewils, an East Prussian gentry scion, living eighty-five years. Luise Henriette Margarethe wed a Hanoverian estateowning country official, who died nineteen years after their marriage. Carolina Sophia, the youngest, married a cavalry captain, dying at sixty-four.

Military service, and Frederick II's wars, delayed the Kleists' sons' marriages. The eldest, Friedrich Wilhelm (also bearing the kingly name), took a wife in 1754, at age thirty-seven. His partner was an army officer's divorced wife and the daughter of a collateral Kleist lineage. She brought 10,000 talers, doubtless her first-marriage dowry-inheritance, recovered upon divorce. They agreed, should her new husband predecease her, she would receive 500 talers yearly interest on this capital, which at her death would fall to her sister and nieces. Friedrich Wilhelm, army-discharged in 1759, lived eighty years, dying in 1797 in west German Minden, where he was the St. John's Knights' local *Commendator.* Several other Kleist sons will figure in later pages. Here we note that Ludwig Leopold (1723–90) entered the army, like his father, as a teenage page. At seventeen he was sub-lieutenant, rising to lieutenant-colonel before his 1766 discharge at age forty-three. He fought in six or more of Frederick II's battles and was wounded twice. At the battle of

[33] Martiny, *Adelsfrage*, passim.

Leuthen he was company commander in an infantry regiment, which "during the whole action was never out of enemy fire and was practically mowed down. In this battle a bullet was shot through [his] mouth."[34] In 1764 he gained a St. John's prebend. With his Stavenow inheritance he bought an estate near Cottbus and his sister Sophie Charlotte, where he later died. In 1762 he entered into a childless union with Saxon Imperial Countess Antoinette Friederike von Schönburg-Glaucha.

Among the Kleist brothers, one attained living celebrity and historical fame. This was shortlived Major-General Friedrich Wilhelm Gottfried Arnd (1724–67) who, as commander of the Green Hussars Regiment, was known, among the myriad Kleist officers, as "Green Kleist." After studying at Halle University, he entered the army at twenty. In 1756 Frederick II elevated him to cavalry major. For intrepidity in the 1757 Gotha "battle of hussars" Kleist won the coveted decoration *pour le mérite*. In 1760 he gained command of twenty-two cavalry squadrons, forming his "Freikorps," which repeatedly distinguished itself in the Seven Years War, winning the king's and his royal brother Prince Henry's accolades. Kleist won a reputation for "humanitarianism" in victory and was popular among his troops. Small and lively, a subordinate described him as "a very agreeable man, who issued orders with a light and fine touch."

"Green Kleist" died on postwar duty in Silesia, where in 1765 he bought four estates. He succumbed to smallpox "owing," as regimental history reported, "to sudden shock at the sight of the disfigured corpse of one of his innkeeper's children who died of this disease." When Kleist's adjutant, following custom, gave Frederick II the departed general's parade horse, "the king was so visibly moved that, turning to the window to conceal his grief, he could say nothing but: 'Keep it! keep it!'" Kleist figures in the frieze on Frederick's statue standing before Berlin's Humboldt University. The unmarried soldier bequeathed his fortune to his youngest brother Hans Reimar.[35]

Seventh son Friedrich Carl Leopold (1731–99), appointed sub-lieutenant at twenty-one, retired as captain at thirty-three. The Austrians captured him in 1759, holding him prisoner until war's end. In Tyrolean captivity he met Marie Irene, Baroness von und zu Wetzel, whom he later married. He bought a Pannewitz estate and lived near his sister and brother Ludwig Leopold. After remarrying, he died at sixty-seven of a stroke, leaving three sons and two daughters. The 1785–6 winter killed his sheep, plunging his estate, with only poor soil, into financial crisis

---

[34] Kratz, *Geschichte des Geschlechts*, Th. III, Abt. III, 365.   [35] Ibid., 365–8.

and impelling him to petition the government for "estate improvement and Royal mercy funds." To equip his son for military service he pawned his wife's silverware for 200 talers at 6 percent interest. But this does not mean bad luck plagued his entire life.

Wilhelm Heinrich and Friedrich Ferdinand were twins, born 1735 and living to sixty-one and sixty-five, respectively. Both joined the same regiment at nineteen, and gained lieutenancies on the same 1757 day. After thirty-four years' soldiering they retired in 1788, aged fifty-three. Wilhelm Heinrich, awarded *pour le mérite* in 1758, drew a good 600-taler yearly pension. Friedrich Ferdinand obtained prebends as a cathedral chapter member in Brandenburg (town) and as a St. John's knight. Both died unmarried in Berlin. Friedrich Ferdinand fathered an extramarital son, C. H. Friedrich Ferdinand von Kleist, who in 1825 received a captain's pension, dying thirty-six years later in Breslau.

Hans Reimar (1736–1806) was "Green Kleist's" and also his childless sister Charlotte Marie's beneficiary. His long career ascended from cavalry officer to major-general, decorated with *pour le mérite*. He gained 1794 discharge with a pension "because Blücher," later famous as the Prussian commander at Waterloo but "who then was only colonel, was advanced in preference to him, which his sense of honor could not tolerate, since he was convinced, and on many occasions had proven, as for example by capturing 20 cannon and taking 1,000 prisoners, that he did not stand behind Blücher in capacity." He married twice, at twenty-seven and, after his first wife's premature death, at thirty-two. His second wife Antoinette Maria Josepha von Dumont (d. 1809), possibly a Huguenot descendant, bore him four sons. He died in Silesia, his first wife's homeland, where, seemingly, he owned land.[36]

Though nine Kleist sons served in the army, only a few made lifetime careers. The rest, like their daughters' husbands, retired in middle age to live on their incomes and estates. None died in battle, and only heroic and gentlemanly "Green Kleist" met an untimely death. If they were the militarized Prussian nobility, most were not loath to lay down their swords.

THE FAMILY INHERITANCE SETTLEMENT, 1758–1763

On the day Frau Kleist died, her second eldest son, Cavalry Captain Wilhelm Adrian, aged thirty-seven, dispatched letters from Stavenow, where he was staying, to each brother. "Much loved brother, Thou most loyal brother," he began,

[36] Ibid., 371–2.

With the greatest dismay and sadness I must report to you that our beloved mother this morning the 27th between eight and nine o'clock, having suffered a stroke, very suddenly passed away, gently and blessedly in the Lord. How we poor [brother and sister] were plunged by this most sorrowful and completely unsuspected death into the greatest consternation that I can up to now ever remember, you cannot imagine.[37]

With him was his youngest sister Carolina, who similarly wrote her four sisters. Their mother would be buried two days later, Blüthen Pastor Bertram pronouncing the funeral oration. Judge Hasse would visit Stavenow soon thereafter.

Conrad Kleist, responsible for Stavenow's administration, drew up a plan, co-signed by the family lawyer Wackenroder, for dispatch to his siblings. With Brandenburg under siege, "present circumstances are critical." Because of "the enemies'" menace, he was immediately sending their mother's costly silver and porcelain, plus cash and interest-bearing notes, to Hasse's son in Hamburg. Someone would need to accompany these valuables, since "they cannot be entrusted to mother's servant Friedrich alone." As for Stavenow's management, "Herr Administrator Böhmer will faithfully fulfill his duties as before, without raising the slightest doubts." From Mademoiselle Charreton, Conrad would request a description – "a true test of friendship" – of their mother's "last days and hours." These arrangements would, he believed, preserve "the good peace in our family [*Famille*]."[38]

Conrad soon wrote from Berlin to his brother and Mademoiselle Charreton at Stavenow. After pausing to recall "our so loving departed mother," he announced that, with Böhmer's concurrence, the lordship's expendable rye reserves would be shipped to Berlin, certified for customs-free passage, as was the nobility's privilege. Perhaps they feared hostile troops would seize the lordship's stores, though the worst Stavenow later suffered was loss of 12 bushels of rye and oats to "the Swedes," presumably raiders from nearby Swedish Pomerania. A "competent employee" should accompany the grain, preventing "theft and secret sale." Conrad's Berlin banker Schultze would find buyers. According to the latest reports in the Berlin press (*"Intelligenz-Blatt"*), rye was fetching 25.6 groschen the bushel. Conrad agreed to a perhaps panicky proposal that 150 cows be sold abroad, though the 1758–9 accounts are silent on this.[39]

Judge Hasse, inventorying the lordship, wrote the absent Kleist heirs, mentioning his "great age," but assuring them that their family's "precious

---

[37] No. 716, fos. 253–4.   [38] Ibid., fos. 263–5.   [39] No. 716, fo. 269; no. 237.

effects" were safe. He expressed condolence over their mother's death, with the pious hope "that Almighty God, Who has caused you a very painful moment, will soon heal you through His unending consolation, and amid the present terrible events take you into His protection, gratifying you with a soon to be expected peace settlement." He could, seemingly, trust the military-minded Kleists to concur in such unwarlike sentiments.[40]

Hasse's weightiest task was the lordship's full-dress appraisal, to determine the cash value of the shares each Kleist son would inherit. Helped by administrator Böhmer, he finished this elaborate document in 1760. But not for three years was a family conference held at which, with higher current commodity price corrections, it was finally approved, setting Stavenow's net value, minus farm inventory and furniture, at 127,483 talers. Hasse having meanwhile died, it was left to the new justiciar and family lawyer, Judge Betich, to register in the "Prignitz Land and Mortgage Book" the "Inheritance Contract and Fraternal Agreement" which the ten brothers signed in June 1763.[41]

"After the restoration, praise God, of peace," the Kleists faced the question, not only of determining inheritance shares, but of how to fulfill their mother's will that Stavenow be held "in common and undivided." Their father, as the 1763 settlement noted, acquired Stavenow "as true allodial property," unencumbered and free of restrictions deriving from any kinfolk's claims apart from Colonel Kleist's direct descendants. The colonel had accepted Frederick William I's 1717 "allodification" of noble property, a non-binding option landed gentry could exercise in bequeathing their land. The royal purpose, as we saw, was to strengthen the property rights of noble estates' immediate possessors, so they might more readily improve them through efficiency-enhancing investments. Previously, as evidenced by the Blumenthals' and Quitzows' competition over Stavenow, feudal law on fiefs bestowed important property claims on landowners' entire male agnatic kin group (brothers and descendants) as well as on their own sons.[42]

To the pre-1717 system the Kleist brothers, with their mother's testamentary blessing, returned in 1763 "in fraternal harmony." They agreed Major Friedrich Joachim, the sixth eldest, should inherit Stavenow, but on condition the property "shall always remain in the Kleist family and be considered as a new fief, constituted by this present act, in all brothers' hands." This was feudal ownership "by

[40] No. 716, fos. 261–2.   [41] No. 58, fos. 34–46.   [42] Ibid., fo. 3. Cf. Martiny, *Adelsfrage.*

collective hand" (*zur gesamten Hand*), to which egalitarian tradition and self-interest strongly inclined the Brandenburg-Prussian nobility into and beyond the eighteenth century, despite royal advocacy of streamlined property rights. As the new possessor, Friedrich Joachim (familiarly named Joachim) would be free to name his successor. "Following his best knowledge and conscience," he would choose among his sons or, lacking them, his brothers, or, should they have died, his male agnates "in equal degree" (that is, among his nephews), selecting a guardian should the heir be a minor. Female inheritance would occur in male heirs' absence, proceeding downward through the brothers' sisters and their descendants, and excluding male heirs' widows.[43]

The settlement decreed that "each owner [after Joachim] will be subject to a fee in the amount of the [1763 appraisal] price of 127,483 talers in prewar currency." Thus the principle of equal inheritance would apply to Joachim's successor, who (in the generation following the ten Kleists) would pay shares of this large sum to his own brothers and to his male cousins too. The ten brothers agreed to establish a "lineage capital" (*Lehn-Stamm*) of 3,000-taler shares which each would invest in Stavenow, and on which Joachim would pay interest at 5 percent, both to his brothers and their unremarried widows, or to inheriting nephews. Upon all agnatic heirs' deaths in the ten brothers' generation and among their children, interest payments would cease and the 30,000-taler capital would merge with the lordship's value. So long as lineage shares remained, their value would be deducted from the purchase price subsequent owners would pay their agnatic co-heirs.

Should the possessor die without a successor son, the next owner would compensate other heirs for new buildings, though only if not built with compulsory labor and unpurchased materials belonging already to the estate. If the predecessor built "a costly dwelling-house and lavish gardens," his successor's liability would be limited to 5,000 talers. Improvements in field agriculture and pasturage would be shared among heirs by "common law." To discourage the despoiling of seigneurial woods, if a possessor sold timber for more than 500 talers in one year, half the excess sum would be deducted from his successor's purchase price. And though the possessor could borrow money against the lordship, he could not mortgage the fraternal shares lodged in it.

[43] No. 58, fos. 36–8.

Joachim agreed to give room and board "to the old aunt residing here," Dorothea von Kleist *née* Kleist, and to "supply food to old Martin Kuhno for the rest of his life on account of his faithful service." Mademoiselle Charreton would receive a yearly 100-taler life annuity, paid from the common fraternal capital. Joachim compensated his brothers with 15,481 talers for household goods and the estate inventory he acquired with Stavenow. "They have already divided the few books." Joachim agreed "to keep permanently at the estate the enameled family boxes" (perhaps bearing members' likenesses) "and the spinet" (evidence of some familial musical competence) along with "the drawings and portraits." He would also "continue the family tree." In these mementos the Kleist heirs invested a collective identity.

The family's interest-bearing investments now amounted to 75,237 talers. At Frau Kleist's death, questions arose about this fund, spurring Conrad Kleist and Hasse to explain "why it has diminished." Its twenty-year decline from some 120,000 to 89,000 talers resulted from 46,000-taler dowry and inheritance payments to four daughters. To balance these debits a 1748 sale of Stavenow timber, "owing to uncommonly heavy wind-breakage," netted 5,000 talers, while Frau Kleist sold "silver service" for 3,000 talers. These gains, plus reinvested interest, raised family capital by 9,600 talers. The brothers concluded that Conrad's administration of Stavenow since 1755, and the capital fund since their mother's death, was correct and properly documented.[44] Subsequent debits – including the fifth daughter's dowry and inheritance, and the brothers' 500-taler annual allowances – drew this fund down again. Thus in 1763, after deducting the lordship's 12,000-taler debts, interest-bearing investments plus the value of the lordship and its inventory totaled 205,773 talers. To a tenth of this sum each brother was entitled as his final inheritance.

Unsurprisingly, the elder sons had not contented themselves with army pay and annual family stipends, but borrowed directly from the "family fund" and by signing binding promissory notes against their inheritances among private lenders. Friedrich Wilhelm, aged forty-six, owed personal creditors over 6,000 talers and the family fund 4,000 talers. Similar were the two elder siblings' debts. The five younger brothers owed much less. Altogether, the ten brothers' individually contracted obligations tallied over 64,000 talers. Joachim would deduct these debts from his brothers' inheritance shares and pay them himself, leaving the brothers, instead of cash, a combination of interest-bearing notes signed into their possession and residual claims on Stavenow. On these Joachim would pay 5 percent interest until requested, with advance notice, to pay out the capital (except for each brother's 3,000-taler interest-bearing investment in the lordship). Thus the family fund sank by 47,000 talers, while Joachim acquired a debt, apart from his brothers' 64,000 talers owed to private lenders, of about 75,000 talers payable to his siblings.[45]

Chief among the Kleists' moneylending benefactors, claiming 10,200 talers, was Hans Otto von Wilmerstorff, District Commissioner and Joachim's brother-in-law. Their relative, "old lieutenant von Wilmerstorff at Buschkow," also lent 2,100 talers. They owed widowed Frau Generalin von Schwerin 2,900 talers, and nearby Lieutenant-Colonel von Karstedt-Fretzdorf 2,500 talers. Other creditors were various unmarried or widowed noblewomen and a certain General von Kleist. Lesser sums derived from local gentry and burghers. Here the noble moneylending network, in which Stavenow's owners were deeply engaged, is visible from the creditors' viewpoint. Though considerations of mutual social or political advantage were doubtless involved, they are not, apart from the Wilmerstorff connection, individually decipherable.[46]

The 1763 settlement left the Kleist brothers with free and clear inheritance claims ranging from 9,800 to 20,500 talers. Yet Joachim embarked on his landlordly career with confidence. In a 1764 letter to his brother-in-law, he promised repayment of his correspondent's loan "properly and in cash," declaring that "I must set the management of my estate on a new footing, and improve it." He asked brother Conrad in Berlin to secure him such agronomic books as *The Relation of Livestock Raising to Agriculture, According to the Improved Mecklenburg System* (1763 [16 groschen]), but also *The Charms of Country Life, Or Guide to Construction of Country Houses and Gardens* (1758 [5 talers]) and *The Cheerful Collection of Natural Lore*, a monthly.[47]

Joachim's character will deepen in further pages, but basic optimism appears in these details, and in his assumption of Stavenow's management. Born in 1730, he rose in his famous brother's Freikorps to major's rank and "green dragoons" commander. The Kleists' genealogist reports that "he advanced 10,000 talers toward the Freikorps' formation [but] when he asked the king for repayment, he got fourteen days in jail instead of the money." The king thought Kleist's demand, in war's

[45] No. 58, fos. 42–4, 81–4.   [46] Ibid., fos. 70–3, 85–7.   [47] No. 717, fos. 133–4.

midst, unpatriotic. Family tradition held that the playwright Lessing visited Kleist and modeled *Minna von Barnhelm*'s Major von Tellheim on him, a play said to have been performed at Stavenow at Joachim's silver wedding anniversary. Another confrontation with Frederick II occurred in 1762, after disbanding Kleist's Freikorps, when Joachim asked leave both to return to Stavenow and to make use of a bath. In a marginal note, the king exclaimed irritably: "No nonsense about baths, and no hightailing it either!"[48]

In 1764 Joachim married Caroline Amalia *née* von Sack, two years older than himself and an estateowner's widow in her native Neumark. She died in 1795 of "cramps and stroke" at sixty-seven. Pastor Friderici wrote in the parish register that she lived "with her husband in a marriage that, though childless, was without disturbance and most tender."[49] Joachim needed such companionship, since he fell into conflict, practically from his Stavenow tenure's start, with both his villagers and a faction among his brothers.

His confidant and closest sibling ally was the long-lived Conrad (1726–1808), who in 1764 bore the imposing title "Privy Councilor and Brandenburg Cathedral Deacon, First Deputy of the Corporate Nobility to the Inner Committee of the Offices Both of the New Beer Tax and the Land and Hearth Tax, and Immatriculated Knight of the Order of St. John."[50] He borrowed 18,000 talers against his inheritance from family capital, "on account of his deaconate," investing in the office for both financial and political yield. His earlier career in the administration of lesser taxes which the absolutist regime left to the corporate nobility's collection lent him a prominence leading to the deaconate and a St. John's sinecure.[51]

The Kleists' genealogist reported that "he lived unhappily in his marriage with Luise Dorothee Julie von Schwerin [1736–79], Lieutenant-General Reimar von Schwerin's daughter." Indeed, he divorced her "because of bad conduct and extravagance." She found a new husband in Artillery Major von Trossel, but Trossel shot himself a year before her own early death. With Conrad she bore three surviving children, including Friedrich Ferdinand Heinrich Emil (1763–1823) who, as General Field-Marshal Count Kleist von Nollendorf, paladin of the Napoleonic wars, attained – alongside "Green Kleist" – the highest military eminence in the Kleist lineage's history, as Berlin's Kleist-Park

[48] Kratz, *Geschichte des Geschlechts*, Th. III, Abt. III, 369.   [49] Begräbnis-Register Blüthen, 1795.
[50] No. 58, fo. 36; no. 717, fo. 219.   [51] No. 58, fo. 44.

recalls. A daughter married a von Trossel, dying at forty-one in Berlin. Another daughter married honors-laden Lieutenant-General von Brauchitsch, Commandant of Berlin and Gendarmerie chief. Their father died in 1808 in Leipzig. Conrad's career shows that social ascent in the nobility was well achievable through a successful career in the civilian and non-absolutist sphere (and despite marital irregularities).[52]

Joachim exchanged friendly correspondence with Conrad, reporting to him from Stavenow such local news as "at *Trinitatis* Herr [administrator] Böhmer is leaving, but for where he still doesn't know himself." Later Joachim wrote that:

young Elias Hasse, [one of Judge Hasse's sons and a notary himself,] died suddenly in Arendsee a few days ago. Next Thursday we are invited to Quitzöbel where there will be a big gathering and a ball. Here the water is very high and has breached the Taubenholz forest dike.

Reading the Berlin newspaper, the *Vossische Zeitung,* Joachim noticed an advertisement for a book on horseriding, and asked that Conrad have it sent to him, if their brother Heinrich thought it good. Payment of siblings' inheritance shares was proceeding, the foggy issues of equalizing prewar and postwar money values having been clarified by edicts. "My wife and the rest of us present here greet you and everyone else with open hearts, and I remain your loyal brother."[53]

As frequently happened when gentry debts needed liquidation, Joachim thinned his forests, selling 400 lots of beech firewood to Havelberg wholesalers. Joachim believed his brothers had assented in 1762 to this step, which led him into the first of his battles with his villagers. Then, in 1764, "the well-known rise in prices," as Joachim wrote, caused the government to bar firewood exports, preventing his buyers from shipping to Hamburg or elsewhere down the Elbe. Kleist petitioned the government for release from this restriction.[54] But already the wood merchants had received a letter from Joachim's elder brother, Wilhelm Adrian, instructing them, in his name and his four brothers' "here in Berlin," to cease cutting, "for this is entirely against our Family Agreement." Stavenow's "present owner" could only act with brotherly permission. Adrian warned the merchants that "the War and Domains Board will be monitoring wood exports closely, and old licenses won't be valid."[55]

In 1772, partly to settle family timber-sale conflicts, Eldenburg crown estate's forester surveyed Stavenow's forests. Excluding lumber and fuel

---

[52] Kratz, *Geschichte des Geschlechts*, Th. III, Abt. III, 369. [53] No. 717, fos. 134, 145.
[54] Ibid., fo. 148. [55] Ibid., fo. 136.

necessary to manorial operations, he valued the woods, "by liberal estimate," at 20,000 talers.[56] This was part of the lordship's fixed capital,
meant to yield steady annual incomes. Whether or not Joachim abused
his rights to forest income, he finally prevailed over fraternal objections,
which Adrian alone seriously voiced. Here, it seems, was the one
Stavenow heir deeply discontented with his lot. His reaction was to lash
out, not only at Joachim, but also Conrad.

Wilhelm Adrian (1721–95) began his military career at seventeen and
retired as cavalry captain at thirty-seven in 1758. In 1764 he was induct-
ed into St. John's Order, later becoming one of its Commanders. He
was present at his mother's death and wrote the above-cited heartfelt
letter to his absent brothers. In 1760 a letter from one sister to another,
written in French, described his gout-induced torments. "We were
seized with fear upon seeing him, for he is terribly swollen. His face is
so big one can hardly see it, and his feet are surprisingly thick." His
sister, perhaps mindful of this affliction's German name ("water addic-
tion"), advised him against drinking mineral waters, but he was insistent, eagerly awaiting his Mecklenburg doctor's arrival. Only this Kleist
generation's daughters, incidentally, but not its sons, learned French
well enough to write it.[57]

Adrian lived another thirty-five years, first on a Prignitz property
which he quitted – possibly under duress and unwillingly – in 1769. He
then lived briefly on a Silesian estate which had belonged to his departed brother "Green Kleist." From his marriage to Anneta von Voss, of a
Brandenburg family (one of whose members would later purchase
Stavenow), one son survived. Altogether one senses that, measured
against his siblings, Adrian's fortunes, and perhaps his talents, were
modest. It is not certain, but very likely, that his was the "von Kleist
bankruptcy" of which a discreetly anonymous documentation survives.
In 1763 his acknowledged debts tallied 8,400 talers, leaving him a net
inheritance of 12,000 talers. Yet his obligations seem thereafter to have
skyrocketed, perhaps because of landlordly misfortune in the postwar
era of depressed prices. At any rate, in 1769 the unnamed, bankrupted
Kleist's debts, unsecured by registration as mortgages on landed property, were officially liquidated at about 9 percent of face value. Among
the losers, apart from Joachim von Kleist, were a widowed Frau
Lieutenantin von Karstedt, probably a Stavenow neighbor, who lent
the ruined borrower 1,043 talers, but recovered only 98 talers.

[56] No. 718, fo. 9.   [57] No. 717, fo. 17.

Worse still were the losses of local non-nobles from whom the anonymous Kleist had coaxed money, or who held his promissory notes. These included "the servant Herr," receiving 14 of 151 talers – quite possibly his life-savings; "the widow Berckholtzin," Premslin manorfarm leaseholder, who lost 950 talers, perhaps her whole capital; the heirs of departed estate manager Christoff Erhardt, who hazarded 472 talers; and blacksmith Bernhardt, Pastor Carsted, and estate laborer Michael Zeggel, who lost, respectively, some 200, 100, and 50 talers. This bankruptcy began in 1767, when Berlin lawyer Maneke wrote Judge Betich that "the poor people are probably going to have to march away with 50 percent" (although finally their losses were much worse). Maneke wrote later to Betich, saying decently he did not wish to press for lawyer's fees: "whoever pays, pays. I'm sorry that such poor people got drawn into these proceedings. I haven't wanted to profit from that."[58] Adrian lived some years at Stavenow and could well have borrowed from seigneurial neighbors and clients.

Adrian's wrath descended not only on Joachim but also Conrad, who was stung into dispatching a complaint to the king. Though nothing, he wrote, could be held against his 1755–63 Stavenow administration, he must "endure the completely unjustified, incredible fate" that Adrian "has now long been spreading, in writing and verbally, all sorts of calumnies," such as that "in the whole Mark Brandenburg a more deceitful inheritance settlement than ours has never been concluded."[59] Yet from 1758 to 1763 Adrian lived at Stavenow "in really excessive circumstances at our, the other nine brothers' expense." Though unreproached, Adrian "started a fraternal quarrel that only spared the eldest by a hair from death by aggravation." Adrian so frequently challenged Joachim in word and writing, said Conrad, "that I have had to remind myself of my duty to obey the Divine and human laws."

In 1760 Conrad offered to let Berlin's Chamber Court scrutinize his administrative accounts, but his brother Ludwig Leopold persuaded him not to punish the other brothers, through bad publicity, for one's wrongdoing. Adrian raged that Conrad owed him 4,942 talers, and stole promissory notes payable to him from the "Stavenow church chest." Recently Adrian submitted Conrad to "an attack," seemingly physical, "such as could hardly be worse in war." Conrad therefore sought governmental inquest and vindication. Later, in a 1766 letter to Adrian, his brother Leopold condemned him for hard and reckless

[58] Ibid., fos. 247–8, 258, 269–71, 293, 295.   [59] Ibid., fos. 115–22.

words. He urged peace with Conrad and Joachim, "for how fine and agreeable is it, when brothers live together in harmony." He concluded this high-flown letter with a greeting from "my beloved other half." Joachim likewise wrote Conrad urging him to settle the quarrel according to the "noble way of thinking," adding that "tomorrow there is a county assembly in Perleberg with a picnic [*Picning*]." Finally, Prignitz District Commissioner Friedrich von Rohr mediated the fraternal conflict in Wittstock, near Adrian's new country home. In Conrad's and Joachim's presence, Rohr proved Adrian's charges groundless. The three brothers signed a protocol ending the "misunderstandings," concluding "with expressions of brotherly tenderness."[60]

In the 1763 inheritance contract, as in this fraternal quarrel, intense sibling sentiment appears, both in the brothers' resolve to maintain common Stavenow ownership and in their strife's vehemence. Yet individual self-interest, and need for ready cash, soon overrode institutionalized solidarity. In 1770 the brothers dissolved the "feudal capital" they promised to establish with non-withdrawable 3,000-taler shares. They retained their rights as agnates and "heirs by collective hand" to inherit Stavenow, against payment to siblings of the estate's 127,483-taler 1763 value. But this act, increasing by 30,000 talers the capital needed for the lordship's acquisition, made such inheritance unlikely except for the richest among them. Joachim, however, as present possessor, could now mortgage Stavenow, without consulting his brothers, to its full 1763 value.

The 1770 settlement included entry in the Prignitz mortgage-register for noble properties (*Lehns-Registratur*) of debts burdening Stavenow and guaranteed by its real-estate value. These totaled 100,030 talers, payable at 5 percent annual interest. They included promissory notes to all Joachim's brothers in their net inheritances' full sums. Between 1763 and 1769 the brothers had all transferred their notes to third parties, gaining cash or landed property of their own. Not enough money had fallen to them, evidently, to encourage 3,000-taler investments in the parental estate. Among other encumbrances, there were the still unpaid 1,530 talers owed the Stavenow churches, leaving these with only 75 talers' annual interest in working capital. There were also 3,500 talers, once payable to Judge Hasse, and now to his heirs. Forty years on the Stavenow bench had led this sober burgher to buy a share of the lordship he so ably served.[61]

---

[60] No. 717, fos. 215, 226, 203–4.　　[61] No. 58, fos. 107–13.

THE SEIGNEURIAL ECONOMY IN THE MID-EIGHTEENTH CENTURY

After Colonel Kleist, in 1728, leased Stavenow to tenant-farmer Hartz, his family settled in Potsdam. When widowed Frau Kleist retired to Stavenow, Hartz left, replaced by salaried administrator Christoff Erhardt. He was the "total outsider" who in 1721 purchased the Garlin free mayorship from its bibulous, creditor-hounded owner. Erhardt rose to prosperity and, winning the Kleists' confidence, entered their service in 1740. He remained until 1756, when Conrad Kleist attested that:

Herr Christoff Erhardt, having with his wife loyally administered the Stavenow estates entrusted to him since 1740, is now, because of his and his wife's old age, no longer able to properly oversee the extensive agricultural and domestic economy. And so they have each on several occasions requested their discharge, to betake themselves into retirement. This request could not be refused, but with good will has been granted.

Conrad confirmed Erhardt's orderly transfer of cash accounts and other inventory to "incoming administrator Herr Böhmer." We saw that Erhardt's savings were in significant measure lost to his heirs in the 1760s Kleist bankruptcy, and later pages will return to him.[62]

Erhardt seemed indispensable. In 1755 the Kleists, seeing that Erhardt's old age required his job's "easing," appointed Martin Böhmer to assist him in his final managerial year. Böhmer previously administered Colonel Kleist's friend Marschall's estates. He came with his assistant Friedrich Leutzow/Lützow, who would oversee Semlin manor-farm while Böhmer kept accounts and Erhardt steered "household economy and fieldwork." Hasse administered Böhmer's "corporeal oath" to "Almightiest God":

that I will carry out written and verbal instructions as duty and conscience command, and will not fail to oversee the estates industriously and loyally, and will loyally receive and disburse money and keep accurate accounts of everything, and pursue as best I can the advantage and benefit of the gracious Lordship, warding off damage and loss in every way possible, and properly carry out what the gracious Lordship commands of me, and in every way act as befits a loyal, honorable and honest administrator, so help me God through his Son Jesus Christ.[63]

Evident again in these ceremonies and rites of passages is the crucial part played in noble lordship's maintenance, especially seigneurial

---

[62] No. 716, fo. 205. [63] No. 716, fos. 75–6.

management, of men (and women) of bourgeois or commoner origins. Their impact on the villagers as authority figures remains for discussion. Here the point, usually overlooked, is that non-noble professionals, not noblemen themselves, routinely administered "Junker estates." How far they were mere instruments of their lordships' quotidian or sporadic management decisions varied widely, but their skills were vital.

Hasse's and Böhmer's Stavenow appraisal following Frau Kleist's death witnessed the innovations and improvements carried out, doubtless with the Kleists' encouragement and conceivably at their initiative, by tenant-farmer Hartz and bailiff Erhardt. In the 1727 *Hausbuch*, Colonel Kleist fixed his sights on then unrealized but, seemingly, achievable output. Thirty-three years later, those hopes were measurable against reality.[64] The boldest stroke was Erhardt's replacement in the 1740s of the ancient three-field grain-crop system with almost fallow-free convertible farming. As one of Joachim von Kleist's agricultural handbooks' titles shows, this figured in Brandenburg as "the Mecklenburg enclosure system [*Koppelwirtschaft*]," because in east-Elbian Germany that principality, where seaborne trade and estate-owners' freedom to innovate were largely unimpeded by princely controls, pioneered it. The 1760 appraisal said:

it consists at Stavenow and Semlin demesne farms of eleven enclosed fields, to which garden land and outlying arable were added to equalize them. Of these fields, each year three are sown with winter and two with summer grain, five remain as pasture, and one lies fallow. And these rotate one after the other.[65]

This system entailed a new settlement of workers' lodgings and farm buildings, christened "Marienhoff," doubtless in Frau Kleist's honor.

In English and the Low Countries' convertible agriculture, clover often served for pasturage, but ecological conditions in eastern Germany were thought unfavorable to it. Later, another English option was the planting of turnips for livestock's stall-feeding. When this spread to east Elbia in the late eighteenth century, potatoes often substituted for or accompanied turnips. But under Stavenow's improved system, livestock were left to graze natural cover and fertilize the fields in non-winter months. At Premslin manor, and at the new demesne farm ("Kleistenhof") in the Dargardt colonists' village, the old three-field system remained partly or fully intact, seemingly to coordinate the

---

[64] 1760 appraisal: no. 259, fos. 1–30. Capitalized values were recomputed in 1763 on the basis of commodity price increases, but production levels remained unchanged.
[65] Ibid., fo. 2.

compulsory labor-service regime with villagers' routines and perhaps to gain seigneurial advantage in communal grazing.

The prime question, from the appraisers' viewpoint, was the new field system's effect on the amount of grain now sowable. The 1727 *Hausbuch* foresaw plantings of 69 tons, though in 1717–19 they tallied only 52 tons. In 1760, real sowings stood at 88 tons, 70 percent higher than when Kleist arrived and almost 30 percent higher than 1727 expectations. Partly this resulted from establishing the Dargardt demesne farm (Kleistenhof), which cultivated 13 tons. Dargardt aside, gains since 1717 (at 44 percent) were lower, though still exceeding the ambitious 1727 projection by 10 percent.

Convertible agriculture also reduced the arable devoted to grain crops (from two-thirds to 45 percent). Its impact was strong on manorial stockraising, and on grain yields. Cropland's increased fertility allowed more seed to be sown. Leaving Dargardt aside, and considering the reduced space devoted to grain crops in convertible farming, one could say – though the appraisers did not make the calculation – that sowings since 1717 had increased 60 percent per surface unit planted. Erhardt's and Böhmer's explanation would doubtless have pointed to the land's better fertilization, achieved through longer use as (periodically plowed) pasturage. Increased harvests were mainly rye, for which market demand was heaviest. Its sowings doubled. Oats plantings rose 40 percent, while barley remained constant, despite this crop's often good price.

The four demesne farms now kept seven four-horse plow teams. At Frau Kleist's 1758 death, there were forty-two seigneurial horses: six work teams, four carriage-horses, three mares with foals, six young stallions, and two riding horses.[66] Neither these horses nor milk-cows provisioning the lordship and its workers with food were capitalizable assets. Instead, the expenses they occasioned figured as production costs. The profit-earning herds were the seigneurially owned animals the dairymen tended on contract.

The Hollanders can indeed give some 6 talers annually per head but, on one hand, the capital embodied in the animals is precarious, because of frequent epidemics and other causes. On the other hand, the provisions of grain and firewood given the Hollanders and the herders require a large expenditure. Considering also the hay and other winter fodder given them by the lordship, [the profit on] milk cows cannot be reckoned higher than 5 talers per head.[67]

[66] No. 10, fos. 36–7.   [67] No. 259, fo. 4.

The dairy herds comprised 330 cows, nearly 60 percent more than in 1717–19. This was expanded pasturage's strikingly positive consequence under the enclosure system. Space remained for 120 calves and two-year-old non-milking cattle, raised for sale and appraised very low.

The new rotational system banished sheep from its enclosures, so they remained only at the Banekow manorial sheep-run and, as a seigneurial prerogative on the Premslin manor's and village fields. The lordship's sheep holdings fell from 1,900 in 1717–19 to 1,050 in 1760. That Kleist in 1727 projected flocks numbering 2,200 suggests he had not yet thought of abandoning three-field agriculture. Pigs the hollanders' leases allowed them to keep on their own account, leaving only 100 for fattening on Stavenow's brewery and distillery by-products (though in 1758 the lordship counted 140). Because of wood sales past and pending, the pigs, besides the lordship's own and its married employees', that could be grazed in the Stavenow forests in exchange for forage fees fell from 196 to 166. Again, 1727's target of 400 was missed. Of seigneurial timber the appraisal remarked:

> This consists of oaks, beech and alder, and although logged-off oak and beech wood can be reckoned as a 4–5,000-taler capital, considering necessary heavy consumption of [Stavenow] wood in the manorial household, brewery and distillery, also in repairing the many buildings and bridges and for use in the castle gardens, no more than 300 talers in wood can be sold yearly, while at Premslin there is only swine-forage income.[68]

The values assigned to seigneurial grain production were not market prices but averages the transactional partners accepted. These rose only slightly between 1717–19 and 1760–3. The average bushel value of the three main crops rose, for appraisal purposes, from 13.5 to 14.5 groschen. For dairy cattle and sheep, the increase, at 25 percent, was larger. The 1760 appraisers observed that "according to eleven-year averages of Stavenow and Semlin sowings, and five-year Kleistenhof averages, rye and oats yields should be reckoned at $3\frac{1}{2}$ kernels, barley at the 4th kernel, but peas only at the 3rd kernel." The best years were 1756–8, when rye yielded 4.5–5.5 kernels, barley 7 kernels, and oats 5 kernels. Only once in these eleven years did combined seigneurial rye harvests fall below 3 kernels (to 2.5). But Hasse and Böhmer took a very cautious view of the lordship's net cereal crop gains:

> It is doubtful that $1\frac{1}{2}$ or even 2 kernels should be capitalized [as profit], because taxes, salaries, and wages at these three estates amount each year to 1038.21.6

[68] Ibid., fo. 6.

talers cash. Just for [the lordship's and its laborers'] household consumption, [married] employees' grain allotments, and [seigneurial] work-horses' fodder-grain a whole kernel must usually be expended. And Premslin yields can be reckoned at no more than the 3rd kernel, so that with certainty no more than one kernel should be brought into appraisal among brothers.[69]

Thus, after reserving the next sowing's seed-grain, $1\frac{1}{2}$ or 2 kernels would be consumed, leaving just one kernel for sale. Adding cash wages to such unmonetized expenses, seigneurial production costs were high, especially measured against the old rule of thumb fixing them at one harvest kernel only. Accordingly, the appraisers set the lordship's net yearly income from grain sales, as table 5.1 shows, at but 1,202 talers. Nor did grain conversion into beer and schnapps much fatten this income. A six-year average showed beer sales at 85 barrels yearly, yielding only some 30 talers beyond what the grain alone would have fetched. Schnapps, selling at almost 3,000 quarts annually, earned by similar calculation 123 talers. The formulas for livestock (cattle, sheep, pigs) generated net profits nearly twice those of grain products (2,295 talers). Seigneurial stream fishing yielded some income, but more important were carp ponds, "somewhat run wild." The manorial household consumed some 360 fish yearly, leaving 720 for sale (2 groschen apiece). Costs were "maintenance of fishing gear and fisherman."[70] The brickyard earned 121 talers on half its yearly sales of 36,400 bricks, debiting the remaining earnings against firewood and wages. Hunting, though unprofitable, was capitalized at 400 talers.

Such was the light in which accounting categories cast seigneurial market production. Examining the lordship's *actual* cash flow, including its wage-bill, yields a different picture. But it remains to consider the 1760 appraisal of the other great source of landlordly income – rents, especially the subject farmers'. Dargardt colonization added eight full-holders to the Kleists' other forty-nine. Among landed smallholders serving by hand, eight more now lived in Dargardt, but the six Sargleben subjects had been reduced to (resentful) landed cottagers, rendering fewer than three days' weekly service. Thus, in 1760 fullhold-ers – the most valuable farmers – numbered fifty-seven, alongside six-teen smallholders and fifteen mini-smallholders.

The appraisal noted that fullholders' "construction services, together with levies for lordship's weddings and contributions to executioner's or feud money, which the *Hausbuch* says all subjects ought to render, are

---

[69] Ibid., fo. 3.   [70] Ibid., fos. 6–7.

Table 5.1 *The Stavenow estates' appraised assets (excluding buildings), 1763, contrasted with values of 1601, 1694, and 1719 (current talers)*

	1694				1719				1763			
	Qty	Price	Total value	%	Qty	Price	Total value	%	Qty	Price	Total value	%
Grain sowings (tons [*Wispel*])												
Rye	24	12t			24	16t			49	17t	825t	
Barley	18	10t			11	14t			16	16t	256t	
Oats	6	4t			17	10t			23	9t	207t	
Total	48		504t	21.4	52		702t	15.4	88		1,288t	21.9
1601/1614:			**77 tons = 363t**	**20.3**								
Livestock												
Milk cows	106	4t	424t		210	4t	840t		330	4–5t	1,600t	
Sheep (100s)	14	10t	140t		19	16t	304t		10.5	20t	210t	
Swine and forage fees			255t				531t				365t	
Total			819t	34.9			1,675t	36.7			2,175t	37.0
1601/1614:			**328t**	**18.3**								
Subject farmers' labor services (appraised commutation-fee value)												
Fullholders	38	12t			48	20t			57	20t		
Smallholders	21				23				31			
Total	59		582t	24.7	71		1,112t	24.4	88		1,282t[a]	21.8
1601/1614:	**74**		**302t**	**16.7**								
Grain rents (rye, in tons)												
Mills	12	12t	144t		22	12t	264t		19	17t	323t	
Villagers	3	12t	30t		6	12t	72t		16	17t	272t	
Total	15		174t	7.4	28		336t	7.4	35		595t	10.1
1601/1614:	**197t**			**11.0**								

	1694				1719				1763		
	Qty	Price	Total value	%	Qty	Price	Total value	%	Qty	Price	Total value	%
Other incomes[b]			272t	11.6			738t	16.1			544t[c]	9.2
1601/1614:			**600t**					**33.7**				
Total 1–5			2,351t	100.0			4,563t	100.0			5,884t	100.0
1601/1614:			**1,790t**	**100.0**								

Leasehold fee or agreed average annual income:
1694: 2,000t = +12% since 1601
1719: 3,800t = +90% since 1694
1763: 5,884t = +55% since 1719

[a] Includes tribute dues and meadow rents as well as labor services.

[b] 1694: cash rents (47t), wood sales (100t), brickyard (50t), hunting fees (50t), court (25t) fees.
1719: alcohol sales (150t), fishery (150t), buckwheat and flax sowings (37t), brickyard (100t), court fees (40t) fees.
poultry sales (44t), house and meadow rents (58t), tribute hens and eggs (11t), millers' rents in cash (24t), barren cattle (35t), incomes from gardens (60t),
1763: garden (50t), peas and flaxseed (43t), non-dairy cattle and poultry (135t), hay sales (30t), wood sales (300t), fisheries (65t), alcohol sales
(15t), brickyard (121t), tolls (15t), house rents (159t), tribute barley (7t). Fixed debits: perpetual leasehold fee at Dargardt and Gosedahl
(342t), administrative salaries (190t).

[c] 1601/1614: wood sales (466t), gardens and fisheries (108t), subject farmers' cash rents (26t).
1,072 talers income minus 532 talers fixed debits.

Sources: no. 255 (1601–14): family appraisal; no. 282 (1694): leaseholder's appraisal; no. 240 (1719) leaseholder's appraisal; no. 259 (1760–3): family appraisal.

not assigned a value." That is, when seigneurial construction work was needed, it required some compensation, while archaic wedding and judicial fees had fallen into disuse. About all-important weekly manorial service, the appraisal said of the fullholder that:

[he] serves three days weekly with second worker and team, supplying his own food, or pays 20 talers commutation fee. But because some subject farmers are used in fieldwork [i.e., did not – or could not – pay commutation], where there are many absences and deficiencies, the weekly service day is not to be capitalized higher than 100 talers, which in interest on three days of capital at 300 talers is 15 talers yearly.[71]

Thus Hasse and Böhmer, recognizing labor services' defects, reduced their value 25 percent. Altogether, a fullholder's labor and other dues (apart from grain rents) comprised assets, capitalized at 5 percent, worth 348 talers. Considering that commutation in 1694 cost 12 talers, or that labor services in 1601–14 were appraised at 5 talers annually, the villagers' obligations had soared in value. But labor-service deficiencies, then as in 1763, necessitated costly investments in fixed capital and wages.

Fullholders' grain rents had remained unchanged since 1727, ranging from 3 to 12 bushels per farm. Capitalized at seigneurial crop values, farmers' tribute grain earned an annual income of 221 talers on a 4,420-taler capital. The three millers' leasehold fees pouring into seigneurial coffers remained a profitable indirect levy on the villagers. The millers paid in kind from their stocks, accumulated in grinding villagers' harvests, 19 tons of rye (capitalizable at 6,460 talers). By the lordship's accounting, average fullholders' annual rents and services were worth 23 talers, or interest on 460 talers capital. Among smallholders, the Mesekowers were strongest. Their three days' weekly manual labor, or 10-taler commutation fee, inspired the same 25 percent discount applied to fullholders' grudging labors. Their exertions, plus 6 bushels' grain rent, were worth 14 talers, capitalized at 280 talers. Mini-smallholders yielded much less.[72]

The nobility's appraisals employed an archaic accounting method designed for leasing estates and settling inheritances. They are revealing

---

[71] Ibid., fo. 9. Valuation of fullholders' supplementary dues and services: tribute payments (hunter's bread, hen, ten eggs, 2 pounds of spun flax) – 9 groschen; six extra days of yearly hand labor – 7 groschen; one seigneurial grain-haul (minus 1½ groschen "beer money") – 6 groschen; "service in rye harvest with second worker and supplying their own food" – 1 taler; plus hereditary meadow leases – 12 groschen.

[72] The Mesekowers' supplemental rents mirrored the fullholders', including grain haulage.

Table 5.2   *Income from grain and livestock – 1601, 1694, 1763*
(current talers)

	1601 Value	%	1694 Value	%	1763 Value	%
Manorial grain sowings	363t	41	504t	34	1,288t	32
Grain rents from mills and villages	197t	22	174t	12	595t	15
Livestock: cattle, sheep, swine	328t	37	819t	54	2,175t	53
Total	888t	100	1,497t	100	4,058t	100
[Increase since previous appraisal]			[+69%]		[+171%]	
Value of labor services	302t		582t		1,282t	
[Increase since previous appraisal]			[+93%]		[+120%]	

Sources: as in table 5.1.

when read between the lines, especially on compulsory labor services and production costs. They also register fairly accurately actual seigneurial capacity in arable farming and stockraising. Table 5.1 shows that, under the Kleists, Stavenow 1694–1763 grain sowings increased 2.5-fold and dairy cattle threefold. Where farmers' 1694 grain rents were worth little, in 1763 the Kleists' restoration of earlier rents and Dargardt colonization multiplied them sixfold in quantity, though their market value was not high.

Contrasting Stavenow's 1694 leasehold fee (2,000 talers) with its 1763 appraisal value reveals a 2.3-fold profitability increase – in years of slow price rises and minor monetary devaluation.[73] This is a long leap forward which, if generalized throughout the land, would represent a dramatic recovery from the seventeenth-century crisis. To the extent that such macro-gains derived (as did Stavenow's thicker grain sowings and more numerous cattle herds) from replacement of open-field with enclosed farming, they could fairly be considered a kind of "agricultural revolution."

Table 5.2 displays net income from grain and livestock alone, showing a long-term rise in livestock's relative importance. If historians sometimes think Junker landlords were cereal monoculturalists, Stavenow's masters do not fit the charge. Unsurprisingly, in the depopulated seventeenth century, labor services' value rose faster than seigneurial income.

[73] To compare 1694 and 1763 incomes, the 1763 value of labor services (1,282 talers) must be subtracted from the appraised annual net income (5,884 talers), since the 1694 lease included a 20 percent discount on total estimated annual value (because labor services, though valuable, themselves yielded no income).

In the eighteenth century, despite realistic discounting of their value, services again appreciated rapidly, but so too did the lordship's wage-bill in cash and kind.

THE TESTIMONY OF THE ANNUAL ESTATE ACCOUNTS, 1746–1759

Leaseholders' and intra-familial appraisals project revealing views of the Stavenow estates. But in 1746 a system of annual accounting was adopted – on whose initiative is unclear, though administrators Erhardt and Böhmer and their assistants actually kept the books. These records, surviving from eight years between 1746 to 1759, yield the finely nuanced picture displayed in table 5.3.

As the judge and bailiff would have hoped, real seigneurial income, averaged over eight years, closely resembled their appraisal's estimate, which for 1763 was 4,602 talers. The eight-year real figures show that actual cash income (5,717 talers yearly), minus all expenses' cash value (1,764 talers), plus cash value of manor-hall deliveries of food, drink, and other goods in kind (778 talers), amounted to 4,731 talers, or only slightly more (3 percent) than the appraisal forecast. The cash accounts show that the appraisers undervalued Stavenow's field-crop income, which equaled (at 37 percent of cash earnings) livestock profits, while money income from rents, dues, and leases made up the rest (26 percent). But the new accounting system, beyond tracking cash sales, recorded consumption within the lordship of its grain harvests, its beer and schnapps, and other in-kind deliveries to Frau Kleist's household. These non-monetized accounts open windows on the lordship's operations and its subjects' lives.

The grain accounts registered threshed yields from sheaves hauled in from the fields, and the seigneurial threshers' pay in kind. In these years eight resident threshers lived with their families on Stavenow's estates, wage laboring outside the harvests. Of threshed rye, barley, and oats they kept every fifteenth or sixteenth bushel for themselves, of buckwheat and flaxseed every eighteenth, and of peas every tenth. Thresher Steder (perhaps with a kinsman helper) took home from 1749's harvests 50.5 bushels and, in 1754, 59 bushels, mainly rye, of which he doubtless sold some, probably to local millers. Occasionally manager Erhardt commented on the harvests, saying of 1748–9 spring plantings that "because of 12 weeks of great heat, when there was absolutely no rain, the barley and oats couldn't be sheaved and counted." In 1752 he wrote that "I haven't been able to count the barley and oats, because of all the rain. As soon as it was bound I had it loaded on the wagons."[74]

The grain accounts tracked payment of millers' and farmers' grain rents, including arrears, unless paid in cash. They registered seed-grain, internal grain consumption for fodder, brewing, and distilling, consumption by resident unmarried workers and supervisors, yearly allotments given various married workers and employees, and delivery as flour or in other milled forms to Frau Kleist. On a seven-year average, the annual rye harvest (after threshers took their shares), plus grain rents paid in kind, totaled 138 tons. Of this, the lordship reserved 24 percent for seed and consumed 15 percent internally. Once (only), a casual laborer – a Stavenow lodger – earned, rather than cash, 2 bushels of rye "for picking 12 bushels of pinecones."[75] When rye harvests were ample and prices low, or when the oats harvest was thin, much rye went for fodder. In 1746–7 the lordship fell short 13 tons of oats, partly offset by feeding 5 tons of rye to manorial work-horses, while in the rich 1749 rye harvest, Erhardt fed the horses nearly 8 tons rather than selling at low prices. Another 10 percent of the rye harvest went for schnapps which, though partly internally consumed, was an important commodity whose sale in 1746–59 earned 7.5 percent of cash income. This left on average 70 tons (51 percent) for sale in the grain trade. Counting schnapps earnings, the lordship commercialized well over 50 percent of its rye harvest.[76]

With other grains it was different. Erhardt and Böhmer sold only 14 percent of an average barley harvest. They fattened pigs and fowl with barley, while over 50 percent was malted for brewing and distilling, whose products they partly sold for cash at the tavern, though mostly these were consumed by workers and the manor-hall. Of oats, on average only 7 percent were sold, the rest poured into the troughs of seigneurial work-horses and Frau Kleist's and her many visitors' carriage and riding horses. The lordship consumed other field crops even more fully, though occasional rich harvests earned some cash. Peas were a rest-day food. As Erhardt noted: "to cook for the workers, one-eighth bushel every Sunday."[77] But seigneurial calves also ate them.

Millet, planted sparsely, put groats on the workers' tables. Buckwheat yielded groats and fed the lordship's geese and even horses, while

---

[74] Nos. 228, 232.   [75] No. 211.

[76] Commercialization rate of seigneurial harvests alone (averaging in six cases 99 tons per year): 53 percent. Grain accounts from 1746–54: nos. 274, 228, 211, 232, 281, 236.

[77] Nos. 236, 211.

Table 5.3 *Actual earnings, expenses, and profits of the Stavenow estates, 1746–1759 (based on yearly cash accounts [current undevalued talers])*

	1746–7 val.	1748–9 val.	1749–50 val.	1751–2 val.	1752–3 val.	1753–4 val.	1754–5 val.	1758–9 val.	1746–59 Average val.	%
I. Income										
From crop and alcohol sales										
(1) Rye	1,730	2,232	620	633	1,775	1,042	667	2,146	1,356	23.7
(2) Schnapps	460	520	300	300	489	444	148	743	426	7.5
(3) Barley	2	0	28	120	48	2	222	107	66	1.1
(4) Beer	178	146	126	144	234	215	208	162	177	3.1
(5) Oats	2	10	55	57	108	2	18	112	46	0.8
(6) Other	6	10	10	43	64	61	10	262	58	1.0
Subtotal 1–6:	2,378	2,918	1,139	1,297	2,718	1,766	1,273	3,532	2,129	**37.2**
From livestock										
(1) Dairymen	1,070	945	500	960	944	1,050	1,035	1,322	978	17.1
(2) Sheep/wool	384	157	367	127	129	141	449	334	261	4.6
(3) Pigs sold	205	158	329	200	160	120	0	231	175	3.1
(4) Forage fees	1,026	729	856	373	144	282	0	771	523	9.2
(5) Other	189	72	170	179	126	64	78	285	145	2.5
Subtotal 1–5:	2,874	2,061	2,222	1,839	1,503	1,657	1,562	2,943	2,082	**36.5**
From dues, rents, fees										
(1) Monetized dues (villages)	499	789	557	603	673	595	592	1,332	705	12.3
(2) House and meadow rents	127	114	138	131	134	140	143	114	130	2.3
(3) Premslin manor lease	650	650	650	650	650	650	650	700	656	11.5
(4) Court fees	16	9	14	13	13	11	15	32	15	0.2
Subtotal 1–4:	1,292	1,562	1,359	1,394	1,470	1,396	1,400	2,178	1,506	**26.3**
Total I	**6,544**	**6,541**	**4,720**	**4,530**	**5,691**	**4,819**	**4,235**	**8,653**	**5,717**	**100.0**

	1746–7 val.	1748–9 val.	1749–50 val.	1751–2 val.	1752–3 val.	1753–4 val.	1754–5 val.	1758–9 val.	1746–59 Average val.	%
Rye price (local yearly average, to nearest half-groschen)	22	25	17	17	18	24	24	20.5	21	
II. Labor and production Costs										
Labor										
(1) Officials and servants										
Cash wages	377	390	391	369	375	372	384	394	382	21.7
Wages in kind	333	375	245	244	258	340	?	312	301	17.1
Workers' food	119	154	116	120	124	159	?	182	139	7.9
(2) Threshers and day laborers										
a. Cash wages	21	42	16	19	64	55	46	350	77	4.4
b. Natural wages	241	265	197	194	195	206	?	360	237	13.4
(3) Artisans' fees	83	81	88	64	92	82	119	190	100	5.7
Subtotal 1–3	1,174	1,307	1,053	1,010	1,108	1,214	?	1,788	1,236	**70.1**
Production purchases and expenditures										
Seed/Livestock	69	315	138	26	36	170	197	97	131	7.4
Equipment	60	49	56	48	52	90	40	278	84	4.8
Work-horse fodder-grain	327	354	219	240	292	397	?	363	313	17.7
Subtotal 1–3	456	718	413	314	380	657	?	738	528	**29.9**
Total II	**1,630**	**2,025**	**1,466**	**1,324**	**1,488**	**1,871**	**?**	**2,526**	**1,764**	**100.0**
Costs (II) as % of gross income (I)	24.9	31.0	31.1	29.2	26.1	38.8	?	29.2	30.9	
III. Value of net income = (I minus II)	**4,914**	**4,516**	**3,254**	**3,205**	**4,203**	**2,948**	**?**	**6,127**	**3,953**	
IV. Owners' Consumption	804	859	860	698	1,172	826	830	171	778	
V. **Net value (= III + IV)**	**5,718**	**5,375**	**4,114**	**3,903**	**5,375**	**3,774**	**?**	**6,298**	**4,731**	
VI. Cash to owners (including cash leasehold fees)	4,200	3,700	2,800	2,300	2,299	0	1,462	6,361	2,903	
VII. Cash surplus[a]	352	561	298	284	1,217	2,538	499	1,178	866	
VIII. Sum VI + VII = **net cash income**	4,552	4,261	3,098	2,584	3,516	2,538	1,961	7,539	3,756	

[a] From yearly cash accounts. In 1752–4, the lordship invested 3,755 talers of yearly net earnings in the Dargardt project.

Sources (in chronological sequence): nos. 265, 207, 208, 229, 270, 233, 262, 237, 259.

flaxseed produced linseed oil and workers' and servants' clothing. Hay harvests, comprising one heavy cut followed later in the summer by a thinner one, yielded 350–450 wagonloads, mostly of the wider "manorial wagon" (*Knechtsfuder*) dimension, though some in the half as small "farmers' wagons" (*Bauernfuder*).[78] Hollanders took most of the hay for their cattle, but in 1746–7 the Stavenow foreman and his wife received 93 wagonloads to feed work-horses and the workers' twelve dairy cows.

Hasse and Böhmer were right in conservatively setting overall grain-harvest commercialization at the low "one kernel" level. As for schnapps and beer, these together earned nearly one-ninth of mid-eighteenth-century real monetary income. Beer was brewed at two-week intervals throughout the year. In summer, from May through September, the brewer's formula of 1 bushel of malted barley per barrel produced a lighter beer. In other seasons he increased malt by one-quarter, gaining a heavier drink. Of 297 barrels brewed in 1749–50, the lordship publicly sold one-fourth at the Stavenow tavern and served one-sixth to the manorial labor-force. Stavenow manor-hall took two-thirds, drinking on average 3.6 barrels weekly, or about 11 US gallons daily. The laborers altogether consumed about 18 gallons weekly on average (with seasonal variations), the tavern's patrons about 30 gallons. In 1758–9, workers' rations were 50 percent higher (76 barrels), while the seigneurial share had fallen by three-eighths.[79]

Frau Kleist's household swallowed beer in deep draughts. As for other recipients, on July 20, 1749, when the rye harvest ended, Erhardt rewarded the villagers with four barrels for bringing in the seigneurial crop, also giving the manorial foremen four barrels to share with their workers. Occasionally hollanders or other employees bought a full or half-barrel, but infrequently. Villagers, who frequently bought beer for life's various rites of passage, purchased it elsewhere, probably mainly in local towns. Erhardt debited the manor-hall 1.5 talers per barrel, but sold beer to the tavern and individuals at the "going market price," usually 1.75–2 talers. Erhardt once sold 4.5 barrels to "tavernkeeper Kettelhayne," one of the farmers entitled to run a modest pub.[80] In 1758–9 the seigneurial inn bought beer for 127 talers and "other inns" for 31 talers.

The brewer distilled schnapps ("brandy") about once monthly, 24 specially milled bushels of rye and 3 of malted barley yielding some

---

[78] No. 184, fos. 75–7.
[79] No. 237. One *Tonne* = 100 quarts; 1 quart = 0.87 liter; 1 liter = 1.06 US liquid quarts; 87 liters = ca. 22 gallons.
[80] Nos. 264, 261.

275 German quarts (ca. 240 liters or US quarts). Sold (relatively expensively) at 2.5–3 groschen per quart, the lordship earned nearly twice what unprocessed grain then fetched. But while schnapps production was profitable, mid-century demand – at eight quarts daily throughout the year – was inelastic, perhaps because of neighboring lordships' competition. In December 1825, Stavenow administrator Neubauer, perusing 1760's appraisal, exclaimed with surprise: "How high since then has schnapps production risen, but also schnapps consumption along with it?!"[81] The appraisal reckoned one-third of earnings as capitalizable profit, twice the beer rate, thanks to higher tavern and public sales. The 1758–9 cash accounts show only 198 quarts of brandy internally consumed, none at the manor-hall.

Food and fodder deliveries to Frau Kleist display the noble household's mainstay diet. Of rye milled to flour the manor-hall consumed 6–7.5 tons annually, enough to keep some 20–5 people in bread. Minor quantities of oat and buckwheat groats, as of field peas, suggest the nobility did not favor them. Barley served, perhaps mainly, as fodder for the sixty hens, sixty-seven turkeys, and fifty-eight ducks the cook tabled, on average, each year. Geese occasionally figured, at thirty-six per year in 1748–9. For meat there were ten fattened pigs, twenty fattened sheep, in some years a fattened cow or two, in others a dozen calves. Eggs averaged only one or two daily, but the manor-hall doubtless had its own supply, as it did of vegetables, fruit, and fish (including two seigneurial carp eaten weekly). The hollanders delivered dairy products separately. In May 1758 hollander Bolhorn collected a sizable 185 talers for butter and cheese supplied to the manor-hall.[82] In 1749–50 Erhardt debited Frau Kleist for 943 pounds of butter and 135 cheeses, and for "milk and cream only 1 groschen daily, though often 2 groschen's worth are fetched."[83] The only drink debited was beer, although the wine cellar was well stocked when Frau Kleist died.

Of oats, deliveries typically amounted to a very considerable 22 tons, mainly to the carriage-driver but also to Kleist sons, local gentry drivers, visiting army officers, and provincial officials, including District Commissioners Platen and Grävenitz. Seigneurial geese, swans, and partridges also ate oats. Occasionally Frau Kleist withdrew rye stocks for her own disposition, as in 1751–2 when she gave 32 bushels to "burned-out people in Nebelin." In 1752–3 she bestowed 3 bushels on

---

[81] No. 259. [82] No. 53, fo. 4.
[83] No. 209. Other manor-hall accounts: nos. 273, 268, 230, 279, 234.

Table 5.4 *Internal food consumption of the manorial workforce, and fodder consumption of seigneurial teams, 1746–1759 (yearly average)*

	Rye Bu.	Value	Barley Bu.	Val.	Oats Bu.	Val.	Buckwheat Bu.	Val.	Peas Bu.	Val.	All Bu.	Value
Threshers' shares	176	15t	50	36t	87	43t	5	3t	4	4t	322	237t
Married employees and their servants	295	253t	39	28t	14	7t	5	3t	10	10t	363	301t
Manorial foremen and unmarried workers	124	106t	2	1t	22	12t	21	11t	6	6t	175	136t
Fodder grain	112	101t	18	13t	357	176t	25	16t	8	7t	520	313t
Total	**707**	**611t**	**109**	**78t**	**480**	**238t**	**56**	**33t**	**28**	**27t**	**1,380**	**987t**

Source: grain accounts 1746–54: nos. 274, 228, 211, 232, 281, 236. Monetized at average local prices (current, undebased talers), as recorded in cash accounts.

"the kitchen maid for her wedding," twice gave 2 bushels to "burned-out men," and sold 21 tons to a certain captain – probably an army provisioner – in Altmark's Tangermünde.[84]

The 1760 appraisal averaged all such manor-hall deliveries of natural provisions at 778 talers yearly. This weighty sum figured, rightly, not as an operating expense but rather as part of net income. The items it monetized could have been sold at prices assigned them. It was otherwise with the manorial workforce's food consumption, natural payments given the lordship's married employees, and crops fed the seigneurial teams.

These were weighty production costs: nearly 58 tons of cereals, with a market value of almost 1,000 talers. As table 5.4 shows, the largest outlay was fodder, mainly for horses, while the smallest share was the unmarried workers', some compulsorily recruited. The threshers earned their wage in their work's thoroughness and cleanliness, which affected the price of the grains they threshed. The lordship never consigned their job to compulsory laborers. Freely contracted, married workers also consumed much grain but, if they were to be entrusted with seigneurial livestock and other property, their good-will was needed.

We can imagine tight-fisted Junkers, complaining that their villagers ought to bear such costs – especially horsepower – more fully, but Hasse and Böhmer only dutifully subtracted them from marketable surpluses. Yet the lordship's labor-force was still more expensive. In 1748–9, the accounts listed forty-seven persons – outside Frau Kleist's own household – receiving, variously, cash wages, food or fodder allotments, free or low-cost grazing, and free house rents. In 1760–3 there were fifty-four such persons, with or without family dependants. At the salary scale's peak stood "administrator and accountant Böhmer," with 100 talers annual cash wages. He and his wife managed the Stavenow manor-farm, housing and feeding three male and three female farmhands. These workers' pay, limited by Brandenburg wage statutes, was 11 and 8 talers, respectively, plus linen allotments for clothing which mid-century accounts debited at local linen-weavers' piece-rate charges. In 1754–5, weavers earned only 3.5 talers, seemingly miserly wages – no natural payments accompanied them – from which the lordship received 258 ells, or over 500 running feet, of "flaxen servants' linen" and "rough linen."[85]

The Semlin manor-farm overseer earned 50 talers and supervised four unmarried workers. Next highest in pay, following Judge Hasse,

[84] Nos. 230, 279. [85] No. 262.

were a seigneurial gardener (33 talers), a forester-hunter (30 talers), a female "dispenser," managing the manorial storehouses, including foodstuffs and liquors (30 talers), a brewer (26 talers), and combined court bailiff, field foremen and nightwatchman Voss (20 talers, plus 28 bushels of grain). The top farmhands (*Häcker*) at Stavenow and Dargardt, working as mechanics and lead plowmen, each earned 15 talers. Dargardt foreman Griese fed, with his family, an unmarried worker from a 45-bushel grain allotment. Among married workers receiving grain shares were four cowherds and a swineherd (5–8 talers), with 25–30 bushels each, and a youthful calfherd and a goose-girl (4–5 talers). Though they took their pay in livestock, the shepherd and three hollanders also received substantial grain allotments. There were also two manorial impounders, the senior with 8 talers and 18 bushels, three seemingly elderly nightwatchmen, and a chimney-sweep (6 talers and 6 bushels).

The resident workers all received free housing. Others paid for housing but enjoyed other perquisites. Innkeeper Haussmann and blacksmith Thormann paid substantial house rents, gaining garden and meadowland and broad grazing rights. Eleven households of threshers and laborers, including one widow, plus a wheelwright and two linen-weavers all paid 6–8 talers rent for cottages and gardens, and most also 2 talers for meadowland. They too had free grazing for a cow and calf and two pigs. Six owed six days of yearly manual labor (appraised minimally at 2 groschen daily). There were, also, two workers' cottages given free to tailor-schoolmaster Fick and widowed Frau Pastor Willebrandt.

In wages alone, these employees cost the lordship 528 talers yearly, though incoming money rents reduced net outflow to 385 talers. Ignoring forgone profits of free housing, grazing, and forage, the entire yearly wage-bill in 1760–3 amounted – adding food allotment values at 1746–59 prices – to 923 talers. Wages and workforce's internal grain consumption together tallied 1,372 talers. Historians agree that east-Elbian landlords shifted production costs onto subject farmers' shoulders. Certainly they aimed to do so, and succeeded significantly. But to ignore, as the literature has done, such substantial production costs as these borne by the Stavenow lordship is not only to misjudge the seigneurial economy and the noble landlords' social power, but also to lose sight of the pressures impelling them to keep up their rent offensives against the villagers.[86]

[86] The standard view's strongest assertion: Kula, *Economic Theory*. Cf. Abel, *Landwirtschaft*; Müller, *Landwirtschaft*; Treue, *Wirtschaftsgeschichte*; Duplessis, *Transitions*. On Kula: Jacek Kochanowicz, "La *Théorie Economique* . . . Après Vingt Ans", *Acta Poloniae Historica* 56 (1987): 197–211.

Let us now, finally, consider Stavenow's income from its products' sale. The mid-century cash accounts offer a rare view of seigneurial dealings on local grain and other commodity markets. Although it might seem that politically regulated and territorially fragmented eighteenth-century European markets produced predictable and routinized sales, Stavenow accounts show managers Erhardt and Böhmer engaged in a shifting array of transactions. Rye yielded the largest earnings. Tactics included sales soon after fall grain was first threshed, but also delays until late winter or spring, when scarcity pushed prices higher. In March 1747, Erhardt could sell 40 tons to nearby Wittenberge's army-operated government grain magazine (*"ins Majecien"*) at 23 talers per ton. But in June – when it was, presumably, evident that the new rye harvest would come in at normal levels – a Potsdam buyer only gave him 21 talers per ton for 31 tons.[87]

In 1748–9, high autumn prices induced heavy early sales, but in 1753 spring sales were best. When prices were very low, as in 1751–2, the lordship withheld sales and let reserves rise, or used rye for fodder. In an average year, Stavenow managers made about forty sales. Apart from favorable prices, they were induced to sell by high-volume bids and good timing for haulage, whether by the lordship's wagons or villagers'. Principal large-lot buyers were grain-dealers of burgher status in Perleberg and Lenzen, army officers negotiating for magazines and garrisons in Perleberg and along the Elbe, local millers, urban slaughterers, and even the Perleberg executioner. A few village mayors purchased small lots of a ton or more, suggesting they might have been petty dealers, but professional merchants and buyers took 5–15 or more tons.

The lordship did not buy for resale its villagers' grain, allowing villagers instead to substitute cash for tribute grain, at a rate sometimes below market prices. This opportunity farmers seized when market prices were high. Nor did landed villagers turn to the lordship to buy grain when they ran short. Instead, smallholders, cottagers, and estate laborers purchased the occasional few bushels at the manor. Grain hauls typically occurred once yearly in a one-day round-trip, but in 1748–9 Erhardt registered no expenditures of beer money for such trips, while in 1749–50, with hauls farther than usual (to Wilsnack in the Prignitz), beer money was quadrupled.

Other crops only sporadically earned much cash. Barley and oats found local town buyers, and "field turnips" (*"Feldrüben"*) were marketed

---

[87] No. 265.

for 4–6 groschen per bushel, while white cabbage could sell at 16 groschen. In 1758–9 Böhmer sold 5,629 quarts of schnapps, doubtless ιο army buyers, for 743 talers. In 1755 Erhardt sold 2 tons of dried pears and apples for 51 talers; in 1758–9 dried fruit earned three times more. Flaxseed sometimes found buyers. Much more important were livestock transactions. The estate managers collected large fees, averaging 523 talers yearly in 1748–59, from local communities and individuals for foraging pigs in seigneurial forests. Administrators also bought fattened pigs, calves, and pregnant heifers and cows from married employees and tenant cottagers, and occasionally from villagers. They sold surplus swine, old cattle and sheep culled from the seigneurial herds, cowhides, the yearly wool-cut (averaging 1,400 pounds), and fishpond carp.

Just as they often bought supplementary seed-grain, Erhardt and Böhmer also replaced livestock lost in epidemics. Erhardt spent 36 talers on a horse "for me to ride."[88] Their partners in livestock transactions were local burghers, especially slaughterers, shoemakers, and saddlers. Altogether, the lordship earned some 1,100 talers yearly on livestock, plus another 1,000 talers in hollanders' fees. As for equipment, tools, and other manufactures, pre-modern agriculture entailed few such capital goods. The 1760 inventory counted ten large and small plows, six wagons, thirty iron and wooden harrows, plus fodder choppers, push carts, metal shovels, hayforks and scythes, "one large earthborer," and sundry tools – along with a "field-cart for Herr Captain Adrian von Kleist's use," required, presumably, because of gout.[89]

Services of such craftsmen as blacksmith, saddler, wheelwright, ropemaker, mason, carpenter, linen-weaver, and chimney-sweep cost the lordship on average 100 talers yearly. Another 84 talers bought salt, lamp oil, anis and caraway seed (to flavor schnapps), distilling equipment, sealing pitch, herring (five per groschen), salt cod (a groschen per pound), lanterns, bricks and other constructions materials, locks, and calendars, though this rubric also counted intermittent fees of such workers as woodcutters, reedcutters, and livestock castrators. In 1748–9, 2.5 talers went to "farmer Beckmann in Blüthen for curing the four brown horses of scale." In 1755, a thresher earned a pound of tobacco, worth 1.5 groschen, for washing the manorial calves.[90]

Average yearly operating expenses of all kinds in 1746–59 comprised 1,764 talers, equal to 31 percent of average gross income. Here is more proof that east-Elbian estate agriculture was far from cost-free (not to

[88] No. 270.   [89] No. 259.   [90] Nos. 207, 262.

mention the noble properties' high price). While Stavenow paid the Kleist family a handsome yearly income, this was but a good return on a considerable investment of fixed and operating capital.

The historical literature usually conveys the impression that east-Elbian estate agriculture was a simple affair of cereal monoculture based on coerced labor. But the picture of the Stavenow estates painted here reveals a complex economic system with a large and expensive workforce, much valuable and vulnerable livestock, and big commodity sales. Its management, under pressure of insubordination-prone villages' and its socially ambitious owners' profit-taking demands, required expertise and authority. Like many other "pre-industrial" economic structures, large-scale east-Elbian estates were more intricate and finely tuned than customarily supposed. Nor were they the expression alone of noble lordship, whether contested or not, but also of the technological and managerial strengths of an array of hard-working and able non-nobles, including administrators Erhardt and Böhmer, the lordship's other salaried officials and leaseholders, and Judge Hasse and the Kleists' bankers and lawyers. Such an enterprise was a highly developed and, in the eighteenth century, rapidly evolving institution of early capitalism.

6

Noble lordship's servitors and clients: estate managers, artisans, clergymen, domestic servants

Scattered among village farmsteads and around Stavenow manor-hall, adding light and shadow to the social landscape, were numerous other households, prosperous and threadbare alike. Their significance in subject farmers' lives, and in seigneurial authority's exercise, was considerable. Some were rural notables' families, others stood beneath village cultivators, for whom both groups' circumstances offered instructive contrasts with their own condition. They are another window onto the Brandenburg-Prussian countryside, though one historians have rarely peered through. These pages display the lordship's agents and beneficiaries, while chapter 7 examines manorial laborers' lives. The actors mustered here testify to the attractions of seigneurial patronage. Unlike dependent farmers, they were legally unconstrained persons, whose well-being hinged partly on settlement terms freely negotiated with the lordship, partly on talent for upward mobility in this society's middling ranks. Their fortunes again measure villagers' liabilities.

ESTATE ADMINISTRATORS AND TENANT-FARMERS

In his first six landlordly years, Colonel Kleist entrusted Stavenow to three successive leaseholders. His own appointees – Meyer and Schmidt – he abruptly fired after they failed to pay second-year rents promptly. In 1728, after aggressively imposing "equalization" and strict new discipline, he hired tenant-farmer Hartz who, assisted by clerk and sub-bailiff Halentz, ran it until 1740. After Frau Kleist's permanent return, Christoff Erhardt was appointed salaried administrator. In 1756 Böhmer, whose family was allied with Halentz's, replaced the aging Erhardt, to be eclipsed in 1763 by Major Kleist, who managed his estates directly, though not without officials' help, until his 1803 death.[1]

[1] No. 200, fo. 16.

Tenant-farmer Schmidt's embittered self-defense projected the clearest voice of any estate manager before the nineteenth century. Of estate lessees' status claims a hint emerges from the address on a letter Meyer received from his counterpart at a nearby estate: "A Monsieur, Monsieur Meyer, Bailiff à Stavenau." The salutation invoked the "Most Excellent Sir, Much Esteemed Herr Bailiff!"[2] Hartz's leasehold terms are unknown, but his belligerent, bare-fisted, and ungenteel methods left documentary traces. Thus, in 1732, six local noblemen wrote jointly to Kleist charging Hartz with violating "public and neighborly law." Captain von Winterfeldt claimed Hartz unjustifiably impounded his subject's horses and wagon. Hearing the aggrieved farmer's threat to appeal to Kleist, Hartz "not only spoke shamefully, but fetched a stick and stoutly thrashed him about." When another nobleman's farmer could not pay Hartz's inflated impoundment fee, Hartz kept the animal, worked it through the summer, and sold it. Hartz ignored jurisdictional lines in fining other villagers, scorned neighboring nobility's and agents' protests, and had a hunting dog traversing Stavenow land shot dead.

When estateowner von Karstedt's workers hauled his grain to the Mesekow mill, Hartz stopped them, ostensibly because low water limited milling capacity. To Karstedt's people's remonstrances, "he answered shamelessly that he s— [shit] on the half-ton of grain, whether it belonged to me or anyone else. Indeed, I am ashamed to report the other gross and unseemly expressions he used."[3] Karstedt's circumlocution reflected the nobility's code of refinement and gentility, which reached its gallicized extreme in the eighteenth century.

Kleists' critics said reprisals were possible, but they desired neighborly friendship with him, and so only asked for an impartial inquiry. Hasse, commanded to investigate, discovered that Hartz's fines were either justified by damages done by offending horses, or exaggerated, as in the allegedly sold horse's case, which was recoverable for 2 groschen, and which Hartz gave to a needy villager, even though it had no teeth. The miller denied reporting Hartz's crude words to Karstedt, while Stavenow hunter Birkholtz shot the dog on Kleist's orders because of repeated trespassing on his hunting grounds and threats Karstedt's hunter uttered against Birkholtz. Thus Hasse, perhaps unjustifiably, acquitted Hartz of all wrongdoing. Whatever the estate manager's faults, the job required aggressiveness and standing up to local gentry.[4]

---

[2] No. 712, fos. 13–16. [3] No. 597, fos. 13–15. [4] Ibid., fos. 16–22.

Garlin free mayor Christoff Erhardt was quite a different figure. He embodied a stratum of rural entrepreneurs of commoner origins, often intermarried, who achieved incomes and material well-being prefiguring what subject farmers might attain if their feudal burdens were lightened or lifted entirely. Before helping pioneer, as Stavenow manager, advanced bookkeeping methods and convertible agriculture, Erhardt rescued his mayor's farm from debt and disorder. He acquired it in 1721, "at Colonel von Kleist's wish," seemingly without having to buy it from his disgraced and absconded predecessor, Christoff Schlohe, but only on condition of paying its debts and supporting in retirement Schlohe's abandoned wife and son.[5] In 1725 she died, leaving her son to her three-quarter-holder father Jacob Kratz's custody. A subject farmer's daughter had not been unworthy to marry into the free mayoralty, however dishonorable Schlohe proved to be. But Kratz lineage members, alternating with Schlohes, had owned the mayoral farm since before the Thirty Years War, while others were millers' kin. The Schlohes possessed kinsmen among dependent farmers, such as the appointed Mankmuß village mayor. Social–legal boundaries between seigneurial subjects and free farmers were fluid. To cross them depended on assets and incomes.

By 1727 Erhardt, expanding with leased land his farm's size to 3 hides, liquidated 225 talers in debt. He successfully fended off his predecessor's siblings' money demands, parrying by charging they seized deceased widow Schlohe's cash holdings and four sacks of linen. Various documents also disappeared, for which the widow's father, possibly wishing to secure his grandson's mayoral succession, stood accused. But grandfather Kratz blamed his absconded ne'er-do-well son-in-law, who allegedly stealthily returned and took the documents, saying he wanted "to go with them to the king, and to show them to the king," presumably to regain his lost property.[6] Whether or not these words were actually spoken, they bear witness to widespread naive faith in royal justice, though it was wholly misplaced when invested by reprobate Schlohe in Pietist Frederick William I, who probably would have stiffly caned Schlohe had he entered the royal presence.

Apart from later having to refute a false charge of sexual commerce with a maidservant – an incident to be considered from the plaintiff's angle – Erhardt avoided legal entanglements until 1751. His predecessor's wife's sister then produced a government order that he document

---

[5] No. 200, fos. 157–62.   [6] Ibid., fos. 69–70.

his mayoral title. He brandished his proprietorship deed, plus proof that he gave his predecessors' children their maternal inheritances, while delivering the earlier-cited harsh denunciation of Schlohe's faults and failures.[7] This routed his foes, leaving him free in 1757, with seigneurial consent, to sell his farm, a power subject farmers – even with full inheritance rights – lacked. The buyer was Hans Milatz, an estate manager's widow's son, perhaps related to the same-named Glövzin farmer who earlier led various opposition movements against the authorities. The new mayor's brothers-in-law, both nearby seigneurial administrators, witnessed this transaction. While Erhardt became Stavenow manager, his mayoral successor was tied by marriage to other landlordly officials: probably common networking wherever in east-Elbia free mayors' farms survived.

Erhardt set his farm's price handsomely at 1,300 talers, "in good, full-valued coins." Milatz had 500 talers plus 200 from his wife's dowry. The remaining 600 he borrowed at 3 percent interest from his mother-in-law, who held them as her three minor children's paternal inheritances. Because the mayoralty was a "man's fief" (*Mannenlehn*), Milatz owed the lordship a 40-taler entrance fee. Doubtless following Conrad Kleist's wishes, Hasse ruled that for Milatz, "out of special regard for Herr Erhardt, an old employee of House Stavenow, even though a complete stranger [to the lordship], [this sum] is set at 20 talers." For 10 talers each, Milatz's brothers-in-law acquired succession rights "by collective hand" for themselves and their male heirs. Milatz's wife could claim, should her husband predecease her, dowry repayment and retirement provisions.[8] They were enacting, modestly, the same feudal rituals the nobility followed in marriage and property settlements.

Erhardt himself had no available heirs. Ten years later, after his death, the Stavenow court settled the estate of his widow, Anna Erhardtin *née* Lemme. Their surviving children were a daughter, married to a town councilor in Mecklenburg's Grabow; a son, a Grabow innkeeper; and another son, "*Candidatum Theologiae*." The Erhardts lost most of the 472-taler promissory note they held from bankrupted Adrian von Kleist, salvaging only 37 talers. Yet Erhardt was worth more than the lost sum, and by 1767 his heirs, though doubtless embittered and perhaps inclined to poisoned thoughts about spendthrift and overbearing nobility, were launched on respectable if modest bourgeois careers.[9]

---

[7] No. 715, fo. 44.   [8] No. 326, fos. 210–11.

[9] No. 717, fos. 193, 195, 267. A Stavenow thresher named Jochen Lemme – perhaps Frau Erhardt's kinsman – died in 1767 at age ninety-seven, having long received the Kleists' "bread of grace."

In 1786, thirty years after buying the mayoralty, Milatz sold it to estate bailiff and accountant Wieneke, but for only 1,085 talers, over 200 less than what he paid. Major Kleist's enforcement to the hilt of his feudal rights is evident in Wienecke's 80-taler entry fee, and acceptance of a 40-taler seigneurial levy on transfer from father to son. Wieneke swore to conduct himself toward Kleist as befitted a "vassal" (*Lehnmann*). His rents were the same as Erhardt's, except that now, like ordinary farmers, he owed one annual Elbe grain haul (antiquatedly called *Junkerfuhre*). In 1791 Wieneke's successor separated his fields from the Garlin villagers', creating an enclosed yeoman's farm that in 1815 bought itself free of all seigneurial charges.[10] Possibly Major Kleist's strife with his subjects undercut the mayorship's market value, though details of assets sold with the farm are missing. Still, such farms were desirable to local estate officials set on social ascent. It was more ambitious to lease an estate such as Stavenow and reap commercialized manorialism's profits, but this called for sizable capital investment and, as tenant-farmers Meyer's and Schmidt's experiences showed, risked painful losses. A middle course was to rent a noble domain farm, such as Stavenow's at Premslin, which had always, except when the Quitzows inhabited it, been leased to tenant-farmers.

Non-noble tenant-farmers rose to wealth, managing crown estate complexes and private lordships much larger than Stavenow, sometimes sub-leasing them. After the 1807 introduction of a free land market, very many prosperous tenant-farmers acquired noble estates. They were also principal buyers of crown estates when the government, facing war-inflicted bankruptcy, sold many in the early nineteenth century.[11] But rising to prosperity required estate managers and leaseholders to muddy their boots, imposing their will on recalcitrant farmers and laborers. The richest could work through hired officials, as wealthy noblemen did. But small operators like the Premslin tenants did not easily overawe villagers, and sometimes found themselves in undignified combat with them.

In 1731, Kleist's Premslin leaseholder was a certain bailiff Schultze. Once, in the presence of six 15–18-year-old farmers' sons whose labors his lease bequeathed him, Schultze stood confronted by shepherd David

---

[10] No. 666, fos. 29–32; no. 720, fos. 32–43.
[11] Hans Rosenberg, "Die Pseudodemokratisierung der Rittergutsbesitzerklasse," in Hans-Ulrich Wehler, ed., *Moderne deutsche Sozialgeschichte* (Cologne, 1968), 287–308. Cf. Koselleck, *Preussen*; Harnisch, *Agrarreform*; Treue, *Wirtschaftsgeschichte*.

Thormann, who sub-contracted Premslin's sheep-run. Thormann, wanting to settle accounts, claimed the bailiff had not given him a promised cabbage allotment. Schultze replied, "Thormann, you [*ihr*] know what you're saying, and what robbery is. You've gone and gotten yourself drunk." Thormann said the tenant-farmer was "not an honest man," whereupon Schultze threatened him with his whip. Thormann "held his elbows before his face and said, 'You scoundrel, you [*du*] want to hit me. But if you do, I'll kick your guts out.'" Thormann ran off, insulting Schultze's wife before getting dead drunk at the tavern and being found later insensate on the road with his rifle at his side. Although Thormann's father-in-law later settled the quarrel, it illustrates the explosions a tenant-farmer faced, including aspersions on his honor, and the challenge to stand firm.[12]

Frau Kleist's Premslin tenant was Friedrich Bergholz and, after his death around 1752, his widow Sophie Magdalene *née* Kehlen. He was doubtless related to seigneurial hunter Birkholtz. He and his wife paid 650 talers' yearly rent, rising in 1758 to 700 talers. In 1749 Bergholz impounded four Premslin farmers' cooking pots, forcing them to settle rent arrears. In 1752 widow Bergholz reported her husband's unmarried brother died seventeen years earlier in Batavia in the Dutch East India Company's employ. She and her six children were his heirs, along with his sister and brother, a Potsdam artisan master. The pastor drew up requisite certificates, which she laboriously signed, for mailing to her Amsterdam lawyers.[13]

In 1757 widow Bergholz demanded swine forage fee increases from farmer Zeggel, who "cursed her and her kin," saying – in an earlier-quoted phrase – they came from "families who deserved the gallows if they had only been caught." Zeggel, summoning the language of insult focused on inhuman diet, called the widow's son a "stubble-shitter and peel-eater." Both sides denied the other were "honorable people." Zeggel spoke also of "gallows and the wheel" – dishonoring modes of execution.[14] A decade later widow Bergholz lost 950 talers to bankrupted Adrian Kleist. Between 1772 and 1775, Stavenow innkeeper J. G. Bergholz, probably her son, who married sub-bailiff Halentz's daughter, lost two children and his wife to disease before disappearing, along

[12] No. 591, fos. 39–41. Cf. no. 296, fos. 1–31.
[13] No. 715, fos. 12, 45.
[14] No. 326, fos. 216, 220. On honor among the popular classes: Andreas Grießinger, *Das symbolische Kapital der Ehre. Streikbewegungen und kollektives Bewußtsein deutscher Handwerksgesellen im 18. Jahrhundert* (Frankfurt/M., 1981); Kathleen Stuart, *Defiled Trades and Social Outcasts: Honor and Ritual Pollution in Early Modern Germany* (Cambridge, 2000).

with his mother, from Stavenow records. After a decade and more of independent estate-leasing, widow Bergholz seemingly fell on ruinous times.

Meanwhile, Major Kleist bargained with a certain Giese, who leased Premslin in 1764–70. Hasse earlier valued it at 1,023 talers yearly, including nine farmers' labor. Giese, lowering nominal grain prices one-third in comparison with the lordship's reckoning, offered 780 talers, probably close to what Kleist accepted, since by his appraisal method past leases had been discounted by some 20 percent.[15] In 1771 Kleist uncontentiously separated his Premslin land from the six small-holders' there, following recent separation from fullholders. The small-holders claimed their land was better fertilized than the estate land they received. Government negotiators agreed to require Kleist to compensate them in manure deliveries. Henceforth the fallow-free Mecklenburg rotation governed the manor's enclosed fields.[16]

In 1783 the major again leased Premslin. Sowings and grain yields had risen considerably since 1764. With the lease went labor services of ten fullholders, one smallholder, and two cottagers, amounting to 216 days yearly. Though nothing was stipulated about compulsorily recruited servants, the leaseholder doubtless would avail himself of such labor as he could squeeze from farmers' households. Kleist touted the manor's additional, unappraised capacity for peas and flax, declaring also that "the fruit garden bears well." There was forage for twenty pigs, and "surplus hay," letting the tenant keep more livestock than the appraisal assumed. "I don't ask for a security-deposit, because you will supply the [livestock] inventory yourself . . . If there is a total die-off of cattle, the dairy lease will be canceled until new animals are obtained." Should crop failure strike and harvests yield less than half the appraised output, Kleist would write off losses below 50 percent. While pegging the manor's annual profit at 1,242 talers, he wanted only 800 talers in the first three years, 900 talers in the fourth, and 1,000 talers in the last two, averaging 883 talers over five years. If the tenant's first three years proved unsuccessful, "you can move away." Kleist offered to come to Perleberg to seal the contract. Twenty-five years later, despite the post-1806 state crisis, the lease stood at 1,400 talers, nearly twice its 1760s' value.[17]

---

[15] No. 717, fos. 153, 155.
[16] No. 458, fos. 1–9; no. 39, fos. 10–20: section IV.
[17] No. 719, fos. 28–9. Estimated cereal yields 1763–4: 1:3.5. In 1783: rye 1:3.7; barley 1:6; oats 1:4. Cereal sowings 1763–4: 18 tons; 1783: 24 tons. 1808 values: no. 39, fos. 10–20, section IV.

Kleist's 1780s' tenant-farmer was a certain Helm, hired as Stavenow sub-bailiff in 1779. In 1811 he testified on disputed hunting rights, saying self-importantly that "in 1781 I established myself in Perleberg." He then leased Premslin, remaining until 1809, when he moved away "to my property at the Striegleben estate." Here was an estate official who rose through tenant-farming to possession of a small manor farm worked by six landed cottagers, of which Helm was already before 1804 listed as "proprietor."[18]

HOLLANDERS AND SHEPHERDS

The Kleists delegated to their tenant-farmers and estate administrators powers of everyday economic decision-making and labor-force control that were quasi-seigneurial. Below such officials stood leaseholding entrepreneurs entrusted only with specific economic functions without wielding landlordly authority. Some figured in a network of non-noble rural notables with ties to estate managers. In villagers' eyes, they appeared in varying degree powerful and privileged.

Hollanders were dairymen who appeared at Stavenow after 1648. In return for housing, gardens, grain allotments, and fodder, they leased the nobility's cattle, and sometimes sheep too. Under the Kleists they paid fees per seigneurial milk-cow, pocketing earnings on milk, cheese, and other sales. In 1700 the Blumenthals' justiciar summoned manorial shepherd Hans Janentsch, since "some weeks ago he let it be known he would lease the lordship's dairy cattle for a set fee." Janentsch requested postponement. "He wants to go down to his house and talk it over with his wife." The next day he appeared with her, saying:

he wants to take the lease for a year, but it's impossible to give 120 cheeses for each cow. An eighth-barrel each of butter and cheese was customary throughout the land. He can't give more. Otherwise he'd suffer losses no one would repay him for.

The outcome is unknown, but the transaction entailed natural, rather than money payments. Hollanders' wives were their husbands' partners, unsurprisingly, given women's centuries-old responsibility for seigneurial dairy operations. Janentsch's reference to "the whole land" (whatever he meant) suggests he was used, as a shepherd, to wandering.[19]

---

[18] No. 655, fos. 27–30. Friedrich Bratring, *Statistisch-topographische Beschreibung der gesamten Mark Brandenburg*, 3 vols. (Berlin, 1804–9), vol. 1, 427.
[19] No. 200, fo. 2.

Twenty years later tenant-farmer Meyer forecast grazing 160 milk-cows, offering 4 talers per head. The 1727 housebook registered the same number, plus 190 heifers and other non-dairy cattle, optimistically projecting the future dairy herd at 240.[20] But in November 1728 newly appointed Stavenow hollander Thomas Hermsen wrote Kleist saying, when he assumed his duties at St. John's (June 24), "one hundred cows were delivered to me, among which almost none was in a condition from which one could derive any gain." In four months he only made three 20-pound butter casks and 150 cheeses. His complaints Hartz "fobbed off with false consolations." If Kleist would not remit Hermsen's winter fees, he wanted the cows replaced with better ones, "meeting hollanders' standards," and his pasture improved. At present "an honorable man" could not survive without making "big debts." Hasse wrote on Hermsen's letter: "he should have patience until the year is over."[21]

When the lordship finally gave Hermsen a new contract, he broke it immediately. Kleist then leased his dairy to Hans Klasen, "the present administrator" – though he signed his name with a cross – at a Blumenthal manor-farm. The annual contract ran, as was customary, to May Day. Klasen would receive 100 milk-cows and run his own sheep on Stavenow land. The annual fee had risen to 5 talers per cow. Klasen could keep two horses "to haul his wares" and ten cows of his own fodder-free. From the lordship's hay each cow would have one wagonload plus necessary winter straw. Klasen could keep as many pigs as he could feed, and drive them into the woods when trees yielded forage. He would "draw six calves [from their mothers] and feed them on sweet milk for six weeks" before delivering them (for eventual slaughter) to the manor-hall. Milk-cows that died Kleist would replace at his expense. Klasen was not liable for animals injured by negligent (or spiteful) villagers performing labor service or by seigneurial oxen. The lordship paid 5 talers toward Klasen's cowherd's wages, but he hired and paid the stable hand who fed and milked the cows. The hollander fed himself and his workers from 23 bushels of cereals and peas the lordship allotted him, and helped clothe them from the flax it sowed for him. For the sheep-run Klasen received food for his shepherds (who could keep 100 sheep of their own) and 10 rye-bushels per 100 sheep, to winter them over. In return, the lordship took half the wool and lambs.[22]

---

[20] No. 240, "Arende Anschlag"; no. 30: 3.V.   [21] No. 184, fos. 2–3.
[22] Ibid., fos. 16–17; no. 184, fos. 4–5.

Such were hollanders' terms, modified case by case. It was an arrangement meant to assure solicitous treatment of seigneurial dairy cattle and sheep while maintaining landlordly control of livestock-raising through herd ownership, though at the risk of losses through epidemic disease. In 1731 Hartz renewed Klasen's contract, with concessions "because of the cattle's bad condition." A young man bearing previous hollander Hermsen's name appeared in 1753, leasing Stavenow cattle with his father-in-law at 5.5 talers per head.[23] By 1740, probably during fallow-free convertible agriculture's adoption, a second dairy-farm appeared. Georg Lohss, previously seigneurial hollander near Ruppin, then signed contracts for both herds, counting 250 milk-cows. Each May Day, ten milk-cows would be culled out, half chosen by the hollander and half by the lordship, to be replaced by ten new manorial cattle. One-fifth the leasehold fee entered Hartz's pocket, while Frau Kleist acknowledged receiving her share at "Micheln" (Michaelmas).[24] Lohss would give her one calf, six weeks old, for every ten cows, or twenty-six altogether. The lordship provided his cheese-making equipment and supplies, including salt, expensive at 5 talers per barrel.[25]

When Lohss later died, his wife drew up in her own hand a list of their furniture and equipment, revealing a house well supplied with copper kettles and brass pots, alongside the usual trunks and chests, and counting – among other animals – two sows, two yearling pigs, and ten piglets. Raising the hollander's household above village farmers' were its four pewter bowls, sixteen pewter plates, six silver spoons, and its two tables, four stools, four chairs, and four servants' beds (suggesting the hollander's family ate at one table, on chairs, and the servants at another, on stools). Metal tableware was not expensive, but it rose above ordinary farmers' (perhaps self-imposed) living standards, which permitted utensils only of wood and ceramic.[26] Another measure of hollanders' comfort was housing. In the 1750s the Kleists built a new dairy-farm at Dargardt. A glazier submitted a handwritten bill for work at the "Hollens Haus": seven shuttered and leaded glass windows, and "in the maids' room one small window [and] two windows in the shepherd's house."[27] Village farmers had windows, too, but references are few.[28] Built in the half-timbered style with oak, and with a thatched roof, the

---

[23] No. 591, fos. 11, 14.   [24] Lohss arrived in 1733: no. 184, fos. 18–19, 32–4.
[25] Ibid., fos. 29–31. For both dairy-farms he kept twelve cows and four horses fodder-free, with free firewood and two pigs forage-free.
[26] Ibid., fo. 104.   [27] No. 715, fo. 306.   [28] No. 200, fos. 65–8.

hollander's house with outbuildings carried 1809 insurance for a considerable 1,250 talers.[29]

A 1760 dispute reveals clashing styles of life at mid-eighteenth century among hollanders and doubtless more widely among rural middle strata, if not ordinary farmers. Administrator Böhmer cancelled the lease of Dargardt hollander H. H. Prittwitz, related by name to Stavenow hunter-foresters and innkeepers. Prittwitz wrote to Conrad Kleist, whose "mercy" he beseeched, that Böhmer had broken the royal ordinance requiring six months' notice. Rival hollander Johann Bolhorn, resident in the lordship, outbid Prittwitz, offering 6 talers per head, but Prittwitz vowed to match it. He warned Conrad that Bolhorn had fled a 200-taler debt in Mecklenburg's Wismar. "Things will end badly with him."

Every day Bolhorn and his wife twice have coffee and always they have rolls and a separate table, and he keeps a servant who fetches fresh meat and butter pastry from Grabow for him. And that takes a lot of money, yet he always complains that he can't manage. But I eat with my workers out of one bowl at the same table.

Prittwitz offered to pay what he could really afford, while still being "just to the lordship, for my soul is more precious to me than the whole world." He had invested 30 talers in the hollander's garden, and planted fruit trees. In this work "blood flowed from between my fingers." Prittwitz was confident "you [*Sie*] will not drive me away, for you have much too much insight and your mercy is too great." But Conrad wrote Hasse from Berlin that the lordship would hold to its (unstated) grounds for dismissing Prittwitz, though his successor was not the allegedly self-pampering Bolhorn, but two partners.[30]

Yet Bolhorn survived and prospered. In 1761 he leased Stavenow's 140 cows at 7 talers per head. The lordship was enclosing a separate field for dairy cattle, but meanwhile Bolhorn's cows would mingle with those of "seigneurial household, herders, foremen, farmhands, impounder, and brickmaker." His grain allotment exceeded 40 bushels, but he had only two pigs forest-free, "when God bestows forage." Seigneurial calf deliveries fell to seven. Bolhorn paid 980 talers' yearly lease, and a security deposit of 1,000 talers "without interest in 8

---

[29] Dimensions (50 × 18 feet) and style: no. 39, fo. 35; no. 294, fos. 1–41. A dairy-farmer's house near the Elbe, appraised in 1817, measured 42 by 34 German feet (including barn, but not the cattle sheds, under the same roof), and had a good brick chimney, two sitting rooms, two bed-chambers, a kitchen, an entry-hall, and a plank floor: no. 252, fos. 1–6.

[30] No. 184, fos. 55–7.

groschen pieces" (3,000 coins). He signed in a good hand.[31] In April 1762, Bolhorn faced three competitive bids: hollander Biller's son's, offering 8 talers per head and 200 talers deposit; hollander Johns' on his son's behalf, offering 10 talers and 500 talers deposit; and the Dargardt partners', offering up to 12 talers. The Kleists hired hollander Johns junior at one farm, but kept Bolhorn at the other two, forcing him to pay 9 and 10 talers. Here the Kleists profited from a seller's market in hollanders' leases.[32]

In November young Johns proposed a lease renewal geared to price fluctuations, offering "10.5 talers per cow if the future [butter] price stays the same as now, and to pay the half-taler [beyond 10 talers] even if the butter price falls, provided it is remitted if the butter price falls to 6 groschen per pound." But Bolhorn, on behalf of his son-in-law, near-by hollander Honig, overtrumped Johns, offering 11 talers regardless of butter price, plus a weighty 2,000-taler deposit. This Conrad accepted, provided Honig's "good behavior" satisfied expectations.[33]

Bolhorn's good fortune soon deserted him. Five months later, he wrote to Conrad, who had asked him to haul butter for sale to Berlin. This he would have done,

if the dear God had not placed me in the sorry state I am in because my dear wife died. When my servant girl came from Stavenaw to deliver Your Honor's gracious letter to me, my wife was in the greatest fear of death, and expired an hour later, blessed in the Lord . . .

It is impossible for me to come now to Berlin. I ask Your Honor to receive this letter of mine graciously, even if I have made mistakes writing it, because my heart is too heavy, and tomorrow the first of May I will have my dear wife buried, which for me is a sad day in this world. Almighty God will give me the necessary power and strength. I beg always to remain in Your High Grace, and remain in deepest submission, Your Honor's most obedient servant, Johann August Bolhorn. P.S. I delivered the inventory of the butter to Herr bailiff Böhmer.

This honest and ungrammatical letter displays emotions stirred among rural commoners by matrimony and spousal death.[34]

The bereaved hollander persevered, and a year later held all three Stavenow leases, at 11 talers per cow. In 1766 Major Kleist paid him 5 percent interest on his 3,000-taler deposit. In 1767 he deposited only 800 talers, which he left with Kleist until his 1781 death outside the lordship. His children's guardian, hollander Bielefeld, agreed Kleist's interest payments should assist their education, until at maturity they inherited

[31] Ibid., fos. 75–7.   [32] Ibid., fos. 90–2.   [33] Ibid., fos. 80–1.   [34] No. 717, fos. 89–90.

the capital. But in 1783 Kleist transferred money and interest payments to Berlin's *"Pupillen Collegium,"* the government agency tending minor children's interests among the propertied classes.[35] So vanished hitherto durable Bolhorn. In 1775, Kleist leased Dargardt dairy-farm to Ulrich Bühring, a relative of former Premslin tenant-farmer widow Bergholz. Bühring's 8 talers per head, compared with Bolhorn's 11, illustrate this market's volatility, where the government made no effort, as they did with grain, to stabilize prices. In 1808, hollanders were again paying 10–11 talers.[36]

If in 1760 Bolhorn's rival Prittwitz did not greatly exaggerate his antagonist's dining habits, Bolhorn was a substantial man, able to pay big deposits on leases, embodying bourgeois tastes and, to some degree, manners and culture. Seigneurial shepherds, by contrast, were more homespun, though much superior in fortune to shepherds of villagers' flocks. At Stavenow, young Christian Möller bargained in 1700 for the seigneurial herd. Crucial issues were the number of his own sheep the lordship permitted him to graze with its flock (he proposed 100) and the fee per head for the "milk-lease" on seigneurial sheep (he offered 4 groschen).[37] In 1729, Hans Klasen's seigneurial flock contract waived the "milk-lease," suggesting dairy profits on sheep were marginal. He could graze 100 sheep of his own, and would give the lordship half the wool-cut and new lambs. He received 34 bushels' rye allotment, housing, gardens, and grazing for household cows and pigs.[38] The 1760 estate inventory registered but 1,050 seigneurial sheep, though the 1727 housebook had foreseen 2,200 cropping Stavenow's grass. The lordship's shepherd's own animals now numbered one-sixth of the entire flock. Other terms were as in 1729. While in 1719 tenant-farmer Meyer paid 16 talers per 100 sheep, in 1760–3 annual rent was 18 talers, but 1746–59 sheep and wool sales on average earned them more (261 talers yearly) than their flock's lease. By 1808, sheep-raising profits had greatly risen, causing the shareholding shepherds' disappearance, replaced by waged herdsmen.

An interesting though not blissful picture of a seigneurial shepherd's familial and material circumstances emerges from Christoffel Möller's estate inventory. Related or perhaps identical to the aforementioned Christian Möller who bid on the lordship's sheep in 1700, he was tending the seigneurial herd at his death, probably in his sixties, at Easter 1742. His first wife predeceased him, leaving seven children. His second

---

[35] Ibid., fos. 149ff; no. 719, fos. 3–4.   [36] No. 718, fos. 34–5; no. 39, fos. 10–20.
[37] No. 200, fo. 2.   [38] No. 184, fos. 16–17.

wife, with whom he fathered two children, aged two and three, was remarrying newly sworn-in shepherd Ludwig Jahncke. The shepherd's house stood alone, 35 feet long, with a large sheep-stall, both thatch-roofed. Möller left behind 118 sheep of his own, appraised at 1 taler each "because there are many bad ones," plus 48 half-taler lambs, making a 142-taler flock. On hand were 15 stone-weights of more valuable winter wool, and 5 stone of lesser summer wool, rated altogether at 36 talers. He also owned three cows and five pigs. The lordship's draft-horses did necessary haulage.[39]

Of his first marriage's children, Hasse noted that "Johann was with the soldiers and is supposed to have deserted." Another was a soldier in the Prinz Wilhelm Regiment. A third soldier son "had a furlough but also went away." Hans Jürgen, eighteen, "is still tending sheep here." There were also Ilse Trine "who was in service with the Herr Postmaster in Lenzen and ran away," and two others, fifteen and sixteen, still at home. Their step-mother, Grete Guhlen, bearing a local farmer's name, settled their inheritances with guardians, including ("represented by his wife") the deceased's brother; Hans Klasen, a former Stavenow hollander but now estate administrator near Berlin; and Stavenow smith Meister Jahncke, the new bridegroom's relative. Evident here is the social intersection of subject farmers, shepherds, hollanders, rural artisans, and estate officials. Seemingly, the shepherds' rootlessness, in contrast with landed villagers, tempted their children to desert the army and flee objectionable masters. One army deserter had already taken, in inheritance, fifty-four sheep and "shearing wages," while the other took eighteen sheep. But these "runaway sons" allegedly received too much, as did the absconded daughter, so that all three were excluded from further shares. Such were family abandonment's penalties. The first marriage's remaining four children would each receive 30 talers in parental bequests, though for now they would only have 1 taler yearly interest, with that of the son still under arms to be sent to his commander. The shepherd son, planning his career, wanted sheep instead of cash. The daughters would each receive 5-taler cows and summer-sheared wool for stockings, testimony to such footwear's sturdy nature.

Shepherd Möller's first wife's father, Andreas Thiel, living near Ruppin, submitted via his seigneurial court a self-signed specification of the marriage portion he had many years earlier bestowed on his daughter,

---

[39] No. 323, fos. 9–13. A heavy stone weighed 22 German or English pounds, a light stone half that amount.

which he proudly termed "dowry" and "bridal portion" (*Brautschaft*). This included "a free wedding at which the young married couple received matrimonial gifts costing at least 30 talers." He also gave her 100 talers cash, 40 talers at the wedding (probably with ceremonial flourishes) and the rest in the next three years. There were also:

3 young cows and 2 steers; a sow with 8 edible piglets; 2 fat pigs worth 12 talers; 10 hens and a rooster; a new oak-framed trunk; a pinewood trunk; 2 spinning wheels; 3 cooking pots; a complete and wholly new set of bride's bedding, plus bedding for two servants; a new dress of honor. His blessed wife supplied the various linenwares, which he therefore cannot itemize.

Measured by village farmers' standards, this dowry was admirable, comprising the same categories but richer than most of theirs.

Of the deceased wife's remaining clothing there were eight dresses and six camisoles. Shepherd Möller left "a gray coat not yet turned," blue and "everyday" jerkins, lederhosen, neckerchief, cap, and hat. The family possessed one weaving loom, suggesting that shepherds wove only for their own needs. Furniture was commonplace, tableware of wood and ceramic. Spiritual sustenance derived from seven religious books, including *Spangenberg's Postille*, the widow Möller's song- and prayerbooks, Möller's first wife's Lüneburg songbook, a New Testament, and two other prayerbooks (*Evangelienbücher*). For food the family had on hand supplies of flour, groats, and preserved half-geese, "which are being eaten by the children and servants." Any cash on hand when Möller died had vanished. Debts, including a Perleberg shoemaker's bill and the servant-girl's wages and shoe money, were minor, apart from 31 talers claimed by the nearby von Winterfelds. This Möller had disputed, saying they "let many sheep" – impounded by the "Hunting Junker von Winterfeld" – "die of hunger."

Nine years later, the deceased shepherd's two younger daughters, now twenty-four and twenty-five and working in Mecklenburg, one in town and the other at a fulling-mill, requested their "inheritance money." To their 30-taler payments fixed in 1742 were added 13-taler estate shares of their now deceased older brother, shepherd Hans Jürgen. From the 60 talers he held for them Erhardt deducted 4 talers each for taking inheritances out of the lordship, and with Frau Kleist's approval paid the balance.[40]

Seigneurial shepherds like the Möllers occupied a lower niche among the middling ranks. Shepherds entrusted with villagers' sheep probably

[40] No. 715, fos. 29–30.

owned fewer animals than their seigneurial counterparts. But the two shepherd types intermarried. In 1746 both the Blüthen village shepherd and his son-in-law, a seigneurial shepherd, died. The younger man's pregnant widow, after a daughter's birth, married the new village shepherd. Her previous husband, as seigneurial shepherd, owned 100 sheep, worth 100 talers, and claimed 40 talers for a large sack of wool sold to a Mecklenburg burgher, who denied the debt and would have to be summoned to court. At maturity, the new-born daughter would inherit her mother's modest dowry: a cow and furniture, minus the twenty low-quality sheep, slaughtered to pay for the christening party. The mother's brother, also a shepherd, would hold his niece's 100-taler paternal inheritance, meanwhile paying 4 percent interest to her step-father. The deceased son-in-law had given a brother ten sheep "because he is poor and a cowherd."[41]

These shepherds were living closer to farmers' levels. Similarly, in 1771, an elderly Dargardt shepherd and his wife bequeathed their estates to each other. Both bore local cottagers' and laborers' names. The husband had already settled with his first-marriage children "and put them in bread." They received maternal inheritances and more than the "obligatory [fatherly] share." The couple's three daughters had married into nearby non-Stavenow villages. Husband and wife signed with crosses.[42] In 1731, among bidders on the flight-vacated Blüthen mayor's farm, there was an extra-jurisdictional unmarried shepherd with 100 talers cash, two cows, and eighty sheep. He requested "lumber for [repairing] the rooms" and a rent-free year. He could "make wagons and the wheeled plow himself." Though he did not get the farm, he was accepted as a candidate, showing that a shepherd might aspire, if in vain, to a village mayorship.[43]

Yet grazing disputes could pit seigneurial shepherds against villagers. In 1724 hollander Klasen said the Blüthen farmers impounded all 300 of his "lords' sheep," leaving them exposed at the mayor's farm "to stand under open sky, so that because of rain and mud they almost died." The Blütheners, acting in unison, denied seigneurial sheep's access to their fields, but Stavenow forester and hunter, Caspar Seyer, testified the lordship had long grazed there, and not only when there were unoccupied farms whose land the lordship, the villagers conceded, could use. Seyer "himself, as a little boy, had during manorial service helped the hollander graze the sheep on the right-hand side by the

---

[41] No. 326, fos. 132–3.   [42] No. 358, fos. 106–7.   [43] No. 591, fos. 19–20.

vegetable gardens behind the village." Three former seigneurial shepherds, now working elsewhere, would corroborate him. Unsurprisingly,
the court was already satisfied the villagers were at fault.[44]

In 1727 Premslin hollander Guthke charged the village shepherds –
"two young fellows" – with setting their dogs on the seigneurial flock
tended by his servant, who "boxed their ears a few times." The young
victims took revenge by ambushing their tormentor as he returned from
the fields, beating him badly. They then repaired to the tavern, later
claiming – with the tavernkeeper's support – they had never left it.
Guthke complained that "the villagers graze their horses so heavily the
sheep have nothing to eat." His servant's beating, he said, would make
it hard to hire other workers. The Premsliners disputed seigneurial
rights on their fields, but young Judge Hasse draconically ordered one of
the defendants to pay a heavy 10-taler fine "or suffer it on his body and
sit it out," that is, to be whipped (or otherwise chastised) and jailed.[45]

Seigneurial sheep, unlike cattle, were thieves' prey. In 1726 a neighboring lordship charged Stavenow smallholder Martin Jetschurki with
having eight sheepskins from its flock, plus two others bearing other
farmers' brands, some allegedly hidden in his bed-straw. His (observant)
neighbors said he owned eleven sheep, of which he slaughtered five in
the winter. Jetschurki averred his wife found one of their own sheep
which "had strangled itself." This they butchered and sold for 16
groschen to a carpenter. She could not appear in court because "she
had a swollen leg and was heavily pregnant." Possibly the accusations
were groundless, for no further hearings occurred and Jetschurki
remained on his holding.[46]

Like other social groups, shepherds often intermarried, but alliances
outside their ranks show they were not shunned as dishonorable, as
seemingly was true elsewhere in Germany. Animal herders enjoyed
esteem for bone-setting skills. Retired smallholder Jochen Seyer once
quarreled with the successors on his farm. Curses led to fighting, during which Seyer broke Marie Schütten's arm. Hasse had him pay her 2
talers and "4 talers medical fees to the herder."[47]

MILLERS

Like hollanders, millers displayed capital strength far beyond village
farmers' horizons. While the lordship supplied millstones and maintained

---

[44] No. 200, fos. 10–11.   [45] Ibid., fos. 78–9.   [46] Ibid., fo. 47; no. 326, fo. 110.
[47] No. 591, fo. 81.

the grinding mechanism, the millers enjoyed hereditary leasehold tenure for yearly rents, payable in tons of unmilled rye. Deliveries fluctuated, from 10 tons total in 1649, down from 24 in 1601 (drawn perhaps from more villages than after the war), to 10 tons in 1711 from Premslin and 9 from Mesekow. By 1719 tenant-farmer Mayer anticipated 22 tons, a sum Kleist's 1727 housebook ratified in vain, for in 1760 mill rents totaled 19 tons, and in 1808 slightly less.

The housebook also recorded millers' cash deposits – "hereditary tenure money" – held, often interest-free, by the lordship. In 1717 Kleist invested Mesekow Meister Friedrich Wiese for the same 200 talers Wiese's father paid in 1704. With the two-wheeled water-mill went meadows and plowland sowable in 7.5 bushels. These assets young Wiese acquired "by purchase," giving him and his descendants "hereditary leasehold's rights and customs" for the 200 talers and 10 tons' yearly rye. He would freely mill seigneurial grain and fatten two pigs, or pay 6 talers, and feed two seigneurial whippets or hunting dogs. Lumber for major repairs the lordship would sell him cheaply. He grazed only such cattle as he could winter over with his own fodder, and raised no more pigs "than he can keep at his trough." He was not to become a livestock dealer. The mill was, "save for the lordship's direct dominion [Wiese's] own," and he alone paid its taxes.[48]

The hereditary tenure money reverted at the possessor's death to his heirs. His successor paid a similar deposit into seigneurial coffers or, if market conditions allowed, a larger one. When thrice-married Anna Wiesen, Premslin miller Friedrich Lohmann's wife, died in 1725, her heirs claimed the 300 talers with which her second husband, Christoff Krantz (or Kraatz), had (as Lohmann said) "bought the mill." The current miller, Anna Wiesen's third husband, said "his blessed wife told him [her second husband] had good money and brought it to her, and that the children would best settle their affairs amicably." Lohmann, who fathered no children with Wiesen nor invested his own money in the mill, leaving his wife's legacy from Krantz there instead, prudently said "for his part he would gladly keep the peace."

Deceased Anna Wiesen, the Premslin mill heiress, doubtless stemmed from the Wiese family operating the Mesekow mill. Her first-marriage daughter also married into a milling family. Two second-marriage daughters became Perleberg master bakers' wives, while their brother was now succeeding their mother's third husband Lohmann, who was

---

[48] No. 176, fos. 19–20; no. 355.

moving into widower's retirement. Here are evident social endogamy among millers and a friendly, doubtless mutually beneficial relationship between rural millers and urban bakers. Anna Wiesen's children each received 90-taler inheritances before her death. Now Kleist sanctioned a final 60-taler payment from the "hereditary tenure money," deducting 6.6 percent tax on funds leaving the jurisdiction. Anna's first-marriage daughter had, with her husband, striven "very hard" – doubtless on grounds of primogeniture – for a larger inheritance share. Though unsuccessful, she gained a 6-taler bonus, her mother's two best dresses and vest ("*Wambss*"), plus "Holland serving dish." New miller Jochen Krantz was to keep the "mill and hereditary tenure money for his own benefit," though actually the deposit was earning Kleist interest.

If larger inheritances and better property rights distanced millers' families from subject farmers, the possessions retiring Premslin miller Lohmann and his wife accumulated signal a narrower gap. Anna Wiesen's burial indeed cost 14 talers, and her legacy included a 2.66-taler ducat and 15 talers in lesser coin, plus seven silver buttons worth 1.5 groschen each. But otherwise there were only two cows and a steer, two pigs, and some fowl. The copper and ironware were typical of farmhouses. Among household goods were four tin-capped mugs, five Holland dishes, a mirror, two old songbooks and "Henricis Müller's *Haustpostill*." The miller's deceased wife's few clothes included a black apron and cap. Bedding was meager and "bad." Meister Lohmann would take the livestock into retirement, "because otherwise he receives nothing," though actually he kept all cash, some silver buttons and household goods, including a mirror.[49]

With savings and inheritances sunk in mill ownership, the early eighteenth-century Premslin millers lived modestly. The Wiese family at Mesekow displayed more prosperity, but also grievous quarrels. In 1721 "senior tenant-farmer" Schmidt wrote in the court transcript book that "after it pleased the All Highest approximately five years ago to summon blessed former Meister Heinrich Wiese, Messekau miller, from this world," the five children Wiese fathered with Christina Lohmannin, Premslin miller Lohmann's daughter, settled their paternal inheritance. Appraisers were "junior tenant-farmer" Mayer, a Perleberg town official named Mayer, and nearby tenant-farmer Böhring. Debt-free miller Wiese's estate tallied 751 talers, including 200 talers "hereditary tenure money," an equal sum deposited at interest with Kleist, and

49 No. 200, fos. 178–80.

another 210 talers in coins, gold, and silver in the widow's keeping and, among other assets, a ducat, a 1.66-taler silver spoon and a 12-groschen spoon someone pawned with the widow. Monetary assets totaled 645 talers, plus eleven cows and heifers and five pigs, but no horses. Plates and dishes, weighing 24 pounds, were of pewter, as was a candlestick and metalwork on three mugs. There were five copper kettles and iron-ware including a meat spit (12 groschen) and – a rare item among vil-lagers – a clock (2 talers). There were but two books: a Lüneburg folio Bible (1 taler) and, again, Müller's *"Postill"* in quarto (16 groschen).

Leaseholder Schmidt wrote that "the mother [Wiese's widow] receives according to ancient law of the Mark Brandenburg half the estate" (375 talers), but because she "is moving out of the land to Mecklenburg" she owed Schmidt, as court administrator, a stiff 10 per-cent "exit fee." So that the new miller, the widow's son Friedrich, would not be "too straitened," he might withhold payment of his four siblings' 75-taler shares until "they should by God's will marry or be able to earn their own bread," to which the minors' guardian, "old barrelmaker Janentz," assented. On this agreement the new miller pledged his prop-erty with the backing of his retired father-in-law, *Pensionarius* – a rarely used estate lessees' title – Böhring in Mecklenburg. To this the parties agreed "in all peace and approbation."[50]

In fact, this settlement ended a bitter conflict between the widow and her eldest son and his wife, who took over the mill after old Wiese's death. Earlier in 1721, the widow wrote as supplicant to Kleist, recalling how she informed him on his previous Stavenow visits, "in word and writing," of her "lamentable condition." Kleist's "great inborn good-ness" had comprehended "my misery, so that you [*Sie*] even took the trouble to solemnly rebuke my son for his earlier disobedience and earnestly admonish him to better observance of filial duty."

> But this bore little or no fruit, for my son and especially his wife persist in their overbearing, haughty, and malicious attitude, and have not ceased to cause me and the other children every imaginable aggravation and heartache, instead of helping us as they should. Nor have they in the least bestirred themselves to better housekeeping . . . If we should live any longer in this condition, the greatest misfortune is to be feared. This mill, upon which I paid the deposit money, urgently needs a better proprietor.

She begged Kleist to appoint an interim miller, until a younger child could succeed him. Signing as Kleist's "humble servant," she promised

---

[50] No. 176, fos. 7–11.

to pray for "Your Most Noble Family's continuous increase." Kleist sent her letter to Stavenow from Potsdam, decreeing that "the tenant-farmer should try to get another miller, who will pay out her deposit money and assume the mill-lease himself."[51]

But Friedrich Wiese kept his mill until his premature death in 1725. Neither his alleged faults nor his wife's are evident. To the household library they added bible, prayerbook, and two hymnals. Perhaps they affected a display the embittered widow resented. Among their valuables, apart from a ducat's "godfathers' money" given to one of their children and 4 talers to the other, they accumulated 32 talers' worth of silver: ten silver spoons and "small pitcher, a large and small pair of belt-buckles, shirt-buckle, 2.5 dozen small buttons and neck button," fourteen silver buttons for both husband's and wife's shirt-fronts, and a pair of small shoe-buckles. Neither Friedrich's nor his wife's garments were inventoried, but were left for the children, so they might have "decent clothing." Among household goods were a "large clothes closet with two doors (3 talers), canopy-bed, somewhat worm-eaten (1 taler)," a mirror and (rarely mentioned) clothes brush, also a rather valuable Spanish cane (16 groschen), a shotgun (1 taler), and a writing slate. The clock no longer ran. There were numerous cattle (ten) and pigs (nineteen).

Subtracting unpaid inheritances, Friedrich's net estate tallied 128 talers, half his wife's, who now married Jacob Arndt, from the nearby Lantz millers' family, into which Friedrich's sister earlier married. Kleist accepted new miller Arndt on the same terms as Wiese's, adding an additional meadow. Arndt paid 200 talers deposit, freeing Wiese's money for his heirs. Arndt promised to raise his step-children "without reducing their inheritances and, like a corporeal father, to provide them with all necessities." Hasse appointed free mayor Erhardt the children's co-guardian, along with their grandfather. The remarrying widow's first-marriage children would have preferential inheritance rights, though they might not have "a liking for the trade" or want to fulfill its obligations, in which case the lordship could appoint another miller. All male parties signed with full names. Here are evident, apart from Kleist's insistence on discretionary powers over subjects' tenurial rights, millers' endogamy and membership in the non-noble rural notables' social network.[52]

Twenty years later, Mesekow miller Jacob Arndt, facing death, traveled to Perleberg to record his last will. He averred that, while "he and

---

[51] No. 596, fos. 35–6.   [52] No. 200, fos. 181–6, 191–2.

Sophie Bühringen produced no heirs during their marriage, she held him in love and respect, and managed his household faithfully and honestly," so that "after his – may God grant! – blessed death" he appointed her sole heir. He signaled attachment to step-children by adding that, should his widow predecease them, they alone should inherit his estate. As for his kinfolk, the 5-taler legacy he left a brother bespeaks frigidity. His step-son Johann Wilhelm subsequently took the mill.[53]

Whether these Mesekow millers prospered is unclear. In 1727 two farmers charged Arndt with mowing for himself a meadow Captain Kleist leased them. Arndt, with free mayor Erhardt's backing, claimed that the Kleists' stream-bed alterations and meadow-building cost him "water over the wheel." The previous summer the mill stood idle for eighteen weeks. He could hardly earn 1.5 tons of grain from Stavenow farmers, depending on "foreigners" for the rest. He sought rent reduction "to avoid complete impoverishment." Kleist dropped one ton's grain rent, reclaiming arable and meadow granted in 1717. The aggrieved farmers gained the second cut on the disputed meadow.[54] Forty years later, Arndt's step-son renegotiated Mesekow's lease with Major Kleist, who took the mill's remaining arable, cutting rent by a half-ton and waiving pig-fattening fees. These terms persisted into the nineteenth century. The downward rent turn suggests sagging incomes. To repair his water-wheel, Arndt's successor borrowed 100 talers from Blüthen Pastor Frederici, rather than spending ready money.[55]

By contrast, Premslin's mill flourished in the mid-eighteenth century. In 1748 Jochen Kraatz was in his twenty-third year as Premslin miller and, with his wife Eva Knacken, was seeking a mill successor and husband for their daughter Eva. Young Eva was betrothed to a Havelberg miller's assistant, but he was drafted into the army and his commanding officer refused him a marriage certificate. Now Hans Schultze, sponsored by a nearby miller related to Kraatz's wife, "presented himself as a bridegroom." Frau Kleist approved this marriage, into which Schultze brought 600 talers, though the money was now held by relatives or lent out. He proposed, until Kraatz retired, "to work a bit longer for his parents-in-law or to lease another mill." When he took the Premslin mill, he agreed – in village farmers' fashion – to give each of his predecessor's two younger daughters 100 talers, two cows, and a half-wedding. All parties signed for themselves, except for bride Eva.[56]

[53] No. 16, fos. 1–5.   [54] No. 200, fos. 77–9; no. 176, fos. 1–3.
[55] Ibid., fos. 5–6; no. 358, fos. 76–7.   [56] No. 326, fos. 153–4.

Two years later both old miller Kraatz and Jürgen Möller, Eva's ill-starred soldier fiancé, were dead, and young Schultze now held the mill. Möller, on furlough, died suddenly while working in Havelberg. His brother, also a mill-worker, was visiting him at his death. In 1749 this young victim of premature death deposited 96 talers with Frau Kleist. Other assets raised his estate over 150 talers plus 4 tons of grain – dealer's stock, presumably. His cash on hand (6 talers) was spent on medical treatment. He left a neckerchief with gold embroidery and pistolette coins sewn into it, worth 9 talers but sold to cover the funeral. He owned two suits of non-work clothes, including a vest with silver buttons, and two pairs of lederhosen. Here was an ambitious and enterprising young son of the rural notable class thwarted in marriage by the Prussian army and claimed by the grim reaper. He left as heir a sister in Stavenow's jurisdiction, who requested her money be held at interest "against a certificate until she can undertake something of her own."[57]

Premslin miller Schultze vanished in the late 1750s, replaced by miller Rogmann who was married to Sophie Hartzen, former tenant-farmer Hartz's kinswoman. She died in 1766, after finding a second husband in miller Adam Lenz, now a widower with three step-children and a daughter of his own. Lenz belonged to a millers' lineage that, in 1711, held this mill. Judge Betich, entitling Lenz "hereditary miller" (*Erbmüller*), settled the estate with assistance from a local free mayor, nearby Pastor Lenz, Frau Pastor Karstadt and her sexton, and a local miller – a social network prominently displaying the clergy. Miller Lenz did not immediately remarry, proposing to raise his children with widow Hartzen, his mother-in-law's, help. Her 400-taler mill share secured her lodging and old-age provisions. Lenz was responsible both for her and aged widow Kraatzen, who had married into the mill in 1725. Lenz promised to conserve the children's inheritances until they went their own way, give them "a Christian upbringing appropriate to their station, free maintenance and daily clothing, and also hold them to school and church." Widow Hartzen would tend them, without asking interest on her money.[58]

The court appraised the dwelling-house and water-mill at a substantial 901 talers, excluding the near-halfholding farm the lordship in the 1750s had allowed to be carved out of a long-abandoned plot. The farm, because "subject to the *Kontribution*," was not mill property, though Lenz held it securely. Here a miller possessed subject farmers' land.[59] The two-story dwelling-house, joined to the water-mill, was

---

[57] No. 715, fos. 19–21, 72; no. 326, fo. 187.   [58] No. 358, fos. 15–26.   [59] No. 715, fo. 9.

"new and in good condition," Half-timbered partly in brick and partly in masonry, it possessed a tile roof, two chimneys, a tiled floor, eleven windows (2 talers each), four external and seven internal doors, one carpeted and one uncovered stairway, one painted ceiling, and three tiled heating ovens (6 talers each). This was one of the best non-seigneurial houses in the lordship. The mill counted two water-wheels (12 talers), two millstones totaling ten hundredweights (10 talers), and a new grinding assembly (150 talers).[60]

In cash, "the widower declares there is no more than 32 talers." He reported such village luxuries as a 2-taler gold ring, "gold-plated silver earrings" (16 groschen), two pounds of silver tableware (14 talers per pound), including a "soup tureen," eleven "ordinary eating spoons," six "teaspoons" – the second reference to this fashionable drink – and "one spoon for the boy," plus women's silver shoe-buckles. There was a "copper teapot" (12 groschen), 39 pounds of copper and brass pots, and 60 pounds of pewter plates, dishes, soupbowls, and candlesticks. Lenz's predecessor left but three silver spoons (9 talers), a tobacco pipe with silver-work (1 taler), and a pewter tobacco canister.[61]

Lenz kept four good horses, worth 95 talers, to work his farm and have his servants perform its one day's weekly labor service. He had five cattle, ten pigs, and eighty-four fowl among 200 talers' worth of livestock, more than all but a few village farmers boasted. His light-weight carriage rated 16 talers. The furniture displayed "two blue iron-bound oaken trunks," five red stools, an ashwood living-room table with two pinewood benches, a chiming clock (6 talers) plus an "old unusable clock" (probably 1725's), still worth 1 taler. Also present were a red and blue painted cupboard, a blue pinewood table with six chairs, an 8-groschen "sleeping bench," two mirrors, a stone writing slate, twelve teacups (18 groschen), five mugs, six beer glasses, and six two-quart bottles.[62]

Linen, beds, bedding, tablecloths, napkins, and hand-towels were abundant and valuable (121 talers). In the second-story room stood a canopied pinewood bed with red, white, and blue bedcovers worth 12 talers, alongside two other beds. The first-story living room contained a bed with blue-striped curtains (7 talers). There were also beds and bedding for a child (1 taler) and a maid (6 talers), and four beds for apprentices and farm servants (1.5 talers each). Among the miller's deceased wife's sixteen dresses, worth 26 talers, were a valuable one of "black

---

[60] No. 358, fos. 27–8. [61] Ibid., pt. II. [62] Ibid., pt. VIII.

flowered silk damask" (8 talers) and one of red and white striped cotton (1 taler). Among her clothes, headgear, and (rarely inventoried) handkerchiefs, valued altogether at 65 talers, blues, reds, and mixed colors were numerous. Miller Lenz's own valuables included a blue woolen coat and vest (8 talers), twelve good shirts (12 groschen each), and two Spanish canes, one silver-plated (2 talers).

Apart from 17 bushels of dried fruit, perhaps for sale, food supplies went unmentioned. "The books stay for the children." Miller Lenz was owed 57 talers, mostly in 3–8 taler sums by eight local village farmers, perhaps for grain advances, plus 47 talers in "uncertain" loans, seemingly to landless villagers. Minus these latter, Lenz's assets tallied 1,583 talers. Debits included 400 talers his mother-in-law invested in the mill "at its purchase," as part of her departed daughter's dowry. A previous miller Rogmann's three orphaned children claimed 100 talers from the mill. Lenz owed his apprentice Rogmann 43 talers for 1.6 years' wages (relatively good, for a young countryman, at 26 talers yearly).[63]

Debit-free, the net estate totaled 900 talers, which Lenz split with the four children, who each would receive at maturity 112.5 talers. Though bereft of his wife, miller Lenz possessed sizable capital and lived comfortably in a bourgeois prosperity distinguishing his household among rural notables. Unfortunately, he too soon died, as emerges from a complaint widow Hartzen brought in 1767 against new miller Lenz. This was the deceased miller's father, who moved in (with unspecified kinfolk) and soon was quarreling with widow Hartzen. She wrote the lordship seeking "protection and aid" against the "so undeserved as well as dishonest and illegal mistreatment" the new miller was visiting on her after the death of her son-in-law, "who has now followed [her daughter] into eternity": "It is not enough for his people that they have my possessions in their hands and enjoy them, nor is it enough that they cause me all imaginable heartache, and wound me with the most painful abuse and malicious remarks both openly to my face and behind my back."

They were, she claimed, endangering the children's inheritances. Nor were the children's guardians, one the deceased miller's brother and another living outside the jurisdiction, observing their duties. "Nature and love" – Rousseauean words – "oblige me as these children's grandmother to ward off great harm to them." Hence, and because of "my own suffering, which these people are inflicting on me,"

<hr />

[63] Ibid., pt. XII.

widow Hartzen sought court intervention, to prevent dispersion of "movable assets" the children would one day inherit. Such goods should be given reliable guardians. She also requested the new miller release her 400 talers to her, "whereupon I wish to vacate and leave the mill for good." Betich summoned the new miller to answer these charges, with the result, seemingly, that widow Hartzen soon departed. The mill remained in Lenz hands into the 1790s.[64] This letter's repetition of the words "all imaginable heartache," which also appeared in widow Wiesen's 1721 petition against her son, suggests a certain legal discourse to which aggrieved mothers or mothers-in-law resorted to protect their interests in such profitable enterprises as Premslin's mill. If, possibly, their antagonists' behavior was less culpable than these letters claimed, such women displayed determined self-defense and confidence in their legal rights.

In villagers' eyes, millers might excite suspicion as monopolists, though millers thought differently. In 1727, after Kleist's "equalizations," Hasse summoned the millers to regulate "the milling-customer question." Mesekow miller Arndt complained his contract wrongly assumed he served Garlin village. He wanted customer redistribution between himself and his Premslin colleague "so both could earn their livings" and because "now the non-obligatory customers are milling elsewhere" – no positive reflection on his own services. Hasse applied the formula, of obscure origin, setting millers' seigneurial grain rent at the (high) rate of 4 bushels per obligatory milling-customer (among open-field farmers). He transferred some farmers from Premslin to Mesekow mill, warning villagers the fine for patronizing "foreign" millers was a confiscatory 1 bushel per bushel illegally milled.[65] Premslin miller Schultze once pressed his luck, charging the usual one-sixteenth per bushel fee for milling sub-bailiff Lützow's grain. Hasse ruled that millers freely served the lordship and manorial economy, including such administrators as Lützow, though seigneurial laborers with freestanding households must pay for milling their grain allotments.[66]

If villagers patronized "foreign" mills, their seigneurial miller was obliged to summon the lordship against them. Miller Krantz once charged four farmers with this misdeed but the court, after hearing their excuses about bad roads, dismissed them with a first-offense warning. Miller Wiese caught Stavenow's blacksmith and a village mayor evading him, for which they each paid 1-bushel fines. But farmers who,

[64] No. 319, fos. 1–3.   [65] No. 200, fos. 63–4.   [66] No. 326, fo. 210.

because of transportation difficulties or other reasons, wished for release from obligatory milling seemingly could do so by paying cash fees, as a smallholder did to the Mesekow miller of a sizable 1.3 talers yearly. Disputes over millers' measures seldom appear. In 1722 a farmer aggrieved on this score boycotted his miller. Though the court imposed a quarter-bushel fine, the miller diplomatically declined to accept. In 1725, a farmer's (dismissed) charge of cheating on measurement earned him one hour in the "Spanish overcoat."[67]

Millers' conflicts with farmers were court rarities. Possibly milling evasion was difficult to conceal and unrewarding, given unvarying charges. Perhaps millers were intimidating figures. A blacksmith charged a kinsman miller with beating him and his daughter. The miller declared the girl had rudely cursed him and his wife, "even though we" – as godparents – "raised her out of the baptismal font." He gave her some lashes with his whip, leading to curses and blows between the two men. Hasse fined the miller 2 talers and the blacksmith 1 taler, ordering them "to reconcile as befits Christians." Whips were authority symbols, never figuring in lesser villagers' quarrels.[68]

TAVERN KEEPERS

These families perched on comfort's and respectability's edges. Often tavern keepers pursued second occupations, leaving daily affairs to their wives, who needed to possess the requisite skills. The character of innkeepers' work, and their proximity to ordinary villagers, deprived them of the social distance reinforcing the lordship's and more prosperous and well-educated notables' authority and prestige.

In 1722 Stavenow's tavernkeeper was Caspar Seyer, who had recently served as seigneurial hunter-forester and whose name occurred among local smallholders. His Mecklenburg-born first wife having died, he now married another outsider. In 1727 the roughly 100 foot long tavern building, also housing Seyer's family, displayed two front sections divided by a wagon-entry onto an inner courtyard, flanked on both sides by stalls curving around to enclose the gated back courtyard. Construction was of plastered half-timber, with tile roofs. On the ground floor in each front section was a large room, with brick or tile floors, plastered walls, fireplaces, and tiled heating ovens. Each room had four four-paned, openable glass windows with shutters facing the

---

[67] No. 589, fos. 4–5; no. 200, fos. 27–8; no. 713, fo. 264; no. 326, fo. 210.
[68] No. 200, fos. 145–6.

street and one window facing the courtyard, plus an adjoining kitchen with hearth and chimney. One wing housed a first-story bed-chamber, pantry and firewood room, while both had plank-floored second-story chambers. A hedge largely enclosed the inn. Behind it were 8-bushel arable land and meadows, with free grazing for four cows and six pigs. Rent was 1694's 22 talers yearly. Seyer recorded 19 talers in wages he paid building repairmen, at 4–5 groschen daily, signing as "Caspar Seiger."[69]

In 1722 Seyer's assets tallied 123 talers, including livestock (but no horses, suggesting he hired cultivators for his cropland, or leased it). In cash he had 40 talers, excluding 4 talers' godfather's money each of his children, aged six and eight, had received, which would be kept in trust for them. His departed wife's clothing, to be held for their daughter, reposed in a metal-bound oak chest, including five dresses and four camisoles of red Frisian, Jersey, and other good cloth, plus four home-spun dresses, three silken caps, and two cotton and two fine linen aprons. She had two good spinning wheels and a loom. Seyer promised to provide his children with "appropriate food" to their fifteenth year, "to hold them to school," and give them their maternal inheritances.[70]

Thus did premature death disrupt a seemingly comfortable house-hold, as again happened in 1726 when Seyer himself died "on Monday before whitsuntide," leaving his second wife, "in blessed condition," to bear a posthumous child. The widow agreed with her step-children's guardians that she would raise them herself, conserving their inheri-tances, educating her step-son in "the trade he wants to follow," and paying his apprenticeship fees from his inheritance. These promises her own pledged capital secured.[71] Seyer's deathbed assets totaled 177 talers, including 71 talers cash, half in small coins. He lent 29 talers, mostly to relatives, a bacon-side to a farmer, and 23 groschen to an outsider "whom carpenter Meister Pagel vouched for when he was working here." Seyer's six cows and one heifer, "which in part are somewhat old and very thin," rated low values, "because of present disease danger." Seyer, once forester-hunter, left behind "coat and vest of green woolen cloth that are still good," two old green-cloth pants, two lederhosen, an old green coat, and a "shooter's bag." He owned five flintlock rifles, three deer knives, a fox trap, and two ammunition cases. Tavern furni-ture, undifferentiated from Seyer's own, included three tables and two dozen wooden plates, seven metal-covered mugs, "an old violin, a white

[69] No. 704, fos. 34–6; no. 30, pt. I; no. 705, fo. 134.   [70] No. 200, fos. 168–71.
[71] Ibid., fos. 193–6.

weasel-skin" and numerous candlesticks. "The victuals on hand were eaten at the funeral."

In 1728, Kleist leased the inn for three years to Conrad Peters, raising the rent to 25 talers but increasing grazing and allowing Peters to clear overgrown land for expanded sowing. Peters agreed to buy seigneurial beer and schnapps "at prices current in neighboring country towns." A draft contract, though not the original with Peters' firm signature, bound him "to render everyone friendly service." But he exhibited no great hospitality in a gambling dispute later that year.[72] A certain artisan master Schmied testified that he had "fallen to gaming" with Peters and the nightwatchman. After Peters won Schmied's money, Schmied "drunkenly" demanded its return, sparking a fight. Peters threw him to the floor and "abused him so sorely" he could not work for eight days. Schmied wanted "satisfaction" and 1 taler recompense for each of his "days of suffering." Peters said he did not force Schmied to gamble. Schmied hit him in the mouth, to bloody effect. In return, he boxed Schmied's ears, but not so "atrociously" as Schmied claimed. In Peters' defense, woodcutter-lodger Schütte, "forty-six years old and probably older," said the nightwatchman stirred up the dice game at six pfennigs per bet, drawing in a soldier and Schmied, who started the fight. Peters only threw Schmied to the ground. Schmied's apprentice, aged twenty, claimed Peters struck his master's eye. Hasse dismissed Schmied's complaint, since he initiated the fight, but fined Peters 2 talers, payable to the lordship, because he "drunkenly" pummeled Schmied.[73]

Yet Peters was ambitious, striving to expand his operations and income. In 1730, as he reported to Kleist ("High Command-Giving Herr Excellency"), he renewed his contract with tenant-farmer Hartz, gaining for doubled rent (60 talers) expanded arable and grazing. Peters' occasion for "incommoding" the Colonel with his "humble writing" was Hartz's "inconstancy."

> He wrote out a statement of how the contract should read and asked if I had any objections. I had to send to Perleberg, where the contract was to be duplicated, for a stamp. And now that I thought I was secure in this arrangement, I got the land ready . . . but then [Hartz] told me in a letter that I should not meddle with the land and that our whole deal was null and void. But I had already equipped myself with livestock and everything else, so I incurred great damage, since now the best leasings have everywhere been concluded and I don't know where to go with my things.[74]

---

[72] No. 657, fos. 1–3; no. 200, fo. 102. [73] No. 200, fos. 108, 110–12. [74] No. 713, fos. 4–5.

Kleist must have calmed the waters, for Peter remained to submit a similar complaint in 1731, charging Hartz with reversing an agreement allowing Peters to clear and plant land. The ten cows and four horses Peters bought "are now useless to me." He asked only pay for his labor, and return of a 3-taler saddle Hartz's son seized from him. "I don't ask for the Semlin land, since he won't give it to me. Tenant-farmer Hartz is a strange [*wunderlicher*] man, and nobody can get along with him."[75]

Possibly Peters aimed to elevate himself to hollander or tenant-farmer dignity, but here he disappears. Several offenses against public morality involving his tavern did not help his cause. In 1727 Hasse found Mesekow village mayor's sister Marie Besen, who worked at the inn, "under suspicion" of pregnancy. She confessed, attributing fatherhood to a carpenter living at the inn: "his name is Frantz, she doesn't know his last name." He gave her nothing, but "promises to take her," except (she self-damagingly added) "he wants to know what he should do if it weren't his fault." Summoned, carpenter Franz Künstel admitted sleeping with her but denied promising marriage. Time would show he was not the father. Künstel harshly said "the woman had whored enough . . . and had already been others' whore before he came to her."[76]

Künstel was doubtless acting out a well-worn script, and when convinced of his paternity he submitted to marriage with Besen. But the carpenter's relations with Peters soured. Four years later, Künstel ordered beer brought from the tavern to his nearby house, but thought himself cheated on quantity. He therefore sent his maidservant to fetch him "a mug of beer from the manor," where it was customary, though resented by tavernkeepers, to sell beer and schnapps to local inhabitants. Peters and his wife appeared, warning Künstel's maidservant if they caught her again buying manorial beer they would "beat her crooked and lame." Armed with "great fence-posts," the Peters couple descended on Künstel's house, cursing him and his wife Marie as "arch-canaille, and there isn't a curse so gross and filthy they didn't swear it." Künstel denied injuring Peters' "heavily pregnant" wife, nor did he climb over Peters' fence to assault him. Weighing these unpleasantries, Hasse let them cancel out. But they again exhibited Peters' bellicosity.[77]

In 1730 Hasse learned a "woman had borne a child in the inn, though who she is or where she's from is unknown." Bailiff Hartz summoned Peters to testify. The woman was not to leave his inn, on pain of a stiff fine.[78] A year later, in Peters' final complaint to Kleist, he wrote:

---

[75] Ibid., fos. 28–9.   [76] No. 200, fos. 92–4.   [77] No. 591, fo. 10.   [78] No. 713, fo. 6.

There also was a soldier's wife living in the inn, because of whom [Hartz] ordered me to pay a 30-taler fine, which is the greatest injustice in the world . .The Blüthen pastor baptized the child, and the soldier showed the pastor his marriage certificate, which satisfied the pastor. Why then should I not take in the woman with her child?

The embittered Peters concluded: "if Herr Colonel hadn't leased his estates and instead were present here, I would have wanted to live out my days under your authority."[79]

As Peters departed, Künstel and his wife took the Stavenow inn, though the carpenter soon died (1732). He left Marie *née* Besen and two sons, aged five and two, whose guardians included a miller. Künstel bequeathed 60 talers cash, though funeral and debts halved them. On his artisanal travels, he had lent still unrepaid sums in East Prussian Königsberg (12 florins) and 2 guilders in Copenhagen to a Strassburger, to whom he fruitlessly wrote. There was some silver jewelry – vest buttons, earrings, shirt-clasps. Künstel gave the court 50 talers in wages due his journeyman, payable on return of certain tools and settlement of the worker's "training fees."

Künstel's household possessed "a small German bible" (*Teutsche Biebel*) – a rare documentary appearance of the national name. There were songbooks, plus – a remnant of Künstel's wanderings – a "guide to traveling and inns," and various building designs. He owned a suit with a white woolen vest, plus everyday clothes, lederhosen, and three pair of shoes, tallying altogether 10 talers. His wife's clothes, unremarkable except for "two silk caps with golden clasps," rated 20 talers. Bedding was ample, livestock adequate. Marie and the children had consumed the grain and victuals on hand.[80] She recovered from her husband loss by marrying Stavenow blacksmith Christoph Jahncke, who took the inn, though doubtless she managed it. She bore Jahncke two children before expiring in 1737. The 1740 inventory, made at Jahncke's remarriage, noted that "since [his] children's birth, household assets which were once appraised at 108 talers have in no way improved, but because of the great burden of raising the children . . . have diminished considerably." Yet Jahncke managed to marry a Premslin miller's daughter, whose dowry must have thickened his wallet.[81]

In these stories, tenant-farmer Hartz refused to help tavernkeeper Peters improve his fortunes, while smallholder's daughter Marie Besen

---

[79] Ibid., fos. 28–9.   [80] No. 591, fos. 62–5.   [81] Ibid., fo. 5; no. 324, fo. 1.

succeeded in marrying twice among minor entrepreneurs despite her rocky start with Künstel. Such courtroom dramas over premarital pregnancy were not uncommon, nor did they stigmatize the contending parties if marriage followed. Apart from personal qualities, Marie probably benefited from membership in a successful village mayors' lineage. In the marital network encompassing these people local millers figured.

Stavenow's inn is ill documented after 1740, but it changed hands frequently. In 1757 Conrad Kleist leased it to Heinrich Haussmann, former nearby estate administrator, on terms similar to Peters', including grazing his cattle "with the little [landless] people."[82] In the early 1770s disease decimated the family of tavern keeper Bergholz, married to a bailiff's daughter. In 1782 linen-weaver Wulff ran the inn, while from 1794 to 1808 and beyond it was blacksmith Künstler's (probably precursor carpenter Künstel's kinsman). After 1770, Major Kleist skirmished with the collectors of the hated excise tax, levied in towns on retail sales, and with Perleberg's town fathers. Both antagonists aimed to halt his schnapps sales by the quart to his lordship's residents and outsiders alike, whether at Stavenow or, after its 1784 opening, Dargardt tavern. On Christmas Eve 1770 the Royal "Gardes à Pied" carried out a Blüthen "house visitation," finding mayor Glissmann in possession of a four-quart brandy cask bought from Stavenow inn. Attendant officials claimed Glissmann ought to buy his liquor in Perleberg, where it was excisable, and accordingly seized it for tax defraudation.[83]

The Blumenthals' lawyers defended Stavenow's ancient right to maintain a tax-free inn, and Hasse successfully argued the case in 1745. Major Kleist was expanding schnapps production, relying on Judge Betich to uphold his right of sale. Betich claimed mayor Glissmann was free to buy schnapps wherever publicly sold, exhorting the excise-men "to leave [Glissmann] in peace and spare him such importunities." Glissmann's predecessor, he added, ran Blüthen's tavern, obtaining his drinks from Stavenow until about thirty years previously, when "the tenant-farmer at the time" – Hartz – "made such a bad beer and schnapps no one wanted to drink them." Blüthen tavern since then bought its stock in Perleberg, but could rightly do so at Stavenow. Undeterred, excise-men in 1771 seized a "quart of grain brandy" from cottager Rohr. Kleist complained to Betich that only since the establishment (1766) of the "Régie" (an excise tax-farm, run for Frederick II by French officials) had his liquor-selling rights been challenged. Betich

---

[82] No. 716, fos. 237–8.   [83] No. 313, fo. 27.

protested again, optimistically invoking the Royal Will to uphold "His Highness's nobility's possessions and privileges." Kleist sourly inscribed his copy of this letter: "unanswered once again."[84]

In 1782, young day laborer and shepherd's son David Weitstrauch was arrested after buying 15 quarts of schnapps and some allegedly illegal tobacco at Stavenow inn. He was taking them to fellow workers at Eldenburg crown estate when "seized" by taxmen. He was conscious of no wrong. "He believed," Betich wrote, "he had taken the straight path." The Régie found him guilty, fining him 11 talers – eight times the evaded excise's value. Weitstrauch said resignedly "he had no property whatever and so would have to await the ruling." Charged with trying to escape arrest, he said he "ran downstairs" because he suddenly felt ill, offering Stavenow's court bailiff a taler, not to bribe him, but to sleep in his office and not the jail. Linen-weaver and tavernkeeper Wulff disclaimed knowledge of Weitstrauch's purchases, saying his wife took care of such business. He was only a "hired tavernkeeper," selling Kleist's schnapps by the quart, without markup, to anyone who wanted it, as the Major instructed him. "He made no profit thereby except on the small quantity" – perhaps it was actually large – "that he sold in the inn by the glass." The taxmen asked Kleist for a quick response since Weitstrauch was sitting, "on account of poverty," in health-menacing jail.[85]

Weitstrauch resolved this dilemma by escaping, presumably with the court bailiff's connivance, and disappearing. Later Judge Gutike, replacing the retired Betich, successfully defended Kleist's rights before Berlin's "Excise Court of Electoral Brandenburg." In 1789 the Major was again under attack, now for quart sales to Stavenow manorial settlement outsiders. Kleist claimed tax conflicts frightened people away from his inns. He averred that Premslin, Glövzin, and Blüthen taverns were "without significance," villagers there fetching drinks from Perleberg. But "from immemorial times" all Stavenow subjects bought schnapps quarts at the manorial seat. Formerly, female seigneurial stores managers sold beer and schnapps directly to the public, but this practice hurt the inn and was discontinued. The farmers, said Kleist, "can brew their own beer at sowing and harvest-time." In 1795 Gutike tried to dissuade Perleberg authorities from suing Kleist, appealing to the Major's "advanced age," to previous pro-Stavenow rulings, and to traditional "good understanding" between lordship and town.[86]

---

[84] Ibid., fos. 28–30; no. 714, fos. 112–13.   [85] No. 313, fos. 8–14.   [86] Ibid., fos. 52–7.

In 1802 the jousting continued, but 1808 estate-sale appraisals were silent on legal difficulties. Dargardt tavern sold Stavenow spirits, paying an annual 19-taler tax assessment to the corporate nobility's beer-tax office rather than the crown's excise-office. In 1790, when this tax was 11 talers, Kleist reported six-year average Dargardt sales of 38 barrels of beer and 2,040 quarts of schnapps. In 1808 they had almost doubled. Stavenow tavern in 1808 sold tax-free 80 large hogsheads of schnapps (14,400 quarts) annually. This quantity would have yielded a yearly income from Stavenow inn alone of 2,400 talers, nearly six times all the lordship's annual schnapps sales in 1746–59. The 1808 appraisers found 65 talers' annual rent from combined smithy and inn too low and advocated an increase.[87]

Major Kleist enormously increased liquor production and sales, despite the combined opposition of absolutist taxmen and local bourgeoisie. He was fortunate in having an ancient tax exemption, originally granted by Mecklenburg but ratified by Prussian authorities at the Kleists' accession. It was inscribed, Major Kleist protested, "in my letter of enfeoffment" of 1722.[88] His liquor sales witness local population growth, rising cash incomes (if not real wages) and, perhaps, more fulsome drinking among ordinary people. From these trends seigneurial tavernkeepers too profited. Nor did Kleist's liquor trade impose feudal burdens on his villagers, since he sold at local prices and they were not captive consumers.[89]

In 1808 the lordship's costly alcohol-processing equipment comprised "three distilling pans and a 12-cask brewing vat," the latter holding about 1,200 quarts. The brewer earned 30 talers yearly, 4 talers more than in 1760. In 1766 Kleist accepted a deposit, cancelable on three months' notice, of 220 talers "in old gold" from brewer Georg Schulze, on which Kleist paid 5 percent interest until Schulze's death in 1782, and for two more years to his widow. Such money's secure possession placed the brewer, who (unlike his wife) signed his name well, among lesser artisan masters.[90]

As for village taverns, they were not, despite Major Kleist's dismissal, insignificant, though his inns' competition doubtless squeezed them. As we saw, the finest farm wife's wardrobe on record belonged to Blüthen

---

[87] No. 39, fos. 10–20, 54. High German = *Oxhaupt* or *Oxhoft*, each containing by 1808 reckoning 180 quarts. No. 720, fo. I. In 1691 the Blumenthals reported supplying the inn with 40 barrels of schnapps, equaling at 100 quarts per barrel 4,000 quarts. The 1746–59 accounts show that, on average, yearly sales amounted to 3,300 quarts, sold at 2.5–3.0 groschen per quart. Major Kleist's schnapps fetched 4 groschen. No. 709, fos. 236–41.

[88] No. 313, fos. 36–7.

[89] No. 200, fo. 101. But in 1728 the lordship fined hired timber-cutters for not buying Stavenow beer.

[90] No. 717, fo. 243.

halfholder-tavernkeeper Ohlert's spouse, who died in 1759: a Lenzen master artisan's step-daughter with 112 talers' cash dowry. Ohlert himself ran a well-stocked farm for twenty years or more, but under his descendants it weakened, and mention of tavernkeeping ceased.[91] In 1760 deceased fullholder-tavernkeeper Christian Diercks' widow Trine ran Glövzin tavern, while continuing to head her farm. She operated the tavern in a cottage for which she paid additional rent. Before Diercks took the farm in 1720, it was managed by "Joachim Neumann's widow, the tavern-mistress," whose daughter Diercks married.[92] In Premslin, fullholder David Hecht ran the tavern from 1718 to 1741. He commuted his labor services to cash, traded lumber, and left his farm in sound condition. He married Anna Niemanns, probably the Glövzin tavern-mistress's kinswoman, with a good dowry and wardrobe.[93]

Tavernkeeping offered women some scope for profits and entrepreneurship. But with it came drunken quarrels, such as one from Trine Niemanns' Glövzin years. On 1731 Whitsuntide holiday's second day, Stavenow senior farmhand Hans Milatz joined his brother (their father's farmhand) and another farm worker, buying at Niemanns' tavern a quarter-barrel of beer – a large quantity, shared perhaps with others. They were, as plaintiff Milatz later testified, "all at peace, and were there [at the tavern] in the evening until nightfall." But then, he claimed, Trine Niemanns began cursing him as a "swindler and rascal. It was because she was drinking." She said, "you sponger, you whore-chaser!" and told him "he should never again set foot in her house, which was impossible for him to accept, since others might hold it against him." This happened when "she wanted to lead him out of the house." This he resisted, without cursing her, saying only "you're not better than me, and nobody who's honest can say so." Milatz's companions backed his story, but Trine testified the three were drunk, Hans wagering with the others for schnapps. Hasse found Trine guilty of cursing, "which as tavern-mistress befits her least of all," and of "illicitly serving beer at Whitsuntide." To satisfy Milatz's pride, she was obliged to shake his hand. Hasse fined her 2 talers, but on her husband's pleading halved the sum.[94]

BLACKSMITHS

Like seigneurial tavernkeepers, blacksmiths were lesser village notables, distinguished by master artisan status and, occasionally, some comfort.

---

[91] No. 513, fos. 51–9.   [92] No. 200, fos. 45–6; no. 259.
[93] Ibid., fos. 228–9; no. 324, fos. 2–3; no. 326, fos 63–5.   [94] No. 591, fo. 17.

They too leased taverns, entrusting them to their wives. Tavernkeeper Marie Besen and her second husband, smith Jahncke, were once worth 108 talers, but many village farms commanded greater capital. Similarly modest were the circumstances of Matthes Cober, a Stavenow smith (bearing a pastor's name) who died in 1730. He left five children from two marriages, inheriting between them only 75 talers. A daughter was a town servant. Apart from Spangenberg's *Hauspostill*, Cober's only books were for church and prayer. He left a "gray woolen coat with camel-yarn buttons," a vest with brass buttons, a blue neckerchief, two pairs of stockings, one pair of shoes, and leather gloves. His furniture counted four wicker armchairs, wooden plates and earthenware bowls, an "oak bacon-box," pepper mill and ginger-grater. His smithy housed tools worth 30 talers, including an anvil and twenty-three hammers, nine tongs, and bellows. He paid the lordship 12 talers yearly rent for newly constructed buildings, garden and orchard, free grazing for three cattle and 3–4 pigs and, for 5 talers more, meadow. He left no debts, nor had he lent money. His food on hand rated 6 talers. The impression is of spareness and self-control.[95]

A generation later, Stavenow's smith was Joachim Thormann, in circumstances markedly better than Cober's, judging by his 1758 marriage to former estate official and current Stavenow tavern keeper Heinrich Haussmann's daughter. An account entitled "the entire dowry that Haussmann has given Meister Thormann for his daughter" totaled 266 talers. It displays comfort unsurpassed by prosperous farmhouses, and more urbane self-presentation by Haussmann's daughter than most village women mustered. It shows, too, some of manorialism's profits passing through estate officials' hands into village notables' pockets.

Haussmann's daughter's clothing counted twelve dresses and jackets or camisoles. Most valuable were combinations of these items in " black *traktedam*" (5.5 talers) and "half-silk" (4 talers), along with "striped five-comb dress" and half-silk camisoles (1.5 talers each). Other dress colors were yellow, black and blue, red and green, brown and white, and gingham ("*ging gang*"). Most valuable among many scarves were those of muslin with lace or embroidery, or flower-printed cotton. The two best bonnets rated 2 talers. There was a "street cap with lace" and "black Moor's cap." Numerous aprons included one of "red gingham." She possessed a good bodice, and twenty-five upper and undershirts, plus "green velvet gloves" (1 taler). There were five Frisian tablecloths and

---

[95] No. 200, fos. 235–43.

one "fine hand-towel" (12 groschen each), apart from "five ordinary tablecloths" (2 talers). Among valuable bedding were "two fine bed-sheets" (4 talers) and three white pillow-cases (1 taler). Journeyman's and housemaid's beds with linen rated 5 talers each, the master bed without linen 7 talers, plus "curtain around bed" (30 groschen) and mattress, pillows, and bolsters (1.5 talers). There were clothes trunks, pots and kettles, four good cows, five pigs large and small, three heifers, plus loom "which they will keep but the father will also use." Finally, "in cash Herr Haussmann has given his daughter 100 talers." Here was a well-dowered young villager.[96]

At Stavenow, the smith's dwelling and workshop belonged to the lordship, which leased it to tenants such as Thormann. In villages, blacksmiths bought and sold their properties, paying minor seigneurial fees. We can follow several generations of smiths in Garlin, where in 1723 Hans Bernhart bought the smithy for 50 talers. A predecessor recently sold it to move "to [East] Prussia." Following a fire, the lordship granted Bernhart building materials and two rent-free years, after which he paid 4 talers rent and 2 talers for meadow.[97] In 1735 he joined village mayor and von Karstedt subject Will, selling in Berlin two wagon-loads of dried fruit they bought on credit for 41 talers from Karstedt's estate manager. Later, Will petitioned the crown against Bernhart, saying that although they reaped "considerable profit," "realizing 56 talers," Bernhart kept most of the money, rather than sharing it. When Will remonstrated, "Bernhart attacked me not only with rudest calumnies, cursing me repeatedly as rogue and swindler, cheating Your Majesty and subject villagers, but he also seized me unexpectedly by the throat, pulled hair from my head, and beat me bloody, as tavernkeeper Gerloff will attest." Will sought redress from his "opponent's overlord, tenant-farmer Hartz, but I got no hearing from him."[98]

Blacksmith Bernhart survived a Chamber Court inquest. Will's and his venture benefited from the nobility's privilege to sell manorial products duty- and excise-free, for the two commoners obtained a certificate from Karstedt's chief administrator, von Knesebeck, verifying they were selling the fruit on behalf of the manor. From customs officials' notations on this certificate it emerges that, to drive a loaded wagon from Perleberg to Fehrbellin, about fifty miles and still another day's journey from Berlin, required three days. Such collusion in noble tax evasion displays villagers' tactical flexibility.

[96] No. 324, fos. 27–8.   [97] No. 200, fos. 39, 45, 202.   [98] No. 597, fos. 132–3.

In 1745, at Garlin's "combined court," representing all manors with villages subjects, "Hans Bernhart in all the lordships' presence dared strike and box the ears of von Winterfeldt subject Ohrtmann, nor would he cease until Herr Erhardt restrained him." Two days later, Hasse harshly sentenced him, as punishment for his "great outrage," to stand two hours in the "Spanish overcoat" and pay the court bailiff's charges.[99] In 1754 Bernhart's son, Christoffel, succeeded as blacksmith. Of Christoffel's five siblings, one sister was a Mecklenburg combmaker's wife, while the other "kept house for the father." Two brothers were journeymen smiths, in Grabow and Berlin, a third was apprenticed to brother Christoffel. Old Hans wished Christoffel to pay each sibling 8 talers from the smithy, plus 4 talers' modest annual retirement income to himself. Hans had built for retirement a "little house," with a cow, four sheep, and a pig. When he helped with smithy work, he would receive 6 pfennigs per job, as Christoffel's brother did.

Christoffel's new wife, of Sargleben blacksmiths' lineage, had delivered a "marriage gift of 100 talers," plus a cow and three trunks of clothes and linen. Christoffel said, optimistically, he did not know what more she might bring. A marriage contract still needed issuance, but "they have pledged each other unto death all their love and marital loyalty and solidarity." Old Hans having approved this "marriage pact," it was to be formally inscribed along with Christoffel's deed of possession. The new married couple signed their names, she quite well. But three days later Hans wrote of his son, both imperiously and cryptically, that:

he promises to give me 8 talers each year and some cabbage land and trees on it, and is thinking after a convenient time to make the change that the person will have free housing after the death [that is, after old Hans's own death]. In this matter I hereby co-decide.

Perhaps "the person" was Christoffel's sister, but it may have been a partner old Bernhart decided to take into his "little house."[100]

Christoffel outlived his father's whims. In 1769 "tobacco inspectors" arrested his son of twelve years, returning from Mecklenburg with a shoulder-basket containing shirts a former servant-girl, now married, sewed for Christoffel. The excise-men, threatening to beat the "frightened" boy if he did not open the basket, discovered a half-pound of tobacco, and so detained him in a nearby "mayor's court." Christoffel went to "take him home, since he is man with a fixed residence" who could be trusted not to abscond. The tax-court heard Bernhart's

[99] No. 591, fo. 127.   [100] No. 326, fo. 202; ibid., 18. X. 1755.

disclaimers of smuggling, agreeing to dismiss charges if he "purified himself with an oath," though the tobacco would be confiscated regardless. The stiff 10-taler fine and 6 talers in court costs that Bernhart finally paid show that he shrank from damnation-threatening vows.[101] Evident here again is the excise-men's ruthlessness. Ordinary people hated them for their joyless zeal.

Despite the Bernharts' faults and vicissitudes, old Hans had persevered for thirty-one years, seeing his four sons trained in his craft, succeeded by an evidently competent son with a well-dowered wife, with whom he swore everlasting love and loyalty and raised a son to age twelve at least. Consistent perhaps with old Hans's domineering tendencies, his wife and daughters only hover in the documentary shadows. But possibly the most aggressive of Stavenow's blacksmiths was Christoff Jahncke, Marie Besen's husband. In 1747 Jahncke's step-son Joachim Künstel sued him for non-payment from Joachim's inheritance of money he needed for fees to advance in Lenzen's smiths' guild. Jahncke said he could have trained Künstel, who instead "furtively ran off." Künstel bridled, saying "Jahncke had practically beaten the eyes out of his head, so his relatives and guardians took him away and placed him with Meister Richter in Sargleben." An uncle and guardian confirmed this, excusing "neglect of their duty" in having their charge's 36-taler inheritance properly paid, thinking this had occurred upon sale of Künstel's deceased father's tools. Hasse held Jahncke to his "very fair" obligations, adding that if the tools could not be found, the guardians to whom they were entrusted must pay the equivalent value to young Künstel. A year later, when smith Jahncke moved away, the debt remained unpaid, leading Hasse to transfer it to the Premslin mill, owned by Jahncke's in-laws.[102]

Here again appear the brutal treatment of minors, behavior both conscientious and negligent on step-children's guardians' part, but also Hasse's perseverance in enforcing contracts. Despite Jahncke's marriage alliance with Premslin millers, he could not amass assets at Stavenow. In 1741 Hasse fined him several talers for wood theft, and later he quarreled with a tailor over the ownership of linen cloth their wives wove.[103] Blacksmiths had difficulty collecting their often individually meager fees.

---

[101] No. 717, fos. 262–4.
[102] Jahncke's father-in-law, the Premslin miller, agreed to pay this debt, but had not done so before dying in 1752. Hasse imposed 10 taler yearly payments on the miller's widow, who was free to seek recompense from Jahncke in his new jurisdiction. No. 326, fos. 140–1, 147; no. 715, fo. 47.
[103] No. 591, fos. 99–100, 123–4.

In 1738–9, Hartz threatened Jahncke with eviction for not settling accounts with the lordship, but Jahncke accused Hartz of reducing his bill from 31 to 26 talers. Though Hartz retorted that the blacksmith mistreated his horses, Hasse ordered Hartz to pay Jahncke's full bill, a scene later repeated with Premslin leaseholder Birkholtz, who countered futilely he had cultivated rented church land for Jahncke. A 1749 list of Jahncke's charges to Erhardt included "shoeing with two old horseshoes, 2 groschen; with one new horseshoe, 3 groschen; hammering out an ax, 1 groschen; making a hatchet for Christian, 14 groschen; bleeding two horses, 2 groschen; making a new kettle-hook, 3 groschen."[104]

More could be earned from treating animals. Jahncke once charged 2 talers for bleeding cattle. Stavenow smith Thormann shakily penned a 1753 bill for treating farmer "Hinst's" [Hintze's] horse, which a nobleman's hunter "shot through the backbone . . . and a piece of bone split off and I took it for treatment . . . and have already spent in cash for medicine 4.16.- talers and demand for my efforts 2 talers."

But the horse can't be brought to shoo the flies with its tail and there's no hope of healing it. Do not think the smith overlooked anything – a man was summoned from Perleberg named Schieberling who has been an army smith for 19 years.

The army smith added his charges for eight visits at 6 groschen each.[105]

Finally, Premslin blacksmith Joachim Völsch's fortunes well illustrate the pressures and burdens untimely death generated within economically hard-pressed families. In 1724 Völsch married the widowed Margarethe Brünings who with her husband Hans Möller was raising four children before Möller's 1721 death. In 1690 Möller took the war-devastated smithy, later also renting an abandoned farm. After his death, Margarethe tried running the smithy with Hans Joachim Wegener, whom she agreed to marry. But Wegener absconded with one of her horses and a carriage, "diminishing the estate," which before this loss tallied 99 talers.

Kleist, reclaiming the rented farm, selected from among the smithy's heirs a daughter to marry incoming smith Völsch, who agreed to pay her siblings modest inheritances and support his mother-in-law while she raised a small son, who would be "educated in the trade." Völsch would also pay for his mother-in-law's burial, but – Hasse added – if she wanted to keep the big kettle, she would have to credit Völsch 4

---

[104] Ibid., fos. 82; 109, 114; no. 713, fo. 270; no. 714, fo. 180.   [105] No. 715, fo. 312.

talers. Völsch swore obedience "with hand and mouth" and received
his "certificate of hereditary tenure," at 4.5 talers yearly rent for smithy
and meadowland. He "shall on the first court day be admitted to his
duties as subject." This was almost the same legal script incoming farmers followed.[106] Later Völsch complained his mother-in-law was maintaining, probably under her children's pressure, that "everything
belonged to her," and that he should pay his brothers-in-law larger settlements. But Völsch retorted that, because his mother-in-law's previous "bridegroom went away, and squandered a horse and cow," his
obligations should not rise. Hasse agreed.[107]

In 1740 Margarethe, Völsch's wife of sixteen years, died leaving him
with four children. He took a new wife with meager possessions. In 1748,
his brothers-in-law asked Hasse to order his retirement and hand over
the paternal smithy to them, claiming it had been given Völsch for only
twenty years. They also accused Völsch's sister of beating their mother.
At least they wanted their long-dead father's clothing and tools (worth 32
talers). In 1750, his elderly mother-in-law having died, Völsch defended
himself, referring to Wegener's "godless" abandonment of "the mother
[his mother-in-law, whom he] fed for twenty-six years." Hasse backed
Völsch, saying Kleist was free to give him the smithy and that "he fed
the mother and children that they might not have to go begging before
the town gates," though Hasse ordered him to pay the 20 talers he owed
his disgruntled and disinherited brothers-in-law. Because of Völsch, in
their view, they failed to gain independent livelihoods. But work-worn
Völsch could reflect that he spent ten years longer supporting his mother-in-law than with his wife, and that – seemingly with little thanks – he
saved the fatherless Möller family from penury.[108]

PARISH CLERGY

If blacksmith's property such as Völsch's was scantier than solid farmers',
local pastors' fortunes towered far above those of cultivators and artisans
alike. Though no Stavenow parsonage inventories survive, their assets
were substantial. Pastors embodied authority as much as they radiated
bourgeois prosperity, but that is another chapter's subject. These pages
look briefly at their material condition before turning to the sextons and
tailor-schoolmasters, whose roles sometimes merged and who figured,
because of their functions if not incomes, among minor notables.

---

[106] No. 28, fo. 67; no. 200 fos. 3, 177.   [107] No. 200, fos. 17–18, 84.
[108] No. 591, fo. 99; no. 326, fo. 147; no. 715, fos. 18–19.

In the Lutheran Reformation's aftermath, it was the parishes' lay patrons' – in rural districts, mainly noble landlords' – responsibility to assure the now-married clergy adequate incomes. These might derive from arable land attached in the medieval colonization to parishes, or from grain rents from farmers assigned to parishes instead of such lands, which the nobility often took for themselves. Lutheran officials' sixteenth-century visitations found Premslin parish with 2 hides, worked by two "parson's smallholders." Besides income from these lands, the pastor received 30 bushels' grain rent the Quitzows assigned him from three villagers. Similarly, in Stavenow parish, including Mesekow village, the parsonage sowed for itself 30 bushels yearly, while collecting rents of 75 bushels of rye and 47 of barley or oats. By 1600 the Quitzows had diverted much of this rent into their various pockets. In sixteenth-century Blüthen, Glövzin, and Karstädt, parishes retained only meager plowland. Instead, Blüthen's pastor claimed 2 bushels' tribute grain from fullholders, one from smallholders, which in 1581 ought to have tallied 54 bushels. Glövzin's pastor should likewise have received 37 bushels. The Karstädt pastor collected 24 bushels from two farmers and a half- or quarter-bushel from remaining fullholders or smallholders. Pastors also collected parishioners' seasonal contributions, such as from fullholders a loaf and sausage at Christmas, and ten Easter eggs. At christenings pastors sat at the dining table. From *Sechswöchnerinnen* – women first attending church after bearing children – a groschen or two were due, as also was the case for marriages and funerals. Funeral sermon charges were extra, depending on eloquence. All households seemingly paid the sixteenth-century "four seasons' penny." Pastors sometimes shared these incomes with sextons, if they had one.[109]

The Thirty Years War and its aftermath played havoc with Stavenow parishes' grain rents, while parsonages' eighteenth-century incomes are not otherwise exactly known. Inequalities had evidently grown worse, for the Blumenthals conditioned Johann Sauerbier's 1702 Premslin appointment on sharing his "rather adequate" income with his Blüthen counterpart, "because his income is very poor." Sauerbier agreed to give his colleague 24 bushels of rye and 10 talers yearly, and if Premslin income proved "plentiful," he would give more, "at [the Blüthener's] request and according to need, as love demands."[110]

[109] Victor Herold, ed., *Die brandenburgischen Kirchenvisitations-Abschiede und -Register des XVI. und XVII. Jahrhunderts.* Band I: *Die Prignitz* (Berlin, 1931), 386–7, 396–7, 404–5, 421–3, 436–7.
[110] No. 710, fo. 9.

Yet by 1748, the Blüthen pastor, now serving Stavenow and Mesekow parishes alongside his home village and Groß Linde, was more prosperous, though not because of seigneurial largesse, which in 1809 yielded but 12 rye-bushels annually. Of elderly Blüthen pastor Kober's retirement the Kleists observed that "with barely 200 talers [annual income] to support this parsonage," it was a question, apart from "necessary good lodgings," what the retiree should receive, especially in cash.[111] Two hundred talers yearly was, if net income, enviable by village standards. We saw that Blüthen pastor Bertram and his "maiden sister" in 1754–6 deposited 1,000 talers at interest with Frau Kleist – valuable capital by any reckoning – while Blüthen's pastor later lent a miller 100 talers.[112] As for Premslin parish, now encompassing Glövzin and Karstädt churches, the pastor in 1757 was cultivating with his two smallholders' labor land sowable in 40 bushels. If he was receiving the 34 tributary bushels credited him in 1727, his income was not inadequate.[113]

Pastors' dependency on parishioners' good-will for rents and other payments doubtless galled them when arrears or disputes arose. In 1715, a new Premslin pastor, studying church accounts, listed among deficiencies to be addressed the question "whether those who do nothing to help the church or parsonage, either with food or labor, and yet enjoy free burials and bell-ringing, aren't obliged to contribute something." The miller had not paid for his church pew since 1705, the smith for his two pews since 1711, and the tailor for his pew since 1714. And should not those who lived there but married outside the parish pay him the "customary offering"?[114] Yet university theological faculty graduates ardently, even desperately, sought appointments to such clerical livings, which alone enabled them to marry and seek further advancement. The parishes' noble patrons could not always dictate succession to vacancies, since higher church authorities rejected implausible candidates. Other lordships with parish subjects might champion their own clients, while village communes might support or quarrel over candidates.

In 1715 considerable agitation accompanied the selection of a successor to a Premslin pastor forced to resign under scandalous circumstances. Stavenow leaseholder Georg Neumann recommended to Countess Blumenthal in Berlin nomination of "Joachim Willebrandt, my children's tutor." In the three parish villages, factions formed for

---

[111] No. 714, fos. 172–3; no. 62.   [112] No. 716, fo. 73.   [113] No. 326, fo. 211.   [114] No. 711, fo. 7.

and against Willebrandt and his rival, the von Kaltenhof family's tutor.[115] The Blumenthal guardians commissioned Perleberg notary Straube to investigate objections to candidate Willebrandt, including his preaching, of which Kaltenhof leaseholder Müller wrote that it was, "by virtue of its good enunciation, very understandable." At issue, seemingly, was the gulf between educated and popular speech. Willebrandt, who entered Mecklenburg's Rostock University in 1697, wrote with calculated self-deprecation to the Blumenthal guardians of his "few studies" and the "unworthy public disputation held by me" upon his graduation.

A letter from Lenzen Church Inspector Hasse, one of Judge Hasse's elder kinsmen, championed Willebrandt, who was "born in Lenzen of a well-known lineage [*Freundschaft*]." He attended "good schools," advancing to

the celebrated *Gymnasio Berolinensi* [where he] graduated competently in *literiis humanioribus* and in his favorite *studio theologico* performed rather *solider*, as he has praiseworthily proven not only in successful private tutoring of other people's children but likewise through learned and edifying interpretation of the Holy Word of God in public sermons to many Christian communes.

It would be hard to find another candidate "hereabouts with similar gifts and grace." His "life and comportment" were "praiseworthy," serving "to edify his fellow men."

A similarly supportive letter arrived from "Wachtel, Pastor and Inspector" in the town of Wilsnack. Willebrandt for several years tutored "my sister's children at Stavenow" – Wachtel was tenant-farmer Neumann's brother-in-law – "and conducted himself admirably well in his station." Knowing Willebrandt well, Wachtel had never observed in him "any *principia enthusiastarum, Fanaticorum, Photinianorum* [statism] or other *Haereticorum,* but rather he has always believed and professed *Theologiam orthodoxam.* He has, moreover, a good grasp of *Theologiae moralem,* which with God's grace will enable him to beneficially exercise the preacher's office." Wachtel "entreat[ed] the Lord to grant [Willebrandt] grace to be worthy of his calling, so as to bless him in it and make him true to it through Christ!"

Tenant-farmer Neumann deepened support for Willebrandt, who lived three years at Stavenow, tutoring Neumann's children "with much profit" and ably preaching at the manor-house in the two-week intervals between Pastor Sauerbier's regular services there. His learning was

---

[115] Ibid., fos. 13, 22–3, 27–34.

"altogether solid," as his record at Rostock "sufficiently verifies." Among Willebrandt's other advocates was von Winterfeldt's Dallmin pastor and Blüthen Pastor Jacob Cober, who knew him from the Berlin Gymnasium, averring he was "pious" and "gifted in preaching with considerable dignity and an understandable manner of speaking."

Such was Willebrandt's triumphant engine of support. But when in 1762 Major Kleist nominated "candidate Hindenburg" to a pastorate, the Berlin Consistory rejected him, "not because of human imperfections, not even because of [Hindenburg's] incomplete university studies, but because of real incompetence to hold the preacher's office." Kleist had four weeks to propose a new candidate, or the Consistory would decide, since his powers were only *ex jure devolutionis*. In 1768, Kleist petitioned the Consistory to appoint Christoph Höpffner in Premslin without the obligatory Berlin interview and trial sermon, arguing that Höpffner, related by name to Stavenow subject farmers, for several years was *Rector Scholae* in Lenzen. The Consistory refused, leading Kleist to deduct the 46 talers expended in Höpffner's (eventually successful) Berlin trip and ordination from Stavenow church funds. Here, as in many other governmental encounters, Kleist suffered rebuff.[116]

A pastor's appointment usually entailed his predecessor's retirement or provisions for his widow, as in Frau Kleist's 1748 regulation of Blüthen Pastor Kober's succession by Georg Samuel Bertram. After Kober's (more than) forty-year service, his "advanced age" and "complete loss in the last year of bodily and mental strength" left no hope for recovery. Bertram had preached for Kober "to the communes' satisfaction" and had "held the three sermons ordained by His Royal Majesty with honor and distinction, as witnessed by the Lords Consistorial Councilors and Provosts in Berlin." Bertram therefore became adjunct pastor, obliged to share with retired Kober (seemingly a widower) lifelong one-third the parsonage's income or its cash equivalent.

Of Bertram Frau Kleist wrote that "I myself am even more satisfied with the Herr Candidate inasmuch as his edifying teaching and spiritual way of life are sufficiently known to me from the many years when he was my children's tutor." She wrote, formulaically, that his charge was:

to teach and preach plainly and purely the salvation-bringing Word of God as it is contained in the Prophetic and Apostolic writings, and also in the Four

[116] No. 717, fos. 77, 281–2, 288.

Chief Symbols no less than in the Augsburg Confession and its explications and Luther's Catechism; to administer the Sacraments as Christ instituted them; to diligently examine catechists; to visit and comfort the sick; and through an irreproachable manner of living to seek tirelessly to shine forth for the edification of all, in which may the Gracious God plentifully bestow upon him His Holy Spirit.

When Kober died, Bertram would become *pastor ordinarius*. After the customary "half-year of grace," during which the Consistory harvested Kober's retirement income, Bertram would enjoy the full living.[117]

Such was a transition favorable to the successor, unlike Countess Blumenthal's 1702 appointment of Premslin's Sauerbier. He replaced Pastor Elias Wilhelm, "a man who has lived out his years" and suffered a stroke. Sauerbier, married and living in Blüthen, would have "free board" and transport, on condition he help care for the old pastor "so that he will not be troubled and dejected." Following Wilhelm's death, his widow would enjoy the "half-year of grace," making arrangements to vacate the parsonage, as widowed Frau Willebrandt would do years later, when the Kleists gave her a rent-free cottage at Stavenow. The Countess signed herself in her appointment letter to Sauerbier as "My Much-Admired Sir's Friendly Patron," words that in future would haunt Sauerbier's mind.[118]

Stavenow pastors employed a language of marital and parental affection reflecting exemplary bourgeois family life as understood in Protestant Germany. In burial-register entries, early eighteenth-century Blüthen pastor Beyer wrote of his "heartily beloved son Achatz [who] passed away blessedly amid our prayers and tears," and later of "my pastoral companion [*Pastorin*] and deeply beloved wife . . . [who] at six o'clock in the morning in the distress of childbirth gently and blessedly passed away in Jesus her Savior, forty-one years."[119] In 1770 Premslin Pastor Emeritus Wolfgang Ludwig Carsted registered in court his marriage agreement of ten years earlier with his second and present wife, "Frau Marriage-Companion [*Ehegenossin*] Catherine Margarete *née* Breitsprach."

These 1770 arrangements again confirm women's comparatively strong property rights. To allay any doubts, Betich confirmed "the marriage companions are, praise God, possessed of good and healthy minds." Medical doctor Gutike, Betich's successor Judge Gutike's kinsman, attested that Carsted demonstrated "right reason with not the

[117] No. 714, fos. 167–8.   [118] No. 717, fos. 78–9; no. 710, fos. 6–7.
[119] Blüthen Begräbnis-Register, 1700, 1706; Wunder, "'*Er ist die Sonn*'," ch. III.

least detectable deviation from the mind's proper workings." Perhaps Enlightenment enthusiasm for psychology was here in play, though some of the elderly Carsted's relatives may have been angling for his legacy. Another witness descended from Premslin tenant-farmers, signaling the local notables' urban–rural network within which pastors located themselves.

Should Carsted predecease his wife, she would recover her dowry in full and, "as some compensation for love and loyalty," also inherit half his estate, the other half going to his first-marriage daughter, "Maiden Marie Elisabeth Carol." If Marie outlived her step-mother, she would receive half of what Carsted left his second wife. Brandenburg Minors' College was holding Marie's inheritance from her deceased mother until she reached maturity. Carsted wished that, if his daughter outlived him, she should – considering "her sickly condition" – bequeath her estate to those who "treated and cared for her most loyally." She should remember the "goodness" of her step-mother, who promised to keep Carsted's daughter "and regard her as her own child" until she could care for herself. Something of the daughter's estate would thus be left to Carsted's second wife or "the Breitsprach family." All this Carsted's wife "thankfully accepted from her dear marital master [*lieben Eheherrn*]." The couple agreed, finally, that, if she predeceased him, he should keep the bedding and dress of honor she brought in, but otherwise return her dowry to her "nearest blood-relations."[120]

THE SEXTON AND THE TAILOR-SCHOOLMASTERS

Sextons (*Küster* [Latin: *custos*]) assisted pastors in singing and scriptural readings during services, and by ringing church bells. Stavenow counted only the Premslin sexton who, according to sixteenth-century visitations, received a house and garden, meadow and arable patch, supplemented by half-bushel rye contributions from fullholders and quarter-bushels from smallholders, plus minor occasional payments.[121] In 1809, he was also collecting 4 bushels of seigneurial rye.

Premslin sexton Barthel Sauber earned extra income penning villagers' documents and helping in their harvests. He married a schoolmaster's daughter bearing smith Jahncke's name and, after her 1730 death, a farmer-tavernkeeper's daughter. He rented bits of cropland, but kept no horses. He owned four cows, twelve sheep, and three pigs.

---

[120] No. 358, fos. 94–7.   [121] Herold, *Die Prignitz*, vol. I, 422, 436.

His deceased's wife's textiles were sparse: five dresses, two camisoles, bodice, two caps, and various linen and bedding, including a "linen coverlet decorated with lambs." Among housewares were a pewter bowl, a pewter-topped yellow beer mug, and an ashwood table with locked drawer. Sauber's debt-free household rated but 42 talers, although his father-in-law owed him 12 talers. While his wife's estate was rightfully Sauber's, "from love of his children" he wanted to leave them their mother's clothes and textiles. As for the 12-taler debt, "since he could not know how it would go with him in this world, in case he might be in need he wanted to share in it. But if God on High keeps him in health," the children should have it all. Their guardian, pastor's small-holder Krumm, vowed "the children shall not be slighted."[122]

Sextons quarreled with schoolteachers over church duties, and hauled parishioners to court for payment arrears. In 1738–40 Garlin sexton Hanncke charged cottager Gerloff with non-delivery since 1729 of his annual quarter-bushel. Hanncke, saying Gerloff evaded payment by playing the Kleists against the Blumenthals, asked Stavenow to cover his losses. For otherwise "I have to run about, and listen to many god-less mocking words." Sextons' arrears, like pastors', counted in farm inventories as secure debts, but rarely appeared.[123]

When schoolmasters emerge from documentary shadows, it is main-ly as tailors – unsurprisingly, since the "school heating money" (*Schulholz*) that parents paid for winter tutelage was but 3 groschen per child, and not everyone paid.[124] In 1809 Stavenow schoolmaster Bernhard, probably the earlier blacksmith's kinsman, received only 5 bushels of seigneurial rye. Yet, as evidenced by villagers' promises to "hold their children to school," schoolmasters there were, and school-houses. In Karstädt cottager-teacher Jürgen Seyers, married to a Mecklenburg gardener's widow, refurbished the schoolhouse at com-munal expense, suffering his cooking kettle's impoundment in a dispute over the 4 talers' wages he demanded. The family's fallen fortunes find reflection in his step-son's efforts to recover 100 talers from a ruined Mecklenburg merchant.[125]

The tailors made villagers' clothes, both from customers' own home-spun linen and town-bought manufactured textiles. They trafficked in second-hand clothing, sometimes sold following premature deaths. "Master tailor" Schmidt occupied a mini-smallholding, owing 1.5 days' weekly manual labor, which he refurbished for 41 talers and sold in 1771

---

[122] No. 200, fos. 250–1.   [123] No. 591, fos. 19–20, 85, 90–2; no. 326, fo. 71; no. 715, fo. 10.
[124] No. 324, fos. 20–2.   [125] No. 512, fo. 31; no. 326, fo. 124; no. 200, fos. 244–6.

for 45 talers.[126] At mid-century, Stavenow's tailor-schoolmaster was Joachim Ficke, whose manorial cottage, though not meadow, he received rent-free. In 1753 his wife died, leaving him with children aged five years and three weeks. The infant had been (in a rare reference to the practice) "put out to nurse at Friedrich Hecht's house."

Ficke's worth – clear of debts (including his wife's 5-taler funeral) – was 72 talers, including livestock. Like sexton Sauber, he rented arable patches to have some bread-grain of his own. Needing cash to remarry, he sold his deceased wife's clothing. Her best dresses and jerkins, some of gingham and poplin, rated 1–2 talers. His own clothes, fit for a tailor-schoolteacher, included a black coat with black vest and stockings (3 talers), a blue coat "already turned," ten shirts (5 groschen each), and a Spanish cane. "Shoes and stockings are old" (6 groschen). He was no intellectual, for apart from schoolroom texts he possessed only a bible and songbook. Two years later, "tailor Ficke" gave the court 17 talers in "children's money," to be safely invested. His youngest son (the nursling) had died the previous year. His remaining son's guardian, Ficke's mother-in-law, "an old woman stricken in years," deferred to Pastor Bertram, who offered to take the boy's 10-taler inheritance and "improve it to 20 talers" before its disbursement, meanwhile paying Ficke interest. Here a pastor benevolently patronized his subordinate.[127]

A decade later, Ficke's successor Johann Buchholz died, leaving a widow with four children aged 2–8. The deceased, smith Thormann's kinsman, owned some stylish clothes, whose 22 talers' worth was his children's sole paternal inheritance, since "he had no ready cash, neither when he married nor when he died." Yet he sported "a black suit with woolen vest, still good, 5 talers; a light blue woolen coat and vest, fine and not yet turned, 6 talers; a light blue percale summer coat with vest (1.8.-); white cotton stockings, old (8 groschen); black woolen stockings (8 groschen); black felt hat, very old (6 groschen), black summer hat of waxed linen (10 groschen); silver shoe-buckles (2 talers), silver pants buckles (20 groschen), neckerchiefs and clasp (20 groschen)," plus detachable sleeves and colored cotton cap (3 groschen). In these clothes, Buchholz was perhaps the best-dressed man among the villagers. His thoughts on spiritual and intellectual matters would be of interest. His wife bore an outsider's name and signed with a cross. Her dowry went unappraised since, as she said, it had "no great value." She was pondering remarriage with schoolmaster Schrader.[128]

---

[126] No. 358, fo. 75.   [127] No. 324, fos. 15–16; no. 326, fos. 191, 201–5.   [128] No. 358, fos. 47–8.

Schoolmasters' pedagogical gifts can only be imagined. During Dargardt's settlement, Jacob Lehn, "cottager no. 7," submitted a copy of his handwriting, "in case," a Stavenow official wrote, "no better schoolmaster turns up." Lehn legibly wrote down a religious verse, though he disconnected syllables and misspelled words. It said, in unrhymed translation:

> He who allows Dear God to rule,
> Putting his hope in Him always,
> He will be wonderfully upheld
> Through all suffering and sadness.
> He who trusts Almighty God
> Does not build on sand.[129]

Lehn was doubtless right to think it a schoolmaster's job to instill such thoughts in pupils' minds. But, when it came to their elders' life struggles, whether among themselves or with the lordship, resigned sentiments often yielded to belligerence.

MANORIAL SERVANTS

Here figure the seigneurial family's domestic servants and certain authority-wielding agents. After Frau Kleist's death, Hasse disbursed servants' unpaid wages, closing Stavenow manor-hall until war dangers passed. In her household Frau Kleist had employed eight "girls," with salaries of 5–16 talers, headed by "housekeeper Friedenberger" (18 talers). All received room and board. None bore village farmers' names, but seemingly were recruited in town. Faithful Mlle Charreton managed the servants. She now transferred four of them, raising one's wages, to other Kleist households' service. She dismissed a senior woman with a bonus plus bedding and linen. Manservant Henning (21 talers) would stay with the Stavenow Kleists, as would Christian Brunn, whom "well-blessed Frau Kleist trained as a cook in Berlin and took into the house at Easter 1753, without setting a fixed salary." Judge Hasse now agreed with Brunn on 3 talers monthly pay in his first two years, rising to 5 talers after Easter 1758. Frau Kleist's wage-book showed she gave Brunn 20 talers cash in his first year and thereafter 10 talers yearly, lowering 1759 seigneurial debt to him to 181 talers. Evident here is what little pocket money such an employee needed, and how he

---

[129] No. 715, fo. 3: *Wer nur den lieben//Gott lest walten//und Hofft auf//Ihn alle Zeit//den wird ja wun//der lich er halten//In allen Creutz//und Traurogkeit//wer Gott den aller//hochsten traudt//der hat auff//keinen Sampt ge//baudt.*

left a growing capital with Frau Kleist. He had been ignorant of his actual salary, trusting to matriarchal benevolence.

Outside the manor-house lived hunter Johann Prittwitz, earning 50 talers yearly plus 10 talers' expenses for his horse. His assistant was his son, serving since 1756 without fixed wages. Hasse now set them at 8 talers for his first year and 10 talers for the second. The hunter was dismissed, but his son stayed on as forest bailiff. Gardener Jahnentz (33 talers), employed since 1752, would remain with administrator Böhmer, supplying the family when in residence with food and otherwise "monetizing the produce," and sharing earnings with Böhmer. Hasse dismissed coachman Schulze (16 talers) with a bonus. His assistant Maass, by collecting only part, saved 31 talers from his 12 talers yearly pay. Nightwatchman Peters (10 talers) stayed. These three men could have stemmed from local farm families. Seemingly elderly livestock watchman Voss earned 4 talers. Hasse added that "old Martin stays until New Year's as before in the castle, and thereafter will be given necessary clothes and food at the manager's office." This was Martin Kubno who died in 1767 at age ninety-seven, of whom the burial register said that he "was Colonel von Kleist's mounted servant [who] subsequently was given his bread in charity by Stavenow lordship."[130]

A series of unrelated men wore Stavenow's hunter's uniform. This violence-beset post will figure in later discussions of law enforcement and the Stavenow court, for in various ways hunters were police officials. In some cases, they prospered. We saw how, in 1720, Caspar Seyer resigned the hunter's post to run the Stavenow inn, reshouldering his rifle in 1726 before dying the same year, leaving some good assets. His 1720 successor was Daniel Gehricke, whom tenant-farmer Meyer rewarded in 1721 with 3 talers for producing evidence, including birdclaws, that he shot, as livestock predators or otherwise troublesome creatures, six hawks, one eagle, three storks, seven owls, twenty-two crows, and two foxes.[131] In 1724 Gehricke suffered severe injuries in a fight with Stavenow's nightwatchman, and by 1726 had been replaced by old Seyer. No doubt Gehricke was related to – possibly identical with – Theiss Gehrecke who at Christmas 1725 disappeared, abandoning his wife and young children. Frau Gehrecke testified he left her with nothing but a cow. "[Her] step-father had taken her in as his own, but what he earned was all his. From butter and linen [weaving] she earned what she needed, but nothing beyond daily expenses."

---

[130] No. 716, fos. 248, 273–5.   [131] No. 705, fo. 141.

In 1727 hunter Johann Friedrich Birkholz took his oath, which hints at how precursor Gehricke attracted suspicion of venality. Birkholz promised to "keep forests, swine-foraging woods, plowland, and borders under good surveillance; to sell or dispose of no forest wood on my own account without the gracious lordship's express order and knowledge; to report accurately what animals I shoot."[132] Birkholz, from whose lineage the Premslin manor leaseholders emerged, survived to 1739 or beyond, replaced by another Seyer, followed by hunter Prittwitz dismissed in 1758. In his place Conrad Kleist appointed Gottfried Glaubitz, who vowed to resist all gifts and bribes, keep a monthly "account-book" of wood sales (after administrator Böhmer approved them), "show appropriate respect and obedience to lordship and supervisory officials," and (finally) observe Royal Forest Statutes. He received Prittwitz's rent-free house at Stavenow, with the usual gardens, meadow, and grazing for two cows with calves; seigneurially sown flaxseed; 24 bushels of oats for his horse; 50 talers in "steady wages," plus half the fines he collected for forest pilferage and other infractions, the other half being Böhmer's. Such extra income may have been minor, since his predecessor's son in one year earned only 30 groschen this way – testimony, perhaps, to infrequent (or successful) forest theft. Glaubitz was paid 5 talers to move to Stavenow. He and his wife would eat at Böhmer's table until Prittwitz's term expired.[133]

Glaubitz lasted eight years, followed by Severin Frickmann, "hunter and forester from Hohenstein," east of Berlin, who died at age thirty-one in the 1771 epidemic year. Hunter Kaden was sacked in 1775 for unspecified reasons, having borrowed 40 talers from carriage-driver Maass to pay for his hunter's equipment but being unable now to repay them. Among Kaden's valuables were a horse (10 talers), an expensive watch, bought in Perleberg for 13.5 talers, two rifles (10 talers), two bacon-sides (5 talers), and a new "meat cask" (1 taler). The court ordered the auction of the horse and watch, directing Kaden to sell the rest to settle his debt.[134] A good view of the hunter-foresters dates from 1790, when Friedrich Dalchow died prematurely, leaving a widow, born of Dargardt smallholders, and two young sons. Dalchow's wood sales, seemingly at his own discretion (perhaps to counteract foresters' collusion in pilferage), left a debt at his death to Major Kleist of 263 talers, which the deceased's liquid assets could not cover. His

---

[132] No. 200, fo. 60.   [133] No. 655, fos. 34–5, 37–9.   [134] Ibid., fos. 17–22.

personal possessions were therefore auctioned, announcements having been called out in local villages and towns. Widow Dalchow asked only for her dowry's return.

She swore a "disclosure oath," identifying "what I actually brought in at my marriage," vowing to "All-Knowing God" she was not concealing nor had she "maliciously misplaced" any of her husband's estate. Her dowry seemingly conveyed no cash, but only a 16-taler bed, loom, cow, sheep, and trunk of clothes and textiles. Her husband gave her clothing as gifts, which her children's guardians argued for including in the dowry, "since in exchange she has worked and must raise the children." Of household goods credited to her husband, she claimed 40 talers' worth, making her too a claimant on the bankrupted estate. Forester Linow had borrowed 32 talers from Dalchow, at no interest "because the deceased had never asked for any." Tenant-farmer Birkholz, possibly Kleist's Dargardt manor-farm leaseholder, repaid 41 talers Dalchow had lent him, also without reference to interest. Five other minor interest-free debts required repayment. Hunter Meyer borrowed 11 talers in 1783, but had disappeared.

Before concluding Dalchow or other villagers sought no return on loans, the symbolic capital should be considered which such cash advances accumulated. They served too as insurance should need on the lender's part arise. Possibly Dalchow expected his debtors to repay him with interest of their own reckoning. Smallholder Key lent Dalchow 32 talers in 16-groschen coins, plainly charging a high annual 12.5 percent interest, officially debited. Among Dalchow's other obligations were 15 talers owed his father-in-law for three years' house rent. His widow also sought 10 talers burial expenses.[135] Auction earnings met Kleist's and other creditors' claims, but the children's paternal inheritances were largely lost in the debacle. The mother would employ what assets she salvaged to help the children "learn a trade or otherwise get ahead." The guardians – Stavenow gardener and Dargardt village mayor (soon to become the widow's father-in-law) – "promise to diligently observe the widow's household, and inform the lordship if she should fall into difficulty; otherwise they will be responsible." Apart from this show of paternalist concern, Kleist took 14 talers cash into keeping for the boys' future. But when the widow remarried the next year he gave it to her "to improve her household."

[135] No. 17, fos. 1–8.

Stavenow manager Quittenbaum conducted the auction. Prices actually paid for Dalchow's goods nearly all equaled or surpassed their court-assigned values, suggesting eighteenth-century appraisals accurately mirrored market values. Kleist's brother-in-law Podewils bought Dalchow's horse, a "fox gelding," for a handsome 61 talers. Podewils also took a "trained dog" (6 talers), while hollander Kersten bought the "multicolored dachshund" for 8 groschen. Miller Lent gained a double-barreled rifle for 6 talers, while ten other guns went to various others (none village farmers). Dalchow's silver deer knife fetched 9 talers. His forester's horn, appraised at 2 talers, earned only 19 groschen. His clothes were good. Three coats and vests fetched 15 talers, and five pairs of deer-skin lederhosen sold well. He owned newly fashionable "Manchester pants," probably Berlin-manufactured (1.5 talers), plus an overcoat (2 talers), eight pairs of gray stockings, riding pants, and five pairs of boots, the best worth 3 talers. His silver pocket watch fetched over 10 talers.

The auctioned household furniture included typical items, plus twenty "eating spoons" and six pairs of knives and forks – these latter utensils' first mention outside the Stavenow manor-house – plus casserole, sugar canister, three sets of teacups, two candlesticks (16 groschen), "shaving knife," whip (4 groschen), some writing paper, and 112 pounds of various linen yardage. Among items the widow kept for herself were a coffee-mill (2 groschen), all the pottery, a cradle, 148 ells of linen cloth, a loom, an oak trunk, and a bedstead. Among her clothes, secure within her dowry and 64 talers, there was, together with the usual eighteenth-century women's dress, a "green silk coat," high priced at 10 talers.

Dalchow's household displays a living standard incorporating norms of dress and cuisine foreign to earlier eighteenth-century village farmers. Probably in solid farm families similar styles were appearing, for widow Dalchow came from Dargardt colonists' village, as perhaps did her husband. In any case, at the century's end forester-hunters, even when they suffered early death and debt crises, belonged among village notables. Prominent among auction buyers were the Kleists, their estate officials, the gardener, a miller, a hollander, a hunter, a smith, and various *Herren* and *Meister*. Dalchow's successor in 1809 was well-paid hunter Erlenbusch, receiving 70 talers yearly; 47 bushels of rye, barley, oats, buckwheat and peas; two pigs' free foraging (now worth 6 talers); plus free grazing of two cows, free housing with gardens, firewood, and "some flax and potato land." One estate appraiser thought his house ill sited. It ought to stand on the estate's boundary with Mesekow smallholders' village, "because most wood thefts are to be feared from that direction."[136]

Seigneurial fishermen early disappeared from the scene. In 1726, Colonel Kleist leased Löcknitz stream access and Premslin millpond for 15 talers yearly to Reimar Hecker, but later the lordship self-managed its various fisheries. Hecker promised "to use [the fishery] responsibly and guard against damage by outsiders and swans; observe the pikes' spawning season; and deliver fish as needed to the manor for cash payment, pike at 6 pfennigs per pound, other small fish at 4 pfennigs." He received a rent-free cottage with garden, fuel, and grazing for a cow. "And when he joins in the hunt he will have his reward like other hunters, and he can keep pelts of fish-otters and foxes he kills."[137]

The manor-hall gardeners grew progressively more important, not only for the food they put on the Kleists' table, but as the prestige value among the nobility of formal gardens rose. The 1809 wage-register shows the gardener's salary, at 40 talers, 20 percent higher than in 1758. The 1809 natural provisions were good: 42 bushels of grain and peas, pasturage or forage for three cows and four pigs, potato land, and fuel. In 1801 elderly Major Kleist visited his long-sick gardener, Johann Ketter, who asked Kleist to take down his last will, "if God was to make His dispensation over his life." The major returned with two officials who put Ketter's wishes to paper, the gardener signing shakily. He named his wife as "universal" heir, not obliged to give "the least thing to their children" (unless she remarried). Two daughters had been dowered with trunks of textiles. The eldest, still unmarried daughter and the two eldest sons would have to await their mother's death or remarriage for an inheritance.

Here again Kleist played the patriarchal role: "as for the youngest son, I, Major von Kleist, have promised to concern myself with his education and learning of a métier." Ketter reported that his eldest son received a "medal from the Royal Danish Agronomy Society, which he sent to his father [i.e., to Ketter] at Stavenow." Worth 14 talers, Ketter wanted it returned to his son at Ketter's wife's death, "if [she] did not fall into extreme need and, to support herself, sell it." While Ketter's attitude toward his children otherwise seems stony, he took evident pride in his eldest son's accomplishments under the Danish crown (probably in nearby Holstein or Schleswig). It was a sign of filial devotion that the son sent his valuable prize home.[138]

---

[136] No. 39, fo. 49.   [137] No. 712, fos. 154–5.   [138] No. 326, fos. 228–9.

Ketter was a Stavenow outsider, while Frau Kleist's gardener Jahnentz bore a local smallholder's name. A woman also named Jahnentz was, until her 1755 death, wife of the Kleist coachman Caspar Schultze. Though resident at the manor-hall, coachman Schultze and his wife kept the usual kitchen livestock, and stored quantities of unthreshed rye, oats, and flax. Whatever her occupation, she possessed ample clothing, tallying 44 talers, including numerous good aprons, many upper and lower undershirts, black plush gloves and "one pair of women's house slippers" (10 groschen). Her bedding displayed a "blue linen bed-curtain." Among housewares, their pewter teapot, five pewter spoons, brass clothes-iron (10 groschen), "big leather chair," "small spinning chair," "herb pestle," and "tin oven-door and ironwares" were missing from village farmers' inventories. There was also a "red painted oak linen chest" (3 talers), with matching table and stools. Twenty-one furniture-maker's oak planks (11 talers) point to the coachman's sideline. They owned but three religious books.[139]

Schultze and his wife were holding 105 talers in cash. Their debt-free assets, including their seemingly comfortable household's furnishings, tallied 273 talers, well above village farms'. It seems that loyal service of competent people – Schulze wrote a very good hand, and undertook lengthy trips – reaped material rewards advertising seigneurial benevolence. The cooks' experience confirmed this. If married, as in 1809, they lived in seigneurial housing, with the customary food allotments and grazing rights, though they otherwise had no ties to surrounding village culture. Like his mother, Major Kleist favored the seigneurial chef. In 1797 cook Heinrich Petry died, leaving a net estate of 363 talers, most in cash. The major owed him half his 60 talers yearly salary, plus 5 talers for sheep and rabbit skins delivered to the lordship. The unmarried Petry's personal effects were sold and his legacy paid to relatives living under the Anhalt princes in Schaumburg an der Lahn, in west-German Hesse. Petry's coffin and burial cost a good 25 talers. Major Kleist patriarchally supplied the funeral party with "food and drink free of cost." He wrote the Schaumburg court that, because of Petry's "loyally rendered service," he waived the customary seigneurial tax on inheritances removed from his jurisdiction, trusting the Hessian court would reciprocate should the (unlikely) occasion arise.[140] Nor should Kleist's solicitude be surprising. What would sour a rich landlord's life more than a sullen and vengeful chef?

---

[139] No. 2, fos. 1–4; no. 716, fo. 287. [140] No. 324, fos. 53–4.

CONCLUSION

The occupations and existences these pages have observed composed a network of seigneurial power and patronage. Those prospering within it were proof that life could be good under the Junkers' parasol. Some upward mobility occurred from ordinary farm households into this sphere. Perhaps the Kleists expected such advancement to discipline their villages, turning their subjects' aspirations toward the manor-hall. If the social groups standing between lordship and village did not all embody delegated authority, most of their members stood on the land-lordly side and could expect seigneurial judicial and police powers to support them in such conflicts as might arise with subject farmers.

Yet such lengthening of the seigneurial shadow did not eclipse the villagers' readiness to assert against the lordship their rights as they understood them. Perhaps they compared their material circumstances with those of their neighbors favored by proximity to the nobility and concluded they were no less entitled to similar comforts. Certainly such neighbors helped introduce into the villages consumption styles associated with urban and aristocratic prosperity, suggesting they were accessible and respectable for farmhouses too.

7

Farm servants, young and old: landless laborers in the villages and at the manor

Stavenow lordship was part of a larger western world, inhabited mainly by family farmers and artisan craftsmen, accustomed to unity of workplace and living space. It was natural to think of society as a hierarchy of households, and of wage-earning workers as servants under surrogate-parent masters' discipline and authority. Just as farmers' children expected, after years of youthful service, to marry into their own landholdings, or as artisans' apprentices aimed to become independent masters, so also young agricultural laborers of humble origins sought to marry and acquire households.

At Stavenow, as elsewhere under east-Elbian manorialism, landless workers followed this path both in villages and at the manor. Villages housed cottagers' holdings, some with arable patches separate from larger farmers' open fields, others with house and garden only. Craftsmen and married agricultural laborers occupied them, while poorer workers lodged on farmsteads, often in empty retirement quarters. At seigneurial manor-farm settlements, unmarried workers, many compulsorily recruited, lived under married estate officials' supervision in workers' barracks or outbuildings with sleeping chambers. The lordship also possessed cottages assigned or rented to various married employees, including agricultural workers.

Although village farm servants and seigneurial laborers have figured in these pages, especially as farmers' daughters and sons, it remains to consider their fortunes more closely, especially lifelong landless workers'. For if the landholding farmers dominating village society measured themselves against craftsmen and rural notables at the social scale's higher end, so did they also against lower-end laborers. Subject farmers stood counterpoised to both groups, who were free (and this also applied to compulsorily recruited workers), on work contracts' expiration, to depart the jurisdiction without needing, as farmers did, to find seigneurially acceptable replacements. To see the world through subject farmers' eyes, lifelong landless laborers' lot requires contemplation.

Farm servants were also the pre-industrial world's most numerous workers, and their condition reflects the minimal well-being that able-bodied people could expect to attain. A judgment of living standards in that world must rest heavily on such laboring folk's experience. Historians incline to infer welfare from wage and price trends, steam-rolling the peaks and valleys of common people's fortunes. Here we follow trails leading, along life paths variously cushioned and tormented by fate, to their dwellings, words, and thoughts.

VILLAGE FARMERS' SERVANTS

Around age fourteen, a service period began for virtually all youth, including even the privileged like the Kleists, whose sons often early joined the army as line officers' pages. For farmworkers and apprentice artisans, release from subordination came only through marriage and their own households' establishment, occurring – if they were fortunate – in their mid or late twenties. Among landed villagers, elder children might remain as farm servants on parental holdings. In law, farmers could retain for their own needs two or more grown children's labor power. Additional children, when not lost to seigneurial or military service, often served on other farms, preferably among labor-short kinfolk.[1]

Sometimes parents hired out children against their will. In 1722 Perleberg lumber dealer Joachim Cuno complained in Stavenow court that Joachim Ladewig "hired himself at Easter" to Cuno, agreeing – as was customary – to begin work at St. Martin's (November 11) and accepting a 6-groschen tip or "hiring money" to seal the bargain. But Ladewig stayed with his previous farmer-employer and "secretly put the hiring-money on the table in [Cuno's] house." Young Ladewig "could not deny his father promised him [to Cuno] . . . but when his father told him this, [Ladewig] took the money back after fourteen days. His weak constitution wouldn't let him work for Herr Plaintiff. He would stay instead with his previous master [*Brod Herrn* (bread-giver)]." Whatever penalty he suffered for refusing to change jobs, this case displays fathers' inclination to dictate children's employment.[2]

---

[1] Lennhoff, *Das ländliche Gesindewesen*; Kurt Hinze, *Die Arbeiterfrage zu Beginn des modernen Kapitalismus in Brandenburg-Preussen, 1685–1806* (Berlin, 1927); Georg Friedrich Knapp, *Die Landarbeiter in Knechtschaft und Freiheit* (Leipzig, 1909), 66–86; Horst Krüger, *Zur Geschichte der Manufakturen und der Manufakturarbeiter in Preussen* (Berlin, 1958).

[2] No. 629, fo. 3.

Perhaps because the court hesitated to interfere with parental authority, this was the only such recorded instance. But severe conflicts might arise from unwilling service, and parents likely sought their children's assent to contracts they negotiated for them. Ideally, such service enabled youth to learn farming skills and accumulate marriage portions that, combined with parents' contributions, would buy them into a household of their own. Young farm servants' money wages were so low that hard-pressed parents could expect little from children's earnings, nor do charges of parental wage confiscation arise, though this may have occurred. Commoner were complaints of unpaid wages that farm servants lodged against employers.

In 1728 ex-farmhand Peter Ebel, having just acquired through marriage a stroke-disabled farmer's debt-burdened fullholding, demanded in court 12.5 talers' back-pay from his recent employer, plus 18 groschen shoe-money. So far he had only collected 2 talers in cash and lumber worth 4 talers. In 1729, Christian Hoth appeared, claiming 10 talers' wages Ebel's predecessor owed him. Ebel complained Hoth "had the effrontery to seek him out at home, to bully the debt out of him. One word led to another, until [Hoth] grabbed him by the head in his own house and scratched his face and pulled out his hair." Hoth retorted that Ebel "cursed him for a scoundrel and seized him, trying to hit him with the clothes-presser, so they both took each other by the hair. Since he thought [Ebel] aimed to kill him, [Hoth] backed away." Ebel denied the charges, but Hasse found him guilty of starting the fight. Still, since Hoth committed violence in Ebel's own house, Hasse fined him a taler, enjoining both to compose their quarrel "as befits Christians." Next year Ebel satisfied Hoth's claim with sheep and a heifer.[3] Hasse annulled another farmhand's wage claim unpaid by Ebel's predecessor on grounds of contract-breaking, since he left service prematurely.[4]

Young men serving village farmers risked many forms of abuse, which might not come to light if the victim's relatives did not defend him. To previous examples may be added Adam Brüggens, who served farmer Reimar Guhl as farm boy. Guhl charged Adam with losing an ax and a hatchet, "but although the court bailiff threatened him with a hard whipping," the youth stood by his denial. This was a rare instance of seigneurial officials intruding into household conflicts. Young Brüggens added that "the mother" – Guhl's wife – "and the proprietor beat him so much he had to say something" to his own mother, whom

[3] No. 200, fos. 113–14, 123–4, 148, 220–2; no. 715, fo. 9.   [4] No. 200, fos. 107–8.

Guhl then "beat very black and blue" after she had thrown Guhl's wife
to the ground in an altercation over her son's mistreatment. Hasse
spared the boy, absolving him of theft for lack of evidence, releasing
him from Guhl's service, and ordering Guhl to return the boy's possessions he had seized.[5] In another case, farmhand Joachim Zinner acted
from fear of his master David Zeggel's punishment when he furtively
released Zeggel's horses from Premslin manor leaseholder Frau
Berkholtz's barn, where she impounded them for grazing violations (for
which servants were responsible). Other farmhands paid her fines, but
Zinner could not or did not. Hasse harshly sentenced him to two days
on bread and water in Stavenow jail.[6]

Doubtless young farmhands suffered more under abusive employers
than the older ones. Farmer Hans Jürgen Zeggel, often himself in
court trouble, reported "his farm boy Johann Huth left again and for
many weeks has been going around begging, and because he won't
mend his ways, [Zeggel] asks he be compelled to fulfill his duty." Hasse
agreed, "as soon as he turns up, to bring him to order through imprisonment," though he left it to Zeggel to find the boy.[7] Similarly, four
young farmhands fought with a nearby estate manager, pummeling his
wife while forcefully resisting his attempt to impound their horses for
grazing violations. Two "furtively ran away," though one returned
next day to face the Spanish overcoat and a fine. The other remained
missing, though probably – as local farmers' kinsman – he eventually
surrendered.[8]

Young men successfully traversing this life stage accumulated marriage
portions – sometimes also a horse or two – and found farm heiresses or
other brides.[9] Village farmers' maidservants faced greater difficulties.
Their wages were much more miserly than young men's, accounting perhaps for the theft charges occasionally surfacing in their conflicts with
employers. Thus Marie Eggerts "ran off" before the expiration of her
yearly contract from farmer Hans Zeggel's service to work for a hollander. Zeggel and his wife asked Hasse to assign her unpaid wages to her
successor, and also punish her. Eggerts said she quit "because the
plaintiffs beat her with a threshing flail, though when they cursed her she
did not curse them back." She didn't want – this was doubtless a stock
phrase – "to serve for blows." In withheld pay she claimed 12 groschen,
shoes, and "half a dress" (worth 12 groschen). Zeggel complained "she
drank him out of his milk and also stole 16 groschen from a money-bag."

[5] No. 326, fo. 214.   [6] Ibid., fo. 189.   [7] Ibid., fo. 127.   [8] Ibid., fos. 122–4.
[9] Ibid., fos. 36–7.

She promised the preacher, Zeggel said, she would return to work. She conceded "she indeed gave [the pastor] her hand, but she didn't want to go [to Zeggel] a second time." Hasse commanded her to return and behave properly, or face bodily punishment. Zeggel deposited her back-pay, in textiles, with the court for safekeeping. Theft charges were dropped and all parties, if grudgingly, shook hands.[10]

Some maidservants' reputations for thievery stalked them for years. In 1722 farmer Jochim Ebel charged his "girl" (*Dirne*), fourteen-year-old Anna Seyers, "whom he'd raised in his own house," with stealing money from his farmhand and sacks from himself, taking them to her "father's brother's wife, who put her up to it." Anna confessed, saying "she great-ly regretted letting herself be seduced into such a theft." Although her aunt claimed innocence, Anna "told her to her face" she urged the theft on her, "because her people" – that is, Anna's employers – "didn't give her spending money as they should." Tenant-farmer Meyer, conducting the court, ordered the aunt's arrest, dispatching the village mayor to search for stolen goods in the farmhouse lodging her.

The court bailiff's wife reported the mayor's refusal to carry out this "visitation." Changing tactics, Meyer allowed the aunt to swear an oath, whereupon "she is declared innocent." Meyer imposed "eternal silence" on the charges against her, threatening violators with impris-onment in Spandau. Young Anna, found guilty by admission of steal-ing from the farmhand and her employer, was condemned to pay all costs or work them off, and also to two days' jailing on bread and water. Meyer demanded the mayor, who was only required to witness the search, explain his non-compliance with "a written order." He thought, he replied, the female bailiff expected him to break through the aunt's door. For this insubordination, suggesting willful non-cooperation with the more or less despised and outcast court bailiff, he paid a half-taler.[11]

Nineteen years later, the same Anna Seyers charged farmer's daugh-ter Trine Zeggels with falsely accusing her of linen theft. Former farm-hand Joachim Witting joined Seyers' complaint, saying Trine claimed he stole 4 talers from her household. Trine said Anna had given Witting, who had confessed paternity in another woman's premarital pregnancy case, a stolen shirt. In general, farm daughter Zeggels said, Anna had "her hands in the wrong places," having also stolen a dress from tenant-farmer Berkholtz's maid. As for Witting, his claims to have gotten his money from Zeggels' father as a worker's bonus concealed theft from her

---

[10] No. 713, fo. 266; no. 200, fo. 142. [11] No. 589, fos. 11–12.

trunk. Witting replied "he earned some money during the harvest playing music." Trine would not allow Anna to swear an oath, saying she
was a "thief" who had stolen other things – beer, brandy, and wool.
Following inquiries, Hasse dropped charges against Witting but found
Anna guilty of linen theft and docked her pay accordingly, also fining
her 12 groschen for theft of "the bottle and crock."[12]

Possibly thirty-three-year-old Anna Seyers was stigmatized for her
early misstep and fell into disrepute. Perhaps she sought Witting's favor,
or hand, with the gift of a shirt. If so, this reveals the implacability of
social censure. As Witting's situation suggests, farm servants' conflicts
could focus jealousies among village youth while exposing the local
hierarchy of respectability. It was the poorest's fate to serve those above
them, and ensuing resentments might come starkly to light.

This is evident in the mutual recriminations of two Blüthen maidservants, neither bearing local farmers' name. Anna Böthling accused
Anna Stuhr of stealing her three new outer shirts, three new undershirts, two aprons, two dresses, a printed silk scarf, a white scarf, a cap
and two bonnets. Perhaps such a wardrobe existed only in her dreams,
but she claimed Stuhr took them from her bedroom, which "her people" normally kept locked, while she was grazing horses and oxen.
Stuhr allegedly hid the clothes in the vegetable garden, from whence
her father Daniel, a local lodger, whisked them away. Defendant Stuhr
counter-charged Böthling with thefts in other villages, though admitting
joining her in stealing apples, for which Böthling's "mother had beaten
her hard." Of Stuhr and her father, Böthling claimed "nobody wanted
to have anything to do with them, since he struck [farmer] Glissmann's
wife" – when his daughter worked for Glissmann – "threatening her
with setting a red rooster on their house if they wouldn't pay [his
daughter] wages enough." This signified arson. Mayor Knippenberg
confirmed the joint apple theft, but said no one knew of stolen clothing. As for Stuhr's father, "no one wanted to have anything to do with
him" – evidently a ritualized phrase – "because he threatened
Glissmann's wife with a red rooster because his daughter should not
have to graze the horses." Hasse ordered the two girls to stand one hour
in public and pay 12 groschen fines. He left the village to deal, seemingly through social ostracism, with the elder Stuhr's arson threats.[13]

Yet conflicts between farmers and their servants did not crowd the
court, while fieldwork at seigneurial manors focused considerable anger

---

[12] No. 326, fos. 68–70, 74.   [13] No. 200, fos. 109–12.

and aggressiveness among village farmhands performing their employers' obligatory weekly service. Prosecution of employers' sexual advances against maidservants was rare, and premarital pregnancies were not commoner among farmhands than other groups. Young people's reputations, upon which their marriage prospects hung, were at risk, while few older single workers toiled on villagers' farms.

One luckless farmhand was Fritz Hoppe, who left farmer Jürgen Kratz's service because, as Hoppe claimed, Kratz "spread the insult that [Hoppe] had been together with [Kratz's] wife." Hoppe produced a statement from Garlin Pastor Eisenhart concerning "the crime of which Georg Kratz accused [Hoppe] in my presence." Kratz, the pastor wrote, "held [Hoppe] in suspicion of having committed adultery with his wife, which when it came to offering proof he could in no way explain, but it all rested instead on pure chatter. This on [Hoppe's] request I wanted to document in my own hand." Hoppe demanded mid-level farmworkers' half-year wages of 3 talers and textile yardage for 1.5 shirts and pants. Kratz complained that Hoppe, whom he hired at the Lenzen autumn market, left his service "without cause, although he asked him to serve out his year." Hasse wrote: "only long after [Hoppe] left [Kratz's farm] did [Kratz's] wife's sister . . . and the old [woman] Wiesekensche spread the rumor, which is why they" – Kratz and, probably, his wife – "went to see Herr Preacher." Kratz challenged the other women to come, but they declined. "It was therefore just gossip, as Herr Pastor Eisenhart attests."

Hoppe complained that Kratz "dismissed him and acted so roughly toward him because he spilled a bucket of milk curds on the linen." Hoppe moved into Hans Gerloff's tavern, "but because [Kratz] gave him no more than 3 talers' pay, he had to work at day labor." Hasse ruled Hoppe "did wrong to suddenly move out of the village for such a poor reason, putting [Kratz] to the inconvenience of hiring day labor." He rejected Hoppe's clothing claims and fined him 1 taler, leaving Kratz to pay him 2 talers' back-pay. Here the lordship enforced labor discipline on village farmers' behalf. Both Hoppe and Kratz turned to the pastor to vindicate themselves against potentially damaging adultery charges. If village gossip initially swayed Kratz, as seemingly it did, Hasse saw no reason in this to favor the ill-starred Hoppe.[14]

Presumably Hoppe survived this mishap. Other young villagers, in service on parental holdings or elsewhere, fell ill and died before marrying,

[14] No. 326, fo. 131; no. 591, fo. 83.

their accumulated savings and inheritances remaining to witness dashed hopes. Fullholder's daughter Margaretha Hintzen died at twenty-nine on her sister's and brother-in-law's smallholding, leaving bedding and linen, two new dress-jackets, and five sheep, together worth 24 talers, plus a 19-taler inheritance lent out to a farmer. Her brother-in-law claimed "nursing costs," the deceased having "lain in misery and weakness" at his house for five weeks. Judge Betich granted him her laboriously accumulated movable goods, leaving the money to her younger brother. Thus, if not in destitution, many unmarried laborers vanished.[15]

Rare, but instructive, was the case of Johann Hintze, fullholder's brother and lifelong bachelor who died in 1735 in middle or advanced age as a smallholder's farmhand. According to his brother, Johann left behind in his trunk 30 talers cash, "two old guns that don't shoot straight," and promissory notes for five loans he made, tallying 116 talers. Here was a laborer of substance. Two of his sisters married townsmen, in the Altmark and Mecklenburg, their sons becoming urban artisans. Another sister married locally, with two daughters in service and another a soldier's wife. Opening the trunk, Hasse found – apart from guns, everyday clothing, and 9 ells of linen – "a pair of still good shoes . . . a coat still good, one pair of new white stockings," a gray woolen jacket with blue buttons, eight shirts, two neckerchiefs, and other jackets and coats, hats and caps. There was a pot, but no money.[16]

Hasse interrogated the deceased's employers, Joachim Nentz and his wife. Nentz admitted they took a "handful of money" from Hintze's trunk, "which put him in such uneasiness of conscience that he almost went crazy before confessing it." His excuse was that he and his wife had had "so much trouble" with the ailing Johann before he died, for which the deceased's relatives had not rewarded them. On Johann's death day the sufferer's half-sister went to town to buy "stroke-water" but upon her return Johann could no longer speak, so she left to fetch his brother. Nentz and his wife then took keys from the expiring Johann's pocket and opened the trunk in his room. This callous deed was, Nentz admitted, punishable. He wanted to return the 9 talers they took, which his wife was keeping in her "bundle." Nentz further conceded he owed the deceased 6 talers in loans. Johann's other trunk, which the half-sister (unedifyingly) broke open, contained only tools.

Hasse sent the Stavenow tailor to Stendal to summon Johann's relatives, while letters were sent elsewhere, whose posting cost tenant-farmer

---

[15] No. 358, fos. 12–13.   [16] Ibid., fos. 266–7.

Hartz 18 groschen. Subsequently the deceased's brother admitted he took, in other people's presence, 10 talers from the trunk, including 1 taler for funeral beer. The deceased's nephew admitted taking a ducat (2.75 talers), spent on funeral meat, herring, bread, and beer. Among the deceased's other goods, some stored in a third trunk, were five religious books, and more clothes. He allegedly lent 60 talers to a Perleberg saddle-maker kinsman, whom Hasse ordered to repay. Farmer Völsch, owing the deceased 12 talers, testified his wife received the loan, of which he never saw a penny, showing that wives took responsibility – perhaps often – for debts and borrowing. The debtor added that "this year too hail destroyed the grain, so he sold his other livestock to buy bread." His creditors "would have to grant him some respite because of poverty." Yet he now paid 5 talers. The Hintze heirs waived 2 talers and agreed to wait until 1740's harvest for the rest. Here is evidence how livestock embod-ied villagers' assets, reducible in need to ready cash.

The saddler claimed to have borrowed 12, not 45 talers, as the deceased's sister, looking the saddler "in the eye," claimed. After mutu-al recriminations, and perjury warnings, the saddler successfully swore an oath. He also owed the deceased 8 talers for a horse. The deceased's Mecklenburg kin borrowed 30 talers from him, but repaid half. Finally, when burial and court costs were paid, 79 talers remained for distribu-tion. Nentz and his wife went unpunished.[17] Johann Hintze, though a landless laborer, had accumulated respectable clothing and consider-able savings. He was a moneylender and occasional horsetrader. What his guns signified is unclear, but perhaps he was once a huntsman. He stands as a successful bachelor farmhand, leaving behind an estate bet-ter than many heavily burdened village farmers'. Of employers and rel-atives who plundered his trunks, the best that can be said is they con-fessed their guilt. This, perhaps curiously, they sought to minimize by pointing to their services to the deceased in nursing him in his illness or honoring his memory – with his own money – at the funeral.

UNMARRIED MANORIAL FARM SERVANTS

These laborers were, in law and local observance, liable to compulsory recruitment for three-year terms from among village farmers' supernu-merary working-age children. Yet there is, before the 1790 government-negotiated Urbarium, no evidence the lordship invoked a right to

[17] No. 713, fos. 271–3.

coerce into service the farmhands and maidservants it needed, though probably it did so. In 1760, it employed at its three demesne farms altogether six single men, earning 10.16.- talers yearly, and five women, earning 8 talers. In 1748–9, only two such farmhands bore local farmers' names, while others shared names with freely contracted married seigneurial workers, whose siblings or children they likely were. There was also "old farmhand Christian," earning 12 talers, though soon he was gone. Three women were milkmaids, one tended pigs, and one served in the workers' kitchen. Turnover between 1748 and 1754 was nearly total. At leased-out Premslin manor-farm, tenant-farmers employed additional compulsorily recruited workers.[18] By 1809, there were (including at Premslin) thirteen unmarried farmhands, most earning 20 talers, and seven maidservants, earning 7–12 talers. Now nearly all bore local farmers' names. Evidently Major Kleist and his successors exercised compulsory recruitment powers to the hilt.

We saw, discussing villagers' diet, that early nineteenth-century manorial workers received, on average, adequate or even good food rations. In 1762, for manorial employees and workers at Dargardt and Semlin manor-farms alone, the lordship kept nineteen milk-cows.[19] They were each given, for clothing, 17–24 ells of linen yardage – some fine, some coarse. A 1756 inventory of manorial workers' bedding discovered, in the building housing both workers and horse-stalls, two beds for unmarried ploughmen-drivers, each having covered mattresses, linen-enclosed bedcovers, two pillows, and a bolster. Here also were individual beds for two maidservants, a brewer, and a cow-herd. Similar beds were found at Semlin and Dargardt, while the hollander also received workers' bedding. For all workers, and for foremen and overseers also boarded within the manorial economy, there were "eight tablecloths still good, two dozen napkins, one dozen hand-towels, one dozen rough napkins for the servants that are still good," and an additional seventeen tablecloths, eighteen towels, ten bedcovers, and five bedsheets. In quantity, the workers were well swathed in textiles.[20]

These details confirm many other impressions of the Stavenow lordship's efforts at paternalist benevolence, aimed to secure its servants' loyalty and acquiescence. Yet recalcitrance and resentment were hard to dispel, and refusal to serve, flight, displays of rebellion, and threats to damage seigneurial property were ever-present possibilities. Absconding was uncommon, for it severed farmers' sons and daughters

---

[18] No. 259; cash accounts, 1748–54 (above).   [19] No. 184, fos. 90–2.   [20] No. 62; no. 716, fo. 196.

from their social environment and inheritances. Yet it occurred, particularly during tense periods, as under leaseholder Hartz's 1730s' regime. In 1739 Hasse investigated twenty-nine-year-old Friedrich Hecht's "flight from service." He was the brother of farmer Joachim Hecht, who apologized for their mother's failure to obey her summons. He delivered her (defiant) message that her sons, formerly under her "discipline," were now "grown up and she can no longer control them," so that she could also not "surrender" the runaway. Tenant-farmer Hartz, accusing the absconder of stealing 1-taler harnesses, claimed he was seen with his mother on Sunday, "and on Monday he departed with a great pack." Hartz wanted the miscreant's inheritance from his brother's farm blocked, but errant Friedrich had already claimed his steer and sold it, leaving only wedding-party claims unpaid. Hasse threatened the mother with a 2-taler fine if she did not appear, but no further record survives, suggesting he dropped the case.

The day before, Hasse summoned Anne Niemanns, charging her with "fleeing service" at the hollander's to return home. Her excuse was that "she couldn't keep working because of pain after her sister, whom she'd quarreled with, threw a rock at her back." Carrying milk pails was impossible. Tenant-farmer Hartz, contemptuously calling her "that person," accused her of conniving with his farmhands, probably vanished Friedrich Hecht, to abscond. She claimed two cows' inheritance from her brother's farm, and had already sold one. Hasse ordered her wages frozen and a second cow impounded until she returned to work. Seemingly, a would-be female runaway shrank before the deed.[21] In a 1747 inheritance dispute, a farmer from whom an ox was claimed said "it belonged to [his] absconded brother who hadn't wanted to move up to the manor-farm here, and so they secretly sold the ox, and this was nine years ago." Hasse ordered an investigation into the furtive ox sale, though in vain. Here was a successful escape, with a little money in his pocket, of a laborer drafted into seigneurial service.[22]

Abscondings did not embroil Frau Kleist's matriarchal regime, and not until 1782 is there evidence Major Kleist lost workers through flight. Three young men bearing local farmers' names fled west across Prussia's border into the kingdom of Hannover. In answer to the major's letter, a Hannoverian court reported the presence of Kleist's subject, Joachim Nagel, working for a farmer. Typically the Prussian state and its neighbors resisted, in rivalrous interest of increasing their

---

[21] No. 713, fos. 266–9.   [22] No. 326, fos. 143–4.

own able-bodied populations, each other's attempts to reclaim non-criminal emigrants. The Hannoverians absolved Nagel of the major's theft charges, saying "he abandoned his trunk and 5 talers' wages at Stavenow," and so was not extraditable.

Major Kleist received a copy of twenty-three-year-old Nagel's testimony. Born in "Glassien" (Glövzin), he had been a Stavenow stableboy. He "betook himself away because they received such bad food and almost nothing to drink." Asked whether he quit work properly or ran away, he replied that "he often spoke to Herr von Kleist about the bad food but found no support, and instead received the answer: if [Nagel] didn't hold his peace [Kleist] would put him under arms," that is, have him enlisted in the army. "Because he feared this, he secretly departed." He was not already an enrolled soldier, working at home on furlough, and so was not a deserter. But did he, the day before leaving, get drunk – it was late July, when harvest celebrations occurred – and beat a maidservant? He denied drunkenness, but admitted boxing her ears: "because she was falsely gossiping he emptied 30 quarts of beer." He and his comrades had split up at the border. They too fled "because of bad food." The Hannoverian court ordered Nagel to promise his present employer, farmer Märtens, with a handshake that he would stay on the job. It proved a mistake to place his pay and personal effects under temporary sequestration, for farmer Märtens soon reported that Nagel, "highly dissatisfied and irritated at having to work for nothing, departed surreptitiously and unnoticed."[23]

Here runaways justified themselves with the argument that workers should receive acceptable food rations, and by fear of Prussian army recruitment. These were both motives, doubtless regularly invoked, that the Hannoverian court tacitly endorsed, while downplaying the seemingly drunken workers' quarrel that catalyzed Nagel's flight. Whether or not Major Kleist threatened punitive army enlistment (probably he did), it was a charge plausibly attributable to him.

The lordship took farm servants' dissatisfaction with working conditions seriously, to ward off worse things than absconding, such as arson or animal mutilation. Seigneurial workers' grievances never issued in such collective actions as the 1700–2 Prignitz rent protest, but they exacerbated manor–village conflict. When, in July 1730, worker flight resulted from protests over food rations, judge Hasse entered the ensuing investigation in his transcript register under the heading "Stavenow

---

[23] No. 602, fos. 7–10.

farmhands, on account of their uprising [*Aufstand*]." The workers, Hasse wrote, "stirred one another up [and] on Friday evening at supper held all sorts of godless talk." Joachim Neumann took the lead: "he carped about the food and drink, cursed about the cream cheese [*Käsebutter*] and especially the [unsatisfactory] butter-box, and next morning," together with two other farmhands, "secretly fled." One returned after the court bailiff arrested his father for harboring the runaway, only to run off again on Sunday. Summoned and asked the reason for their son's "insubordination," Jochen Ernt and wife said "their biggest worry was they didn't know why [their son] ran away. He was always an obedient son and never let any work irritate him. It hurt them that he went away and caused them such tears [*Schnupff*], because he had no reason to do it."[24]

Hasse interrogated twenty-four-year-old Erdmann Mentz, manorial horse-driver and stable-hand, who said that ringleader Neumann started complaining about the "soup, and then he cursed the other food, and he babbled about the stewed plums, that they were no good and he didn't want to eat them." He cursed the "sow-drink" poured into their mugs, and told the others "they should speak up, and he signaled them with his eyes, and said they were rascals and dirty cowards if they didn't speak up for themselves." Hartz's wife, "Frau Amtmannin," testified Neumann "explicitly said that, with this food, he wanted to take his stuff and work not another lick." He also cursed field bailiff Halentz and his wife for "insolent blather." Hasse asked Erdmann Mentz if he lacked for food and drink, and heard that "they always ate their fill, and when they brought in the hay the tenant-farmer gave him beer, which otherwise they didn't receive." Halentz's wife, asked how she treated the farmhands, said "she never gave them beer but they got the drinks she made, and Jochen Neumann could have had his four measures if he'd wanted, but no more. And she had given them cream cheese more than once."

Friedrich Schütte, twenty-two years old and another manorial laborer bearing – like most of his mates – a local farmer's name, corroborated Erdmann Mentz's testimony, saying he told Neumann at the table "he wasn't smart to curse them all" and that he would not take his bundle and go, as Neumann urged. Schütte was in his seventh year at the manor, and "he didn't complain now of food and drink; often there was food left over." He added that another worker, Wilhelm, "tried to tell

[24] No. 200, fos. 143–5.

[Neumann] that he should be quiet, but he wouldn't let himself be controlled." Under interrogation, Wilhelm, bearing an outsider's last name, said he and the others "warned [Neumann] to be patient." But Neumann "said it was their fault that things were as they were, and he wanted to turn the tables on the big talkers so they would suffer for it." Finally, Neumann declared – doubtless referring to Colonel Kleist – that "if the old man came tomorrow recruiting for the army, he would say the same thing." Wilhelm was satisfied with manorial food. They received cold soup earlier in the day, and ate their fill. "Jochen Ernt had also shot off his mouth, and wanted to eat the cream cheese by the spoonful and have his bread and butter to boot." When Neumann urged them to leave their jobs, "Friedrich said he wouldn't do that, but was going to loyally serve out his year and that they should have patience." In Wilhelm's view, "they couldn't complain about food and drink, nor could he. They always had it good."

This story's ending went unrecorded. Perhaps Jochen Ernt disappeared for good, but ringleader Jochen Neumann returned, inheriting a smallholding to which in 1739, as we saw, his sister, disaffected from manorial service, temporarily fled. The workers' 1730 rage over food under leaseholder Hartz's regime, though hardly an uprising, shows that for most, if not all of them, seigneurial work required them to be "smart" and "patient" – and that they viewed the threat of "the old man" consigning them to active duty in the hated army as real. The incident spurred maidservant Anna Milatzen, who had tried to mollify Neumann, to leave manorial employment. But "because [she] herself said it didn't matter whether she stayed another year, she can't give notice now, but will have to continue in service" – it was late July – "until a year from next Michaelmas" (September 29). Though not an exercise of the lordship's compulsory recruitment right – Anna could have quit earlier – Hasse's ruling exemplifies seigneurial power to rule workers by fiat.

Disaffected laborers could threaten the lordship with furtive reprisals other than flight. In 1733 Hartz charged twenty-four-year-old farmhand Hans Peters, Stavenow swineherd's son, with having "let himself be heard that, if he didn't get his [fourth-year] pay, he wanted to ride off with a pair of Herr tenant-farmer's horses or stab a few cattle to death when no one was looking." Sub-bailiff Halentz had reprimanded Peters for giving animals the wrong fodder, provoking Peters' curses and attempted blows, though Peters called them "self-defense." Stavenow cowherd Geier called Peters "a godless young fellow" who had long declared "he wanted to go away." A young maidservant, "born after the hard winter [of 1718–19] and therefore fourteen years old," said she heard of Peters' threats from the hollander's wife.[25]

Although Halentz repeated his charges, looking Peters "in the eye," the farmhand denied threatening to steal or kill livestock: "never in his life had such things been in his thoughts, and they never came forth from his mouth." If cowherd Geier (who also accused Peters of threatening Hartz's older son with a pitchfork) swore otherwise, Peters would suffer the consequences. He protested that "I still haven't, thank God, stolen any horse or cow, but" – speaking of Halentz and Hartz – "I wasn't born in their barn" – he was not one of their beasts of burden. "Peters behaves," Hasse wrote, "very badly and vehemently denies he had the thoughts, from which [he says] may God preserve him." Hartz finally "declared that he wanted to forgive Hans Albrecht Peters, hoping he blurted it out because of stupidity and anger and would better himself in future, so long as he could be sure improvement would really occur and that [Peters] would not assault him or his family or the herders." Peters' father stood surety to his son's improvement "with his goods and blood," while young Peters swore to it "with hand and mouth," whereupon Hasse waived punishment and ordered the disputed 2 talers' wages paid him "immediately in cash."

Field bailiff Halentz and Hartz seemingly provoked Peters with blows and withholding pay, before shrinking back from threats targeting Hartz's son along with livestock. In a society where damaging violence lurked near life's surface, mollification of unpredictable hotheads such as Peters evidently could seem advisable. Peters, though a humble laborer, was not lacking in pride and self-assertion. Yet no farm servant, whether working for villagers or manor, could do his job without fear of employers' or seigneurial officials' physical abuse, which to suffer undeservedly must have been maddening. The principal constraints upon overseers' whiphands were the lordship's patriarchal efforts to present a benevolent face to its subjects and the wish to avoid the losses it and its farmers suffered through farm laborers' flight or shoddy work. The number of court cases involving violence between farmworkers and employers was, from the 1720s to the 1760s, not great, though it is clear from villagers' household histories that quarrels exploded at the workplace and doubtless many similar physical altercations at the manor went undocumented.

---

[25] No. 591, fos. 60–2.

Though the theme of seigneurial violence will reappear below, a few examples involving farm servants will illustrate their exposure to it. In 1728, Kleist's field bailiff Hahn discovered mini-smallholder Jochen Koltzer's grown son asleep on a harvest wagon. Before Hahn could "reprimand him," Koltzer fled. Later Koltzer testified "he worked himself into a sweat that day and was very tired," and lay down while the boy he had with him fetched something. Hahn appeared "and struck the boy with his whip and cut a piece out of his knee, and when [Koltzer] saw how enraged [Hahn] was, he went away." Hasse proposed to discuss the matter with Hahn, who subsequently disappeared from the records.[26] Thirteen years later Koltzer was still working as a farmhand.

In 1731 field bailiff Hans Witring charged manorial laborer Daniel Guhl with striking him on the head with a whip's butt. Witring was arresting another farmhand and ordered Guhl to depart. When he hesitated, Guhl said, Witring "hit him on the head and seized him by the hair," so that Guhl's reaction was justifiable self-defense. Witring conceded he gave Guhl "a stroke of the rod," adding that Hartz's wife vainly commanded Guhl to stop fighting. Ignoring Guhl's call for witnesses, Hasse fined him a quarter-year's pay and threatened worse, should Guhl again attack the bailiff. Evidently bailiffs, who might wield clubs or canes instead of whips, were sometimes worsted in fights. Workers' assaults on them earned severe, though not in this case physical, punishment. Twenty years later Guhl, too, was still a laborer, though no longer at the manor.[27]

It would have been consistent with Kleist's 1720s' new order that field bailiffs grew more aggressive, while tenant-farmer Hartz, burdened by villagers' enmity, was likely to buttress his authority with coercion. Still, there are not many court cases of seigneurially sanctioned violence, especially not under Frau Kleist, suggesting she and her administrators applied the rod sparingly. Yet in 1760 Hasse harshly punished fullholder Reimar Guhl and his farm-boy, Hans Ebel, whom field bailiff Birkholz accused of assault and defiance during manorial service. Farmer Guhl claimed that "neither he nor his boy said more than that they had no barley and the horses were hungry and couldn't be coerced, whereupon [Birkholz] straightaway struck [young Ebel], as he also did without cause the previous year, which [Guhl] hadn't forgotten." Guhl admitted they let their horses get into seigneurial pastures,

---

[26] No. 200, fo. 107.   [27] No. 591, fo. 28.

but were leaving when the fight began. Bailiff Birkholz said he did not strike young Ebel until he provoked him with "good-for-nothing talk," saying "'come on, if you have the courage,' and he kept cursing like that, and the farmer, instead of controlling him, ran at [Birkholz's] throat with club in hand."

Hasse ruled "it was clear, and plaintiff [Birkholz] takes it on his conscience," that young Ebel started the quarrel, justifying Birkholz's blows. Farmer Guhl, thrice warned to control himself, instead assaulted Birkholz.

[Guhl] well deserves to be punished with three days [!] in the Spanish overcoat, but for now he will be spared and instead punished with spending only this one [June] night in the tower here. But the boy will be brought by the bailiff to better obedience and disciplined for his coarse and unwarranted talk with the whip, and will first ask the plaintiff [bailiff] for forgiveness.[28]

Here is a rare instance of a judicial whipping unequivocally ordered and doubtless executed. There is no unambiguous record before 1763 of such a penalty inflicted upon adult farmers, though they sometimes faced the choice of money fines or corporal punishment, which might include lashes. But Hasse's court avoided imposing inescapable floggings, except (rarely) in youthful transgressions such as young Ebel's. Possibly the ill-will and resentment generated among farmers by such humiliations seemed too high a price to pay.[29]

As for unmarried women farm servants, violence sometimes engulfed them, but not seigneurially provoked. In 1729 fullholder's servant Marie Niemanns, on the same day she was found guilty of practicing minor witchcraft, stood accused by kinswoman Vey Niemanns of throwing a rock at her, moving Vey to hit Marie with a broomstick. Marie retorted that Vey taunted her with "whoring, and that she had lain with a farmhand. The plaintiff [Marie claimed] was completely falling down drunk." But Hasse, though he ruled the two women's actions canceled each other out, warned Marie that "if she should further cause any such trouble, she will on a Sunday be displayed in the pillory to the whole commune." Both women, probably, were kinswomen of the Glövzin tavernkeeper, and of the Niemanns who fled her hollander's job in 1739.[30]

---

[28] No. 326, fo. 240.
[29] On laws governing servants' and laborers' corporal punishment, see Lennhoff, *Das ländliche Gesindewesen*; Koselleck, *Preussen Zwischen Reform und Revolution*; Lüdtke, *Police and State in Prussia*; and Richard J. Evans, *Rituals of Retribution. Capital Punishment in Germany, 1600–1987* (London, 1996).
[30] No. 200, fos. 126–7.

In 1728 farmer Hans Milatz appeared with his daughter Anna, who charged seigneurial maidservant Marie Schütten with accusing her, when Anna worked at Stavenow manor, of stealing seigneurial textiles and refusing to give administrator Halentz her trunk keys so he might investigate. Defendant Schütten claimed the other servants spoke of how Halentz finally found the textiles in Anna's trunk. But she knew nothing of Anna, as the formula went, "but honor and goodness." Although Anna wanted written confirmation of innocence, Hasse ruled Schütten had delivered the requisite "[oral] declaration of honor . . . and if anyone should hold such gossip against [Anna Milatz], the [written] certificate of honor will be issued at the defendant's expense."[31]

In both cases, Hasse adjudicated quarrels involving servants, rather than disciplining seigneurial workers for misdeeds. Defense of young servant-girls' reputations was a serious matter. The life stage of service was one that both sexes needed to traverse with honor as unscathed as possible. Though the lordship sometimes physically punished farm servants, runaways and reprisals were disruptive and dangerous. Many former servants remained in the jurisdiction as farmers or other householders whose deference toward the lordship was preferable to defiance.

MARRIED LABORERS IN THE VILLAGES: COTTAGERS

Demand for intermittent agricultural labor was high enough to enable some landless villagers to escape celibate service into life as married cottagers (*Kätner*). Apart from craftsmen and minor notables, Stavenow settlement housed married day laborers, some guaranteed winter work as threshers, others not. Villages also housed such laboring cottagers, some with small arable plots, others with gardens only. Below such householders stood married lodgers, who could do no better than rent farmsteads' unoccupied rooms. Some were able-bodied workers, others were old or impaired. By renting some seigneurial cropland, as was possible before Dargardt's colonization, some cottagers gained incomes, supplemented by wage labor, allowing them (rarely) to accumulate savings and possessions superior to larger farmers'. We earlier encountered a modestly successful cottager in Hans Bahlcke and his widow Anna Schulten. Hans rose from 1744 lodger status on a cottage holding to its purchaser. After his 1768 death, his widow reported her dowry at 330

---

[31] Ibid., fo. 110.

talers and present assets at 142 talers. The cottage itself, which in those years lost its Dargardt lands, declined in sale price from 70 to 60 talers. One of Stavenow's cottage holdings endured unhappier fortunes. In 1724 it was in Reimar Häwecke's hands. Appraisals in 1718 and 1727 found it "in bad condition." Colonel Kleist attached some arable to it, setting annual rent at 6 talers, plus seven days of seigneural harvest labor. Taking the usual farmer's oath, Häwecke received his deed of hereditary tenancy. In 1731, though, his female relative (probably sister) Anna Hewekens' husband Stoffel Buck, a nearby fullholder, went mad. Reimar Häwecke took Buck's farm while the deranged farmer and his family moved onto the cottage holding. Buck died in 1737, his wife in 1742, leaving proprietorship to their 20-year-old son Christoffel and his new bride. Christoffel gave his younger brother a sheep and "cow with halter," keeping for himself a sheep and two calves, their sow having died. Of furniture and equipment, including ax, shovel, and threshing flail, Hasse observed "it amounts to little because the father drowned miserably and thereafter the mother headed the household only with difficulty."[32]

Twenty years later, Christoffel was dead, but not until 1771 did his widow, now physically impaired, pass the cottage to her daughter and new son-in-law, Christian Zeggel. But because Zeggel was an active-duty "rank and file musketeer," one of two other daughters was seeking to marry, so a man might be present as household head. The holding, its physical condition still "bad," could sow but 6 bushels annually. It possessed two steers, a sheep and a pig, plus minimal equipment, a kettle, and a 5-taler bed. It carried 13 talers' church debt, and two years' back rent (12 talers) to the preacher, to whom the Kleists had assigned this minor income.[33] Whether because of the post-1763 manpower shortage or this holding's poverty, the only man prepared to marry into it was a soldier who, though without discharge papers, might hope his new dignity would gain him them. Meanwhile a widow with four children would have to survive on her daughters' earnings and 6 bushels' harvest, which could yield only a bare minimum for such a household. Here we glimpse a cruel version of the fate of village farmers' married kinfolk who could not gain proper farms, for Häweckes, Bucks, and Zeggels were all fullholders' descendants or relatives.

Threadbare too was Trine Havemanns' household. In 1766 she entered her third marriage since 1752 when, with Frau Kleist's approval,

---

[32] Ibid., fo. 174; no. 326, fos. 103–4; no. 323, fo. 8.   [33] No. 358, fos. 111–12.

she and a shortlived soldier-husband succeeded her parents on a landless holding owing but 2 talers rent yearly and one day's weekly hand labor. Six of Trine's siblings, including her twin, had claimed meager legacies, the parental holding displaying only a bed, "one good table," a cupboard and two kettles, plus "mother's clothes and body-linen, in bad condition." On behalf of the widow's eleven-year-old son, his new step-father, Tobias Marwitz, promised "to raise [him] to Holy Communion, give him in winter necessary sustenance and support" – suggesting he would in other seasons fend for himself – "and send him to school." The boy would eventually inherit the cottage. As for his step-father, "if after his wife's death the children should press for property division, he will be given free housing in the small living room as long as he lives."[34]

The lordship drew little advantage from its humblest subjects. Hans Ohlert's self-built cottage ought to have rendered manual labor, but "because he is feeble he has been released for life from service, and now gives the lordship only a tribute hen." In 1757 Ohlert and wife charged neighbors with invading their garden. Resulting quarrels led to Ohlert's cooking kettle's impoundment. Conrad Kleist, "in consideration of the plaintiff's poverty," gave him "from his own funds" 1 taler to recover the kettle, directing the pastor "to charge plaintiff and wife earnestly to keep the village peace."[35] Other less troublesome but similarly unprofitable cottage tenancies, especially of widows, occurred.

Some cottagers were furloughed soldiers, whose settlement as laborers in their native jurisdictions helped relieve widespread soldierly poverty in the Prussian kingdom.[36] Possibly just-mentioned Ohlert was a disabled war veteran. The lordship gave Michael Zeggel, a soldier in Colonel Kleist's former regiment, "the place by the Glövzin churchyard to build his cottage," in exchange (after two free years) for one day's weekly hand labor, waived during the annual military review. In 1753 Zeggel and his wife moved into the cottage, taking hereditary possession. Rent was 1.5 talers, payable after two more free years, during which they would "bring construction to complete perfection." Zeggel later sold this holding, becoming a permanently employed Stavenow cottager-laborer (eventually losing 50 talers entrusted to bankrupted Adrian Kleist).[37]

[34] Ibid., fos. 13–14; no. 326, fo. 186.   [35] No. 259, fo. 16; no. 326, fo. 210.
[36] See Büsch, *Militärsystem*; Menge and Wilm, *So lebten sie alle Tage*; and Krüger, *Geschichte der Manufakturen*.
[37] No. 715, fo. 46; no. 326, fo. 190.

In 1759 Conrad Kleist permitted invalid soldier Hans Linow, non-locally named, to build a Mesekow cottage. This led to conflict with the farmers. Mayor Biermann warned that grazing was limited and Linow would have to pay for his cow. Linow appealed to "the law of the land" which, Hasse agreed, allowed him free grazing if he paid the herder's fee. Because Biermann cursed and threatened Linow at the verdict's announcement, Hasse sentenced him for "gross excesses" to two hours – doubtless uncomfortably shackled – in the dungeon. Later Mesekow miller Wiese gave Linow and his wife some arable and garden land, in return for inheriting their cottage after their deaths. Linow penned his name.[38]

Here is evidence of landed villagers' resistance, widespread in eighteenth-century Germany, to the settlement of landless cottagers with claims on such communal resources as grazing.[39] Yet Frederick II's government advocated giving landless villagers in perpetual leasehold the arable attached to churches, sometimes communally cultivated but often leased to prosperous villagers such as millers. In 1778, upon this policy's announcement, Joachim Schlow successfully petitioned for land sowable in 2.5 bushels, where he would build a cottage, paying Blüthen commune 1 taler yearly. As churchland, the holding was tax-free. The lordship granted Schlow life release from manorial service, obliging him to repair the church and parsonage.[40]

Resistance to such settlements persisted. In 1797, when soldier Hans Nagel sought a perpetual lease on Premslin churchland, the farmers invoked (apart from poor soil) their grazing rights, also warning that a new cottage built there, where the village had planted a pinewood, would be prey to robbery. This was a rare allusion to highwaymen and other wandering malefactors disturbing German tranquility in the French Revolutionary era, but it was doubtless meant to discourage Nagel. Perhaps because a rival lordship backed the soldier, Major Kleist endorsed his subjects' counter-proposal to lease the land instead to a farmer short-term.[41] Conversely, the Premsliners saw their self-interest served by laborer-shepherd Georg Ebel, who with his wife in 1790 paid 25 talers to renovate the communal shepherd's house, earning lifelong occupancy.[42]

Major Kleist's aggressive assertion of seigneurial power, manor–village relations' advancing judicialization, and rising eighteenth-century land

---

[38] No. 324, fos. 42–3.   [39] On Hesse: Taylor, *Indentured.*   [40] No. 718, fo. 94.
[41] No. 720, fos. 73–5.   [42] No. 603, fos. 9–10.

values manifest themselves in the 1791 perpetual-lease contract he signed with Crown Prince Regiment musketeer Jahnke. The soldier purchased "in hereditary possession" for himself and his descendants, "also lateral and other relatives," half a newly built house with a garden. He paid 120 talers, fully due by 1795, on pain of being "thrown out." Rent was 4 talers which, if left unpaid for three years running, would justify eviction, provided Stavenow paid the owner the fair property value. Kleist could preempt other purchases by paying third parties' prices, while "at every death, whether lordship's or perpetual leaseholder's, 1 taler will be levied as feudal charge, in recognition of [the lordship's] feudal property rights [*Obereigentum*]." Jahnke and his successors would be obliged to work for the lordship or its tenant-farmers at the "customary day wage," and patronize Premslin mill alone. Major and soldier signed, Jahnke with a cross, "whereupon Jahnke, as a born [Stavenow] subject, further submits himself to subject status both for himself and his descendants." This clause, of dubious legality, seemingly aimed to compel Jahncke's heirs to take the cottage.[43]

OTHER VILLAGE LABORERS: LODGERS

A step below worker-cottagers stood lodgers (*Einlieger, Einwohner*), living in rented quarters. The able-bodied day laborers among them did not always fare badly, but the seigneurial quest for unpaid labor and farmers' preference for unmarried resident servants constrained their numbers. The lordship had long resisted harboring impoverished lodgers who, because of age or disability, were a source neither of useful labor nor money rents. In 1744 Hasse summoned the mayors to report on lodgers. These numbered twenty-one, fifteen of them men, including one soldier. Six bore local farmers' names, while the others were evidently outsiders. Two, and probably more, were married, including Kohn, the tavernkeeper's lodger, "but he is deaf and lame and the wife too, and they are nourished in Glövzin and Premslin where they beg their bread." The survey assumed the other men performed seigneurial hand labor as required. Mesekow housed two female lodgers identified as old women, living together in the "herder's cabin," but other women appear employable. Hasse warned against taking in lodgers without landlordly approval, threatening 2-taler fines.[44]

[43] No. 720, fos. 51–2.   [44] No. 326, fo. 109.

A 1724 ruling required lodgers to perform one day's weekly labor service with meals, or one day twice monthly without. Such labors possessed little value, for the 1760 appraisal failed to mention or monetize them. In the 1780s, lodgers in three villages protested paying the increased "protection money" Kleist demanded, having abandoned his claims on their labor and even forbidden them to offer it. When in 1785 the village mayors remonstrated that other local lordships collected but 1 taler yearly per lodger, whether single or married, Kleist backed down, agreeing also that lodgers confining themselves to nursing elderly or sick retirees were exempt.[45] Curiously, Berlin's Chamber Court handed Kleist a 1785 victory in his 1777 suit against a worker miller Lenz employed to cultivate the farm attached hereditarily to his mill. Aggressively, Kleist viewed Lenz's cultivator as a lodger liable to the usual charges. The court agreed, saying the 1769 Statute on Laborers entitled Kleist to two days' weekly hand labor – or however many were locally customary – in exchange for meals. The major settled for protection money.[46]

The lordship earlier often waived its demands on lodgers' unpaid labor, as when in 1731 a farmer housing a woman argued successfully that she neither worked for pay, "nor lived in his outbuildings," but was his housekeeper. In 1727, two widowed lodgers gained release, one because of illness and the other, a mother raising young children, because she was needed to nurse her farmer landlord's old mother "and protect her in her weakness from fire and candles."[47] Yet, while Major Kleist insisted on his right to protection money, its collection may have been half-hearted. In 1830 State Minister Voss's son, now Stavenow's master, wrote estate manager Neubauer saying the 1751 Servants Ordinance and later legislation entitled him to "protection services" or cash equivalents from lodgers, though they were now going unpaid. "But in protection money's collection lies a means to discourage poor people's crowding into Stavenow's villages, who then become charges on them." This was the more necessary, Voss thought, because of Stavenow's location near the Hannoverian and Mecklenburg borders. Individual cases suggested "the poor from other places seem only to have settled here because of opportunities for contraband." Hence Neubauer should collect 1 taler yearly from married lodgers and a half-taler from the unmarried, waiving charges where appropriate. Though this was the voice of the nineteenth-century propertied classes against people stigmatized as the undeserving and

---

[45] No. 200, fo. 22; no. 602, fos. 1, 18.   [46] No. 719, fo. 63.   [47] No. 591, fo. 38; no. 200, fo. 90.

criminal poor, smuggling at Stavenow was a temptation, and not only for lodgers.[48]

Unmarried male laborers might accumulate some good assets, but most married lodgers left meager estates. Their initial possessions were often scant, as were a recently wed lodger's wife's who died in 1768. Her smallholder father rather than laborer husband paid the debts occasioned by her death and burial, reclaiming the dowry while giving the husband 2 talers and some bedding in place of his childless deceased daughter's dress of honor. The widower was left to pay a 3-taler debt on a cooking pot bought on credit.[49] Older couples also might have little to show for life's exertions. In 1754 Pastor Karstedt inventoried the goods of day laborer Joachim Hintze, a fullholder's lodger. His wife had died, leaving some creditable clothing: six dresses and four camisoles, twelve bonnets and caps, twelve upper- and undershirts, and three scarves, one "wine blue," plus linen. They owned four kettles, including "one to warm up a meal," plus bed and bedding, and spinning gear. His tools comprised two axes, a hatchet, and two spades. He had, Hintze said, no money.[50]

Another lodger, Hans Heitmann, renting the tavernkeeper's quarters, in 1725 found himself (again) widowed, now with an infant daughter. He said "his and his child's circumstances required him to marry Ilse Braun, retiree's daughter in Quitzow. Through this he expected to acquire, apart from her clothes, one head of cattle." He had secured an inheritance for a grown first-marriage daughter, depositing a chest with her guardian containing two dresses, "one for Sundays and one for workdays," plus bedding and linen "in a bag." Of the same daughter's two cows, one had been "sold and drunk up," perhaps at her mother's wake, but Heitmann promised to replace it.[51]

Eloquent is the 1770 testament of Joachim Ebel, "retiree and day laborer on Ditten's holding." Ebel summoned Pastor Höpfner, who found him "exhausted but mentally sound."

Upon my arrival he expressed his longing for the end, though resigning himself entirely to the Divine will, and after requisite examination of his soul's condition, he averred, as he did last Sunday when taking Holy Communion, that he wanted to make his wife, with whom he had gone through a great deal, his modest estate's sole heir. And since he had heard that his brother had laid claim to the inheritance [he wanted Höpfner to record his will], because he could not countenance that she, who was closest to him, should lose the slightest part.

[48] No. 349, fos. 1–2.   [49] No. 358, fo. 45.   [50] No. 716, fo. 11.   [51] No. 200, fos. 190–1.

Höpfner agreed, calling a local mason, because no one else was at home, as witness, and then writing "from the mouth of the dying man,"

that his wife Anna Maria Schultzen should alone keep what little there was, because he could in no way complain about her. He didn't have any 100 talers, but only the small amount his wife would have to reveal . . . but that wouldn't amount even to 10 talers.[52]

The dying man had given a farmer a trunk, in return for the farmer sowing for him and his wife 5 bushels of seed-grain. Here again is evidence how landless prevailed on landed to raise crops for their sustenance. Among his possessions were two kettles, an ax and a hatchet, and various pieces of furniture. His wife needed it all, for at Michaelmas she would pay house and garden rent (they lived in a retirees' cottage), plus 16 groschen to the kettle-repairer.

Though elderly, Ebel and his wife possessed their own rented dwelling and had secured a food supply. But this depended on continued income, which during his final illness was faltering, leaving his wife to a widowed lodger's uncertain fate. Some paired with other single elders, as Louise Neumann seemingly did with a retired farmer, to whose son and successor in 1793 she willed her possessions in return for his agreement to bury her.[53] Some persevered in rented quarters, as apparently did Elisabeth Ekkardt, who in February of famine year 1771 was found dead in the fields. In her room were goods later auctioned for 13 talers, of their claim to which her relatives in Mecklenburg were duly notified.[54] Or the landless poor remained in rented quarters until terminal illness, when relatives took them in, as happened to farm widow Catharina Kratzen, living in old age as a miller's lodger. Her heirs wrangled over her estate. It was slight, for her cow died and she sold its calf. She left two jackets, but one of two dresses vanished. She left half-worked flax and linen, a bed and kettles, an old loom, other household goods "all very old and mostly worn-out," and 9 talers lent out. A daughter claimed 2 talers for the funeral. Her son Jacob demanded "much" for her residence with him during an earlier fourteen-year period, "and likewise for his mother's nursing and cleaning . . . when she lay for fourteen weeks with dysentery and especially during her last illness."[55]

For some, lodger status denoted social descent, as with Johann Key, "former Wittenberge burgher and master smith" renting quarters in a Stavenow village. Another lodger charged him, together with "the Schenck woman," with stealing 50 talers, saying that "Meister Key

[52] No. 358, fos. 90, 93.   [53] No. 326, fo. 223.   [54] No. 358, fos. 137–42.   [55] No. 200, fos. 225–7.

hasn't been sober for three days."[56] In 1742, blacksmith Richter clashed "shortly before Christmas" with Christian Volcken over money Volcken owed him. Richter charged Volcken and his wife, who were someone's lodgers, with behaving "very unfittingly." Volcken's wife, believing the blacksmith's wife

had publicly denounced them for being dissipated and slovenly, pounded on the table and said [to Richter's wife] that she would hold her to be a whore and trash [*Canaille*] until she proved her charges. And then she ran out of the living room and was shouting in the entry-way about whores and trash.

Richter's wife only conceded saying that Volcken had not repaid the grain he borrowed six years previously and that Volcken's wife's stepparents "were slovenly people in the way they kept house."

Volcken's wife admitted a 4-taler debt, but blamed Richter's wife for reproaching her and her husband with "eating up" their assets and for saying "now you think you can pay off [your debts] with weaving," and that they were a "dissipated pack," and her relatives were "slovenly stink-women" and people who squandered their patrimony. She called on her father for support but he, a sixty-three-year-old, could only remember hearing the word "dissipated." Hasse imposed a debt-repayment schedule, fining Richter's wife 1 taler and Volcken's 12 groschen. Here, seemingly, Frau Volcken's shame over poverty, especially when publicly condemned for it by village notables, boiled over into rage.[57]

Poverty inclined other lodgers to crime, besmirching their law-abiding counterparts' reputation. Tenant-farmer Hartz accused a lodger's wife of furtively milking manorial cows. The accused proudly, if implausibly, claimed she owned seven cows "and got what she needed from them." Hartz countered that the accused had given "the old Hecht woman some butter," but she replied that "she does indeed give something to the poor people, without asking anything in return."[58] The outcome is unknown, but that lodgers might raid seigneurial resources was clear to the belligerent Hartz. As for village farmers' suspicion of lodgers, of which some evidence concerning wood thefts emerged earlier, in 1757 a farmer charged a lodger he had employed with "ruining a lot of his things," stealing eighty-four plum and three walnut saplings – signs of orchard tree trade – plus a window frame. Hasse ordered impoundment of the 1-bushel crop the defendant, now outside the jurisdiction, had gotten a farmer to sow for him.[59]

[56] No. 591, fos. 90–2.   [57] No. 326, fos. 75–6.   [58] No. 591, fo. 66.   [59] No. 326, fo. 211.

SEIGNEURIALLY HOUSED LABORERS

Married workers renting the lordship's cottages and laboring exclusively or primarily for it were, apart from resident craftsmen, either livestock herders or workers threshing for harvest shares in the winter and otherwise living from wage labor. In 1724 Hasse summoned Stavenow's cottagers to announce new rules. Seven appeared, while four others, including the blacksmith and linen-weaver, were absent. They were to "keep up their cottages," whose rent stood at a fairly stiff 8 talers yearly. Their lodgers, if any, must render requisite unpaid service. They could freely graze two head of cattle, and pay for more. "Whoever pilfers lumber or fencing shall pay 2 talers beyond the wood's value or wear for a whole day Spanish overcoat or fiddle, depending on whether it is man or woman, but gathering of loose boughs is unforbidden." A day of such punishment seemed to the lordship (at this moment) endurable punishment.[60]

In 1741 a manorial official, probably a forester, wrote Hasse saying "the cottagers here keep too much summer livestock. I think one cow would suffice, for the profit [the animals] yield they burn up in [winter] firewood, if [the people] were to pay for it." This remark, without detectable effect, suggests the cottagers were engaging in livestock-trading, wintering over more animals than they could otherwise have done without cheap or free firewood.[61] Apart from pursuing profit, such villagers sought through livestock-breeding (and gardening and flax-work) to emulate the farmer class. Cottager-thresher Kober once complained that neighboring carpenter Wiese's wife falsely accused him, among other things, of wrongly slaughtering a sheep. Though the fault is obscure, thresher Kober had a sheep to slaughter. The carpenter protested innocence, retorting that Kober cursed him and his wife as "whore-pack" and "landless folk." Landlessness could be reproachable.[62]

Midway between salaried seigneurial officials, contracted entrepreneurs, and craftsmen, on one side, and married and unmarried manorial workers, on the other, were various foremen. One was the overseer (*Statthalter*) and his wife, who at each manor-farm housed, fed, and supervised unmarried workers. At Stavenow in 1809 there stood, alongside seven salaried employees' cottages and two large houses with nine married workers' apartments, the "administration building" with six large and three small rooms, and "a capacious kitchen." Here lived overseer Schnell and wife, together with the unmarried laborers they boarded. At

---

[60.] No. 200, fo. 22. [61] No. 591, fo. 103. [62] No. 200, fo. 60.

Dargardt, overseer Struve (earning, like Schnell, 30 talers yearly) received for himself and his few workers "6 talers instead of the third pig for fattening, the yearly quarter of beef, and the 120 herring," plus 68 bushels of cereals and peas. He grazed cost-free four cows, three pigs, four sheep, and received free potato-land, salt rations, sown flax, and firewood.[63]

In 1771 Stavenow overseer Jacob Hasselbring's widow married Johann Schamp. Both, like hers, were outsiders' names. Her three children stood under schoolmaster Tendt's guardianship. She was a refugee from Mecklenburg, where she lost everything in "war's upheavals." She had no money, Betich noting its theft "a few years ago." Her husband had lent, to the miller and the yarn-weaver, 55 and 40 talers, though neither claim was properly "secured" and would require litigation. With smaller loans owed her, plus a cow and calf, clothing and household goods, her assets tallied 173 talers, half of which her children would share at age twenty-five. Neither she nor her new husband could sign their names.[64]

The second type of married foreman was the *Häcker*, or head ploughman-mechanic. Traditionally, he led seigneurial laborers and farmers and farmhands in fieldwork, but the eighteenth-century trend was for senior unmarried workers to assume this job. By 1809 only one such field foreman remained, at Stavenow, earning 15 talers cash, receiving 23 bushels of food, and keeping a cow, two pigs, and sheep, with a free cottage, garden, and fuel. In 1768 there was a Dargardt field foreman, Joachim Griese, whose wife died, leaving four young children. Griese, related to Dargardt smallholders, said his wife's estate amounted to "only a little, and out of love for his children" he wanted them to have her textiles. Her clothing had been ample and varied, including four silk kerchiefs and three pairs of new blue woolen stockings. There was also a brass flat-iron and a good array of copper and brass kettles, plus three cows, a sow, and four pigs. Griese had 130 talers in cash, entrusting 100 talers on behalf of his children to the court, though retaining the right to draw upon them if "worldly circumstances" required. He and one of the smallholder guardians signed with crosses. Here we see, again, that the lordship's village-born senior employees might attain a comparatively comfortable and secure social station.[65]

Married livestock herders lived under poorer conditions. In 1809 there were four such employees receiving the usual food and other provisions, though only earning 8–10 talers cash. In 1758 Semlin cowherd

---

[63] No. 39, fo. 28; no. 62.   [64] No. 358, fos. 121–4.   [65] Ibid., fos. 50–2.

Knaebeler died, leaving his wife with three children aged 14–18. She carried on as a widow for thirteen years until, debt-free but holding assets of only 22 talers, she married a village lodger.[66] Herders also lived with animal violence. In 1724 two Stavenow cottagers charged seigneurial swineherd Daniel Tiede with beating and driving their pigs to death. Tiede said one pig "could hardly walk anymore; another must have eaten evil weeds, because it was stretched out on all fours and lying all blue next to the stream; the third his dog bit to death," for which he would pay minor damages; "the fourth, a sow, the plaintiff himself ate." One plaintiff claimed he "foddered the first sow four weeks at his house, and the defendant himself said she was so comfortable that he couldn't push her around." The second plaintiff said Tiede's dogs "had torn both ears from [his pig's] head and bitten her neck to pieces." For all this Tiede paid only 1.5 talers.[67] In 1726 farmer Nagel charged a field bailiff with a young herder's loss of control over a seigneurial bull, which invaded the farmers' horse-grazing pasture, where "it gored [Nagel's] best horse to death." The field bailiff supported the herder's charge that Nagel's son let the farmers' dogs bite the bull, enraging it. Hasse heavily fined the herder 3 talers' pay, but left Nagel to suffer, by his reckoning, an 11-taler loss.[68]

Among married threshers-laborers, some were long-term Stavenow cottagers. All were capable, with sound health, of earning fair shares of threshed grain, some of which – in bounteous years – they sold. But thresher Holtmann's estate, inventoried at his 1757 death when he was in his mid-thirties, shows that he and his wife lived very modestly. Assets totaled 61 talers, including 11 talers cash, 3 bushels of rye, a calf and two cows. Holtmann's brother, the Glövzin mayor, still owed him 10 talers from the parental farm. The thresher's clothing was simple but not disreputable. Of his burial, which apart from the coffin cost 4 talers, it was noted that "the old linen pants were taken by the Voss woman who dressed him." His boots fetched 6 groschen. He left behind axes, flails, scythes, rakes, hammers, and tools worth 2 talers, plus tobacco worth 2 groschen. His wife's wardrobe was unimpressive. Her "daily clothing," appraised at a mere 1 groschen, "isn't worth much." They owned an old loom. "The bed is also old and was used for twenty-four years by her father and mother and four years by them." With bedding it rated but 3 talers. Unlike most childless partners in non-landed workers' first marriages, they had not named each

---

[66] Ibid., fos. 124–6.   [67] No. 200, fos. 18–19.   [68] Ibid., fos. 59–60, 85.

other as exclusive heirs, obliging the widow to divide net assets with her mayoral brother-in-law.[69]

In 1729, four Stavenow threshers stood accused of workplace rye theft. Michael Kober was the only one among them not bearing a local farmer's name, though he shared the Stavenow blacksmith's and swineherd's, and the Blüthen pastor's. "He added he has a couple of children at home, and had neither bread nor grain, so he should be pardoned for what he only did out of poverty. He has always been loyal." Kober surrendered his booty, one-eighth bushel (ca. 12 pounds). Hasse accepted the protestations of innocence of two others, but not the third, who with Kober "shall be banished from the threshing barn" and would work three wageless summer days as punishment. Kober, for his "furtive pilfering," would also stand one hour in the Spanish overcoat.

The lordship then swore in a new four-worker team, including the two found innocent, whose oath bound them to report thefts and be "loyal and hard-working threshers." The six Semlin and Premslin threshers, some farmers' sons but other not, also took the vow. "The punishment of the Spanish overcoat was carried out against Kober, and after he promised improvement he was dismissed," his name then disappearing from the thresher-cottager ranks.[70] Here, soon before the manorial workers' 1730 food protests and flights, the lordship cracked down unforgivingly on threshers' pilferage.

Twelve years later, thresher Christoffel Wille was still at the manor when his wife's brother Jürgen Heerden and Heerden's wife both died. Reporting as heir and co-claimant was a man, born in 1716, whose mother now appeared, claiming he was the deceased Heerden's extramarital son. Thresher Wille's wife, speaking for herself and three other siblings, harshly said "whore-children don't inherit, and the plaintiff couldn't legitimate himself to do so." Wille's wife further argued that, according to the church certificate the plaintiff's mother produced, the father named in 1716 was not her brother. Speaking of the extramarital mother, Wille's wife said "she hasn't raised the claim [concerning the plaintiff's father] in twenty-six years, although she's been living in Blüthen in [farmer] Jürgen Ohlert's cottage." Hasse tried to persuade Wille's wife and her siblings to give their would-be natural brother 1 taler each, but they refused, whereupon he dismissed the plaintiff's claim, because he "can in no way prove that he was fathered by Jürgen Heerden."

[69] No. 326, fos. 214–15; no. 358, fos. 43–6.   [70] No. 200, fo. 115–17.

Deceased Heerden was a Stavenow laborer of some sort, possibly a thresher. Manager Erhardt appraised his not threadbare estate at 64 talers, including 34 talers cash, plus textiles and bushels of grain, a good cow, calf and pig. His shoes sold for 12 groschen. Among burial costs were 1.5 talers for the coffin, 2.5 talers for beer and a bushel of peas for soup, 3.5 groschen for a burial shirt, 6 groschen for the corpse's dressing, 6 groschen to "transport the body to Stavenow," 2 groschen for black ribbon, 6 groschen to the sexton and 1 taler shared between two presiding pastors.[71] For a landless worker, this was a respectable exit from the earthly vale.

Doubtless wage laborers fell into debt in times of dearth and led lives punctuated by crises and trouble. Of this a glimpse emerges from some experiences of Erdmann Mentz, a smallholder's son and 1740s' seigneurial thresher. In 1731 he was found guilty, together with fullholder's daughter Anna Milatz, of committing, seemingly while both were in seigneurial service, "the gross vice of whoring." Since they agreed to marry, their heavy 15-taler fine "shall be remitted in holy matrimony's honor." Ten years later, following 1740 food shortages, Mentz and his father-in-law Hans Milatz confronted sexton Bartelt Sauber in court. Sauber testified he lent the thresher 2 rye-bushels against one of his wife's dresses and a bedsheet, while farmer Milatz said he pawned with the sexton his daughter's "dress of honor," which had cost him 5 talers, to give his needy daughter and son-in-law a sheep and a lamb. Since Sauber had not been repaid (while thresher Mentz owed him money from earlier loans), Sauber sold the dress of honor for 1.5 talers and sought court approval to sell the bedsheet as well. Hasse agreed, with a month's grace period. This story shows the sexton playing pawnbroker and moneylender, and threshers and farmer fathers-in-law reduced to pawning and thereby losing a worker's wife's most valued textiles.[72]

In 1749, Erdmann Mentz was missing, having absconded. His wife put their youngest child in the care of Mentz's extra-jurisdictional sister, who took this as a pretext for coming to farmer Milatz's house and seizing the child's "maternal inheritance," whatever it was. The absconder's older child was in a farmer's service. A year later, Mentz had returned to live with his wife and younger daughter Anna Grete. They appeared again in court, charging a neighbor with accusing Anna Grete of stealing apples from the garden of Pastor Cober's "maiden daughter," who lived in her own cottage with a maidservant who was

---

[71] No. 326, fos. 75, 78–9.   [72] No. 591, fos. 35, 101–2; no. 326, fos. 71–2.

the child of Anna Grete's accuser. Mentz said he and his wife had sent their daughter at 5:00 A.M. to the Stavenow administration building with "a brandy bottle and 1 groschen," plus nine shirts for her brother in seigneurial service. Carrying these things in her apron, Mentz's daughter appeared suspicious to mistress Cober's maidservant. Hasse, after interrogating various witnesses, fined both parties 12 groschen "for their ill-considered babbling." Mentz and his family subsequently disappear from the records, though they may have stayed at Stavenow. These incidents show that periodic upheavals afflicted their rather turbulent lives, but they persevered, raising children and placing them in service as best they could.[73]

CONCLUSION

Lodgers and seigneurially housed married laborers led more mobile lives than farmers and cottagers with hereditary tenures (though non-inheriting children of both household types often dispersed widely). Landless workers with supervisorial skills or other advantages could, especially in landlordly employment, find positions of some stability and respectability. But for many such workers, separation from land-holding and farming was the more galling in that it was rare, though not – as we earlier saw – impossible, for mature workers with savings to buy their way into landed households. On Stavenow evidence, landless workers were not condemned to poverty and misery, but could with some luck live in modest sufficiency, though hard times periodically struck. From village farmers' perspective, a married laborer's existence, spent in one's own housing or rented cottage, might seem acceptable for non-inheriting children, if marriage portions conveyed some assets. But, despite all disabilities and aggravations, holding a farm must have seemed preferable to landless laboring in those villagers' eyes whose hopes and talents did not impel or admit them to higher spheres.

[73] No. 326, fo. 157; no. 715, fo. 27–8.

8

Policing crime and the moral order, 1700–1760: Seigneurial court, village mayors, church, state, and army

In worst light, European seigneurial courts appear as theaters of cynical injustice: from the judge's bench, half-educated squires tyrannized defenseless and cowering villagers. Absentee landlords callously entrusted the enforcement of abusive rights to ruthless bailiffs and lawyer-agents, or leased their estates to tenant-farmers who milked manorial jurisdiction's incomes dry. Only when Enlightenment liberalism replaced legal feudalism with independent lower courts could justice dawn in the countryside – if room was left by the modern state's social discipline and resource extraction. Nor, seen negatively, were villagers' self-government and customary law more satisfactory, embodying the rule of the landed few over the land-poor many, the elderly over the young, men over women. Here, too, liberalism promised improvement, but faced the obstacle of village oligarchy.[1]

In Prussia, Frederick II's judicial reforms limited feudal corruption and arbitrariness. Where previously noble lords were largely free to entrust manorial courts to such judges as they saw fit, whether lawyers, bailiffs, or themselves, they were after 1747–8 obliged to employ only government-approved, university-trained jurists. While, earlier, costly fees impeded appeals beyond courts of first jurisdiction – in Brandenburg, to Berlin's Chamber Court (*Kammergericht*) – Frederick's Justice Minister Samuel von Cocceji's reforms cheapened and accelerated appellate justice, the one legal path to challenge seigneurial rulings[2]

---

[1] This was long the liberal view both of seigneurial courts and village self-government, e.g., Blum, *Our Forgotten Past*, and Jerome Blum, *The End of the Old Order in Rural Europe* (Princeton, 1978). For strong emphases on village oligarchy see Rebel, *Peasant Classes* and Hoch, *Serfdom and Social Control in Russia*. A positive view of German village institutions is to be found in Blickle, *Deutsche Untertanen*. More measured is Heide Wunder, *Die bäuerliche Gemeinde in Deutschland* (Göttingen, 1986) and, at the European level, Scott, *Peasantries*.

[2] Otto Hintze, "Preussens Entwicklung zum Rechtsstaat," *FBPG*, 32 (1920): 385–451; Otto Hintze, "Zur Agrarpolitik Friedrichs des Grossen," ibid., 10 (1898): 275–309; Otto Hintze, "Die Hohenzollern und der Adel," in Otto Hintze, *Regierung und Verwaltung. Gesamelte Abhandlungen zur*

Most lordships had long depended on local burghers trained in law to handle their weightier affairs. Prudent seigneurial courts resolved difficult cases by soliciting appeals courts' and university law faculties' opinions. As legally constituted corporate bodies, village communes could rightfully appeal to princely power against their landlords, resulting in high court rulings not always to villagers' disadvantage. But parsimonious early absolutism burdened communal lawsuits with heavy fees funding judicial salaries, while for individuals, among villagers and the poorer classes generally, legal expenses virtually annulled appellate rights in civil suits beyond courts of first jurisdiction. Criminal defendants could only hope for fair hearings, and to benefit from Frederick's abolition of judicial torture, complete by 1754.

Current research is much interested in seigneurial courts and the justice they dispensed. There is agreement they must be understood as enforcers of social discipline, less through sheer compulsion than power to impose discourses of social and civilizational order. Agreement also prevails that such courts, like all early modern institutions, were sites of negotiation, variously subtle, between lordships and subjects. Negotiation's failure led to the myriad early modern European revolts and rebellions which historians have impressively analyzed. Equally important was the capacity of legal institutions to channel social tension, a process German historians, addressing the 1525 Peasants' War's long-term legacy, characterize as judicialization (*Verrechtlichung*), especially between seventeenth- and eighteenth-century manor and village.[3]

At Stavenow, no evidence suggests the seigneurial court played a pivotal role in the commercialized manorial economy's pre-1648 ascent. Instead, the lordship–village power-balance, reflecting varying demographic-economic constellations, yielded, through Quitzows' commands or concessions, terms more or less endurable to the villages. Occasional disputes between Stavenow's Quitzows and neighboring

---

Staats-, Rechts- und Sozialgeschichte Preussens, ed. Gerhard Oestreich, 3 vols. (Göttingen, 1967), vol. III, 30–55; Hermann Weill, *Frederick the Great and Samuel von Cocceji* (Madison, WI, 1964); Mittenzwei, *Friedrich II*, 95ff; Grossmann, *Über die gutsherrlich- bäuerlichen Rechtsverhältnisse.*

[3] See above-cited literature on "peasant resistance," especially relevant works authored or edited by Peter Blickle and Winfried Schulze; Peters, *Konflikt und Kontrolle*; Gleixner, *"Das Mensch."* On Brandenburg court transcript registers and seigneurial courts: Bernhard Hinz, *Die Schöppenbücher der Mark Brandenburg, besonders des Kreises Züllichau-Schwiebus* (Berlin, 1964). Cf. Heinrich Kaak, "Untertanen und Herrschaft gemeinschaftlich im Konflikt. Der Streit um die Nutzung des Kietzer Sees in der östlichen Kurmark 1792–1797," in Jan Peters, ed., *Gutsherrschaftsgesellschaften im europäischen Vergleich* (Berlin, 1997), 325–42; Axel Lubinski, "Gutsherrschaft als lokale Gesellschaft und Konfliktgemeinschaft," in Lubinski et al., *Historie*, 237–60; Lieselott Enders, "Nichts als Ehr', Lieb's und Gut's. Soziale Konflikt- und Ausgleichpotenzen in der Frühneuzeit," in ibid., 141–61.

lordships and villages brought princely commissioner-mediators to the scene. But with the Blumenthals' and especially the Kleists' arrival, the seigneurial court acquired new institutional power, exemplified in Judge Hasse's forty-year tenure and preserved in the reams of case protocols that flowed from his pen. Colonel Kleist employed Hasse's court to "equalize" his villages in the 1720s. Subsequently, Hasse's rulings gave voice to landlordly authority on all fronts. After 1760, under Major Kleist, the court's role grew weightier still, representing Stavenow's seigneurial interests before royal tribunals to which the villages' lawyers appealed against the major's imperious demands.

This chapter appraises Stavenow court justice before 1760: its charges against the villagers, the pleas it heard for redress, its verdicts, punishments, and disciplinary tendency. These pages examine also the pastors' role in upholding seigneurial authority, and the village mayors' powers and actions, asking whether they served landlordly interests alone or also buttressed village autonomy. They consider too villagers' use of judicial procedure to pursue their own ends, and their conception of state rather than seigneurial power, especially as it flowed from the army and their service in it. Finally, they look at the Stavenow court's adjudication of manor–village conflict over rents and labor services during the seigneurial economy's considerable expansion between 1717 and 1763. These paths converge on lordship's and villagers' ideas of social order and justice. On what morally acceptable plane, rising above the lordship's superior power, did manor and village seek to coexist? Or did such a gulf yawn between the two that the question could not meaningfully arise?

MANORIAL COURT AS LEGAL INSTITUTION

In Brandenburg-Prussia, as elsewhere in Germany and Europe, a provincially variegated body of common law, sprung from medieval roots, acquired in the sixteenth century an overlay of new procedural codes, as well as substantive civil and criminal laws, inspired by Roman Law tradition. These innovations of Renaissance humanism strengthened judges at juries' expense, and mandated the keeping of verbatim transcripts of testimony heard by seigneurial and other courts of first jurisdiction. To this eclectic edifice absolutists later added wings housing voluminous administrative codes and new laws they unilaterally promulgated. By Frederick II's age, bureaucratic power to resolve by administrative fiat disputes involving the government was formidable. But civil suits between private parties took their course, steered by disputants' lawyers through the courts. Under criminal law, defendants' rights were glaringly weak, especially descending the social scale.

At Stavenow, as elsewhere in rural east-Elbia, manorial courts virtually never confronted defendants armed with legal counsel, though extra-jurisdictional plaintiffs often engaged lawyers or scribes to write letters seeking redress. Many of Hasse's cases pursued charges of wrongdoing the court itself or its agents, including occasionally local pastors, brought against the jurisdiction's inhabitants. But myriad cases also arose from intergenerational property transfers among seigneurial subjects. Numerous too were villagers' contentious charges against one another, or those of outsiders against Stavenowers.

Princely legislation empowered manorial judges, within moderate limits, to levy fines, impose physical punishments, and issue local jail sentences in a wide array of civil and criminal cases. But if defendants faced extended incarceration or death, they were surrendered to higher jurisdiction and transported to a royal fortress. Among Hasse's hundreds of cases, few were of such gravity. In his forty Stavenow years he did not once try a murder case. The crimes he punished were, mostly, bodily assault and theft. Premarital sexual relations and pregnancies provoked hearings and rulings, as did rare allegations of magic and sorcery. Numerous, though usually minor, were individual Stavenowers' offenses against the lordship, particularly in rendering seigneurial dues and services. Most common among villagers' offenses against one another were conflicts over debts, inheritances, retirement provisions, and other grievances issuing in quarrels and blows.[4]

The court spoke for the lordship, summoning villagers to hear seigneurial pronouncements on work rules or communal usages. Only rarely and indirectly did it represent state power. In taxation and troop recruitment, power rested with the three Prignitz District Commissioners (*Landräte*). In consultation with noble landlords, they dealt with village communes over payment or remission of direct taxes and enrolled farmers' sons in locally based army regiments. These weighty matters' documentation in the Stavenow archive is, unfortunately, extremely sparse. Thus the manorial court was both seigneurial authority's arm and village dispute-resolution agency. In individual villagers' eyes, its authority was effectively unchallengeable. But its punishment powers, whether financial or physical, faced limits in princely law

---

[4] The cases of 1724–53 are individually registered in chronological sequence in no. 63, and for 1754–7 in no. 326. Transcripts: nos. 200, 326, 328, 591, and the many scattered among the miscellany of nos. 710–19.

and, more importantly, the seigneurial interest in maintaining properly manned subject households capable of fulfilling their obligations.

Still, a manorial court might act despotically, as tenant-farmer Schmidt did while interrogating fullholder Heinrich Lent on the Stavenow forester's 1723 accusation that Lent, under a false name, sold stolen wood to a Wittenberge merchant. At the first hearing, Schmidt wrote that "the fellow himself didn't appear," but two other farmers, Lent's enemies, testified he tried to recruit one as an accomplice. Later twenty-six-year-old Lent appeared. Schmidt asked him "whether he diligently goes to church and takes communion, and also whether he knows the Seventh Commandment?" Lent answered "'Yes,' and he then prayed the Seventh Commandment." Did Lent seek Samuel Höpfner's complicity? "He didn't know as how he could remember this." Did he steal the wood? "No, he never did this, and people must have said otherwise out of hatred." After noting Lent's meager livestock holdings, Schmidt wrote: "Because the witness will admit nothing, he is thrown in jail." After three days' long confinement Lent emerged from the frigid dungeon. Schmidt failed to persuade Wittenberge's mayor to compel the merchant receiving the stolen wood to testify. Soon Lent absconded, permanently and unpunished, taking his livestock and possessions. His weakness, apart from relative poverty, was antagonism of village foes. He benefited perhaps from landlordly reluctance to long imprison farmers, since both their households and health suffered. But Schmidt did not hesitate to assume Lent's guilt and lock him up.[5]

The first protocol young Judge Hasse penned recorded Lent's farm's 1724 transfer to a new proprietor. He continued transcribing and sentencing uninterruptedly until his 1763 death, holding two or three sessions a year but often otherwise appearing to settle various matters. Perhaps the court functioned similarly under the Blumenthals and Quitzows, for certainly both lineages employed local lawyers' services, but few case transcripts survive from earlier times. In 1722, tenant-farmer Schmidt summoned an extrajurisdictional judge to settle a subject's estate.[6] Possibly this was standard practice, leaving to bailiffs and tenant-farmers such cases as they felt entitled or obliged to handle, including issuance of occupancy deeds.

Old custom lingered on. Teams of farmers or mayors appraised villagers' and seigneurial farm assets, and elders' testimony settled disputes over boundaries and other usages. In 1724 nearby estateowner Karstedt

---

[5] No. 593, fos. 1–7. [6] No. 200, fos. 168–71.

appeared, demanding from Kleist farmer Daniel Mentz annual grain rent
for land long attached to Mentz's farm. Mentz claimed he never in ten
years paid this charge, nor his parents before him. Summoned by Hasse,
"Bartelt Krumm, eighty years old, says in person that he indeed heard
from old people that the defendants' ancestors held land . . . from the lords
von Karstedt, but it may have been 300 years ago, and he couldn't identify the actual piece." Karstedt appealed to a 1579 contract, but Mentz said
"it's well known he doesn't have more land than his neighbors, so he
couldn't agree to pay five bushels when they didn't. He calls for an inspection," which the court undertook, finding the disputed land too small for
the rent claimed. Hasse ruled "the defendant holds his land within his
farmstead." Sensing defeat, Karstedt did not stay for the verdict. Mentz
was a turbulent subject, recently found guilty of joining his wife in physically abusing his mother. Before his 1745 retirement, he faced many
charges of rent and debt arrears, and provoking violent altercations. Yet
here, backed by Kleist's court (inclined to minimize its farmers' obligations
to other landlords), and invoking history and logic, he prevailed.[7]

Judicial oaths carried great weight. In the pious mind, perjury risked
perdition, while transparent falsehoods doubtless besmirched forswear-
ers' honor. Moreover, the court – and sometimes the plaintiff too –
decided whether defendants might exculpate themselves with oaths, for
which fees were levied. Laborer-lodger Hagelstein challenged his
farmer-landlord, against whom he raised various financial claims, to
clear himself and a partner with an oath. The accused agreed, if
Hagelstein paid the oath's not inconsiderable 1-taler cost. To his double
misfortune, Hagelstein paid, while the defendant's convincingly sworn
oath exonerated him. Hasse deepened the laborer's defeat by having
him pay each defendant 8 groschen for time lost. Here, again, the court
manifested its punitive inclination toward workers challenging employers.[8] But while the lordship imposed vows of obedience and industriousness on new farmers and other subjects, it rarely used oaths to establish fact or guilt, usually leaving disgruntled plaintiffs to demand them,
as when farmer Peter Ebel accused neighbor Andreas Appel of "hack-
ing his horse to bits with his scythe, [rendering it] useless." Appel admitted chasing the horse out of his barley, but denied injuring it. When he
satisfied Ebel's demand for an oath, Hasse closed the case.[9]

Lower courts' power to summon extrajurisdictional defendants was
weak, leading to impasses or violence. Hasse might order a burgher to

---

[7] Ibid., fos. 24–5.   [8] No. 591, fo. 128; no. 326, fo. 121.   [9] No. 591, fos. 98–9.

pay horsetrading debts, but whether the town authorities would support him was uncertain. The "Zeggel brothers" once complained that a von Karstedt servant "tried to pull [Stavenow farmer] David Bussen's wife from her horse on the public thoroughfare, and attacked her with drawn sword, drunkenly cursing her as hangman's trash [*Recker Canaille*]." Striking her with his flat sword, the servant aimed to seize her horse for Karstedt, but "David Hecht's former farmhand" halted him, wrestling away the sword, with injuries on both sides. Hasse later settled with Karstedt. Noteworthy here are the farm wife on horseback, doubtless a routine sight, and farm servants' willingness to defend employers' wives, whether because of kinship, common village loyalties, or intraseigneurial rivalries.[10]

As for litigation's sport, tenant-farmer Hartz once congratulated Hasse on besting a local notable: "there wasn't no fat left on the gentleman."[11] When a sexton drowned in a pond, administrator Erhardt sent two villagers to guard the body, but neighboring landlord Knesebeck, claiming jurisdiction, ordered his subjects to pull the body from the water and lay it on his land. Erhardt gained the corpse's possession and asked permission to deliver it to the widow, inspiring Hasse to ask whether Knesebeck "shouldn't be rapped a bit on the knuckles?"[12] In big cases such as Blüthen equalization or Dargardt colonization, Hasse displayed skills and self-confidence perhaps not every provincial lawyer possessed. Nor did he shrink from ruling occasionally against seigneurial administrators. Sub-bailiff Halentz failed to appear to answer a livestock dealer's 1731 demand for 69 talers for sheep sold to Halentz's brother-in-law partner Gottfried Böhmer, probably a tenant-farmer. Halentz's wife said her husband "had gone out," but Hasse ruled he must pay. Meanwhile "his possessions will remain here in arrest."[13]

Hasse's services grew indispensable to the Kleists, who drew him into their family circle. In a 1756 business letter, Conrad Kleist renewed his standing invitation to the family's "usual Saturday dinner." In 1758, the judge, untypically yielding to fashionable Francomania, pledged the Kleists his "lifelong *attachement*."[14] Considering his exertions, his 40-taler yearly salary was modest. But the Kleists' 1760 court fee capitalization at 200 talers shows that, assigning themselves only 10 talers yearly, they conceded most fines and other incomes to the judge. Pocketing statutory fees on court business was the recognized mode of judges' payment throughout the monarchy.

[10] No. 326, fo. 121; no. 200, fos. 51–2.   [11] No. 597, fo. 126.   [12] No. 714, fos. 55–6.
[13] No. 200, fo. 16.   [14] No. 716, fos. 180, 276.

In 1725 young Hasse penned a list of "court fee arrears." Among twenty-four entries, totaling 94 talers, were 40 talers in "whoring penalties," men paying 10 and women 5 talers. Inheritances removed from the jurisdiction, mainly by rural notables' children, yielded 34 talers' duty. A shepherd owed 10 talers for assaulting a hollander's worker. Several farmers had not yet paid their 1–2 taler entry fees. There were fines for minor violence, resistance to livestock impoundment, cursing, and disobedience toward the bailiff. Liese Seyers, a lodger's wife guilty of theft and collusion with runaway servants, would, in serving a stiff eight-day jail sentence, "suffer the penalty on her body." Though Hasse would not pocket all fees undivided, a good share was his. He also collected money for written documents, such as 2 talers a farm widow paid him for two letters.[15]

Monies deposited for safekeeping, such as 17 talers' children's inheritance tailor Ficke delivered to be "securely invested at interest," Hasse locked in the "court cabinet" in Stavenow's courtroom. He conducted an orderly tribunal, punishing unruly defendants. Von Karstedt bailiff Haussmann charged middle-aged farmer Hans Zeggel with cursing him "on the public thoroughfare as a fleabag [*Lausewentzel*] and dog's ass [*Hundsfott*] and poking him in the nose." Zeggel pleaded self-defense, but Hasse promised to sentence him to two hours' Spanish overcoat if Haussmann would swear to Zeggel's words and actions. Haussmann declined, saying he did not want Zeggel "punished too hard, but rather treated with mildness." Since Haussmann requested "corporal punishment be waived," Hasse sentenced Zeggel to one day's jail. But "as the defendant was taken to the dungeon he spoke with godless mouth, saying 'now he sees that [Haussmann] should have sworn the oath.'" Zeggel added that "he must receive something for his days of suffering," possibly a revenge threat. For this "insolent talk" Hasse prolonged Zeggel's sentence to two days, advertising the imprudence of protesting his rulings.[16]

Apart from private parties' cases, the lordship supplied Hasse with a varying array of misdeeds to investigate and punish. A list survives from the 1750s, from a field bailiff's pen. Among eight plaintiffs was a town-dwelling non-commissioned officer's wife, who claimed Mesekow's "old mayor" was her father, and had not paid her full inheritance. Estateowner Knesebeck wanted a Stavenow smallholder's repayment to Garlin church of 12 talers, donated by Knesebeck. Widow Berkholtz,

---

[15] No. 596, fo. 26; no. 591, fos. 12–13.   [16] No. 591, fos. 116–17.

Premslin manor-farm leaseholder, charged that three farmers assigned to her "don't perform manorial service as she wants it done." Crossed off the list was the charge that a young woman had stolen seigneurial harvest grain sheaves. Three farmers faced accusation that "one afternoon they hauled in but one wagonload of grain before going home." Ten other farmers failed to report for harvest haulage. Docketed also was a millers' quarrel. Finally, "I myself have to charge that the people in Glövzin and Premslin don't arrive for manorial service before eight o'clock in the morning."[17]

About Johann Erdmann Hasse's life apart from Stavenow duties little is known. His family long figured among Perleberg city fathers. A seventeenth-century Bürgermeister Hasse dealt with Stavenow as a timber trader, and in the town museum an elaborate family tree with oil portraits survives, though antedating Stavenow's judge. He held mayoral title, lived, and kept office in the riverport of Lenzen. He schooled his several sons in Berlin. In 1738 the school rector wrote, saying that they, with other classmates, had played with gunpowder, causing an explosion and mildly injuring themselves. The rector thought burns and fright penance enough, but it concerned him that Hasse's sons would not confess to their part. The judge promptly wrote the boys in a stricken tone, admonishing them to seek "God's grace" and repent, and to cultivate Christian love. His religious temperament appears also in his correspondence with the Kleists. Noteworthy in this prankish incident, perhaps, is the absence of threats of physical punishment. In 1764, one of Hasse's sons, a lawyer, died suddenly while traveling. Another legally trained son, *Hof Rath* Carl Ludwig, resident in Neu-Ruppin, died in 1772. Their father died in May 1765, bequeathing (as we saw) an obligation of 3,500 talers payable by Major Kleist at 4 percent (140 talers) annually. In 1777 his wife transferred it to a third party, who agreed to pay 5 percent.[18]

The mentality of Hasse's successor, Samuel Ludwig Betich, a Perleberg city councilor and taxman, will emerge below.[19] Though his prosecution of Major Kleist's cases against his villagers was aggressively partisan, his conduct of routine business appears conscientious. This was less true, as will be seen, of Betich's successor Gutike. In 1798, the eight lordships with interests in Blüthen village appointed Perleberg attorney Schroetter communal judge, handling all legal issues apart from their own subjects' farm transfers and inheritances. Schroetter

---

[17] No. 715, fo. 49.   [18] No. 166, fos. 27–8, 33–4; no. 122, fos. 66–8.   [19] No. 343, fo. 300.

would earn 20 talers yearly plus "court fees and charges flowing to him." In 1809, in the midst of the post-1806 economic crisis, he resigned, writing to Judge Gutike that since Kleist's death he had not regularly received his salary, and that the other lordships' judges forced cases on him they should have handled.

"With the almost general poverty in Blüthen," wrote Schroetter, "I received no compensation; during my tenure I handled almost all my work there as poverty cases." Under satisfactory conditions he would return, since "I have gained a reputation in the community for strict justice," making work easier, a statement showing that judges might seek legitimacy in villagers' eyes. Stavenow estateowner Voss ignored this gambit, and Schroetter's office vanished. Not until 1848 would revolution abolish landlord-administered courts entirely.[20]

STAVENOW COURT'S POWERS OF PHYSICAL COERCION AND PUNISHMENT

As part of its self-prescribed civilizing mission, Prussian absolutism gradually abolished witchcraft prosecution and judicial torture. Public spectacles of barbarous executions were slower to disappear, but came under enlightened criticism, as did the physical punishment of villagers by lordships and soldiers by superiors. The 1794 Prussian Law Code specified the type and frequency of lashes under which seigneurial laborers might lawfully be disciplined. Yet justifiable suspicion remains that such reforms concerning Junkers' subjects languished on paper. Nor did the 1807–19 Reform Era break cleanly with feudal violence, for the 1810 Statute on Servants sanctioned large-estate laborers' physical disciplining until its abolition in the 1918 revolution.[21]

Seigneurially imposed coercion and violence in eighteenth-century Brandenburg-Prussia require grass-roots investigation. Physical pain's infliction was certainly a rural commonplace. The Stavenow court confronted numerous serious, if non-lethal, assaults among villagers. We have also encountered estate officials' violence against servants and farmers, about which more will follow. Here we consider manorial court punishments, imposed by legal process on guilty defendants. While historians have not yet addressed this question in depth, there were various possibilities – from mildness to despotism – flowing from

---

[20] No. 326, fos. 226, 230–1; no. 604, fos. 4–5.
[21] Koselleck, *Preussen*, 52ff, 641ff; Lennhoff, *Gesindewesen*, 28ff.

landlords' considerable autonomy in exercising judicial and manorial authority. Stavenow lordship cannot stand for all, but only for such relatively large, professionally administered, prosperous (and not uncommon) noble enterprises as itself.

Stavenow court levied many money fines on miscreant villagers which, even when not exceeding 1 taler, represented sizable losses, considering that many adult wage laborers pocketed no more than this sum weekly. Occasionally Hasse let the defendant choose between paying the penalty in cash or labor, as in winter 1744–5, when he allowed a tavernkeeper, already twice fined for wood theft and liable again for restitution costs and a 3-taler charge, to work it off, presumably for communal benefit.[22] Such concessions undercut Hasse's income, and were rare. More often, the choice was less palatable. In 1753, two farmers of the oft-cantankerous Zeggel clan, seconded by their wives, exchanged curses and blows over farmstead boundaries. Hasse ordered immediate re-fencing, condemning each side to 2-taler fines or "suffering [punishment] on the body." The quarrel's resumption would lead, he threatened, to jailing on bread and water.[23]

Doubtless, behind the invocation of corporal punishment, threats of court-ordered lashes sometimes lurked. In 1752, a Zeggel farmer defied and cursed the village mayor, refusing to surrender his cooking pots to impoundment. For this, Hasse doubled the 2-taler impoundment fine and then, following renewed defiance, redoubled it to "8 talers or bodily expiation."[24] It is unlikely irascible Zeggel paid such a heavy fine. But, with one exception, nowhere do the documents speak plainly of judicial floggings, though they are clear about disputed lashings during fieldwork. The whip was an instrument of domestic disciplining, of which servants' and soldiers' flogging was an extension. It was also a weapon sometimes wielded in suspects' capture and other exercises of police power. Yet in seigneurial court practice, "bodily penance" seemingly usually signified not the lash (though court bailiffs might lawfully be instructed to lay it on), but jailing or public display in pain-inflicting devices. The one case in which Hasse plainly ordered whipping supports this conclusion. It was the 1760 case, discussed above from another angle, in which a farmer and his young farmhand fought with an administrator and field bailiff, despite triple warnings to desist. The boy suffered whipping precisely because he was a youthful servant. Three years earlier, the same farmer cruelly beat another farmhand he

[22] No. 326, fos. 116, 123, 126.   [23] Ibid., fo. 190.   [24] No. 591, fo. 122.

suspected of stealing tools. "Although the court bailiff severely threatened [the boy] with his whip," he stuck to his claims of innocence,
which Hasse then accepted, releasing him from his violent master's
service.

Yet, court sentences locking or "laying out" prisoners "bent" in
Stavenow jail signal the pain that might accompany incarceration. This
and similar procedures entailed shackling inmates in painful postures,
and was doubtless the point of Hasse's occasional sentencing of both
men and women to "a few hours in the tower," as befell Mesekow's elderly mayor when he ignored a summons to avoid facing his incensed
family's complaints against him. In 1724 Hasse threatened Daniel
Mentz's wife and mother, if they did not cease fighting, that they would
"lie [in the tower] and, beyond that, spend a half-day in the fiddle" –
publicly sited, pain-inflicting devices for women.[25]

Hasse once fined twenty-six-year-old Anna Guhl 12 groschen for
throwing a rock at her step-father when he berated her brother for
smoking in their barn. This sum she could either pay into the village
poor-relief fund (*Armen Casse*) or "suffer bodily" during several days in
the tower. This threat seems meant to frighten, for the judge reduced
the fine to 6 groschen.[26] In 1750, one of the trouble-prone Zeggels
furtively hauled away field fencing for firewood at one o'clock at night,
for which Hasse fined him 1 taler plus 4 groschen impoundment money
owed court bailiff Johann Hartenberg. Because Zeggel denied the "misdeed" Hasse also sentenced him to two days' jail, though next day – it
was icy January – the chastened prisoner "promises improvement and
is dismissed from dungeon."[27]

As for the Spanish overcoat, Hasse in 1731 sentenced farm servant
Johann Hecht, for assaulting the field bailiff during manorial service, to
stand in the shoulder-crushing device a half-hour before the church
door, doubtless – as other sentences made plain – on Sunday, the better
to be publicly seen.[28] In 1742, Hasse quelled unseemly fighting that
erupted during a farm transfer between a reluctantly retiring interim
proprietor and his step-daughter's new husband. Hasse, branding the
older man as troublemaker, sentenced him to the Spanish overcoat, fining the younger man. But, tempers calmed, the judge reduced the punishments to fines of 1 taler and 12 groschen, respectively (showing it was
worth a fair sum to avoid the overcoat's pain and ignominy).[29] Renitent

---

[25] No. 200, fos. 17, 35; no. 591, fos. 127–8.   [26] No. 326, fo. 153.   [27] No. 715, fo. 17.
[28] No. 591, fos. 14–15; no. 200, fo. 71.   [29] No. 326, fo. 100.

villagers wore it most frequently in the 1720s. There were two sentences for wood theft and one for impoundment resistance. In 1724 Hasse sentenced villagers who had raided a seigneurial alderwood to two hours in the overcoat. This was a scare tactic, for Colonel Kleist, present at the hearing, reduced the penalty to a few groschen. Two hours were, perhaps, the limit of endurable suffering.[30] In 1757 manorial-service insubordination brought the overcoat down on farmer Christian Nagel, and in 1760 old Hasse was still threatening delinquents with its torment.[31]

Insubordinate and unruly women faced the fiddle but, though oftener threatened, its application is recorded but three or four times. In 1731 a quarrel between a mayor's wife and a farmer yielded one-hour sentences in overcoat and fiddle, respectively.[32] In 1740 smallholder Schenck's wife, who as the congregation left church rudely insulted the miller and his wife, faced a 2-taler fine or two hours in the fiddle. But "because Schenck's wife behaved very unfittingly in court, the punishment of the fiddle has been immediately imposed on her." Hasse warned her, "if she doesn't curb her tongue, she will be punished [in jail] with neck-irons."[33]

If there were other punishments with overcoat and fiddle, they ceased after mid-century. Incarceration, with or without chaining, supplanted the physical pain they inflicted, while money fines grew commoner. From the landlordly angle, the most efficient punishments were brief jail sentences, entailing no injury, or money fines which, though painful, did not cripple villagers economically. It was not in the manorhouse's interest to embitter subjects with deadly resentment, corroding their fragile willingness to labor for the lordship, if not firing impulses of revenge in their breasts. Fear of transportation to Spandau fortress, and of gruesome punishment for capital crime, held local violence within limits in a rural society displaying frequent physical conflict and petty theft, but little major crime.

THE LORDSHIP'S POLICE POWERS (AND VIOLENCE EXERTED DIRECTLY BY LANDLORDLY HANDS)

Bearing opprobrium for executing punishments and jailing delinquents were the court bailiffs (*Vögte*). Apart from their occasional testimony against refractory villagers, little can be said about them. In 1760

---

[30] No. 200, fos. 23, 82.   [31] No. 326, fo. 216.   [32] No. 591, fo. 25.
[33] Ibid., fos. 94–5; no. 200, fo. 113.

Stavenow bailiff Voss earned 10 talers plus housing and 25 bushels of food-grains. He had a counterpart at Semlin manor-farm. In 1809, "court servant" Witte earned 12 talers cash, alongside two forest wardens, paid 4–5 talers. Seigneurial hunters-foresters held much better-paying jobs, as did sub-bailiff clerks, estate managers' seconds in command.[34] Such officials, alongside village mayors and livestock impounders, sufficed to maintain law and order. Reinforcing them, when serious crime or insubordination occurred, were the Prignitz sheriff and nearby garrison soldiers.

Some of the worst violence ordinary people suffered came at the hands of bailiffs and huntsmen, and even – though there is little trace of it at Stavenow – Junker landlords. This usually exploded when delinquents committed or, though innocent, were arrested for transgressions for which they later answered in court. An instance of a nobleman personally assaulting humble villagers occurred in 1746. Nearby landlord Captain von Kaphengst wrote to Frau Kleist, saying he discovered Marie Möllers in his forest with an "unknown fellow." When he summoned them, "the woman came running [at him] with a cudgel, crying 'beat him, beat him.'" Kaphengst was confident Frau Kleist would "disapprove this thieving woman's excesses."[35]

Hasse later heard the case against Marie Möllers, a farmer's lodger's wife. She admitted she entered Kaphengst's pinewoods with Hans Ohlert, another lodger. She filled one sack with pine needles, while Ohlert took two. As she pushed them on her wheelbarrow, Kaphengst appeared. "She earnestly pleaded [with him] to pardon her husband," referring misleadingly to Ohlert. "But he was not to be moved, so she left the sacks lying there and proceeded with wheelbarrow alone." Kaphengst pursued them "and beat Ohlert on the head with a stave until the stave broke in two." Kaphengst then "pulled Ohlert to the ground by his hair. But she did not incite to violence. She had a blind old husband, and only thought to make a forkful of manure." It was her first time in the woods, "and she thought a sack of pine needles wouldn't matter, since others took whole wagonloads without hearing a word." She did seize a stick from a nearby fence, "but for nothing more than self-defense. She had no thought of hitting him." Though she assumed Kaphengst would care nothing for "such a bagatelle," he took her sacks to his new manor-farm. Having lost them, she pleaded for no further punishment.[36]

[34] No. 259; no. 62; no. 513, fos. 31–5.   [35] No. 321, fo. 383.   [36] No. 326, fos. 127–9.

But Hasse ruled that "since Valentin Möller's wife admits to wrong-doing, not only going into the woods with another fellow and falsely presenting herself as his wife, but also taking up a fence-cudgel against the Herr Captain, so will she be punished as an example to others with one hour in the fiddle." He added: "this punishment was immediately executed and the defendant, after promising improvement and paying court bailiff's fee, was dismissed." Accomplice Hans Ohlert neither tes-tified nor faced separate charges. He figures a decade later as a cottager with a physical disability (not inflicted, one hopes, by Kaphengst's blows). Kaphengst's belief in his right to recklessly thrash male – if not female – interlopers on his property doubtless found other landlords' assent.

More often hunters and forest wardens delivered the blows, though they suffered them too. Hunter Birkholtz charged Johann Hecht with attacking him and seizing his hatchet. Hecht said "Birkholtz beat him so much for the bit of [brush] he carted off, even though he hadn't cut anything down, that he was totally dazed – and didn't know what he was doing." Hasse sentenced Hecht to 3 talers' fine within eight days or "to suffer it on his body."[37] Nor were local villagers alone at risk. A Lenzen blacksmith wrote Colonel Kleist that Birkholtz charged a tree's illegal burning to a "workman who made charcoal for me." When the smith came to collect his charcoal, Birkholtz cursed him as "canaille and murdering arsonist, and beat me bloody with a cudgel." Birkholtz confiscated the smith's horses and wagon, and when he recovered them, "one horse was starving and finally died." Whether Kleist released the smith's impounded charcoal and refunded his losses is doubtful.[38]

In 1728 Birkholtz suffered a beating at the hands of nearby estate-owners lieutenant and non-commissioned officer von Knesebeck, seem-ingly father and son. A Kleist-commissioned surgeon documented the hunter's injuries: two head wounds and "severe cranial contusion," shoulders and back "brown and blue" from blood under the skin, ribs and arms marked by blows.[39] In his own hand (and dialect), Birkholtz wrote that he visited the Knesebecks seeking a lost hunting dog. The elder Knesebeck denied having it and, irritated that the (non-noble) Eldenburg crown-estate leaseholder was accompanying Stavenow's hunting party when the dog vanished, said that, if the Eldenburg manager hunted again, he would seize Stavenow's dogs.

[37] No. 713, fo. 261.   [38] Ibid., fo. 53.   [39] No. 596, fo. 90.

"To this I replied that we would be there again in eight days. Just let him come and take the dogs. We'll see. Then he called the manager a scoundrel."

I answered that if we were doing wrong he should report it to our masters, who would punish us for it. But he began to curse me for a dog's-ass, villain, rascal, and that last winter I killed two rabbits his dogs had flushed, and cursed still more, and I begged him not to curse so much. Not even my master says such things, and that's not what I serve for and that's not what my master keeps me for.

Old Knesebeck summoned his son, who arrived fence-stave in hand. The hunter said "if he wouldn't stop cursing, then I would take him for what he took me for. I'm the younger one and he's the older." Young Knesebeck struck Birkholtz, who tried to ride away, but

Lieutenant von Kniese beck jumped up and seized my horse . . . and pulled me off . . . and thrashed my body with the club and they took my deer knife from its sheath and beat me with the bare blade, and broke it on my body . . . and scattered my money, how much it was I can't say for sure, and how they treated me God knows and they cut my hat to pieces. And what exactly happened I don't know because of pain and days of suffering, but a King's farmer saw it from afar.

The Knesebecks impounded Birkholtz's horse and deer knife. "I crawled more than I walked back here." The lieutenant

says I was drunk and . . . [that] he beat me sober. But I say let the Herr forester of Ellen burg and also the Herr crown bailiff speak of drunkenness, and I will say nothing. And later [Lieutenant Knesebeck] offered me a groschen and said I should keep quiet like a man, but I replied that if he wanted to give me 4 or 5 ducats I asked nothing, I would let my master take care of that.

An unknown hand recorded the hunter saying that before the beating "he swung his whip about him so as to ride off, but they pulled him off his horse."[40]

Unfortunately for Birkholtz, the "king's [crown-estate] farmer" testified only that young Knesebeck "very badly pummeled" the hunter. Old Knesebeck claimed the hunter was drunk and threatened him: his blows, moderate enough, were dealt in self-defense. Further witnesses were a carpenter and farmer then repairing Knesebeck's manor-gate. The carpenter heard the elder Knesebeck dismiss Birkholtz, saying "on your way, fellow." The hunter replied, "the devil is your fellow."

[40] No. 605, fos. 24–5.

Knesebeck cursed him as a "scoundrel." "Who knows who's the oldest scoundrel," Birkholtz replied, whereupon Knesebeck called his son to "fetch a cudgel and help rid him of the fellow." The son told Birkholtz to leave, saying he was drunk. Whether intentionally or not, the carpenter reported, when Birkholtz lashed his horse he struck young Knesebeck, who then pulled him down and beat him.

Perleberg garrison commander, Christoph Heinrich von der Goltz, respectfully wrote Frau Kleist, saying he had arrested young Knesebeck, whose claim of self-defense against the allegedly drunken hunter's whip the two workers corroborated. Goltz was hopeful that:

> My Gracious Lady will kindly wish to consider that [young Knesebeck] could not let this insult go unavenged. I do not doubt she will acquiesce, allowing the junior officer to be released from arrest. Incidentally, I hear with much *plaisir* that Herr Colonel will soon arrive. I shall be delighted to have the honor of embracing him in the good health we wish for him. My wife, who sends Your Grace her best regards, still suffers daily fever.[41]

Here the story ends, though Birkholtz kept his job. It highlights violence lurking along the seigneurial boundaries hunter-foresters patrolled and defended, tensions generated by non-noble participation in hunting, and the dangers of (armed) huntsmen's disputes with neighboring noblemen. This conflict's resolution, given the Knesebecks' soldierly status, lay in the military rather than civilian sphere, where an officer's honor outweighed all else. The verbal and physical excesses of old Knesebeck, seemingly a retired officer turned country squire, went unpunished. Birkholtz spoke with divided voice, aggressively asserting his own authority, but also humbly invoking his master's protection.

The Kleists' aggressive imposition of their new lordship entailed a rapid succession of seigneurial hunters. In 1724, after hunter Daniel Gehrcke recovered from wounds nightwatchman Jürgen Hedder inflicted on him, Hedder emerged from a nine-week imprisonment – the longest on record at Stavenow. Gehrcke admitted he began the fight with Hedder, who regained freedom with a vow to keep the peace (*Urfehde*):

> I, Jürgen Hedder, swear to God Almighty in Heaven a corporeal oath that I will not seek revenge for the arrest and punishment I have suffered, whether in word or deed, by myself or through others, either on the government of the land [*Landesherrschaft*], its officials, servants, and subjects, or on this seigneurial jurisdiction and its members, and especially not on huntsman Daniel Gehrcke, but instead will fully pay what I still owe of [this case's] expenses.

[41] No. 596, fos. 91–100.

At Colonel Kleist's written order, the hunter swore a similar oath, whereupon the enemies shook hands.[42]

Two years later, hunter Joachim Metzki lost his post through malfeasance and corruption charges that seigneurial fisherman Reimar Hecker reported to Kleist in Potsdam. Hecker complained the hunter stormed into his house, denouncing him as a "scoundrel" and a "spy." Unruffled, Hecker warned Metzki the Mesekow farmers should be patrolled more closely for wood theft. Pressed by Hasse for details, Hecker remembered seeing "a tall man with a completely white head" pilfering alderwood. Hecker lectured the hunter he "shouldn't be so negligent with deer and other game," the fisherman having found two deer carcasses the martens had eaten, "whereupon [Metzki] cursed him still more crudely, threatening, if he found him in the forest, to break his rifle over his head." Hecker claimed the hunter forced farmers to drive game, putting livestock herders to this work almost daily, so he could illicitly sell the meat in Perleberg. Hecker claimed knowledge of five deer thus sold.

Hunter Metzki complained that Hecker "spread it all over the Prignitz" – their geographical universe – "that he [Metzki] didn't do his job right and that he [Hecker] would get him one way or another." The fisherman's wife testified damagingly that Metzki, in her house, said of her husband that "if he were a proper hunter he wouldn't have given himself into such beggarly service [*Betteldienst*]." Hasse ordered her to repeat this, looking Metzki in the eye, which she did. Metzki weakly excused the words "spy" and "beggarly service," which insulted the lordship, pleading forgetfulness. Though the swineherd denied the hunter used farmers to drive game, the lordship dismissed Metzki, Hecker disappearing as well. Two months later hunter Birkholtz was hired, promising not to furtively sell wood or game.[43]

No further charges of improprieties or corruption arose against Stavenow hunters. Such incidents illustrate this society's violent and law-breaking propensities, showing law-enforcers both abusing their powers and suffering attack for possessing them. Nor were humbler seigneurial agents free of danger. In 1756 bailiff Böhmer recorded an assault on hunter Prittwitz's forest warden, Hans Jacob Ballhorn (the Stavenow hollander's kinsman). The twenty-five-year-old warden said Dargardt farmer Heinrich Peters burst with an ax into his lodgings on a smallholder's farm, crying out, "You dog! You betrayed me and I'm

---

[42] No. 200, fos. 11–13.   [43] Ibid., fos. 53–60.

going to kill you!" The farmer then struck Ballhorn's head, "so that he fell to the ground copiously bleeding." A Perleberg "registered surgeon" treated the wound, about 1.5 inches long, bleeding Ballhorn on the foot, housing him until he healed, and later visiting him in Dargardt. At 7 talers, his fee was stiff. Assailant Peters ignored the court bailiff's summons, delivered – menacingly – in the battered Ballhorn's brothers' company, whom farmer Peters recklessly insulted before fleeing. Plaintiff Ballhorn testified that, before the assault, he informed hunter Prittwitz that Peters was selling pilfered wood, whereupon Prittwitz rode off and seized the contraband. Next morning at five o'clock, while Ballhorn was eating breakfast with his hired hands, Peters attacked him, knocking him off his chair. Peters's penalty is unrecorded, but four years later this ax-wielding Mecklenburger was still running his farm.[44]

The later eighteenth century witnessed, seemingly, tighter law enforcement, further judicialization of conflict, and resultant pacification. In 1767 the lordship appointed hunter Lindow, mainly responsible for woodland surveillance, supervising two forest wardens rather than one. The previous year, hunter Glaubitz complained to Betich that, when he was hiring wood-haulers in a nearby village – Stavenow farmers were on strike against this work – Baron Bredow's hunter Meisner accosted him, saying "he was canaille and a dishonorable [*infamer*] neighbor because he shot and killed his dog." Rather than responding with violence, Glaubitz mildly said, "in the most friendly way," he was innocent, but Meisner "boxed his ears and pulled a considerable piece of hair from his head." Yet, after securing witnesses, Glaubitz departed. Not wishing "uproar and long drawn-out proceedings," he bypassed Bredow's "foreign jurisdiction," asking Betich for legal satisfaction. Glaubitz's writing displays a more correct German, and better hand, than his predecessor Birkholtz's of 1727. Later he reported that, in his absence, Bredow's dogs were driven into Stavenow's woods. Bredow's behavior was "unbridled and brazen . . . This matter is getting violent and going too far."[45]

Perhaps Glaubitz did not go far enough himself, for soon, after seven years' employment, he was gone. But, if brawling was declining, other hunterly faults remained. In 1811, former Stavenow field manager and Premslin leaseholder Helm reported that Kleists and Karstedts had abolished their ancient reciprocal hunting rights, but continued to hunt the "Premslin farmers' land in common." In Helm's day (1779–1807)

---

[44] No. 577, fos. 3, 5, 7–14.   [45] No. 717, fos. 206, 208–9.

the two lordships lived "in the greatest harmony." Later, the Karstedts hired hunter Krohn, who "does as all other hunters do, that is, he doesn't respect boundaries. But," said Helm, echoing (or coining) a proverb, "no plaintiff, no judge."[46]

PASTORS' SOCIAL AUTHORITY AND VILLAGERS' RELATIONS WITH THE CHURCH

If the manorial court and its few enforcers upheld the Kleists' judicial lordship, it was not because they embodied irresistible repressive force, though historians have assumed otherwise. While, ultimately, Prussian military power stood behind them, its deployment in landlords' interest required negotiation and the Berlin government's sanction. The Junkers' intellectual partisans, countering bureaucratic reformers' challenges to seigneurial authority from above and the French Revolution's from below, fashioned after 1789 patriarchalist ideologies justifying noble power over the villages.[47] The Kleists and doubtless too their Stavenow precursors similarly represented their authority in everyday practice. Among them, Frau Kleist and her son Conrad acted most skillfully on the principle of *noblesse oblige*. How well this served the Prussian nobility after the early nineteenth-century emancipation remains an open question, but in the eighteenth century worldly-wise acquiescence among villagers in benevolently exercised seigneurialism did not prevent communal resistance when it seemed unjust. Neither discourses nor everyday theatrics of aristocracy, whether feudal or absolutist, by themselves engendered obedience.

Nor did Christianity perceptibly deepen Stavenow villagers' bow toward manorial authority, though doubtless successive pastors extolled it. Here, too, historians have usually argued contrariwise.[48] Communal insubordination, though hardly so strong as to render seigneurial power impotent, was a susceptibility challenging the Stavenow lordship which the Lutheran pastors could not banish from their flocks' minds and hearts. Certainly villagers respected pastors and hoped for their guidance toward Christian salvation. But, in the realm of villagers' secular concerns, pastors often appeared captives of their own interests, if not also the lordship's.

[46] No. 655, fos. 27–30.
[47] Berdahl, *Politics*; Bowman, *Planters*; Melton, "The Decline of Prussian *Gutsherrschaft*.
[48] Otto Hintze, "Die Epochen des evangelischen Kirchenregiments in Preußen," in O. Hintze, *Regierung und Verwaltung*, vol. III (Göttingen, 1967), 56–96; Wehler, *Gesellschaftsgeschichte*, Band I, 268ff. Cf. Kittsteiner, *Die Entstehung*, 293ff.

Parishioners, we saw, sometimes withheld services and tributes they owed their pastors. But villagers might also feel deprived of spiritual attention. After Premslin Pastor Sauerbier's 1702 appointment, his flock in neighboring Glövzin pleaded for more ministration. They were bitter over their own pastorate's post-1618 loss and their subsequent reduction to Premslin village filial, entitled only to occasional preaching in their own church, though it physically survived the deluge. In 1711 a royal commissioner negotiated an agreement between Sauerbier and the Glövziners adding four new quarterly masses and sermons to Easter, Whitsuntide, and Christmas services there. Sauerbier resented this "extra work," seeing it as concession and not duty. He agreed "solely out of Christian freedom and the desire to win over his auditors."[49]

A year later Sauerbier sent the Blumenthal trustees a new settlement, which the Perleberg Church Inspector renegotiated to end "the farmers' persistent insubordination." Of them the disgruntled pastor wrote: "It seems they are holding aloof because of evil people's urgings, and are collecting much money to take the matter to lawyers, which will embarrass me in the Most Laudable Consistory's eyes, but also ruin them, so they won't be able to render seigneurial authority its dues." Sauerbier singled out fullholders Hans Milatz and Jürgen Zeggel as "instigators, preferring to reject Holy Communion and absent themselves if I do not, yielding to their demands and obstinacy, administer mass in their church." Communion's refusal was a potent sign of disaffection, here aimed at forcing Sauerbier into concessions to "win over" his flock.[50]

Three years later Sauerbier fell into a worldly abyss. The story reveals the law's workings, while its consequences again agitated the villagers.[51] As bailiff Neumann wrote the Blumenthal trustees in 1715, Sauerbier's recently discovered impregnation of his servant-woman "has given great offense to all of his auditors." Upon learning Neumann knew of the scandal, "a weighty offense" that must be "gravely expiated," Sauerbier's wife hurried to Berlin, "to beg for pardon both of His Royal Majesty and My High Commanders and Lord Trustees." They ordered an investigation, one remarking incredulously, "I always regarded [Sauerbier] as a pious and God-fearing man." If he admitted guilt, "the village subjects were to guard him in a well-secured room or bed-chamber." Neumann then informed the trustees that "the priest" took flight when his wife returned with the

[49] No. 711, fo. 1.   [50] No. 595, fo. 1.
[51] No. 527, fos. 1–3, 7–14, 16–25, 31, 35–43.

impending investigation's news. Though his destination was unknown, Neumann was (wrongly) sure it would be Mecklenburg. Assuming the pastorate now vacant, Neumann began lobbying for his replacement candidate.

Letters from Sauerbier, both to the trustees and Countess Blumenthal, arrived in Berlin. They had been posted in Magdeburg, still within the Prussian monarchy though near its Saxon border, and delivered through a Berlin intermediary, to conceal Sauerbier's where-abouts. Admitting his "misdeed," he said of his wife's recent Berlin trip that she aimed "to seek grace and mercy for her fallen and trans-gressing husband." But, "in her great grief" she fell ill and could not reach the countess's advisers. Sauerbier now spoke for himself, "in humility and woe, for the sake of God's mercy, Who does not wish the sinner's death, begging for pity for your servant as a poor sinner betrayed by the world, the devil, and flesh and blood." Sauerbier pleaded on behalf of

my poor and miserable wife and little children . . . not to be treated according to the laws or otherwise adversely and violently handled, but rather dismissed with a fatherly punishment. Let your mercy, O gracious Patrons, distinguish itself even against the lawcourt!

Sauerbier promised "heartfelt penance" before "God, the Patrons, and the community." His "resurrection" would, he sanguinely predicted, be edifying. He asked the trustees to intercede with the king, so that he might keep his office or, failing that, stay "in these lands" and not be rendered "unfit" for other employment. Choosing words delicately, he said that "out of fear I have absented myself a bit," for which he also asked pardon.

To Countess Blumenthal, Sauerbier wrote similarly, sparing painful details "so as not to trouble and disturb you." He emphasized the mis-ery of his wife and three young children, "whom I deliver into Your High Countess's loving lap [*Liebes-Schoos*]." About his flight, he wrote that "to compose myself in my present distracted state I have under-taken a journey to my fatherland," the Magdeburg District. "Please do not take this amiss." His wife would see that all his parish work was properly done – a remark his partner might have thought heaped injury on insult. Sauerbier pleaded his own case since, although his wife went to Berlin, "she did not trust herself, because of fear and terror, to wait upon you, and the weakness that overcame her drove her away." If accurate, this portrayal of a humiliated parson's wife's inability to face her husband's grand patroness is eloquent. Yet, judging from Frau Sauerbier's good handwriting, evident in a receipt she penned, she possessed some advantages.

Sauerbier soon wrote again, brandishing biblical citations and hopeful reference to a sinning Saxon pastor's retention in office. The trustees, sternly summoning him to return, left mercy to the king. The pastor asked a Berlin lawyer to intercede with the countess, conceding to the trustees that "*Homo sum*, and through inattentiveness to myself I have fallen into error, yea, like a foolish lamb I have run away. But now as I see the Wrath of the Highest before me, and disgrace at your hands, I find anguish, fear, terror, and misery overwhelming me like thunder and lightning." Such words did not foreshadow Sauerbier's return, which indeed never occurred.

The trustees composed a proclamation, publicly posted at Stavenow, Premslin, and Perleberg, recounting the "disgraceful crime" Sauerbier committed with "Sophia Hechts, serving-wench." "Irresponsibly forgetting his office, his wife and children, [Sauerbier] stole away secretly, driven by conscience and fear of worldly punishment." The thoughts about their spiritual shepherd such words inspired among his flock would be interesting to know. Now charged both with adultery and unlawfully impregnating his servant-woman, Stavenow court again summoned Sauerbier. But he had fallen silent and disappeared.

In June 1715 a Berlin lawyer petitioned the king on the injured wife's behalf. He noted that, were Sauerbier a layman, the matter could be settled, given wifely readiness to forgive, by banishment from the land of two or three years, which with royal assent could be "bought off" with a "moderate fine." Speaking in Sauerbier's wife's name, the supplication said that "only through lust and Satan's temptations, and his maidservant's self-prostitution, was he misled in my absence to this misfortune, his only false step." She pleaded for a money-fine and permission for him to remain, if not at Premslin, in some office in the Prussian kingdom, if only as a Pomeranian schoolteacher. Months later, the government solicited the trustees' views. They supported her petition, saying Sauerbier had been "pious and good" before his crime. They felt "hearty compassion" for him, for in losing his parish he was paying a much heavier price than usual. Recognizing it would cause "great offense" were he to return to Premslin, they seconded a Pomeranian schoolteachership. But in November 1715 a "special order of the king" arrived, signed by Frederick William I's ministers, saying "We are not of a mind to pardon the delinquent, but rather wish him to shun our lands for the rest of his life," a judgment the trustees were to communicate to him, "so he may observe it."

Soon after Sauerbier's flight, Stavenow lawyer Samuel Straube deposed impregnated servant Sophia Hechts, whom estate manager Neumann drove to Straube's Perleberg chambers. She testified she was "nearly thirty years old," and "had served the Premslin preacher going on five years, and took her bread in his house, and now she nourishes herself living with her father ['little' Peter Hecht] in his retirement quarters" on his former Premslin fullholding. Her mother was "long dead." She admitted pregnancy, saying it occurred "when the preacher came to her at night in her bed." This happened six weeks before Perleberg's summer market of July 2, 1714. She had not slept alone, but shared a bed with the children's maid. "How," Straube asked, "was it possible for another person to lie with her?" "The bedstead," she replied, "was big enough that three persons could well lie on it." Did the children's maid not wake up? Sophia did not know, "but she didn't speak of it with her." Had Sophia "been together" with the preacher before? "Not in all her days." What did the preacher say to her? "Only these words: Still! Still! By which he meant I shouldn't make any noise, so as not to wake the other girl." What was the preacher wearing? "Nothing more than his sleeping gown." Did she refuse his advances? "As much as she could, but he overmanned her in bed," where he remained "no longer than it took for him to carry out his business."

Did the preacher promise her anything? "He promised, provided it remained secret, to give her 3 bushels of rye every year for three years." In fact she received nothing, nor did she again sleep with him. When she revealed her pregnancy, he callously said "he hadn't had enough to do with her that she could be pregnant by him." Subsequently she left his house. Later she sent Johann Krümmes to him with the message "that she would like to take evening communion, if it was fitting, and that he should administer it to her in the church alongside the others." He refused, saying "her time was getting too short, and someone could be found who would give it to her in her house." Had she already "sat in penance in church?" This she had, five weeks previously, on command of "the preacher's wife and the preacher himself." Of this encounter, she recounted these words, exchanged in the pastor's "little front room":

Oh, why [Sophia said] should I sit in penance? You know, Sir, how it was with us together. You [*Er*] are guilty for my plight. To which the preacher said, [she] must sit in penance and he, the preacher, deserved to sit in penance with her.

The three spoke again, after Sophia saw bailiff Neumann. Reluctantly, she told Neumann she was pregnant and "the preacher was guilty."

Doubtless some of Sophia Hechts' testimony concerning her seduction represents stylized discourse, required to dispel suspicion she initiated the affair.[52] But Sauerbier's confession lends credence to the words notary Straube attributed to her, whether they reflected realities or – as perhaps with the preacher's promise of bushels of rye – wishful thinking. Sophia Hechts' subsequent fate is unknown. Viewing her as a seduction victim, the court may only have fined her. Sauerbier's incapacity to face the authorities was pusillanimous, but evidently also reflected debilitating guilt. The legal process did not utterly rule out salvaging something from the wreckage, but he could not seize it. Perhaps unsurprisingly, in this case of a master's violation of his maidservant, both his wife and the Blumenthal trustees forgave him, with little thought, seemingly, of Sophia's misfortune.

Sauerbier's disgrace and flight opened competition among rival candidates to succeed him which, as chapter 6 showed, witnessed the triumph of Joachim Willebrandt, estate manager Neumann's children's tutor. The villagers in Premslin, Glövzin, and Karstädt, not all Stavenow's subjects, split into parties, one supporting Willebrandt, the other von Karstedt tutor Gebhardt. Their rivalry throws otherwise rare light on villagers' understanding of the church's role in their lives. In April 1715 Gebhardt's village backers recommended him to the trustees, noting how Sauerbier had "of his own free will abandoned his office (presumably because of a certain offense)." The pro-Willebrandt party protested that the April statement did not represent them, but was composed by "deputies" who "were the Karstedts' subjects, leaving it an open question whether they were acting, against our views in the matter, at their overlord's instigation or for other reasons." They concluded with the assurance that "we remain, in a submission fitting your subjects, your obedient subject communes."[53]

A third group surfaced, writing to Countess Blumenthal in the name of the three villages' mayors and communes. Neumann had warned them "they shouldn't even contact her if they didn't want to be severely punished, but we, Your loyal subjects, live in firm hope that we may indeed represent our needs and concerns without punishment." Of Willebrandt – "Hildebrandt" to them – they wrote that he "strained for

---

[52] Gleixner, *"Das Mensch."*   [53] Willebrandt candidacy: no. 711, fos. 13, 17–21, 24–5, 36–42.

[the pastorate] with hands and feet, for he is supposed, and wants, to marry the estate manager's niece." Moreover,

because of his weak enunciation we cannot hear much of what the aforementioned Hildebrandt says and consequently we understand less than nothing. Besides which, we can place absolutely no love or trust in him, which in the future will only give rise to conflict and constant disunity, so that nothing will be built up, but instead everything will more and more from day to day be torn down.

By contrast, candidate Gebhardt's preaching "pleased us very much," and "through his exemplary way of life he will rightly lead and graze his flock." The Glövziners wanted biweekly church services, since old people could not go to Premslin and hence must frequently "miss the Word of God." Glövzin must once have had its own pastor, "since there is still a deserted parsonage there."

The Perleberg Church Inspectorate informed the trustees that Glövziners' "trust in Willebrandt is poor because he will conclude no agreement with them about their own church services." The Inspectorate thought that preaching there once every 3–4 weeks was reasonable. Neumann called a meeting at Notary Straube's house of the "mayors, church elders, cultivators, farmers, and pastor's small-holder" to discuss the memorial whose dispatch to Countess Blumenthal he warned against. Those present said the memorial was sent on the initiative of two Karstedt subjects and Stavenow's opposition-minded Glövziner Hans Milatz, whom the village chose as negotiator. This was perhaps the same Hans Milatz who helped organize the 1700–2 anti-rent movement.

As for the offending memorial's other assertions, no one present, wrote Straube,

knew whether Herr estate manager wanted to have his former tutor Herr Willebrandt as their pastor, much less whether [Willebrandt] strove for it hand and foot; nor had they heard from Herr estate manager or anyone else that Herr Willebrandt would marry Herr estate manager's niece. [Nor had Neumann forbidden them to contact the countess.] They knew of no fault in Herr Willebrandt, whose enunciation was good and understandable, so that the commune could well understand him, and was also, so far as they knew, sound in teaching and comportment.

The villagers wanted only a good preacher, so they "could get along in peace and friendship." Neumann wished such views officially recorded, seemingly both to advance Willebrandt's cause and dispel any impression in the countess's mind that nepotism was involved or that he sought to block villagers' access to her. Though in compelling such testimony he was indeed muzzling them, by taking the opposing memorial so seriously he lent dissenting villagers' voices a certain strength.

The Glövziners provoked their Premslin neighbors' counter-attack. In the Premslin mayor's and commune's name, a petition reached the countess praising Willebrandt's trial sermon and urging his appointment. The Glövziners, it claimed, had occupied separate pews in the Premslin church for more than 200 years, with only quarterly services in their own village. Should changes be contemplated, the Premsliners wanted to oppose to them their own "weighty needs." The Glövziners fired off a third petition, their first two having gone unanswered, saying that, in "runaway preacher Sauerbier's" post, candidate Gebhardt would preach biweekly in their village, while Willebrandt made no promises. The trustees asked lawyer Straube to investigate the villages' conflicting positions.

The Glövziners argued anew for their own pastor, citing church visitation records from before the Thirty Years War showing their village then *mater* and not *filial*. "And if we had our own preacher we would gladly surrender and hand over to him whatever exists and may be found here in our commune in the way of land and incomes." In Berlin, village deputies Jochim Niemann and Hans Milatz had recently tried to gain the countess's hearing. But "when they reached Her Excellency the Countess's Secretary, He said to them they were agitators and deserved to be put in the Spanish overcoat. And when they returned home, the estate manager told them she hadn't even been there [in Berlin], and they couldn't have accomplished anything." They hoped the trustees, "from simple love for the spread and maintenance of the Word of God," would sanction either biweekly services or a separate Glövzin pastor.

In September 1715 Blüthen Pastor Cober reported he could not continue performing both his own duties and those of the Premslin parish, where "from commiseration and love for the abandoned Frau pastor I took most of the office's business upon myself." He urged the Premslin pastor's appointment before winter. His own was a "most arduous and laborious pastorate," all of whose filials were a good five (English) miles distant. Willebrandt soon took the job, agreeing to preach monthly at Glövzin. But he wanted the trustees and the countess to stipulate on which Sundays, to avoid getting caught between the two villages' "considerable strife and unrest."

The agitation attending Willebrandt's appointment unveils villagers' ardor for God's Word and other ministrations of a pastor of their own, whose absence endangered spiritual health. But they also demanded to be heard in pastors' selections, according to whether they understood their sermons and could "love and trust" them. They did not hesitate to criticize candidates, making it clear that passive subordination to an unsatisfactory preacher was repugnant. No theological disputes are detectable here, hardening the point that, within the established Lutheran order, subject villages strove for pastors of their own liking, and pressed for institutional changes in their favor. Here Glövziners' protests considerably improved their spiritual services. But the hopes they reposed in Countess Blumenthal came to nothing, for, as in Sauerbier's case, though she may have consulted with the trustees, facing her Stavenow subjects she kept a sphinx-like silence.

Villagers' assertiveness in church affairs was not matched by pastors' intervention in parishioners' secular concerns, especially not the tug-of-war over seigneurial rents and labor services. Documentation of pastors' relations with the villages is too thin to permit definitive conclusions, but in manor–village strife's dense documentation they are absent; nor did lordship or farmers appeal for their support. Instead, the clergy displayed considerable dependency on seigneurial authority, readily deferring to it, while the lordship was confident it could prevail through its worldly powers over subjects' obstinacy and insubordination. In 1727 Pastor Willebrandt saluted Judge Hasse as "Highly Honored Sir and Patron!" He wrote that, in meeting earlier with Colonel Kleist, he agreed to offer "weekly children's instruction" to his lordship's numerous progeny at Stavenow manor-hall. He also accepted the duty, which his predecessors had borne, of weekly preaching there. But now he protested these burdens, invoking the 3–4 weekly village catechism classes he was already holding. Seemingly, confronting the imperious colonel, his powers of self-assertion failed him, and he sought, with unknown outcome, Hasse's intercession.[54]

The manorial court alone could implement certain pastoral proposals. It ratified the nominations of parishioners – seemingly always farmers – as church wardens, summoning them for appointment, if "according to its finding" they were fit for office and acceptable to the lordship. If a warden complained that, through computational error, he owed the parish 10 groschen, it was Hasse who denied his request for

[54] No. 712, fos. 203–4.

reimbursement, saying he must pay for his "negligence." In 1729 Willebrandt reported that Premslin needed a midwife (*Wehmutter*). He interviewed candidates from three villages, and proposed one with "most experience." Hasse then recommended her to the state-appointed rural physician (*Landphysicus*), whose judgment would prevail. Willebrandt also submitted for court investigation such reports as that "it has been learned Vey Ebels, Jürgen Nagel's maid in Karstedt, [delivered] Michael Schultzen's whore-child in [Nagel's] retirement quarters."[55]

Stavenow's church patronage powers extended far beyond pastoral appointments. Of minor import were such seigneurial gestures as allowing Garlin's pastor to fish the Löcknitz to stock the table for his father's wake. "Through God's blessing," the cleric thankfully wrote, "I caught as many as I needed."[56] In 1726 Colonel Kleist built Stavenow's church, since the chapel there could not accommodate both Stavenow community and Mesekow villagers, who lost their "house of God," as Kleist wrote the king, "in the Thirty Years War." To cover his expenditures, he sought to direct Mesekow church revenues to Stavenow parish.[57] While the lordship might borrow money for secular purposes from parish funds, it sometimes endowed or strengthened them with grants of its own.

Weighty also was Colonel Kleist's effort to mediate a dispute between Groß Linde commune, where he had no subjects but exercised church patronage, and tax officials, who wanted to cut wood on communal churchland to pay tax arrears. And of quasi-doctrinal importance was Major Kleist's 1782 resolution of a quarrel pitting Blüthen Pastor Friederici, obliged by his superiors' orders to introduce a new Lutheran songbook, doubtless expressing the late Enlightenment's fashionable rationalist theology, against his parishioners' obdurate opposition, who – in the spirit of Goethe's *Sorrows of Young Werther* – defended the older hymns. The villagers threatened to boycott church services, until Kleist dictated a compromise alternating new and old hymns, refusal of which would bring hard punishment upon them.[58]

Often, pastors relied on the lordship to enforce and defend their authority. In 1745 Garlin's pastor, bearing a farmer-tavernkeeper's name, complained to estate manager Erhardt of the "godless" treatment he

[55] No. 200, fos. 123, 141; no. 591, fo. 2.   [56] No. 595, fos. 18–19.   [57] No. 711, fo. 44.
[58] No. 713, fos. 86–8; no. 719, fo. 12. On eighteenth-century Württemberg songbook conflicts: Medick, *Weben*, ch. 6. On Prussian Enlightenment theology: *inter alia*, Brunschwig, *Enlightenment*.

suffered from a parishioner defying the pastor's command not to send his son to the village's cabinetmaker-schoolmaster. Whatever their feud–perhaps doctrinal (pitting Lutheran orthodoxy against Pietist heterodoxy)–the cleric could not prevail on his own authority.[59] In 1748, Frau Pastor Willebrandt, evidently a retired widow, charged a farmer with refusing to continue her 1-taler lease on his land. He claimed her payments were in arrears. They quarreled over livestock in each other's gardens. On Sunday, walking to evening communion, she greeted him, but he snubbed her, saying only "Pfui." Hasse ordered more evidence, warning against further "gross discourtesy."[60]

In 1757 Premslin Pastor Carsted elegantly penned a letter to Hasse, his godfather, about the "quarrelsome and unjust people in my Premslin parish," disputing his right to graze on common pasture the riding horse he needed "for my trips to Stavenow" (where his pastoral duties' scope seemed to rankle him, as it had his precursor). His village antagonists "threaten, if they can't lay hands on the horse, to goad one of my cows to death, as they once before did with my livestock." Facing such "INSOLENCE," the pastor remonstrated "in all friendliness" with the mayor, explaining "that the gracious lordship, whose interest it is that I keep a horse, will lend me support." He invoked "natural law" (*dem natürl. Rechte*), though not as Enlightenment savants understood it. The parsonage's arable open-field holdings entitled him to keep five head, while he grazed but two cows and a riding horse. This right he also possessed "under the civil law and the law of the land" (*dem bürgerl. und Land-Rechte*).

He might graze a horse-team for cultivating his land, as precursors Wilhelmi and Sauerbier did, but instead he hired farmers to work it. Pastor Carsted reviewed his parsonage's grazing rights, going back to "the MOST NOBLE" Hans Dietrich von Quitzow's late sixteenth-century improvement of pastoral incomes. Because of the grazing dispute, manorial leaseholder Frau Bergholtz had recently "been so good as to take my horse." The village mayor, "accustomed to take the bull by the horns," supported the pastor, but since "others in the parish were hostile and jealous toward me" the mayor wanted Hasse's ruling. The court could then discipline anyone who should "yield to the desire to disturb the preacher in his rights."[61]

Hasse, assembling the villagers at the parsonage, upheld Pastor Carsted's grazing rights, but later Carsted complained that mayor Ebel

---

[59] No. 591, fo. 125.   [60] No. 326, fo. 152.   [61] No. 321, fos. 56–7.

failed to prevent farmers from seizing one of his cows. Ebel said he "couldn't force" Hasse's ruling on the other farmers. The village "had no quarrel with the previous preacher, but this preacher has done them injuries, and won't even hold an hour of Sunday prayer with their children." Ebel begged release from mayoral office "because it causes him so many losses." Hasse announced he would again instruct the village in Carsted's rights, but "because the mayor must take responsibility when in the village such misdeeds occur," and because Ebel now sided with the villagers, Hasse jailed him for a day.[62]

Here a grazing conflict served as a lightning-rod for villagers' dissatisfaction with Pastor Carsted's ministrations. Parsons' comparative prosperity, like millers' and other local notables', provoked some degree of village hostility. Their moral policing, including indictments of punishable behavior, may have deepened such feelings, at least among more easy-going villagers. Suggestive of these attitudes was Pastor Willebrandt's 1737 charge against his former housemaid, Trine Kusels, of "much injuring him" by gossiping that the pastor's eldest daughter had a "whore-child." Trine replied that, on visiting her native village of Seetz, she was told of a child there "living at the young mayor's house that belongs to a priest's daughter." Trine denied proclaiming it Willebrandt's daughter Dorothea's child. No one knew whose it was. Nor had she told Dorothea "she didn't deserve to be called a maiden."

Willebrandt had summoned witnesses to his house, before whom Trine was expected to testify. When she balked, "Herr Pastor grew angry and wanted to strike her." She then declared, formulaically, that "she knew nothing but good and honorable things" about Dorothea. "She did say that 10 talers and all sorts of victuals had been sent to Seetz [for the baby's care], but not that Herr [Pastor] sent them." Hasse questioned Trine about "her condition,"

and she admits that she has a child and no husband. The child was fathered by a farmer's son in Nebelin and is in Seetz with her mother, widow and lodger . . . Next St. Jacob's Day the child will be four years old. Herr Preacher cursed her as vagabond's whore, but that's not true.

She said a farm servant and the court bailiff overheard how "the tutor," presumably Stavenow's, called her "any man's whore" while Willebrandt again condemned her – the cruel words were cutting – as "vagabond's whore." The pastor again denounced her, when she visited

---

[62] No. 326, fos. 211, 215.

his family on a Sunday to ask forgiveness, "if she had said anything unwarranted."

Willebrandt admitted Trine then spoke well of his daughter, "but as soon as she left their living room she said to the other servants that it was true all the same." As witness he called his nineteen-year-old servant, likely blacksmith's daughter Liese Thormanns. She said Trine told her of the pastor's daughter's overnighting in Seetz to bear the child, and how the mother promised 10 talers "and lots of groats and other food" for the baby's wet-nursing. Liese claimed Trine was telling this story to many people, and that Trine "wanted a pair of women to inspect" Dorothea (to determine whether she was a virgin). If Willebrandt's were a farmer's house, Trine allegedly said, she would address Dorothea by name only, and not, as she did, "for God's sake" in the pastor's house, as "maiden."[63]

The outcome is unknown, but it is clear the pastor's and seigneurial tutor's moral censure stung Trine, as did the contrast between her fatherless child's sorry condition and the mysterious baby's well-being. If Trine's story was believed, it would have inhibited Willebrandt's daughter Dorothea's marriage prospects and otherwise discredited her. The social and cultural gulf separating clergy from humbler folk yawns again. Pastors' personal virtues and the respect villagers paid them doubtless yielded happier social interactions. Villagers prized the clergy's spiritual services, sometimes asking them to record their last wills. But, in the secular sphere, pastors' words carried little weight independent of such sanctions as lordship or state might marshal behind them.

VILLAGE MAYORS' FRAGILE AUTHORITY

As sixteenth-century east-Elbian noble lordships adopted commercialized demesne farming, they reduced village mayors (*Schulzen*) largely to seigneurial instruments. But absolutism, using mayors to draw taxes and soldiers from the villages, challenged landlordly dominance. The 1765 Stavenow mayors' office-taking oath said "I swear, first, to His Royal Majesty in Prussia, my most gracious King and Lord, and then also to Herr [Major] Friedrich Joachim von Kleist, my High Jurisdictional Overlord and Seigneurial Lordship, to be loyal, faithful, and subject." Yet, though historians usually leave mayors standing

---

[63] No. 591, fos. 70–2.

obscured in the Junkers' shadow, to judge authority's structures it is vital to know whether mayors were sharp or dull tools in noble hands.[64]

Negotiations accompanying Stavenow's mayoral appointments are indiscernible. On the same 1742 day that Hasse sacked Premslin's mayor for brutally beating a farmer in a tax dispute, he wrote "Peter Ebel is appointed mayor by the gracious Frau Colonel and accepted in office." Ebel's colleagues were a newly appointed alderman (*Schoppe*) and assistant mayor (*Beystand*). Seemingly there was no fixed service term. Appointments might last a working lifetime, and be passed from father to son. Peter Ebel was still in office fifteen years later. But, while one particular holding might be called the "mayoral farm," the lordship might also appoint any fullholder, granting him the small perquisites that were his sole recompense.[65]

In 1749, Joachim Holtmann, who in 1737 at age twenty-two succeeded his mayoral father, gained reappointment as Glövzin headman after his earlier dismissal, perhaps for joining others in 1743 wood pilferage. Now the Kleists admonished him "to keep better order in the village." He received an arable patch that previous mayors had held, and whose possession other villagers were warned to respect on pain of "bodily punishment." In 1760, despite Holtmann's commission of severe misdeeds, he was still mayor.[66] His neighbors opposed landlordly largesse for good reason, not wishing to see headmen as the manor-hall's paid agents. In 1777, Kleist gave Blüthen's mayor a "piece of pasture" without consulting the village's other lordships and over farmers' protests there. Complaints having reached the "Royal Prussian Altmark-Prignitz War- and Domains-Board Office in Stendal," Kleist said Stavenow's jurisdiction over village roadways empowered his action. But the government ruled that, while he could grant the mayor an "emolument," he must gain fellow lordships' assent, and not infringe communal village property.[67]

Mayors' jobs, troublesome at best, grew harder in wartime. The headmen of Stavenow's four major fullholders' villages plus three others had lawyer Stappenbeck compose a 1745 petition to the Prignitz

---

[64] No. 358, fo. 1. At Stavenow, Kleist usually bore the military title of major, having been promoted from Obrist-Wachtmeister ("sergeant-chief"). For debates over the east-Elbian village commune's autonomy or subjection see Hartmut Harnisch, "Die Landgemeinde im ostelbischen Gebiet (mit Schwerpunkt Brandenburg)", in Peter Blickle, ed., *Landgemeinde und Stadtgemeinde in Mitteleuropa. Ein struktureller Vergleich* (Munich, 1991), 309–32; Lieselott Enders, "Die Landgemeinde in Brandenburg. Grundzüge ihrer Funktion und Wirkungsweise vom 13. bis zum 18. Jahrhundert", *Blätter für deutsche Landesgeschichte* 129 (1993): 195–256.
[65] No. 326, fos. 94–6.   [66] Ibid., fo. 157.   [67] No. 601, fo. 1.

District Commissioners. It was a litany of mayoral burdens. In wartime, they organized army hauling services. They mustered men on inactive duty (*Enrollierte*), delivering them for review and war service, sometimes losing 2–3 days' work plus heavy travel expenses. They hunted down deserters, "and in the rush of pursuit our horses must be first." They were responsible for supplying mounts to carry officers and troops from one army station to the next. They demarcated the equal shares their villagers could cut from communal woodland, while their "fellow farmers" went about their business, yet mayors received no more wood and brush than others. "Lord High Commanders! Thus are we much-plagued people, since we must alone care for everything concerning the whole commune, and without any help from it we contribute *ex propriis* all work, trouble, losses, and costs."[68]

Since (they claimed) they received no pay, they wanted their offices, as in other villages, to rotate "one by one among the proprietors." "For weighty reasons," unnamed but doubtless referring to seigneurial fiat, this was not possible. They therefore asked for "moderate compensation, to no one's disadvantage," since "a worker is worthy of his pay, or at least tends everywhere not to suffer losses because of it." Specifically, they wanted immediate release from wartime haulage requirements, double communal firewood portions, and grazing rights "at Whitsuntide and in autumn days" for two additional livestock head. The commissioners acknowledged that mayors should have "a small enjoyment," but directed them to seek it from their "jurisdictional overlords." Thus the government washed its hands of the matter. The mayors' demands show they boldly sought to unshoulder a major wartime burden while considerably improving fuel and animal stocks, usually already their villages' best. This gambit's failure does not warrant concluding they were tottering on ruin's brink, or that no advantages flowed from mayoral office (though seemingly they lay more in prestige and command-power than material benefit).

The mayor with his assistants presided over their village's "mayoral court" (*Schulzengericht*), settling violations of communal order through minor fines in cash paid into the village coffer or quantities of beer, drunk by landed householders. In 1747, Premslin fullholder David Busse, one of Stavenow's most debt-plagued and least law-abiding farmers, stood before Blüthen's mayoral court accused with his step-son of stealing young trees from the communal woods. Busse interrupted

---

[68] No. 611, fos. 2–4.

the mayor to denounce him as a scoundrel and a swindler, even though admitting the theft and having resisted mayoral search of his premises. The court heavily fined Busse and his accomplice 20 groschen for the trees, 1.4.- taler for a half-barrel of beer, and 1.4.- taler to recover pot, pothook, and tools impounded for this offense. The mayor protested Busse's defiance to Hasse's court, which sentenced the delinquent to four hours' jail for treating the mayor "very rudely." Like pastors, mayors sometimes needed the lordship to enforce their authority. Next day, Busse ungrudgingly sought Hasse's help to recover a 6-taler kettle Stavenow's hunter had impounded two years previously. The hunter having left the jurisdiction, Hasse told Busse he would, for a fee, write if given an address.[69]

Another institution of village self-rule, alongside the mayor's court, were periodic meetings concerning parish funds. When a women complained to Hasse's court about her son-in-law's military status, the judge instructed Karstädt mayor Nagel to investigate and report at the Friday church-fund meeting. Here requests for loans were heard or decided, in church warden's, interested villagers', and pastor's presence.[70] But mayors might themselves assemble their villagers, as when Mesekow mayor's wife Trine Besen sounded the "farmers' bell." Andreas Ebel, not a local farmer, asked why she was ringing, but she told him to wait for the others to arrive. He then cursed her as a "whore" and a "lordship's toady." Had the villagers not arrived, she claimed, Ebel's son would have struck her. Ebel told Hasse she began the cursing, but Trine's witnesses testified the pastor earlier condemned the Ebels' behavior toward her "from the pulpit" – a reminder of church services' practical function – so father and son suffered one-hour terms, respectively, in the Spanish overcoat and the fiddle, a rare subjection of a (young) man to female punishment.[71] Ebel's taunt about toadying – he spoke of a "snail sticking to the lordship" – exemplifies the rhetoric of class betrayal that, unsurprisingly, some villagers hurled at headmen.

Mayors themselves sometimes suffered public reprimand, as when in 1728 Hasse instructed five Stavenow headmen to watch for fires and forbid tobacco smoking on farmsteads or in the streets, on pain of imprisonment in Spandau. The mayors themselves would be "doubly watched."[72] Far more drastic was the lordship's action before Christmas 1748, when it summoned the Glövziners and Premslin mayor and his assistants. Hasse called roll among Glövzin farmers: six of twenty-one

[69] No. 326, fos. 133–4.   [70] No. 713, fo. 260.   [71] No. 591, fo. 25.   [72] No. 200, fos. 103–4.

were unexcusedly absent. One of the three assistant mayors' wives represented her husband, who had gone "to the Elbe." Hasse noted the presence of two farmers with their wives. He then proclaimed of Glövzin:

The previous great disorder in the village has gotten out of hand, and no small blame and explanation for this lies with mayor Jürgen Nagel, who in his advancing age can no longer shepherd the village's common needs. This has been shown again today by the commune's late appearance in court. Although it was agreed to arrive in the morning, no one came until midday, and even then five [sic] stayed away. Another mayor will therefore be immediately appointed, while the assistant mayors are warned not to be neglectful of village order.

For lateness, Hasse fined each farmer present 1 groschen, and absentees 2 groschen, payable into the village's poor-relief fund. "Further, anyone who doesn't obey the bell when the mayor orders assembly shall pay 6 pfennigs." And if workers, "as before, arrive so late for manorial service instead of at eight o'clock, plow or wagon will be sent back" to return next day punctually, while the guilty farmer's "disobedience" would earn him two hours in the Spanish overcoat. For those failing altogether to report for manorial service, the back-straining punishment would be "two hours in the morning and two hours in the afternoon." Hasse issued the same threats to the Premsliners. Alluding, seemingly, to favoritism in the communes, he declared that "in future, village penalties [*Bauernstraffen*] will be rigorously imposed without regard for persons involved, so all disorder may be avoided and remedied with true earnestness."[73]

It took nine months to replace mayor Nagel with Joachim Holtmann, one of this meeting's absentees. These proceedings again display the seigneurial court buttressing mayors' weak authority, while pointing to factionalism and favoritism dividing the villages. How fault-lines ran is unclear. Possibly they separated kin-based alliances. If a new mayor could emerge from an absentee faction's ranks, it probably was no more anti-seigneurially minded than the majority. In any case, Holtmann did not prove very authoritative, complaining in 1750 of two farmers who flouted his orders on hauling and grazing. Hasse commanded them to obey or face "painful punishment."[74]

One of headmen's most contentious tasks was enforcing rules on grazing, woodland access, and other communal usages. Daily policing

---

[73] No. 326, fos. 150–1.   [74] No. 715, fo. 27.

was the work of impounders (*Pfänder*), usually landless villagers, middle-aged or older, who like village shepherds received from landholders annual rye portions: in 1731 a mayoral farm paid an impounder a quarter-bushel (and a shepherd one-fifth).[75] Doubtless impounders also shared in fines imposed on those they apprehended, while performing other wage-earning work. Jacob Otto encountered physical resistance from David Busse "*et uxor*" when he attempted to seize their geese, probably for illegal grazing. Embittering the confrontation was Busse's debt to the impounder of 14 groschen unpaid wages. Hasse ordered payment of the fine and wages "or execution" (seizure and sale of equivalent possessions).[76]

Impounders enforced villages' collective will. When in 1722 impounder Hans Hecht seized Hans Röhr's horses and delivered them to the mayor's farm, where impounded animals were held, he invoked "the wish of the whole commune," which "ordered him" to seize livestock discovered grazing in the woodland, where he found Röhr's horses "in the acorns." Röhr's fine was only 3 pfennigs per horse, but he refused to pay, later retrieving his animals against the mayor's wife's opposition in her husband's absence, rudely denouncing her as a "fat-bellied whore" and impounder Hecht as an "old rogue." Though Röhr woundedly claimed she called him "hunch-backed scoundrel," the seigneurial court was unmoved, adding to impoundment fees a half-taler fine.[77] Similarly, Premslin's mayor later charged David Busse's wife before Hasse's court, saying she cursed his wife and "tried to seize him by the head when the commune wanted to impound [Busse's possessions] for plowing up the pasture." Debt-ridden Busse sought to expand his arable at village cost.[78]

Village fines could be stiffer, as when in 1727 Stavenow's blacksmith let his four horses get into the Blütheners' rye, for which he owed them 3 groschen. But because he "secretively" removed the horses from the mayor's farmstead, Hasse fined him an additional 12 groschen, payable to the seigneurial court on pain of bodily punishment.[79] Again, landlordly power was needed to enforce mayoral will. Impounders, too, often brought charges against delinquents to Hasse's (rather than the mayoral) court, especially when physical violence arose. In 1730 a young farmer resisted his horses' confiscation, striking the impounder on the head and seizing his hair. His offense's occurrence "on seigneurial premises" heightened its gravity, and Hasse condemned the impecunious

<hr>

[75] No. 591, fos. 19–20. [76] No. 200, fo. 80. [77] No. 629, fos. 4–5. [78] No. 200, fo. 104.
[79] Ibid., fo. 84.

defendant – sentenced already to two days' labor for wood theft – to a 6-groschen fine or "working it off."[80]

Impounders sometimes suffered worse abuse. Joachim Schultze charged Glövzin mayor Nagel's son with drunkenly beating him in a 1744 grazing dispute "with a manure-rake." Schultze claimed he bled all night. His brother said he "screamed piteously." The mayor did nothing to punish his son "and that's where the malice in the village comes from." Hasse sentenced the son to a heavy 2-taler fine or bodily punishment, the penalty to be doubled should he attack anyone else in future. The mayor's behavior would be investigated – though four years passed before his sacking.[81] A Perleberg surgeon's 1734 affidavit described the Winterfelds' impounder's grievous suffering, seemingly inflicted at Stavenow subjects' hands: in the head "a deep wound of about a finger's length; an eye heavily swollen with blood," and arm wounds, including "a severe contusion, and on his side two large sores full of blood."[82]

In 1753 Stavenow court bailiff Friedrich Voss, also seigneurial impounder guarding manorial grounds and borders, charged Glövzin mayor Holtmann with attacking him in the Stavenow manager's office. Holtmann cursed him as an "old scoundrel and thief" and "like a madman fell on [him] with an ax." He would have killed Voss, had Frau Erhardt – evidently a woman of authority – not restrained him. These charges Holtmann, complaining Voss had unfairly seized his horses for a minor infraction, could not deny. But Hasse was the more unforgiving for having earlier reinstalled Holtmann as mayor to pacify an unruly village, only to have him now threaten a seigneurial official's life. He suffered a heavy 5-taler fine, payable in a month on pain of four weeks' imprisonment on bread and water.[83]

Sufficiently agitated, villagers might act collectively to enforce impoundment regulations. Premslin farmer Daniel Mentz complained in 1732 before Hasse's court, in Colonel Kleist's and Captain Karstedt's presence, that both lordships' subjects attacked him on his own farmstead. The defendants said "because [Mentz] wouldn't come to the commune on charges of harmful grazing, the whole commune went to his farm." Hasse ruled Mentz's "disorderly actions" did not justify "such a beating." Kleist, intervening personally, draconically sentenced one of his subjects, and Karstedt two of his, to three days' imprisonment, Mentz escaping with a warning.[84] Here neighboring landlords cooperated against communal turbulence issuing in (rare) mob action,

[80] Ibid., fos. 138–9.   [81] No. 326, fo. 117.   [82] No. 713, fo. 75.   [83] No. 326, fos. 190, 222.
[84] No. 591, fo. 47.

but multiple lordships' presence in many villages complicated other impoundment cases. Winterfeldt farmer Porepp retaliated against Stavenowers' 1737 seizure of his horses by taking two horses from one of them. Porepp, armed with "two big dogs and ax in hand," falsely claimed his lordship authorized his action.[85]

A 1724 case dramatically illustrates the pressures manor–village grazing disputes exerted on mayors. Blüthen farmers seized some 300 seigneurial sheep from hollander Klasen and impounded them for three days at the mayor's farm, "letting them stand under the open sky so they almost died of rain and mud." Hasse summoned two suspect farmers, neither Stavenow subjects, "but in the course of [my] writing further they went away together." Hasse interrogated eleven others, also non-Stavenowers, asking "how it happened they rebelled against their lordship." They said Stavenow had no such grazing rights as the hollander exercised. "They carried out the impoundment together, and stood" – here they employed a phrase common in Germany and Europe to acts of village rebelliousness – "all for one and one for all."[86] Hasse replied it was "very punishable [that] they acted as their own judges," and fined each one a taler. If they could prove Stavenow lacked grazing rights, even though still having unresettled farms, they must "submit their complaint properly and await legal decision." Next day, mayor Jacob Meyer "finally appeared," along with twenty-eight fellow farmers. The judge asked Meyer why he let the farmers impound the lordship's sheep. Meyer replied "he couldn't do anything about it. The farmers did it on their own." Meyer was against it, "but that was no help. They even told him today if he brought the sheep back . . . they would kill him like a mad dog." The sexton had read them Hasse's previous day's resolution, "but that didn't change their minds, and they wouldn't surrender the sheep without getting impoundment money."

Why, Hasse asked, had the mayor kept the sheep at his farm? "He had to do it, otherwise the farmers wouldn't leave him in peace." "Did he fear the farmers more than his overlord?" Meyer replied "he couldn't set himself against the farmers. They had already threatened him enough." Meyer conceded the lordship's sheep always grazed where impoundment occurred. Why then had he not returned the sheep? "He wasn't allowed to." For Meyer's "disobedience," Hasse sentenced him to two hours' jail, demanding the sheep's prompt return on pain of redoubled punishment and threatening the other farmers with

---

[85] No. 597, fo. 116. [86] No. 200, fos. 10–11. Göttsch, *"Alle für einen Mann."*

"execution" if they did not also comply. Later the same day, Hasse noted Meyer had "acknowledged his misconduct and promised improvement," vowing to return the sheep immediately, whereupon Hasse ordered him freed. Soon thereafter mayor Meyer absconded. This incident, so revealing of the mayors' weakness facing their insubordinate communes, occurred during Blüthen's "equalization" and finds no subsequent echo before Major Kleist's post-1763 conflicts with his subjects. But later in 1724, another seigneurial hollander charged the village impounder had "beaten [the hollander's] sister-in-law black and blue when she was grazing his cattle," as "his women workers" could attest. This quarrel too involved disputed manor–village grazing boundaries. On encountering the herdswoman, the impounder said, "you old cat [i.e., witch], who ordered you to graze here?" and then lashed her with his whip.[87]

Mayors too sometimes abused their powers, as when on Penance Day (*Busstag*) 1742 Premslin mayor Joachim Hecht summoned the commune to discuss "improper grazing." The mayor "twice boxed [Hans] Ebel's ears because he wouldn't pay the [direct] tax," that is, the share the mayor assigned him, based on Ebel's grazing allowances, of increased wartime *Kontribution*. Ebel "seized [the mayor] by the hair," but the mayor's brother joined in hurling Ebel to the ground and "kicking him in the face until blood ran from his nose and mouth, so that he still detected blood three or four days later."[88] The mayor blamed Ebel for starting the fight, and Ebel's wife for cursing him as "swindler, devourer [*Auffresser*], [and] werewolf," and also for chasing "whores." So he gave her too "a few blows." Hasse ruled Ebel and wife owed the mayor "Christian reconciliation," and the warring parties shook hands. "But because of his excesses the mayor is, not unjustly, relieved of his office," whereupon Hasse appointed Peter Ebel mayor.

About the tax dispute, Hasse wrote Ebel's Karstedt lordship that "after the tax increase *de anno* 1733," Ebel's monthly rates (measured by grazing usages) should have risen. The new higher payments Ebel's wife had accepted (a point underscoring women's co-management of farms). But Ebel himself "departed" the courtroom rather than acquiesce, though later he relented. The tax payments followed, Hasse noted, the "settlement" Karstedt's father reached with his Premslin subjects, which was "in the farmers' hands" and which should be kept intact "so

---

[87] No. 200, fos. 21–2.   [88] No. 326, fos. 80, 93–5.

as to preserve the village in peace and calm." Here are Prussian subject farmers entering into tax agreements with their lordships, the texts of which they kept among village records. If this was a sign of communal vitality, it was a tribute to the collectivity, not the mayors. Hecht's sacking was one of three mayoral demotions in the 1724–48 years, to which Meyer's absconding might be added. Doubtless communal leaders often performed their duties peacefully and effectively, but the conflicts embroiling them speak loudly.

One of their chief – and uncontroversial – functions was to serve with their assistants as farm appraisers in generational transfers. But they might be slow in redressing villagers' grievances. Cottager widow Buck once complained to Hasse that two local farmers' horses damaged her crops, and that mayor Jürgen Nagel would not help her. Nagel then wrote – or had written for him – a letter to Hasse, saluting him as "learned," "wise," and "high-commanding." Nagel confirmed the widow's losses, recommending compensation for 1.5 barley sheaves lost. "Hans Zechel's child let the horses in, because he's of no use. [Zeggel] was ordered before to mend his ways, and paid impoundment fees once already for this, but he's a good-for-nothing." Hasse awarded her 2.5 sheaves from each trespasser, suggesting the mayor was inclined, despite his low opinion of the Zeggels, to let farmers guilty of such offenses off lightly.[89]

The impression left of mayors' weakness, combined with petty corruption and cronyism, overshadows better qualities. The resentments they inspired radiate from a 1738 letter to Hasse from farmer Jürgen Ohlert. He admitted his son wrongly cut firewood on his brother-in-law's wood parcel.

But although I amicably settled with the mayor, he and the commune nevertheless went to the tavern and drank a quarter-barrel of beer at my expense. And I only learned that Your Honor sentenced me to a 6-groschen fine – nobody told me about this – after my harnesses' impoundment.

Ohlert protested the double penalty and asked redress. "But I must next report to your High Nobleness that our mayor upholds such disorder it's almost unconscionable." With two other farmers, he harvested firewood belonging to the whole community, and he unfairly "parcels out [other] wood as he pleases."

And he associates with such disreputable people [*losen Leuten*], always causing village trouble. And also he claims the swine-forage for himself, and gives his

[89] No. 591, fos. 112, 114.

pigs the acorns whenever he likes, even though they belong since long ago to the community.[90]

Although Hasse ordered Ohlert's harnesses returned, mayor and commune later counter-charged Ohlert with violating the "village rules" (*Dorfordnung*), leading Hasse to decree that because Ohlert "seldom [observes] good order," he was dismissed as assistant mayor.[91]

Another villager who clashed with his mayor was Johann Kiecks, a lodger Colonel Kleist installed in an absconded fullholder's place. In 1728 mayor Knippenberg complained to Hasse that "Kiecks keeps a dangerous fire, and threatened to strike [the mayor] dead when they wanted to impound his goods, and [Kiecks] was supposed to give the commune a quarter-barrel of beer, but it didn't happen. And because he doesn't hold with the commune, no one helps him, [so] his roof is still not up." Hasse promised Kiecks' punishment, but also ordered the mayor "to help [Kiecks'] building as much as possible" – showing that villagers sometimes supported each other's construction projects. Here again, the mayor sided with the majority.[92]

Sometimes mayors (and their wives) suffered rude physical attacks in meetings, as when in 1726 Christian Diercks cursed Glövzin mayor Holtmann, a future mayor's father, "publicly before the commune assembled at the mayor's house." Hasse required Diercks to render the mayor a "declaration of honor" and pay 1 taler or suffer the Spanish overcoat for an hour.[93] Karstädt mayor Hans Nagel complained that, when he summoned the commune during the 1737 harvest, non-Stavenow farmer Brunst, whose son was among those guilty of grazing infractions, "tore the shirt off his arms and cursed him in the worst way as a swindler and scoundrel." Nagel's wife, who "wanted to rescue him," suffered Brunst's and a henchman's blows to eye, nose, and mouth. Brunst's son "held her by the hair while Brunst lay atop her." Meanwhile, Nagel complained, "the other farmers just stood and watched." Hasse promised to write Brunst's lordship, meanwhile issuing a "directive" to Stavenow farmers to render mayors "necessary assistance." Nagel later gained a lordship-brokered peace between himself and his tormentors.[94]

Mayors' frustrations as mediators between lordship and village appear dramatically in a 1727 rage seizing mayor Holtmann senior. Unidentified assailants furtively grazing their horses on the lordship's

---

[90] No. 713, fo. 139.   [91] No. 591, fo. 79.   [92] No. 200, fo. 104.   [93] Ibid., fos. 52–3.
[94] No. 591, fos. 73, 75.

pasture attacked seigneurial impounder Hecht by night. Suspicion focused on Glövzin farmers' junior farmhands. To penetrate their silence, Captain Kleist summoned the commune. "The old impounder," Hasse wrote, "is heard, and because he cannot stand up, Herr Captain and I went to him." Hecht said after midnight he encountered two black horses tended by two male servants and a boy. They

> had made a fire by the pond, and when he spoke to ask why they were grazing horses there, one of them immediately struck him from behind on the head, so that he fell down, and then the other two fell on him and all three beat him so pitiably that he was all black and blue, and didn't come to his senses for an hour.[95]

Hasse identified three farmhands who could not verify their whereabouts when the assault occurred and ordered their detention. They were local farmers' sons, including communal opposition leader Hans Milatz's. Defying Hasse's order, young Milatz and his comrades left the mayoral court – the hearing's scene – and marched to the tavern. Hasse ordered mayor Holtmann to take young Milatz in custody.

> Upon hearing that mayor and commune should place Hans Milatz under arrest, the mayor says he won't let himself be attacked by the commune. He wasn't that kind of a fellow, he would take a rifle and shoot somebody, he had defended himself before against cavalrymen and soldiers. He too was a royal servant [*königlicher Diener*].
>
> Asked how he knew he would shoot, he says he doesn't know for sure, but because [Milatz] wouldn't willingly come and stay, he feared he would take a weapon and resist.

Hasse berated the mayor for "this violent talk," about which Colonel Kleist's judgment would be sought. Yet Holtmann remained in office until his 1742 death, while young Milatz, whatever punishment he suffered, faced Hasse again in 1730 for assaulting the field bailiff during manorial service before disappearing from the records.

Here the court found a mayor's threat to assert his authority gun in hand no less objectionable than the farm workers' beating of the impounder. Hasse and Captain Kleist did not wish to see mayor Holtmann armed with real authority and acting decisively, but rather wanted him to be their own power's docile instrument. The lordship could not rule villages directly with its own officials, yet neither could it rely on mayors to represent it effectively. This placed village domination

---

[95] No. 200, fos. 73–5.

in the landholding farmers' collective hands. Their opposition could nullify mayors' authority and sometimes inspire resistance to the lordship of real force. In this sense, the village commune, though bent under seigneurial domination, remained unbroken.

SOLDIERS IN THE VILLAGES

The historical literature's emphasis on seigneurial domination leaves the absolutist regime's presence in the villages in shadows. Yet District Commissioners and their subalterns wielded mighty power over tax collection and army recruitment, while an influential argument holds that the absolutist army militarized Prussian rural society. This is one version of the thesis of early modern social discipline, imposed from above by political and cultural elites, stressing subject farmers' youthful service as soldiers in regiments recruited from their rural localities and often commanded by their own or nearby landlords or noble kinsmen. Short-term annual summer maneuvers following initial years of active duty tightened the disciplinary bonds that Prussian militarism fastened on the soldiers, deepening villagers' subjection in civilian life to the Junker landlords, many of whom – as in the Kleist lineage – served as army officers.[96]

Stavenow villagers' insubordinate inclinations cast doubt on the militarization thesis, but the question remains of army service's impact on communal life and manor–village relations. The records, patchy though they are, suggest that soldiers disrupted communal and seigneurial order more than they reinforced it. Soldiers were, when present in the villages, less an embodiment of social discipline than a force for indiscipline, working against seigneurial – and sometimes also village – interest.

Soldierly status entailed many disadvantages, including inability to marry, constraining not just active-duty soldiers but those on furlough leading civilian lives except when called to annual review or war. Without marriage permits from their commanding officers, such men were condemned to celibacy, though some furloughed soldiers impregnated unmarried women, hoping to escape through marriage into civilian life. In 1733 Hasse summoned farmer Häwecke's daughter Grete, who was "rumored to be pregnant." Her father appeared, conceding she would bear the child "at any hour and moment." Its father was soldier Ruhn, a former thresher on Frau von Platen's estate where Grete worked. Old Häwecke said, hopefully, that Ruhn "wants to

---

[96] Büsch, *Militärsystem*, passim, and related literature cited above.

marry her."[97] Nor were relatively privileged millers' sons exempt. In 1748, miller's apprentice Möller's commanding officer rescinded his marriage permit, preventing his union with a mill heiress, who then married another man. Möller had a brother, also a miller's apprentice, who "seven or eight years ago" – at the Silesian wars' outbreak – "became a soldier on the Imperial side" – possibly through impressment – "and wasn't in his right mind, because he chopped up his own gear with an ax and so is also no longer present."[98]

Soldiers perished in battle, or fell captive. In 1759 Friedrich Tihlmann wrote from Austrian-held Silesian Breslau to Cavalry Captain Kleist, saying he was a grenadier in von Retzow's battalion and a Stavenow subject (a seigneurial cowherd's kinsman). To Kleist "I appeal as to a father," asking for 20 ducats (55 talers) to buy himself free, promising to "be of service at any time." Whether Kleist ransomed him is unknown.[99] Other villagers, forced under arms, disappeared from view, like smallholder's "son Nichlas who served eighteen years as a cavalryman and didn't write, so it's not known whether he's alive or dead."[100] Other soldiers were mustered out as invalids, unfit for farming and eking out lives without pensions, like Joachim Höpfner, who lost his claim on his father's fullholding, but hoped for the yearly harvest from it of 2 bushels' sowings.[101] We saw that Frederick II's pressure on villages to settle invalid soldiers as cottagers on church or other communal land met frequent resistance.

Army service, among other defects, was ill paid. Rarely did deceased soldiers leave much behind. Typical was the estate of Christian Nagel, "*Mousequetier,*" who in famine-epidemic year 1771 willed his possessions to his three siblings. Though disputed, they amounted but to clothes and linen worth 8 talers, including two overcoats.[102] The poverty of active-duty common soldiers in Frederick's Prussia was legendary.[103]

Mesekow mayor Ketelhöhn prided himself on escaping youthful army service in his native Mecklenburg. He recalled his home village's "farmers wanted to make him a soldier," but he "bought himself free" for 30 silver talers, perhaps his inheritance, fleeing then to Brandenburg.[104] Here village oligarchs decided who should be sacrificed to the recruiters.

[97] No. 326, fo. 39.   [98] No. 715, fos. 19–21; no. 326, fos. 153–4.   [99] No. 324, fo. 41.
[100] No. 326, fo. 242.   [101] No. 715, fo. 100.   [102] No. 358, fo. 135.
[103] See, *inter alia*, Krüger, *Manufaktur und Manufakturarbeiter*, and Ulrich Bräker's account of his impressment in the Prussian army and subsequent life in Berlin in *Das Leben und die Abentheuer des Armen Mannes im Tockenburg* (Zürich, 1788).
[104] No. 715, fo. 41.

In post-1733 Prussia all able-bodied young men were registered and could be drafted into active service at local regimental commanders' and District Commissioners' behest. But in Frederick William I's days, high-handed army actions were common. In 1729 Hasse mentioned "the farm-servant the soldiers took away to Pomerania."[105]

In 1789, the Prignitz District Commissioner solicited a report on Stavenow's "absconded cantonists": young men enrolled for military service who had left their legal residences under Kleist's jurisdiction without giving new addresses, thereby evading impressment – in a renewed age of central and eastern European war – into active service. Sub-bailiff Quittenbaum informed Judge Gutike there were thirty such draft-evaders, some farmers' but most lodgers' sons and all, so far as Quittenbaum knew, living beyond Prussian frontiers, mainly in demilitarized Mecklenburg. This large number witnesses the fear in which ordinary villagers held active army service, especially those with no great inheritance prospects. For evasion of military duty entailed loss of farm succession rights and marriage portions, though doubtless families conniving in sons' flight gave them such portable assets as they could. Possibly noble lordships resented the labor-pool depletion such illicit migration caused – the documents are silent – but otherwise they probably welcomed impecunious youthful rebels' and troublemakers' departure.[106]

The social-discipline argument holds that subject villagers internalized military values and acted on them. Yet household inventories say nothing of military clothing or memorabilia, though doubtless some men wore tattered army-issue dress in workaday life. There is but one recorded incident of one villager's repressive deployment of the ethic of military discipline against another. In 1729 Pagel Hecht, a farmer's servant, charged Andreas Koselleck, seemingly a furloughed soldier and perhaps also farmworker, with beating him. Hecht was harrowing seigneurial land when he stopped to fix a broken harness. Soldier Koselleck approached, Hecht claimed, and struck him with his sword, "cutting a deep wound on his shoulder." Hecht's father, an elderly lodger, said his son "is very unhappy [since] he has been made unfit to work and has to suffer want."

Two other Hechts witnessing the incident – one also a furloughed soldier – declined to support their nominal kinsman, saying Koselleck only injured the plaintiff after he threatened him with a stone. The soldier-defendant claimed:

---

[105] No. 200, fos. 117–18.   [106] No. 719, fo. 94.

Pagel Hecht has a habit of always smoking tobacco and quitting work. Because he was one of the worst tobacco-smokers and idlers, whom he [Koselleck] had so often encountered [while malingering] but had [until now] left alone, on Saturday he [Koselleck] hadn't been able to control himself when he saw him stopping work once again, but gave him a few blows.

Koselleck had taken early supper (*Vesperbrot*) and drunk a brandy at the tavern, while plaintiff Hecht and his comrades sat at the table's other end smoking their pipes. Hecht said defensively that foreman Halentz permitted them to smoke at suppertime. Hasse now banned all smoking at work. He pronounced laborer Hecht wrong to threaten soldier Koselleck, dismissing his sword wound as "of no account." Yet he fined Koselleck 12 groschen, including 2 groschen paid the swineherd for treating Hecht's injury, while 10 groschen went to the tavern, where the soldier caused damage in his fight with Hecht.[107] Koselleck seemingly viewed lackadaisical Hecht through drill-sergeant's eyes, punishing him, as soldier-king Frederick William I might have done, with the flat of his sword.

More often, active-duty soldiers furloughed to their villages proved disruptive and, because the army retained jurisdictional rights over them, difficult for seigneurial courts to punish. In 1739, a von Winterfeldt official charged two Stavenow soldiers and farmers' sons with beating his impounder, occasioning fines and medical bills of 14 talers. The issue went unresolved for five years, probably because the defendants, who now pleaded self-defense, were beyond legal reach.[108] Some furloughed soldiers sought to play their military status against landlordly authority, as did Hans Ohlert when Stavenow farmhand Caspar Schultze claimed Ohlert beat him "at the manor-farm" where Ohlert was working while on military leave. It happened when they were last served beer, probably at harvest's end. Ohlert admitted the charge, saying they were both drunk and that Schultze had insulted him, which the plaintiff admitted. Hasse, ruling that Schultze's "disgusting talk" helped trigger the fight, fined him one taler and Ohlert two.

Upon this verdict's announcement, soldier-worker Ohlert indignantly rejected it, saying he wanted to "get some defense, and with that, he left." Though ordered to return to the courtroom, he refused, appealing to his "company papers" (*Compagnie-Brieff*) which, he thought, gave him the "right" (*Recht*) not to return and immunity from the court bailiff's

---

[107] No. 200, fos. 127–8.   [108] No. 713, fo. 265.

coercion. Hasse resolved to report Ohlert's actions to his commanding officer.[109] Possibly this resulted in the defiant soldier's recall to active duty, an outcome he probably would have regretted. But the incident shows that Hasse trod lightly in disputes involving the army, while Ohlert, a subject farmer's son, believed his military status shielded him from his lordship's verdicts.

A much more serious incident occurred in June 1770, when musketeer Peter Glissmann, twenty-four-year-old Blüthen mayor's son, faced Stavenow field bailiff Johann Röwer's court charge of insubordination during manorial service.[110] Röwer testified that the compulsory workers, engaged that day in manure-hauling, "lazily" started work after the midday break. He told the lead wagon, "Get moving, and don't stand around like you were at the fair." From behind someone said, "But today is the fair." Without looking around, Röwer replied, "'Shut your trap, dog's ass,' so as to stop the mouth of the wise-guy [*raisonnier*]." On the wagons' return, musketeer Glissmann asked bailiff Röwer if his words were aimed at him. Yes, said Röwer, if Glissmann had spoken "out of the crowd." Glissmann replied, "You [*Du*], fellow, are a dog's ass," repeating this four or five times. The other wagons halted. Though Röwer knew this "insubordination" called for action, he only told Glissmann to get back to work. But he could not let it pass, "because otherwise he wouldn't be able to say a word of warning to them during work without exposing himself to curses or even to mob action." It had been "impossible to revenge himself physically on Glissmann, because the manorial workers later on would have accused me of beating them." The lordship sought to present a peaceful face while royal commissioners were mediating other conflicts with its villagers.

Defendant Glissmann observed that Wilsnack fair was actually being held. To Röwer he had only said "Yes, today is fair-day. If we were only there." Röwer replied, "Dog's ass, shut your trap until you're asked to talk." Glissmann's words were not meant to be hostile or insubordinate. When he asked "his comrades" whether Röwer's words were aimed at him, they said "They must be for you," leading Glissmann, returning from his haul, to say, "Herr Röwer, you [*Er*] called someone today a dog's ass. Who did you mean by that?" Röwer said it was for whoever answered him. When Glissmann said that had been himself, Röwer replied, "Then you [*ihr*] are one." This provoked Glissmann's uncreative retort: "If I'm one so are you [*ihr*] too." Glissmann continued:

---

[109] No. 591, fos. 77–8.   [110] No. 718, fos. 1–5.

Then plaintiff [Röwer] started calling him "du," so [he] called him "du" as well, and matched each of his words. He can't let himself be cursed as a dog's ass, nor let it pass. Neither his army officer nor Herr Major von Kleist have commanded any such thing. No other person has addressed the defendant this way . . . He has enough understanding of his own [*er habe aus sich selber so viel Verstand*] that he can't allow himself to be cursed.

When Röwer told Glissmann to move on, he replied, "If you want to give me orders, come here." But Röwer "sat still," so Glissmann did nothing. If Röwer had attacked him physically, he would have defended himself. "He can't allow his honor to be taken away by being cursed. Therefore he asks for absolution." He performs his manorial service "loyally." He meant his remark about the fair not for Röwer, but his brother. Röwer shot back that "in manorial service he had nothing to do with soldiers, but rather with the person of a farmer." If Glissmann did not want to obey orders, he could stay away. Judge Betich concluded that Glissmann "called [Röwer] to account . . . and repeatedly vented curses at him." But such "behavior on a manorial servant's part is punishable, because he must refrain from all insubordinate back-talk [*wiedersetzlichen raisonnirens*]." If he felt abused by supervisors, he could appeal to the lordship. Betich would therefore request that Glissmann's army commander, Major von Winterfeldt, punish him. Betich ordered Glissmann not to report again for manorial service, threatening his arrest "as a willful insubordinate" and return to his regiment. Glissmann's father would have to send another "competent man" to perform his labor services.

This incident reveals the modes of address current between lordship and subjects: on one hand, patronizing, on the other, indirect and deferential, but in anger's heat shifting to the egalitarian "du." Manor–village relations were balanced on a knife-edge, stilling for fear of villagers' collective responses (through lawyers, if not fists) the bailiff's lash as a disciplinary instrument. The confrontation shows how a self-confident villager could invoke his honor, understood militarily, and his "understanding" (or "reason") in aggressively challenging an imperious seigneurial field bailiff. Peter Glissmann may have suffered military punishment for his defiance. In 1771 a son-in-law succeeded Peter's father, retiring after twenty-nine years as mayor, though Peter's expectations concerning the family farm are unknown. Undoubtedly neither Prussian kings nor Junkers intended that subject villagers' military service should weaken landlordly authority over laborers, yet clearly it sometimes did.

Soldierly training also sporadically heightened violence and disorder in the villages, as a 1747 wedding fight shows.[111] Present in sword-bearing uniform were two Hintze brothers, furloughed but active soldiers in the Prinz von Preussen Regiment Colonel Kleist once commanded. It was they who in 1734 allegedly beat the Winterfeldt impounder, and disrupted the 1747 wedding couple's pre-nuptial betrothal by exploding hand grenades. Glövzin mayor Jürgen Nagel now accused them of severely injuring his bridegroom son Joachim at the pre-wedding dance-fest. Klaus Hintze admitted he "cut" young Nagel, but in self-defense. The Hintze brothers had earlier quarreled with Nagel, but they made peace at the party, drinking beer with the bridegroom and his entourage.

Mayor Nagel said Hintze struck his son with a saber "such a blow to the left arm that he immediately fainted." He was taken to Perleberg, "where he now lies in the army lazaret without hope of recovery," or if he did recover, he would be a lifelong cripple. "And it's not for this that the king gives the soldiers their weapons." Old Nagel, outraged, wanted legal satisfaction, and even to inform the king's court of the incident. Another witness, Hans Nagel, Karstädt mayor's son and soldier in the Hintzes' company, said the bride's father offered the guests "another pot of beer." Assault victim Joachim Nagel danced with his fiancée. Defendant Hintze joined in, colliding with Nagel as they "danced around." Beer spilled and complaints arose about "comrades" and "invited guests" treating one another so. Hintze contemptuously told Nagel, "you fool, you can't keep to the dance as well as I can." Fighting words were uttered, but the host decreed that "whoever doesn't want to keep the peace should leave." The Hintzes went home, the insulted Nagel followed, fighting broke out, and cries resounded that Nagel was dead. But Nagel, though injured, revived and assaulted Klaus Hintze. Pretending to offer him his hand, he struck him in the face and "seized him by the head and threw him down," triggering more fierce battling. The wounded Nagel recovered, and finally, though acrimoniously, succeeded his father on the farm. The day after the fight, following the wedding ceremony, the two Hintzes and four Nagels "settled among themselves that they didn't want to be enemies any longer and so departed in peace."

While drunken fights doubtless sometimes marred earlier weddings, the addition of young men trained in the military code and armed with

111 No. 326, fos. 144–6.

swords made them more dangerous. Here militarism strengthened, not village order and discipline, but rather violence and disorder. Village custom – the host's right to dismiss unruly guests, family conferences to end feuds – limited damage. But, as mayor Nagel bitterly told Judge Hasse, "if the soldiers destroy the farmers, things will be bad in this land." This was not a militarized world-view, but rather a remark conjuring twentieth-century war's devastating impact on east-Elbian Germany.

GRAVE OFFENSES: THEFT AND ABSCONDING

Though they loomed in the background, it was neither state bureaucracy, church, nor army that maintained social order in noble jurisdictions, but rather the seigneurial court. At Stavenow, it imposed the Kleists' – and, indirectly (and selectively), the Prussian state's – will, though in a manner usually consistent with communal values, especially as expressed in the landholding farmers' way of life. Most of the conflicts these pages have so far discussed ranked low in criminality, however explosive they otherwise were. Quarrels among kinfolk and neighbors, boundary violations and pilferage, physical assault, individual villagers' violation of seigneurial work rules or expressions of disrespect for landlordly authority: these were far from trivial matters, yet they were also common occurrences leaving social and political order intact.

Unlike in large eighteenth-century cities, and modern urban-industrial society, major crime's incidence in the Stavenow lordship was extremely low. This is clear from the dense documentation of Hasse's forty-year judgeship, and seems true of subsequent decades too. Murder and permanently crippling assaults were virtually unknown. Property theft, uncommon in itself, rarely involved large values. There were but a handful of livestock thefts, mainly of horses. As for grave offenses against the lordship, the villages' collective resistance rested on legal claims. Though infuriating to seigneurial authority, they did not figure as crimes, though "excesses" committed in their course led to individual punishments.

But when desperate farmers absconded, carrying off any valuables on hand, the seigneurial interest, both economic and political, suffered flagrant violation. There are a few such cases. Otherwise the court dealt mainly with moral issues – especially illicit sexuality – and infrequent magical practices. Here the only severe punishments fell upon several adulterers, and one ne'er-do-well magical treasure hunter who, on charges of sheep theft, suffered removal to Spandau. In the numerous instances of premarital impregnation, the court sought to salvage such honor as it could, and minimize economic losses. In villagers' eyes, the seigneurial court was more than landlordly authority's threatening instrument. Mayoral weakness and inclination to play village favorites made of the court a vital forum of dispute resolution. Apart from adjudication of villagers' material conflicts, it resolved quarrels over villagers' dignity. Though historians have neglected it, subject villagers' sense of honor was important to them. Especially during Judge Hasse's tenure, the court sustained, not just seigneurial but village order too, though mainly as landed householders understood it.

Theft by itinerant outsiders, such as horse thieves, inflicted painful losses on individual villagers. But larceny in their own midst was likely to trigger communal upheaval and provoke seigneurial vengeance, since such crimes, apart from their material significance, flouted local morality and challenged noble authority. Exemplary was the case of sixty-year-old former nightwatchman Caspar Seyers and his wife. They had been Glövzin lodgers for nine years when in 1724 the new nightwatchman, twenty-one-year-old Joachim Wulff, reported he saw Seyers' wife bringing home a sack at eleven o'clock one Sunday night. Though she claimed it contained only cabbage, "the farmers" later demanded the mayor perform a house-search, which turned up 6 bushels of fresh and three of dried fruit, also nuts, but no cabbage. Worse, the empty trunks of two of four compulsorily recruited manorial servants who had earlier absconded turned up in Seyers' possession.[112]

Other testimony, recorded by the von Karstedt judge to whom the Glövziners sent outspoken Hans Milatz to report about cabbage thefts from their gardens, had Caspar Seyers carrying the sack, occasioning the house-search that discovered the fruit and nuts. The investigators wanted to open Seyers' own locked trunk, but his wife, who kept the keys, was away performing manorial service. When finally the trunk was inspected, in a Karstedt official's presence, it contained nothing suspicious.[113] Yet agreement was general that the absconded laborers had stolen seigneurial goods. Defendant Caspar Seyers said when they brought their trunks to him, they emptied them of ill-gained wool, gloves, and leather leggings. Other evidence showed that linen yardage,

[112] No. 200, fos. 14–16.   [113] No. 655, fo. 16.

coats, shirts, and hats were also among the booty. Seyers received nothing. The fruit he claimed to have gotten honestly from "the farmers" and his daughter, who picked it from trees overhanging fences along the streets: seemingly arborial no-man's land.

Seyers took the trunks because one of the runaways was his wife's nephew. He charged farmer Michael Zeggel with having recently received a furtively visiting absconder and transporting the stolen goods to Mecklenburg, delivering them to the runaways at a baptismal celebration for the child of Zeggel's daughter, who lived there. Zeggel conceded meeting a suspect, but denied transporting the booty, though his wife admitted giving him two shirts to deliver from an absconder's aunt. Farmer Joachim Möller, from whom elderly suspect Seyers rented quarters, testified that, after "the commune" carried out the house-search, "Caspar Seyers wanted to revenge himself on the village," threatening arson. Seyers said to Möller: "when things are going well for you people here in the village, you should remember me," adding that "who knows if I'll ever come near Glövzin again." To these elliptical but menacing words Möller laconically replied that Seyers "had better think things over."

The Karstedts' judge asked Seyers "why he had [recently] disappeared into the dust." Seyers did it "out of impatience," because "the farmers" were treating him "hard." He went to Lenzen "to do day labor," but returned when "his friends" (relatives) told him of his court summons. "Had he not threatened to revenge himself on the village?" Seyers replied:

The farmers wanted to make him by force into a thief, and he wanted to give them something to think about. And besides, when he was nightwatchman, the sheriff read the regulations to him about how nightwatchmen must now pay attention that farmers not thresh by candlelight, nor do flax-work, and that he should report such actions. For the king had severely forbidden such things, and he wanted to report them to the sheriff.[114]

Seyers told Hasse his story, adding – as extenuating circumstance – that "the farmers" had "torn up his mattress." But Hasse concluded Seyers and wife had stolen "much fruit and then carried it away from here." They also "manifestly seduced the young people [into absconding] and carried their things off, and also engaged in suspicious talk" of fire. Farmer Zeggel, his wife, and daughter would suffer penalties on Kleist's return for collusion in absconding. Hasse delivered the Seyers

---

[114] Ibid.

couple to Karstedt's court for sentencing. It ordered "the fellow" and "the woman" harshly punished with eight days' (early October) imprisonment in neck-irons for theft and concealing runaways and their booty, menacingly promising to torment the absconders "as severely as lies in its power."

Here were villagers abetting runaways, some sharing in their seigneurial loot. One cultivator, still on his land three years later, admitted a fugitive to his house. A rare glimpse emerges of "the farmers'" struggle to defend their possessions – here, gardens and orchards – from nocturnal thieves of landless status. The lordships' courts visited harsh punishment on two elderly miscreants, partly as scapegoats for absconded youths. Old Caspar Seyers gained nothing appealing to his former humble public servant's role, invoking the king's will and authority while denying – probably mendaciously – his embittered threat against "the farmers" of fiery revenge.

The proximity of Mecklenburg's ill-guarded and porous border worked against Stavenow's arrest and prosecution of mobile lawbreakers. They readily fled Brandenburg-Prussia, especially since the two neighboring states competed for immigrants to boost their populations and were loath to extradite minor lawbreakers to the scene of their misdeeds. Sometimes veritable border raids occurred, such as one led in 1731 by resolute widow Margarete Bühring, "who lives here [at Stavenow] in the cottage."[115] She was the Mesekow miller's sister-in-law. Her deceased husband had been brother to Mecklenburg estate administrator H. J. Bühring. In court, farmer Porep's wife, in whose house the widow's spouse expired, testified that Margarete "lamented greatly before [her husband] died, and demanded money. First he answered that he had nothing, but later he told his wife he had 100 talers in his brother's keeping." She should, the dying man said, take it "and buy bread for the children."

Bühring in Mecklenburg later charged his widowed sister-in-law with stealing a valuable horse and selling it in Perleberg, and suspected her in the loss of a cow, allegedly "slaughtered at the [Stavenow] tavern." Margarete admitted taking the horse, saying it was the only way to fully get the inheritance – 100 talers, an ox, a horse, and a foal – the administrator wrongly withheld from his brother. This the plaintiff denied, conceding only keeping some pigs his brother put into forage on his estate as recompense for his brother's

[115] No. 591, fos. 33–6, 48–50.

burial expenses. Hasse's mediation led the Mecklenburger to grant the widow the horse, though her other claims required better documentation.

A year later she wrote Hasse, saying that in response to her further efforts to gain her husband's inheritance, Bühring cursed her "with the most insulting words, so then I had to be on my guard." He was, she claimed, also holding another deceased brother's legacy, in which she "as a poor widow along with my many orphans would have liked to participate." Petitioning her brother-in-law's arrest, she signed as "a poor and abandoned, unhappy widow." But Bühring was now charging her with stealing, together with her daughter and son-in-law, soldier Heinrich Fröstel, 444 sheep. They allegedly beat his shepherd, forcing him to accompany them across the border, where they allowed him to sort out his own from Bühring's sheep and depart. Two other soldiers were their accomplices, one on horseback "who wore a long overcoat with deep pockets and whose hair was bound together on top and loose below, and who otherwise was not of strong constitution, but had very swollen cheeks." Bühring's shepherd Zecker, "some thirty years old," identified Fröstel and two other "Brandenburg soldiers" as the thieves, while "the old Bühring woman" and her daughter drove the sheep. Administrator Bühring said he followed Fröstel and demanded his sheep back, but Fröstel

kept totally still and [Bühring] well saw that things weren't right with him. Fröstel then insulted him most vilely, threatening to beat him and shoot him dead. And he called to the women [accompanying Bühring] and bared his hindside to them.

On Margarete's behalf her kinsman-in-law Christian Wiese took her claims to Bühring. But he called Wiese a "swine" and set a soldier on him, who "beat him to pieces with a thick Spanish cane on arms, back, and body, and also knocked a few holes in his head, so he had to engage a Lenzen barber-surgeon to cure him." The case's outcome is unknown, but it illustrates the violent, lawless, and insolent character of many Prussian soldiers – again casting doubt on the social militarization thesis. It shows how a middle-aged widow, failing to gain satisfaction in Mecklenburg courts, could commit serious thefts to gain a disputed inheritance. Probably because of her connections to local notables, Hasse treated her with forbearance, though perhaps her son-in-law the soldier, if not she herself, paid heavily for her high-handedness.

Livestock theft was a rare peacetime occurrence, but high horse prices during the Seven Years War spurred thieves to action. In 1760 Hasse wrote to nearby Mecklenburg lordship Jessenitz on behalf of Blüthen tavernkeeper, widow Ohlert, from whom a thief stole a mare, selling it to Jessenitz's tavernkeeper for 38 talers. The widow's brother, armed with a testimonial from Blüthen's pastor, located the horse, but could not recover it. Hasse appealed to Jessenitz's noble proprietor, saying his innkeeper bought the stolen horse for a "derisory price" and should be punished. "For if there were no such buyers, the godless horse thefts couldn't get so disgustingly out of hand." Two Stavenowers who could testify to the widow's loss delivered Hasse's letter. One aimed to search for another horse, robbed from his brother and sold in Mecklenburg. Hasse also wrote to nearby Mecklenburg's Eldena, where a horse stolen from once-turbulent soldier, now civilian farmer Joachim Nagel, was reportedly sold for 5 talers by a vagabond, who also plundered reins and a saddle from Stavenowers. Hasse again lamented the theft wave, saying "almost no one can feel secure in his property." Eldena lordship replied that Nagel's horse turned up at an inn, but "the tavernkeeper is one of the most prosperous residents here," who would never "stoop" to illegal trafficking. He bought Nagel's horse, now court-impounded, from a knife-dealer to be interrogated upon returning from his rounds. The Kleists could be confident of Mecklenburg justice.[116]

Perhaps so. In 1785 Stavenow sub-bailiff Grotian wrote Mecklenburg princely officials that a thief they sought, Germer, was under lock and key, along with two horses he allegedly stole from a Mecklenburg farmer, and was available for extradition, which followed. The delinquent was "a fellow about fifty years old of haggard, tall stature." When arrested he carried, apart from 4 talers cash, various papers, including a petition he submitted to the Prussian king, "purchase deed of the house Germer bought, and the knife with which *Inquisit* cut himself in the hand."[117] Stavenowers observed that Germer was not unknown, the Dargardt wood bailiff having seen him in the tavern and riding along the fields. Another tavernkeeper also reported his presence. Germer's letter to regal Frederick would perhaps make interesting reading. Like widow Bühring, he was, seemingly, someone with a grievance, though house-ownership positioned him better than her. Evident here is various Stavenowers' cooperation with the court to catch a horse thief.

---

[116] No. 717, fos. 2–6.   [117] No. 719, fos. 65–9; no. 602, fos. 2–3.

Germer's subsequent fate was probably unpleasant, to judge from Hans Heinrich Richter's, whom Stavenow officials arrested in 1769 in possession of magical treasure-hunting paraphernalia and other people's sheep. Richter was the Sargleben blacksmith's elderly but still vigorous, foot-loose brother. He pursued treasure-hunting to repair his fortunes, which sagged after a disabling accident as a youthful journeyman smith. The magical formulas he transcribed from various books invoked benevolent spirits, some Christian and some from the early modern magicians' pantheon, to combat malevolent supernatural guardians of buried treasure. Stavenow's investigation of his excavations found no evidence he was swindling partners, mostly artisans and minor estate officials, and a few village farmers. His dabbling in magic – whose efficacy the enlightened Prussian regime dismissed as superstition – was not a crime. But Richter was an adventurer uninterested in settled life and respectable employment, while the sheep in his hands, despite his explanations, led him to Stavenow's dungeon. After consultation with higher authorities, Kleist delivered him to a military patrol which transported him to Spandau fortress, where perhaps fatally hard labor awaited him.[118]

It was outlaws or the itinerant poor who committed horse theft, since settled folk could not steal each other's livestock with impunity. Horse thieves' testimony illuminates its practitioners' social world, otherwise hard to reach. In 1762 Hasse interrogated arrestee Christoff Schmidt, son of a Wilsnack town shepherd's servant.[119] His mother bore him in nearby Vehlin village, where "she lived with the lodgers." She had, Schmidt said, been "three times impregnated." She was still alive, as was his half-sister, a farm servant, though his soldier half-brother had disappeared. When he was ten years old, "his mother gave him to the farmers, sharing his upbringing's cost, and when he was older" he worked three years for other farmers as a servant-boy.

His soldiering half-brother helped him enlist and they campaigned together in Bohemia. Wounded and captured at the battle of Collin, Schmidt gained release and tried to return to his regiment, walking through Bavaria, the Harz mountains, and Hannover. But then he worked at farm labor before landing in Lenzen, where he "again went on day labor" before becoming an official's servant. When he fell ill in 1761, "he received his dismissal." Recuperating, he lodged with a farmer, then with a nailsmith, and later a linen-weaver. After drinking

---

[118] William W. Hagen, "Glaube und Skepsis eines magischen Schatzgräbers. Ein Fall aus der Prignitz und Mecklenburg aus den 1760er Jahren," in Lubinski et al., 175–86.

[119] No. 600, fos. 1–3, 14.

"a glass of brandy" he stole a horse at a tavern, later buying a saddle "and a black dog's-hide blanket" in Mecklenburg. In Wilsnack he tried to sell the horse to a Jewish buyer, but when they disagreed on price, he sold it to an estate bailiff for 82 talers. He also bought a watch from a Mecklenburg soldier and sold it to a Jew, perhaps the same one, for "8 groschen profit."

Stopping at Glövzin inn, he fell sick with "great side-pain," lasting ten weeks. Thinking he would die, he asked Pastor Carsted for the Holy Sacrament, handsomely paying him 6 talers and also giving him 5 talers "for the poor" – a rare instance of generous almsgiving. Schmidt also paid doctor Gutike 9 talers for treatment and medicines, plus 7.5 talers to the apothecary, 3.5 talers to the barber-surgeon, and 7 groschen for bleeding. "The woman he met in the inn with her children he hadn't known previously, and paid her 1 taler weekly for her ministrations, [or] altogether 10 talers." After recovering, he bought a farmer's 8-taler horse and gig, but then sold it and traveled on foot. He stole another horse from a tavern and sold it in Lenzen, where he "served a butcher" for six months. He worked with a partner as thresher and harvester. The year 1761 he spent employed at Lenzen army magazine. His cash, in a money belt, was almost gone. Changing money in Perleberg "with the Jews," he acquired "4 Saxon Pistolettes." Returning to his farmhouse lodgings, he again fell ill, and then was arrested. Anna Marie Kleiden, the thirty-seven-year-old widow of a Prussian soldier who died in battle in 1758, tended Schmidt at Glövzin inn. Of her three children she said she wanted to send one to a married sister, another to a married sister-in-law, and keep the third.

This was the world of the landless laboring, soldiering, and mothering class, in which horse-theft with its seemingly easy profits tempted the rootless and desperate. Poor and semi-orphaned children were surrendered "to the farmers." Like treasure-hunting Richter, Schmidt moved from job to job, kept solvent by occasional livestock thefts into which Richter too was, seemingly, finally tempted. It is a picture of a segment of the poor that still persists today. Absconding described a different pattern, in which occupants of settled and respectable, potentially productive farmsteads stole away into lives resembling Schmidt's and Richter's. Exemplary was the aforementioned free mayor Schloh, whose bibulousness and other failings led him to abandon farm and family for disreputable refuge among soldiers.

Laborers, both on manor-farms and village holdings, broke their contracts and ran away. Young men illegally fled to evade military service. But very few Stavenow subject farmers absconded. In 1700–11 a farm stood uncultivated because of its occupant's flight. In 1749, Joachim Mentz, successor on a poor smallholding to his debt-plagued father Erdmann, disappeared. His wife complained that his sister, who for a year had raised their youngest child, carried off the Mentz children's (unspecified) maternal inheritance. Pastor Carsted reported that Mentz left a 20-taler church fund debt, whose annual interest Kleist paid (though he soon found a new tenant who assumed the debt, keeping the farm nineteen years). Such aftermaths were likely when householders fled, especially alone.[120]

Absconding might be temporary, as when in 1747 a smallholder's wife and daughter, accused of stealing six geese from the local blacksmith's wife, "ran far away." Hasse ordered their beds' impoundment pending payment of a 2-taler fine, which probably duly occurred, since their family still held their farm in 1760.[121] But male householders' flights were one-directional and, despite seigneurial efforts, punishment-free. During Blüthen "equalization," three fullholders absconded. In 1723–4, Heinrich Lent junior disappeared, followed by his father, who left retirement to run the farm his son "shamefully abandoned." They "hauled off" such livestock and goods as were transportable, leaving the holding "fully ruined," in debt and devastation. As we saw, the lordship interrogated and punished young Lent for wood theft, at which time he spoke of his neighbors' hatred of him.[122]

In 1726, Blüthen mayor Jacob Meyer, in debt and under fire from neighbors because of the equalization controversy, absconded. Following his flight, new mayor Kniepenberg found the farm "completely devastated." He slaughtered one of the cows Meyer left behind "because he found nothing on the holding to live from."[123] Apart from Mentz's 1749 disappearance, subsequent records speak of no other farmers' flight, though some suffered eviction for debt. Probably deterioration of relations with village neighbors, rather than debt alone, triggered the Lents' and Meyer's departure. But these events ignited Colonel Kleist's wrath. He wrote, indignantly and threateningly, to a Mecklenburg ducal estate manager, quaintly entitled "kitchenmaster," saying the Lents had "secretly run away" with all farm stock, including two unpaid-for oxen tenant-farmer Meyer gave them. They found refuge in Mecklenburg's Brunow village, followed by fugitive mayor Meyer, who "likewise took everything away." Worse still, wrote Kleist:

[120] No. 326, fo. 157; no. 640; no. 358, fos. 53–4. [121] No. 326, fo. 139.
[122] No. 200, fos. 9–10. [123] No. 240; no. 200, fos. 18, 64.

the [Brunow] farmers fetched these faithless subjects away, even transporting Meyer from his farm with five wagons, and later collecting his sheep from the pasture. This outrage is all the greater because [Brunow] farm servants help carry out such raiding and robbery in this land with weapons in hand. And now mayor Meyer is reportedly working at day labor in Grabow. It is impossible that this village should get away with this violent outrage.

To "get behind the truth of the matter, recover the farm stock robbed from me, [and] punish the evil-doers as they deserve," Kleist demanded immediate arrest of the absconders, "who are staying together in Brunow with Lent's kinfolk."

Since this is a matter of utmost consequence, I would not wish to doubt that legal compliance will occur, so that I shall not have to take reprisals against this village for its raid and ask His Royal Majesty to issue requisite orders to the nearest Regiment.

To this warlike threat, non-noble Mecklenburg official Warnecke replied coolly and pleasantly that he would devote "all possible diligence to investigating [the Lents'] whereabouts" and to arresting them and Meyer. But the absconders moved, leaving Kleist with knowledge alone that Meyer was later seen near Grabow, where he sold his animals to a farmer and bought a horse. He was, it was rumored, headed for Swedish Pomerania. The Brunowers denied they assisted Meyer's flight.[124] Kleist could only issue a 1727 announcement saying that "after Jacob Meyer . . . together with his family maliciously ran away from the farm he occupied, leaving it encumbered with many debts," new mayoral candidates, and Meyer's creditors, should assemble at Stavenow.[125] Kleist's vision of armed Mecklenburg villagers invading Brandenburg to assist runaway farmers reveals an awareness both aggressive and fearful of villagers' disposition to reject seigneurial authority. Seemingly he sensed that Mecklenburg officials, despite protestations, would not apprehend his subjects, who – they perhaps hoped – would contribute to their underpopulated land's economy and fisc.

STAVENOW'S HARBORING OF RUNAWAY SERFS FROM MECKLENBURG

Long after the Thirty Years War, east-Elbian principalities competed for immigrants. They preferred free and unencumbered settlers, properly released from previous jurisdictions. But the lure of farmer-colonists'

---

[124] No. 712, fos. 178–83.　　[125] No. 691.

good tenures and favorable rents attracted disadvantaged and disaffected villagers, especially those living under personal serfdom (*Leibeigenschaft*), existing (alongside freer statuses) in some northeastern, southeastern, and trans-Oder Brandenburg districts, in Prussian and Swedish Pomerania, Holstein, Mecklenburg, and farther east. Yet princely or seigneurial interest counseled against penniless settlers. Usually only immigrants arriving with startup capital could hope to gain colonists' farms. Such conditions impeded massive absconding of legally hobbled villagers to lands of freer tenures. Yet along the Mecklenburg–Brandenburg border, flight with livestock and other farm capital was, if risky, not impossible. The question arose how Prussian authorities should handle successful border crossings of Mecklenburg serfs whom Brandenburg landlords wanted to accept as subject farmers. Early in his reign Frederick II pronounced personal serfdom an affront to humanity, ordering that runaway serfs should be protected.[126]

Compensating absconders' lordships for losses remained a thorny issue unresolved by Frederick's enlightened principles, nor did local officials and landlords always esteem them, loath though they were to provoke royal ire. In 1743 Stavenow farmer-soldier musketeer Reinecke, drafted into war, arranged that Joachim Botz, a runaway Mecklenburg serf, cultivate the farm he had inherited. Mecklenburg officials demanded Botz's extradition of Perleberg's magistrature, seemingly because he first settled there after fleeing. Unwisely, the town fathers arrested Botz, prompting Reinecke to protest to the crown. Orders from Berlin informed the magistrates their actions were "very displeasing" to the king. "Farm servant Botz" was to be immediately freed, on pain of "heavy punishment" and "highest royal disfavor." Botz's "reclamation" (extradition) was forbidden "because it violates the king's sovereignty and the land's prerogatives." Here the bourgeoisie failed to play the role, assigned them by liberal theory, of championing runaway serfs, colluding instead, seemingly against their own interests, in their capture.[127]

Frederick II's "populationist" zeal required the Kleists to settle their new Dargardt village with immigrant farmers. Predictably, Mecklenburg fugitives appeared. In 1755 Conrad Kleist wrote nearby Mecklenburg estateowner von Ditten, courteously objecting to Ditten's

---

[126] Stadelmann, ed., *Könige*, vol. II, 14ff, 101ff; Knapp, *Bauernbefreiung*, 49ff; Otto Hintze, "Zur Agrarpolitik Friedrichs des Grossen," *Forschungen zur brandenburgischen und Preussischen Geschichte* 10 (1898): 275–309.

[127] No. 714, fo. 65.

hunter's seizure of horses and wagon of fullholder Joachim Kuhpass, whom the Kleists had settled in Dargardt. Kuhpass had driven to Mecklenburg to buy straw, but Ditten claimed him as a runaway serf. Kleist wrote:

Among 14 Mecklenburgers living here only two serfs, so far as I know after making precise inquiries, have landed unwelcome on our doorstep – namely Peters and Matthaus, both of whom I heartily wish and have every intention to extradite once I obtain a royal cabinet order permitting it. This I have written to both their lordships.

Kuhpass would swear an oath, Kleist told Ditten, that "he was released cost-free from personal serfdom at your own blessed brother-in-law's verbal behest when [the latter's] sickness was worsening." From his parental farm Kuhpass received, "apart from the usual gift of a half-barrel of wedding beer, not three-pence."

Conrad wrote nearby Mecklenburg estateowner von Jahn, Ditten's neighbor, expressing confidence based on long friendship that Jahn "would rather be inclined to mediate a beneficent peace between [Ditten's estate] Werle and Stavenow than see actual war break out, particularly as such conflicts are, among us as close neighbors and people of rank [*vom Stande*], unusual." Of luring away illegal emigrants, Kleist said that "in settling our Mecklenburgers I always guarded myself as much as possible against such unjust dealings." He wanted to avoid lawsuits, which are, "as the proverb says, irksome at best," adding jovially that "the melon seeds I recently sent you" – signs of gentlemen farmers' innovations – "will not, I hope, impede your mediation or seem suspect."

The aggrieved Ditten wrote that, since his hunter was unable to seize Kuhpass's person, he took the horses and wagon. Kuhpass "secretively and undutifully fled." If arrested, he would have deserved "imprisonment in Dömitz fortress," while law allowed Ditten to keep Kuhpass's horses and wagon. But "should aforementioned Kuhpass pay 20 talers for release, he will gain both horses and wagon and complete liberation from subjection [*Unterthanenschaft*], with the usual release certificate." Kleist replied that Kuhpass, even when Ditten's hunter confronted him, had not changed his story or withdrawn his unfulfilled demands on his parental farm. But Kleist, according to Ditten's word precedence over Kuhpass's oath, offered his neighbor 10 talers, "following the fashion now spreading everywhere," – referring to Frederick II's judicial reforms – "to cut controversy short instead of burdening it with a lot of pro's and contra's on my part and Kuhpass's." Sweetening his offer, Kleist added that "the unpaid balance on the higher price you asked I defer on credit until coming autumn when I will discharge it with a half-hundredweight of carp." Kleist apologized on his and his mother's part for "unwittingly and unwillingly, in this one case alone, injuring our friendship."

Ditten accepted, asking only that "the now freed man avoid frequent visits" to former Mecklenburg haunts. Ditten wanted Kleist to impress this on Kuhpass, so that, as he delicately put it, "the unpleasant consequences that are to be feared from the tempting effect" – of liberated, favorably tenured Kuhpass's presence among enserfed former neighbors – "might be avoided."[128] This episode reveals the awareness of noble landlords living along the Brandenburg–Mecklenburg frontier of their interlocking interests. Conrad Kleist affected to care more for the landed nobility's solidarity than enlightened government, though he valued Kuhpass enough to buy him free of his landlord. The incident also shows how the personal serfdom Mecklenburg's nobility fastened on many subjects weakened dealings with Brandenburg colleagues, who could reckon on heavier runaway flow in their direction.

Conrad Kleist, asserting seigneurial independence, settled Kuhpass's case without recourse to Judge Hasse or royal regime. But in the one other instance in which Stavenow harbored a contested Mecklenburg runaway, Prussian officials played a crucial, if ambiguous, role. The affair began in 1753, when Mecklenburg estateowner Captain von Koppelau at Möllenbeck angrily wrote Conrad that "tonight one of my subjects named Ernst Madaush [Maddaus] secretively and knavishly broke his oath and with livestock and chattels ran away." Should the fugitive enter Kleist's jurisdiction, Koppelau requested he "be detained as a thief" to prevent "the scoundrel" from selling anything, "since I want to recover my stolen goods": nine horses, four cattle, two wagons, and the rest of "what belongs to a farmer's enterprise." Koppelau darkly demanded the escapee's extradition "so that I might have the opportunity to administer justice upon a perjurer and thief."[129]

Koppelau also wrote Frederick II, invoking the king's "world-renowned love of justice," which would move his majesty to "disapprove" Maddaus' flight "together with wife and children, also maid-servant, all my subjects in personal serfdom [*leibeigene Untertanen*]." These were terms whose harshness Ditten delicately refrained from applying to absconded Kuhpass. Maddaus "threshed all his grain and took it with him," along with livestock and other movables, "which are any estateowner's

---

[128] No. 716, fos. 93, 95, 107–8.   [129] No. 715, fos. 348–9.

property." Stavenow was now shielding the fugitive, appealing to royal policy. But Koppelau believed Frederick would not find Maddaus worthy of "protection."

The Brandenburg War and Domains Board informed Frau Kleist the king's cabinet had entrusted Koppelau's claims to it. "In our opinion, Your Highborn Grace will do well, should alleged circumstances obtain, to seek to silence the supplicant's complaint by return at least of purloined farm stock and grain." Later the Board retreated. Since it had no specific royal instructions, "we wish also to command nothing, but only express our opinion, especially since in other cases His Royal Majesty has gone so far as to charge the Board with extraditing both such subjects' persons and the inventory they hold by theft." The Board therefore "wishes to leave everything to Frau Colonel's own consideration and disposition." Conrad wrote privately to a government colleague, seeking advice while citing the 1743 Perleberg "*casu paralleli.*" His correspondent concluded from the crown's exchange with Koppelau "that it is not the king's intention that Maddaus should be extradited." If Maddaus knew he was to be arrested and deported, he would "disappear into the dust." Kleist should therefore pressure Maddaus to pay Koppelau 10 talers for a release certificate.[130]

Koppelau gathered testimony about Maddaus's flight from Adam Platt, the fugitive's seventy-six-year-old father-in-law, whom Maddaus succeeded on his farm, and from the runaway's brother-in-law and half-brother's son, both Koppelau farmers. Old Adam averred that Maddaus took six good horses with harnesses, wagons, harrows, two good plows, and "everything else a farmer must have for his trade, in good condition, plus seed- and bread-grain along with all garden vegetables." He also took three horses and five cattle "but these were his own." If true, Maddaus was both an enterprising farmer and an intrepid absconder. Koppelau sent this testimony to Frau Kleist, whom he also asked, seemingly in vain, for a personal hearing in Stavenow's court. He was, he said, following Frederick's instructions, who in November 1754 wrote Koppelau with characteristic stringency, saying:

Since you know where the fellow [*Kerl*] is, you must proceed against him through the court there and so settle the matter with him legally. For you can well conceive that I cannot allow his extradition on the basis of your one-sided representations without hearing the man [*Menschen*] and his counter-explanations. I remain your well-affectioned etc.

[130] No. 716, fos. 6–7, 12, 92.

Conrad wrote Koppelau several friendly letters. Of Maddaus he wrote:

Because of his great and constant fear of extradition back to Mecklenburg I don't much trust him not to abscond again. But I've talked sharply enough to him that he now wants, in exchange for a binding release certificate, to give three good horses and 10 Reichstalers for himself and his dependants.

This was "the surest and shortest way to attain public satisfaction with greatest deterrent effect on your other subjects." Kleist invoked Ditten's example, who "was paid 10 Reichtalers for a certificate of freedom [*Frey-Schein*] by a colonist here named Kuhpass, who claimed to have been verbally released from serfdom by [Ditten's] departed brother-in-law, and served for some twelve years as coachman in Hamburg." Kleist insisted there were but two fugitives among Dargardt colonists, including Maddaus. The "vexation and troubles" their unwitting acceptance as colonists occasioned "we would have wished to spare both you and ourselves."

Nearly two years after Maddaus's flight, Conrad Kleist wrote Koppelau that he had sought intervention by the royal Commission of Colonist-Settlement, at work nearby. It too disclaimed jurisdiction, recommending before extradition "a full court hearing of Maddaus's counter-position" for forwarding to the Criminal Tribunal and the king's final decision. After conjuring up such formidable legal obstacles, Kleist again proposed private settlement, referring misleadingly to "the absence of our judge, who lives ten miles away and also is not a native to these parts." Again, the Brandenburg nobleman preferred dealing directly with his Mecklenburg counterparts, excluding his otherwise esteemed bourgeois justiciar. Kleist himself had heard Maddaus's story: "I spoke straight to his conscience, that he should either go back or properly settle with [you]." Maddaus rejected Mecklenburg testimony against him, saying "he mainly fled because of the vexations his father-in-law caused him, and excessive labor service demands." Maddaus denounced his brother-in-law, saying "he got the farm [Maddaus] abandoned, and exaggerated stock removed to his own advantage. Moreover the maidservant went back."[131]

In 1756, countering Koppelau's charges, Maddaus told Hasse's court that "Adam Platt was indeed his father-in-law, but [Platt] stood in greatest conflict . . . and was at odds with him in everything, just so he could get his son Adam Reimar Platt on the farm and drive him [Maddaus]

[131] Ibid., fos. 91–2.

away." The horses he got with the farm were so old they ate only bread, were of little use, and then died. "And because his father-in-law was so hostile to him, and because Herr Captain [Koppelau] took away his farmhand and gave him to [Koppelau's] brother-in-law Herr von Plothow, he had to go away, because he couldn't work alone." Maddaus detailed the defects of other farm stock he received, denying he had taken seed or grain. He paid 10 talers' farm debt, as he could document. "The barley he threshed the first year he devoted to his father-in-law's children, clothing them with [its proceeds] and buying bread-grain and malt." He spent more on the farm than he carried off, and therefore rejected Koppelau's claims.

In a last salvo, Conrad informed the War and Domains Board he had consulted District Commissioner Grävenitz, but he too evaded a firm stand. Seemingly exasperated, Kleist wrote: "I would have no reservations or the least sense of guilt in immediately extraditing aforementioned Maddaus, with all his boorishness [*Grobseeligkeit*]." But this appeared to contradict royal policy. If Maddaus's property were given to Koppelau, he couldn't run even a "small farm" at Stavenow, and so would be beggared and burden the land. Referring delicately to Maddaus's support among fellow villagers, Kleist warned that extradition without "military backing" was inadvisable. Official decision was essential, for another Mecklenburg landlord had petitioned to recover another Dargardt colonist (Peters) as an alleged runaway serf.[132]

Here the record ends. Like Kuhpass, both Maddaus and Peters remained on their Dargardt farms, suggesting the Mecklenburg lordships settled for 10 talers and whatever more their faithless subjects surrendered. Conrad's views lie partially hidden behind diplomatic veils. Probably he did regret settling the fugitives, while his scorn for Maddaus's alleged low-mindedness was doubtless genuine. Yet the thought occurred to him fleetingly (though he repudiated it) that guilt might flow from returning runaways to such vengeful landlords as Koppelau. Stavenow was facing communal rent resistance from the Dargardters which the runaways' deportation would only have stiffened. Prussian officialdom's stand on extradition was strikingly noncommittal, but Conrad clearly wished to avoid such disfavor as Frederick threatened to shower on the Perleberg magistrates.

Still, the king's letter to Koppelau, displaying his own rough composition and gruff address, is unequivocally opposed to pro-landlord

---

[132] Ibid., fos. 193–4, 242–3.

partisanship in fugitive controversies. Maddaus, like Kuhpass, humble runaways though they were, received court hearings helping them justify flight and resettlement in Prussia. Seemingly, mercurial Frederick usually was adamant in protecting fugitives (who populated his land), while his officials and landed nobility (including the very royalist Kleists) wavered between compliance with their feared sovereign's wishes and desire to avoid litigation and social rifts with their Mecklenburg neighbors. It seems suggestive of Junker yearnings to silence subaltern troublemakers that the urbane civilian Conrad in 1759 entertained the idea of military coercion of the villages, just as his soldierly father did in 1726. But perhaps Conrad was subtly signaling the government that, in the midst of the Seven Years War, deploying troops to expel Mecklenburg colonists was self-defeating.

POLICING THE MORAL ORDER: EXTRA- AND PREMARITAL PREGNANCIES

In twenty-four cases, records survive of Stavenow villagers charged for acts of illicit sexuality. In ten of these, premarital pregnancy occurred, but the erring couples were prepared to marry. In nine cases, the man the pregnant woman identified as the future child's father denied the charge, or disappeared. The remaining cases concerned adultery and incest.

These litigations illuminate official attitudes toward sexual transgressions and villagers' values and behavior in this realm. At issue were the institutions of marriage and family, and property rights. Questions of poor-relief could also arise. To this subject historians have applied the social discipline theory, emphasizing religious, political, and social elites' imposition on the common people of a morality of puritanical self-control and abstention from sex before marriage. Though recognizing certain Rabelaisian traits among ordinary people, especially on holidays, historians tend to think that material and physiological circumstances – such as cramped quarters and diseases – conspired with psychological repression, in part church-induced, and with male authoritarianism to limit positive expressions of sexuality among ordinary people. Especially the upright and God-fearing among villagers, bowing to higher authority, might seem to have held such attitudes, unlike more easy-going householders, or the desperate and defiant poor.[133]

---

[133] Gleixner, *"Das Mensch"*; literature cited in the introduction and chapter 3 on social disciplinization and popular culture; Christiansen, *A Manorial World*.

Certainly Judge Hasse took a dim view of sexual delicts. Yet his rulings were often pragmatic and even helpful to embarrassed defendants, often in need of mediation to channel and resolve their conflicts. Although sometimes the court, spurred by local pastors' or seigneurial officials' denunciations, sought out sexual transgressors, rumors often triggered its intervention. Doubtless one of village rumor's functions was to provoke investigation, so that injuries to the moral order might be repaired. Thus in 1729 Hasse wrote that "after it was heard that Grete Ebels mingled in dishonor with Hans Reinecke," he summoned her.

She immediately admitted it, saying it happened six weeks before Michaelmas. But she added it pains her heart [*Hertzen Leyd*], and she would be glad if it hadn't happened. She wants to cover over with marriage the indecency she committed, and has arranged for banns to be posted tomorrow, and requests a marriage license.

After hearing her partner Reinecke's assent, Hasse halved the usual heavy fine – from 10 to 5 talers for men and from 5 to 2.5 talers for women – and issued the license. The pastor could, he added, be brought to accept the hastily publicized banns and marriage. But, unfortunately, this happy ending failed to occur. Grete was a 17–18-year-old fullholder's non-inheriting daughter, entitled to no more from her farm than wedding-party provisions. Farmhand Reinecke must have backed out, for in 1740 Grete was home, tending her retired father and still, as her brother-in-law and household head unfeelingly complained, unmarried. She had failed, through rushed marriage, to neutralize her "dishonor" and "indecency."[134]

In 1730 "the rumor rang out" that Anna Tostorffen, a farmer's maidservant, was pregnant. She confessed, saying the father was seigneurial farmhand Muchow. "Her time" came two weeks before Whitsuntide, but two weeks later she missed it. Meanwhile Muchow "had to do with her." Muchow granted "he had to do with the person after Whitsuntide, when Herr bailiff gave him beer, and he left his bed to go to her on fast-night [*Fesselabend*] but she also left her bed to come to him. Although he was so drunk he couldn't have done anything to her, he wanted to take her."

Well-known linguistic codes were here in play. The pejorative term "the person" (*das Mensch*) morally devalued the woman, as did the claim she had come to him, while absolving the man of suspicion of overpowering or raping his partner. Drunkenness likewise mitigated the

---

[134] No. 200, fo. 117; no. 712, fos. 44–5; no. 591, fos. 93–4.

offense, or even cast its performance in doubt. Again, despite the "wrong" of their "indecency," Hasse halved the fines, "if they would, as they requested, marry," while for "improvement and true [Christian] conversion" he remanded them to the pastor. Whether this union succeeded is unknown, for both parties disappear. Anna's relations with her employer were tense. Soon after impregnation, she petitioned release from her service contract, saying her master falsely accused her of plum theft, but Hasse ruled she must serve out her year. Muchow descended from a family that once held a farm. Conceivably they settled down as married lodgers.[135] Similarly, as we saw, in 1733 Hasse summoned Grete Häwecken, who stood "in repute to be pregnant." The child's soldier-thresher father proposed marriage, and perhaps, if he obtained army discharge, it occurred.[136]

Marriage could mitigate premarital sex's sinfulness, but still it was punishable. Hearing that village cowherd Theis and his wife, a nearby cowherd's daughter, recently christened a child though only married six months, Hasse summoned him. The cowherd conceded "he impregnated his wife, which he wanted to excuse by saying she was already his engaged bride. But that this is unsatisfactory was made clear to him" by imposing 7.5 talers' fine, payable in cash or labor. He chose labor, "and promised betterment."[137] Theis's belief that engaged couples could rightly have sexual relations was old, deep-rooted, and long combated by European churches.

The misery and desperation that pregnancy without subsequent marriage could elicit in women appear in the 1733 case of seigneurial servant-girls Marie Schütten and Vey Ebels. Marie was pregnant by Claus Ewert, who promised marriage. But Vey claimed Marie also slept with "stable-boy Christoffel."

Vey Ebels alleges in person that she lay in the cabin with Marie Schütten, and Christoffel came and lay down between them, and after he had done it with Marie, [Marie] said that he should now do with Vey what he'd done with Marie. At this, she [Vey] sprang up and ran out of the cabin. And what she now said she would always maintain. [But] if Marie hadn't held her foolishness against her, that she [Vey] was going to have a baby, she wouldn't have said anything against her.

Hasse found Vey's accusations false and injurious, expressing retroactive "enmity" against Marie. He sentenced her to one hour in the fiddle, and to shake hands with Marie and absolve her of the charges.[138]

---

[135] No. 200, fos. 142, 145.   [136] No. 326, fo. 39.   [137] No. 591, fo. 45.   [138] No. 200, fos. 59–60.

While maligned Marie duly married her child's father Claus, it was not until later that fullholder's son Jürgen Seyer admitted his paternity of tale-telling Vey's child. But he would not marry her, agreeing only – if she dropped further claims – to pay her 2 talers now and 10 talers next Easter.[139] On her fate the record is silent. In 1738, a certain Jochen Seyer quarreled with Marie and Claus, breaking Marie's arm. Hasse fined him 2 talers for her "loss" and 4 talers payable a herdsman for "medical fees." Quarrels were not new to Marie. When in seigneurial service, she accused Hans Milatz's daughter of theft of manorial textiles, a charge she was obliged to retract publicly.[140]

Carpenter-innkeeper Künstel's above-discussed case showed that harsh denials of paternity did not prevent eventual acceptance of marriage, however much such conflicts cooled the couple's ardor. A farm heir's marriage to an impregnated woman who did not please his parents could portend family trouble, as with ill-fated foreman Seyer, who (as we saw) died falling from a tree, leaving a widow on his farm mightily resented by his mother and sister. And, among couples guilty of premarital intercourse but wishing to marry, there were men under arms or draftable into military service who could not obtain marriage licenses. The court might show considerable forbearance, as it did in 1745 toward Heinrich Fischer, who two years earlier impregnated Eva Seyers, a twenty-eight-year-old retiring farmer's daughter and eldest child. Because "he was still not free of the soldiers," Heinrich had not married Eva, despite his promise. Meanwhile, Hasse ordered him to pay her 2 talers yearly in child support, and 1 taler to her father, who was keeping mother and child in his retirement quarters. Fischer resigned his and his "fiancée" Eva's claim on farm inheritance, leaving it to Eva's newly married sister. To "insure his marriage promise," Fischer gave her father two steers, doubtless inherited from his parental farm, to be grazed for her. Here, among landed households' children, Hasse refrained from punitiveness, though Eva lost succession to a good fullholding.[141]

Unhappier was Heinrich Fischer's sister, Anne Liese, pregnant in 1741 by farmer's son Joachim Hecht, who then was drafted into war. At home on leave, Joachim conceded he and Anna Liese had been "engaged, but then she rejected him, and not he her, so he wanted cancellation of his obligation to her." She, supported by her retired father, said they had been long engaged when, "nine weeks before [spring]

---

[139] No. 326, fo. 39.   [140] No. 591, fo. 81.   [141] No. 664, fos. 1–6.

Perleberg market, they knew each other carnally, which led to a little boy's birth at Perleberg fall market time." She demanded child support, but he claimed "she had taken another bridegroom," farmer Koltzer's farmhand, "so he could well seek another bride." "The court's persuasion" produced a support agreement. Hecht later admitted "having proceeded with her outside marriage." He "wanted to marry her and take her on his father's farm, if he can only get free of the soldiers." Hasse would discuss this with the "gracious lordship," but the couple then vanishes from record. Possibly Hecht died under arms.[142]

Luckier, if not happier, was mayor's son Joachim Nagel, combatant in the bloody 1747 wedding fight. In 1742 he admitted to fathering two extramarital children with Trine Hechten. Nagel proposed marriage, asking "to be helped get free." Hasse sternly imposed two halves of a 15-taler "whoring fine," but agreed to petition the District Commissioner for a discharge. Joachim's 1747 wife was, seemingly, Trine, but neither she nor their two children long survived. Following his contentious 1750 farm inheritance, Joachim remarried.[143]

Despite its coercive and persuasive powers, the court could not compel all single fathers to marry the mothers. The pregnant women, if without hope of marriage, sought child-support payments, but their former partners in intimacy could be harsh and heartless. Marie Wittings, a nineteen-year-old seigneurial maidservant, charged Caspar Schultzen, a twenty-six-year-old manorial farmhand and non-inheriting halfholder's son, with fathering her child, born four weeks before Christmas 1739. Four weeks before the preceding Easter, she said, he came to her "in the old cottage out there where he leaned her on the grain sacks, and had to do with her three times, namely on fast-day evening and later." He told her "it can't harm her, and she should just tell him" if pregnancy followed. Marie added:

On a harvest-time Sunday and again after Michaelmas he came to her in her room, during the sermon, and lay her on her bed. And it was already all over with her, because she well knew she would have his child. But since he had said so many good things to her, she trusted him. And because she had already spent what she had on the child, and it belonged to him as well as her, she asked for child-support payments, or she would have to leave the child at his doorstep.

Caspar sharply rejected her appeal. "She came a good twenty times to him in the stable, meaning to draw him into her indecency," but he resisted. "And when at Whitsuntide they had a quarter beer-barrel at

---

[142] No. 326, fo. 73.   [143] Ibid, fo. 79.

the manor, she came to him at night and lay in his bed." She visited him altogether three times, "but whether he slept with her he didn't know, because he was drunk. And the person gave him no peace." He denied visiting her housing, and "because of his drunkenness he couldn't be held responsible for her child. Her mother said herself that [Marie] whored with the tailor's brother behind the stall, and that [the mother] found the two there, but [the tailor's brother] was now in service in Potsdam."

Marie denied sparking the affair. Her mother said Caspar told the barrel-maker the baby "would have to come on fast-day before Christmas," otherwise "it wouldn't be his." Therefore – presumably because the child was born then – "he was responsible for her daughter's fall." Barrel-maker Henning disclaimed this testimony, but said "this much is true, that he saw defendant [Caspar] one night in late winter coming and going at [plaintiff] Wittings' place. And he asked him where he had been so late, and he answered he was sitting by [her] stove and fell asleep." Hasse sought amicable resolution, but Caspar protested Marie "did him wrong. He wanted to take Holy Communion next day to prove he was innocent." Hasse lectured Marie that she must prove her case better, imposing 5 talers' "whoring penalty" for her "indecency." He warned her to cease "her thoughtless talk of setting out the child on pain of corporal or, if warranted, capital punishment."[144]

Here the court seemingly protected a lifelong seigneurial laborer from a lodger's daughter's claims. Her invocations of innocence and gullibility, and the circumstantial evidence against her antagonist, left Hasse unmoved. Other women's fear of premarital pregnancy's dishonoring effect led them to pursue marriage with hostile men toward whom they harbored no such tender sentiments as Marie expressed for Caspar. Agnese Ebels, a twenty-four-year-old fullholder's daughter and seigneurial maidservant, charged Jürgen Peters, a twenty-year-old male co-worker at Premslin manor, with impregnating her. Peters, like his relative Hans who once threatened to kill tenant-farmer Hartz's livestock, was a rough and penurious character. "He admits that eight days after Michaelmas [he and Agnese] committed their shame in her bed," and if the baby came at a corresponding time, "he would have to suffer accordingly and accept it." Agnese replied that it happened six weeks before Michaelmas. Peters gave a false date "to get out of it, but since

---

[144] No. 591, fos. 89–90; no. 326, fo. 74.

he dishonored [*verunehret*] her," he would have to take her. Peters said, if the baby came at proper time, "he will return her to honor, but otherwise he'll break her arm and her body for trying falsely to give him the child." Agnese threatened, if he would not take her, "to lay the child on his doorstep." Hasse delayed proceedings until the baby's birth, imposing the usual fines and encouraging marriage. Meanwhile, for his talk of violence, Peters "is properly punished with eight days' imprisonment on bread and water." This tough sentence likely reflected apprehension that Peters would act on his threats.

In March 1741 Agnese bore twins. She pleaded that, when first children are girls, they often come "four weeks earlier than usual." Although her case was crumbling, she held to her dates, saying "although Peters often came to woo her [*sie gewitzet*], he only committed his shame with her that one time." In Peters' self-exculpatory view, the babies arrived only thirty weeks after the alleged event. Hasse ruled that, "before taking an oath, Pastor Cober will be asked to sharpen Peters' conscience and impress on him the oath's and his transgression's importance." Six months later, Agnese, protesting she couldn't alone "feed the children," pleaded for "protection and help." Young Peters rejected Hasse's suggestion that he and Agnese seek the Perleberg Consistorial Inspector's mediation. Peters instead wanted each to swear an oath. He was prepared to pay 10 talers so she might "revenge her [lost] honor [*Ehren Rache*]." But "strangers' whore-children he couldn't accept." They quarreled again over timing. She said Peters "sprang into her bed and put out the light, so she wouldn't know who he was." She also claimed he offered her a sack of rye. Hasse decided the Consistory should intervene, though meanwhile Peters, having admitted his "whoring," was ordered "to give her something from good-will for raising the children."[145]

Three years later, Agnese appeared in court, claiming 20 instead of 40 talers' child support (one twin having died). Peters' counter-offer, following his insulting demand she swear "she had not let herself be carnally known by anyone else," was 12 talers. Again "negotiations broke down." But Agnese survived. In 1748 she became a fullholder's second wife, bringing in 30 talers, two cows, and her seven-year-old daughter, whose unpaid 12-taler claim on her recalcitrant father (whose name she bore) figured as a legal asset. Agnese had her own virtues to thank for this fortunate outcome, and her brother, who helped fund her dowry

---

[145] No. 591, fo. 109; no. 326, fos. 70–1.

from their parental farm. Her husband Jürgen Hecht was about forty years old, with two children, including an infant who died after their marriage. At Hecht's 1755 death, Agnese retired at thirty-eight on his economically sound farm.[146]

The belligerent Peters faced 1741 charges of fighting with Dorothea Hellbrings, an artisan's maidservant. He beat and set dogs on her, cursing rudely and saying "now go and tell this to [her employer] the great Meister." Peters admitted only roughing her up for calling him (at Agnese's birthing-time) a "whore's stallion." This reputation rankled Peters, who subsequently disappeared from documentation. Perhaps it tarnished his lineage's standing that Stavenow subject Gertraut Peters, "who let herself be slept with by a Perleberg clothier's apprentice," bore a 1729 "whore-child." While the father wandered off, Gertraut's mother pleaded against fining her, saying several local daughters escaped payment, as had the "shepherds' wenches" recently in the neighborhood. Gertraut and her parents had also recently lost everything in a fire. Hasse relented somewhat, imposing half the fine and leaving Gertraut to petition the lordship to cancel the rest.[147]

Men sometimes forced women into sex and then spurned them, crassly exposing status and power imbalances. Anne Stechen, twenty-seven, charged Stavenow miller's son Joachim Richter, twenty, with "impregnating her two days before [St.] Catherine's market [1744] in Reckenzin while she was milling."

Then he summoned her to Peter Theis's farm, where she should get another one, and when she didn't want to, he struck her with his hand and fist in the face, and with a cane, while the doors and everything were shut so no one could come to her.

She demanded payment and "satisfaction." Richter said contemptuously "he didn't hit her more than twice" with his fist and twice with the cane. He mocked her for disclaiming, even when obviously pregnant, having had "to do with any man [*Mannesmenschen*]." She said "she denied it because her employer would otherwise have chased her away." The court postponed ruling on Richter's liability until the baby's birth, fining him 2 talers for beating her and threatening redoubled penalties for further violence.[148]

Richter succeeded his father as miller, while Anne's fate is unknown. Noteworthy are his arrogance and belligerence, her fear of being fired,

[146] No. 326, fos. 112, 153, 201–2, 205.   [147] No. 591, fo. 114; no. 326, fo. 63; no. 200, fo. 132.
[148] No. 591, fo. 115.

and Hasse's readiness to punish him (mildly) for abusiveness. Similarly, the Mesekow miller's brother-in-law admitted impregnating the miller's maidservant, though the 1727 child born "in dishonor" died. Pastor Cober gained the father's agreement to cover her 5-taler fine, and give her 12 talers for her injury. Because the delinquent still owed her 2 talers, and had not paid his own 10-taler fine, Hasse held miller Arndt responsible.[149]

In another case of forced sex, Hasse asked farmer Schenck whether his maidservant Liese Seyers "had borne a child." "Yes," Schenk replied, "on the fast-day before Christmas [1726]. The person had neither father nor mother." Why did he hire "the person without a certificate?" She had, Schenck said, worked for a neighboring farmer, "though she also had a bad reputation [*bösen Schneck*]." What kind? "Various things were said among servants," and Schenck noticed – one wonders how – that Liese missed "her time." She had lived, Liese said, with parents in Karstädt, "and then they had to come down here [to Stavenow] as lodgers," where they died. She said "she didn't know her age." Seigneurial worker Heinrich Besen, Mesekow mayor's son and future successor, fathered the child. "She didn't want to say anything about it, because she feared he would go away like the others," meaning perhaps like other men facing such charges (or as her other suitors had done).

He first impregnated her at the Banekow pond, and the priest rode by on his way from Stavenow to Blüthen. [Other times followed.] She resisted long enough and finally got tired, and then he overpowered her. He didn't say whether he would give her anything, or whether he would take her.

About her 5-taler fine, she said "she had nothing, and the fellow would have to pay it."

Besen disputed the timing. "They were fetching lumber for the carpenters, [when] he met her sitting in the vegetable garden. She asked him for money." He admitted having to do with her that once, "but not so that he belonged to her." She should divulge the real father's name. "She had whored around so much." Previously "the old Brüning woman saw her lying with the farmhand on the manure [*auf dem Mist*], and one knew who was responsible for that." Because they admitted "indecency," Hasse fined Heinrich 10 talers and ordered that Liese "should suffer the penalty on her body, while both parties are remanded to Herr Preacher for church penance." If she better proved her dating

---

[149] No. 200, fos. 63, 67.

of the incident, "she could expect another ruling concerning the child's provisions."[150]

The case ends here, but Liese soon married fullholder Joachim Ebel. Seventeen years later, quarreling over theft, the mayor's son cursed her as a "whore" and "marriage breaker." A reputation evidently stalked her. But she "wanted to pledge her body and soul" they were innocent of theft, and Hasse dismissed the case for lack of evidence. She died three years later.[151] The story displays many stylized elements of paternity disputes, including male defendants' harsh condemnations of plaintiffs' characters. Liese's charges of physical coercion were also conventionalized, but she may be given the benefit of the doubt. Her lowly status worked against her, especially in the physical punishment – whatever it was (not excluding flogging) – she suffered. Yet she too proved a survivor who found a husband she defended with "body and soul."

Another woman suffering seduction and character defamation was Trine Wöhlckens, twenty-four, a fullholder's sister whom their farm's manservant impregnated in 1725. She admitted he "lay with her shortly before harvest. He came into her house, so she could mend his clothing. They wanted to marry, [but] she didn't know what she had coming from the farm." Hasse debited her 5-taler fine against her dowry. Unfortunately, in 1731 she found herself again pregnant, by the son of Stavenow's brickmaker, who promised marriage. But while his family acknowledged their son's responsibility, "now they stay away." Hasse agreed to help gain her inheritance from her brother.[152]

Trine Wöhlcken's name arose in 1737, when Hasse asked Glövzin mayor Jürgen Nagel why his maidservant (not Trine) had "run away." Nagel said she was pregnant "and didn't want to work any more for him, nor could she." A swineherd's step-daughter, she was "a dissolute person" who accused Nagel's son of seducing her. After leaving Nagel, "she stayed with the whores [*Hurenweiber*] and with Wöhlckens, where she worked last year and where her things were stolen from her." Perhaps unmarried mothers branded as disreputable lived together. But because Nagel let "the person secretively flee," Hasse fixed her fine on him, while summoning his son for "bad behavior during manorial service" and the pregnancy. Next year mayor Nagel's brother Christian denied maidservant Grete Preissen's claim he impregnated her while

---

[150] Ibid., fos. 62–3.   [151] Ibid., fos. 125–6; no. 326, fo. 108.
[152] No. 200, fo. 39; no. 326, fo. 40.

his parents were at Perleberg market. Further ox-stall encounters occurred. Later, he took "the little girl" into his bed – a concession, in Grete's view, of paternity. Hasse imposed an oath on him, but the case remained unresolved a year later. Here, seemingly, was another instance of the village oligarchy's sons working their will on servant-girls.[153]

Singular, finally, was a 1751 incident in which an estate foreman's wife from Prignitz's Kyritz town charged retired Mesekow mayor Caspar Ketelhöhn with fathering her before fleeing Mecklenburg to escape army conscription and settling under the Kleists. Allegedly he promised to support her, but never did. He retorted that the woman's mother "was such a dissolute creature [*Nickel*] no man wanted to have her, and that's why she falsely accused him." Hasse accepted Ketelhöhn's testimony, warning the woman to silence her charges.[154]

In these contestations over premarital relations and pregnancy, apart from the Ketelhöhn case, all parties were, unsurprisingly, young people, mostly in service or working on parental farms. Of those whose parentage is known, thirteen were farmers' children with inheritance prospects, while eighteen were progeny of the landless or non-inheriting offspring of smallholders. Another five men bore artisan status. Thus distribution of offenders between landed or craftsman class, on one hand, and landless laboring class, on the other, was equal. In two cases, single mothers married into landed households, but they themselves derived from such families.

Landless laborers did not, then, face premarital pregnancy charges more often than the propertied villagers. Nor, considering that of such cases only nineteen records survive, were they frequent. Probably close demographic analysis would show that many women suffering no legal penalties were pregnant at marriage. Evidently illicit sex was often consensual and pleasurable, if risk-laden. The Kleists remained aloof, leaving Judge Hasse to apply the law, though doubtless he sometimes consulted their wishes. He ruled stringently, but neither inflexibly nor flagrantly favoring men. Although no men unwilling to admit paternity, or to marry, found themselves forced into matrimony, Hasse sentenced many to share costs of extramarital children's upbringing. Compelling recalcitrant men to marry was a likely recipe for disaster. Mothers forfeiting marriage prospects paid a much higher price, but some eventually found husbands and

---

[153] No. 591, fos. 73–4, 78.   [154] No. 715, fo. 41.

others survived as single women to raise their children under
Stavenow lordship.

ADULTERY AND INCEST

Dishonoring and impoverishing though they often were, pregnancies
among unmarried youth were civil, not criminal offenses. As Pastor
Sauerbier's fate showed, adultery was much graver, but – like incest –
rare. Stavenow records present only five such cases, three fragmentarily,
two intact with verdicts from Berlin's Criminal Court (*Criminal-Collegium*).
The latter illuminate Brandenburg-Prussian rural society from many
angles, but the others also repay brief attention. Among these, two deal
with adultery charges against married fullholders. One was Glövzin
mayor Joachim Holtmann, aged thirty-six, whom Anne Meyers in 1751
accused of fathering her eighteen-month-old twins when she was his
maidservant. Three months pregnant, she revealed her plight to
Holtmann's wife, who with her errant husband promised Marie support
if she would maintain she was raped on the road by a non-commissioned
officer – a man of power and authority, though not a nobleman.

This explanation she offered to Pastor Carsted and his successor
Pastor Höpfner when she gave birth. Now Holtmann cut off aid. Anne
Meyers needed child support but, as she knew, the poor-law (*Armen-
Ordnung*) would not confer it should she move to another lordship. She
revealed her plight to Frau Kleist, who evidently encouraged her to
speak out, which she did, charging Holtmann with sleeping with her in
his own "living room and bed" and, later, elsewhere. Of her concocted
rape story, Pastor Carsted said "her tenacity [in professing it] was
remarkable," considering she "spent eight days in labor pains." She
might have died perjured. Mayor Holtmann, condemning her as a
seductress, denied paternity, charging her with other dalliances.
Holtmann's wife said the twins arrived too early to prove her husband's
guilt. Nevertheless, they showed Anne "so much goodness," rooming
and boarding her nearly two years, when she worked very little, that
they now owed nothing more.

Hasse proposed Holtmann provide 4 bushels of rye yearly until the
children reached age ten, or half should one die. From the village poor-
relief fund 1 taler would be paid yearly to house mother and children.
The affair provoked Holtmann's neighbors to fine him 1 taler in the
village assembly. Their "reproaches" led Hasse to order him to find a
replacement in the mayoral office or manager Erhardt would do so.

Holtmann's wife expressed forgiveness for his "transgression," fearing she and her five children would "suffer for it." Hasse ordered Anne Meyers and her "two adulterous children" removed to non-Stavenow village housing. Skies darkened over Holtmann as Hasse announced the Berlin Criminal Court's opinion would be sought. Whatever his punishment, he survived the storm, occupying again in 1760 the mayoral office and farm.[155]

Holtmann was lucky his parsimony, in refusing Anne Meyers further aid, did not cost him more. In this rare instance of Kleist involvement in their subjects' domestic grief, the seigneurial matriarch cannot have viewed him kindly, yet Hasse sought pragmatic resolution not unfavorable to the errant mayor. As in Pastor Sauerbier's case, the betrayed wife was too terrified of losing the familial livelihood not to forgive her husband and fight for his survival. The ill-funded poor-relief system comes into rare sight, and it appears again how shaky mayoral authority was, and how few were willing or able to wield it.

Another fragmentary case, from 1760, involved now-familiar Joachim Nagel who, after marrying the woman who bore him premarital twins, took his paternal fullholding. Now forty-six, remarried and father of five children, he faced an unnamed, husbandless, probably widowed mother's claim he added a child to her household. Nagel admitted visiting her dwelling, but denied "having to do with her in that manner." She had, he claimed, "gotten her children and other people to summon him ten times, and when he arrived he didn't know what she wanted." She said he promised some support, urging her to attribute paternity to a wandering journeyman tailor or blacksmith, "and, finally, that she got [the baby] on her trip to Magdeburg." Defeated and cornered, despite his protestations, Nagel agreed to child support if she swore she had "corporeally mingled" with no one but him. She agreed, but Hasse decreed waiting for Pastor Carsted's "admonition to avoid perjury." Whatever the price, Nagel remained on his farm, dying there in 1765. By then his second wife had died and he was again remarried. In 1770 his second eldest son obtained army discharge to take the farm. None of his premarital children attained adulthood.[156]

Still-young widows were protagonists in the two illicit sexuality cases Hasse forwarded to the Criminal Court. The first, from 1725, involved married laborer Christian Nagel, a Premslin lodger, and widowed Glövzin lodger Marie Hechten, *née* Seyers. A thirty-five-year-old fullholder's

---

[155] Ibid., fos. 32–4.   [156] No. 326, fo. 239.

daughter, Marie had married laborer Jochen Hecht, who died at Easter 1725, "having lain ill only five days," leaving her with four small children. Now, in November 1725, pregnant, she received Hasse's summons after rumors "went around" that she and Christian Nagel "were living in adultery."[157] Asked how she fed her family, she painted a poverty-streaked picture:

The bit of grain she sowed with her manure had now sprouted, [but] she has been living wretchedly. She scooped up the manure on the roads, and Herr Captain [Kleist] permitted her to gather some composting leaves, and hadn't ignored her in handing out work ["didn't disdain her in her work"].

She admitted Christian Nagel visited her at Whitsuntide, after her husband's death. Not knowing his aim, she let him in her dwelling. He was drunk, "and wanted to throw her to the floor and commit his shame upon her." She resisted, whereupon he told her to go to bed. "He wanted to lie down outside [her bedroom] on the trunk." But he followed her into bed and "threw himself on her, and in the narrow bed she couldn't move." It happened but once, and with him alone. "She couldn't actually say" when she missed her period "because she was laboring hard all summer" (making periods irregular). Nagel "forced himself on her [and] committed a great sin against her." She only met him when her husband sickened and she replaced him at work, threshing alongside Nagel in the barn her husband had contracted. She condemned Nagel's drunken "foolishness," though he was "clever [i.e., sober] enough to carry out his pranks [since] otherwise he would have gone to his wife." Though she "told him to go home, he'd said it wouldn't do her any harm."[158]

Was she sober? "She had never her livelong days gotten drunk." Why hadn't she cried out for help against Nagel's coercion? "In the night there was no one she could have called to." When pregnancy followed, she told the preacher. She could not pretend her departed husband was the father, "because [impregnation] was nine weeks after his death." Why was she now living with Glövzin's schoolteacher? "She resisted [taking him in] long enough, and wanted him out of the house, but he wouldn't leave." Hasse asked "whether she didn't recognize she did wrong in committing indecency, and thereby deserved worldly and eternal punishment?" She agreed, "but if he hadn't brought her to it, they could have avoided it." Did she wish to offer a "written defense"? "She had no money, and asked for a merciful punishment."

[157] No. 571, fos. 2–3.   [158] Ibid., fos. 3–4, 10–12.

Adulterous Christian's wife, Ilse Schultzen, "at most thirty years old," said her husband confessed his "misfortune" before "the woman-creature ['*Weibestück*'] drunkenly told people" what happened. As he sat in the Premslin pub, Marie invited him to visit her to advise her on "getting a bridegroom." He wanted to go home, "but she kept him there, and took him to bed, because she said her husband's mother told her she wouldn't have a child by him, but it would belong to her blessed husband, should she have one" (i.e., Marie thought any child she bore would be the departed Jochen's). Ilse's husband's drunkenness reduced his guilt. Meanwhile "that person was courting the schoolmaster and was even living together with him in one household in the school." Ilse had four young children with Nagel.

And because she couldn't raise them alone, she wanted finally to forgive him. He would better himself, and regretted his transgression very much . . . In all her livelong days she had never seen him act this way, and she had also had a peaceable marriage with him, for in all her days he had still not beaten her, and they hadn't squabbled either . . . That person, who had been sober, should have been smarter. Satan [*Satanas*] wanted to play his games, letting a fellow get seduced like that.

But "they wouldn't leave it at that," giving the Tempter the last word.

Satan's victim Christian, like other accused parties, was allowed a pre-interrogation statement. To visit a single women to discuss her remarriage prospects was not disreputable, though Nagel excused the late hour by work pressures. He conceded drunkenness. "She got him into her house and into bed, and laid the children on the side, [who] are already big enough to guide the plow." "That person [Marie Seyers] couldn't truthfully say he coerced her with force. He was instead in such drunken condition that the littlest child could have overpowered him." When she knew she was pregnant, "she told the midwife [*Bademutter*] and the preacher."[159] Nagel said he was a fullholder's son who "had to feed himself by the labor of his hands." He "doesn't really know" whether he was thirty-seven or thirty-eight years old. Asked about his acquaintance with Marie, he said "her home was Karstädt and his Glövzin," where they grew up, though both moved to other villages. Had Marie visited him? "Yes, now and then she came around to his wife and said she'd like to talk with him, but nothing more." Marie told him "he should arrange for her to find a bridegroom, so that she'd get her hands on a good fellow." As for drunkenness, "he had definitely drunk up a few groschen of beer."

[159] Ibid., fos. 2–3, 5–6, 12.

An oath would "witness with his free conscience" – a spiritual attribute rarely invoked, but doubtless important – that he had not coerced her. If he knew he alone "had had to do with her," he would accept paternity, but perhaps there were others, such as the schoolmaster, of whom Nagel said he and Marie "wanted to have each other." Hasse asked Nagel whether he had not promised his wife, "before God's eyes, marital loyalty" and now broken that vow? "Yes, but he didn't want to leave his wife, nor she him. God had" – here Nagel showed passivity about responsibility for sin – "bestowed this misfortune on him, and he wanted to ask God day and night to forgive him." He knew he deserved "worldly and eternal punishment," but waived written defense. "He leaves it to Royal mercy and . . . his overlordship, which would" – he hoped – "join in his plea on behalf of himself and his wife and four sons, the oldest of whom was just nine years and the youngest six months."[160]

Marie Seyers' farm wife step-mother, sixty-six, pleaded against "hard punishment" for "her daughter's" four children's sake. Nagel "had once again wanted to come to her one night in the harvest, though she didn't want to let him in. Thus she came to her misfortune." David Richter, a sixty-year-old schoolmaster (bearing a local blacksmith's name) said he took Marie into his house "to care for him in his old age." If the "overlordship and his children" agreed, he wanted to marry Marie. One son was a village schoolmaster, another worked for a Perleberg merchant, while the daughter was Stavenow's tailor-schoolmaster's wife. Richter added:

> [Marie] couldn't say he had had to do with her. He'd spoken with her about marriage. They were indeed in one living room, but not in one bed. The person had three children with her in bed, and the fourth child her sister's husband took in place of children of his own, and he [Richter] sleeps alone. When he became engaged to the person he decided to accept [Marie's] children as his own, and still would do so if his children agreed.[161]

Richter's schoolmaster son, "Meister Joachim," wrote to Marie an outwardly respectful letter in a good hand, asking to meet with her at the Perleberg Church Inspector's office to discuss old Richter's proposal. Addressing her as "right honorable Frau Hechten," he said he understood "that things were not right with her," and that she planned to marry his father, who was allegedly ignorant of the idea. Rather than that the old man "should have to plague himself with other people's

---

[160] Ibid., fos. 6–10.   [161] Ibid., fos. 4–5.

children, we two brothers have come forward to take our dear old father in his hard old age under the arms." Should she miss the hearing, Joachim threatened her with unspecified costs he would incur in his determination "not to abandon my old father." Yet, with his brother, he "conveyed friendly greetings." Perhaps this intimidating intervention (by previously indifferent sons) explains Marie's disengagement from Richter, whose readiness to marry a poor and beleaguered pregnant woman, still raising three children, highlights the need some elderly men felt for female ministrations.

Hasse sent the case's documentation to Berlin's Criminal Court, whose verdict he proclaimed in January 1726, noting attendance and gaining signatures of the Glövzin mayor and alderman representing the village. Court costs tallied 24 talers, of which Christian Nagel managed to pay 5.5 talers.

Marie Seyers recalls that she consumed everything she had in [schoolmaster] Richter's house, and he also lived from it. She had four bushels of rye and five of barley, of which David Richter offers to replace two of rye. On Jochen Ebel's land they both have one bushel of rye planted with manure supplied by them.[162]

This was the extent of their resources.

The Berlin Court sentenced both defendants to six months' imprisonment in Spandau, "the fellow at hard labor ['the wheelbarrow'] in the fortress, the woman-creature at work in the spinning-house." Hasse ordered their departure that very day, transported by three fullholders, driving their own wagons, selected by Colonel Kleist. The court would reimburse their travel costs. "They must also keep good watch over the arrestees or expect to be punished in their place, to which end the court bailiff will accompany them." The prisoners were to equip themselves against their impending ordeal. Hasse's letter for delivery to the Spandau governor said the sentence "required Stavenow noble court to give the *Inquisiten*, or let them take, necessary clothes and underwear so that, especially during the present [winter] season, they should not be naked and bare."

Hasse ordered schoolmaster Richter to repay Marie the provisions she gave him. Richter would house and care for her "biggest girl" until Easter and "the little girl" thereafter, while farmer Jochen Ebel would care for them in reverse order. Her other young child would accompany Marie. Nagel's wife Ilse "is ordered to keep [their] children, as

---

[162] Ibid., fos. 14–15.

before, in school, and since she interceded for her husband, she cannot now back out, but must follow him." Ilse – either housing her children with kin or taking them with her – would live near Spandau, working to support herself and supplement her husband's prison rations, which otherwise would hardly keep him alive.[163] With this ruling, Christian Nagel and his family vanished from Stavenow records. If he survived imprisonment, he must have moved away. Marie Seyers returned. Fourteen years later she was widowed in a new marriage with a disabled retired farmer, whom she – as she said – "carried about and cared for and fed like a baby." After his death, her farmer-landlord expelled her, arguing coldly that she had married into retirement quarters without right to remain as a widow. Marie left, with food and livestock provisions for her life's next stage.[164]

This adultery case illustrates Frederick William I's regime's punitive moralism, and its exploitation of incarcerated labor. Will to draconic punishment on Stavenow court's part is not detectable, but neither did it plead for mercy. Marie Seyers' landholding relatives and schoolmaster Richter's employed and housed children did little or nothing to alleviate their landless kinfolk's miseries. At thirty-five, Marie Seyers was not resigned to widowhood, and may have yielded to Nagel for companionship, thinking eventual pregnancy ascribable to her departed husband. Nagel perhaps grew interested in Marie when they worked together threshing. Facing disgrace and Spandau's terrors, they succumbed to mutual recriminations and their friendship dissolved. Nagel's wife and children perhaps suffered the greatest loss, while Seyers' single status enabled her, following imprisonment, to start a new, if celibate, life as a retiree's married caretaker. The "good fellow" she had wanted had not yet appeared.

The second case of criminalized sexuality exemplifies the spirit of Frederick II's regime. Widow Liese *née* Hintzen had been Karstädt fullholder Hans Wöhlcke's second wife. In 1757 Hasse summoned her to explain, in estate administrator Böhmer's and assistant manager Lützow's presence, why she was pregnant when her husband died six years earlier. She said "her husband was some sixty years old when he died and she was now thirty-three," and "when her parents forced her to marry the old man she was just eighteen." Her husband's son Hans, with whom "she had grown up," was but one year her junior. When she married, he was a soldier. But when his father died, Hans, "as the eldest

---

[163] Ibid. fo. 16.   [164] No. 591, fos. 93–4.

son," returned from military service to inherit the farm, "under which circumstances he took the opportunity to impregnate her, having long pursued her, though she long kept on guard." In 1752 she bore son Jochen.

In 1757 Hans, once again a soldier, was home, "proposing again to marry her, just as when they were children they courted one another." He had in 1756 "again led her astray so that she became pregnant by him once more." Back at his regiment, he knew of her condition and "aimed to come home, but couldn't get a discharge, though Major von Dequade promised him one."

> But because she wasn't able to manage the farm herself, her step-son was now content she should marry another man. So she wanted to ask the overlordship, since she now has proposals, to permit her [to marry] Johann Nagel from Karstädt.

She proposed to place her two teenage daughters from her marriage with old Wöhlcke under the guardianship of smallholder Hans Seyer, "as her closest living relative ['friend']."

> The people in her house proposed she attribute the first extramarital child to a plum buyer. Hans Wöhlcke especially proposed this, knowing well the child was his. She had already previously told Herr Pastor that he should enter the child's proper name in the parish register.

After the second child's birth, she wrote Hans immediately, but without reply. "She prayed often enough to God to forgive her sin, and hoped the overlordship might do the same." Her suitor, Johann Nagel, declared readiness to marry "widow Wöhlcke," provided she settle with her children's inheritances and, "concerning her transgression, puts the matter right."[165]

Liese hired a scribe or attorney to compose a memorial on "her twice-suffered impregnation," which she submitted with "most doleful gratitude." She would never have yielded to Hans's "incessant entreaties" had he not inspired "firm hope he would certainly marry me." "Only so could I remain on his father's farm." Since 1752 Hans' military superiors repeatedly assured him "he would gain discharge to take his paternal farm, or at least a marriage license." Liese accepted Hans's proposals. "Otherwise I would have been acting against my own welfare." To this rational calculation she added self-deprecatingly "I am too simple not to have believed [him]." Though she had "hoped from

---

[165] No. 496, fos. 2–4.

day to day" for her "sorrow's" end, she now saw that by obeying his will "she only brought herself to disgrace and shame."

Thus have I been plunged in the deepest misfortune. My simplicity – and here I call all my neighbors' witness – was too great and the cunning of my step-son too deep. I bewail my misery.

Her father eagerly married her off despite her youthful friendship with Hans. "Thus a thoughtless father plunged immature and uneducated children in the deepest ruin." She begged that mercy might override law, asking again to marry Johann Nagel.[166]

Soldier Hans was trapped in the Seven Years War's flames, but from Bautzen, in Saxon Lusatia, he dictated on September 3, 1757 a letter to Liese. Here is a rare opportunity to hear a Stavenow villager speak of his personal life, and of soldiering in Frederick II's army. Addressing Liese Hintzen as "my dear mother," he wished her and "my dear son Joachim Heinrich" good health. He was, "amid much uproar, marching, and exhaustion, still healthy." He implored God to "stand by us," including also his brother Johann, "whom I lost at [the battle of] Buntzlau in Bohemia."

Whether he died of sickness or was shot I don't know. But it's certain he's dead, and because he had most of the money with him, that's gone too, so I'll soon be in need myself, and that will last a long while. And though I wanted to ask you to send me something, I didn't let myself do it, because the roads are unsafe, and we move around from one place to another. Now I'm in camp at Görlitz, in Winterfeldt's corps, where the whole army has gathered, except for the king, who advanced with a corps on Dresden, since the French have entered Saxony along with the Imperial army. At the moment it looks dangerous for us, as it was already when I was at the battle and siege of Prague, when in the winter more bullets than snow flew around us. But God protected me, and he'll keep doing it.

Hans turned to the future. "So I can again pursue my livelihood, please take good care of everything – the horses, the pear trees." If God didn't spare his life, "and if I don't come again to what is mine," it was his "earnest will that the property should fall to my son Joachim Heinrich, and be given him."

At the moment I'm in Bautzen on mission, since we're bringing the baker's unit back to Görlitz. My dear mother, if it hasn't already happened, I leave it to you [*euch*] to select another man you have a mind to live with, as long as he takes good care of the farm [*Nahrung*], as if it were his own. I greet you many

---

[166] Ibid., fos. 8–11.

thousand times, also my father's brother, my half-sister, Herr Hantschuch and all the good friends, I commend you to God's protection and remain, your true son, Hans Wöhlcke.

A postscript asked that his tools "be kept in a box so they don't get lost or ruined," and relayed messages from other Stavenow soldiers. "Niklaus Hintze was wounded in the chest at Prague, but has been cured, although he now has a fever, and greets his wife many thousand times." Mathias Hintze was still healthy, and likewise greeted his wife, "but he doesn't know what he should think that she hasn't once written to him." Heinrich Brunst greeted wife, father, and son, and all his good friends (in that order). Four others, one sick, sent similar greetings.[167]

In November 1757 Berlin's Criminal Court ruled in this case of "reiterated incest . . . in first degree of affinity in the direct line, which tends for the most part to be punished by public whipping and banishment from the land." Damningly, Liese Hintzen admitted to multiple encounters, and "had in no way proven her allegation of seduction by the step-son." But in her favor spoke "her straightforward confession and demonstrable remorse, and further that as simple farm woman she cannot fully grasp her crime's enormity." She was sentenced to pay 3 talers' verdict fee and serve a six-week prison term. As for Hans, his regimental commander would at war's end receive court documentation "and punishment shall be left to him." In August 1758 Hasse noted that "after harvest here has, praise God, mostly ended, and other circumstances hindering execution of the sentence against former widow Wöhlckens . . . have ceased, she has today been brought to the jail . . . and her husband shall be informed accordingly by the court bailiff."[168] In 1760 the former Wöhlcke farm was in Joachim Müller's hands, who was, presumably, her new husband. Hans disappears from the documents, fate unknown. He may, like his brother, have died at war.

This case illuminates the villagers' psychological universe, including their inclination to pair up affectionately in youth (as Liese's reminiscences show) and their strong attachment (as Hans' attitude reveals) to parental farms. Frederick's punishments of sexual offenses were, seemingly, milder than his father's, assuming Hans's commander would have counted long military service in his favor and not disciplined him, as a man, harder than Liese suffered as a woman. The court's allowances for female villagers' alleged moral defects reflect enlightened officials' condescending views of the common people, while Liese's invocation of

---

[167] Ibid., fos. 6–7.   [168] Ibid., fos. 16–20.

unwilled marriage to explain her misfortune mirrors Enlightenment critique of irrational institutions. Liese's light punishment, measured against earlier sanctions, exemplifies the (imperfect) Frederickian rejection of torture and judicial savagery. The court's deferral to military authority in Hans' judgment, though pragmatic in wartime, also illustrates the army's independence of civilian control, a problem that would long persist in Prussia.

Another (brief) case of alleged incest remains, revealing drastic emotions and perceptions both among Stavenow officials and villagers. Premslin Pastor Höpfner in 1777 reported his service tenant Caspar Porep's allegation that the baby his wife had borne the preceding November was someone else's. They had only married shortly before and Porep "was not the father, and could and would never recognize the child as his own." His wife, Porep said, "claims an unknown man, who paid her 3 Reichstalers, committed indecency with her on the road."

Pastor Höpfner studied his parish register, recording Porep's first wife's death in April 1776: "found dead in her living room. Because the deceased's father expressed suspicion her husband may have killed her, her corpse was opened on court orders by Herr Dr. Gutike and Surgeon Genrich, but no signs of violence committed upon her were found." The pastor's broodings conjured suspicion Porep may have "lived in adultery" with his second wife before his first's demise, which allegedly would invalidate the present marriage, "if he didn't also intentionally promote his first wife's death."

But later I heard a rumor, which grew ever more widespread: old Peter Ditten had committed the sin against the blood with his own daughter Agnese, now married to Porep. If only this time the rumor had been a lie, as rumors almost always are, but to my not inconsiderable damage [Porep farmed the parsonage's fields], I am now convinced of its truth. The most despicable deed – that I must write this! – has been committed.

Yet Agnese came to Höpfner to take Holy Communion, an assertion of innocence. He subjected her to "instruction and admonitions," but "because she was not in the requisite frame of mind, she was told to report next day for further rectification."

She came, and because she said nothing on her own initiative, was asked: whether she knew what the whole village was saying about her and her father, and if it was true? The answer was: she knew what was said about her, and it wasn't wrongly alleged: the child she bore belonged to no one else than her own father. Upon further questioning, how this had become known, whether she told anyone about it, she answered: she had told her husband, her sisters knew it too, presumably also their husbands, her step-mother, and who knew how many others.

The pastor had not spoken with Agnese's father, "to avoid the appearance I wanted to conduct an investigation."[169]

Judge Betich interrogated Agnese, twenty-six, about "preacher Höpfner's denunciation." She said the child was the result "of sleeping [*Beyschlaf*] with a traveling craftsman on the road from Perleberg to Premslin in the pinewoods." Simultaneously, her sister returned to live at home, and since they lacked sufficient beds, the sister took Agnese's, while Agnese slept with her father. This arrangement gave rise to the rumor. She had not admitted to incest to the "priest, [for] she was not aware her father had committed the actual sexual act with her." "It is necessary to note," Betich added, "that the summoned party showed herself to be a very simple-minded and insignificant person." Her husband Porep, forty-six, supported the wandering artisan story, denying she ever ascribed paternity to her father. To this he would swear, but he refused to call the child his own. Agnese's father, sixty-two, said they shared a bed because his other daughter came home sick. The scandalous rumor was false.[170]

These actors' subsequent fate is unknown, but the story shows how both pastor, professionally preoccupied with sinfulness, and some villagers leapt to lurid conclusions about their neighbors. Possibly the incest was real. Paternity ascriptions to wandering apprentices were common and, if believed, convenient escapes from difficulty. But Betich rejected the pastor's denunciation, and seemingly dropped the matter, leaving the Porep household, if not the village, in turmoil. Porep's case leads to this chapter's final subject, concerning witchcraft accusations and other honor-besmirching offenses among villagers. Here, too, the court resolved conflicts outside seigneurial self-interest's boundaries, maintaining or restoring normative order, though not without revealing the widening gulf – evident in the foregoing adultery trials – between governing-class views and values and the common folk's.

POLICING VILLAGERS' HONOR

The village quarrels and fights the seigneurial court so often settled and punished frequently arose from alleged violations of communal morality. Curses and insults usually accompanied physical abuse, challenging

---

[169] No. 718, fos. 83, 88.   [170] Ibid., fos. 84–7.

the antagonists' good reputation or honor, sometimes severely. Sexual transgressions, real or imputed, might trigger gross insults and fisticuffs. When seigneurial laborer Jürgen Peters, denying paternity in an embittered impregnation case, found himself taunted as a "whore's stallion," he addressed his mocking antagonist, a maidservant, as "you troublemaking shitter." Her response, Peters complained, was to announce that "she wanted to shit something for him, and he could kiss her ass." Because Peters turned his dogs on her, he was fined, but her "loose trap" disqualified her from further satisfaction. Here good reputation made no entry.[171] But when an impounder publicly accused a hollander's sister-in-law of assisting another couple's premarital affair, she indignantly branded him an "honor-besmircher" (*Ehrenschneider*).[172]

Among common, now familiar insults were "dog's ass" (*Hundsfott*, referring to female dogs, and connoting cowardliness) and "fat-bellied whore." There were "Frenchman's," or "drunken," or "any man's whore." A farm wife once insulted a farmhand as "ass-barer" (*Aftblecker*), while physical imperfections reaped scorn in such terms as "crooked-backed scoundrel" (*krummpuckelter Schelm*). Among insults alleging poverty and poor diets were "stubble-shitter," "peel-gobbler" (*Pehlfresser*) and "dirt-eater" (*Erdfresser*). Cleanliness defects were imputed by "louse-bag" (*Lausewentzel*, derived from *Wentzel* [servant], rooted in Czech).[173] These and other, less sexually or bodily oriented epithets (e.g., *Canaille* [trash]), comprised antagonization's repertory, but did not alone suffice to dishonor.

Village mayors suffered rough language. One was cursed by a woman he whipped as "devourer" and "werewolf." A farmer resisting impoundment denounced another as "scoundrel and church-thief," married to a "fat-bellied whore."[174] But mayors retaliated. A Garlin free mayor assaulted farmer Kratz for his son's allegedly reckless horse-grazing. A witness claimed the mayor cursed Kratz's son, calling him "harebrained idiot" and saying "your father's a fool, a scoundrel, and he cheats his workers." The last of these insults (*Leute Vertreiber*) charged the boy's father with driving servants away, and when Kratz appeared, he threw it back at the mayor. The Mayor and his wife then broke Kratz's scythe and pummeled him. A pro-Kratz witness, whom the mayor's wife cursed as "canaille" and "lout" (*Lümmel*), said "Kratz's

[171] No. 591, fo. 114; no. 326, fo. 63.   [172] No. 200, fos. 21–2.
[173] No. 589, fos. 9–10; no. 200, fo. 84; no. 200, fos. 133–4; no. 629, fos. 4–5; no. 326, fos. 216, 220; no. 200, fos. 117–18; no. 591, fos. 116–17.
[174] No. 326, fos. 80, 93–4; no. 591, fos. 117, 119.

teeth were all bloody, his eye black and blue, and his shirt torn apart." Kratz endured this abuse stoically, returned home to fetch a new scythe, and later petitioned for satisfaction, though with doubtful success.[175]

Just when quarrels seriously damaged reputation is difficult to detect, but many sentences entailed guilty parties' formal affirmation of acquitted defendants' honor (*Ehrenerklärung*). Antagonists shook hands, the accuser declaring he or she "knew nothing" about the defendant "but goodness and honor." Impugned parties might even request issuance at the plaintiff's cost of written "certificates of honor" (*Ehrenscheine*), as when one servant-girl falsely accused another of stealing from the lordship.[176] Any unfounded charge likely to diminish reputation, particularly for honesty, called for a "declaration of honor." An ill reputation could be described as a *Schneck*, a word also for rumor, perhaps suggesting it stuck to the victim like a snail (*Schnecke*).[177] Miller Arndt charged farm wife Schenck with "much cursing him on the first day of Whitsuntide" as he left church with his wife, daughter, and maidservant, calling him "groats-thief" and his wife someone's illegitimate daughter (*Treffe*). Schenck insultingly told the miller's maidservant "her Frau was initiator of all rumors" (*Schneckereyen*). These words obliged the farm wife to beg the miller's wife's pardon and affirm her honor.[178]

Blacksmith Jahncke blusteringly insulted a village tailor in a tavern during town market. Jahncke seized tailor Key's Spanish cane, worth a taler, and broke it, loudly proclaiming "where [Key] was sitting no honorable fellow should sit, nor drink from the mug he was drinking from, because he was a cheat." Jahncke threatened, if Key protested, "he won't take scissors in hand for the next three months." The quarrel's source were 30 linen ells the two men's wives had jointly woven, most of which tailor Key claimed, but for which smith Jahncke refused to pay. In court Key demanded payment and satisfaction, "because he must have his honorable name." Jahncke claimed his brother-in-law told him Key threatened to "shoot him dead." About linen Jahncke knew nothing, since his wife had died. Hasse ordered an investigation, directing Jahncke to replace Key's cane and apologize for his insults.[179]

Millers and other artisans were touchy about honor, but all villagers understood its significance, both for themselves and others. Free mayor Erhardt charged farmer Müller with mowing his hay when Erhardt forbade it. Erhardt impounded Müller's plow, whereupon Müller

[175] No. 712, fos. 8–10.   [176] No. 200, fo. 110.   [177] Ibid., fos. 62–3.   [178] No. 591, fos. 94–5.
[179] Ibid., fos. 123–4.

"shouted at him today in front of the Stavenow administrator's office that he had not acted toward him as an honorable fellow [*ehrlicher Kerl*]." A witness said Müller mowed hay before the barley was harvested, and so "acted against [communal] prohibition." Müller claimed "he could do what he liked with what was his. He also told the mayor it was wrong to take his plow, and he stands by this." Administrator Schmidt, running the court, fined him 12 groschen for breaking village rules and because "he spoke contemptuously of the mayor."[180]

In 1746 two farmers accused each other of "defamation" (*Diffamation*). Hans Zeggel complained that, at market in Mecklenburg, Peter Ebel struck him with his staff and cursed him as "cheat and scoundrel," later hitting him, in a village tavern, "above the eye with a pitchfork." Zeggel admitted having "drunk a bit." Ebel woundedly said that, while playing dice with two cavalrymen, Zeggel forced him to defend himself with a pitchfork he had bought at market. Zeggel, a Glövziner, sneered about Ebel's village that "Premsliners couldn't even pay for a few pitchforks." Hasse fined Ebel one taler and Zeggel (whose drunkenness mitigated his guilt) a half-taler. Ebel affirmed Zeggel's "honor and goodness" and they shook hands "as befits Christians." Here imputations of poverty figured in defamatory speech.[181] Men could also offend women's honor, as when Jürgen Zeggel called Hans Schultze's wife, who was standing on her porch, a "mold-bag" (*Muffsack*). He complained "she wouldn't even say good morning to him," once even snubbing him going to Holy Communion. Hasse said Zeggel deserved the Spanish overcoat "for his quarrelsome tongue," but the "declaration of honor he has made" spared him punishment.[182]

Association with certain seigneurial functions could be dishonoring, but recriminations risked court displeasure. Working in manorial service, farmer's son Joachim Bahlcke and his sister Marie clashed with Peter Hagelstein, another farm servant, over precedence in hauling. Hagelstein beat Joachim with a doubled-up horse-whip. Hagelstein complained Marie cursed him as "bailiff [*Voigt*] and rascal." Marie disclaimed the bailiff reference, which implied contempt for executors of overlordly punishment. She claimed he denounced her as "letter-deliverer [*Brieffträgersche*] and blabbermouth," the first epithet recalling the enforced and derisorily paid walking tours noble lordships imposed on subject villagers, especially smallholders. Hasse ruled Joachim's beating at Peter's hands just punishment for aggression. But for epithets

---

[180] No. 596, fo. 44.   [181] No. 326, fo. 126.   [182] No. 200, fo. 93.

impugning seigneurial authority Hasse fined Peter 1 taler and Marie 12 groschen, payable in eight days or expiable "on the body."[183] The lordship had other occasions to defend its agents. Following a murderous mayoral assault on bailiff Voss, Hasse ordered the offender to make "a fitting declaration of honor."[184] It was very disrespectful when farmer David Zeggel insulted Premslin leaseholder Frau Berkholtz, saying, as we saw, "she came from families who long ago deserved the gallows if they had only been caught." Adding insult to injury, Zeggel dismissed Frau Berkholtz's son as "stubble-shitter and peel-gobbler." A witness agreed Zeggel defamingly mentioned "gallows and scaffold," sparking mutual denials of Zeggel's and Berkholtz's status as "honorable people."[185]

As for accusations of commerce with demonic powers, Frederick William I early abolished capital punishment of alleged witches and sorcerers, ending their judicial prosecution in Prussia. But local courts continued to confront popular belief in occult forces. While judges rejected resultant charges as superstition and ignorance, their effects were serious, since persons branded by them, or otherwise brought into contact with diabolical practitioners, were at risk of losing their honorable reputations.[186] Yet the mere epithet "witch" (*Hexe*) did not necessarily defame. During a neighbors' quarrel over children's alleged misdeeds one farmer called the other's wife an "old witch." She countered with "gray-headed, left-footed scoundrel," while many other rude expressions – "thieving rascally people," "Jürgen Nagel's whore," "the children ought to be kept in cages" – flew about. Yet, finally, "all was forgiven."[187] An enraged farmer, as we saw, cursed his widowed mother as "witch and Frenchman's whore," though this quarrel too ended in (brittle) reconciliation.[188] More offensively, a farm wife, complained little-loved leaseholder Hartz, "branded him witch-rider [*Hexenreiter*]," while her daughter added the epithet "gray-haired rascal."[189]

For witch charges to become serious, some evidence of occult practices was needed. At Stavenow, this appeared in three cases. The first pitted in 1729 Glövzin farmer Jochen Ebel and wife, Liese Seyers, against sometime communal opposition leader Hans Milatz, his wife

---

[183] Ibid., fos. 133–4.   [184] No. 326, fo. 190.   [185] Ibid., fos. 216, 220.
[186] Hagen, "Glaube." Cf. Jan Peters, "Hexerei vor Ort: Erfahrungen und Deutungen in einer Klcingesellschaft der Prignitz. Saldernherrschaft Plattenburg-Wilsnack (1550–1700)," *JBL* 49 (1998): 38–74; Lieselott Enders, "Weise Frauen – böse Zauberinnen: Hexenverfolgung in der Prignitz im 16. und 17. Jahrhundert," ibid. 49 (1998): 19–37.
[187] No. 200, fos. 21–2, 84.   [188] No. 326, fo. 150.   [189] No. 591, fo. 44.

Marie Hechts, and his maidservant Marie Niemanns. Amid harsh criticism of her character, Liese Seyers, as we saw, earlier waged an unsuccessful premarital paternity suit. Now, having married, she faced Milatz's household's accusations that her diabolical activities caused livestock to die, and that she spread evil rumors against Milatz's wife Marie, who said Liese Seyers "denounced her as a witch, and whispered about her [that] she claimed she got the old Bock woman to die and wanted to get the old Milatz woman" – possibly Marie's mother-in-law – "to die also." Liese Seyers went to Marie's house, protesting "she was innocent of the rumor" and knew nothing of the Milatzes but "goodness and honor." But Milatz's wife, "without waiting to hear her, immediately broke a bowl over her head," saying "'you child murderer! you witch! I'll kill you.'" These charges suggest Liese's premarital child had not lived (and, indeed, Liese died in 1747 a widow without direct heirs).

Liese Seyers said of Milatz's maidservant Marie Niemanns that "the girl started this rumor [against her own mistress] at the village well." The magical technique involved was furtive use of sewing needles and hat pins to pin to barn and stall walls animal organs, especially calves' hearts previously collected in bags, as well as to hang charms on calves. Amulets were also hung around sheep's heads to guard against epidemics and other disease. Liese Seyers accused Milatz's maidservant herself of these practices, "though she doesn't say who [they're] aimed at." One of the parties – possibly Seyers' husband Jochen Ebel – was charged with believing, of witchcraft protecting animals, that "if it doesn't help him, it also doesn't hurt him." Finally, maidservant Marie admitted to "nailing up the heart, but she didn't do it as witchcraft, much less directing it against a human being." Hasse sentenced her to two days' imprisonment for "chattering against her own mistress" (not – or not explicitly – for practicing witchcraft). "For his superstition" Jochen Ebel owed 12 groschen, "payable to the school fund," to help spread enlightenment and extinguish popular credulity. Hasse found the two farm wives innocent of occult practice. It seems Hans Milatz's rebellious soul also housed fear of demons.[190]

A second case displayed charges raised against Glövzin farmer Hans Zeggel and his wife Trine by Ilse Griesen, fourteen, their maidservant whose landless parents lived nearby. Ilse suffered convulsive attacks, possibly epilepsy. In 1733 Hans and his wife charged Ilse with bringing

---

[190] No. 200, fos. 125–6.

them into "groundless ill-repute" and "putting them in fright" by claiming her mistress Trine Zeggel "had done something evil to her." They recounted how Ilse, "in her fear," accused them of wishing her harm because of enmity between Ilse and their young daughter. Ilse's public denunciation of Trine Zeggel during her seizures seemingly provoked the Zeggels to punish her, for Hans (damagingly) added that "now, for fear of blows, [Ilse] can no longer talk, and [her mother] is blaming [Trine] for making her dumb, so that she'll never get well."

Hasse concluded rationally and dispassionately that "what the girl babbles in her great emotion and pain comes from pure ignorance" and that "all [her] problems stem partly from heavy bleeding and obstruction of her natural functions and partly from her false imaginings and hostility to Zeggel's wife." Ilse's parents "did not wish to leave her any longer in superstitious delusions but will send her to the preacher for necessary instruction." Ilse shook hands with the Zeggels, of whom Ilse's parents declared they knew nothing but "honor, love, and goodness." Hans and Trine declared themselves

ready and willing as Christians to forgive . . . But Hans Zeggel and his wife have requested a court certificate and proof be issued, so no one might, whether sooner or later, bring them into dishonor . . . The present declaration of honor and attestation of their innocence under this court's usual seal is therefore issued, while the Glövzin commune is to be informed that whoever offends against this ruling and insults Hans Zeggel or his relatives with such foolish slander will be punished with the Spanish overcoat or fiddle.[191]

Here the enlightened state worked with rationalized Christianity to dispel popular benightedness – but also the "fears" and "frights" that suspicions and accusations of witchcraft still provoked among villagers, whether or not they believed in diabolical forces. Defamation's danger was real enough.

While Ilse blamed her torments on Zeggel malevolence, in other cases mental illness opened the door to demonic powers. The mentally impaired relatives farms sometimes housed were often able to work, and parents and siblings showed good-will in promising to feed and clothe them. But sometimes the picture was unhappier. A 1730 inventory described Johann Huth, thirty, one of a deceased smallholder's six children, as "imbecilic." Twenty years later, Hasse commanded a landless couple, seemingly lodgers entrusted with the handicapped man's care, "not to let Johann Huth wander about in his misery." They should

[191] No. 326, fo. 36; no. 597, fos. 5–6.

report "if he didn't want to stay," so provision could be made for his "further care."[192]

Mental derangement could inspire groundless but honor-threatening sexual charges. In 1738 free mayor Erhardt reported that his disturbed niece and former maidservant, Anna Steinbecks, "shamefully defamed him," charging "he was together [sexually] with old Grete," while she also said about herself that Erhardt's farmhand Pankow lay with her. Anna, twenty-six, claimed she learned from her mother the upsetting rumor about Erhardt going about the village. She entered Erhardt's living room and told him and his wife about it, though without ill intent. As for her saying old Grete let Pankow into the house after eleven o'clock so he could sleep with her:

> she woke and said it out of agitation [*Unruhe*]. After the harvest [it was now December] she had out of agitation secretly gone off with a bundle of her things to Eldenburg ... The Eldenburg tavernkeeper talked her out of it, and she came back here, and she had scolded herself for leaving.

Anna's father, a blacksmith's lodger, excused his daughter's allegations, saying "she's sometimes not right in the head" and that she ran off for three days – to Perleberg, Lenzen, and Mecklenburg's Grabow – before he found her again. Erhardt paid her comparatively well – 9 talers with two pairs of shoes annually – but now he had a new maidservant.[193] Hasse noted that Anna "couldn't deny her slander." He sentenced Anna's mother, as the gossip's originator, to 8 talers' fine, while Anna was to pay 4 talers or "to suffer it on her body." Anna owed "Christian apology and declaration of [Erhardt's and Pankow's] honor, without prejudice to her own honor." These heavy sanctions aimed, seemingly, to drive the Steinbecks, whose names disappear from record, from the jurisdiction.[194]

Sometimes madness engendered religious delusions, as with Glövzin fullholder Stoffel Buck, whose miseries some villagers derived from sexual and demonic realms.[195] In 1727 mayor Holtmann told Hasse that "Buck has gone on a rampage again and broken everything to pieces." He should be treated as a "madman [and] locked up or otherwise detained, for no one's life is safe in his presence." Buck's wife, Anna Hewickens, said "she had him bled from his main arteries, but he only got worse." The "misfortune" (*Unglück*) returned on Wednesday. Thursday he suffered twelve attacks, but Friday and Saturday "he

---

[192] No. 715, fo. 19; no. 200, fos. 148–9.   [193] No. 591, fos. 82–6.
[194] No. 321, fo. 27.   [195] No. 200, fos. 65–8.

quieted down completely, and said nothing." Saturday night he visited his Premslin farm-wife sister. At four o'clock in the morning he "knocked on the priest's farm door, but they kept it shut." At the sexton's house he "cursed the people there."

He was crotchety about the priest because a few years ago he was censured from the pulpit when he quarreled with old schoolmaster David Richter's wife, [who] took his hat and wouldn't give it back unless he answered her question whether he had to do church penance before being admitted again to Holy Communion. He took this so much to heart and became so melancholy that he finally got the misfortune. He often said he'd rather meet a black man in the forest than a black-clothed priest [*Pape*].

Sunday morning he came home, changed clothes, and returned to Premslin, where in David Hecht's house he behaved, as the mayor said, "very unfittingly. He threw everything about and broke it, and tore down the walls and doors and smashed out the windows." His wife said he then "went into the church and started quarreling with the preacher until the farmers seized him and brought him home," where again he broke everything, "so that she couldn't let him out of the bedroom anymore."

Nine years ago he ran at her with an ax and hatchet and she barely saved herself by climbing over the fence at her father's house. Which is why she can no longer trust him, but must fear he'll harm either her or himself, for now he said plainly he wanted to strike her dead. Either she'll die or he will. Finally she went home and was spinning when he broke out of the house and took a rope with him to the barn, where he wanted to hang himself. Her maidservant noticed this and ran to him with other people and rescued him. He would have broken her father's arm with a shovel from the barn, and he said [referring probably to his madness] that it would last until the devil got his booty.

Anna pleaded for help and protection. "She prayed to him, but he didn't want to hear anything about prayers." He would eventually grow exhausted, but then start again. "Now he hasn't slept in 8 days." Her father supported her, saying if Stoffel "in his rage got hold of a knife or something like that, or fire, he might cause a great misfortune."

Farmer Hecht said when Buck arrived at his house, he tried to send him to church service, "to get him off the farmstead." Buck first resisted, hurling himself "terribly" against Hecht's closed gate-doors. Finally he entered the church

and went to the altar. He had a short club he flailed about with, and said to the preacher, 'what are you [*du*] doing here?' The preacher looked around at the other people, and finally a few of them seized [Buck] and took him home, but on the way he kicked so with his feet that five people could barely take him away. He also cursed the sexton as a lousy dog, so they couldn't continue the service.

Buck's wife reported he "now frequently says if they want to hold him, they'll have to cut him in roasting pieces." He was tearing out wall-plaster with his bare hands. "If he gets more out he'll pull down the wood-frames and no one with be able to deal with him." Hasse directed the bailiff to fasten Buck to his room's standing beams. After hearing the preacher's and county physician's report, "His Royal Highness should, if circumstances warranted, be consulted."

Buck's "rage" eventually subsided, but he could not continue farming. With his wife and two young sons he moved in 1731 to his father-in-law Reimar Hewicke's Glövzin cottage holding, while Hewicke took Buck's farm. In 1737, Buck, probably then about fifty, was found dead. Hasse reported:

Stoffel Buck, afflicted many years with epilepsy [*Jammer*], went last Friday into his garden to pluck leaves from the cabbages, and had the misfortune, seized by this illness, to fall into a ditch and miserably drown . . . Herr administrator attests that a few months ago, in a seizure, he fell into the fire and burned himself badly.

Buck's wife told Pastor Willebrandt "he has recently been having very strong attacks." At the death scene, farmer Koltzer testified he saw Buck "stumble into the ditch, just as on Sunday 8 days ago he was struck down in church." Buck's wife reported five seizures in their bed, three within an hour. "On Sunday he prayed very earnestly, and repented, to which the whole community along with the Herr Preacher could attest." She and the mayor and four other farmers averred his death had been natural.

The thought was unavoidable that Buck perhaps killed himself, but Hasse concluded, "since it is notorious in both [Glövzin and Premslin] that Stoffel Buck was burdened with epilepsy, and that he died accidentally in the ditch, the body is hereby delivered to the widow for appropriate burial."[196] She and her sons managed the poverty-ridden cottage holding until her 1742 death, when the elder son, having married, took it for himself, giving his brother a cow and sheep.[197] Buck's wife showed considerable forbearance, and the couple shared the same bed until his death. Having shed his earlier deranged anti-clericalism, Buck somehow made peace with the church, and even found solace in

[196] No. 591, fos. 68–9.   [197] No. 326, fos. 103–4; no. 200, fo. 174.

prayer and repentance. The community accepted his presence, despite his earlier rampages.

After Buck's 1727 explosion, Johann Koltzer charged Buck's former farmhand Jochen Zeggel with beating their son and calling Koltzer's wife Grete "an old witch." Zeggel said he had heard Koltzer's son was calling him "Buck's bastard [*Triffel*], which he couldn't put up with, because he wasn't any bastard child but an honorable child [*ehrlich*]." He only told Grete "if I'm a bastard then you're a witch." But the Koltzers claimed Jochen went farther, calling them "Buck's devil," and saying "you two are devils [*Düfels*]." Hans Milatz testified Koltzer's wife murderously ran at Zeggel with a scythe. Milatz heard talk that Zeggel was publicly calling Grete "Buck's devil" (*Deibel*). Zeggel's fullholding father said the affair arose because the Koltzers "told the Kleists and other gentlemen about it in church, which was a great sin." Hasse concluded farmhand Jochen wrongly struck Koltzer's son, since "Buck's bastard" were Grete's words. One of her unfriendly neighbors claimed she publicly said "the Zeggels lie and deceive their way through the world."[198] Hasse fined the Koltzers and the farmhand, who meanwhile had "reconciled themselves," 12 groschen each.

This conflict reveals that many interpreted epilepsy as devil possession. The Koltzers' charge about Buck's extramarital son, and Buck's wife's testimony about his disorder's origins in aggravation and humiliation over church censure, suggest people saw his unhappy fate, as perhaps he himself did, as the consequence of sexual missteps in early life, though other evidence of them is lacking. Whether or not the Koltzers sought the Kleists' intercession, the idea of doing so seemed to their neighbor a "great sin." Beyond besmirching the Zeggels, it drew the lordship into a discursive realm in which, as the rationalizing Christian Prussian state's representative, it did not belong. Whether villagers aggrieved over local quarrels and rivalries accosted the Kleists at church at other times is unknown, but not unthinkable.

Such were the few cases under Hasse's judgeship concerning demonic powers and madness. It seems witchcraft charges' judicial weight, if not seriousness in villagers' eyes, plummeted after the 1730s. In 1743 a farmer demanded the Karstedt lordship discipline a farm wife "for defamation by witchcraft allegation." Karstedt replied he would punish her if Hasse satisfied his own subjects' grievances. Here witchcraft accusations were mere subjects of judicial horse-trading.[199]

[198] No. 200, fos. 81–3, 91–3.   [199] No. 326, fo. 105.

CONCLUSION: DEFENDING THE LORDSHIP'S HONOR
AGAINST THE VILLAGERS

The villagers lived under Brandenburg-Prussia's laws, as Stavenow court and higher royal tribunals applied them. They were subject also to local customs and usages in the Prignitz District, army regulations, Lutheran church prescriptions, and their own villages' rules. This chapter's transgressions were individual – not communal – violations, whether of codes of powers superior to the villages or of the villagers themselves. Such rules, as they governed property or morality, were in some measure legitimate in villagers' eyes, whatever they thought of punishments inflicted for their violation. In his long tenure, Hasse acquired considerable authority among the villagers, though they perhaps feared his decisions as the enforcer of Stavenow's seigneurial power. But his court also served their interests, giving fair form to the property transfers and inheritance settlements, quarrels and strife among themselves that comprised so much of his work and so deeply affected their fortunes and honor.

But what of defending seigneurial honor against besmirchment by villagers? Mostly this was, in Kleist eyes, a question of the collective communal struggles against the lordship's authority that chapter 9 will address. But, as prologue, it is worth considering one curious case, in which one of Colonel Kleist's subjects gravely insulted him. The occasion was the 1731 post-harvest celebration at Stavenow manor-hall, called the *Erbessen*, to which the lordship invited its subjects for food and drinks. Among the guests was fullholder Hans Jürgen Schultze. He later accused Trine Möllers, blacksmith Völsch's wife, of grossly slandering him at the celebration, causing his exclusion from it. Triggering the conflict was Schultze's beating of Trine's young brother, whom Schulze employed as a farmhand.[200] Schultze summoned as witness Liese Besen, who testified she heard Trine say, to all within earshot, that he "had skinned the boy [through punishment] and her little brother wouldn't be able to hold out [against such treatment]." Trine further accused Schultze of saying:

Herr Colonel ordered they should all bring the young boys when they came to the supper. So it was better that he punished the boy instead of sending him . . . Herr Colonel might take him to Stavenow and he might boil him or roast him.

[200] No. 591, fos. 24, 28–9.

Upon hearing these words, Liese Besen claimed to have said to the blacksmith's wife, "Oh my dear girl, don't say that! The man [Colonel Kleist] still has his own food. He wouldn't boil him or roast him."

Blacksmith Völsch, Trine's husband, marshaled witnesses minimizing the clash, one quoting the blacksmith as saying, after Schultze had beaten his wife's younger brother, "no harm done. They should bring the boy along, or give him something to eat at home." But farmer Schultze claimed, because of the remarks Trine libelously put in his mouth, he suffered "the greatest damage." Trine Möllers publicly defamed him as "flayer" (*Schinder*) of farmhands, while his alleged insult to Colonel Kleist deprived him of food and drink at the fest, and the hay and straw allotments with which the lordship rewarded harvest workers.

Hasse directed witness Liese Besen to swear she heard the blacksmith's wife ascribe to farmer Schultze the words "that Herr Colonel might take [the boy] to Stavenow and might boil or roast him." Defendant Trine now confessed that "if she said it, it was unwittingly and from excitement. She couldn't imagine it was said against the overlordship . . . But if she uttered it against Herr Colonel, she wanted to beg forgiveness." Hasse ruled that, since she couldn't deny that, "on a public street," she had "maliciously mocked the lordship," she must pay 6 talers or "expiate it on her body." She would also "be locked in the fiddle on three consecutive Sundays in front of the church." She was obliged to reimburse Schultze's losses, which he put at 2 talers in fodder he owed four harvest workers, one of them Trine's younger brother, whom he had sent to the lordship's fields. Trine would also beg Schultze's forgiveness and make him a "declaration of honor." She died nine years later, leaving her unprosperous husband to raise four children.[201]

Farmer Schultze proved innocent of suggesting Colonel Kleist might cook and eat his subjects' children. Why the blacksmith's wife put such words in his mouth can only be surmised. Nor can it be known how many minds other than hers held the fearful image of Kleist as his villagers' devourer. Yet the event itself, and Trine Völsch's humiliating punishment – including perhaps a public whipping, for 6 talers was a heavy fine – broadcast the heretical vision across the countryside. It was, like witchcraft, an idea any villager's head might have harbored.

---

[201] No. 591, fo. 99.

9

Policing seigneurial rent: the Kleists' battle with their subjects' insubordination and the villagers' appeals to royal justice, 1727–1806

In western Europe and British North America, eighteenth-century landlords drew rents, mainly cash, from legally unbound tenants. In east-Elbian northern Europe, the legally encumbered farmers' labor was the landlords' prize. Their claims were ancient, but profitable enforcement was a challenge, as this chapter will show. Colonel Kleist's farmers tested the new discipline he imposed in the 1720s with varying results until his son's accession in 1763. The economic pressures squeezing young Major Kleist, an inexperienced landlord, led him to decree heavy new labors. His farmers' obduracy triggered a conflict which, through royal court intervention, landed on the state's doorstep, without quelling local insubordination, strife, and minor violence. In 1785 the villages petitioned for a contract (Urbar or Urbarium), enforceable in appellate courts, cataloguing precisely their seigneurial obligations. In 1797 it was signed and sealed, though with rough edges discomfiting both sides until the major's 1803 death and beyond.

Here beat the heart of the manor–village relationship. Without unpaid labor services east-Elbian landlords' engagement in villagers' lives would have been as businesslike and remote as the French nobility's or English gentry's. East-Elbian farmers would have been free to sink or swim, like their French and English counterparts, in a sea of cash or product rents, market forces, taxes, tithes, and kinfolk's demands. Instead, east-Elbian labor rents tied manor and village together like partners in a strife-torn but indissoluble marriage.

When conflict erupted, the manorial court sought to quell it, but finally royal commissions and higher courts stepped in. These pages depict the mediation styles of Frederick II's regime and his successor's. About such government intervention, vital to the country-dwelling majority, little is concretely known. By far the best-known instance was the famous "miller Arnold case" of 1770–9. Here Frederick II reversed the Berlin Chamber Court's ruling against Arnold, a mill lessee like Stavenow's, who charged a neighboring nobleman with interference with his water supply, preventing his earning enough to pay rent to a noble landlord who refused to aid Arnold against his upstream tormentor. Frederick's seemingly liberal championship of the miller entailed royal intrusion in the judicial process that belied the enlightened king's adage that, in the halls of justice, the law must speak and the ruler hold his peace, while Frederick's dismissal and jailing of the recalcitrant justices exposed a despotic fist under the philosophical glove.

Miller Arnold's fate mainly illuminates the rocky road from royal absolutism to a bureaucratically stabilized rule of law (*Rechtsstaat*) antecedent to nineteenth-century constitutionalism.[1] How Frederick's regime routinely dealt with landlord–village conflict is a text that until recently escaped close reading. Historians looked at royal legislation and administrative reports on provincial enforcement or neglect, and accordingly pronounced rural policies good or ill. Marxist scholars little doubted the efficacy of the "feudal mode of production's" politically grounded "extra-economic coercion." Their empirical research, which was valuable, strengthened inquiries in other directions than everyday labor relations. In the 1990s German scholars launched imaginative new investigations into grass-roots manor–village turmoil, but Anglo-American historians have scarcely faced this work's challenge, which these pages aim to heighten.[2] They cast strong new light on landlord–tenant relations, conflictual and quotidian, yielding many insights into village mentalities and values. They offer a Brandenburg-Prussian model of rural labor disputes' "judicialization." Because the Berlin government and judiciary were divided over the Stavenow conflicts, they offer a revealing picture of Prussian late absolutism.

Labor strife such as Stavenow's triggered structural changes in the seigneurial economy that, together with market pressures and opportunities, hastened early nineteenth-century "emancipation" – especially from labor rents – in favor of village freeholds and noble estates worked by landless wage-earners. This dynamic was strong at Stavenow, and doubtless widely across Prussian east Elbia, contradicting the still prevalent idea that the "Junker economy," in its dependence on coerced, unpaid labor

---

[1] David Luebke, "Frederick the Great and the Celebrated Case of the Millers Arnold (1770–1779): A Reappraisal," *CEH* 32 (1999): 379–408.
[2] See the literature discussed in the introduction.

and aversion to capital investment, vegetated in low-productivity backwardness until Prussia's 1806 defeat by France instigated modernizing
reforms. The evidence is strong of profit-heightening, productivity-
enhancing innovations in Stavenow's pre-1763 seigneurial economy. It
remains to show that village obduracy and insubordination helped drive
innovation forward toward the final demise of the regime, born in the
late fifteenth and sixteenth centuries, of marketized manorialism.

PERFECTING MANORIAL SERVICE: THE KLEISTS' NEW WORK RULES OF THE 1720S

In 1723 young Judge Hasse, inexperience evident in egregious mis-
spellings, penned a proclamation to the farmers and their servants:

> Herr tenant-farmer [Schmidt] is leaving, and Herr Colonel is taking over his
> own estates. Therefore, everyone who comes to service for the master [*Herren
> Dienste*] shall work industriously and competently, especially in sowing season.
> All subjects shall perform good manorial service, reporting at proper time, and
> work, by hand and with teams, just as well as they do for themselves, using the
> same size wagons.

No villagers, on pain of redoubled punishment, should ignore court war-
rants as, seemingly, occurred under the tenant-farmers. "Much less shall
they remain away when summoned to service for the master, or they will
be punished with two days' work instead of one, or one day's jail."[3]

In 1726 Colonel Kleist, following his reforms in Premslin, Glövzin,
and Blüthen villages, affirmed to the assembled inhabitants his will
"that the subjects carry burdens on equal shoulders and, in return, have
the same farmland and meadow. This will be upheld strongly and firmly in future. Farmers opposing this order and arrangement should leave
their holdings." Exceptionally, Kleist signed this protocol-book entry.[4]
Later the farmers arrived to be rewarded for acquiescence in "equalization." They "immediately made their way to the [Löcknitz] meadows" where their new plots of this valuable seigneurial land "were
divided among them by lot and fenced."[5]

Chapter 2 displayed Colonel Kleist equipping his lordship with new
church bells, the better for his subjects to heed his officials' summons to
fieldwork and assembly. It is worth recalling here, too, Judge Hasse's
courtroom proclamation to them of 1728 on labor services. None more
detailed appeared before the late eighteenth century:

---

[3] No. 704, fo. 32.   [4] No. 200, fos. 48–9.   [5] Ibid., fos. 68–9.

Many disorders have been observed in the performance of manorial services, since some people bring such poor horse-teams they can't finish the job, while others work so unconscientiously and disobediently that nothing gets done. His Excellency Colonel von Kleist has ordered this state of affairs corrected, if only by having those who cannot bring a serviceable team do their work manually. Those who do possess teams with a good wagon and other equipment will serve from Easter until three weeks after Michaelmas [29 September] from six o'clock in the morning until returning home at six o'clock in the evening, with a rest at midday of two or three hours after unharnessing and feeding the horses. From three weeks after Michaelmas to Easter they will report for service at eight o'clock in the morning and leave again at four o'clock, stopping at midday for one to one and a half hours. They must demonstrate the greatest possible diligence in their work or, if they do not, expect to be removed from their holdings and replaced by better farmers. Manual labor services must be performed by farmers themselves, or they must send able people in their place, or otherwise expect the same punishment. They must also report for service at sunrise and leave only at sunset, and not rest at midday longer than one hour. In the harvest, there can be no fixed hours for service with horse-teams, which must be regulated according to the work that needs doing.[6]

Though these work rules were meant to be tolerable, villagers sought, unsurprisingly, to evade them, apart from buying free of one or more days, by slacking at work. In 1741 the field foreman complained to Hasse that "the subjects come too late to manorial service, and benevolence toward them does no good." The outlying Karstädters were reminded of their hours, from 7:00 A.M. to 6:00 P.M. in summer. Hasse warned them "on pain of punishment not to leave work without the foreman's directive," which clearly they had been doing. He fined three farmers for wood theft, ordering them to appear for manorial service "at the right time or expect to be locked ['laid'] in jail and ordered the next day to work," a warning extended to all Glövziners.[7]

Three years later, Hasse complained of Glövziners' "negligent service" and that "they all come to work too late and even then send small children." He decreed early arrival, seven o'clock at latest, midday rests of but two hours, sundown departure, and farmers' dispatch of "able people," two if with a team, or that they "come themselves to serve." If tardy, laborers would be sent home and called again next day. If they did not then report willingly, "they shall be fetched" by the court bailiff.[8] With swelling irritation, the lordship in December 1748 menaced Glövziners and Premsliners collectively, "should they in future come so late to service and not at eight o'clock."

---

[6] No. 200, fos. 97–8.   [7] No. 591, fos. 102–3.   [8] No. 326, fo. 116.

Wagon or plow will then be sent back, and directed to come punctually next day, and for disobedience [the farmer] will be punished with two hours in the Spanish overcoat, or if he should absent himself entirely from work, four hours – [two hours] morning and [two hours] afternoon.[9]

Yet in 1751 ten farmers skipped seigneurial harvest haulage, which "this time" they requited with an extra plowing day, though in future jail sentences loomed. Three others, "furtively" leaving after hauling but one wagonload, scorned to appear in court. The field foreman, reporting these derelictions, repeated the charge that "the people in Glövzin and Premslin don't arrive [in summer] for work before eight o'clock in the morning."[10] A few wagonloads of hay could not, it seems, buy villagers' zeal for working lordship's land, nor did judicial threats long quicken their pace.

INSUBORDINATION IN MANORIAL SERVICE UNDER COLONEL KLEIST AND HIS WIDOW

We have observed violence erupting at the manorial workplace, including fights pitting farmers or their servants, or both together, against foremen, as well as lashes and floggings overseers administered to compulsory laborers. Here we look more closely at such conflict, gauging its frequency and seriousness and judging the lordship's success in enforcing work rules. It might seem that individual resistance yielded fewer gains and more pain than collective action, and that group strategies of slacking and evasion were more congenial to villagers than one-to-one confrontation.[11] Yet anger or pride stirred them to stand up alone against physical abuse. A case opposing villagers to a townsman is revealing. Mecklenburg Grabow's municipal judge asked Hasse to interrogate day laborer Joachim Porep for "crudely berating" Grabow burgher-baker Georg Martinss, leading to blows and Martinss' later death. Porep, with three other Stavenow farm laborers, allegedly confronted Martinss for beating a servant-girl who visited Porep against the baker's orders.

The Grabow judge wanted Hasse to ask Porep (long-windedly and biasedly) whether Martinss' prohibition of his maidservant's visit had not "offended" him. Had he not publicly said: "'Martinss is not only notorious in town, but also in the countryside for beating his servants?' Whereupon Porep punched [Martinss] and trampled him with his feet,

---

[9] No. 591, fos. 150–1. [10] No. 715, fos. 42, 49. [11] Scott, *Weapons*.

saying he wanted satisfaction [of his honor], and that Martinss accused [Porep] of collusion with the maidservant in cheating him?" The deceased's witnesses said Martinss – displaying Sabbath calm – warned Porep "not to trouble him on Sunday." The baker "wanted to eat something and go to church," and led Porep by the arm out of his house. Porep resisted, saying Martinss abused him as he did his servants, unleashing the fight.[12] Porep's witnesses said Martinss caned him, mitigating Porep's guilt. However it ended, this incident shows that employers gained evil reputations for violence, and (whatever the baker's real faults) might suffer outraged workers' blows (whatever the cost).

The lordship's field foremen and bailiffs likewise could not count on villagers' docility, even though the court might harshly punish assaults on seigneurial officials. From mid-1720s until tenant-farmer Hartz's 1740 departure, bitter, if ill-matched, conflict occurred between individual villagers and their overseers. Thus in 1726 communal opposition leader Hans Milatz's two sons stood accused of defying the field foreman. Jochen Milatz "charged at the foreman's throat with a club," while brother Hans disputed villagers' obligation to cut water-reeds. Jochen said he normally labored "loyally and industriously," but the foreman "wanted all the [villagers'] draft-horses to go belly up." Jochen allegedly threatened to strike the foreman with his reins, saying "the dog" – the foreman – "wouldn't shit him any new horses."

The brothers' father testified that, when Captain Kleist was last absent, the field foreman got "totally drunk" at farmer Hecht's house, and then struck Hecht's son on the head. The foreman, dispelling suspicion of socializing with villagers, said he was only settling money accounts with Hecht. He struck young Hecht "because he didn't want to come when I called him." Judge Hasse, ignoring the Hecht incident, sentenced Milatz's sons to "one hour in the tower," doubtlessly locked in a painful posture. Their father, ordered himself to mow the controversial rushes, defiantly left the courtroom. "He sent word he wanted to go to the king," that is, appeal to royal authorities against Stavenow's rulings. Hasse postponed the case until Colonel Kleist's next visit.[13]

Whatever the outcome, Hasse, though accompanied by Bernd Kleist, tolerated the elder Milatz's defiance, awaiting consultation with Stavenow's master. Villages often disputed liability to various seigneurial tasks, which common law understood principally as work entailed by noble lordships' grain-crop agriculture. Yet Hans Milatz was the only

---

[12] No. 598, fos. 22–7.   [13] No. 200, fos. 47–8.

known Stavenow farmer to threaten, as an individual, appeal to higher authority against manorial work rules. Seemingly he gained such assertiveness as the leader of earlier protests, which evidently left his faith in royal justice undimmed.

In 1728 a farm servant accused of negligence suffered, apparently at newly installed leaseholder Hartz's own hands, "a few blows of the cudgel ['*Kerbatsche*']," a brutal instrument, otherwise unmentioned in Stavenow sources, whose use in punishing workers the 1794 Prussian Law Code outlawed. Hartz ("the bailiff") claimed the laborer defied him, telling him "he shouldn't come any closer." The worker, pleading equipment breakdown, protested he only said Hartz "should just stop beating him, since he'd already hit him five times." The farm servant's master promised "he would improve," but Hasse, likely under Hartz's goading, decreed the victim willfully caused his work stoppage. "Since blows hadn't improved him, he shall as an example be locked in the tower on bread and water." Here the bailiff and judge imposed maximally hard discipline. From new leaseholders villagers could expect the worst, and probably at their arrival each side tested the other's toughness.[14]

Hasse also cracked down on newly installed fullholder Peter Ebel for reaping grain on Sunday, and "also because he recently sent a child worker to the lordship's harvest." Ebel apologized for the child incident while claiming that, though carrying a scythe, he was not working on Sunday. Field foreman Halentz said Ebel "sent his [under-aged] servant several times to manorial service, and though they sent him back, he came again, or no one appeared." Hasse found Ebel guilty of "disobedience . . . and dishonoring the Sabbath." Instead of paying a heavy fine of 1 taler, his punishment, the judge noted, "was atoned through corporal punishment" – possibly a flogging – "and jail." Hasse threatened any future violations "with the hardest imprisonment," warning "the others" to take notice.[15]

Conflict between Hartz and village farmers intensified, while estate laborers, as chapter 7 showed, bridled under his reins. In 1730 Hans Milatz junior (again) and another farm servant exchanged blows with field foreman Pelz, to whose aid hunter Birkholz rallied. Milatz's partner complained the foreman struck him with a birch rod, while the hunter chased him on horseback and "broke his nose with his whip." These injuries sufficed as punishment, but Milatz, "because he so grossly defied the foreman," sat in jail three days as "the insubordination's instigator."[16]

[14] Ibid., fos. 96–7.   [15] Ibid., fos. 102–3.   [16] Ibid., fos. 146–7.

Soldiers or ex-soldiers further challenged Hartz's regime. Foreman Pelz, supervising villagers' work in Stavenow's gardens, discovered farmer Hans Hecht with his pipe in his mouth. Hecht defied both Pelz's command to cease smoking and his effort to seize the pipe. "Hecht charged at him," Pelz complained, "tearing up his coat and smashing his hat, which he also produces [as evidence]." Hecht said the pipe was unlit and its cover down. He held it in his mouth "because his teeth hurt" (a rare reference to dental pain, doubtless widespread). The lordship's gardener always, Hecht claimed, permitted outdoors smoking. He was ten years a soldier before discharge for "severe disability." He ripped Pelz's coat in self-defense, because "he wanted to seize the whip [Pelz] meant to strike him with." Laconically, Hecht said "he would rather not come to manorial service at all." He was waiting for two soldier-brothers to be mustered out. Meanwhile Colonel Kleist ordered him to run his parental farm. But the court bailiff, backing Pelz, affirmed Hecht's aggressiveness. Hasse concluded, because his smoking endangered "noble outbuildings" and he attacked "the lordship's official," he deserved "severe corporal punishment, as deterrent to others." But owing to his disability, punishment would await Kleist's next visit, whom Hasse evidently preferred to entrust with refractory ex-soldiers.[17]

Once, when Hartz's son was serving as field foreman, "soldier Hintze," reporting for seigneurial labor, jumped from his wagon and beat the young man with a whip-butt, despite the victim's shouting at Hintze from his horse, "stay back, fellow." The overseer had announced, "today you're doing construction service," a demand villagers (rightly) thought illegitimate unless related to manorial agriculture. To Hintze's question, "what kind?" young Hartz replied, "at the baking oven." Hintze retorted, "if that's construction service, it's the devil who says so," sparking the fight in which Hintze gave the foreman "3–4 blows." Despite the unknown outcome, the incident illustrates the explosive potential of all but the most routinized and customary tasks.[18]

Hartz's off-the-job relations with farmers and farm servants were also tense. In 1733 village farmhand Joachim Zeggel complained that, when trying to deliver a Perleberg mayor's letter seeking "justice" for him in a disputed horse sale, Hartz refused to accept it, beating Zeggel

[17] Ibid., fo. 142.
[18] No. 704, fo. 161. In 1732–3, Hartz employed unpaid manorial service in bridge repair (sixty-seven workers) and well-digging (twenty-three). No collective protests were recorded. No. 343, fos. 263, 265.

instead. Hartz claimed Zeggel was so drunk he could not explain himself. He told him to come back the next day. When Zeggel would not leave, Hartz "had to push him off the grounds to put an end to his swaggering." Only then did Zeggel mention a letter, which Hartz thought might be from Colonel Kleist. Since Zeggel would not surrender it, Hartz gave him "a few lashes."

Zeggel resisted, lying on his stomach until Hartz's wife intervened. His parting words were, "You [*du*] villain, you bailiff Hartz, the way you treated me not even Colonel Kleist treated me. May God strike you with plague for all the wrongs you inflict on me and the other subjects." Zeggel denied saying, when Hartz tried to seize the letter, that Kleist "shits on the letter, and he shits on me and the [Perleberg] mayor." But a manorial employee was prepared (unsurprisingly) to corroborate Hartz's testimony. Hartz said this was the same Zeggel who ran away from an apprenticeship Kleist arranged for him at an Altmark brewery, who was once drunk in the seigneurial harvest, and whose brother stole a neighboring lordship's horse. After inspecting Zeggel, Hasse found his claim false that a surgeon removed gravel from his back after Hartz's beating. Hasse wrote Kleist for instructions.[19]

Though Hartz and Hasse showed no patience with Zeggel, the case was delicate, since the Perleberg mayor and city council earlier wrote Kleist in Potsdam charging the Jänicke brothers, two farmhands under Stavenow jurisdiction, with stealing from town impoundment a horse that, Zeggel claimed, the Jänickes swindled away from him. When, as the magistrates complained to Kleist, they sought Hartz's cooperation in enforcing their jurisdiction, "instead of his doing us the slightest justice, he not only threw back unopened our letter, with harsh, filthy and highly insulting words we shrink from citing, but also treated Zeggel, to whom we entrusted the letter, mostly brutally, though this we leave aside here." The burghers forbore intruding on seigneurial disciplinary powers.

Zeggel, despite his lowly status, had a lawyer write to Kleist rehearsing Zeggel's newly acquired horse's theft and his attempt to deliver the magistrates' request for Hartz's legal cooperation. Though Hartz claimed Zeggel grossly defamed his seigneurial overlord, Zeggel said only that:

the bailiff refused the letter, saying (pardon the expression) he shits on it and on the mayor. When I then verbally asked to have my horse handed over, he attacked me with a great cudgel, saying "you rascal, I'll give you the horse,"

---

[19] No. 326, fos. 37–8.

and beat me on the arms, ribs, and hands until I was black, blue, and bloody, and finally he beat me on the head until I fell to the ground, as Perleberg surgeon Barnau, who examined and treated me with ointments, must attest.

Zeggel's lawyer put the following words in his mouth, offering rare insight into the language a laborer might, in a petition, employ to address his own lordship:

I am so entirely persuaded of Your Highborn's merciful attitude toward Your subjects that I have not the slightest doubt that Your Highbornness will not approve Administrator Hartz's barbaric treatment of me, especially since I was but pursuing my own just cause. You will instead sharply reprimand him, reminding him that such matters are to be decided at law and not with the cudgel, and to earnestly command him that Your loyal subjects are to be treated as human beings and not as dogs.

Zeggel's letter ended with lawyerly requests for a court hearing, a decision against Hartz, and restitution of his horse and legal expenses.

Hasse wrote the Perleberg authorities, confirming the Jänicke brothers indeed spirited off the disputed horse, though they sought excuses in "their rusticity [*RUSTICITATE*] and simple-mindedness [*lieben Einfalt*]," saying they misunderstood the council's orders. The magistrates' complaints about Hartz, Hasse wrote, "very much ill-pleased the Colonel," but Hartz and a witness would swear they were false, though Hartz did give Zeggel "a few blows with the staff to get the letter." Hasse and Hartz suffered "heartfelt pain that this malicious man [Zeggel] caused the magistrates vexation." Hartz did not want the burghers to think "he failed in his duty in such an unreasonable [*IRRAISONABLE*] manner." He was astonished at the "charge of brutality [*BRUTALITE*]" which Zeggel "godlessly invented as revenge for his blows."[20]

Joachim Zeggel appears no further in the records, though possibly he remained among his numerous local kinfolk. The language of the European Enlightenment glimmers through these documents, with their references to human beings' right to a fair judicial hearing, and their condemnation – on a village laborer's behalf – of barbarity, brutality, and irrationality. Despite Hartz's aggressive and violent behavior, he wished to be seen as judicious and reasonable, while Hasse presented his court's workings as scrupulous and correct. As for Zeggel, his curse on Hartz, with its implied condemnation of Colonel Kleist's harshness, voiced bitterness toward the seigneurial regime reflected in his lawyer's juxtaposition of justly treated human beings and mishandled dogs.

[20] No. 321, fos. 13–19.

Occasionally a farmer's contrariness and belligerence partially disarmed estate officials. In 1739 Hartz sought court action against chronically indebted and conflict-prone David Busse. Charged with missing four consecutive days of manorial service, Busse said "the village mayor's son so roughed him up that he couldn't hold rake or pitchfork in his hands." Though Busse offered to make up the missed days, Hartz said Busse "couldn't easily be brought to obedience without punishment." He earlier evaded manorial service and was behind on partial commutation payment. "Indeed, his wickedness goes so far that when [Hartz] sends the village mayor to summon him, both [Busse] and his wife reply with vicious words, so [Hartz] can no longer get anyone to go to him." Busse's daughter cursed Hartz as a "gray-bearded villain" while Busse's wife "defamed him before harvest as a witch-rider." Busse's livestock "do much damage, and when impounded he recovers them by force." Hasse stiffly fined Busse 8 groschen for each absence from work. Despite his truculence, Busse, already twenty-four years on his farm, kept it some eight years more.[21] Possibly Hasse and even Hartz showed leniency toward farmers, however troublesome, in authentic difficulties. Yet, also in 1739, farmer Hans Schütte, 11 talers in rent arrears, faced Hasse's eviction threat, despite Schütte's previous illness, failing payment soon. Here Cornet von Kleist, one of the colonel's elder sons, was present in the courtroom, perhaps inspiring Hasse to exemplary severity.[22] But in the war-torn 1740s and 1750s, court punishment of individual farmers for manorial service misdeeds were rare and minor.[23]

Farmers especially resented seigneurial demands for long hauls with horses and wagons, apart from their grudgingly acknowledged once-yearly obligatory grain-hauls. When "before the [1727] harvest" field foreman Halentz ordered wool-hauls to Potsdam, farmer Jürgen Nagel claimed he missed the summons delivered on Sunday by traveling partner farmer Hintze. Nagel had gone "into the woods with his people," leaving Hintze to travel alone on Monday. Hasse lectured assembled villagers that "short and long trips shall be done by each subject in turn." For scorning haulage orders, Nagel faced a 12-groschen fine or corporal punishment.[24]

In 1738 Hartz ordered nine Premsliners to haul 400 heavy "hollander cheeses" for sale to Berlin. His wife and maidservant packed them for transit. On arrival, Hartz's relative receiving them discovered pilferage, the farmers having stolen and sold some 100 pounds, worth 4 talers.

---

[21] No. 591, fo. 44.   [22] No. 713, fo. 264.   [23] No. 715, fos. 7, 28.   [24] No. 200, fos. 85–6.

Confronted, they threatened Hartz's "cousin" with violence, but later quarreled among themselves over guilt. Hasse pronounced them collectively responsible for compensating Hartz with 6 talers. Appointing two temporary aldermen (*"Forderschoffen"*) from among the seemingly innocent, he ordered them all to remain in court until they settled payment among themselves. Several then confessed, one admitting saying to another about cutting up the cheeses, "do it so you can justify it. If you do it right, you'll get away with it."[25]

Hartz later charged other farmers with failing to complete Potsdam cheese-hauls, stopping half-way there. Still others pilfered their loads. One farmer pleaded injury to his horse, which travel's rigors reduced to 1.5 talers' value. Others blamed a tavernkeeper for stealing cheese and the roads for failure to reach Potsdam. Hasse imposed fines to reimburse Hartz for lost goods and toll money he had given the farmers, threatening the villagers with a day's jail on bread and water should they repeat this "insubordination." This was, clearly, deliberate sabotage and passive resistance to demands for unpaid labor they rejected as illegitimate.

"As this judgment was proclaimed," Hasse wrote, "Hans Zeggel stepped out in front of the others and said, if they must pay costs, then let their eviction notices be written up, because they could no longer head their farms." Hasse retreated from this threat, however improbable, of mass resignation, saying he would consult with Colonel Kleist. Zeggel remained on his farm until his 1750 retirement. The lordship evidently decided stretching farmers' transport obligations was counter-productive, and imposed no further controversial hauls before 1763, though in 1749 two villagers faced fines for stealing seigneurial grain, probably to feed their horses, from loads they hauled to nearby Lenzen.[26]

The lordship sought to impose its work rules alternatively through condemnations of collective defects and offending individuals' punishment aimed to deter others. There was underlying seigneurial consensus that manorial services were badly performed, as the 1760 appraisal's discounting of their monetary value as capital assets showed. In 1735 Colonel Kleist wrote Hasse that "Herr Hartz is very irritated with the farmers because of their insubordination, and I would gladly have Your Wellbornness go to Staveno [sic] to decide everything equitably and punish the guilty as circumstances dictate."[27] Earlier Kleist was more belligerent. In 1727 the lordship informed Mesekow smallholders that,

---

[25] No. 591, fos. 79–80.   [26] No. 704, fos. 30–1; no. 326, fo. 157.   [27] No. 713, fo. 98.

after "the Löcknitz stream's improvement and very expensive clearance," they must contribute two days of "meadow service with plows" if they wanted to keep certain streamside meadows. They agreed, provided they retained a nearby wood-grove. The lordship assented, saying the Mesekowers could also lease swine forage there for "a few years" if they raised their offer of 10 talers. Yet in 1733, the villagers engaged a lawyer to petition Kleist. Excusing themselves "for incommoding [him] with this forthright but submissive letter," they complained Hartz had diverted stream flows onto their fields. They would not have "emboldened themselves" to protest, except that Hartz's action threatened them with "the greatest hardship and misery, especially since this piece of land is the best from which we must live." If Hartz acted on Kleist's orders, they would submit, "although total ruin stands before our eyes." But they pleaded with Kleist, "our most benevolent, justice-loving overlord," that "we poor people be left as before undisturbed in this land's peaceful possession."[28]

Kleist wrote Hartz from Potsdam, addressing him as "honorable [*wohledlen*] and much esteemed Herr *Amtmann*." Kleist praised Hartz's renovations, directing him to explain to the Mesekowers (*"Meschauer"*) "how this does not injure them."

Hopefully they will let themselves be amicably instructed. Previously they had to render two days' haulage and otherwise didn't have any grazing rights there. [Hunter Birkholz will draw new boundaries.] If the farmers don't accept this explanation and won't follow orders properly, I'll have to send a few to Spandau, for I'm there to judge them.[29]

Doubtless the villagers struck the most doleful tone possible, while Kleist believed abolishing their previous two days' haulage offset their losses. No transportations to Spandau occurred.

Villagers were conscious of Hartz's pressure on them. In 1732 he charged Stoffel Zeggel with "willfully" failing to report for barley-harvest work, causing him "great damage." Zeggel was "so impertinent" as to tell Hartz "he had to bring in his own grain first, for if he and his children had no bread, [Hartz] wouldn't give him any." When Hartz sent the court bailiff to impound Zeggel's horse, the defendant and his wife fought him off. Hartz "could still less remain silent about such insubordination since it would inspire evil consequences." Zeggel said "he thought [Hartz] wouldn't care about one day," especially since villagers had just spent six weeks working in the seigneurial rye harvest. He denied the hostile statement about bread. Because his neighbors

---

[28] No. 200, fos. 61–2; no. 713, fos. 43–4.   [29] No. 713, fos. 45–6.

were bringing in their barley, "he wouldn't have gotten a handful" of his own if he had not sent his workers to join them. Nor did he threaten the court bailiff, though "otherwise he didn't let himself be intimidated." One more day's service did not matter that much: "he didn't want to be summoned to court, and would rather work two days than be absent one." Hartz denied they had worked six weeks in the rye harvest, saying it was only nine days. He charged Zeggel with later missing two weeks' service, an example seven other farmers followed. If he had to wait about until farmers decided they could work, he would never get anything done. Hasse ruled Zeggel's actions a "crime," earning him a fine and the Spanish overcoat.[30]

Twenty-five years later similar conflicts were occurring. In September 1757 field foreman Lützow charged farmer Christian Nagel with allowing his and his neighbors' horses to graze during the seigneurial harvest on the sheaves and uncut grain. Nagel defied both Lützow's and the impounder's efforts to intervene. Later Nagel's farm servant Johann Paustein left off plowing in manorial service "before quitting time [*Feyerabend*]," and when Lützow protested, "Paustein mouthed off maliciously and talked the other farmers into leaving work as well." Nagel tried to excuse this by saying they intended to come back to work in the evening, but because Lützow was "so angry" he could not talk to him. Hasse sentenced Nagel to the Spanish overcoat and a fine, reserving separate judgment on Paustein. Here, seemingly, villagers tried to revenge themselves for unwelcome exertions by commandeering seigneurial fodder and quitting work early to attend to their own fields.[31]

Yet, in the 1740s and 1750s, the preceding decades' conflicts abated under the scaled-down expectations of the hard-driving Colonel's and Hartz's successors. Villagers contributed labor adequate to the manorial economy's transition to convertible farming, while the lordship refrained from novel demands. In 1750 a farmer complained "because he has it so hard with labor services and commutation payments." Hasse replied that "no more will be demanded of the petitioner than what he previously owed."[32]

THE KLEISTS' STRUGGLE WITH THE DARGARDT COLONISTS

Into the workaday arena where lordship and subject farmers roughly contended, Stavenow's 1750s resettlement of long-abandoned Dargardt

---

[30] No. 591, fos. 52–3.   [31] No. 326, fo. 216; no. 321, fo. 66.   [32] No. 715, fo. 9.

village introduced new actors. From fullholders and smallholders, eight apiece, the lordship aimed to draw labor to cultivate its new Kleistenhof manor-farm. But the Dargardters proved turbulent, especially negotiating tenurial terms. Their tug-of-war with Stavenow was a prologue foreshadowing, perhaps triggering, the 1760s outbreak of the old-established villagers' bitter struggle with Major Kleist over labor services. Historians, while lauding Prussian kings' "populationist" zeal in inviting "foreign" colonists into their lands, overlook their settlement's disruptive effects on noble subjects. Joining native villagers were newcomers enjoying better tenurial terms but who, like Dargardters, might display the opposite of humble gratitude toward their new overlordships.[33]

In 1752 the government empowered the Kleists "to negotiate as best they can the dues and services the settlers will render." Earlier a certain Friese wrote Frau Kleist. Knowing she wanted to settle "Mecklenburg subjects alone, I have the honor to RECOMMEND to Your Gracious Highbornness four good subjects and request most obediently that You, if possible, accept them. I send two of them with this letter."[34] Such freelance agents witness a strong demand for the perpetual-leasehold farms which Prussian colonization policy required noble landlords to offer. Colonists and heirs were exempt from army conscription and their farm titles were, eventually, freely sellable. By 1753 the Kleists faced eighty-six Mecklenburg applicants, including such fortune-seekers as "Johann Kraash, thirty-three years old, one daughter aged two years, one cow, ten sheep, 40 talers cash," or "Jacob Kraash, unwived, one cow, one calf." Two married Elbe river-boat workers applied, one with eight cattle and horses. Claus Rohr, a lodger with five children, one twenty years old, was a straw-roofer, "hard of hearing," with but a cow and calf. Many were landless laborers, ex-soldiers, and petty artisans, seeking smallholdings joined to tavernkeeper's or schoolmaster's posts. Others were personally free farmers on short leases, such as Hartwig Behrens, who "according to the accompanying attestation of his overlord," a noble Frau, "wants, with eight horses, ten cattle, two sons, to take occupancy at Trinitatis."[35]

Stavenow's "desiderata concerning colonists" exempted first-generation settlers from taxes, church levies, and tolls, abjured tithes or feudal tribute payments, and waived entry fees on jurisdictional newcomers. The lordship wanted the settlers to freely help construct the necessary seigneurial buildings, and bring their own iron stock and seed for first

---

[33] On Brandenburg colonist-farmers: Peters et al., *Bauerntagebücher*; Stadelmann, *Könige*.
[34] No. 715, fos. 135–8, 144.   [35] Ibid., fos. 393–5.

sowings, though concessions were negotiable. It would provide them "considerable grazing land" immediately.[36] By 1755 the Dargardters had built and begun cultivating their farms. With government commissioners' mediation they settled rents with Conrad Kleist. Their property rights in perpetual leasehold (*Erb-Zins-Eigenthum*) were restricted inasmuch as neither the first owner nor his heir could sell the holding. They would render two days' manorial service and pay commutation for the third, plus working four days in the seigneurial rye harvest. Fullholders would pay in cash yearly levies of 12 bushels of rye and 6 bushels each of barley and oats, which at current appraisal values tallied 14 talers.[37]

Hasse's draft deeds show the fullholders gained extra grazing land, giving them communal pasturage for nine horses or oxen, six cattle and two calves, four pigs, sixteen sheep, and two "mature geese." The lordship also granted some of them initial start-up seed-grain and money (30–50 talers) to buy livestock. But in 1756, Conrad Kleist, "for himself and in the name of his brothers serving in the army," petitioned the king, through the Brandenburg War and Domains Board, "for remedy against Dargard colonists' insubordination." Despite earlier government mediation, they refused their deeds, "remain in irresponsible opposition, and will not accept the stipulated dues and services." The smallholders did not believe they had received sufficient land for winter and summer sowings of 6–7 bushels, although "four sworn mayors and experts, among whom one . . . leased and cultivated the land for some twenty years," assured them their plots could bear 6-bushel sowings "without counting the bad land." Previous cultivators only sowed less because they lacked livestock and manure. Yet despite "all exhaustive explanations" they refused their deeds, spurring fullholders into opposition.

Exasperatedly, Conrad said he yielded to "these disruptive and noisy colonists' complaints," even though in 1753 they accepted terms which had now been "in various ways infinitely reduced." Yet "they only do and give what they please or, through false suppositions about the most graciously extended royal order, want to enjoy the years free of dues and services continuously." Resolution was impossible so long as they thought themselves "indispensable." Here Kleist pointedly referred to Mecklenburg runaway serfs Peters and Maddaus, whom Stavenow had "until now unwillingly protected" from extradition. Dargardt colony arose, he protested, "at our heavy cost . . . and we assisted these miser-

---

[36] Ibid., fos. 238–9.   [37] No. 716, fo. 31.

able [*armseligen*] people with seed and bread-grain, and also money." To inspire obedience, he asked authorization, "in reality, or to frighten them," to announce that those who did not accept their deeds and conform to their provisions would be dismissed, and "in their place loyal and obedient children of this land, who cannot otherwise make a living here and who therefore would like to go abroad, will be settled."

The government unbendingly declared the Kleists free to "remove insubordinate colonists, if incorrigible, and put others in their place, but they must also be foreigners." In 1757 Kleist publicized this ruling, "but since [the colonists] still would not conform to their obligations," he gave them eight days to reconsider. With some remaining defiant, Kleist selected replacement colonists, asking the government to instruct Prignitz sheriff Schumann to evict the recalcitrant in favor of the "loyal and obedient."[38] Kleist forwarded transcripts of two court sessions where the colonists heard these ultimatums. At the first, sickness absented seven colonists but three were represented by their wives. Those present demanded the abolition of the third day of manorial service and more pasture. Because none broke ranks, the court later summoned them individually, asking if they would accept their deeds. The first to appear, smallholder Friedrich Brusse, said

he had no objections to the deed if only they were granted another head of livestock on the pasture. He wants to accept the deed if the others do so also, but he can't cut himself off from the other farmers, because then they would revenge themselves on him, saying he was a scoundrel and a village-wrecker [*Dorfverderber*].

Other smallholders said nothing of communal solidarity. Several wanted larger hay meadows. Another said "he can't keep himself in bread because he hasn't enough arable, and so can't accept the title." Christian Wilcke likewise said "he has already this year bought 6 bushels of rye and will have to buy more, and so can't manage on the farm." Jochen Stock's "wife says her husband is sick, and they heartily wished to stay but they can't manage on the farm because the land won't bear, and when her husband gets better he will also report." Fullholders sounded similar tones. Jochen Heinrich Kuhpass said "he can't feed his livestock with his eight loads of hay because the horses consume it, and the land doesn't bear and their pasture is bad and grows no grass, and so he can't accept the deed." Another dispiritedly

---

[38] No. 716, fos. 128–53, 182–5, 197–8, 219–20. The Kleists dropped claims to smallholders' grain rents, and conceded them good grazing rights.

said "he has nothing to live on, rye he's already purchased, the bread's gone, and he has no money."[39]

Two years later settlement emerged between lordship and settlers, none of whom, seemingly, were evicted, though several died. The "reflection period" had been repeatedly extended, but the settlers still refused their titles. Resignedly, Kleist announced various concessions on which "the gracious lordship, from pure good-will and to clear away all further complaints and to preserve the colonists more securely, has resolved." The lordship dropped fullholders' grain rents to 12 bushels of rye only. It canceled commutation arrears for the third day's service, though this levy would in future prevail. Yet the colonists had minimized labor rents for three years after the initial three free years, while earlier expanding pasturage and later profitably halving grain rents.[40] Doubtless labor shortage during the Seven Years War worked against the Kleists' initial hard line, but Berlin also held them to its terms. Even in 1776, when Major Kleist requested formal title to Dargardt, having settled all sixteen farmers plus a hollander, schoolmaster, shepherd and two livestock herders, the government balked until he recruited the three additional cottagers his mother promised to settle. Judge Betich advised Kleist to comply, for the government would not relent.[41]

ORIGINS OF MAJOR KLEIST'S CONFLICT WITH HIS SUBJECT VILLAGERS

The spectacle of the Dargardters' successfully deflating overweening seigneurial demands must have strengthened old-established villagers' communal instincts. Perhaps it convinced young Major Friedrich Joachim von Kleist, taking managerial reins in 1763, that stiffer discipline was wanting in his villages. We saw that pressure of debts within and outside the family led him, soon after inheriting Stavenow, to sell much timber and, on the cleared land, to extend seigneurial grain plantings. This ignited two struggles with the villagers, one over the cut timber's haulage, and the other over labor services on the expanded arable. Major Kleist had exhausted his small reserves of diplomacy and conciliatoriness by 1766, when he began handling his farmers with a violence, aimed at groups rather than individuals, previously unrecorded. As a young man unused to landlordly authority, he wielded all too quickly the weapons of coercion. But as a regimental commander's son

---

[39] Ibid., fos. 222–3.   [40] Ibid., fos. 293–301.   [41] No. 718, fos. 91–2.

and veteran of Frederickian war, it is not surprising he took up the lash against his subjects.

This first skirmish was a 1766 clash between estate officials and Stavenow's five Sargleben cottagers. They were embittered at losing to Dargardt colonists lands the lordship had rented them, supplementing their meager hereditary arable and raising them to smallholder status. Now declassed and poorer, they bridled at long-controversial milling fees, which Major Kleist ordered the court bailiff to collect through impoundment of the Sarglebeners' goods. Estate administrator Fygel informed Hasse's successor, Judge Betich, that the villagers "resisted and drove the court bailiff away with curses." Kleist, on a trip's eve, ordered the five brought before him and commanded their compliance. This having failed, he "wanted to bring them to obedience" – punish them physically – "but they resisted and fought back, repelling the court bailiff; in short, in Monsieur the Major's presence and with the highest degree of disobedience, they flaunted all respect and reverence."

They wanted, too, to run off, and tailor Schmidt actually did, but the court bailiff brought him back. And as Your Wellbornness may imagine of such an event, it could not be otherwise than that a few blows decided the matter, until it was possible to throw them in the hole [*Loch*, or dungeon] to bring them to obedience. This unpleasant event caused Monsieur the Major much vexation and exasperation, and today at departure he ordered that they be left to sit in jail, on bread and water, until changing their minds.

Still, Kleist would be happy if, in his absence, Betich settled the matter. Fygel offered horses to fetch Betich, but asked:

What if the arrestees rebel again, and even storm against us? What then to do? Wouldn't we have to heave to with the sword? I don't see anything good coming of it. There'll have to be rough canings. And among the five there's a woman, and she sits with those fellows. But I think that's of no importance. (She can [Fygel maliciously added] defend her honor herself down in the hole.)[42]

Whatever Fygel's background, the Sarglebeners' desperation and defiance unnerved him.

By 1769 Kleist's importunities drove his three principal fullholders' villages of Glövzin, Karstädt, and Premslin to pool resources, engage a lawyer, and petition the king. The government appointed a Perleberg-seated commission to investigate, initiating a thirty-year battle in courts

---

[42] No. 600, fos. 5–6.

and on the ground. Chief among villagers' grievances was Kleist's order to haul his cut timber, in regular weekly manorial service, for sale to the Elbe, some fifteen English miles distant. Because, as villagers believed, such haulage was never admissible, at Stavenow or elsewhere, and because "we ruin our teams with timber-hauls," they refused compliance. In 1767 Kleist tried to break resistance with "illegal impoundments" but, since they paid their fines, in vain. "Most recently he attacked us even harder, having his domestics harshly beat us and putting us into such an unhealthy jail that even the strongest nature runs the danger of ruin within 24 hours, and where we sometimes have to hold out several days." The king must consider "whether such methods can well be approved among Christians." They claimed that, "though innocent, he often cruelly beats us without cause, and even the advanced age of one or another does not cause him to desist, or to have mercy." They expressed awareness (referring perhaps to Frederick II's abolition of judicial torture) that the king had often forbidden such un-Christian and illegal treatment. Moreover, Kleist arbitrarily demanded two days' manual labor if they were not called for one day's work with teams, and compounded their six "extra days" (*Beytage*) of rye harvesting with the two non-commuted days they otherwise owed in any particular week, though the six-day obligation should cancel out the two.[43]

After receiving his farmers' petition from the government-appointed investigator, Perleberg burgher Senator Lamprecht, Kleist and Judge Betich replied to Berlin's Chamber Court. The major read "with greatest astonishment" how the villagers "heaped untruth upon untruth." The more concessions they received, the more "malicious and refractory" they became. His powers of "reasonable explanation" exhausted, Kleist asked the government to enforce his rights and their duties. Forest incomes were, he held, a seigneurial "usage," whose "enjoyment" villagers' labor service made possible. He recalled the Chamber Court had already in 1766 ordered Stavenow farmers to haul wood in regular weekly service or suffer punishment as "insubordinate subjects." Kleist threatened them with two days' jail, including two hours daily in irons. Though obliged by law to return them for harvest work, he impounded their draft-animals. While some wood-hauls had occurred, resistance revived. The Chamber Court sanctioned the sheriff's arrest of the leaders and their imprisonment in Perleberg. "But this was no help," requiring Kleist to pay at "heavy cost" for haulage. He proposed

[43] No. 343, fos. 3–6.

the "ringleaders," including Premslin mayor Holtzmann and Glövzin's "Zeggel brothers," be transported to Spandau fortress until swearing to perform the hauls.

Kleist recited his "disorderly" farmers' other faults, following field foreman Kraatz (who shared Stavenow's free mayor's name). Though manorial service elsewhere started at sunrise and ended at sunset, "I observe moderation," Kleist declared, asking only that from Easter through September villagers report at 7:00 A.M. and otherwise at 8:00 A.M., work ending at sundown. But it was "custom" to arrive thirty or sixty minutes late. The field foreman spoke more bluntly: "despite all reminders they still come too late. Blows do no good [*Kombt Schlage ist es auch nicht recht*]." Kleist said that, though the farmers possessed big four-horse wagons, they brought to the manor small ones with two horses for manure-haulage. "They always bring [their] worst plows," so worn-out (the field foreman added) "that they constantly fall apart, so they can halt work." And to perform manual labor "they send the worst people, indeed even children" ("useless stuff," Kraatz said). "Last harvest small-holder Jahnecke was so bold as to send a maidservant for mowing," though by law he should do it himself. "Mowing grain and hay, they ruin half, because they don't cut hay flush to the ground or leave grain-stubble but a half-ell long, nor will they heed any corrections." Often, Kleist complained, "according to whim and without good reason," they ignore summonses "to present themselves before me, their overlord," at the manor-house, "although their subject condition [*Unterthänigkeit*] and respect should cause them to appear."

Nor could Kleist get them to obey smoking and school regulations. "To preserve farms," villagers were forbidden to fell trees without seigneurial approval, but the Glövziners cleared a whole woodstand on their arable without asking permission. Villagers, when called for unpaid construction services, made only two hauls daily, loading wagons so "disgracefully" they carried only 200 pounds, requiring summoning them oftener. Though agreeing to make 18-bushel grain-hauls, they would not carry 20 bushels of barley, even if weighing less than 18 of rye. Their farmhands did not protect young trees planted along Kleist's driveways, but pulled up the stakes and threw them about the roads. "I would never finish listing all forms of their insubordination and malice, which often go so far that they resist those appointed to oversee their work, threatening and even assaulting them." Foreman Kraatz noted it was the villagers' farmhands who were guilty of such turbulence, but of farmer and servant alike he said, "they resist while

making gestures of working, when they should be in jail instead."
Tacitly admitting his disciplinary limits, Kleist sought government rein-
forcement.[44]

Senator Lamprecht, sending Kleist more villagers' grievances, summoned him to a Stavenow tavern hearing. Kleist's subjects charged him
with "enervating" them with fines and punishments. They instanced
foreman Kraatz's command that farmer David Zeggel "soundly thrash"
his twelve-year-old son who let Zeggel's horses into seigneurial pastures.
Since the boy promptly recovered them, Zeggel refused, provoking
Betich to jail him one day and fine him 30 groschen. When villagers
reported for haulage to Stavenow's ice-cellar, Kleist raged over their
small wagons, ordering four cut to pieces. Kleist ignored the once-yearly
limitation on local grain-haulage, commanding other such transports in
regular service. Villagers protested his orders to break rocks and haul
them to Stavenow to rebuild bridges. Before the major's day, they never
made more than three hauls daily of seigneurial firewood. Recently,
"from good-will and to live in peace, we did four hauls," but now Kleist
demanded five, "so that we quit only at nine o'clock in darkest night."
They had to bring a worker to load wood, breaking the "well-known
law" that when they served with horses, they need not bring a second
hand, since that equaled adding a day's manual service.

On Kleist's punishments the villagers' lawyer cited mayor Peter
Ebel's testimony. In the previous winter, after refused wood-haulage
to the Elbe, "some of us were thrown in [Stavenow] jail, where I,
Peter Ebel from Premslin, a sixty-three-year-old man, after sitting
there five days, fell so ill I was taken out for dead, and was only
restored somewhat by a purgative given me by field foreman Kraatz,
who by profession [here Ebel erred] is surgeon." Resistance unbroken, Kleist secured the three renitent villages' mayors' and aldermen's imprisonment in the Prignitz sheriff's Perleberg jail, "where
otherwise delinquents condemned to death sit." It was an evil place.
"Only when our group arrived was it scrubbed and various holes
plugged up."

Naturally we fell into danger of our health in this jail, in itself unhealthy,
through the air's fouling by these repairs, made worse by bailiff Dattel's burning wet pinewood in the prison stove during the first two days. This created
such terrible smoke we had to lie flat on our stomachs with our faces to the
earth to avoid suffocation.

[44] Ibid., fos. 13–23, 39.

After five days Ebel again sickened, gaining release into surgeon's hands for bleeding and medicine. His jailings left him with "feeble body" and he still could not "breathe properly." Other comrades also fell ill and were discharged. One stayed two weeks, being freed only when his livestock succumbed to hunger. A horse died and other animals could no longer stand on their feet, "so that he had to ride around everywhere begging for fodder." Two others endured "three full weeks." "Certainly these dealings with us overstep humanity's bounds." The king would not approve them, "and never will Herr Defendant be able to answer for his behavior toward us before God's judgement seat." The villagers, "on our knees and with hot tears," implored the king for hearing and redress, including payments for time lost and "torment" (*Marter*).[45]

FIRST COURTROOM DUEL, JULY 1769

Kleist's subjects' plea invoked both "humanity" (*Menschlichkeit*) and divine retribution, holding that seigneurial (or higher) sanctions should not imperil their health or livelihoods. In July 1769 Kleist and Perleberg burgher and city councilor Judge Betich faced the villagers in a two-day hearing held in Senator Lamprecht's chambers. The farmers – perhaps confined to mayors and other leaders – were "all present in person," represented by lawyer Bürgermeister Gutike, from Brandenburg's somewhat distant Rathenow.[46] Though an instance of judicialization of manor–village conflict through royal courts, the session also vented wounded and outraged feelings on both sides, issuing in seemingly heartfelt if shortlived semi-reconciliation. Betich addressed each villagers' charge. The two lawyers then rebutted one another. No one else spoke, though doubtless Kleist guided his counsel's moves. Senator Lamprecht later undertook an on-the-spot investigation before sending his recommendations to Berlin's Chamber Court, which eventually delivered its own binding, though appellable verdict. The lawyers referred to no legal source except Friedrich Müller's *Practica Civilis Marchica Rerum Forensium* (Berlin, 1678), a Brandenburg civil-law handbook authoritative on village subjection and its obligations.[47]

Betich, invoking Müller, proclaimed wood-hauls in regular manorial service to the Elbe – only 7.5 English miles distant – entirely legal, even if Stavenowers had never before performed them. He aggressively

---

denied all brutality charges, blaming the villagers for incurring punishment. "It is false that the plaintiffs were driven with blows into an unhealthy jail. They were brought into the ordinary tower-dungeon, the villagers' jail [*Bauren-Gefängnis*], and because they resisted, they were thrown in earnest." Such jails might properly be unpleasant, while resistance to arrest deserved rough treatment. Villagers' lawyer Gutike countered that commercial wood-buyers' past arrangement of their own hauls told against Kleist's attempted innovation. Nor should Kleist justify his demands by instancing villagers' readiness to haul wood and other goods for free-time hire. "Just to pay rent to the Herr defendant they have to seek out all possible side-earnings, because they can't take anything away from their crops and livestock." Gutike left taxes unmentioned, but doubtless no one forgot them. Betich retorted that Kleist had good reason to care for "his subjects' conservation," whose "stubbornness" (*Eigensinn*) rather than threat of "ruin" opposed them to wood-hauls. Kleist often granted "remissions to the incapacitated," and substituted manual labor for work with villagers' easily exhaustible teams.[48]

Stories of "horrible beatings" without cause or consideration of age Betich denounced as "libel," for which "ringleaders and agitators" should be punished. Gutike declared the villagers ready to make sworn depositions, "but if in future they may be assured such things will not recur – because otherwise it's very difficult to hire farm servants – they will drop the charge." Saying Kleist would never punish the innocent, Betich, doubtless heeding the major, brusquely declined this olive branch. Defending Kleist's demand both for six days' harvest work and regular manorial service in the same week, Betich said Kleist let villagers harvest their own rye before having them reap his fields. At the manor they spent "half their time loafing," explaining why it took six days to bring in his crop. Reducing the seigneurial view to its nub, Betich declared:

The plaintiffs have their farms in exchange for labor services, and it would be misplaced compassion toward these insubordinate people if Herr Defendant were to show them indulgence in performing the labor they themselves acknowledge as their duty.

If he wished, Kleist could put everything "on strictest footing," cancelling third-day cash commutation. Gutike claimed his clients worked in Stavenow's harvest "with all industriousness," but because Kleist's grain sowings were now, because of forest clearing, twice their former extent,

[48] No. 343, fos. 53–8.

work lasted much longer. They proposed hearing two senior day labor-ers, who would swear that formerly Stavenow's rye could be harvested in three days, leaving time the same week for regular labor service. Moreover, in law manorial service was not deferrable, but must be per-formed on schedule or waived.[49]

Kleist bristled at the charge he excessively punished David Zeggel for refusing to discipline his son. When "willful violations" occurred, Kleist needed to "apply serious measures." But he was more concerned his vil-lagers bow to his authority than to punish them for errant grazing. "As is his custom, Zeggel was impertinent, so [Kleist] had no choice but to have him thrown in jail. In such cases Herr Defendant can't be expected to put the respect he commands at risk." Likewise Kleist had his court bailiff demolish undersized wagons "to end this abuse." It was false that they used the same wagons in their own work. They brought them to the manor "only to perform service as badly as possible." Once, "when the subjects made their wagons too narrow, [Kleist's] father had them burned." About other disputed work, Kleist said scornfully it was "a marvelous inspiration" that farmers should decide such matters instead of himself. Servants were not summoned to the manor "to loaf, but to work."[50]

The Perleberg jailings were, Betich said, unobjectionable, the Chamber Court having sanctioned them. The farmers were lucky to be released when they fell ill. Yet, despite his combativeness, Betich struck some conciliatory tones. About wood-hauls he said, "to show [the farm-ers] that [the major] is more mindful of their conservation than they imagine, he wants to repeat the proposal he recently made outside court, that if they voluntarily perform the haulage," he would accept during the same week their second service day in manual labor rather than with horses. Possibly putting words in the farmers' mouths, Gutike said they would consider the idea.

The farmers, Gutike averred, dutifully drove to the manorial work-place at 6:00 A.M. in summer and 7:00 A.M. in winter. Betich retorted that "for some time they've made it their habit to arrive late." They now promised punctuality, "but hoped that if sometimes a quarter-hour were missed it wouldn't immediately be held against them." About careless mowing, they applied "requisite diligence," but occasionally erred. "Nor is it any wonder, since [Kleist's] foreman determines how much a man shall mow daily and often assigns more than is manage-

[49] Ibid., fos. 60-1, 63, 76.   [50] Ibid., fos. 67-8, 72, 74-5, 79.

able." Kleist replied dismissively that workers sent to mow "don't want to be held to their task, but engage in all kinds of mischief."[51]

The farmers denied sending children to the manor who "weren't up to the work," whether "merely leading the plow" or more demanding tasks. "They weren't able to keep farm servants [just to do labor service] and they thank God their children can come to their help, here and at home." They added that, "so far as domestic circumstances and manorial service allow, they would send [children] to school, but it's easy to see this can't occur day in and day out throughout the whole year." Kleist agreed, insisting only on the short winter and summer terms. About heeding seigneurial summonses, "they would never refuse obedience, but if recently they sometimes hadn't appeared, it was because they feared a bad reception." Kleist righteously replied that "if they did nothing bad, they need fear no bad reception, and bad deeds gave them no right to stay away." If one or another farmer did not always promptly pay his rent, Gutike said, "it was simply because of poverty," toward which Kleist "could show Christian mercy." Kleist claimed this virtue for himself, in past and future, "but there can be no insubordination."

Finally, the villagers protested Kleist's punishment of Johann Heinrich Zeggel for his daughter's negligence with fire, which allegedly threatened Glövzin with incineration. Kleist said Zeggel shrugged off his daughter's offense, saying to Kleist's face he hoped "this whole beggar's life might go up in flames [*der Bettel in Feuer aufgehen möchte*]." Zeggel pleaded innocence, but Kleist, said Betich, "knows that denials are Zeggel's specialty," and said three witnesses would swear he had expressed the "wicked wish."[52] Certainly Zeggel's words are imaginable, especially following the Seven Years War's furies and facing Kleist's aggressiveness.

LAMPRECHT'S INVESTIGATION AND CHAMBER COURT VERDICT

Senator Lamprecht visited Stavenow with nearby Kletzke lordship's bailiff Breuel as oath-sworn "economic expert." The villagers' lawyer was Perleberg city councilor Engel, while Kleist and Betich also attended. Inquiry turned first to Elbe wood-hauls, to determine whether they would cause farmers' "ruin and demise." The plaintiffs said their horses "were poor at best."

---

[51] Ibid., fos. 77–80.   [52] Ibid., fos. 79–83.

Their pasture and hay harvests were well known to be much worse than in other villages. They can't give their horses grain, but let them feed in summer on the scarce grass, and seek to bring them through the winter with but meager fodder.

Lenzen hauls would take two days, and horses would then need a half-day rest. Few villagers possessed two four-horse teams. Most kept one team plus a pair of oxen. Kleist was skeptical, but conceded that "ruined farmers were no good to him."

Some Glövziners performed a test haul with wood loads Kleist had approved. The others accompanied the haulers, timing the journey, which without stops, and traveling slowly, as befitted the work, took on average 4.5 hours each way. The experts could not agree on distance traveled. Lamprecht wrote, "in this region the mile's measurement is completely indeterminate, and generally depends *ab arbitrio et opinione vulgi.*" Still, most views held it was slightly more than two German (ten English) miles one way from Stavenow to Lenzen river-dock.[53]

Turning next day to other controversies, three farmers loaded their wagons with manure and presented them for inspection. Bailiff Breuel measured them and, finding loads "very meager" and wagons "too small and narrow," stipulated appropriate dimensions. Concerning construction services, the investigators studied Stavenow manor-seat. The lordship generally Lamprecht found "very considerable ['*impor-tant*'] and its economy correspondingly large and far-ranging." They noticed the 1546 date Lütke von Quitzow had carved into the manor-house stone. They mapped seigneurial buildings, including, 300 paces from the manor-hall, the "*Amtmann*'s or administration house," which was "indeed large and livable," though "in the lordship's view it isn't sufficiently big and suited to its station." Kleist opined that, with fifty-one fullholders to perform construction services, these could not fall on anyone too heavily. Lamprecht's description of the Stavenow "villagers' jail" was sober and detached:

This jail, in which the plaintiffs were thrown, is located in Herr Major von Kleist's dwelling-house, down below in a rather deep basement constructed of stone. It has, up front facing the courtyard, a sufficiently large opening, though without windows, through which adequate daylight, as well as fresh air, can enter. It is not too moldy or small, nor was it noticeably damp or otherwise unhealthy. It is, rather, what a villagers' jail, whose purpose does not aim at pleasure, ordinarily must be.

53 Ibid., fos. 83–4, 90.

Lamprecht recorded various elders' sworn testimony about the seigneurial rye harvest prior to the Kleists' arable expansion. A sixty-six-year-old day laborer remembered working the harvest around 1719–1720, when it could be finished in three rainless days. Seigneurial sowings then were not even half what they were now. Another, Perleberg day laborer Hans Schultze, said he was "near on eighty years old," born a Premslin farmer's son. Like other witnesses, he was asked whether he had village relatives with interests in play. Schultze only claimed a tailor-cottager nephew. He helped harvest seigneurial rye around 1707, and remembered working not more than 3–4 days. He was ignorant of present conditions, not having returned to Stavenow "for a very long time, over fifty years." Here was a migrant to the town who did not look back.[54]

Seigneurial field foreman Carl Kraatz, a twenty-nine-year-old glazier's son from Middlemark's distant Treuenbritzen, testified concerning Kleist's alleged "punitive impoundments" that Glövziners caused much grazing damage, and resisted by flight Kraatz's efforts to seize their livestock. David Zeggel's punishment for refusing to discipline his son was justifiable. "Zeggel, as he was taken to jail, put up much resistance, and so had to be forcibly thrown in, whereupon he threatened that was going too far with him." Peter Piers, a forty-four-year-old Perleberg day laborer, but until recently Stavenow court bailiff, said when Kleist ordered Zeggel to pay 1 taler for not punishing his son, Zeggel replied, "I don't deserve it." After Zeggel's wife came next day with the taler, Kleist told him, "if you [*ihr*] don't want to pay, then it's right back to jail [*dem Gehorsam*]." Rostock-born Johann Brandt, twenty-eight, the new court bailiff, reported that, when upon Zeggel's jail release the major told him to "improve himself," Zeggel retorted sarcastically: "Yes, everything is fine. It's ruination the way things are set up here. It's too much. It's ruination. I've sat here so long I might as well have sat the whole night." Brandt recalled that when he jailed Zeggel, along with Peter Ebel and Heinrich Zeggel, for refusing wood-hauls, "they absolutely didn't want to go in, and resisted with force, and Heinrich Zeggel grabbed the bailiff and wrestled around with him."[55]

Senator Lamprecht took further testimony about jailings. Field bailiff Kraatz denied administering purgatives to the allegedly dying Peter Ebel upon his emergency release from Stavenow dungeon. "Ebel

---

[54] Ibid., fos. 92–6, 102, 117. [55] Ibid., fos. 103, 108–9.

got somewhat sick" because "he was previously inclined to [physical] obstructions." Kraatz took Ebel into a warm room and gave him "elixir drops," restoring him. When Kraatz visited the Perleberg prisoners, he again found Ebel "somewhat sick." Surgeon Grob told Kraatz that Ebel was suffering "febrile attacks" because of "obstructions," but "it was of no importance." Kraatz considered it "no wonder that a man always accustomed to motion should get obstructions from sitting." In Perleberg, surgeon Grob told how, on Betich's orders, he visited Ebel in jail. Grob "found Ebel sitting in a chair, with sweat running heavily down his face." Testing Ebel's pulse, he diagnosed him as sick but not "deathly ill," giving him a "resolving mixture." Following Ebel's jail release next day, Grob opened a vein, easing Ebel's side-pain. After 3–4 days, Ebel told Grob he was "tolerable" but not "fully better," requesting and receiving more medicine. Grob would not ascribe his illness to the jail, because there was "enough air" and the others did not sicken. Whatever the rigors of the Stavenow and Perleberg jailings, seigneurial and urban authorities would not concede such incarceration was physically harmful.[56]

Finally, Lamprecht investigated Johann Heinrich Zeggel's alleged arson incitation. Zeggel's cousin, Glövzin mayor Joachim Holtmann, thirty-nine, said he heard Kleist say, "Zeggel, you must send me your daughter to be punished because of the fire." Zeggel told the major "he needn't take it so seriously. Quitzow village burned down and nothing happened to the woman who caused it. He should leave things be." Zeggel then added, "if only the beggary – meaning his farm [Holtmann added] – would burn down." Holtmann would swear Zeggel did not mean the whole village. Two other witnesses agreed they had not heard the alleged imprecation. As one said, "he had pondered it much, but could remember nothing at all."[57]

Lamprecht's and Breuel's investigations cost 32 talers, split equally between Kleist and the villagers. Lamprecht composed a draft compromise, much favoring Kleist, though not without recognizing some village complaints' justice. Neither side endorsed it, wishing instead definitive judgment from Berlin. Lamprecht dispatched the documentation and in May 1770 the Chamber Court ruled Elbe wood-hauls admissible in regular manorial service, since the villagers had not proven them "an absolute impossibility," nor even that they would "ruin their teams." Müller's lawbook accepted such hauls within a

---

[56] Ibid., fos. 106–7, 114–15.   [57] Ibid., fos. 112–13.

radius of two German miles. Though Lenzen was slightly farther, the hauls took but eleven hours, including a two-hour midday pause. This day was shorter than the usual service day with horses, the plaintiffs gaining "a few hours." It was not relevant whether hauls were "somewhat harder than service *in loco*."

The Berlin court did not find Kleist guilty of authorizing "violent beatings," but reprimanded him mildly, ruling that "when infractions occur, the lordship must allow the seigneurial justiciary to adjudicate them as law prescribes." If a week were required to harvest his rye, Kleist could not also claim regular weekly service, "because accumulating unperformed manorial services is impermissible, tending to subject farmers' oppression." Kleist must limit seigneurial impoundings to fines of 1.5 groschen per offending animal, plus the appraised value of illegal grazing losses. This ruling implied Kleist's fining of David Zeggel was improper because excessive and arbitrary. Kleist's effort to transform farmers' annual grain-hauls, should he not need them all, into a regular service day with team was unacceptable. Hauls must be used or lost.[58]

The court ruled too that fullholders should haul stones for Kleist's legitimate building projects, but not break them, which was smallholders' work. Farmers needed only send one man with a team to haul firewood, nor could Kleist work them beyond sundown. Villagers' complaints over their leaders' jailing were groundless, since they resulted from their own "stiffneckedness." In law, farmers were personally responsible for labor service but, if "hindered," they might send "competent servants." Kleist was left to adjudicate various issues, including Heinrich Zeggel's "alleged wish" of arson. The verdict cost the parties 12 talers.[59]

FURTHER JUDICIAL STRUGGLE, 1771–1774

The Chamber Court judged Kleist's interests benevolently, though not uncritically. The villagers' resort to royal justice gained little except respite from execrated wood-hauls and, perhaps, lighter corporal punishment. Neither side was satisfied, and both immediately entered appeals. Kleist refused defeat on all subsidiary haulage and labor-service issues. The farmers justified continuing non-compliance with wood-haul commands by their appellate action, although Kleist's

[58] Ibid., fos. 137–58, 158–63.   [59] Ibid., fos. 163–6.

Berlin lawyer won a royal cabinet order requiring the transports' interim performance. This was *Hoff Fiscal* ("court fiscal investigator") Berends. He addressed Betich as "cousin" (*Vetter*), meaning – seemingly – "colleague," and advocated toughness. "In past years the subject villagers must have been running very wild. It's unbelievable what bad consequences flow from showing farmers too much indulgence." In 1770 he observed to Betich that the villagers' appeal contained massive "complaints about beatings," which Kleist later rebutted in a letter Berends drafted. Nothing short of "painful pressure" would stanch the flow of financial losses Kleist suffered through his villagers' "shamelessly insubordinate" behavior. "Sheriff Bartz should squeeze money from them to cover commercial haulage."[60]

About physical brutality, Kleist self-righteously said "truly, from love of virtue the farmer does nothing, at least not in manorial service." The major defended his officials' blows and lashes. Since law forbade punishment with money fines,

nothing remains but coercion through jailing which, however, the farmer completely ignores, while his work and his overlord's necessarily suffer. A serious word, a sharp reminder, most efficiently counter the farmer's laziness and least harmfully promote work and uphold discipline. Their effects are felt on the spot while jailing only causes more negligence and loss. Far be it from me to take serious coercive steps without urgent cause . . . Much less have I myself personally engaged in the cursing and beating the farmers complain of.

Kleist commented on several of sixteen physical punishment charges. In one case, even the chastised farmhand's employer complained "that the slacker couldn't be got to move." A farmer's daughter earned punishment because her "idle chatter" distracted herself and others. Another farmhand capriciously stopped hauling manure and went home. "The fellow is feeble-minded, and his employer was earlier told this incorrigible fellow is unacceptable in manorial service, but still he sent him." A maidservant likewise "lacks requisite understanding" and was unmovable "with gentleness."

Farmer Nagel's son had to be rejected because he always puts himself in first place and thinks he can do anything because he's a soldier. He's a hothead always looking for opportunities to stir up the others and keep them from working.

Kleist defended "moderate disciplining" (*mässige Züchtigung*), denying it drove farmhands to desert employers. If only farmers themselves performed their service "honorably, loyally, and properly." But with

---

[60] Ibid., fos. 169–71, 176, 181, 183–4, 187–8.

"7–8-year-old children, good-for-nothing servants, the deaf," and other misfits, "unpleasant results" were unavoidable. "My estate manager assures me he served sixteen years as field bailiff on various Prignitz estates and never encountered such insubordinate, disobedient, and unbending people as at Stavenow." The alternative to Kleist's own "lawful coercion in service" was court-ordered "severe bodily punishment."[61]

A royal order followed, warning villagers to work as the Chamber Court prescribed. Otherwise the "stiffnecked" would be transported to Berlin for two weeks' imprisonment on bread and water. But an earlier private rescript in the king's name sharply reprimanded Kleist for on-the-spot physical punishments. Though villagers must obey,

We cannot forbear saying the circumstances you adduce in no way justify you or your overseer in administering blows to subject farmers or their servants during manorial service, or in otherwise forcibly handling them. This must in future, on threat of sternest requital, cease entirely.[62]

Here we observe – as historians have not – Frederick's regime altering the landlord–villager relationship, not by substantive changes in farmers' seigneurial obligations, but by administrative methods restraining landlordly coercion.

Nevertheless, Kleist commanded village mayors and aldermen in January 1771 to assemble their neighbors for wood-haulage next day. They agreed to announce the order, but said plainly "they were not able." A month-long non-compliance followed. Kleist wrote the Chamber Court of "irrecoverable losses" during "the present frost-weather," when firewood prices were highest. Finally, though the royal cabinet denied Kleist's proposal to hire commercial haulers with fine monies, the Berlin court ordered four village leaders' to be imprisoned at Perleberg for eight days, "half on bread and water," but still they refused the transports. "Indeed," Kleist wrote the Perleberg magistrates, "co-arrestee Zeggel told the sheriff that they, the subjects, wouldn't perform wood-hauls even if the execution tribunal, with gallows and wheel, stood on Perleberg market square."

Kleist secured their reimprisonment, petitioning their transfer to Spandau fortress, but the Chamber Court ordered their release. In famine-stalked April 1771 it wrote him that,

as is notorious, there is now great fodder shortage. Under these circumstances, and so long as this hindrance persists, you must show understanding and, without prejudicing your rights, spare your subjects the [disputed] labor services.

[61] Ibid., fos. 187–9.   [62] Ibid., fos. 190, 194.

The Berlin jurists cited the prisoners' testimony, given the Perleberg magistrates, that "with their already heavy labor services" they could never manage wood-hauls. This year "fodder was bad and grain too expensive." Their "horses and livestock were so exhausted" they could not even pull a small wool load to Perleberg. Without release they would "be reduced to beggars." Heinrich Zeggel had a wife and eight young children, the eldest performing his farm's labor services. Christoph Zeggel's wife was struggling with sick children. Jürgen Ebel's young farmhand could not manage alone, while Christian Nagel's son would soon leave for Potsdam military exercises. Freeing them over Kleist's protests, the magistrates plainly took the villagers' side.[63]

It was Kleist's (well-deserved) bad luck to be struggling with his subjects during the 1770–2 harvest crises, though it was the farmers' worse luck then to be draining their resources fighting an aggressive landlord. Lawyer Berends regarded the prisoners' freeing as a blow. He wrote Betich and Kleist: "Shall representations be made at court? Swift and secret." He feared spring planting's arrival would give the villagers a further pretext for evasion. An angry letter from Kleist to the king's cabinet followed, saying the farmers' wood-haulage refusal was undermining labor services generally. "The subjects are already getting defiant. They don't want to plow anymore, or haul manure. In short, they don't want to do anything in manorial service." Kleist feared "the farmer" would cite the (questionable) fodder shortage alleged by the jurists in refusing other labors requiring well-fed draft-teams, such as plowing. Again, he pleaded for transporting the "ringleaders" to Spandau, complaining too that the villagers refused to pay for the sheriff's several jailings, leaving him with the bill.[64]

Kleist soon savored victory. In May 1771 the appellate bench within the Chamber Court ruled his farmers responsible for losses their wood-haul refusals caused him, and for performing during the same week both six days' harvest labor and two days' regular manorial service. Royal cabinet orders also commanded the Chamber Court to cancel its ruling that fodder shortage prevented wood-hauls, leading the judges to inform the villagers that, with pasturage now available, all labor services and transports must be performed. Attorney Berends had, seemingly, pulled the right strings. The farmers nevertheless spurned the wood-hauls.[65]

Kleist now wrote personally to the king. At first he employed the language of Enlightenment rationalism and humanitarianism. "I am far

[63] Ibid., fos. 192–3, 197–203, 205, 207–11.   [64] Ibid., fos. 206, 215–18.
[65] Ibid., fos. 219–22, 224, 226.

from the unreasonable thought that I should embitter my subjects' lives or demand services of them inconveniently when they could comfortably be performed at another time." But now that farmers could feed their animals, and had finished spring planting, they had no grounds for refusing haulage. After their further non-compliance, he exploded in another letter that all decrees and warnings "produced not the slightest effect." Blaming them for "the present great lawsuit," he lamented,

It is impossible that I should lose time, and watch years flow by, until the farmer is finally held to his duty. Since 1766 the subjects have enjoyed more than lawful clemency . . . They are litigating their way through every stage of this chicanery.

Kleist then conjured with the nobility's special relationship to the crown. "It would cause me extraordinary mortification, whatever the outcome, were I to find myself obliged in this matter to take the final step of approaching Your Royal Majesty's Most High Person." This meant, among other things, that personal supplication of royal protection against his farmers would diminish Kleist's dignity as wielder in his own right of lordship's power.[66]

The Berlin Court commissioned Perleberg Bürgermeister Grave to enforce its newest orders, but Kleist and his advisers were skeptical. In July 1771 Berends counseled the preparation of letters of arrest in Spandau, remarking determinedly to Betich that "I confess, I take the matter much to heart [*au coeur*], so that the farmer doesn't set himself above the courts." Here two bourgeois lawyers, in a nobleman's pay, advocated seigneurial repression of villagers in judicial rectitude's name. But soon Kleist wrote Bürgermeister Grave recalling that, on July 9, the Elbe had flooded at Lenzen, so that "because of high water" he could no longer market firewood there. He resolved, resignedly, to forgo imprisonment orders and await a more propitious haulage time.[67]

Nature's wrath nullified Kleist's judicial triumphs. Worse still, in November 1771 the Royal Supreme Appellate Tribunal (*Ober-Appellations-Tribunal*), responding to the villagers' petition filed by their Berlin lawyer Manecke, unexpectedly reversed the Chamber Court's previous rulings. It declared that, since Lenzen lay farther than two German miles from Stavenow, and since it took the farmers some time to drive from their villages to the manorial workplace, and since the winter day lasted but from eight to four o'clock, one-day hauls were impossible. Kleist could

---

[66] Ibid., fos. 230–1, 240.   [67] Ibid., fos. 232ff.

have the transports, but at the cost, minimally, of crediting his farmers with two days' labor.

Berends wrote Kleist that experience showed the supreme appellate judges "apply the letter of the law, especially when, as in the present case, it eases subject farmers' circumstances [*Soulagement der Untertanen*]." He assumed (though Frederick never proclaimed it) that government policy aimed to lighten villagers' seigneurial burdens. "The tribunal's *rationes*," Berends added, "will hardly be obtainable," but one could write to a "High Privy State Councilor."[68] Kleist indeed complained to a high official how the "Royal Tribunal, against all human expectation," denied him Elbe wood-haulage. Its ruling was bad for Kleist, and for "the whole land." To overturn Chamber Court decisions "is a power which, according to law, it is inadmissible and illegal even for the law-giver to exercise." Here the major was perhaps echoing public discussions of Frederick's sensational intrusion into the Chamber Court's handling of miller Arnold's case. Why Kleist thought Chamber Court rulings were not appellable to a higher jurisdiction is unclear. The Supreme Appellate Court consisted of four ministerial officials reviewing Chamber Court decisions. To Betich it was simply the "council of state" (*Staats Rath*). Kleist and his lawyers may have been implying, as anti-absolutist Enlightenment liberals agreed, that such executive-branch controls on the judiciary imperiled law's autonomy.

Kleist requested clarification, saying he was prepared "to yield" and grant two days' credit for one haul. He spoke impassionedly on behalf of the nobility as a class:

Or should I make no use whatever of a labor service customary throughout the land? If the subject farmers' most familiar and oft-employed services, which are noble landed properties' important prerogatives, should be so unexpectedly abolished, the nobility's decline is unavoidable. Yet their conservation should not be a matter of indifference to the lawcourts and royal administration, since the nobility must, primarily, form the military estate, that chief branch of the State, and are also appointed to the preeminent civil offices. Everyone knows how much they need to support themselves in these offices from their own resources.[69]

In 1774, Kleist irritably wrote the government, complaining that no grounds for the Supreme Appellate Tribunal's decision had yet been

---

[68] Ibid., fos. 243–4. The villagers' lawyer, Chamber Court Advocate Manecke, was, presumably, the same Maneke representing Adrian von Kleist's creditors in the 1767 bankruptcy, who forbore charging the "poor people" fees.

[69] Ibid., fos. 249–50.

offered. He referred to a 1754 royal edict enjoining obedience in manorial service. About Stavenow villagers, he wrote:

For some time now, highly serious events have shown clearly that the subject
villagers' insubordination, so habitual with them, has been not inconsiderably
enlivened by the court judgment in question. [They were refusing various
other services.]

If I want to enjoy my estates' prerogatives, which the land's customs and tradition uphold, I must [now] presuppose incessant, eternal lawsuits, the favorable outcome of which, even concerning the most liquid of assets, I find myself
moved to doubt.[70]

The Supreme Appellate Tribunal finally replied it found wood-hauls
to violate Brandenburg's "laws and custom." Looking back to Stavenow's
original 1766 ruling, the Tribunal judged it non-binding because Betich
had not communicated seigneurial demands to the villagers in advance,
leaving them unable "to defend their rights properly through prior consultation with a counsel versed in the law." Moreover, "lordships are not
entitled to demand from their subjects wood-hauls for commercial sale."
Kleist would have to "calmly accept" this final judgement, a point under-
scored by the accompanying letter from powerful Minister of State von
Zedlitz, fully endorsing the Tribunal's ruling.

Berends, forwarding the "disagreeable resolution" to Kleist, said "I
know nothing more to propose against it. Labor-service questions are
daily becoming more doubtful because, according to a recent royal cabinet order, proposals are being considered for easing manorial service."
Seigneurial powers' defenders again displayed apprehension and pessimism about Frederick's regime's cautious and halting essays to
improve villagers' condition.[71]

NEW STRUGGLES IN THE 1770S

The wood-haulage dispute illuminates both seigneurial repression and
the state's judicial and police responses to insubordinate villages.
Kleist's disciplinary will was strong and, in these meteorologically miserable years, it bruised his subjects. Yet correct judicial process, including punishment, meant something, holding village leaders' imprison-
ments within survivable bounds and finally yielding them legal victory
toastable in the taverns. The 1770s' other labor service conflicts do not
invite close scrutiny, partly because the 1790 Urbarium reformulated

---

[70] Ibid., fos. 272–3.   [71] Ibid., fos. 267–9, 270–1.

their outcomes, but they cast revealing light on seigneurial, village, and governmental mentalities.

A 1770 suit addressed the labor service regime's adaptation to agricultural improvements underway at Stavenow and elsewhere. The Glövziners' lawyer Manecke argued that, while they agreed they must harvest the seigneurial rye outside regular weekly service, this formerly took only three days. Now, because Kleist had planted cleared timberland, six days would not suffice, "no matter how much [they] sweated." Judge Betich wrote in this document's margin, "they're slackers." To work a full harvest week meant they had either to reap their own grain unripe or overripe, losing half the overripe kernels in mowing. To these "lies" Betich replied that either farmer or farm servant worked the lordship's harvest, but not both.

Manecke charged Kleist with violating royal and public interest in forest conservation, while endangering villagers' tax-paying capacity. Employing rarely expressed economic logic, he noted that, as woodland was converted to arable, grain prices would fall, while ever scarcer firewood would grow dearer. Betich's marginal notes countered that "in the enclosed agriculture introduced at Stavenow the fields are used first for grain crops and then for pasture," so that surface area under grain was not vastly greater than before. Manecke held that (admittedly unlimited) harvest services applied only to old-established seigneurial arable. Consistent with Enlightenment political economy, he argued the villagers' self-interest in quickly harvesting seigneurial crops belied Kleist's reproach they were slackers: "in the harvest, every hour is precious to the countryman." Betich conceded this of the farmer "working for himself, but not for the overlordship."

Manecke's clients added that Stavenow formerly paid wage-earning scythemen, but four were now gone, requiring them to "hang their own work on the nail" for a whole week. The Chamber Court declared these complaints invalid. If "better cultivation" widened Kleist's arable, villagers' harvesting liability must rise. Still, as Müller's codex emphasized, landlords could not ignore equity (*Billigkeit*), leading the jurists to reiterate their earlier ruling that villagers should have two free weekdays to reap their own fields. "For it is indeed very hard and unfair if farmers should busy themselves for six days or more with their lordship's harvest only to see their own grain ruined." In this case, since villagers refused to mow a field carved from former woodland, they owed Kleist for wage labor he employed in their stead.[72]

---

[72] No. 424, fos. 1, 4–5, 10–12, 17, 23.

Meanwhile, other court battles flared. In 1772 Betich wrote Berends that the three principal service villages "have through liberation from wood-hauling become so refractory" they refused construction work at Premslin and Semlin manor-farms. They were "under the delusion" they owed such service only at Stavenow manor-seat. "With this rough horde [*rohen Haufen*] explanations are of no help."[73] The Berlin jurists rejected Kleist's claim to various labor services his father allegedly commanded, but which subsequently fell into disuse. Kleist challenged his villagers to swear the disputed work had not been performed since Kleist senior acquired Stavenow. The Chamber Court permitted oaths to be sworn and then pronounced Kleist's claims "expired," ordering him to pay his subjects' testimony's costs.[74]

It irked Kleist that the four Glövzin smallholders had joined the fullholder-led resistance. For their refusal of building services they offered, Betich said, the "paltry excuse that the fullholders forbade them." The Glövzin mayor and aldermen testified they earlier performed them only "because the lordship forced them." The smallholders said they stood together with fullholders over harvest labor "and so could not separate themselves from them now." They held that, "according to the [1686] cadastre, Premslin and Semlin manors are only dairy-farms" and not "knights' seats" which alone, according to old custom, could command construction services. Here the villagers – through their lawyer – presented, if self-interestedly, a historically informed legal argument. Premslin's mayor declared his village's "common cause" with neighboring Glövzin, because the disputed labors were "too hard." Karstädt's mayor admitted his village performed them, but was now "joined with the others because of previous lawsuits."[75]

In 1773, the Chamber Court collected evidence about Kleist's double demand that farmers perform building services at all old-established manor-farms and transport grain long-range in regular service, as allegedly they did in his father's day, when "they unquestioningly hauled grain, fruit, and so forth to Potsdam." Hans Nagel, Karstädt mayor, testified that, while farmers recently performed construction work at a disputed site, they now refused "because their advocate told them [to]; which lawyer it was he didn't know, because he had never been with him." They also, two years previously, made some long hauls, but otherwise never, except in the 1730s they transported "cheese and butter for tenant-farmer Hartz" to Potsdam. "Herr Colonel von Kleist

[73] No. 343, fos. 279–80.   [74] Ibid., fos. 246–7.   [75] No. 601, fos. 2–6.

later forbade this, to preserve the subjects, because they couldn't endure it." Now they would only transport grain to nearby markets.

Peter Hintze, a Karstädt fullholder, said they refused contested services, in a formulaic phrase of self-defense, "because their lawyer forbade them." Hintze said he "doesn't actually know how things stand, because though he has always been in this village, only last autumn did he become a farmer," so entering landed proprietors' closed councils. He knew some villagers, rather than performing long hauls, bought seigneurial grain at "the market price." As for himself, "he would always do what his neighbor did" – doubtless a stock phrase expressing village solidarity's iron grip. Glövzin's Christoph Zeggel conceded they performed some building services, "but they came too often and hard." Lawyers Gutike in Rathenow and Manecke in Berlin informed them of such work's proper limits. They once consented to long-range grain-hauls "because forced to," Kleist having imprisoned two farmers. Premslin's mayor Hecht said that "whatever their neighbors the Glövziners and Karstädters did, they the Premsliners want also to do . . . [T]hey couldn't endure any more long hauls."

Kleist's Semlin manor-farm foreman, sixty-eight-year-old Jürgen Jäger, who said "he looks after the people and works alongside them," remembered that, before entering Stavenow service twenty-eight years earlier, his manor-farm was rebuilt using villagers' unpaid haulage. He added, unhelpfully for Kleist, that since then no such work had occurred, nor any long grain-hauls in regular service. On farmers' disobedience in 1773's harvest, mayors conceded villagers arrived one day late to reap seigneurial rye, also missing an obligatory "extra day" harvesting Stavenow's flax. They said they needed to store their own grain first, and that "extra days" were claimable only in winter and fall. Farmer Heinrich Zeggel, who sent but a manual worker to the rye harvest, said he hauled "a stranger's linen cloth" to the Elbe and, returning home the next morning, confronted an unexpected summons. Since he could not send exhausted horses, in good faith he dispatched his farm servant instead. "God preserve him," he piously said of himself, "from insubordination."[76]

In December 1773 Kleist complained to the Chamber Court that, since his farmers "miraculously" won the wood-haulage case, they had begun "all sorts of new insubordination," misleading smallholders into "disobedience, so that every step in their labor service performance has been

---

[76] No. 343, fos. 289–97, 300.

made difficult for me." From fullholders he could, at best, extract one day of construction service every two weeks outside planting and harvest seasons. Even then they agreed to but one haul daily of no more weight than a man could carry. Other disputed services they refused or subjected to "arbitrary reductions."[77] The following autumn Kleist informed Berends "that the Premsliners are often absent during the [present] summer harvest," now one person, now three, now six. "They excuse themselves, saying they must earn some tax money hauling Perleberg burghers' crops."

If I send a bailiff to make a seizure, they mutter menacing words, leave their horse in impoundment or pay to recover it and then do what they please. Manorial service here can't be so burdensome if they can get their livestock back like this.

Kleist forwarded the three rebellious villages' complaints, "which I very much laugh at, since they do nothing, and only get concessions." Here refractory villagers played off the king, with his insatiable tax appetite, against the nobility, with their more resistible demands. Betich ordered absenteeism's end "on pain of corporal punishment," but government scrutiny weakened seigneurial coercion. He asked Berends to obtain a court order that villagers perform disputed services during litigation. Kleist would soon need contested haulage and, as Betich candidly admitted, "in case of further refusals, Herr Major cannot bring repression to bear [*nicht repressiren kan*]."[78] Berends complied, saying of villagers' work stoppages that "well-known agitator Heinrich Zeggel of Glavetzin expended the day on which he had been summoned to seigneurial harvest haulage in transporting a load of rags" (the above-mentioned linen).

The Chamber Court appointed Judicial Councilor Noeldechen, resident in Neuruppin, to investigate Kleist's charges and settle them through mediation, saying Kleist must limit demands for construction services and make concessions to obtain long-range hauls. "You must make [the farmers] grasp that their insubordination is indefensible, and that we will not permit any lengthy litigation, but will hold them to their obligations through punishment and seizure of assets." Mainly, though, the jurists wanted Noeldechen to act with "your great skill, well known to our court, to lay this matter amicably to rest."[79] In 1775 Noeldechen held Stavenow hearings pitting Kleist and Betich against the three refractory villages with their Perleberg lawyer.

---

[77] Ibid., fos. 260–2. [78] Ibid., fos. 275–6. [79] Ibid., fos. 313–14, 320, 326.

Ordinary Prussians

Both sides seemingly accepted Noeldechen's landlord-friendly proposal that, instead of previously "indeterminate construction services," Kleist should have from each farmer eight construction days yearly, outside plantings and harvests. Kleist promised to treat them "justly and fairly, so that at sundown they may be back at their farmsteads." About long hauls, all once-yearly grain transports should first be made. Thereafter, hauls in regular service as far one way as eight German (forty English) miles might occur, if for every two German miles one service day's remission were granted. But when the farmers complained about haulage beyond the Elbe, and pressed for smaller loads to make room for necessary fodder, Kleist angered, saying "his subjects appeared to be very much abusing his previously announced willingness to compromise and thereby were being misled into wholly unfair and illegal *praetensiones*." Noeldechen and their lawyer tried to persuade them their demands were unsustainable, citing local practice in other lordships. "But they wouldn't accept any remonstrances," until Kleist "contented himself," in hauls beyond two German miles, with smaller loads.

This mollified the outmaneuvered villagers, though the haulage agreement ceased if Kleist leased his estates. Under tenant-farmers they could expect "to be treated with less consideration [*Menagement*]" – "their condition would be harder" – while leaseholders' lesser "consumption" would yield larger marketable surpluses for hauling. Kleist promised, should he lease, to see that "the tenant-farmer doesn't ruin the farmers," but to tie his hand "is completely unheard of." Noeldechen wrote that "because of this minor circumstance the whole compromise negotiation for today came to a halt." He sent the farmers home, warning against "litigation fever."[80] Next day they rejected all hauls beyond two German miles, and accepted but four construction days yearly. Kleist agreed to the latter but, claiming eight-mile transports were Prignitz custom, said only "incompetent farmers'" horses were not fit for such trips. How could they complain "when their horses are mostly capable, in and outside harvest season, of hauling grain in Perleberg, and of making distant trips for hire"? They had, admittedly, recently made long hauls for Kleist, but only because he clapped two farmers "in irons in jail." They did their best to keep their horses strong, "because this tends to their own advantage," but the animals still could not withstand long treks.

[80] No. 573, fos. 6–8.

About hired haulage, "they wouldn't even accept these transports if they didn't lack means to otherwise earn enough money for the King's monthly *Kontribution*." They wanted to settle, "if only strings weren't stretched too tight." They agreed to "the hardest point," accepting four construction days. They "regretted" the compromise foundered over grain-hauls, but this was "an unavoidable stroke of fate [*Fatalité*]," necessitating Chamber Court ruling. Cavalierly noting that grain-hauls, "this small matter," blocked amicable settlement, Noeldechen ended his mission, booking a 50-taler fee. Only six of forty-four farmers signed the protocol by name, the others making crosses.

For these hearings Kleist made some interesting notes. He recalled his parents' day, when Stavenowers "hauled milled grain and all sorts of victuals, received at the White House" – the Kleists' Potsdam residence. Even after leasing Stavenow to Hartz, Potsdam shipments of "fodder and fruit" still arrived. Recently mayor Holtmann tried to persuade Kleist of farmers' horses' weakness, "but they wait for hours on Perleberg marketplace until they're hired." Farmer Christoph Zeggel admitted he hadn't made a long haul for ten years,

which is a big proof of how seldom they make the round. One isn't going to ruin one's own farmer. If he has no team, I lose in my own work and finally I'll have to give him horses so his farm doesn't stand run-down and empty.

On construction haulage: "I've put them in jail, but they persist in insubordination and laziness." Other lordships' farmers did such work, while his shirked it, "and yet the rascals complain of heavy and hard service."[81]

The Chamber Court imposed a four-day construction service by a 1775 fiat, and set terms, including reduced loads, for long hauls.[82] Yet in 1777 the Stavenowers were refusing grain transports to semi-distant Wittstock and across the Elbe to Salzwedel, saying once-annual grain hauls had not yet been demanded. Kleist pronounced this irrelevant, because such hauls were, by common consent, limited to short trips, while he claimed his right to long transports. But mayor Zeggel said "the commune so decided." Betich asked the Chamber Court to dispatch the Prignitz sheriff, saying Kleist, selling his grain locally, had not asked for 1776 long hauls, and indeed since 1763 had gotten none from his farmers. This year he could not profitably sell nearby. Though ten farmers obeyed a recent long-haul command, some by buying the major's grain

[81] Ibid., fos. 11–17, 346.   [82] No. 363, fos. 2–11.

themselves, others refused. Justifying the sheriff's impoundment of villagers' goods, Betich cholerically wrote:

It is futile to hold these stormy people to their duty with jailings, as I know from experience. At most they sit for a while, ruining their own farms, and then persevere in their insubordination, of which I see no end.

In April 1777 Glövzin mayor David Zeggel acknowledged in writing receipt "from the Stabno court bailiff" of the Chamber Court's menacing command to comply. But Berlin denied Kleist's plea for the sheriff's intervention:

You have to hold the renitent farmers to their duty, and with the court bailiff's help, whose authority if necessary is to be strengthened, force the recalcitrant farmers to perform the transports, and in this way through your own jurisdictional powers enforce your rights.

After warning Kleist against using force, the Chamber Court now invited him to get tougher.[83]

ESCALATION OF PHYSICAL FORCE

Kleist began his landlordly career with coercion. As embittered lawsuits progressed, he and his refractory farmers yielded to symbolic and real violence's temptations. This signaled his authority's deterioration and seigneurial overlordship's waning strength and legitimacy in the late eighteenth century. The major personally policed his villages with some brutality, as emerges from his 1772 steps against three farmers he caught illegally smoking tobacco on their farmsteads. Christian Schütt, fifty-one, testified that, while recovering from fever, "he wanted to warm himself up with some work," and drained a puddle while smoking his pipe. Suddenly Kleist appeared, "took the pipe from his mouth, and beat him with a whip." Kleist retorted that when "he found [Schütt] smoking, he gave him 6–7 lashes with the whip, because he deserved it" for ignoring all warnings against "godless tobacco-smoking."

As for David Zeggel, forty-nine, the Glövzin leader who previously defied Kleist, the major caught him smoking as he left home for his fields, but only tongue-lashed him. Kleist also surprised retired farmer Joachim Wulff, fifty-one, who was carrying out his wife's commission to feed their pig. The major entered the stall unannounced, prompting Wulff to cast his pipe into the straw, where Kleist found it. Wulff's

[83] No. 343, fos. 334, 339–43.

excuse was that "he was thinking." "It happens that a person doesn't always have his thoughts together." Nevertheless the Chamber Court draconically sentenced him to three months' labor in Spandau fortress. Zeggel escaped with two weeks' imprisonment at "public labor," while Schütt, because his smoking did not threaten fire, gained acquittal.[84]

Here Kleist zealously poked about village farmsteads, impulsively whipping one offender, and seeking harsh punishment of all. A decade later, he physically coerced three farmers active in the 1780s' contentious negotiations. Of them he wrote the Chamber Court: "some time ago they got it in their heads to deny me the submission and obedience one expects of subjects." They fell into money-rent arrears and "even imagined they needn't appear when summoned." Finally they came, saying "'they had nothing and would give nothing.'" Kleist continued: "I sought to employ my power of judicial compulsion and ordered them into jail, to dissuade them from their malicious refusal to pay commutation fees."

Prisoner Jochen Ebel's wife promptly brought Kleist the money, proving they were not incapable of paying but only refusing from insubordination. He was about to release her husband when he noticed "the punishable act of all three subjects, who had broken away the iron from the jail window and were sticking their heads out." Later, unguarded, they staged a "breakout, even taking the irons binding them and, leaving their farms, disappeared, going to Berlin." Upon their return, Kleist encountered escapee Ebel, who displayed the "insubordination one can expect from my very refractory subjects." Ordered by Kleist to fetch newly appointed seigneurial Judge Gutike, Ebel refused, "making dreadful cries and throwing himself to the ground." Kleist summoned "my people," namely, his brewer, cook, foreman, and servant.

They hurried forward, but Ebel redoubled his strength, kicking servant Günther in the head, injuring brewer Ladewig on the shin, and accompanying his blows in my presence with these curses: they were all scoundrels, a pack of rogues, rats; Heaven would lend him the strength to resist them all; he sh_t [sic] on his farm.

Kleist and his servants bound Ebel, but next day he fell ill, gaining release on promise to return when called. Meanwhile the two other escapees ignored written summons. When the court bailiff went to fetch them, "they disappeared in the dust." Kleist demanded the sheriff return them for trial.[85]

[84] No. 510, fos. 1–6.   [85] No. 340, fos. 2–4 (1781).

Three months later the three stood before Judge Gutike. Jochen Ebel, thirty, said "it baffled him" why Kleist dunned him and his colleagues for arrears. Ebel had never in seven years of farming fallen behind, and only recently missed a half-yearly commutation payment, "which is always a burden on him, but now almost impossible because times are so bad and [he and other farmers] have so many dues to pay." He did not obey Kleist's summons "because he feared that, if he came without money, he'd have to go to jail." He did not say he had nothing and would pay nothing, but that "they had nothing, and couldn't do anything about it. Herr Major should have patience until harvest was over, because they wanted to thresh their crops and pay." Kleist should realize "no one will lend them any money, because if anyone lent without the lordship's approval, he wouldn't get his money back." Although in law Stavenow possessed prior approval rights over farmers' borrowings, particularly outside its jurisdiction, his predecessors had not exercised them repressively. If his court was disallowing creditors' claims on these grounds, his farmers could no longer easily borrow money.

Gutike asked whether Ebel's wife's payment did not disprove his claim. "No, she lamented to people that he'd gone to jail, and they took pity on him and lent her some money." A smallholder gave 16 groschen, a fullholder 2 talers, and the tavernkeeper 5 groschen. About the jail escape, Ebel denied the window was iron-barred. He was first to break out, "in which enterprise he was interrupted by Herr Major, who seized him by the head, boxed his ears and pushed him back into jail, whereupon they were all put in irons." The next morning they fled through the open jail window, "but it was very difficult, since they effected flight while in irons." Later breaking off the chains, they took them to Berlin to protest Kleist's methods to the Chamber Court. Returning home, they threw them in the bushes near Premslin.[86]

When Kleist later caught him, "Herr Major seized [Ebel's] whip from his hand, took him by the throat, and said, pulling him from his horse: 'It's good, you scoundrel, that I've run into you [*dich*] here. Just come along.'" Ebel testified "he lost his breath, fell to the ground and couldn't move." He knew Kleist's workers bound him, but could not remember hurting them. "When Herr Major seized him by the throat, he lost all consciousness." Gutike, who – as we shall see – was working through the court to weaken Kleist's farmers' hereditary tenures, then formulated in these words Ebel's reply to the question whether he cursed his captors:

[86] Ibid., fos. 8–10.

It could well be that he did, but he can think of nothing more than that, right off, when Herr Major took hold of him, he employed the expression: "Herr Sergeant-Colonel [*Obristwachtmeister*], just leave me my health, for I don't claim your [*Ihren*] farm any longer."

Seemingly Gutike sought, perhaps with Ebel's eviction in mind, to fabricate villagers' acceptance of Kleist's ownership of their holdings, on which they were but tenants-at-will, even though in Hasse's and Betich's day court documents routinely acknowledged a given farmer's holding as his own by unquestioned hereditary tenure.

Asked for his self-defense, Ebel said he did not believe the jail-break was punishable, because the Chamber Court earlier instructed Kleist "not to impose punishments [*Exekution*]" on him and his colleagues. Here Ebel interpreted Berlin jurists' earlier pronouncements to rule out, not only the sheriff's seizure and sale of assets, but also Stavenow jailings for debt. Ebel added that "also from Herr Major's physical treatment of him he suffered after-effects he couldn't get over, preventing him from working like his neighbors." After Gutike read Ebel's testimony back to him, he signed with crosses.

The testimony of Ebel's partner Christian Maass, thirty-seven, revealed hardships facing many farmers. He could not pay commutation money because he was "too poor. He's always had to borrow money to pay it." This year, "as happened to him several times already, he had to purchase seed and bread-grain." He ignored Kleist's summons for fear of jail, "whose unpleasantness he didn't wish to undergo." He would swear they had not said they would give nothing, but only that they had nothing to give. Gutike asked him if he could prove he could not pay.

He has only meager livestock that he couldn't sell to gain money. [Nor could he sell other iron stock.] Arable and meadows were bad and only yielded essential seed and bread-grain and pasturage for animals. He couldn't mortgage his lands. Therefore his inability to pay commutation money was clear as day.

How had he managed to pay in his preceding seven years of farming?

He then had money lent out to various people. But this he has little by little recalled to pay commutation. Now it was gone. Therefore he didn't know how he could help himself.

Kleist earlier imprisoned Maass (at Christmas) for missing a commutation payment, at which time Maass admittedly broke the window bars. In the recent jailing, Kleist, by leaving the window unbarred, "tricked them." As for the jail-irons, they took them to Berlin, where they "denounced this event to the Honorable Chamber Court, which had ordered Herr Major that 'he should not impose [sheriff's] execution on them.'"

As usual in multiple interrogations, the defendants followed a common line on what they took to be crucial points, which here included denial they flatly refused to pay Kleist and conviction that Berlin forbade coercion for debt. In self-defense, Maass said "sheer incapacity" (to pay) explained his behavior, and "would have to protect and defend him." His precursor once-removed "was also not able to keep himself in bread on [Maass's] farm, and on behalf of his immediate predecessor, Hantz Milatz, [Maass] had been obliged to pay his final commutation fee." Maass signed with his own name. As for co-defendant, farmer-tavernkeeper J. G. Hecht, thirty, he too said he was obliged to purchase seed and bread-grain, "because no one wanted to lend him anything. He was, besides, a new farm-proprietor who needs many things at the outset. His livestock was also too poor to yield any money."[87]

The Chamber Court instructed Gutike to seek amicable settlement or, otherwise, pronounce judgment. He assembled all parties in October 1781. Kleist heatedly declared the three defendants "the most insubordinate of his subjects." He demanded they pay arrears and the jail-irons' cost, at 1.5 talers each. Unpunished, they would only become "ever more stiffnecked."

Moreover, the three accomplices' [Premslin] commune, which along with Glövzin commune does not render its dues at all properly, must for once be given a warning example, since they think they are entitled to renounce the obedience they owe their overlordship. It's impossible he should compromise with the accomplices . . . Otherwise he might as well waive his rebellious subjects' justly deserved punishments and so give them new occasion for further insubordination.

Though Gutike urged the defendants to pay, they said "they too could not compromise," agreeing only to look for the lost jail-irons. The judge sentenced them to eight days' jail, "half on bread and water," and immediately to pay what they owed, plus 9 talers' heavy court costs. The three appealed to the Chamber Court, which in January 1782 ruled the appeal inadmissible, the case being a "minor matter." Gutike's ruling stood. The Berlin judges lightly chided Kleist, pronouncing the

---

[87] Ibid., fos. 11–18.

jail-break less culpable because he locked them up without engaging his seigneurial judge in the process. "But still it remains a very punishable undertaking, deserving requital to uphold the respect owed the lord-ship."[88]

With government backing, Kleist struck out at his villagers, not because of their individual offenses' gravity, but to restore his greatly reduced authority and, as the Berlin jurists pointedly added, his "respect." In February 1782 the three served their prison sentence in Perleberg, "because Stavenow jail is not fit." Gutike warned, if they did not now pay their dues and fines, including the cost of the Perleberg jailer's meals, he would prolong their imprisonment. They said "they had nothing, and impoundment and sale of their goods would only prove the bad state of their assets." Gutike offered extended deadlines, but they said "they couldn't." Jochen Ebel reported that "during his incarceration he has gotten a bad and thick arm." Gutike ordered them back to jail, and impoundment and auction of their salable possessions, except farming essentials. A surgeon would inspect Ebel's arm. Gutike asked if they had "adequate heating and were otherwise properly treated by the jailer." He quoted them, perhaps falsely: "yes, there was proper heating. They also each received 1 groschen's worth of bread daily, and had no complaints about the jailer."

Gutike ordered court bailiff's seizure of the defendants' possessions sufficient to pay their fines, warning prisoners' wives not to conceal assets. He soon released the three, who had three weeks to redeem their goods before sale. The deadline passed, and Gutike ordered Perleberg book-binder Eiching to conduct the auction, which the town crier announced three times, while Stavenow's court bailiff called it out in the villages. Jail fees, for bread and lamp-oil, amounted to 2 talers. The auction yielded, on the three delinquents' behalf, 12.5 talers for but three metal cooking pots, two heifers, some linen yardage, and a half-cotton dress. Nearly as much remained unpaid. Meanwhile Kleist pressed for the lost jail-irons' return. Gutike petitioned further Chamber Court sanctions against the three. "If it seems," he wrote, "that their landlord [*Grundherrschaft*], Major von Kleist, is dealing harshly, his [earlier] treatment of them" – the extra-judicial jailings – "was recently condemned." Kleist also deserved under-standing since these were his most turbulent subjects in villages "whose disobedience and rebelliousness grow from day to day."[89] Yet the three survived their ordeals, signing the 1790 Urbarium.

[88] Ibid., fos. 27–9.   [89] Ibid., fos. 38, 42ff.

In 1786 controversy arose over transporting to Spandau delinquents condemned to hard labor whose poverty prevented their paying the costs themselves. Kleist had somehow managed to steer his old antagonist, the Glövzin mayor David Zeggel, into the dreaded fortress, and not for unpaid arrears. Kleist claimed such transports derived from village duty, "customary throughout the province," to guard prisoners. The villagers bridled, "because we have never done this" (actually they had). Gutike posed the biased question whether Zeggel had been too poor, "which is improbable, since he possesses [*besitze*] a farm and therefore must have assets enough that he could pay the court bailiff for a tour of eighty [English] miles." They said Zeggel "fed himself and paid court costs and therefore we cannot regard him as without means." He was absent from the 1790 signatories, incarceration possibly having broken him, though perhaps he returned to retirement.[90]

In 1788 seigneurial punishment targeted four farmers' manservants. Field foreman Quittenbaum ordered the workers to haul manure in the seigneurial gardens, but they refused, "on the pretext," he testified, "that the Glövzin commune had promulgated for itself a regulation" providing that the fullholders would perform the disputed haulage by rotation. The recalcitrant workers proposed changing places with others whose turns had not come, but Quittenbaum insisted he alone set manorial service rules. The workers departed, and "whistled to the manure-loaders" to follow.[91] Gutike told the villagers "the ordinance allegedly prevailing among them does not bind the manorial lordship." H. G. Zeggel, twenty-three, testified that when court bailiff Kluber ordered them back to work, he and his comrades said "they couldn't go back like this, the farmers [their employers] would have to go with them." J. J. Glissmann, eighteen, said "his farmer" counseled that, in manorial service, "he must take his cues from the others and do what they did." Like his mates, he denied whistling to the loaders. One of these, a Stavenow cowherd's wife, thirty-one, could not say whether the servants signaled to stop work, but the court bailiff said "the four manure-loaders whistled back and followed." Bailiff Kluber, fifty, added that defendant Zeggel exasperatedly said, "Devil take manure-hauling. I can't get away from this manure. Let someone else do it this afternoon."

Gutike brutally sentenced the obdurate workers to eight days' jail on bread and water. The two alleged leaders, both Zeggels, "shall each be

---

[90] No. 335, fos. 1–2.   [91] No. 507, fos. 2–3.

locked up cross-wise for twelve hours" in the painful chaining also known as "locked bent." All would pay court costs, with ten days to appeal. In Kleist's absence a brother approved the sentence, but punishment waited seven months, until the workers' employers protested to Kleist himself. They would hold their servants to their "duty," but the punishment was too hard. Kleist said "I have suffered most from the farmers' negligence and malice, [but] I will forgo gaining my satisfaction if their servants receive only a moderate disciplining." The farmers dropped their appeal to Berlin, suggesting that Kleist accept lesser sanctions, having blocked the horse-exhausting haulage's communal regulation.[92]

Kleist was irritably aware that mayors and aldermen whom he himself appointed led the vociferous village opposition he faced. Since no village official could withstand pressure to fall in neighborly line, Kleist could gain little by firing officeholders in hope of appointing more compliant ones, especially since the mayor's job was otherwise burdensome. In 1777, as we saw, the government vetoed Kleist's recent gift to the Blüthen mayor of rent-free pasture. Doubtless he aimed to buttress his influence in this seigneurially divided village, whose Stavenow subjects had not joined the lawsuits against him, perhaps because they owed only two days' weekly service and feared assimilation to the other villages' higher obligation.[93]

The Stavenow lordship's punitive zeal contrasts dramatically with the turbulence and disrespect it encountered in December 1789 from Altmark farmers, from across the Elbe, who that autumn contracted with Kleist's field foreman to fatten their pigs in Stavenow woods at 3 talers per animal. When, before Christmas, they came for the pigs, they found them unacceptably scrawny. Kleist's estateowning neighbor Captain von Podewils was representing him in his absence. The Altmarkers refused to pay full forage fees. Podewils, as Kleist explained to one of their overlords,

wanting to reprove them for their improper and rebellious behavior, was met by them with the crudest expressions, such as, that (pardon the expression) he couldn't command shit, he should shut up, and similar crudities that are impossible to mention without shame . . . Herr von Podewils and my field foreman judged it unwise to meet these raging people with violence.

They therefore accepted the proffered 2.5 talers. Podewils declined to press charges, "since he is only too convinced his honor can in no way be diminished by such people." Quittenbaum reduced the forage fee

[92] Ibid., fos. 4–15, 17ff.   [93] No. 601, fo. 1.

"to pacify" the Altmarkers, who behaved "with the greatest violence . . . so that the most unpleasant scenes were to be feared."[94]

Later the disrespectful farmers' own seigneurial court ruled against
them, saying they had not proved Kleist's herders had not properly fattened their pigs. "The piece of bacon they produced," the judges
solemnly wrote, "does not constitute legal proof, since on one hand it
is not certain that [it] comes from one of the foraging pigs and, on the
other, conclusions about all pigs cannot be drawn from one." The
farmers appealed to the Altmark Provincial Court, whose judge (a von
Bismarck) softened the verdict, remitting 6 groschen per animal and
dividing court costs equally among the parties. "Even if," Bismarck
philosophized, "the promised condition of fattening has no precise
definition, and is always relative," so that even butcher Schulze's testimony was ambiguous, it remained clear that Kleist's bailiff pledged but
failed to deliver properly fattened pigs.[95]

This incident reveals another aggressive display of the disrespect for
seigneurial authority which outraged the aging Kleist, though Altmark
courts left it unpunished. The major's expectation that his and other
landlords' villagers treat him with deference and submission was rarely
gratified. The Prussian government had in mind such events as Kleist's
long struggle with his villagers when, in July 1787, it commanded a royal
proclamation's reading throughout the kingdom, "especially to the
lower orders [*niedere Volks-Classen*]."

"We are," said Friedrich Wilhelm II, "compelled to observe, with the
highest displeasure, that in recent times lawsuits and quarrels between
landlords and their subject villagers have greatly multiplied in many of
our provinces." The common people "very frequently" succumbed to
an "unbridled passion for litigation," no matter how hopeless their case.
Shady petition-writers forced themselves on villagers, and on "common
burghers" too, goading them into the courtroom. So did other third
parties, venting "hateful insinuations and stirring up unfounded mis-
trust towards higher authority." The king menaced such troublemakers
with "one, two, or more years of prison." He ordered complaints be
presented only to licensed attorneys, who must not allow "laziness [!] or
fear of other people [!]" to subvert their duty to accept all admissible
cases. Persons unable to pay lawyers' fees could have the nearest court
take their testimony free of charge, whereupon justice would promptly
and fairly be done.

---

[94] No. 719, fo. 99; no. 720, fos. 3, 8–9ff.   [95] No. 720, fos. 22, 30.

Addressing "our loyal nobility," the king reaffirmed his "well-founded confidence" they would not commit "any illegal oppression of Our subjects."

But if any estateowner abuses his rights and jurisdictional powers to harass his subject villagers wrongly with demands for labor services and fees beyond what they properly owe; or if he in any way encroaches on their property or their prerogatives; or if he is guilty of other forbidden exactions or violent mistreatment of his subjects; then not only will such wrongful breach of Our trust in the nobility be punished by the laws of the land, but it will also incur special signs of Our deepest displeasure and disgrace at Our hands.[96]

Here was royal recognition of a kingdom-wide crisis of seigneurialism and village subjection running parallel to Stavenow's struggles.

RECONCILIATION AND HARMONY AT STATE COMMAND: PROLOGUE TO THE 1790 URBARIUM

In 1784 yet another embroilment arose between Kleist and his subjects over their labor obligations in building a sexton's barn. When the Chamber Court ruled against them, the villages petitioned the Ministry of Justice for a rent and work-rules contract, or Urbarium, such as Frederick II had that same year publicly recommended in cases of severe landlord–village conflict.[97] Kleist wrote the aging king that his farmers "can have no other purpose – since dues and services are fixed, and old manorial registers exist recording them – than to gain advantages in the course of [the Urbarium's] formulation. But these they will not attain." Kleist forbore protesting "only so as not to draw upon myself the suspicion that I wanted to set myself against a proceeding that, according Your Royal Majesty's All-Highest Person's intention, shall and must take place." Kleist could hardly, without abandoning all diplomacy, have registered his embittered opposition more emphatically. Yet he was losing ground, since his farmers refused certain labors even when court decisions ordained them. In 1781 they began a boycott

---

[96] "Publicandum, wegen Bestraffung der muthwilligen Querulanten", 12 July 1787, *Novum Corpus Constitutionum Prussico-Brandenburgensium*, vol. VIII (1791), no. LXXV, cols. 1497–1508.

[97] No. 719, fos. 70–5. In 1783 Frederick II ordered Silesia's provincial administration to negotiate registers (Urbaria) for each seigneurial jurisdiction unambiguously fixing subject villagers' labors and rents, together with landlords' reciprocal obligations. In 1784 he extended this policy to Brandenburg "to prevent and redress the numerous lawsuits and grievances between landlords and their subjects". Royal order of September 11, 1784, in Stadelmann, *Könige*, vol III, 206ff, 619. Frederick later ordered Urbaria compiled in East Prussia, but the nobility there, like their Silesian brethren, largely evaded the command. Ibid., 637–8.

of commutation fees, depriving him by mid-1785 of 1,011 talers' cash income.[98]

Among the farmers, the sexton's barn conflict, minor in itself, stoked consternation. Fifty of them, led by ill-fated mayor David Zeggel, declared "they will not give their names until assured their farm tenures will not be collectively abolished." Why fear of mass eviction arose is unclear, but perhaps had some relation to the government-appointed urbarial negotiator Weber, who conceded "he had indeed been charged with investigating their economic condition." He noted that the farmers rejected previous mediators' 1783 findings as, presumably, too favorable to Kleist's cause. In 1784 the major, ascribing his subjects' recalcitrance to "insubordination, stubbornness and laziness," supplied the Supreme Appellate Court with documents "showing the farmers, judged according to economic principles, are excessively well-off."[99] Unfortunately, these appraisals of the farmers' material condition, however biased, have vanished. It is unsurprising, considering pro-seigneurial sympathies among Prussian officials, that judicial mediators produced reports villagers repudiated. As for the Urbarium, the Chamber Court's Prignitz District agent Weber laboriously negotiated it through five years before Kleist and his fifty subject farmers signed it in 1790.

We need not follow their dealings too closely, nor pause over all the Urbarium's 191 paragraphs. Yet the most important of them form a mosaic picture of landlord–farmer relations in which, after three hundred years of intermittent contention, both sides agreed to recognize themselves. Like Prussia's 1794 Law Code – a compilation, launched by Frederick II, of the Prussian monarchy's laws – the Stavenow Urbarium attempted to systematize and rationalize deep-rooted custom. It sought to impart legal order to a tributary-labor relationship that, reaching back to medieval German east-Elbian colonization, eighteenth-century Enlightenment minds easily condemned as outmoded and irrational. In the often pedantically precise limits it set to seigneurial power it vindicated the villages' costly and painful struggle with the lordship, though they failed to gain every point. For Kleist, as for other landlords signing Urbaria, negotiating with his subjects as juridical equals meant surrendering to state arbitration a seigneurial authority his predecessors, including his father and uncle, thought themselves entitled to wield far more freely.

Commissioner Weber's 1786 hearings illuminate both Kleist's previous struggles with his villagers and his self-understanding. Seeking to compel

---

[98] No. 719, fos. 71–2.
[99] No. 312, fos. 7–8. The farmers' words require the addition of "nicht." No. 719, fos. 53–4.

farmers to haul larger sheep-manure loads, he dismissed the objection that smaller wagons were usual before and after his inheritance of the lordship. If he tolerated them, it was because "he then lacked knowledge of economics, since he only left war service in 1763." The villagers' lawyer retorted that smaller wagons had been used "from time immemorial" and that Kleist could not inherit more rights than his father possessed. Weber called witnesses to determine whether a "special observance" prevailed at Stavenow nullifying Prignitz custom permitting larger wagons.

Two retired farmers testified that in Frau Kleist's day "ordinary" (small) wagons worked to seigneurial satisfaction, when manorial teams and workers did not perform this heavy toil alone. Old Christian Nagel speculated that perhaps only during his twenty-fifth year, which he spent "in the company," were farmers asked to use larger wagons. Economic Commissioner Sauerland, whom the Justice Ministry assigned to report on farming practices, confirmed that many Prignitz estates performed this work with seigneurial teams alone, but where villagers joined in, they used larger wagons without detriment. Finally, the Urbarium sanctioned heavier loads.[100]

As for whether Kleist could rightfully command farmers to haul his grain to local mills during regular weekly work, they conceded they had done so "out of obligingness toward our lordship . . . But it's well known grain-hauls are subjects' hardest service." Weber determined such transports were of recent origin, but that farmers had agreed to perform them with lighter loads, which Kleist accepted, "to avoid any conflict." Having earlier gained limited haulage in regular service, he now successfully extended it to milling transports.[101] Similarly, Kleist argued that, since Berlin decreed villagers must transport estate goods within forty English miles, "this obligation may be extended" to driving seigneurial passengers equally far. The villagers would only recognize hauls within ten English miles. Kleist said personal transports would occur only "extremely seldom," but insisted on them, though the Urbarium ruled otherwise. Villagers' fears of precedents set by court rulings and their own concessions were not groundless.[102]

Controversial too was whether Kleist could transfer his farmers' seven annual "extra days" of manual labor, hitherto confined to seigneurial flax-work, gardening, and sheep-shearing, to his summer harvests. He argued that "in most places in this province a six-week period of extraordinary harvest service is customary and the subject

[100] No. 316, fos. 2–8.   [101] No. 334, fos. 1–3.   [102] Ibid., fo. 2.

farmers must help their overlordships nearly every day of the week."
The villagers invoked a thirty-year rule, whereby conditions established or suspended for that time-span were correspondingly either
legally valid or had expired. Three retired farmers testified. Hans
Nagel farmed a fullholding from 1752 to 1784, and remembered mainly doing the traditionally assigned tasks on "extra days." But in Frau
Kleist's time and later, they sometimes also worked in the harvest.
"However, such was done only out of good-will, and it has been well
known in the commune from old and immemorial time, and always
said, that originally only the four above-described manual labors of
the extra days might be performed by the subjects." Nagel knew of
farmers who, when summoned to perform extra-day labor in the harvests, refused to go and were not punished, either by Frau Kleist or her
son the major.

Christian Nagel, a farmer from 1740 to 1776, said in his day "we
weren't too particular, but reported [for extra-day work] when we were
summoned," except during harvest, since by obeying then they "would
have wrongly accepted it and set a precedent." Jochen Müller said of
1756–84 that they occasionally performed extra-day work in the lordship's harvests, especially of flax, "when our own reaping was finished,"
but only from "good-will and not obligation." The Urbarium granted
Kleist his point, extra days counting merely as seven days' manual labor
by one person, though the Chamber Court ruled he could only demand
them in harvests if villagers' own reaping did not suffer.[103]

Another contentious 1786 issue was whether the Löcknitz pastures
ultimately belonged to Stavenow or the villages and so also whether villagers' meadow rents were revocable or hereditarily fixed. Kleist self-
importantly said that "in 1716 my deceased father the Colonel von Kleist
acquired my estate Stavenow as a gift from the most blessed king." In
1727 his father, who (he sentimentally imagined) "stood on good terms"
with the villagers, gave them the meadows "to provide them with a more
comfortable livelihood." Major Kleist was content to leave the "completely insignificant" meadow rents unchanged, but rejected his farmers'
argument that he could neither raise them nor reclaim the lands for himself. The villagers believed their predecessors long held the meadows in
exchange for grain rents, which Colonel Kleist only equalized and supplemented with money payments. Kleist retorted that grain rents were
levies on arable land alone. The 1727 *Hausbuch* clearly stated the meadows

---

[103] No. 345, fos. 2–8; no. 700, fos. 65–6.

were given for cash alone. His subjects, countering that their hereditary farms could not lawfully be diminished by loss of "appurtenances," petitioned "to be protected in our ancestors' possessions."[104]

Elders' testimony revealed their views of the long-deceased Colonel Kleist's regime. Retired farmer Hans Ebel, seventy-four, reported:

> I was born in 1712 in Glövzin. When I was a lad of about fourteen, and could already help loading hay, or do other similar work, the meadows were shared out, about which I still remember much . . .
>
> There was then great inequality among subject farmers, both in lands and payments. Some farmers had comparatively little land but high dues . . . [F]armer Hecht, whose farm Christoph Zeggel now cultivates . . . then had no meadows at all, but nevertheless paid considerable dues in grain. So it was with others. Now because frequent complaints and grievances were voiced about this, Herr Colonel von Kleist's brother, who in 1727 was managing affairs for his brother on the estate here, ordered redistribution to take place, whereby subject farmers of every type would be made equal among themselves.

Commissioner Weber asked "whether the land hadn't belonged before 1727 to the lordship, since otherwise it couldn't very well have engaged in such a high-handed redistribution, taking the subjects' property away from them?" Ebel replied:

> I never heard anything about that, but only always that they were village meadows. *Also, in the olden days the subjects had to submit to such coercion* [Drükkungen], *and they didn't know anyone they could have complained to about it.* The just-mentioned Captain von Kleist *was a hard master, who took control of everything and spared no one* [my emphasis – WH].

Farm rents owed the church the Kleists "bought away" in their equalization. "I can remember that the Holtz and Hecht farms . . . which previously had to give the preacher here 12 bushels' rent, got this high quantity reduced by half." Weber pressed Ebel to admit that, if villagers paid grain rents to the church, they could not have been for meadows. Ebel's response was that:

> he can offer no elucidation of this. He has only set forth the circumstances as known to him, and *cannot know the reasons for them because, as a subject, no one would have revealed them to him* [my emphasis – WH].

Signing with crosses, he was prepared to swear an oath.[105] Here, from an evidently articulate and intelligent man, were illusion-free views of subject status and the limitations of knowledge and action it entailed. Villagers must have sensed a considerable release from powerlessness

---

[104] No. 318, fos. 2–6.   [105] Ibid., fos. 10–14.

once it was practicable to appeal beyond the seigneurial court to royal adjudication of conflicts with the lordship.

Peter Ebel, eighty, had, he said, farmed fifty-four years, and "am now sitting for ten years in retirement." Since he returned in 1731 from the army to succeed his father, his fifty-four-year claim suggests that, as a retired patriarch in 1786, he still ascribed managerial powers to himself, not improbable in a man of such experience and endurance. Abjuring, as usual, kinship-based interest conflicts, he said that:

Farmer Hans Georg Ebel is my corporeal son. Otherwise I have no relatives in [Premslin] village. At the meadows' allotment in 1727 I was a proper young person, working with my father on the farm, and I could already do any kind of farm work.

It was Captain von Kleist's "high-handed regulations" that brought meadow redistribution to pass, "as I can remember exactly."

These were in no way seigneurial meadows, but the subject farmers' actual possessions. At least, for as long as I can think, I never heard differently. And I can truly say it would have occurred to no villager to call these lands lordship's property. Before allotment they were in but a few subjects' possession, and others had no meadow hay whatever. That was often discussed in the village.[106]

The communes claimed the meadows "from time immemorial." Since 1727 redistribution they had "silently become hereditary leaseholds, and they hoped the lordship would leave them so." Kleist said "the subjects, especially in recent years, have not proved by behavior so deserving that he should surrender such considerable prerogatives and cede his property to them." His father would not have diminished the Stavenow fief to his heirs' disadvantage.[107]

Yet the appellate court, sidestepping original ownership, eventually blocked Kleist from raising meadow rents or enclosing villagers' meadows in his properties – undoubtedly an unpleasant defeat, even if he abjured seizing the land.[108] The issue carried more symbolic weight than immediate menace. As in other skirmishes, he had insisted on maximal powers, to force his villagers into obedience with threats of painful losses, however theoretical.

THE 1790–1797 URBARIAL NEGOTIATIONS

The Urbarium confirmed the picture of the villagers' juridical condition earlier pages drew from evidence of everyday practice: "by legal status, the subjects are ordinary usufructuary farmers [*Laßbauern*]. But a

---

[106] Ibid., fos. 15–16.   [107] No. 353, fos. 63–4.   [108] No. 720, fos. 65–6.

deceased farm proprietor's children have the right to succeed their parents in managing the farm." When death left minors on the holding, the lordship was obliged to find an interim proprietor "and conserve the farm for one of the children." The lordship could choose the "most capable" heir, but only where direct heirs, male or female, were absent could it appoint successors "according to its own arbitrary wishes." Since families without mature children were rare, Kleist's intervention powers in village property transmission were narrow, though in disputed successions he could sway the balance.[109]

"Any subject farmer may move away and leave his farm," provided he recruited a competent successor. In general, "subjection clings to the farm" (*Untertänigkeit klebt dem Hofe an*). But "subjection is bound to a farm's cultivation, and subject parents' children are also to be considered subjects." This was old law, as was a non-inheriting son's obligation to take a vacant farm if the lordship so decreed – a seigneurial power never demonstrably invoked at Stavenow, because of self-interest, against a prospective young farmer's will. Farmers' children could not marry without the lordship's consent and written license, but this "may not be denied them." In its 1796 review of the Stavenow agreements, the Justice Ministry's Urbarial Commission included among obligatory revisions the point that seigneurial permission to marry was granted "gratis." Service at the manor of unmarried children inessential to family labor was "compulsory" at statutory wages, if the lordship so chose, "but by local custom lasts only three years." If compulsory servants "can, through marriage or otherwise, make their fortune [*Glück machen*]," the lordship had to release them upon acceptable substitutes' recruitment or at their current service year's end.[110]

The village headman was an "ordinary seigneurial mayor," whose office neither "clung" to a particular farm nor alternated among fullholders. He gained "no other freedoms or emoluments" than use of a small arable plot (sowable in less than a bushel) and release from "short journeys the villagers must undertake." Unless these previously unrecorded mayoral perquisites long existed, Major Kleist seems to have succeeded, though without apparent effect, in giving insubordinate mayors more to lose. Lordship-appointed aldermen "enjoyed no emoluments, advantages, or freedoms."[111]

---

[109] No. 353 (*Urbarium von dem zum Stavenowschen Hause gehörigen Dorfe Premslin* [23.II 1790]). The Urbaria for Glövzin and Karstädt mirrored the Premslin document. Ibid., fos. 6, 16.

[110] Ibid., fos. 12–14; no. 51, fo. 4.   [111] Ibid., fos. 60–1.

The first condition of a new farmer's "appointment" was the ancient "oath of allegiance" (*Huldigungseid*), personalizing landlordly authority in the feudal manner. Tributary rents and labor services a farmer's son or son-in-law owed the lordship could not exceed what the retiring farmer himself rendered. In 1790 Kleist successfully pressured urbarial officials to allow future rent hikes by their ruling that, "if in an [inheriting] child's absence a foreign person is accepted on the holding," the "modality" of dues and services could be renegotiated. Though this menacing paragraph aroused no recorded opposition, in 1796 the Justice Ministry's Urbarial Commission expunged it, on the long-established grounds that "no lordship in any place may raise and increase subjects' dues and services," barring assignment of new lands or incomes.[112]

Similarly aggressive, though not unlawful, was Kleist's insistence on collecting high exit fees of 10 talers from men and 5 talers from women when they quit Stavenow's jurisdiction, even if only to fall under another jurisdiction in the same village. In 1786 the villagers said they did not dispute the charge, "only we have never paid [it] here, and also cannot pay, because we are poor people and can't produce such a big sum. Our children are supposed to get as much from their [parental] farms as the exit fees amount to." If they married beyond Stavenow jurisdiction, exit fines would consume their cash inheritance. Kleist magnanimously said "it was indeed true that in particular cases the exit fee had previously been remitted, and it wasn't intended in future to oppress poor people without resources, but rather he would make them a gift of it in cases of proven poverty." So he had written on departure certificates, as he expected other lordships likewise to do. But villagers could not derive from this "complete liberation."

In 1790 Kleist held that, though exit money was not actually collected, "it never came to subjects' refusal [to pay] nor had he abandoned his claim." In the last decade he had demanded its payment while waiving it. Villagers' lawyer Meyer, the property-law judge, denied payment had previously been demanded. Though "a few departing subjects" had recently paid, villagers should not, in view of "their bad circumstances," be held to it. Commissioner Weber recorded as fact that exit fees were neither claimed nor paid "in older times." Whether villagers' "miserable [*armseelige*] conditions," as he condescendingly (but perhaps protectively) described them, justified collecting them the appellate

---

[112] Ibid., fo. 65; no. 51, fo. 5.

court should decide.[113] To Kleist's outrage, it ruled against him, seemingly because the fee had lapsed through disuse. In 1797 he instructed his Berlin appellate lawyer Michaelis to protest this "highly prejudicial point" at the "high Justice Department," if only to await final vindication by the anticipated (but never issued) Brandenburg Provincial Law Book.[114] Kleist could only have displayed such intransigence to punish village insubordination and show he would not surrender theoretical prerogatives.

He also pressed for fuller eviction powers. Weber's 1790 formulation allowed the lordship, facing villagers' "negligent management" or incapacity to replace missing iron stock, to dismiss a "disorderly farmer," after "summary investigation by a [seigneurial] judge, [and] to make provisions for the holding's further cultivation without formal eviction proceedings." Nor would an evicted farmer's children retain inheritance rights. But, as the appellate Urbarial Commissioners later ruled, Prussia's 1794 General Law Code governed evictions, granting farmers appellate rights, binding on Kleist, against seigneurial rulings.[115]

Urbarial prescriptions "On the Lordship's Duties Toward its Subjects" occupied but one paragraph. In "cases of misfortune," such as severe hail, animal epidemics, crop failures, and war devastation, or when farmers generally could not maintain themselves from their own resources, seigneurial responsibility was to grant labor service remissions or money or grain advances. "But it goes without saying that, as soon as the farmer returns to better condition, he will requite advances received and dues remitted with equitable final payment." This formulation too the Urbarial Commissioners later voided, citing a 1721 statute prohibiting lordships from demanding repayment of aid rendered in "great misfortune."[116]

Subjects' "General Duties Toward the Lordship" were more numerous. When a member of the "overlordship," including children, died, villagers had to ring the church bell daily for four weeks in three fifteen-minute "pulses" between 12:00 noon and 1:00 P.M. Though it hardly encouraged commiseration in seigneurial mourning, villagers received in return one barrel of beer for their "amusement." As for "holding vigil" at sick lordships' bedsides and aristocratic biers, "even if this is customary, the lordship wishes to surrender its rights." Kleist did not

[113] No. 498, fos. 1–3.   [114] No. 720, fos. 63, 65–6, 77–8.
[115] No. 353, fos. 67–8; no. 51, fos. 6–7.   [116] No. 353, fos. 68–9; no. 51, fo. 7.

want villagers with whom he had so long struggled to witness his family's intimate agonies and sorrows. Nor did he demand they "cradle" seigneurial children during their lives' first six weeks, as old custom allegedly prescribed. Yet he allowed the Urbarium to bind his subjects "to carry departed lordships and their children to their burial places, for which they will be given food and drink."

Kleist quoted from Lindt's 1649 housebook, and from a 1731 farm occupancy deed, to claim his villagers' payment of the "so-called maiden's tax," theoretically collectable at seigneurial daughters' marriages. "Since the subjects know nothing of this, and without court order will not agree," higher authority would decide but, after asserting this shadowy claim, Kleist let it die. He also demanded his villagers not only transport seigneurial judges to Stavenow on court days (counting as regular labor service), but likewise when they audited church accounts, and to drive Perleberg Church Inspectors to Stavenow's villages at new pastors' installation or ecclesiastical visitations. Farmers refused non-court journeys, nor did later rulings compel them. They rejected driving prisoners to fortresses, again claiming they had never done so. Kleist's invocation of another ancient charge, that in cases of executions among their ranks they should pay "hangman's money," they likewise opposed. As for supplying the lordship's temporarily employed artisans with bedding, "they only delivered the bedding in question in recent years under compulsion, and this cannot establish the lordship's right."

Enclosure, in all three villages, of seigneurial land, whether arable, meadow, or pasture, simplified the "Reciprocal Rights of Lordship and Subjects," for "thus no conflict can arise." The lordship could exercise its hunting monopoly on villagers' fields, but this provoked no evident controversy. Kleist's hard line brought even the two Premslin "parson's farmers" under attack. These smallholders each paid the parson 4 talers cash rent yearly, "for which they receive a meal," and worked two unpaid days bringing in his harvest, "for which they get food and drink." Their farms, Weber wrote, had existed "since time immemorial," but "one doesn't know whether their tenures are hereditary or for life only." Though this threatened their successors with heavier burdens, no objections arose.[117]

Seigneurial fullholders' iron stock counted forty-four entries, from seed-grain and livestock to humble housewares. Smallholders, as was

[117] No. 353, fos. 69–74, 81–5, 90–1.

usual, were entitled to receive and obliged to keep four horses. Farmer Krumm, serving the Premslin pastor, described smallholder stock's thirty-nine components as "necessary and indispensable, but his predecessor hadn't transferred these items to him by far, as his occupancy deed would show. For he got only two horses instead of four, and only one goose instead of two, etc." Krumm wanted to give his successor only what he had received. Kleist wanted Krumm, like all smallholders, to keep four horses so he could perform yearly the seigneurially coveted grain-hauls. Krumm protesting they were "beyond his power," Kleist promised him the two missing horses. The major sourly claimed that when, because of "slovenly economy" outgoing farmers failed to give iron-stock items to their successors and could not pay for them themselves, the lordship "for its own advantage" replaced them. He later agreed to bring any farm's iron stock up to urbarial level if the occupancy deed showed it had not originally been properly equipped.[118] To limit seigneurial fire liability, the Urbarium required villagers, if their buildings burned down, to rebuild at their own cost, Kleist only suspending labor service obligations for half the time "the king remits their taxes." When buildings "collapsed because of age," villagers claimed free landlordly lumber, but Kleist refused, the appellate commission upholding him.[119]

Kleist gained his points about farmers' lodgers. If "wived" they owed him twenty-four days of yearly manual labor, if unwived only twelve. They also toiled in the seigneurial rye harvest for food and drink. About unmarried couples, seemingly not uncommon: "should a lodger have a female person with him, who if she were a single lodger would owe manorial service, she is not free of it, but such a man must perform the twenty-four days' labor with the female person's help." As for retirees and such "indispensable caretakers, male or female," as they might with seigneurial approval have, they were free of manorial service.[120]

When Weber recorded the ancient three-day weekly service quota, the assembled farmers complained it "exceeded their strength," as the lordship knew, "since it has, from time immemorial, converted for their relief the third day into an equitable commutation fee of 6.16.- talers."

This does not, however, wholly suffice, but the lordship must instead, if they are to survive, remit the whole 6.16.- talers fee. They cannot rest until, in view

---

[118] Ibid., fos. 8–11, 87; no. 354, fo. 1.   [119] No. 354, fo. 12; no. 51, fo. 4.   [120] No. 51, fo. 15.

of their incapacity, their regular manorial service is in future reduced to two days weekly.

The major said these points "deserve no consideration, since court decisions have confirmed that manorial service is fixed at three days, and the subjects took their farms on this condition." Commissioner Weber explained, "drawing in their legal counselor, their demand's groundlessness," making his account "as plain [*sinnlich*] as possible, but they would pay no heed to reasonable [*vernünftigen*] remonstrances." Here, doubtless, the villagers were pressing, however unlikely the prospects of appellate success, their maximal demand.[121]

Kleist wanted a summer work schedule from seven to seven, but the fullholders held they need not harness their horses and leave their farmsteads before 6:00, bringing them to the seigneurial workplace at 7:30. Likewise, if they should be home at 7:30, they would have to leave service at 6:00. Winter hours – from eight to four or five by the lordship's reckoning – should be correspondingly shorter. The farmers thus aimed to cut the maximal hours from twelve to 10.5 hours. Kleist "will not agree to these unfair claims."

Midday breaks for traction workers were two hours in summer and one hour in winter, manual workers taking one hour throughout the year, except in the rye harvest, when two hours were granted, plus half-hour pauses for "morning bread" and "vespers bread." The barley and oats harvests included the same short breaks, but only one-hour lunches. Fullholders entered appeals for two-hour midday breaks throughout the year. Had they gained both and their starting and quitting time demands, their maximal workday would have shrunk to 7.5–8.5 hours. Seigneurial officials needed to announce manorial service obligations before sundown one day before work. Days not served were lost, unless villagers were pressed into government-mandated work. If weather interrupted a given day's task, the foremen could switch to other work.[122]

Though the courts previously required fullholders to haul seigneurial grain, fruit, vegetables, and potatoes in regular service within a forty (English) mile radius, with a twenty-mile round-trip comprising one day's limit, the farmers again claimed "impossibility." Weber warned that obduracy would lead the Chamber Court to punish "capricious litigants." During sowing and harvesting seasons, they were exempt from hauls beyond a twenty-mile round-trip, and always free of return loads.

---

[121] Ibid., fos. 17–18.   [122] Ibid., fos. 19–20, 23, 42–4.

When hauling to local towns, they had to arrive before 12:30 P.M., before markets closed. Compromise load limits, depending on crop, were fixed for the once-yearly grain transport outside manorial service to Perleberg or Elbe ports.[123]

The urbarial commission meticulously specified load sizes for seigneurially consumed firewood, which the farmers need not cut. Experts would set limits to lumber haulage for seigneurial building. Weber reminded Kleist the courts had vetoed transport of "commercially marketed firewood." Irritably replying that this verdict "had greatly injured him," he demanded notation that an appellate court might in future reverse it. In grain harvests, loads would not exceed five sheaves. Because of hay's variable weight, the farmers rejected normative quantities, Kleist finally acquiescing. He first demanded straw loads of 1,800 pounds, but they stuck at 1,200, which he conceded. He and the economist Sauerland thought 18-bushel grain-hauls to the local mill reasonable, but the farmers wanted only 12, "especially since the road is very bad." The parties meticulously regulated grain-haulage from seigneurial fields, villagers promising to avoid traffic jams at the barns. Among many other hauls, farmer agreed to transport no more than 110 pounds of live fish, with necessary water.[124]

Kleist wanted them to plow on service days two small *Morgen*, here called "Rhenish" but later known as "Magdeburg," amounting together to a half-hectare (1.25 acres). They balked at more than 1.5 *Morgen*. While Sauerland advised plowing furrows 8 inches (*Zoll*) wide and 4 inches deep, they lamented "their teams are so weak," agreeing only to dimensions of 6 by 3. Finally, Commissioner Weber gained Kleist's agreement, considering the seigneurial arable's variable qualities, to drop daily quotas and retain the "old constitution," with the field foreman defining work goals. The lordship's laborers used seigneurial horses to harrow the plowed fields. Farmers did not need to serve personally. The workers they sent could be, at the lordship's discretion, females but if conflict arose over farm servants' competence, the crucial measure would be whether or not they were fifteen years old.[125] The lordship refused to reward with food, drink, or coin farmers performing labor services or rendering feudal dues (such as the annual spinning of 4 pounds per household of seigneurially supplied flax), though fullholders' teams grazed at midday on seigneurial pastures. The one happy event the Urbarium recorded followed rye

[123] Ibid., fos. 22, 45–7.   [124] Ibid., fos. 25–31, 36–40.   [125] Ibid., fos. 32, 88–9; no. 51, fo. 4.

harvest, when each village received "one barrel of beer, which they must fetch themselves from the lordship's brewer" though "they may not return the empty cask," perhaps because the lordship did not wish to face demands for more beer or see farmers whose inhibitions had been loosened by drink criticize its product. "Further, the two head mowers [from each village] receive floral wreaths made by the girls serving at the manor, along with clay pipes and 2 groschen of tobacco each," the flowers being for the women working as head mowers' sheaf-binders.[126]

Smallholders' obligations included ten-mile round-trips on foot as seigneurial messengers and taking turns sowing seigneurial seed at (seemingly heavy) 18–24 bushel daily rates. Kleist succeeded in burdening them both with once-yearly grain-hauls and other transports in regular service and during harvest, though against manual labor cancellation and, sometimes, with lightened loads and permission to pair up their teams. They forbore protest.[127] The last paragraph registered the parties' agreement they had formulated "a properly grounded legal statute . . . valid for all time." At Premslin, only one of eighteen fullholders signed with his name rather than a mark, while but one smallholder could write his name. Six years later negotiator Weber received the Justice Ministry's Urbarial Commission's instructions on bringing the three Stavenow Urbaria into conformity with the 1794 Law Code and other preexisting statutes, and eliminating minor variations among the three villages' Urbaria.[128] Apart from aforementioned 1796 revisions, several Justice Ministry objections remained, including that "nothing definite has been settled concerning the poor." For "even though a farmer must assume care of the children on his holding, this doesn't extend to the village poor who might be living with him." The 1701 Statute on Paupers and Beggars required the establishment of village poor-relief funds administered by mayors and aldermen under seigneurial supervision.

In March 1797 Commissioner Weber reassembled Kleist and the three communes, citing the 1794 Law Code's relevant sections. The villagers replied "that they do not see and understand all of this," and wanted to fetch their legal adviser, Assistant Justice Commissioner Schrötter, forcing postponement until next day. The farmers' high suspiciousness appears in the refusal of two mayors to sign a simple statement of the day's proceedings. Next day both

---

[126] No. 353, fo. 49.   [127] Ibid., fos. 53–5.   [128] Ibid., fos. 92ff; no. 51, fos. 3, 5.

sides' lawyers objected to recognizing the 1794 Law Code's higher authority, fearing it might cancel one or another favorable provision already negotiated. The Prussian government's projected Provincial Law Book might in turn override the 1794 code. Weber mollified them by decreeing that higher law should govern only presently disputed points.

About poverty, Kleist's subjects expressed themselves with laconic cold-bloodedness:

The farmers first observed that for a considerable time there have been no village poor among them. For this reason no one has thought to set up a special poor-relief fund. Should a case arise in future, they will give the poor man natural provisions, if he is not taken into the Wittstock poorhouse.

They had no intention of harboring indigent persons requiring public relief (as distinct from locally born poor aided by kinfolk and neighbors). The poor should fend for themselves or enter poorhouses. Only exceptionally might deserving persons remain, making farmhouse rounds for food.[129]

The Justice Ministry also required stipulation of the age at which farmers' sons might be compelled to take the family holding. The farmers "declare the case could hardly arise that someone would refuse to take a paternal farm." But if an age were set, it should be twenty-four. The farmers regarded farm succession as self-evident, whether because it was materially desirable or for socio-cultural reasons. Age twenty-four appeared to them the ideal moment for marriage and entry into self-sufficient farming.[130] At the 1797 hearing Kleist explicitly renounced his effort, already disallowed by the Justice Ministry, to force higher dues and services on "foreign" subjects taking over farms without heirs. On this inflammatory theme, no doubts could linger that previous rents did not apply. As for evictions, Kleist conceded the 1794 Law Code governed them. He dropped his demand that disaster relief be repaid. On maintaining the Premslin church, Kleist said, to Pastor Höpfner's approval, that "the churches here are so well endowed that their resources' exhaustion is not lightly to be feared." The villages would have to acquire communal fire-spraying devices, instead of possessing only gear for each homestead.[131]

---

[129] No. 51, fos. 8, 25. Cf. Jan Peters, "Das unbarmherzige Dorf. Eine verhaltensgeschichtliche Studie aus dem südlichen Fläming (1728)," *JbBL* 42 (1991): 65–77.
[130] No. 51, fo. 18. [131] Ibid., fos. 20–2.

The farmers rejected the Ministry's blanket ruling obliging them in regular service to haul, without exception, everything necessary to seigneurial economy and household within twenty English miles. They recognized only a ten-mile radius, but Kleist, pointing to three verdicts favoring him, held the law had spoken. This was one of the preceding three decades' fundamental conflicts. Until now his subjects had refused the long hauls. Whether before the collapse of old Prussia in 1806 Kleist and his successors imposed them in full measure surviving records do not say.[132]

Finally, the farmers questioned the urbarial assertion they were "ordinary usufructuary farmers" whose children possessed hereditary claims on the parental holding.

If this statement [*Sag*] is interpreted literally, the conclusion could easily be drawn that inheritance right applied only to children, and that other descendants including [the farmer's] siblings and siblings' children were excluded. [The farmers] therefore want to request that [such collateral rights] be clearly established.

Kleist replied conciliatorily, accepting "the subjects' entirely correct interpretation," though any heir "must be competent to manage a farm."[133] To these final March 1797 negotiations six among fifty farmers affixed written signatures, the others making crosses.

CONCLUSION

The Kleists' long struggle over their villagers' labor services and rents ended, in the colonel's son's old age, in embittered compromise. The major won some points. He intensified exploitation of his farmers' horsepower both in long and short hauls, though not for commercial sale of seigneurial timber. But during most of his long landlordly years, he did not benefit greatly from such slowly and litigiously established power, since the farmers frequently refused the hauls. Most of his other legal offensives the courts dismissed or confined within narrow limits, leaving him in 1797 with little to show for decades-long contention. Neither could the villagers boast of burden-lifting victories. Yet they minimized the damage threatened by Major Kleist's quest for new powers, including rent increases and evictions, that, if gained and used, might have been crippling. In an age of expanding commodity markets

---

[132] Ibid., fos. 5, 28–9.   [133] Ibid., fo. 30.

and rising prices and real wages, it was an accomplishment to hold rents at early eighteenth-century levels, and to gain royal courts' guarantee of this and other tenurial rights.

These pages have shown that the villagers accepted the Kleists' seigneurial authority or lordship (*Herrschaft*) as a fact of life, often dangerous, sometimes needing placation by acts of "good will." The Kleists, especially during the colonel's widow's mid-century tenure, were capable of a milder regime, allowing farmers to conserve strength despite manorial service. Nor was the lordship unwilling to display indulgence or forbearance of its weaker farmers' inability to pay one or another fee, though it always pressed them when times improved for repayment of arrears. But nothing this study has revealed of the landlord–village relationship suggests that the Kleists' subjects viewed manorial authority with any reverence or deference independent of motives of self-preservation and self-interest. No mystique or charisma of noble seigneurialism is detectable among them. Instead, the evidence shows they experienced it unmediatedly as domination or overlordship (*Obrigkeit*). Nor did they display more deference to the institutional Lutheran church, though doubtless they accorded their preachers the respect owing to personal virtue, while Christianity's hopes and solaces were real enough to many a soul.

The picture that comes into focus is of a profoundly divided society: rent-averse villagers facing estateowners tempted by the pressure of seigneurial debt and market-oriented profit-seeking to raise demands on subject farmers. An existence tolerable or advantageous to both parties depended enormously on the tact and judgment of all leaders involved in such a localized society as Stavenow lordship, and particularly on the semi-independent authority and legitimacy of seigneurial judges such as Bürgermeister Hasse. Possibly Hasse's long tenure and resultant prestige were not unusual in the east-Elbian lands. Without such a compromise-enforcing authority, Junker lordship rested at best on inertia, at worst on coercion and violence.

Though nothing in commercialized manorialism's logic required a strong centralized government's intervention – as witness the anti-absolutist, aristocratic El Dorados of the Polish Commonwealth and German Mecklenburg – the Prussian kings' state-building zeal worked momentous changes in rural society. This could hardly be clearer than in Stavenow's case. Here widened access to royal jurisdiction afforded by Frederick II's legal reforms enabled village communes to mount a judicial campaign against their lordship that before 1740, though not wholly unthinkable, would have been procedurally and financially endurable only as an act of the greatest desperation. In the villages and at the manor-hall, both at Stavenow and widely throughout Brandenburg-Prussia, the Frederickian state entered as a revolutionary force, disciplining and constraining but also enlightening and liberating.

10

Seigneurial bond severed: from subject farmers to freeholders, from compulsory estate labors to free, 1806–1840

Prussia's defeat at Napoleon's hands broke the ice immobilizing late absolutism. In the ensuing Reform Era (1807–19) liberal-minded ministries steered state and society into cross-cutting currents of nineteenth-century free-market capitalism, careers open to talent, mass education, citizen armies, equality before the law, and electoral politics. These beginnings, though tentative and elitist, marked a departure forever from eighteenth-century corporate hierarchies and authoritarianism, however enlightened.[1]

Central to this transition was the abolition of Brandenburg-Prussian villagers' personal legal liabilities, whether slight, as at Stavenow, or heavy, as wherever serfdom existed. Chief reform minister Baron Karl vom Stein's 1807 October Edict accomplished this without compensation to villagers' overlordships. The edict also opened a free land market, so that estateowners might now emerge from any social class. Though landlords could retain compulsorily recruited servants until 1810, villagers otherwise acquired full legal independence and could quit their villages and seek their fortunes as fate decreed.

But what of subject farmers' land? In two crucial laws, the 1811 Regulation Edict and the conservative revisions encoded in the 1816 Declaration, Prince Karl August von Hardenberg's ministry established the principle that largeholding farmers (those performing manorial service with teams) should receive the lands they tilled in freehold. The price they paid was surrender to their lordships of one-third or half their arable or the cash equivalent, depending on whether their tenures were hereditary or non-hereditary. Old-regime villagers with

---

[1] On interpretive traditions: Levinger, *Nationalism*; Koselleck, *Preussen*; Wehler, *Gesellschaftsgeschichte*, vol. I, 397ff. Cf. Carl von Clausewitz, "Observations on Prussia in Her Great Catastrophe," excerpted in Peter Paret and Daniel Moran, eds., *Carl von Clausewitz: Historical and Political Writings* (Princeton, NJ, 1992), 30–84; Magnus Bassewitz, *Die Kurmark Brandenburg im Zusammenhang mit den Schicksalen des Gesamtstaats Preussen*, 3 vols. (Leipzig, 1852).

largeholdings and strong tenures, such as Stavenow's Dargardt colonists, like the many crown-estate farmers who before 1806 gained hereditary leaseholder status, won release from seigneurial rents and gained freeholds for cash payments with no land loss. Other provisions governed division between manors and villages, and among villagers themselves, of non-arable common lands.[2]

The 1816 Declaration excluded from freehold conversion intermediate or smallholding farmers who could not pay compensation without sinking to the level of cottagers unable to maintain draft-teams. Yet their lordships might negotiate land settlements privately with them, before the 1848 revolution bestowed freeholds on all once-subject farmers tilling arable holdings, regardless of size. The 1816 revision's purpose was to offer estateowners – resentful of seigneurial losses, fearful of free labor markets, or merely driven by possessiveness – the opportunity to confiscate ("enclose") lands of smallholders on shaky tenures or to continue drawing unpaid labor from "unregulated" villagers by perpetuating their accustomed manorial service. Landowners often prized labor more than land, for very many such smallholdings survived to be converted after 1848, for cash, into freeholds.[3]

Nineteenth-century writers later rhetorically elevated Prussia's "regulation process" into "the subject farmers' emancipation" (*Bauernbefreiung*) – in common English, "peasant emancipation." It entailed the east-Elbian countryside's massive restructuring, including the final disentanglement of village and estate land and the cultivation of much formerly untilled but now privately distributed and enclosed common land and forest. It required armies of agricultural and judicial

---

[2] Hartmut Harnisch, "Die agrarpolitischen Reformmassnahmen der preussischen Staatsführung in dem Jahrzehnt vor 1806/07," *JbfWG* 3 (1977): 129–53; Hartmut Harnisch, "Vom Oktoberedikt des Jahres 1807 zur Deklaration von 1816. Problematik und Charakter der preussischen Agrarreformgesetzgebung zwischen 1807 und 1816," *JbfWG*, Sonderband (1978): 231–93; Klaus Vetter, *Kurmärkischer Adel und preußische Reformen* (Weimar, 1979); Schissler, *Preussische Agrargesellschaft*; Christoph Dipper, *Die Bauernbefreiung in Deutschland 1790–1850* (Stuttgart, 1980); cf. Stefan Brakensiek, *Agrarreform und ländliche Gesellschaft. Die Privatisierung der Marken in Nordwestdeutschland 1750–1850* (Paderborn, 1991).

[3] Rudolf Berthold, "Die Veränderungen im Bodeneigentum und in der Zahl der Bauernstellen, der Kleinstellen und der Rittergüter in den preussischen Provinzen Sachsen, Brandenburg und Pommern während der Durchführung der Agrarreformen des 19. Jahrhunderts," *JbfWG*, Sonderband (1978): 10–116; Hartmut Harnisch, "Statistische Untersuchungen zum Verlauf der kapitalistischen Agrarreformen in den preussischen Ostprovinzen (1811 bis 1865)," *JbfWG* 4 (1974): 149–83. Cf. Erich Langelüddecke, "Zum Grundsatz der Entschädigung und des Loskaufs bei den Eigentumsregulierungen und Dienstablösungen der ostelbischen Bauern Preussens im 19. Jh.," *ZfGW* 4 (1960): 890–908; Dietrich Saalfeld, "Zur Frage des bäuerlichen Landverlustes im Zusammenhang mit den preussischen Agarreformen," *Zeitschrift für Agrargeschichte und Agrarsoziologie* 11:1 (1963): 163–71.

officials and most of the nineteenth century to complete. Historians have still not fully weighed its impact. Politically engaged writers long dwelt on the advantages the Junkers derived from the land cessions and other modes of seigneurial compensation imposed on fullholders; on landlords' enclosure into their estates of large and small farms ineligible for regulation because of weak titles; on the exclusion between 1816 and 1848 of landed smallholders from freehold conversion and on the Junkers' degradation of many of them to cottage-worker status by their lands' partial or total confiscation. Georg Friedrich Knapp stamped these concerns into his paradigm-setting 1887 book's title: *The Peasant Emancipation and the Origin of the Rural Laborers in the Older Parts of Prussia*.[4]

East-Elbian estates' survival into the twentieth century created grave political problems. Yet modern research has proven inaccurate Knapp's (and Max Weber's) view that Prussian "peasant emancipation" fatally undercut, through compensation payment inequities and noble engrossment of village land, the emergence of a healthy class of freeholding family farmers. Doubtless early nineteenth-century Prussian reformers retreated, faced with the landlords' aggressive campaign to relinquish feudal privilege as profitably as possible, from initial positions more favorable to villagers. Still, on World War I's eve, villagers held two-thirds of east-Elbian arable land, including, alongside large and middle-sized family farmers, numerous smallholders and cottagers who gained their land through regulation, inheritance, or purchase. East-Elbian Prussia was not, as textbooks still hold today, a landscape defined alone by large estates and cottage-laborers' settlements, but equally a land of village-based family farmers. Nor have they and their villages disappeared today, when most manor-houses lie in ashes or ruin.[5]

---

[4] Knapp, *Bauernbefreiung*; Kaak, *Gutsherrschaft*. Knapp's perspective survives in the work, among others, of Max Weber, Hans Rosenberg, Barrington Moore, and H.-U. Wehler.

[5] In 1906 large estates encompassed some 35 percent of east-Elbian Prussian agricultural land; 24 percent belonged to middleholders with 5–20 hectares, the average farm comprising 9–10 hectares (ca. 25 English acres); large-scale village farmers with 20–100 hectares owned a further 31 percent, with the average farm around 36 hectares (ca. 90 English acres); the remaining 10 percent encompassed cottagers and smallholdings under 3 hectares (7.5 acres). Calculations are based on *Statistisches Jahrbuch für das deutsche Reich* 51 (1932), 51, reflecting the state of affairs in 1907 within the borders of 1925. This leaves the Polish regions of Imperial Germany out of account, but their agrarian structure was similar to the Prussian–German pattern, except that Polish village farms were smaller than their German counterparts: William W. Hagen, *Germans, Poles, and Jews: The Nationality Conflict in the Prussian East, 1772–1914* (Chicago, 1980), ch. 6. Cf. Berthold's and Harnisch's statistical inquiries (note 3); Sigrid Dillwitz, "Die Struktur der Bauernschaft von 1871 bis 1914. Dargestellt auf der Grundlage der deutschen Reichsstatistik," *Jahrbuch für Geschichte* 9 (1973): 104–6; Hagen, "The German Peasantry in the Nineteenth and Early Twentieth Centuries"; J. A. Perkins, "The Agricultural Revolution in Germany, 1850–1914," *Journal of European Economic History*, 10:1 (1981): 71–118.

Apart from genealogists and local historians, German scholars have rarely – and English writers never – explored Prussian village emancipation at grass-roots level. The mountainous documents the regulation process generated make the task laborious. Instead, the literature squints down on rural emancipation, so central to nineteenth-century German life, from the heights of statistically framed macrohistory, or takes the view of the Prussian officials who drafted and administered the laws. The pages below ask instead how the lordship and subject farmers at Stavenow negotiated the divorce of their centuries-long, strife-torn union. They offer a noble landlord's and his officials' commentary on Stavenow's daily administration, and on their objectives in negotiating the emancipation process with the villagers, whose voices speak back.[6]

The farmers proved no less battle-ready and obdurate in this last collective struggle against their seigneurial overlord and his agents than in previous clashes. Baron von Voss, the Kleists' successor at Stavenow, demonstrated that the nobility's post-1806 campaign for their own interests might display little of the desire, apostrophized by conservative ideologists and emphasized by later historians, to retain for political purposes patriarchal hegemony over the countryside. Instead, Voss and company displayed a tough-minded and unsentimental determination to secure his economic advantage as they completed the epochal shift from reliance on unpaid manorial service to modern wage labor.

THE KLEISTS' SUCCESS IN RAISING STAVENOW'S PRODUCTIVITY AND PROFITABILITY

Colonel and Major Kleist may have been arch-Prussian, militarized noblemen of imperious temperament toward village farmers and other underlings. But they prized their estates' income, which structural reorganizations and innovations carried out by their non-noble officials greatly magnified. Like other noble landlords, the Kleists understood the logic of eighteenth-century, Prussian-style agrarian capitalism, and sought with the help of bourgeois talent to profit from it. Pursuit of aristocratic prestige and pressure of family debt inclined them in that direction, but their profit-maximizing quest was nonetheless real. Had

---

[6] Cf. Christoph Senfft von Pilsach, "Bäuerliche Wirtschaftsverhältnisse in einem neumärkischen Dorf (Land Sternberg) vor der Regulierung der gutsherrlich-bäuerlichen Verhältnisse und der erste dortige Regulierungsversuch," *FBPG* 23:2 (1909): 127–91; Hans-Jürgen Rach and Bernhard Weissel, eds., *Landwirtschaft und Kapitalismus: Zur Entwicklung der ökonomischen und sozialen Verhältnisse in der Magdeburger Börde vom Ausgang des 18. Jahrhunderts bis zum Ende des ersten Weltkrieges*, 2 vols. (Berlin, 1978–9).

Table 10.1   *Appraised income of the Stavenow lordship under Kleist ownership (1719–1808)*

	1719				1763				1808			
	N	Value[a]	Sum	%	N	Value	Sum	%	N	Value	Sum	%
1. Sowings (in tons [Wispel])												
Rye	24	16			48	17			54	24		
Barley	10	14			16	16			7	20		
Oats	17	10			23	9			85	20		
Sum	51		702	15	87		1,288	22	146		3,136	29
2. Livestock (leasehold fees)												
Milk cows	210	4	840		330	5	1,600		288	10	2,880	
Sheep (100s)	19	16	304		10.5	20	210		13	50	650	
Pigs/forage fees			531				365		(see note b, below)			
Sum			1,675	37			2,175	37			3,530	33
3. Labor services (in full commutation fees)												
Fullholders	48	20	960		57	20	1,140		57	2	1,625	
Smallholders	23	7	161		31	5	155		25	11	275	
Cottagers									6	6	33	
Sum	71		1,121	24	24	88	1,295	22	88		1,933	18
4. Grain rents (tons)												
Mills	22	12	264	6	19	17	323	5	19	24	456	5
Farmers	6	12	72	2	16	17	272	5	16	24	372	3
5. Other incomes[b]			738	16			544	9			1,284	12
Sum 1–5:			**4,563**	**100**			**5,884**	**100**			**10,711**	**100**

6. Annual lease value of all incomes (excluding wood sales, the hunt, and other noble perquisites) **or** average annual appraised income

		3,800				**5,884**				**14,043**	
		(+90% since 1694)				(+55% since 1719)				(+139% since 1763)	

[a] Value according to the corporate nobility's appraisal schedules (*ritterschaftliche Taxordnungen*) in Prussian-minted talers. The 1764 Prussian currency reform devalued the Prussian current taler (*Courant Taler*) by one-ninth.
[b] 1719 and 1763: see table 5.1; 1808: brewing/distilling/swine forage fees – 500 t.; wood sales – 500 t.; housed laborers' rents and unpaid manual labor – 154 t.; gardens and orchards – 250 t.; fishery and hunt – 220 t.; poultry – 30 t.; bridge-tolls – 40 t.; other – 4 t. = 1,763 t. Annual taxes and fixed charges (excluding wages and salaries) = 479 t. = net 1,284 t.
Sources: no. 282 (*Pachtanschlag 1694*); no. 240 (*Pachtanschlag 1719*); no. 259 (*Anschlag unter den Erben 1760–3*); no. 39 (*Verkaufsanschlag 1808*).

their economic ambition been fainter, their struggles with the villagers would have made little sense.

The rapid eighteenth-century growth of the Stavenow estates' physical output and cash earnings is evident in table 10.1.

Table 10.2 *Stavenow lordship's income from grain and livestock production (compared to labor-service values), 1694, 1763, 1808*

(in current talers	1694 t.	%	1763 t.	%	1808 t.	%
a. Grain sowings	504	34	1,288	31	7,133	60
b. Grain rents (mills, farmers)	174	12	595	14	816	7
c. Livestock (cattle, sheep)	564	38	2,142	51	3,530	29
d. Brewing/distilling/pigs	255	16	156	4	500	4
Sum	**1,497**	**100**	**4,181**	**100**	**11,979**	**100**
Percentage increase since previous appraisal			+179%		+187%	
e. Appraised value of labor services	582		1282		1933	
Percentage increase since previous appraisal			+120%		+51%	
Proportion a–d:e	**2.6:1**		**3.3:1**		**6.2:1**	

Sources: as in table 10.1.

In the near-century 1719–1808, seigneurial grain-sowings nearly tripled. Enclosed convertible farming raised bushel yields, as will be seen, by some 50 percent. Annual income's appraised value multiplied across the century 3.6-fold. This reckoning follows seigneurial accounting procedures, treating villagers' labor services as incomes, since tenant-farmers leasing noble estates acquired them as assets (convertible through commutation fees into cash). Eighteenth-century grain crops rose more rapidly in value than livestock or labor-service commutation fees, reflecting intensifying demand for bread-grains in a growing Prussian and European population and for horse-fodder (oats) during the French Revolutionary and Napoleonic wars.

Table 10.2 displays the appraised annual value of Stavenow's incomes from grain and livestock alone, and these assets' value compared to labor services. Seigneurial output's marketable value in these main production branches steeply rose eightfold over the century, and almost fourfold in 1763–1808. In proportion to the prime agricultural commodities, labor services declined as a landlordly asset.

These tables testify to impressive growth, conjuring up the much debated European "agricultural revolution," long viewed as a precondition of – or accompaniment to – the "industrial revolution." Whatever this concept's limitations, it was thought to apply only to England, the Low Countries, and highly commercialized pockets elsewhere in western and southern Europe. It pointed not to extensive agricultural growth, but to gains in productivity of land, labor, and capital achieved through such technological improvements as new fodder crops and convertible husbandry based on land enclosures, higher-value food and industrial plants, improved livestock strains, and free land markets open to leasehold farming based on capitalist ground rents and wage labor. How widely English and western European agriculture achieved such intensified production remains controversial, but historians have always assumed its absence east of the Elbe, where – ostensibly – reliance on cost-free compulsory labor undercut interest in technology-driven efficiency gains.[7]

Stavenow's growth was partly extensive, as in Dargardt manor-farm's establishment, but also, and importantly, intensive, as in convertible husbandry's pre-1763 adoption. The 1808 appraisal, highlighting Major Kleist's and his administrators' management, reveals further productivity-enhancing innovations. In 1763 three-field farming still prevailed at Premslin and Dargardt manor-farms, while at Stavenow-Semlin headquarters the arable comprised eleven enclosures following a cycle of three annual rye sowings, two years of summer grain, five of pasture, and one of fallow sown with flax or peas. By 1808 enclosure and convertible rotations prevailed everywhere.

Premslin manor-farm continued to be leased, yielding 1,400 talers yearly in 1808, twice its 1755 rental value of 650 talers. The 1808 appraisers wrote of this once mediocre manor-farm: "the soil is of mixed composition and fertile, unexposed to flooding, and well fertilized."[8] Stavenow and Dargardt followed seven-year rotations of better-yielding "inner fields" and five-year rotations of less fertile "outer fields." "Long years of experience" showed in 1808 that inner-field seed-yield ratios here and at Semlin, comprising more than two-thirds of all seigneurial arable, averaged 1:5 for rye, barley, and oats. In the outer fields and at Premslin, they were only slightly lower at 1:4–5.

Thus Major Kleist raised grain yields some 50 percent, while increasing sowings 69 percent. Intersecting with rising prices, these accomplishments elevated seigneurial income from grain production more than fivefold, from an estimated net annual 1,266 talers in 1763 to 7,133 talers in 1808. Kleist's livestock herds did not grow much, but rising prices boosted income nearly 50 percent. The brewery and distillery in 1808 consumed 50–60 tons of grain annually, yielding above 500 talers' annual profit from liquor sales and pigs fed on by-products – threefold

---

[7] Ogilvie and Scribner, *Germany: A New Social and Economic History*, vol. II, ch. 3. Cf. Hagen, "Capitalism"; Duplessis, *Transitions*; Overton, *Revolution*.

[8] No. 39, pt. IV.

the 1763 earnings from alcohol. Wood sales reaped 300 talers yearly in 1763 but, because of Kleist's heavy cuttings, 1808 annual income, despite soaring prices, was but 500 talers. The 1808 appraisers predicted 3,000-taler sales in ten years.

In 1808 farmers' rents and labor services comprised only 14 percent of total assets, compared with 21 percent in 1763. Seigneurial income's impressive market- and technology-driven expansion lowered the relative value of feudal imposts greatly. But the probable cost of replacing compulsory unpaid labor with wage labor was high enough, even with great labor-efficiency improvement, to invest labor services with continued strong value landlords would be loath to surrender without handsome compensation. Debits in 1808 comprised the crown's feudal levy on Stavenow of 60 talers and its perpetual leasehold fee of 342 talers for Dargardt's possession, plus the 20-taler tavern license. Grain given various pastors amounted to 28 talers, plus Stavenow schoolmaster's 5-taler share. Only 6 talers went for poor-relief (*Armen Geld*).[9]

To achieve Stavenow's considerable expansion of production and profitability, Major Kleist was obliged, facing his subject farmers' obduracy on labor-service expansion, to invest considerably in fixed capital and wage labor. Between 1763 and 1808, Stavenow added to its seven four-animal teams of draft-horses thirty-five new plow-oxen. Seigneurially housed families of day laborers and threshers increased from eight to fifteen. Unmarried compulsorily recruited workers and steadily employed married estate laborers and officials rose by seven to forty-seven. Their wages, both in cash and food provisions, expanded, when monetarized at current prices (rising rapidly for bread-grains), from 818 talers annually in 1763 to 1,702 talers in 1808. These production costs were high, but they were advancing profitability's price.

The seigneurial workforce's post-1763 shape foreshadowed nineteenth-century patterns. Four new ox-drivers joined the previously employed eight plow- and wagon-drivers, six livestock herders, and six maidservants. Additions occurred in the middle stratum of married foremen and unmarried workers' female supervisors, whose pay rose, though less than estate managers' and field bailiffs'. Kleist hired a "*Doctor Medicina*" at 40 talers yearly, offering, perhaps benevolently, his seigneurial employees a kind of social insurance. Judicial and police

---

[9] Ibid., fos. 5–20.

officials enjoyed improved pay and provisions, including a judge (*Justiz Direktor*), his assistant, the court bailiff and impounder, two wood bailiffs, and a forester-hunter. On one side, estate laborers' and servants' numbers rose while, on the other, rural professionalization and middle-class formation advanced.[10]

Against this background of economic growth and social complexity, historians' picture of a technologically backward "Junker economy" (*Junkerwirtschaft*), in which authoritarian rigidity and coercion stifled market-generated incentives, is a caricature, obscuring far more than it reveals. Stavenow was an ambitious and well-managed, but not untypical east-Elbian large-estate enterprise. Among many people administering and working in it there was but one nobleman. To label such an agrarian system, next to which bourgeois-leased crown estates loomed large, as feudal or unqualifiedly aristocratic is to misunderstand its socio-economic intricacy and trajectory.

STAVENOW'S SALE TO BARON VON VOSS, 1808–1819

Major Kleist died in 1803, eight years after his first wife's death. As a widower nearing seventy, he married a noblewoman "of the house of Dessau" bearing the family name Wahlen Jürgas. She was a wealthy heiress, owning three Prignitz estates and one in the Altmark. She bore the major his only children; two daughters, one (1800–72) marrying a Mecklenburg officer. After Kleist's death his widow married neighboring Major von Rohr, living with him at her nearby Bresch estate.[11] Kleist's remarriage dashed whatever hopes his brothers and other agnatic kin nurtured of inheriting Stavenow, for his widow and minor children had first claim. At his death, 41,530 talers' debts encumbered the lordship, mostly at 5 percent. He had retired 85,000 talers' debt originally owed his brothers.

In 1808 the eminent and powerful statesman, "Royal Minister of State, Knight of High Orders, Otto Carl Friedrich, Baron von Voss," acquired Stavenow for 255,000 talers. He was an important member of post-Frederickian Prussia's ministerial bureaucracy and, before 1806, advocate of cautious reforms, including improvements in subject farmers' condition. But after 1807 Chancellor Hardenberg's rise eclipsed him, and in 1809 the king dismissed him from his influential post in the noble self-administration system. Voss had risen into the

---

[10] No. 62; cf. Hagen, "Working."　　[11] No. 65, para. 4; Kratz, *Geschichte*, vol. III, Abt. III, 369–70.

leadership circle of the anti-reform nobility's "feudal party." He also
trusted too much in Prussia's French occupiers' benevolence, bringing co-responsibility upon himself for their exactions. When, in 1809,
he took possession of Stavenow he was ensconced in embittered and
reactionary-minded Havelberg exile, busying himself with the
numerous estates which his inherited and self-earned riches won
him.

In the atmosphere of post-1815 Holy Alliance conservatism, Voss's
political fortunes revived. His impassioned opposition to Hardenberg's
Prussian constitutional plans won him the backing of Crown Prince
Frederick William, who in 1821 included him in his advisory council,
which successfully advocated the limitation of representative institutions to noble-dominated provincial assemblies. Even King Frederick
William III restored his once brusquely withdrawn favor, after a visit at
Voss's Altmark Buch estate, "where he lived in quiet retirement, taking
his greatest pleasure in musical diversions." In September 1822 the king
appointed Voss vice-president of both cabinet (State Ministry) and
royal Council of State, second only to the aging Hardenberg, upon
whose death in November Voss succeeded to the Prussian government's
leadership. "The hopes of the feudal party were high." Even Baron
vom Stein approved Voss's ascension, not only because of anti-
Hardenberg antagonism. Stein wrote: "I view Herr von Voss's appointment as a favorable event. He is a skillful and experienced man of
affairs – industrious, religious, morally upright, with a family of dignified persons worthy of respect." Voss's biographer added that "it was
indeed a salutary prospect to return, after Hardenberg's irregular and
extravagant ways, to a frugal and strictly regulated administration."
Yet, only a few months after taking the state's helm, Voss died in
January 1823 at age sixty-eight.[12]

Voss acquired in Stavenow a distinguished property. In 1805, the
economist Leopold Krug rated Stavenow the twenty-fourth most valuable noble estate in Electoral Brandenburg. He credited it (at its 1763
127,000-taler value) with only half the price Voss paid in 1808, but probably his other data fell similarly short. Among the Prussian state's 8,925
noble properties, which in 1805 also included largely non-German
noble properties in the provinces seized in 1793–5 from expiring Poland,
Stavenow ranked among the most valuable 3–5 percent, below the
upper category of 197 estates appraised above 150,000 talers (nearly half

[12] Heinrich von Petersdorff, "Voss," *Allgemeine Deutsche Biographie* (Leipzig, 1896), vol. XL, 352–61;
Levinger, *Nationalism*, chs. 6–7.

Table 10.3   *The Stavenow estates as surveyed in 1810 (in hectares)*[a]

	Arable		Meadows/ reeds	Pastures	Forest	Total
Stavenow manor	607		115	71	380	1173
Semlin manor	322		29	54	–	405
Premslin manor	166		35	28	–	229
Dargardt manor	213		63	53	290	619
Gosedahl field	–		–	115	17	132
Mesekow village	–		–	–	78	78
Total	1,308	50%	242 9%	321 12%	765 29%	2,636 100%

[a] One hectare = 2.47 acres.
Source: No. 258, fos. 9–10.

Polish).[13] In 1809 Voss commissioned Stavenow's first areal survey, proving it by modern measurement a gratifyingly large property. Economically valuable land encompassed 2,636 hectares, or 6,511 English acres. As table 10.3 shows, half lay in arable (3,231 acres), almost a third in forest.

Despite much rebuilding since the seventeenth century, the Stavenow manor-hall, once called a castle but now a "dwelling-house," retained an ancient tower, moat, and drawbridge. Its "very agreeable" site looked down on the Löcknitz stream meadows and cropland beyond. Constructed wholly from stone and masonry, it was "in good shape," with "large and spacious rooms," though "not comfortably furnished." The manor-house road the major succeeded, despite vandalism, in planting with oak and linden trees. His garden, protected by a moat and a high

---

[13] Krug's data on estate values:

Talers	No.	%
Over 500,000	17	0.2
150–500,000	180	2.0
100–150,000	266	3.0
50–100,000	1,151	12.9
20–50,000	2,911	32.7
10–20,000	2,536	28.4
5–10,000	1,864	20.8
Total	8,925	100.0

Leopold Krug, *Betrachtungen über den National-Reichthum des preußischen Staats, und über den Wohlstand seiner Bewohner,* 2 vols. (Berlin, 1805), vol. I, 452; Kurmark values, ibid., vol. I, 444.

hedge, boasted an elaborate greenhouse. Across the drawbridge, administrative and farm buildings stood in solid array, with stone or brick foundations, half-timbered walls, and thatched or reed roofs. The building housing the chief bailiff or estate administrator and unmarried, permanently contracted laborers counted six sitting rooms, three bedrooms, a "spacious kitchen," and a baking kiln. Among the lordship's married employees' numerous dwellings were two buildings for day laborers, one for five families and one for four, each in "fairly good condition" and bearing tile roofs, with a common baking kiln. The half-timbered inn was in good repair, as were the other manor-farm buildings. The Löcknitz bridge was of solid masonry. Pines, lindens, and red beeches lined local roads. Altogether, the picture was of solidity, prosperity, even some noble grandeur and luxury.

The Kleists struggled, like Quitzows and Blumenthals, to avoid Stavenow's sale outside their kin group. By 1808, none of the departed major's brothers were still alive, but five nephews, "his last descendants," claimed inheritance. Like eight of their nine fathers and uncles, they were all Prussian army officers, chief among them the celebrated "Royal Infantry General, Commanding General of the [newly annexed] Province of Saxony, Knight of Many Orders, Friedrich Emil Ferdinand Heinrich, Count von Kleist Nollendorff." Although Voss acquired and occupied Stavenow in 1808–9, lawsuits which these disgruntled Kleists instigated, and the state-proclaimed war moratorium on debt collection, delayed agreement on Voss's final payments until 1819. The defeated Kleist heirs then dissolved, with the major's surviving collateral female descendants' approval, the 1763 family trust vesting Stavenow's ownership in Major von Kleist's agnatic kin, restoring its earlier status as individualized, freely transferable (allodial) property.

In the 1819 Allodification Agreement, Major Kleist's nephews showed little respect for his memory. The 1763 family trust, they recalled, aimed to maintain the Stavenow Kleist lineage "at all times in exceptional bloom." They painted the major's management in implausibly dark colors: "The forests . . . have been in part completely logged off" (though the 1808 appraisal valued Stavenow's woodlands at 80,000 talers). "Advantageously laid-out manor-farms [have been] torn down while . . . buildings that are either superfluous or inappropriately situated have been constructed." A "costly lawsuit" they waged against the major's widow over "deteriorations and improvements" under his management had, allegedly, proven these points. Yet none of his five nephews could meet the terms for acquiring Stavenow following the major's widow's remarriage: paying the 1763 entry price of 127,483 gold

talers, purchasing current inventory (30,000 talers), correcting "deteriorations," and paying Kleist's widow's and daughters' shares.[14]

In 1808 Voss paid 144,200 gold talers, in 5-taler Friedrich d'or pieces,
and 110,800 talers in current Prussian coinage. Gold talers fetched a 10
percent premium over current silver talers. Voss owed Kleist's widow,
apart from 12,000 gold talers, seemingly representing her dowry's cash
component, 60,000 talers both gold and silver as her share of sale earnings. In the major's two daughters' names, Voss deposited 10,000 talers
as interest-bearing capital with the Brandenburg Wards' Trust Fund,
agreeing to give them their 60,000-taler joint share of sale profits later,
meanwhile paying 4 percent interest on it. Voss also liquidated 34,000
talers' debt circulating as Kleist's promissory notes, leaving a residuum
of 66–72,000 talers, payable as agnatic inheritances to the five nephews,
as another interest-bearing debt in Voss's hands. In 1808, with the post-
1806 debt moratorium already in effect, the major's widow, Frau
Majorin von Rohr, announced that "while she does indeed request her
capital's immediate payment in gold," she was willing to accept, "but
only as a favor to the buyer's person," one-third in cash and the rest
when the moratorium ended, meanwhile collecting 5 percent interest.[15]
The moratorium expiring on New Year's Eve 1818, Voss undertook in
the 1819 contract to retire all outstanding debts from 1808 by 1824, as
well as to pay interest arrears, by then swollen to about 20,000 talers.
Among Voss's creditors, General Kleist Nollendorff had lent various
sums totaling 3,000 talers to his cousins, suggesting that, among the co-
heirs, only his finances were comfortably in the black.

Noble fortunes still depended, in centuries-old fashion, on credit
dealings backed by estate land. Voss may have been a frugal State
Minister, but he readily plunged into debt to add Stavenow to his investment portfolio. Nor was he inclined to surrender the least advantage to
his new subjects. Doubtless he aimed to make Stavenow pay a good
profit so that accumulated debt would not discomfit him.

VOSS'S INSTALLATION AT STAVENOW AND THE PRIGNITZ
VILLAGES' 1808–1809 RENT STRIKE

The lost war's burdens on villagers, especially horse-requisitioning and
tax levies to support the French occupation, provoked discontent that

---

[14] No. 122, fos. 1–7; no. 39, fos. 10–20. The 1808 appraisal capitalized 14,000 t. estimated annual net
earnings at 5 percent = 280,000 t. Voss's 255,000 t. = ca. 10 percent less (but note premium on gold).
[15] No. 65.

the 1807 October Edict brought to the boil. Stein's emancipation proclamation triggered rural protest in the Prignitz District between 1808 and 1811 that gripped noble lordships with fear and indignation. The villagers' aim in this ill-documented action, which might well have built on memories of the 1700–2 protest and petition movement, was the end of the hated regime of unpaid compulsory labor services. Minimally, the farmers sought the replacement of physical labor by full commutation payments, a path previously open only with seigneurial approval, and not an unequivocal right.[16]

At the Prignitz nobility's meeting of May 1808, eighteen influential estateowners petitioned the District Commissioners, complaining that "subject villagers' insubordination in performance of the labor services they are obliged to render grows daily more out of hand. The formerly usual coercive measures, applied by court bailiffs and the sheriff, offer no further help whatsoever." They pleaded for deployment of "the local military," to force villagers back to labor service through military execution – billeting of the villages and seizure of renitent farmers' assets. Chief District Commissioner von Rohr, who himself signed the petition, forwarded it officially to Berlin's Chamber Court. He wrote that war taxes and requisitions had already reduced Prignitz estateowners "to a very sorry state," and if villagers now left "manorial fields uncultivated," their overlords would become, "unavoidably, totally insolvent." Rohr added reassuringly: "the subjects are also in no way incapacitated to render labor services, which in this province are by no means oppressive."[17] About these events, Stavenow's Judge Gutike wrote in January 1810 that "in summer [1808] the subjects refused to perform labor services, whereupon on Chamber Court order various among them were brought to jail." Simultaneously, the Berlin court dispatched a commission to investigate villagers' plea that, because of wartime losses, they be released from seigneurial dues and services. Whatever the commissioners decided, the Stavenow villagers were subsequently prepared to render nothing more, of their own free will, than full commutation fees.[18]

At Voss's assumption of command at Stavenow in July 1809, the judge formally released village farmers, in the presence of the departed major's

[16] Bassewitz, *Kurmark*, vol. III, 675–7; Gerhard Albrecht, "Die Gutsherrschaft Freyenstein" (dissertation, Pädagogische Hoschschule Potsdam, Historisch-Philologische Fakultät, 1968), 137; Schultze, *Die Prignitz. Aus der Geschichte einer märkischen Landschaft*, 238ff, 277; Hagen, "Servants," 89ff.

[17] GStAPK, Provinz Brandenburg, Rep. 6A: Ältere Kreisbehörden: Prignitz, No. 11, 13–14. Mai 1808.

[18] No. 314, fos. 1–3.

five nephews, from their "previous obligations as subjects." Gutike presented them to their new "landlordly authority" (*Grundobrigkeit*), admonishing them to render Voss the dues and services prescribed by "urbarial agreements, occupancy deeds, and manorial constitution [*Gutsverfassung*]." The regime change was also a conceptual shift, for neither "landlordly authority" nor "manorial constitution" figured previously in seigneurial rhetoric. But the "customary subject's oath" had hardly changed:

I swear to God Almighty and Omniscient a true corporeal oath, that I will be true, obedient, and subject to my overlordship, His Excellency Herr State Minister von Voss, and will comport myself as befits and behooves an obedient, true, and honest subject, so help me God to blessedness through his son Jesus Christ.

Beyond intoning this oath, seemingly collectively, each farmer signed it, one in four in handwriting, the others by crosses. Insofar as written signatures spelled passage beyond passive literacy (or inability altogether to read), adult male education made some modest eighteenth-century strides, for a century earlier the farmer who could write his name was a rarity.[19]

There followed festive eating and drinking, including six barrels of beer, many quarts of schnapps, 30 pounds of butter, and possibly also the two "large pigs" which seigneurial accounts recorded as having been – exceptionally in summer – consumed "in the household economy."[20] Three days later Voss's Stavenow administrator, *Oekonomie-Inspektor* Neubauer, received a visit from Premslin's mayor and fifteen other fullholders. They were "of a mind" to negotiate "an agreement with the manorial lordship," because they wanted "to give service money in place of the now obligatory labor services *in natura*, which are still difficult for many of us to perform." They offered 15 talers, although full prewar commutation cost 20 talers.[21] Voss must have been forewarned, for Premslin manor-farm administrator Hackradt had just rated his village's farmers' condition, finding nine of twenty fullholders and smallholders in "good condition," judging by possession of four "good" or "serviceable" draft-horses. Three were in "fair," six in "bad," and two in "very" or "totally bad condition." Voss approved their petition, despite the reduced commutation money, but only for a year.

Soon Neubauer wrote Voss that, when recently the nine Stavenow farmers in Blüthen village quit seigneurial fieldwork in protest, he

[19] No. 27, fos. 24–6.   [20] No. 202, fos. 35–42.   [21] No. 196, fos. 2–3.

summoned "and earnestly exhorted them to return." Judge Gutike
"severely reprimanded them" for speaking in Voss's presence "about
their economic condition and whether they possessed the strength to
serve or not."[22] Voss had promised, doubtless at his landlordly installation, "all possible alleviation" of Stavenow villagers' burdens.
Neubauer wrote that, "according to administrator Hackradt's testimony, the Blütheners belong to the neediest of the whole lordship, in
every respect much worse situated than the Glövziners, whose service
Your Baronial Excellency reduced for one year by 10 current talers."
Neubauer and Gutike therefore put them too on commutation
money.[23] The Glövziners had suffered an 1809 village conflagration
for which a farm woman was found criminally guilty. Four days after
Voss's installation, Neubauer gave each of the twelve burned-out
farmers 10 talers and 2 bushels of rye, with Voss's approval, provided
they repaid the sums into the "fire-insurance fund."[24]

The lordship seemingly sought to avoid current harvest interruptions
by disputes over future services. In early August 1809 Neubauer wrote
Voss that "everywhere here the rye is good, [but] harvest work so far
completed has entailed for me a very unusual high cost in food and
drink," suggesting the risk of losing compulsory and perhaps also paid
workers to the prevailing strike mood was high. Neubauer, who signed
his numerous and voluble letters to Voss with the words "most submis-
sively" (*gantz untertänigster*), was new to the Prignitz district. Though his
previous employment sites are unknown, here he found much that was
foreign. He read the laboriously negotiated Stavenow Urbarium, obliging the farmers to bring in the entire seigneurial rye harvest, yet encountered in every village "the unanimous claim" that farmers never contributed more than five days' harvest service. Neubauer wanted to hire
as the new mistress of manorial stores and maidservants a pastor's
daughter, at 40 talers yearly. He asked Voss to agree also to give her a
half-bushel (ca. 30–40 pounds) of flaxseed, sown and harvested by the
lordship, since this was "everywhere customary hereabouts." Neubauer
counseled closure of Major Kleist's orangerie, kept warm in winter in a
"very respectable greenhouse," adding that "firewood consumption here
must be frightful." He pronounced the manorial sheep-flock "miserable," asking Voss whether he wanted to introduce improved breeds.[25]

The next week Neubauer wrote Voss that it was mistaken to pay day
laborers hired in late summer's hay harvest "with every third stack,"

---

[22] Ibid., fos. 4–5.   [23] No. 342, fos. 2, 5; no. 202, fos. 13–14.
[24] No. 342, fo. 3; no. 314, fos. 2–3; no. 202, fos. 13–14.   [25] No. 202, fos. 13–16.

instead of giving them cash and keeping the hay. But that too was locally customary. The Mesekow smallholders asked for release from their two (formerly three) days of weekly manual labor against 16 talers' service money in current wartime coinage, about equalling 10 prewar current talers. This year their harvests were bad, and they petitioned, with the lordship's backing, the District Commissioners for tax remissions, though fruitlessly. Mesekow's mayor told Neubauer that from their earnings on this bad harvest "they didn't believe they could keep servants" to perform manorial service, and were counting on being put on commutation fees. Neubauer was undecided, "because manual labor from such a nearby place" was useful. "But they have a reputation as the entire lordship's best subjects, a view, so far as I've gotten to know them, I must confirm." Again he asked Voss to decide.

Neubauer was orienting himself to local prices, which in manorial schnapps production and sales were especially important because of brisk competition. With rye prices low, Neubauer was considering dropping his schnapps quart price of $5\frac{1}{2}$ current groschen, or 9 groschen in circulating coin, "because here people look very much to Mecklenburg, where [schnapps] is selling at $4\frac{1}{2}$ groschen." He decided, because liquor stock was low, to keep the higher price, but asked Voss whether he was free to alter Stavenow's price. About the harvest he observed that "here [the workers] bind up very small sheaves."[26]

Writing later to Voss, Neubauer discussed seigneurial dairy prices, which competed with those charged by Stavenow's two hollanders, who "make nothing but great cheeses of 20 pounds and more, selling them until now at $1\frac{1}{4}$–$1\frac{1}{2}$ current groschen per pound." Neubauer tried to sell 400 pounds of Premslin manor-farm cheese to a merchant who bought his Stavenow butter, but he declined, saying products of such "small dairies taste old." Neubauer complained he "consumed" much milk in the harvest, feeding it to fieldworkers. His monthly accounts recorded seigneurial gifts awarded at harvest's end to head mowers and female assistants: three pipes with tobacco worth 4 groschen each and three flower wreaths, assembled by kitchenmaid Schulze who for this and, presumably, other services received 1.5 talers.[27]

Neubauer exercised full autonomy directing seigneurial fieldwork and in manorial products' routine sales, but turned to Voss on weighty matters. It hobbled him that he was obliged to deliver most cash earnings immediately to Voss, leaving himself chronically short of working

---

[26] Ibid., fos. 17–18.   [27] Ibid., fos. 19–20; 35–42; 82–9.

capital. To improve the sheep-flock he asked Voss for an 800-taler advance. The animals would have to be good "if the Berlin butchers are not to lose interest in them." From liquor Neubauer did not earn much. It was an "annoyance" that Stavenow's innkeeper only paid for schnapps deliveries when each oxhead (180 quarts) was finally emptied. The estate's best beer he sent to Voss in Havelberg, while few from outside the seigneurial jurisdiction sought to buy the rest. Travelers who wanted to drink beer at Stavenow's inn "will have to put up with it."[28]

On August 16 Neubauer wrote that, if villagers' dues and services were "properly rendered" and prices were not "too wretched," Voss's expectations from Stavenow would be justified. Of manorial farm servants and day laborers he remarked that "after the harvests here the people were always given a harvest feast that used to be pretty lavish [*flott*]." If Voss wanted this changed, he should say so. From Neubauer's next letter, forwarding July and August accounts, it is evident the estate manager felt obliged to follow the "lavish" tradition from his note that "because of the harvest, beer and schnapps expenditure was very high." But he repaid Voss's 800-taler sheep advance, having received the Berlin slaughterers' payment.

Voss was dissatisfied with Stavenow harvests, but Neubauer thought that "for the soil here" they were "unusually good." At Stavenow itself there could be no better cultivation than "the pure Mecklenburg" system of alternating multi-year pasture and grain-crop cycles. The soil was problematic and there were weeds that even three years of grazing could not eliminate, particularly "*Gurkke*," which in 1809 grew so abundantly it seemed "as if the field were strewn full of white wigs." Neubauer tried burning off weeds, but they still hindered harrowing. There was no "certain success" with barley and peas, whose cultivation would "always [be] a game of chance." Improvement depended on livestock. The three manorial domain-farms' soil was superior to Stavenow's, though "it seems better than it is."

About Voss's acquisition of Stavenow in general Neubauer bluntly wrote:

The whole lordship has only a theoretical value [*inmagenirten Werth*]. In these times when the precious material cash money is worth so much, it cannot be called a successful business . . . Incidentally, I am of the opinion and conviction that those enterprises are the best which earn the most money, and

---

[28] Ibid., fos. 23–5.

I am very much in favor of limiting all expenses whose benefits cannot be calculated.

This affirmation that any economic activity's chief aim was maximization of net cash returns shows that the fashionable economic liberalism of Adam Smith and his German followers, including the then-celebrated agricultural economist and theorist Albrecht Thaer, had stamped Neubauer.[29]

From two reports he commissioned before purchasing Stavenow, Voss already knew improvement was needed. One was the customary estate appraisal in monetary terms of assets and incomes, the other a description and critique of the manorial economy and forests written by Havelberg crown-estate administrator Stubenrauch. The appraisal, as this chapter's tables show, painted a positive picture, even though Major Kleist "carried out great timber sales." It observed that, while seigneurial meadows were "rich in excellent grass," more hay could be won if harvest workers were paid in coin alone. "For the custom here has been to hand over the fourth part of meadows harvested once yearly, and the third part of the fall cut of meadows harvested twice yearly, to nearby farmers and day laborers, who strive mightily to get it."[30]

By contemporary progressive agronomy's measure, administrator Stubenrauch found Stavenow wanting. He advocated improved field-drainage and clover-planting for the seigneurial cattle's stall-feeding, a technique for maximizing soil-fertilization. Stubenrauch hardheartedly criticized the Stavenow blacksmith-tavernkeeper's low rent, and thought one of the seigneurial day laborers' houses "spacious enough that four [instead of the present two] dwellings could easily be made of it." His final "judgment," delivered with a government expert's self-confidence, was "that it is not managed in every respect as it could be, given its location and the resources it commands as a whole":

The chief aim of every farmer must be to draw the highest yield possible from his lands . . . [But] under the present management the livestock and their distribution stand in no proper relation to arable cultivation. Manure shortage is evident everywhere here, and yet the distillery by-products are fed only to swine that produce little or no manure. And yet, too, great dairy-farms are maintained, which produce little manure in winter and nothing at all in summer, while the sheep flock has been limited to 1,000, when it would be, without harming cattle-raising, the most effective and useful means of soil fertilization if . . . its numbers were raised to 2,500 . . . [If clover were planted and

---

[29] Ibid., fos. 30–1. On economic liberalism: Abel, *Landwirtschaft*; Müller, *Landwirtschaft*.
[30] No. 39, fos. 5–20.

meadows properly drained], there could never be any lack of fodder and hence of manure. To this revolution [*Umwälzung*] in management, given its great scope, very considerable capital investment would be necessary, whose benefits could only be realized after some years.[31]

Whether Neubauer read this is unknown but likely. His appraisals of Stavenow, both in 1809–1810 and later, pointed in the royal agronomist's direction. Their views show that east-Elbian estate complexes such as Stavenow had become market-oriented operations, based on technological improvements and aimed at maximizing cash income – in a word, capitalist enterprises. This was the work of numerous non-noble administrators and experts, who like Neubauer cooperated closely with well-informed, sober-minded and pragmatic, if also politically conservative, noble estateowners such as Voss.

This picture leaves little room for noble–bourgeois class antagonism in the countryside, particularly once the (imperfect) noble monopoly on estateownership fell in 1807. The noble landlord's relationship with his managers and officials seems comparable to modern firm owners' or directors' ties with their well-paid business executives and higher salaried employees. Such entrepreneurs and executives form "teams" with largely common interests in opposition to others, including their own subordinate workers. They constitute socially diverse interest blocs, though not necessarily class alliances, since in other life realms, including the political, their interests or inclinations might diverge. So it may have been in Voss's and Neubauer's day, though nothing is known of Voss's officials' political views.

THE VOSS TEAM'S FIRST YEAR OF STAVENOW MANAGEMENT

The emancipated farmers' resistance to continued labor services threatened to undermine Voss's efforts to raise Stavenow's profitability. He and his managers needed to adjust production to wage-labor conditions while negotiating with farmers who, soon after the November 1811 Regulation Edict's proclamation, petitioned for freehold conversion and liquidation of all feudal rents. This sub-section further analyzes Voss's 1809–10 correspondence with his officials, who grappled with the intertwined issues of farmers' rent strikes, recruitment of substitute workers, agricultural improvements, and earning the profits Voss expected in

---

[31] Ibid., fo. 50.

ringing coin. A rich documentation captures, from a landlordly view-point, an everyday perspective on this axial moment in Prussian history.

In negotiating with the villages, Voss and company pursued a hard line. We observed Neubauer's hesitation to make concessions to Mesekow's farmers, though he knew them to be "good" – cooperative and industrious – subjects. Neubauer told Voss he summoned the Mesekowers to inform them of Voss's decision to set them on full commutation, a "relief" the administrator privately conceded they deserved. He announced they would still need to perform the seven "extra days" of harvesting and four days of construction work, a "small matter" to Neubauer, though contested under Major Kleist. The Mesekowers' declaration that they would rather render all services in person than agree to construction days startled Neubauer. Perhaps he relented, but he soon noted the Mesekow smallholders' fulfillment of one "extra day" as beaters in the seigneurial hunt – a task that, if imposed by the Kleists, left no trace. Neubauer also informed Voss he had bought many new sheep, while the two "Spanish rams" Voss sent to upgrade the flock arrived safely. Because of "terrible drought" sheep were yielding little wool, while rye and swine prices were low. He was waiting for grain markets to improve before selling. "If prices stay where they are, may God have pity." Meanwhile he bought in Lenzen 60 bushels of "big rye" seed, a new variety he aimed to test. [32]

In fall 1809 Voss, as church patron, mediated a conflict between villagers and pastors. Blüthen Pastor Winter and Premslin Pastor Nehre wrote him, recalling that at his Stavenow installation "he abolished farmers' labor services, transforming them into commutation money." This was not Voss's intention, but seemingly villagers so interpreted it. "We are," the pastors said, "far from denying this change's goodness in general," but it threatened their "subsistence." "Since time immemorial" they cultivated their parsonage farms with the help of villagers' labor services, even paying Stavenow to hire them. They could not afford to keep their own draft animals. They had both been serving, for nine and five years respectively, as adjunct pastors, obliged to give retired precursors one-third their farming incomes. For years village farmers refused to deliver tribute grain, and now were charging them 12 groschen per bushel. If Voss did not assuage their troubles, he could only expect "religion's still deeper decline because of its servants' ever more pressing worries about their livelihoods."

[32] No. 202, fos. 32–3, 73–4, 112–25.

Voss denied abolishing labor services. He gave the farmers one year of full commutation owing to Glövzin's fire and because "most subjects suffered so during the French invasion and under subsequent burdens that they were not indeed able to perform services." He knew nothing of the pastors' difficulties, but promised assistance at his next visit.[33] They turned to him again in May 1810. The sheriff had collected tribute-grain arrears by "execution," but only in Blüthen. The Glövziners twice repulsed him, saying "straightaway that they wouldn't agree to deliver the payments demanded no matter how many times he came." This was "unpleasant and painful," not least because of their "debtors' . . . wounding judgments and utterances about us." Judge Gutike proposed installment payments, but the pastors feared "there is no willingness in the communes." "Coercive means" were again necessary, "through which we will unavoidably fall into the most strained relations with our communes and our offices' efficacy and usefulness will be infinitely hindered." Yet, unaided, they would "suffer, in these so dire times, the most oppressive need and most painful wants." Blüthen's pastor had indeed succeeded in having 1805–9 grain-rent arrears from one farm written into the new proprietor's occupancy deed, promising eventual recovery. But Glövziners rejected such solutions, arguing Voss had forgone collection of seigneurial grain rents. Since the pastors' tribute grain derived from earlier seigneurial revenues, it followed that farmers' deliveries to ministers also lapsed. This was historically grounded, if self-interested, reasoning. In May 1810 the pastors, seconded by Gutike, petitioned for intervention by the sheriff who, pleading sickness to excuse earlier inaction, promised prompt seizure of the delinquents' goods.[34]

At Semlin manor-farm administrator Friedrich Hackrath sent Voss his monthly accounts for September 1809. Hackrath was newly married, with his wife pregnant. He reported their renovation of the sitting room in the manager's house, and that his wife was busy drying fruit. Earlier Hackrath told Voss apologetically that "in her condition strenuous women's work is somewhat awkward." Hackrath signed his letters to Voss "in deepest subjection" (*Untertänigkeit*) as a "most submissive, loyal and obedient servant."[35] Premslin manor-farm's manager was a certain Hollefreundt. Sending Voss his first monthly accounts, he revealed his outsider status by observing that while the harvest, measured against seed sown, was perhaps not so impressive, "here it is

[33] Ibid., fos. 76–7.   [34] No. 314, fos. 10–13, 16.   [35] No. 202, fos. 30–1, 50.

custom to sow almost twice the seed as in other regions." The tenant-farmer Hollefreundt replaced also left the farm in disarray. Because he had only two settled day-laborer families,

I was very short of harvest hands, and at times during the finest weather could do nothing because I absolutely couldn't get any workers, even from other villages. At other times there's no lack of workers here, but at harvest they only go where some hay is promised them.

Hollefreundt finally decided "to offer the fourth stack of hay from a meadow here . . . and then I got enough people."

The [Premslin] farmers did indeed mow and bind up the rye, but they didn't want to do it without receiving beer, and when I sometimes made it too thin and weak, they lay down and wouldn't mow any further. So I found myself compelled to give them a few measures of schnapps just to get them back to work. Six barrels of beer were drunk up, even though I filled them half with water. But people here are so accustomed to getting their fill that they won't allow the slightest thing to be taken away. They are, though, exceptionally industrious and competent workers.

In his work-register, Hollefreundt noted that "fifteen farmers raked oats (but only as a favor)." Now he told Voss that the Premsliners refused to perform their seven yearly "extra days" in the harvest. They claimed these days were only for "digging ditches, harvesting root-crops, etc." If this view was "justified" – which the Urbarium said it was, though Hollefreundt seemingly had not read it – then he wanted cash payment for the "extra days," to have money for hiring wage laborers when needed.

In future Hollefreundt planned to offer each day laborer, for five days' harvest work, some potato-land, plowed and manured by the lordship. "This method is customary everywhere here and I think it is advantageous." Potato-land was inferior arable, while paying workers in hay was inadvisable, "because then there's no fodder to spare." Hollefreundt's dairy-cattle were yielding little milk. He would slaughter for manor-farm consumption an old cow, fattened on distillery by-products. The sheep-flock was "particularly bad." He planned to sell culled-out animals, despite their meager value, "because they can't all be eaten here." Wagons and other equipment needed replacement. "The first time I ordered the crops hauled in, four wagon wheels broke." He needed two new farm servants' beds and one for the female overseer (*Wirtschafterin*), who was presently using her own bedding "for which she demands compensation." She had also asked for "some salary supplement." "She admits she only received 30 talers from the previous tenant-farmer, but got so many presents her pay was almost 50 talers, plus 2 pounds of wool. This is a bit much." Hollefreundt asked Voss to decide. As for draft-animals, Hollefreundt found ten manorial horses too few. He intended to add two ox-teams and, in summer, two more of horses. The fruit crop was "fairly good," but he could not dry it for lack of ready firewood. Because fodder was scarce, he kept only as many pigs as he needed for food for himself and six workers, plus the sow.[36]

At Stavenow Neubauer wrote Voss in mid-November of growing difficulties with farmers and manorial workers. He ordered the delivery of grain rents and other natural payments at St. Martin's (November 11), but the farmers said they rendered these at Christmas. Blütheners claimed they had not reaped enough rye to pay rent, while Mesekowers appealed to their earlier (rejected) plea for tax-remission. Farmers in Stavenow's three other villages "have until now agreed to nothing" except meadow-lease payment. They would not deliver "hunter's bread," which Neubauer called a "trifle," ascribing their refusal to "human caprice." Yet tribute bread was a symbol and remnant of the once-feudal subjection abolished in 1807 – a fact whose significance escaped Neubauer.

Neubauer refused the meadow rents, telling the villagers they held their meadows "thanks to the lordship's goodness alone" (though they possessed them in perpetual leasehold) and could "very likely again be [seigneurially] enclosed." Neubauer expected Karstädt's farmers, who continued performing labor service, would pay all dues, "since they have still got some reasonable means." But Glövziners and Premsliners "are known from earlier times as insubordinate people and they completely justify the old reputation." Premsliners would not pay cash for the third weekly labor-service day, nor would they give money for the seven "extra days," claiming that in Voss's one-year "exemption from service in person . . . all other exemptions were included."

Neubauer believed that, if Voss visited Stavenow before Christmas, it would be better to avoid any "coercive means that might secure Your Highness's just demands," since "a reprimand from Your Highness will have more effect than if Herr etc. Gutike holds court for days on end." Here is evident Neubauer's faith in seigneurial charisma (and the coupling in his mind of coercion with protracted court hearings). To illustrate, Neubauer reported that, the previous week, Gutike spent two days investigating the impoundment of horses and wood thefts. Two compulsorily recruited manorial servants were also found guilty of

---

[36] Ibid., fos. 58–61, 68–70.

"flour theft that was, to be sure, insignificant." Neubauer added, "I chastised them myself," doubtless by flogging or other blows, "whereupon they refused further obedience." He held them two days "in the court bailiff's jail" while Gutike pursued the matter. This led to excessive "formalities," so after four days' jail and further "bodily chastisement" Neubauer fired them. This procedure "makes the strongest impression these days," because many farm servants had fled Mecklenburg military service and sought Brandenburg refuge. They "had no roof over their heads and were putting laborers here in the same predicament." Neubauer replaced the dismissed servants with two other local farmers' sons, both "reliable people."

It came naturally to an estate official and not uncivilized man like Neubauer to personally administer blows to insubordinate workers. But the hopes he placed in Voss's pre-Christmas visit suggest the incident with the two farm servants somehow failed in its purpose. He also reported he had fulfilled Voss's instruction to take an unpaid apprentice into estate management, a seventeen-year-old deceased building-contractor's son, who evinced "much good-will and strong inclination toward the field that will provide him with his future livelihood [*Brodwissenschaft*]." The young man had already "written up the wood auction," in which Neubauer had to lower prices to find buyers. Dairy output was "miserable," yielding little butter for transport to Voss. The following month would be better, because "the people" (manorial servants) would be eating lard instead of butter.[37]

In December Neubauer and Gutike visited Voss in Havelberg to discuss lordship–village conflicts. Gutike expounded the Urbarium, noting that certain controversies were never resolved. Neubauer later sent Voss two fattened Christmas pigs. Voss had sought government aid against the villagers, as emerges from District Commissioner von Petersdorf's letter, promising Voss army discharge for Dargardt farm widow Mardausch's son. Mardausch would have been spared this year's draft, Petersdorf added, if "Dargardters' behavior toward their lordship" had been better. "I hope," he wrote, "that through a complete change in their deportment these people will make themselves worthy of Your Excellency's favor." Conscription as social disciplinization could hardly be better documented, though it did not break the villages', including relatively well-situated Dargardt's, refractoriness.[38]

---

[37] Ibid., fos. 141–3.   [38] Ibid., fos. 176, 178–9.

On January 2, Neubauer wrote pessimistically to Voss. Many piglets had died because of dairy by-products' shortage and their inability to digest substitute distillery wastes. Fodder shortage made milk scarce, so Voss would not have much Stavenow butter. Though Voss approved cheaper schnapps, sales were weak. Neubauer fired the brewer-distiller: "his oft-violated sobriety required [me to act on] my warning, if such were to have any effect in future." "These are altogether wretched times that I find highly repugnant, because I believe only utterly bad people can be indifferent to the results of the tasks set before them."

Neubauer had farmers in mind. Dargardters alone had delivered grain rents, while Glövziners and Premsliners were withholding them, many even refusing to pay commutation. Neubauer heard that "on the second day of Christmas the Prignitz farmers held a meeting in or near Pritzwalk [town], with the outcome that manorial service was to be refused starting at the new year." Neubauer summoned for this letter-writing day all Stavenow's farmers. The Mesekowers arrived, "but now it is noon" and the Dargardters were still absent.

Hopefully everything will remain as before. At Semlin, instead of the expected workers the Karstädt farmers appeared in a body and announced that the whole Prignitz District had agreed from today on to perform no more manorial services.[39]

Voss forwarded Neubauer's letter to the District Commissioners, saying he would indict the Karstädters before the Chamber Court and pressing the Commissioners to request government investigation "to punish the ringleaders." "It is impossible to let willful meetings of whole corporate bodies [*ganzer Corporationen*] aimed at resisting their duties go unpunished."[40]

Neubauer and Gutike urged the villagers against the strike. The Karstädters said they supported the Pritzwalk meeting's decisions, where their "deputies" included Stavenow farmer Georg Nagel. The meeting acted "on the basis of the Royal Ordinance to quit rendering manorial service" referring, presumably, to the 1807 October Edict, which actually made no clear provisions for liquidating seigneurial rents. The Karstädters would at most pay commutation. Even the usually compliant Mesekowers were resisting but Gutike, summoning them to his Perleberg chambers, mollified them. Neubauer told the Karstädters they must render actual field labor because their village bordered on Semlin manor-farm and they were "by unanimous

---

[39] Ibid., fos. 180–1.   [40] Ibid., fo. 211.

testimony in more prosperous condition." Neubauer indicted them before Gutike, but doubted "either jail sentences or sheriff's action would be sufficient or appropriate." Instead, only "soldiers' deployment," which Gutike promptly requested, "would restore the overturned order here." Though the District Commissioners might "storm" Berlin with calls for judicial help against work stoppages, the Chamber Court was still occupied with "the [farmers'] tumultuous meeting earlier [1808] in Perleberg," concerning which "identification of the ringleaders and rebels, so that appropriate punishment may be meted out, is still awaited."

Neubauer informed Voss that January schnapps sales were "extraordinarily good." Since New Year's he had sold almost 2,000 quarts, suggestive of heavy holiday revelry among laborers and farmers. Demand threatened to eclipse supply. The new brewer and distiller knew his trade better than his bibulous precursor. His product's higher quality "much contributed to the [present] impressive turnover." Much money was going into laborers' wages, since the weather was good and many improvements necessary. Premslin manager Hollefreundt hired a carpenter "whose daily wage of 9 groschen during these short days, and with the price of life's necessities so low, is a great deal, but he won't let himself be had for less." The Stavenow shepherd died, which was "no disadvantage for sheep-raising," since he received a "much higher income than the job required." Now wages could be cut.[41]

Neubauer wanted forcible suppression of the Prignitz farmers' strike against manorial service. Whether the "ringleaders" of 1808 or 1809–10 suffered punishment is unknown, but the coercion he and Voss sought duly occurred, with results doubtless favorable to Stavenow. In February Neubauer told Voss that "after the sheriff applied execution against them, the Karstädters returned and yesterday again performed manorial service." As compensation for their unserved workdays Neubauer would petition Gutike for cash penalties.[42] Gutike confirmed that the sheriff's "severe execution measures" forced the Karstädters, now also owing sheriff's fees, back to work. Gutike requested seizure of a refractory Premslin lodger's goods, but the "executor" said "he was too busy with commissions and cannot handle everything, especially since disorders among the farmers have spread so far." Voss's notes for answering Gutike insisted the judge treat the farmers "with severity," since "friendly warnings have been

---

[41] Ibid., fos. 212–15; no. 314, fos. 2.   [42] No. 191, fo. 38.

fruitless." One might then (self-righteously) hope "that benevolence to be shown in future will have still greater effect."[43]

Neubauer soon informed Voss he was negotiating commutation fees with the Glövziners and Premsliners. He conceded "most of them" were not equipped to perform service, but they would have to meet his demands for 15–16 talers even if this sum would not cover labor replacement. Because of fire losses, the Glövziners refused the "war-contribution tax," prompting the government to threaten military execution. This Neubauer sought to avert, so they might pay commutation instead. He asked Voss to aid two farmers whose horses the army requisitioned. They could not grasp that recompense would come only when the government settled all such claims. But without horses they could not continue farming. Neubauer likewise asked District Commissioner Petersdorf to postpone military execution, probably also for unpaid taxes, against Dargardt village. Plunderers also beset the Prignitz countryside. "Adding to the countryman's extraordinary torments is the need to guard against thieving scum from Lenzen. It is not unusual for a village, depending on size, to have to pay three, four or more guards 9 groschen each."[44] Here, the intertwining of seigneurial and village interests is evident, requiring Voss and Neubauer to help their subjects stay on their feet. Voss soon learned from District Commissioner Rohr that Glövziners gained remission of 769 talers already paid in taxes, and that execution to raise 930 talers' current arrears would cease pending refund. Voss jumped to have Gutike issue the Glövziners, as the 1794 Law Code prescribed, a "command to pay" rent arrears which, if not "obeyed" entitled Gutike to petition for execution. Judicialization of manor–village conflict marched forward.[45]

In May Neubauer told a Perleberg court his employer directed him to petition for execution to extract commutation arrears, "especially since forbearance only strengthens the subjects' insubordination, which has already become second nature to them."[46] But Gutike advised Voss not to seek legal redress. The villagers, he said, were stricken with "litigation fever." Their lawyer, Bürgermeister Krippenstapel, would fight the case through both appellate courts, costing Voss "a not insignificant outlay." Most Glövziners possessed little more than iron stock, seed, and fodder, which the law shielded from confiscation. It was "highly probable" they had already sold surplus livestock or grain to avoid impoundment. Thus Voss could gain

---

[43] No. 314, fos. 4–5.   [44] No. 191, fos. 67–8.   [45] Ibid., fo. 72; no. 314, fos. 7–8.
[46] No. 314, fo. 14.

little, even if – as was doubtful in current hard times – the Chamber Court authorized execution.[47]

In June Neubauer informed Voss the Premsliners were still withholding commutation fees while the Glövziners refused annual seigneurial grain-haulage. Voss knew this already, having angrily written the government protesting the Chamber Court's rejection of his military-execution petition. Yet, despite his farmers' litigiousness and "evil advisers," Voss temporarily abjured execution, since by mid-year "the countryman usually has divested himself of his reserves."[48] Neubauer said he was "more content with Stavenow," though the purchase price was too high. As he clumsily wrote:

If this acquisition is considered as if the subject farmers with all their obligations were a free gift, and if they're dealt with more cold-bloodedly and a few are evicted, that will be an essential step toward securing the others' obedience and willing submission – then the purchase may be considered a successful one appropriate to present conditions.

In other words, if the gold coin Voss expended for farmers' dues and services were ignored and seigneurial rents extracted with uncompromising severity, Stavenow would begin to pay profits justifying the purchase price.[49]

Neubauer soon reported that, although the government recently authorized District Commissioners to apply military execution against rent arrears, Neubauer advised waiting until St. John's Day (24 June), hoping the villagers would pay to avoid "that misery's" repetition. About compulsorily recruited manorial servants, he observed: "Numerous lordships hereabouts are making no more use of compulsory service and according to various assurances given me it will be totally abolished at St. Martin's [11 November] 1810." Stein's 1807 October Edict said as much, but Neubauer missed the message. "Here servants come and go at Michaelmas [29 September], and now the girls in compulsory service don't want to stay any longer than until then."

Meanwhile Glövzin's mayor was "overrunning" Neubauer with pleas to replace diseased horses requiring slaughter. As for 2,000 gold talers Voss needed to pay his Stavenow neighbor Major von Rohr (on Kleist's widow's behalf), Neubauer said "exchange rates aren't always the same here as in Berlin." There was no "money exchange in the provincial towns" that could convert Voss's 2,000 talers into gold. He should pay Rohr in ordinary silver, plus 10 percent surcharge for gold's

[47] Ibid., fos. 18–19.   [48] No. 191, fos. 131–3; no. 314, fo. 20.   [49] No. 191, fos. 161–2.

higher value. Voss scolded Neubauer for selling Stavenow wool too cheaply, but the manager claimed he did "good work," since local prices were still lower. The government having requisitioned Stavenow's grain, hay and straw, Neubauer asked Voss to replace his indispensable lost fodder with cash to buy more.[50]

Voss's correspondence during the accounting year 1809–10 with submanagers Hackrath, Hollefreundt, and (at Dargardt) Kielemann portrays both daily routine at old-regime's end and economic transformation. Hackrath reported in September 1809 that Semlin's day laborers duly paid rent for their cottages, meadows, and garden. He had bought two new servant's beds at 7.5 talers each. His calendar showed manorial servants working two seigneurial horse-teams alongside the Karstädt farmers', while the laborers' "women" (*Frauens*) toiled with Karstädt smallholders. Fields were plowed for winter sowing, wood hauled, fodder chopped and fed to draft-animals, plums shaken down and apples picked, fieldstones gathered and hauled away, manure carted to the arable, drainage ditches dug, arable harrowed and sown, rye hauled to the mill, linseed threshed, flax broken, potatoes dug.[51]

In October Hackrath slaughtered a calf and sheep for his own and his workers' consumption. In November 150 quarts of thin beer, 3 quarts of caraway-flavored schnapps and 3 quarts of ordinary schnapps were drunk. Hackrath sold two dressed geese, each 26 pounds, for 2.4.- talers apiece. Local farmers sold the manor-farm 136 young plum trees. The Karstädters dutifully performed yearly unpaid grain-hauls. Hackrath bought a farmer's cow for 22 talers, and the sexton's five pigs for 22 talers. He slaughtered a cow and three pigs for Christmas, and gave the hollander a quart of schnapps as a present.[52]

From Premslin, manager Hollefreundt reported that in October he drove the cattle into winter stalls. Manure shortage delayed his rye sowings, but the seed had now "come up and is standing well." In this work-filled season he fed each of ten seigneurial horses roughly 6 pounds of rye and 10 of oats daily. This costly foddering shows why so many lordships clung jealously to their villagers' labor services, despite farmers' teams' small size and weakness. In December Hollefreundt sought Voss's advice on getting better rye prices. He was looking to buy red and white clover seed, but his brother-in-law Stubenrauch (the Havelberg crown-estate official, presumably) could spare none and it was otherwise unavailable. "In this region no clover is planted whatsoever."

[50] Ibid., fos. 164–5, 191–5.   [51] No. 202, fos. 97–100.   [52] Ibid., fos. 131–5, 200–5.

Hollefreundt bought himself a 26-taler bed and took his 37.5 talers' quarterly salary. In November he and his workers consumed 12 bushels of potatoes ("*Knollen*"), while fattening pigs on 12 more. In December he paid a butcher 18 groschen to slaughter a Christmas cow and pig.[53]

Dargardt's manager Kielemann, earning 80 talers yearly, bought 185 mutton-sheep from local villagers for 570 talers, and sold forty-six fattened sheep to a Berlin slaughterer for 222 talers. His labor-force comprised eight Dargardt fullholders and eight smallholders, a manorial farmhand and cowherder, and seven day laborers and their "women." His married foreman Struwe, who with his wife supervised the workers, received three annual pigs at the lordship's expense, and four quarts of Christmas schnapps. In the four fall months day laborer Kai worked forty-eight days plowing, earning 9 talers altogether (4.5 groschen daily).[54]

At Stavenow, December 1809 meat consumption, including at Christmas, comprised two calves and two hens, these delicacies presumably for managers alone, plus eight "large pigs." In alcohol, 8 quarts of brandy and 800 quarts each of full- and half-beer were drunk. A "vermin hunter" earned 3 talers yearly pay "driving out the rats," while a livestock herder earned a taler for curing a servant-girl. The "messenger-woman" received at Christmas her yearly pay of 4 talers (suggesting the lordship abandoned old claims on smallholders' services as unpaid letter deliverers). The labor calendar noted that the eight Stavenow threshers' wives loaded manure for hauling to the fields in manorial service. Neubauer sent two horses to Perleberg to fetch "the midwife for the forester's wife."[55]

In January Neubauer pocketed 115 talers, half his yearly salary. He collected 2.5 talers' exit fee from a farm daughter who permanently departed Stavenow's jurisdiction (showing the lordship again levying this charge, said during urbarial negotiations to have lapsed). Neubauer bought three expensive new draft-oxen, at 55 talers each. He paid the ancient cavalry money Stavenow owed the government (30 talers) plus the newly instituted seigneurial income tax (32 talers). He bought a villager's cow for 27 talers. In manorial service farmers hauled firewood to Stavenow schoolmaster Burckhardt, while day laborers "bind up the hay to be given the farm servants," showing (again) that manorial workers raised livestock, for sale or marriage

---

[53] Ibid., fos. 101–8, 136–40, 167–8, 206–10.   [54] Ibid., fos. 92–3, 126–30, 157–61.
[55] No. 191, fos. 10–21.

portions. Neubauer paid day laborers' wives 3 groschen daily, two-thirds a man's wage.

At Dargardt, manager Kielemann acquired some improved "Vierländer" rye-seed. In May he hauled large quantities of grain to the Elbe, including some bought from local villagers. Farmers' servants and day laborers sheared the seigneurial sheep and cut sod for composting fields. In January 120 herring arrived for foreman Struwe and the workers. Easter holidays and Whitsuntide suspended fieldwork. Between April and June aforementioned wage laborer Kai worked fifty-nine days, apart from helping thresh seigneurial grain for every sixteenth bushel.[56] At Premslin, Hollefreundt wrote Voss he had dismissed a farm servant after a few months' service, paying him his miserly year's wages (7.5 talers), suspecting but unable to prove that the fired laborer infected fellow workers with "the itches." Hollefreundt gave "other ill-doing" as grounds, spending 20 groschen on "itch-salve for all the maidservants." Voss indignantly underlined both these expenditures. Hollefreundt also dismissed his cowherd. At his Premslin tenure's beginning, he tried to "hold [servants] in line by benevolence," but recently he applied "physical" (*thätlich*) measures, as in the cowherd's case, who twice stole seigneurial fodder. Hollefreundt punished him exemplarily, which the cowherd found "too insulting" – evidence again of villagers' sensibilities – "and demanded his pay on the spot." Hollefreundt replaced him with "a very good person," subtracting from the miscreant's pay the cost of two weeks' intervening day labor.

Hollefreundt confessed that, with grain prices low, he would be hard-pressed to turn a decent profit for Voss. This was "painful," because he "earned a not inconsiderable salary" and was "an upright man." Premslin manor-farm was too small to benefit both manager and land-lord. "Under best management" it might earn Voss 500 talers net annual income. "A sensible married foreman or overseer, providing workers with meals, could very well head the whole works under Stavenow's or Semlin's administrator's supervision." Hollefreundt recommended Premslin's dairy, except for kitchen cows, be shifted to Stavenow, reducing maidservants from four to one. Sheep would never flourish because seigneurial grazing was inadequate and Stavenow could not graze adjacent village land. The proposed "foreman and all his servants can make do with one living room," sparing many of the present thirty-five wagonloads of firewood.

[56] Ibid., fos. 38–49.

Seigneurial arable, because of its "unfavorable location," could only be improved within limits. But if the farmers exchanged "land for labor services" – Hollefreundt already in 1810 envisioned this resolution of the crisis accompanying village subjection's breakdown – the manor-farm could be enlarged and redesigned. To make many necessary repairs Hollefreundt hired, with Voss's approval, a "foreman or top hand" competent in carpentry, roofing, and fieldwork. He was "very satisfied [with him] . . . and he receives only very cheap pay, namely 28 talers and 1 pound of wool but no linen." Hollefreundt supplied tools. Semlin manager Hackrath's wife told Hollefreundt her sister, in service in Kyritz town until St. John's Day, would gladly take the Premslin female manager's job for 30 talers and 20 ells of linen yearly. The current woman manager, about whom Hollefreundt earlier complained, earned the same money plus 2 pounds of wool "and unspecified Christmas gifts." He was "unsatisfied [with her] because we very frequently quarrel about her indolence."[57]

In recommending his own job's elimination, Hollefreundt showed himself Voss's honest advocate. In March 1810 Neubauer sent Voss his "brief plan how Stavenow's administration can be made less costly." It was agreed Hollefreundt would be "transferred" at year's end, his manor-farm coming under Stavenow's supervision. Neubauer wanted it run by a "female manager and an unmarried foreman or top hand," fed at seigneurial expense, to avoid having to give a married foreman yearly provisions. A single stove could heat both the female manager's and her servants' rooms. Premslin should keep its dairy and sheep, while Semlin manager Hackrath, boosted to 150 talers' salary, should keep its accounts. Neubauer proposed that he assume Dargardt manor-farm's administration, dismissing manager Kielemann. With savings from Kielemann's pay and fodder provisions, Neubauer would hire a chief accountant for Stavenow and Dargardt, leaving him to spend more time, as he wished, on daily production matters. Here is evident the gathering trend toward the managerial rationalization of east-Elbian estates and the replacement of married laborers receiving yearly (*Deputat*) provisions with unmarried wage workers.[58]

In March Neubauer's brewer began making expensive "bitter beer," requiring long aging. Berlin slaughterer Broesike inspected Neubauer's fattened sheep, but found them "still not usable and made such bad offers I couldn't make any deals with him except at great disadvantage."

[57] Ibid., fos. 60–2.   [58] Ibid., fos. 69–70.

The animals would sell better in Perleberg and Mecklenburg's Grabow. Berlin livestock prices' decline was a "disgrace." He regretted he had not bought and fattened oxen or piglets instead of sheep. In May he reported his bitter "double-beer is earning applause everywhere." Rain and favorable weather caused the rye to grow "very mightily," especially a new strain (*"Meeschroggen"*) he sowed on land whose peat cover he burned off. Never had he observed such growth except in the "most fertile river-bottoms." Before sowing here he twice tamped down the soil with rollers, with the results proving the process's "unbelievable value." No one in the neighborhood had previously experimented with it. The cows still would not milk because pastures were "terribly bare." He fed 200 new-born lambs, against his shepherd's advice, with oats, to such good effect the shepherd was now asking for more.[59] Neubauer was introducing agro-technological improvements on all fronts. His 1809–10 seed-register showed that half the seigneurial rye was sown on manured land. The remaining fertilizer went for potatoes, peas, broad beans and flax, while barley and oats were cultivated without fertilization in their multi-year rotations. Neubauer also planted, for the first time in the Stavenow lordship, 550 pounds of clover-seed, half among the peas and beans and half among the barley and oats.[60]

His innovations did not always win Voss's favor. In May he responded to landlordly admonition not to make costly improvements with the observation that stream diking at Stavenow was urgently needed. He admitted to paying out too much in day laborers' wages, but many repairs were unavoidable. There was still more bad news:

A horse died of intestinal rupture. In the morning it was still healthy and worked to noon, but then wouldn't eat and its condition grew so bad that in two hours it was dead. Opening him up revealed an unbelievable intestinal knot. This horse belonged to the black team and was in very good working condition.

A good horse's loss was serious. Worse still, Neubauer had again paid (though in everyday coinage) 226 talers' emergency income tax. In April he entered in his debit accounts, under the heading "plagues on the land," 96 talers in *Kontribution* taxes, 52 talers for a "disputed [government] delivery of hay, oats, and straw," and 189 talers "for *Kontribution* levies on various items." He also spent 1.5 talers for "six pairs of forks and knives," probably to replace, for his and his fellow managers' use, the previous century's wooden utensils. Manorial

---

[59] Ibid., fos. 70, 130.   [60] Ibid., fos. 1–5.

employees received 47 pounds in butter allotments. Neubauer lent Glövzin farmer Zeggel 10 talers in connection with an unspecified investigation, but Neubauer assured Voss there was no default danger, "since the defendant's circumstances belong among the best."[61]

In May 1810 Neubauer also sold 20 tons of rye to grain-dealer Hillebrandt at 24 talers per ton, half in full-value coinage and half in widely circulating depreciated currency. He aimed to soon sell what remained, beyond internal consumption needs. He drove cattle to market in Altmark's Seehausen, pocketing 555 talers. But he still had no spring wool buyers, nor takers in Berlin of fattened sheep at profit-earning rates. He asked Voss about sheep prices elsewhere, again revealing the difficulties managers then faced surveying markets. With seeming pride Neubauer reckoned that, if he sold his wool and sheep advantageously, he could soon pay Voss 3,000 talers' yearly net profit. That was, as Neubauer had philosophized, agriculture's chief purpose.[62]

NEGOTIATING VILLAGE EMANCIPATION (I): MESEKOW'S "GOOD SUBJECTS"

Neubauer stayed at Stavenow many years, until Voss's 1823 death and, under Voss's sons – Count Friedrich Wilhelm Maximilian and Privy Superior Court Councilor Carl Otto Friedrich – until 1834 and beyond. Only in 1842 does his successor, *Oekonomie-Inspektor* Eichs, appear in the records. Neubauer's voluminous annual accounts and correspondence survive to 1817. Their further study would illuminate Stavenow's technological transformation and adaptation to wage labor and freer markets whose beginnings in 1809–10 the preceding pages sketched. Many innovations followed after 1810, including the establishment of a new manor-farm, patriotically named Waterloo. But the following pages concentrate instead on Voss's and company's negotiations with the villages over freehold conversion. Here too Neubauer rendered valuable service.

Neither Voss nor Neubauer clung inflexibly to the old regime. They grasped, after the November 1811 Regulation Edict's publication, that the ancient system was unsalvageable, though through the sheriff's and military coercion they had roughly succeeded, in the 1808–10 village protest movement's aftermath, in holding the Stavenowers to commutation payments or physical service. But even before the 1811 edict,

---

[61] Ibid., fos. 102–14. [62] Ibid., fos. 131–3.

many or perhaps most farmers anticipated labor rents' end. In July 1811, while approving another year of Karstädters' commutation fees, Neubauer recorded that, "should in this period, as is the subject farmers' obsession [*Wahn*], a formal abolition of physically rendered manorial service occur," the fees would be refunded, though the November edict later required payment until local "regulation contracts" were signed.[63]

The lordship's hard bargaining comes to light in the Mesekow smallholders' case. It was no help that Voss and Neubauer acknowledged them as "good" or even "the best" Stavenow subjects. In June 1812 lordship and village formulated an "amicable agreement" giving Voss, in compensation for the abolition of labor services and other rents, one-third of these small farmers' arable and meadows, each of whom held 1 hide (17 hectares/42 acres). The November edict allowed villages to retain woodlands undiminished so long as they supplied fuel and other needs without yielding marketable surplus. More controversial was the disposition of farmers' iron stock, or basic farm inventory, consisting minimally of wagons, plows, horse-team, cow and sow. To the iron stock of villagers who before October 1807 held farms by proprietary title (*eigentümlich*), lordships had no ownership claim. As for conditional (*lassitisch*) tenures, even though usually hereditary, government jurists assumed the lordships supplied their tenants' forebears with new iron stock during post-Thirty Years War resettlement, and so could claim compensation under the 1811 law. This one and only significant difference between proprietary and non-proprietary tenures assumed great symbolical importance in villagers' eyes, for they believed the lordship was wrongly claiming property they themselves, or their predecessors, acquired by their own efforts. It was, under Stavenow conditions, an emotion-charged controversy over subject farmers' private space and seigneurial power's boundaries.

Under the "amicable agreement" the lordship sought to impose on a commune bereft of legal counsel, the Mesekowers would pay Voss their iron stock's full value. They abandoned all future claims on seigneurial aid in case of collective misfortune, considering that – as Voss's negotiators suggested they acknowledge – "freehold rights' conferral on them will increase rather than diminish their farms' value." But at the text's reading, the assembled farmers rejected its iron-stock provisions. They claimed Voss had agreed, in earlier discussion with their deputies,

[63] No. 342, fo. 9.

to seek recompense only for "original" iron stock. "We acquired from our parents, as we can prove, far more iron stock than our ancestors originally received" from the lordship. Every Mesekower now held iron stock worth, they claimed, 120–30 talers. "Such a big sum we are not able to raise." Instead, they each offered 50 talers. Neubauer agreed to discuss the matter with Voss, whereupon the eight farmers signed the protocol, six in their own hand.[64]

Neubauer wrote Voss that Mesekowers were "peaceably minded people, properly rendering dues and services." If Voss was inclined to reduce claims on any villagers, "they are best suited." Neubauer reckoned the average Mesekower's iron stock at 135 talers. If each paid 100 talers compensation, Voss would lose 280 talers. But even less might be charged "if some small fieldwork obligation in the hay or grain harvest could be preserved . . . I rate cash savings above cropland gains . . . For grain cultivation, Stavenow has more land than it can keep in good cultivation." Neubauer clumsily summed up village feelings: "The desire expresses itself everywhere to want to be free."

One must just act as if [seigneurial-rent liquidation] were of no importance whatever. They seem to hold government-negotiated settlement in much fear, if only because of costs . . . One must for now take no notice of anything. I think they'll come around of their own accord.

Voss demurred, writing to Judge Gutike that "I myself am inclined, in view of the praiseworthy and peaceable behavior by which, as you say, this commune has distinguished itself, to be as obliging as possible." Still, in the iron-stock question he could not "concede too much," because it would be negotiated with all villages, each of which "at the first sign of yielding" would "infallibly" claim similar treatment. Voss would, therefore, accept 75 talers for each Mesekower's iron stock, provided they surrendered some woodland for conversion into seigneurial meadow.[65]

Summoning the Mesekowers, Gutike archly told them Voss found their 50 talers iron-stock offer "too insignificant." Neubauer voiced Voss's 100-taler claim. The farmers countered with 70 talers, saying they would prefer, rather than paying more, to petition Berlin's General Commission, responsible for freehold conversion, to intervene. Agreement settled on 75 talers plus some woodland. Gutike noted that both parties expected the "higher authorities" to ratify their agreement, "since they regard this contract as corresponding to their respective

[64] No. 408, fos. 1–8.   [65] No. 409, fos. 4–5.

interests." The lordship had made "a few sacrifices" to avoid "expensive negotiation by [government] commissioners."[66]

Gutike and Neubauer represented the farmers' concession to Voss as a minor victory. They assured him their reference to sacrifices was but a phrase to win government approval. Neubauer recounted how the Mesekowers feared they were losing too much woodland. It was "peculiar to every farmer's character that he can only be convinced by his own eyes." After Neubauer showed them exactly what land they were surrendering, they declared themselves satisfied. He praised the new land's quality. "Nonetheless I zealously sought to demonstrate to the village what an advantageous contract I thought they were concluding," advising Gutike to highlight this point "starkly" in his written text.

Although he "only managed to get 75 talers iron-stock money," Neubauer believed interest on the combined 600-taler Mesekow capital, plus fodder from the lordship's small but "fine" new meadow, would offset wage labor costs incurred through the loss of smallholders' unpaid services. Wage-bills were again on Neubauer's mind. The year 1812 posed marketing difficulties. He dropped his schnapps price, but "it still doesn't want to sell in the taverns." To pay wages he was considering a further price reduction, "just to get some cash together!" In the coming year he aimed to buy and fatten as many beef cattle as possible. War in Russia would cut down Ukrainian exports while "the armies' increased consumption" would drive beef prices "up very high." Since arriving at Stavenow, Neubauer had introduced, as yet another progressive innovation, the stall-feeding of seigneurial cattle. He advised Voss, in parallel negotiations with Dargardt colonists' village, to pursue a hard line on iron stock, since these farmers, owing to their favored tenure as hereditary leaseholders, were not liable under emancipation legislation to land cessions to their overlordships. In Machiavellian reference to this once-abandoned village's 1750s settlement, he wrote, "if the ink on the occupancy deeds and colonization papers weren't so dark, more could be achieved."[67]

In October 1812 all parties signed Mesekow's freehold-conversion agreement. A few controversial points remained, such as determining who should supply the village schoolmaster's holding with the small arable allotment that the 1811 edict, aiming to raise elementary teachers' income and standing, prescribed. Mesekow was also locked in a court battle with the local miller over his grazing rights. Neubauer

---

[66] No. 408, fos. 9–15. [67] No. 409, fos. 9–12.

wrote Voss in 1813 that he was talking "with farmer, alderman and church elder Janenz," who was "not so dumb and seems to exercise some sway." Neubauer was offering Mesekow 2 hectares of seigneurial arable if it granted the miller his claim on communal meadows. A Perleberg lawyer told Neubauer the villagers could never win their suit, but "they're acting as if crazy" and would accept no compromise.[68] Later obliged to yield to the miller, they accepted Voss's 2 hectares "as their property and gift with all thanks." Voss mused that the Mesekowers were anciently descended from "small fishermen." Because they were "a small and not prosperous commune," he donated a patch of land to improve the sexton-schoolmaster's holding. In December he spurned as "misunderstanding" the idea the villagers were rejecting these arrangements, "for the Mesekowers are not deceitful."[69]

They had, however, recently dispatched a petition, which their lawyer Justice Commissioner Fromm penned, to the chief regulation agency, the General Commission for the Kurmark Brandenburg, arguing Voss's responsibility to satisfy the miller's grievances. Fromm told the villagers the General Commission had not yet ratified the 1812 "amicable agreement." Their petition said that, because of their "inexperience in legal affairs," they did not know whether in their negotiations with Voss they had been "injured," but if so, they asked the General Commission to draw up a new and more equitable settlement. Later Judge Gutike learned they posted the petition before receiving Voss's land grant. Now satisfied, they regarded their complaint "as not written down." They lamely excused themselves for saying nothing about their petition when Voss's gift was announced, probably because they were either ashamed of acting against their lordship or feared their uncharacteristic insubordination's consequences.[70]

In 1832 the Mesekowers petitioned the General Commission for dissolution of the communal open-field system in which their arable until then lay, so that each smallholder might have an enclosed farm. Resultant documentation shows the 1814 cost of satisfying the miller's claims had been very high: 175 talers cash, and 5 hectares in meadow and pasture. The farms, when finally enclosed, each encompassed some 12.5 hectares of arable, 2 hectares of meadows, and 7.5 hectares of pasture and woodland (altogether 55 acres). This outcome, measured against eighteenth-century holdings, indicates that in 1812 they ceded to

---

[68] Ibid., fo. 49.   [69] No. 408, fos. 68–73.   [70] Ibid., fos. 74–9.

Voss one-quarter rather than one-third of their lands. By 1842 one of Mesekow's eight farms had been parceled among its neighbors, while Stavenow had acquired the mill and its lands. Among Mesekow farmers four bore surnames new since 1812 and previously unknown in Stavenow's jurisdiction (though some may have married old-established farmers' inheriting daughters).[71]

Historians customarily measure the emancipation process's equity by farmers' land cessions and other compensation payments to former lordships, and according to whether or not regulated freeholds were viable farms enabling possessors to remain on familial lands – if not to prosper, at least not to suffer misery because of emancipation's cost. In Mesekow, nearly all farms survived to 1842, though some emancipated farmers probably faltered and surrendered their properties to outside buyers. While the new freeholds were not large, this had always been a smallholders' settlement, and by nineteenth-century European standards 12.5 hectares even of mediocre arable was land enough to sustain hard-working families. Voss took somewhat less land from his "good" Mesekowers than was his right, yet he and Neubauer put Stavenow's advantage above all else, including this "not prosperous" village's survival. Neubauer sometimes acted misleadingly, to confuse the Mesekowers about their concessions' value to the lordship. He would have squeezed the Dargardters if their property rights had been more ambiguous. It was profitable, future-oriented business, with nothing paternalist about it.[72]

NEGOTIATING VILLAGE EMANCIPATION (II): "REFRACTORY AND LITIGIOUS" GLÖVZINERS

Voss's dealings with these most numerous and troublesome villagers stood in eighteenth-century conflict's shadow. In April 1813 Neubauer and Gutike pressed twelve of them for commutation arrears. The debtors appealed to war's burdens – compulsory army haulage and crop requisition, billeting of army reservists – but promised payment after harvest from earnings on "grain and fruit." Voss denied he had extended Glövziners' "freedom from dues and services" until Christmas. He only promised "I would show some indulgence with your" – here, unlike Major Kleist, he employed the respectful formal mode of address (*Ihren*) – "current year's labor services and perhaps be

[71] No. 198, fos. 1–10.
[72] Recent arguments favoring Junker paternalism: Berdahl, *Politics*; Bowman, *Planters*.

satisfied with the previous commutation money," but only if, "in amicable agreement with me," a regulation contract exchanging land for services were promptly concluded.[73]

Yet on New Year's Eve 1813 Gutike repeated to Voss his "personally expressed sentiment" that, "in this refractory and litigious village's case, it was highly advisable" to proceed with government-mediated rather than privately negotiated settlement. Voss assented, asking whether Glövziners were hereditary tenants or tenants-at-will, a point previously uninteresting. Gutike, Stavenow judge for "almost thirty-four years," said they were "conditional tenants with hereditary tenures [*erbliche Laßbauern*]" whose iron stock was exempt from claims by non-inheriting siblings.[74] Voss asked Havelberg Royal Municipal Court Judge Henning, the Berlin General Commission's local representative, to serve as mediator. Voss invoked the "fickleness, well known to me, of this village," and cited Gutike's views, "in which I fully concur, about this extremely difficult commune's customary antagonism to any reasonable understanding with its overlordship." Henning replied subserviently that Voss's wish was his command. Voss privately noted that he aimed to amass the village lands Glövzin and Premslin ceded him into a "self-sufficient manor-farm" (the future Waterloo). To gain it he was prepared to demand less than the one-third of his villagers' land the law allowed.[75] In March 1814, Henning, aided by two royal agronomic experts, opened the negotiations' first round. Voss was present with his lawyer, Havelberg City Councilor Wehrmann, while the Glövziners relied again on Bürgermeister Krippenstapel. Representing the von Karstedts' village interests was their tenant-farmer Ferdinand Hackrath, the Stavenow administrator's kinsman. Here is evident the prominent role of non-noble state and landlordly officials in the manor–village divorce.

The farmers would cede one-third their lands only "if what the lordships are now obliged to provide us" – especially cheap wood and emergency relief – "continues, although we do not dispute that our dues' and services' value may exceed the one-third our lands yield." More likely they did dispute this idea, which Voss's side seemingly pressed on them. But their effort to perpetuate the small advantages they drew from seigneurial obligations collided with the 1811 edict's blunt language abolishing them. Instead tedious conflict arose over Voss's claims to village woodlands and one-third of the meadows the Kleists leased

[73] No. 314, fos. 25–8, 32.   [74] No. 451, fos. 8–10.   [75] Ibid.

their farmers in 1727. The Glövziners lamented that, should they lose their communal possessions' third part, "they could not survive."[76]

Voss's reaction to their renewed renitence found reflection in Neubauer's demand that on St. John's Day 1814 they begin labor services in person instead of paying commutation. The village announced compliance's "impossibility" and intention to defy the order. Judge Gutike petitioned for the sheriff's "execution," but in December 1814 Voss indignantly noted "the Glövziners have resisted execution in a body! [*in corpore*]." Voss ordered Gutike to act immediately "so the barns aren't emptied" through the villagers' sale of crops and excess livestock to evade confiscation. On December 21, Gutike requested sheriff Wunsch to act "against Glövzin and consorts with redoubled forces and urgency."[77] For the villagers, "redoubled execution" was no pleasant seigneurial Christmas gift, but Voss and Gutike could hope the villagers would now have something worth impounding. Their success seems doubtful, for in July 1815 the Chamber Court ruled that if Glövziners persisted in refusing to perform service they would have to pay commutation while seeking legal succor. This Voss already knew. Neubauer offered a compromise, whereby villagers would work twice weekly rather than thrice. The farmers complained that after 1809's fire, in which thirteen lost farmsteads, the lordship gave them neither lumber nor new iron stock. They still could not afford to buy draft-teams necessary for manorial service. To these laments Neubauer and Voss's lawyer coldly advised seeking redress from Kleist's heirs.[78]

In November 1816 the parties settled. The General Commission favored Voss, ruling he could take one-third both of the disputed meadows and any former woodland brought under the plow. The villager's two appeals only caused the Royal Supreme Appellate Court to fine them 20 talers for losing their case (*Succumbenz-Gelder*). They had also to buy their iron stock, for 3,050 talers cash, or 147–262 talers per farm. There were many other legal fees. Stavenow's four Glövzin smallholders each gained unpartitioned but meager freeholds for 500 talers cash.[79] The fullholders gained the single concession that Voss took two-ninths instead of one-third their cropland, pastures, and meadows. In 1836–42 they disbanded their communal open-field system, creating individualized farms. Since 1816 one fullholding had been bought out and parcelized, while four new family names figured among the fifteen remaining largeholders. Among twenty-nine participants in 1842's

[76] No. 427, fos. 1–10, 24.   [77] No. 408, fo. 73; no. 314, fos. 20ff.   [78] No. 533, fos. 1–9.
[79] No. 483, fos. 1–8; no. 428, fos. 10–13, 30–3, 41; no. 433, fos. 1–22.

enclosure settlement, including cottagers, twenty-five signed their own names. These details testify to Glövziners' endurance and capacity to learn. At emancipation's end, they could thank their insubordination and obstinacy for some small gains and Stavenow lordship for less.[80]

Voss mused over his newly won village lands' future yield. Neubauer reckoned in 1817 that every *Morgen* represented 30 talers capital. Voss's minute calculations fixed this value, capitalized at 4 percent, at 33 talers. In 1815 Voss sold some former village land for 26 talers per *Morgen*, but he assumed such land, improved to estate quality, would rise in value. Neubauer promised Voss profit from buying up seigneurial rights over several of the von Karstedts' unregulated smallholders, saying "their wish to be free of manorial service" – for which they would trade land – "is very lively." Altogether Voss, doubtless like other landlords, relished the opportunities the emancipation process afforded of broadening his acres.[81]

FREEHOLD CONVERSION IN STAVENOW'S OTHER VILLAGES

In light of Voss's negotiations with Mesekow and Glövzin, his other villages' release from seigneurialism is quickly recountable. The Premsliners, with lawyer Bürgermeister Krippenstapel, entered government-mediated discussions in December 1812. When the noble lordships "demanded one-third of all communal lands . . . the said commune would not agree to their cession. Finally, it declared it wished to be given an account of its lost possessions, should it cede one-third." The lordships compliantly mapped the proposed annexations, "but they said they could not do without so much land if they were to survive," yet also hinting that one-third cessions might be acceptable if iron-stock compensation were halved.[82]

Later the parties agreed the village would retain woodlands undiminished and pay half the iron-stock values, while also either ceding one-third of its 1727 meadows or paying the iron stock's second half. Some farmers refused, until in 1816 Voss gave the village 4 hectares of inferior cropland for planting in wood. In 1817 Voss signed the final agreement. Speaking in the villagers' presence, he advised against formally defining rents and obligations now being abolished. There had been "many conflicts over manorial services and a unanimous declaration would not be attainable." Half the farmers brought their occupancy

---

[80] No. 426, fos. 1–7; no. 425, fos. 9–23.   [81] No. 451, fos. 45, 65–7; no. 342, fo. 22.
[82] No. 449, fos. 16–19.

deeds, to prove their iron stock's value. Others produced none, maintaining "they have misplaced them, but want to submit authenticated copies." Two von Karstedt farmers said "they didn't want to present their deeds, [and] they couldn't make iron-stock payments, because unlike Stavenow fullholders they hadn't received seigneurial land in return" – a reference to Voss's woodland "gift." The other farmers without deeds agreed "they couldn't pay iron-stock money and, despite all efforts, could not be instructed otherwise." Voss accused them of reneging on earlier agreed-on installment payments for meadows and iron stock, goading the farmers, led by Stavenower J. G. Hecht III, to vote unanimously to reject iron-stock payments. "Although every possible attempt was made, into the late evening, to enlighten them, they were not to be moved."[83]

In 1818 the iron-stock payments' bitterest opponents wrote Voss's lawyer Wehrmann, admitting that in 1813 they agreed to this provision, but on a promise the emancipation would not cost them more than other Stavenow villages. "But if these are not" – they inaccurately held – "to pay for their iron stock"

and if, through cession of one-third our lands, we lose, according to the government agronomist, half our cropland, and if in our land quality's official appraisal there was a glaring error, obliging us to surrender far too much land, then we hope the lordship will drop claims on our iron stock, especially since most of us can prove we replaced with our own money iron stock our predecessors sold to pay for illnesses or lost because of debts.

The villagers' fear of seigneurial deceit, and their quite plausible argument that newly installed farmers often replaced iron stock lost or sold by precursors, left Voss cold. He instructed his lawyer to seek court enforcement, since "the Premslin commune for completely insignificant reasons" was refusing iron-stock payments.[84]

The contract finally signed in 1818 showed the farmers bowing to Voss's will, though iron-stock payments averaged only 40 talers. Six farmers signed with their own names, but sixteen (including four women) only made crosses. Voss gained 182 hectares (454 acres) of arable and 16 hectares of meadow, while the Karstedts took 24 hectares altogether. This was a stately addition to Voss's properties, against which the 10 acres he surrendered for village woodland may be judged. At 30 talers per *Morgen*, Stavenow's new arable alone tallied 22,000 talers. By this reckoning, each of Voss's eighteen Premslin largeholders

---

[83] Ibid., fos. 50–60.   [84] Ibid., fos. 61–6.

gained his freehold for the equivalent of cropland worth 1,100–200 talers.[85]

In Karstädt village, Voss's six fullholders paid him, without surrendering land, "release money" (*Loskaufsgeld*) of 1,000 talers "free and clear," in full-valued "ringing Prussian coin." Though they had rendered three days' weekly service and 11 bushels' annual grain rent, they cultivated the lordship's best-yielding village land. Doubtless they borrowed from local moneylenders to pay by 1815's end the full sum in two installments. Voss's four Karstädt smallholders each paid 600 talers. Two fullholders and three smallholders could sign their names. Twenty-seven years later, one fullholder had slipped to three-quarters status, and one smallholding had been parcelized. Among the other nine, five had headed their holdings in 1815, and but one bore an outsider's name. Despite the 1820s' agrarian slump and difficult adjustments to fully marketized conditions, Stavenow's Karstädters nearly all retained their freeholds, whose value was slowly rising, undiminished. Compared with neighboring villages, they gained advantageous release from seigneurialism.[86]

The few Stavenowers in Garlin also bought themselves free. Halfholder Schütt gained for 500 talers "his farm's free ownership and use," although Voss could still claim "hunting rights, ceremonial services, and court jurisdiction."[87] From each of six Sargleben mini-smallholders Voss gained 150 talers "release money." Voss noted they earlier owed but seventy-eight days' yearly manorial service, which "was only called garden service and badly performed by women and often children."

These smallholders possess no land; cession of arable could not take place. They are very poor and since the above-mentioned services were badly performed, I have appraised them at only 2 groschen daily for an [annual value of] 8.10.-talers.

Capitalized at 5 percent, this yielded 150 talers, whose payment "the Sargleben cottagers accepted only after much negotiation." Voss noted mockingly that "these manorial servants never wanted to work at Dargard, closer to them [than Stavenow]: because this manor-farm was

---

[85] No. 441, fos. 1–46. In 1814–15 Voss calculated fullholders' rents' and labors' market value at 85 talers, which at 5 percent interest = 1,700 t. capital (or, at 4 percent, 2,125 t.). He appraised compulsory labor with teams at 12 gr. daily and compulsory manual labor at 4 gr. For free labor these values were fair, but they overrated unpaid compulsory labor. No. 341, fos. 1–6.

[86] No. 390, fos. 1–4; no. 391, fos. 1–27; no. 392, fos. 1–28.   [87] No. 342, fo. 20.

a new addition!" These cottagers had asserted their common-law right not to have their services transferred to unaccustomed seigneurial sites. Voss conceded nothing to his "very poor" Sarglebeners. In July 1815 Neubauer booked cottager Milatz's "release money," adding he was now "completely free" (*ist ganz frey*).[88]

Finally, the Blüthen farmers maintained they were proprietary tenants rather than hereditary tenants-at-will. As personal property, their iron stock required no compensation payment. Voss and Wehrmann argued before Judge Henning's commission that Blüthen farms were "conditional holdings" (*Laßgüter*), granted "only for cultivation." They denied that Prignitz farmers were, "as a rule, proprietors." But after studying occupancy deeds, Voss wrote his lawyer in 1819 that their position was "not really tenable." Wehrmann concurred, pointing to many eighteenth-century deeds designating holdings as "hereditary and proprietary." Among deeds Judge Gutike had issued since 1780, Wehrmann noted damningly "they appear to indicate, more than previously, that . . . farms belong to the lordship." Gutike had been applying Major Kleist's hard line, even though Blüthen stood aloof from strikes and urbarial conflict.[89]

"In the Prignitz," lawyer Wehrmann concluded, "it is not certain that farmers are proprietors, but the presumption is for them, and the lordship must prove the opposite, for which in the present case I do not think sufficient evidence is available." Perhaps Gutike thought some villages were anciently settled with conditional tenants, but Wehrmann believed such farmers acquired this legal status "only in more recent times," after 1648 and not in every village. He superciliously opined that Gutike was ignorant of Chamber Court verdicts on village tenurial rights published in *Stengel's Beyträge*. Gutike might instead cite Stenger and Lange, but both were "notoriously very weak jurists." Wehrmann added, "I admit the matter is very unsettled, and almost everything depends on the judge's personal view." Still, it was probable, even if Voss won in the first instance, that the General Commission's and Board of Appeals' verdicts would go against him. Voss agreed, saying the iron-stock question was "in itself not significant." Here the seriousness is evident with which legal questions concerning subject villagers might be debated and disputed among landlords, lawyers, and government jurists.[90]

Voss earlier insisted Blütheners should pay rent arrears before he signed any regulation agreement. In 1816 sheriff Wunsch reported he

---

[88] No. 440, fos. 1–5; no. 342, fo. 18.   [89] No. 513, fos. 60–1, 66–70.   [90] Ibid., fos. 70ff.

had collected 30 talers cash instead of grain arrears. Against three other farmers, Wunsch said, "I applied execution, but could find no *Objectum Executionis* in their possession, particularly since hail ruined their summer grain this year and they are having to buy seed-grain, so I could accomplish nothing with them." As elsewhere, Voss's pressure was relentless, if here unprofitable.[91] He signed the Blüthen agreement in 1820, though two farmers separately protested inclusion of 1727 perpetual-leasehold meadow among lands ceded the lordship. The courts ruled against them, and the resultant legal fees forced one, mayor Fick, into bankruptcy. In an 1825 court-ordered auction his farm fetched 1,400 talers, perhaps representing a fullholding's value in those years of sagging markets. In 1827 Fick's lawsuit partner, halfholder Ohlert, pleaded with Wehrmann for more time to settle his 8 talers arrears: "It is completely impossible for me to manage this from my own resources and I can borrow money from no one." He requested "in present circumstances, so unfavorable to the countryman, an extension until Perleberg autumn market," for which, if granted, he promised "lifelong" thanks. Wehrmann agreed, and Ohlert later paid.[92]

In the Blüthen settlement lawyer Wehrmann appears favorably, unlike Gutike, who sought to undermine farm tenures and was, evidently, a superficial jurist. In 1830 a Chamber Court order dismissed Gutike, on unspecified grounds, both from his seat on Perleberg's municipal court and from Stavenow's judgeship. Gutike was refusing, on pretext of illness, to surrender current files to Wehrmann, who recruited a new government-appointed judge, instructing Stavenow's accounting office to ignore Gutike's orders and bar his access to court records.[93]

Freehold conversion left Voss and his sons richer men. Stavenow's former subject farmers emerged as owners of individualized and enclosed middle-sized family landholdings of some value, most free of regulation-incurred debt. These were outcomes Hardenberg's legislation, crafted under noble landlords' pressure, envisioned. It is otherwise hard to detect a governmental bias favoring Voss any stronger than what might be expected wherever superior classes, whose arguments easily appear reasonable, face subalterns on professionally administered judicial grounds. As for landless laborers' fate in *laissez-faire* capitalism's dawning light, it was indistinct, but insights emerge from some evidence from the 1820s and 1830s.

[91] No. 314, fos. 29–30.   [92] No. 475; no. 519, fos. 48, 63.   [93] No. 347, fo. 4.

NEUBAUER'S MANAGEMENT STYLE IN THE
POST-EMANCIPATION YEARS

Neubauer grew more self-confident in his authority's exercise, though the aggressiveness he exhibited toward farmers and workers upon arrival in 1809 did not entirely disappear. In 1821 landless Premslin cottager Sauber wrote plaintively to Voss that Neubauer charged him for 1811–17 rent arrears of 37 talers. But during village regulation Sauber unjustly lost the right to freely graze his cow, four sheep, pig, and goose, "whereby I incurred such heavy costs I lost all movable goods and became a very poor man." Sauber blamed "my lordship," which failed to specify and protect his grazing rights. He appealed to Voss's justice, "about whose generosity of heart everyone may rejoice." The village, Voss replied coldly, successfully contested Sauber's grazing rights, a judgment Sauber accepted "in silence" rather than appealing, as he should if he thought himself injustice's victim. Voss backed Neubauer.[94]

Neubauer could be more accommodating. In 1819 landless cottager Henck, resident outside Stavenow's jurisdiction, wrote him:

As brother of sick widow Wichmann in Nebelin village I feel obliged to bring her to me in Milow. But I cannot suffer to take more than one person, who will be burden enough, if only because of my dwelling's limited space. Her two children the Nebelin lordship [which acquisitive Voss recently bought] will have to keep.

In response, Neubauer, "as the lordship's deputy, binds himself to take in the two boys, fourteen and nine, and also care for their schooling, in return for which Henck assumes the obligation of keeping his sister, widow Wichmann, with him as long as she lives." Though this case engaged landlordly interest in avoiding poor-relief expenses and pooling cheap labor, Neubauer nonetheless exhibited some charity.[95]

In 1828 Neubauer noted that Voss's son, "the Cathedral Prebendary," had ordered the small arable plots the Stavenow and Semlin day laborers cultivated "enclosed" in the seigneurial demesne. Against this ruling the Stavenow sexton and schoolmaster, also tailor, Kobs, who like the laborers rented Stavenow arable for 3 talers yearly, protested. Neubauer reminded Kobs the land was not part of his salary. His retention of it would "totally disturb the lordship's projects." Still, Neubauer gave him another plot. The lordship delivered Kobs' yearly

[94] Ibid., fos. 10–11.   [95] Ibid., fo. 1.

firewood allotment and lent him oxen to haul in his own grain and hay, "since he is very familiar with agricultural work and indeed possesses more skill and handiness than some day laborers whose entire livelihood depends on it." The lordship consented to help him "because with rare considerateness, and rather voluntarily than because he was asked, he has sent [his sons], who are also tailors' apprentices, to work unpaid in the seigneurial harvests." Neubauer expressed confidence that Kobs would perform such services in the future. But should his successor evince "less love and zeal for the lordship's interest," and instead "quibble about churchly rights and how nothing can be detached from his [sexton's] office," such that "the present concession, made from good-will and in recognition" of Kobs' services, "could come to be seen as a prerogative stemming from olden times," Neubauer asked Kobs to verify in writing that he would frequently send two persons to Stavenow's harvests. Kobs assented, saying when his sons were grown and he could send no further workers he would cease requesting "hauling services." Both men signed this agreement, sent to Voss's son for approval. Here, apart from ancient suspiciousness toward establishing unfavorable precedents, is evident the give-and-take that established reciprocal rights and obligations between lordship and laborer.[96]

In dealing with Kobs, Neubauer exhibited a stern but benevolent patriarchalism that appeared again in 1834, when he hired "day laborer and stable-thresher" Hartwich Graget, who "on St. Mary's Day [25 March]" would receive one of the "vacated dwellings."

The aforesaid Graget remarks upon appointment: he has his mother-in-law, widow Arendt, with him, whom he must keep. Disagreeable though this circumstance is, the aforesaid Graget is nonetheless [hired], subject to the explicit vow, to which he has affixed his signature: that should he wish or be obliged to vacate the estate cottage, he will unquestioningly have to take his mother-in-law along, should she still be alive.[97]

Neubauer's last recorded words appear in the text of a remarkable speech he delivered in October 1834 to assembled day laborers. He told them that, "among day laborers' countless abuses hereabouts, one in particular has crept in, namely, that almost every day laborer's family keeps a breeding sow." Its piglets were "not driven out to forage by the swineherd," but rather "roam about without supervision in their owners' livestock pens" or even their gardens. "This prohibited branch of industry" had also arisen on Stavenow's estates. "By law," day laborers

---

[96] Ibid., fos. 8–9.   [97] Ibid., fo. 6.

could keep only one pig for fattening and slaughtering in the current year, and another for the following year. "But since day laborers here must keep servants to help them in their work, while I willingly permit them to take in lodgers, it is therefore permitted" that every day laborer could keep "two pigs for slaughtering and two to replace them," though they might not breed these themselves.

If things follow their previous course, all day laborers will become swine deal-ers, and the purpose of their existence will be lost . . . [This new regulation] is just as important as that a seigneurial thresher should thresh for every sixteenth bushel, or that he should work for fixed wages which, for ordinary labor and mowing of hay and grain, have their graduated schedules and which, when the work is properly performed, are paid out each week. Once again I repeat that, as a free man, no day laborer is bound to remain in one place. [If he is dissat-isfied with work rules, it would be better] to give notice on his cottage and look for a happier place.

At this text's end Neubauer wrote, as if proud of his handiwork: "on this day slowly and deliberately read, accompanied by requisite figures of speech," as witnessed by administrator Hackrath who also, after twenty-five years, was still in Stavenow's service.[98]

Neubauer's speech to the day laborers shows he had mastered the liberal discourse of "the free man" and "the happier place," in contrast to the still half-feudal, menacing language of his first Stavenow years. This transformation captured ideologically the socio-economic transi-tion from the absolutist age's coercive manorial lordship to nineteenth-century estate management, governed by the free market. It was a shift that also occurred in the thought and practice of Minister of State von Voss and most of his fellow noble landlords.

This chapter has shown that Voss and his officials viewed the aboli-tion of the old regime in east-Elbian agriculture and social organiza-tion, and its recasting in nineteenth-century liberalism's mold, as unavoidable necessities. Their prime goal was to gain from emancipa-tion and freehold conversion the strongest economic weaponry for the future. Necessary to this end were the cool and ruthless calculation and pursuit of seigneurial interest that Voss, Neubauer, Wehrmann, Gutike, and other Stavenow administrators displayed. They formed a manage-ment team operating by capitalist logic. The former subject villagers faced the necessity of using corresponding tools, including work stop-pages, to defend themselves as best they could in the feudal dusk and capitalist dawn. Amid the daily realities and financial practicalities

[98] Ibid., fo. 7.

these pages have examined, the political and social ideologies that historians assume were of such interest to the Prussian landed nobility, whether feudal or liberal, make no appearance. Voss and his officials sought, within a new political-economic world not of their own making, their narrow self-interest, and looked to the state's police powers to enforce it. In economic life, economic interests usually come first. This was no less evident to old-regime noblemen such as the Kleists than to modern nineteenth-century estateowners and administrators such as Voss and Neubauer.

THE SUBJECT FARMERS' FUTURE: ONE HOUSEHOLD'S CONDITION IN 1858

The villagers' nineteenth-century fate and fortune lie beyond these pages' scope. But an 1858 fire insurance policy issued to Glövzin mayor Peter Hinze illuminates such material comfort as his household attained two generations after emancipation. Doubtless many other new freeholds fared worse. But Hinze's case is interesting, and perhaps typical, in the continuities it displays with eighteenth-century village life. What most obviously changed was the farm's productivity and its stock's value, but there are also tell-tale signs of advancing middle-class consumption and culture among Stavenow lordship's subject farmers' descendants.

The "Mecklenburg Household-Goods Fire Insurance Society" issued the policy, which excluded Hinze's cursorily described buildings. All still bore thatched roofs. Hinze's main barn measured 100 by 34 feet, with a height of 19 feet and two entrances 14 feet wide. It was set behind and separated from his dwelling-house by a big orchard and garden, 260 feet in length and some 200 feet wide. Hinze's house, walled off from the garden, lay behind and separated by an inner courtyard from other buildings fronting on the village street, including the retirees' and a day laborer's cottage. It was a traditional farmstead layout.[99]

In 1821 Prussia revised its coinage, retaining the taler in the silver value established in 1750 and reconfirmed in 1764 (whereby 14 talers were struck from a 233-gram mark of silver). But now the taler counted 30 "silver groschen" rather than the previous 24. This reform eliminated the devalued coinage brought into circulation during the 1806–13 French occupation. In 1858, the Prussian taler retained its Frederickian

---

[99] No. 465, fos. 27–30.

value, while price rises had not much reduced its purchasing power. Rye prices, measured in constant silver-gram values, stood in Berlin in the 1850s at levels similar to the mid-eighteenth century's, and much lower than in French Revolutionary and Napoleonic years. The insured values of Peter Hinze's possessions are therefore directly comparable with eighteenth- and early nineteenth-century values figuring in the pages above.[100]

Hinze's livestock did not vary greatly from eighteenth-century holdings, except that sheep, at 100 head, were much more numerous and, at 3 talers per head, several times more valuable. His team of four horses was worth 220 talers, signaling high quality earlier found only among seigneurial animals. His four milk-cows (20 talers each) and six younger cattle (15 talers each) were somewhat more numerous than his ancestors' and, again, of better quality. But his sow with piglets and two pigs for winter slaughtering resembled late eighteenth-century holdings, though their value (50 talers altogether) was higher and weights doubtless better. Hinze's farm indicates that post-emancipation conditions did not so much inspire village farmers to expand livestock holdings on which they depended for their own sustenance as to raise more livestock for sale, especially sheep but perhaps also dairy cattle. The cessation of unpaid seigneurial labor may also have allowed them to reduce the number of their work-horses.

Hinze worked with the same equipment his ancestors used, but of better quality. His three wagons rated 20–40 talers. His heavy and light plows, harnesses, harrows, scythes, sacks and measures, and fodder-cutting machines tallied 85 talers. There were two "standing" servants' beds worth 30 talers. Yet, though his farm displayed no important new technology, his two barns were bursting with harvested grain and hay: 102,477 cubic feet, according to the insurance agent's calculations, worth 1,536 talers, plus 183 talers' threshed grain and seed. In value, this was vastly more grain than Hinze's eighteenth-century precursors ever singly accumulated. Doubtless higher yields from enclosed fallow-free land, and seigneurial rents' cessation, accounted for Hinze's bounty.

Summing livestock and equipment yields 935 talers – working capital five or six times bigger than the most solid eighteenth-century farms possessed. Adding harvested grain and hay elevates this sum to 2,654

---

[100] Aubin and Zorn, *Handbuch*, vol. I, 668–70, vol. II, 934ff; Abel, *Agrarkrisen*, pp. 301–10. Abel's scale of decennial Berlin rye-price averages (in grams silver): 1750s – 48; 1760s – 50; 1770s – 57; 1780s – 56; 1790s – 63; 1800s – 103; 1810s – 79; 1820s – 50; 1830s – 60; 1840s – 69; 1850s – 42; 1860s – 87; 1870s – 96; 1880s – 83; 1890s – 80; 1900s – 88; 1910s – 106.

talers – more than twice the compensation value the fullholders paid Voss for freehold conversion. Not every regulated farm survived to attain Hinze's solidity, but many did. This suggests the concessions halfholders and fullholders made to escape seigneurial overlordship, however unjustifiable in equity's light, repaid themselves repeatedly, once the transition to fully marketized conditions was successfully weathered. Another question, unanswerable here, is how to draw the balance between nineteenth-century village farmers who gained, as Hinze did, and those who could not survive on their new freeholds.

In their dwelling-house, Hinze and his wife possessed – among items they cared to insure – eight cooking pots of the eighteenth-century sort, five food and clothes cabinets, four trunks, two tables, and six chairs. There was a loom and the customary mountain of household textiles, plus "bed feathers in reserve" worth 8 talers. All these bore values somewhat higher than the previous century's, as did the house's three "standing" double beds (20–5 talers each). New among furniture, though, were a sofa ("*Sopha*"), worth 10 talers, and a wall-clock (6 talers) – both minor indicators of middle-class commodities' spread to the villages.[101] Similarly, the Hinzes' insured clothing largely corresponded to eighteenth-century categories and values. Unassuming shoes and boots (1–3 talers); ordinary shirts (15–20 groschen); workaday overcoats, suits, and dresses (2–8 talers): these testify to modest self-presentation. New, alone, was an umbrella (1 taler). As for food on hand, it was unspecified, but valued, substantially, at 70 talers. Altogether the Hinzes' movables, insured (at unstated premium) for 80 percent of their value, tallied 3,110 talers. The policy bore a stamp of approval from "Stavenow lordship police" (*Polizey des Dominii Stavenow*), as law and order's local arm was now known.

Mayor Hinze's 1858 insurance policy does not transparently reveal his material circumstances. Such savings or debts as may have attached to his name are invisible. Of kin nothing is revealed. Yet, after entering all caveats, the picture is a positive one. Any farmer under old-regime Stavenow jurisdiction whose post-emancipation progeny landed in positions similar to Peter Hinze's would have counted them fortunate. In this sense, too, the pre-1806 Stavenow villagers' struggles to defend their holdings against degradation at seigneurial hands were worth the hardships and reprisals they provoked. Refractoriness and insubordination proved to be Prussian virtues.

---

[101] On nineteenth-century village embourgeoisement: Peters et al., *Bauerntagebücher*.

Conclusion

These pages have conveyed a narrative account of a Brandenburg-Prussian noble lordship and its subject villages which, from the sixteenth to the early nineteenth century, passed through epochal changes. They have also drawn a portrait of a slow-moving social and cultural world. The narrative dimension offers explanations of origins, transformation, and dissolution; the synchronic dimension reveals deep-rooted structures and identities, and is a source of imaginative insight and intuitive understanding. To explore and join these dimensions, investing the particularized human experience preserved in them with meaning, is the historian's challenge. It is only finally surmountable through comparison of the story and actors on hand with those of other historical settings and trajectories. The empirical social science that cannot flourish within these limits will model a world that never existed. Similarly, the epistemological and ideological critique that refuses to grant the past's power to speak will entomb itself in a monologue.

This book has aimed to construct its narratives and conjure up the social realms it explores to the greatest possible extent in its human subjects' words, as preserved in the Stavenow estate archive's voluminous manuscripts. Such a technique, though available to any historian, is optimally fit for a study such as this, whose local scale creates a stage on which ordinary actors easily move, and whose documentary sources record a myriad of voices. When the last of these has sounded, a chorus, by no means harmonious, has been heard that conveys as much of the quality and spirit, the psychology and mentality, of the world evoked here as seemed possible.

It is short-sighted to think that exploration of human subjectivity cannot proceed hand-in-hand with study of forward-moving structural change. The great impediment in earlier thinking about this latter life-dimension was the assumption that structural change somehow embodied a teleological logic of development toward one or another historical end-state, whether "modernity" or "post-modernity," the rational-bureaucratic state and society, capitalism or post-capitalism, freedom or alienation, civilization or its eclipse. The heavier the emphasis on such trajectories' fixity, the more irrelevant human action became. At best, the dichotomy loomed between people positioned to advance history's dynamic thrust and those standing in its way. But human change through time is, except in historical retrospect, directionless, and nothing whatever can explain it but the concatenation of human actions.

These pages have sought to identify and explain structural change, applying quantitative analysis, within the evidence's limits, as a strong tool of social and economic description. But I have steered clear of the danger, to which this method's exclusivist practitioners expose themselves, of supposing that quantitative analysis contains within itself its own causal explanations. Quantitative patterns in history yield only (and rarely beyond any doubt) to explanation in non-quantitative terms, for which one-dimensional concentration on numerical data unfits the researcher.

The epistemological challenges this book faces are no different at bottom than any other historical study's. Nothing can be known about the past that is not known empirically. No deduction from abstract principle is possible (though inferences from evidence are a different matter). There is no better solution than to take one's cue from Immanuel Kant in resolving to think the thing-in-itself, that is, the historical past in one or another of its infinite forms, while acknowledging it cannot be definitively known in any essential (noumenal) reality. Historical knowledge is the best construction presently put on relevant and available evidence to answer questions of historians' own choosing. The most insistent skeptic, or most fervent apostle of "robust" ("nomothetic") social science, cannot escape these limits and still claim to speak accurately and non-mystically of human reality, which is inescapably historical.

These pages have aimed, among other things, to intertwine quantitative and narrative analysis in an account of the emergence, permutations, and dissolution of the socio-economic system here termed commercialized manorialism. This was, beyond the level of biological reproduction, the most important of all structural contexts encompassing east-Elbian rural society's inhabitants. It was not a creation of abstract forces giving birth to capitalism, whether embodied in markets or classes, but emerged instead from an incessant three-cornered tug-of-war, driven by (subjectively understood) self-interest, among landlords, villagers, and princely officialdom. Though the point is impossible to establish with mathematical precision, these pages show that each of these three sets of actors exerted roughly equal force in the struggle, and likewise shaped the outcome with rough equality. As will emerge from some reflection on the manifold historical trajectories of the many other central, eastern, and southern European lands where post-medieval noble manorialism took root and spread, the Brandenburg-Prussian outcome, as sketched in this book's final two chapters, was utterly unforeseeable from the vantage point of the system's origins.

Yet this book's claim is not only to have offered a reconceptualization, at a local but yet generalizable level, of the landlord–village–state relationship in Brandenburg-Prussia from the sixteenth century to and beyond the Prussian Reform Era, with strong relevance as a model to the study of neighboring central and east European societies. More vital to its purpose was to paint the fullest and most vivid portrait possible of this rural society from the late seventeenth to the early nineteenth century, when the Stavenow documentation flows most copiously. It is a fortunate coincidence that this was a historically coherent and crucial period, defined by the rise of the absolutist state in Prussia. It can fairly be said that no such portrait was ever previously drawn.

Instead of summarizing the arguments advanced in these pages, it seems worthwhile to conclude by recalling some of their most important findings, especially those contested or unanticipated in the existing historical literature. At the economic level, this study has analyzed the incomes, living standards, and material culture of the Stavenow lordship's village farmers and other plebeian subjects. It has likewise demonstrated the force and constancy of the subject farmers' resistance to landlordly demands beyond what they thought tolerable. It was a central argument that such refractoriness was not only effective in holding village living standards well above misery's boundary, but also historically significant in steering Brandenburg-Prussian society in a direction relatively (though – obviously – not wholly, greatly, or primarily) favorable to village interests. These pages have, I submit, successfully made these points, neither of which the earlier historical literature ever seriously entertained or accepted. Instead, it emphasized villagers' immiseration under Junker lordship and their passivity and paralysis as historical actors. The Potsdam school's recent work, discussed in the introduction, is changing this picture, but it has not linked material life and popular resistance as these pages do.

A new picture of noble landlordism likewise emerges here. Rather than a technologically backward, undercapitalized system of inefficient labor coercion, east-Elbian commercialized manorialism, in its not untypical Stavenow form, entailed at its sixteenth-century emergence weighty seigneurial operating and labor costs. Yet it achieved massive extensive growth. In its eighteenth-century expansion, the adoption of enclosed convertible agriculture produced heightened yields and other productivity gains, alongside soaring profit margins, that justify talk of agricultural revolution. Nor was this achieved through village labor's redoubled exploitation, whose extent subject farmers' obduracy held to early eighteenth-century levels. Instead, seigneurial investments in wage labor and fixed capital were the price of improved efficiency and earnings, propelling the large-estate economy into a transitional phase leading through village emancipation and freehold conversion into the nineteenth-century liberal market economy. This was an early modern path to agrarian capitalist development no less real for having been followed by the Brandenburg-Prussian nobility. But these pages showed that commercialized manorialism engaged the administrative, managerial, and judicial energies of numerous commoners and bourgeois. Its social character requires reconceptualization in multi-class terms.

The evidence marshaled here establishes, particularly among landholding farmers, the primacy of kin-ordered lineages (one's "friends") and the family concept's absence in a household life nonetheless lit by positive bonds, if also shadowed by dissension and untimely death. The centrality of elders' retirement provisions emerges very strikingly, as do women's strong rights over dowries and remarriages, and the scrupulous enforcement of inheritance claims of all sorts, including orphaned children's. This rural society possessed social-welfare arrangements that, imperfect though they were, the historical literature largely overlooks. Villagers' material culture, though not opulent, displayed clothing, household goods, and diet that, in best form, might have prevailed among western European and North American middling countryfolk. Stavenowers' mortality and longevity reveal both pre-modern weaknesses and unsuspected strengths. In their emotional lives, they were accustomed to friendship, loyalty, solicitude, and passion, along with the opposite impulses, though these stopped short of crippling violence or murder. The more fortunate of landless laborers, apart from those for whom servant status was but a life-cycle stage, attained married cottagers' status animated by landholders' values. Rural notables of common origins increasingly embodied bourgeois ambitions. The housed and settled landless poor were not numerous within Stavenow lordship's boundaries. In part they are lost in lodger status's shadow but, as burial registers show, they were few in number and often recipients of communally resolved or court-ordered aid. The itinerant poor moved across the Stavenow landscape leaving but few, though often telling, traces.

As for noble families, Stavenow's archive illuminates legal, economic, and seigneurial issues more brightly than personal ones. The fusion of kin-ordered lineage values with marriage arrangements balancing strategic gain and emotion-fraught expectations was nonetheless striking, as were, again, women's strong property rights. While the Stavenow Kleists epitomized the militarized Prussian service nobility, their membership in a propertied and leisured upper class wary of the centralizing and bureaucratizing absolutist monarchy's widening reach stamped them no less – and in individual cases even more – than martial identity. Nor does Stavenow documentation bear out the historical literature's hypothesized efficacy of Prussian militarism in fastening surer social control on the common people, whether directly through the state or indirectly through noble lordship's association with the officer corps.

On popular and elite culture these pages cast scattered light. Religion figures sometimes as real piety, more often as individual and social life's conventionalized setting, and sometimes as a site of popular protest fusing church politics with resentment at elite domination. The authorities, resolve stiffened by Prussian sobriety and neo-Stoicism, methodically, though without ferocity, discouraged common people's illicit supernatural anxieties, though these only infrequently come to light. Honor, another ill-plumbed issue, proved one of the villagers' vital concerns, salient especially in matters of money and extramarital sexuality. Literacy, though advancing, left no traces of revolutionary reorderings in mentality, though it may have lent greater efficacy to anti-seigneurial village mobilizations. Xenophobia and the scapegoating of outsiders are only faintly discernible among Stavenowers, though doubtless "foreigners" encountered difficulty, much reducible with sufficient ringing coin, in breaching walls enclosing long-settled landed kin groups. Wary and combative realism, rather than passive fatalism or otherworldly fervor, seems the right description of villagers' predominant mentality.

Village politics reveal, unsurprisingly, a kind of oligarchy of landholding farmers, who overshadowed both their landless neighbors and seigneurially appointed mayors. The lordship could not steer villages from within through coercion or patronage, partly because subject farmers' hereditary tenures were largely unmanipulable. It relied instead on the seigneurial court, whose workings over long years these pages have analyzed. While the point was, again, unforeseeable from the existing literature's perspective, the court, though doubtless often a seigneurial tool in manor–village conflict, otherwise possessed considerable utility in villagers' eyes. Adjudicating affairs among themselves, it played a necessary and valued, if often stern, role. In mediating the subject farmers' quarrels with the lordship, such judges as Johann Erdmann Hasse, if not his successors, acted to maintain a precarious balance between parties, each deeply, though not wholly, dissatisfied in its way with existing conditions.

The princely – later royal – government at first embraced the seigneurial regime as it found it, benefiting from it itself on crown estates. But in the absolutist age it competed with landlords by taking a sizable tax-bite from villagers' surpluses. Through Frederick II's judicial reforms, subject farmers gained collective power to contest novel seigneurial impositions, forcing their overlords farther down the road of technological innovation and wage-labor recruitment. Princely policy likewise acted slowly to halt impulsive seigneurial violence against servants and workers, unleashed by bailiffs' or landlordly canes and whips, though the state's judicialized punishment of the common people in such institutions as Spandau fortress ushered new menaces into being. Yet, in the longstanding and heated discussion over the Janus-faced Prussian state, the evidence offered here adds weight to the positive view, revealing the equalizing and enlightening effect of the government's increasingly frequent and decisive interventions in the stormy manor–village relationship.

The once common view that the Prussian state rested on the two long legs of bureaucracy and army, and one short leg of a noble-controlled countryside, appears in these pages' light, especially after 1740, as untenable. Liberal historians misunderstood or exaggerated the disabilities with which subject status hobbled the villagers and judged the old-regime Prussian state too exclusively according to its policies on villagers' tenurial rights or personal status. For the great majority of country-dwellers, subjection (*Untertänigkeit*) was much less a personal attribute than a consequence of residence under noble (or crown-estate) jurisdiction and occupancy of farms entailing seigneurial dues and services. These pages show that villagers' access to royal courts to enforce existing rights and guard against their degradation was, before 1807, the decisive improvement they gained from the enlightened absolutist regime. At Stavenow the subject farmers, who after 1763 appealed with some significant if intermittent success to Berlin courts against Major von Kleist's aggressions, trusted the government to hear their pleas, though they also insubordinately defied unfavorable rulings. Sometimes they shifted into illegal, region-wide collective action against state taxes or seigneurial overlords, or both, as in the 1650s, 1700–2, and 1808–10. In these and other confrontations, their leaders risked, and sometimes suffered, the royal regime's carceral torments.

In the post-1811 freehold-conversion process, villagers' stiffneckedness and litigiousness rendered them significant defense, if only in forcing restraint on seigneurial appetites. Even subject farmers with smallholdings or usufructuary tenures emerged with individualized farms worth sacrifice, however undeserved were noble gains. Among landlords, the negotiations inspired them to drive hard bargains to arm themselves for the next round of market and technological challenges. Of noble interest in paternalism, whether genuine or postured, there was little Stavenow evidence, whether before or after 1807's abolition of subjection. Nor did villagers betray any propensity to mystify themselves with ideas of landlordly legitimacy. The bond linking manor and village was wholly practical and, if clouded by sentiment, then more by wary fearfulness than trusting reverence. Over the centuries the two parties approached one another as combatants, probing for weaknesses and opportunities for gain, now accepting truces, now breaking them to pursue strategic advantages with the court bailiff's lash, at the strike front, or on the judicial battlefield. These findings, too, ill fit prevailing views of seigneurial–princely domination and village passivity.

This book dissolves many stereotypes of "Prussian Junkers" and subject villagers. It argues for abandoning, except in its geographical and descriptive utility, the dualistic east-Elbian/west-Elbian approach to German social and political history. Seigneurial rent, noble lordship, and villagers' legal subjection – or their equivalents – were ubiquitous in both west and east before the early nineteenth century. Comparisons need drawing not at formalistic levels, but between the actual lifespheres of kinship and household, property, rent and taxes, and material and popular culture explored in these pages. Certainly the lives many Stavenow villagers led yielded material gratifications superior to those of many west or south Germans, a point stretchable to Iberia's far reaches and the British Isles. Nor need the Prussian state shrink from comparisons with western European governments as an agency of earthly justice and enlightened reform, hobbled though such projects were by interests of class and self.

This study's forward-reaching implications are weighty. Estateowners and landed villagers need rethinking as market producers open to the nineteenth and early twentieth centuries' technological, material, and political opportunities. In pre-1848 years, as in that year's revolution and the Prussian Constitutional Conflict of 1858–66, many Prussian country-dwellers, whether eminent or humble, stood in political liberalism's ranks. The Prussian countryside's subsequent political conservatism followed the drift of agriculturalists throughout the western world, and did not drive all villagers, whether landed or not, from liberal or democratic or populist camps. If politicized Prussian agrarians of the ages of Bismarck and William II increasingly brandished demagogic ideological weapons, including anti-semitism, they were doing so far more for radically modern reasons than as a manifestation of an unbroken tradition of "Junker domination" (*Junkerherrschaft*). The countryside's embrace of National Socialism after 1928 amounted to a rebellion of the young generations, of both villagers and landlords, against the elders, and so was rather "old Prussian tradition's" end than culmination. Lamentably misguided though rural east-Elbian entry into Hitler's camp was, it yields better to an interpretation focused on populist and nationalist mobilization, and conflicts within modern German society and politics, than one focused on survival into the twentieth century of pre-modern authoritarian structures.

The reader preoccupied with the world beyond German central Europe has encountered here one among the early modern world's myriad agrarian societies. The questions these pages have explored of grass-roots power and resistance, wealth and poverty, innovative profit-seeking as against complacent rent-collecting, naturalism and supernaturalism, justice and injustice, rationalization and state-building are variations on universal themes. The consequences appear here, in the Brandenburg-Prussian setting, of the growth-accelerating, capitalism-strengthening long sixteenth century, the crisis-ridden seventeenth century, and the technology-revolutionizing long eighteenth century. In the social and cultural as well as the economic perspective, the continuities and slow transformations these pages highlight strengthen the argument, championed by French historians, that the French Revolution of 1789 was a political event, on the order indeed of a newly arrived comet, but not otherwise a division along all historical axes between modern and pre-modern.

The picture painted here may seem too favorable to its subjects. But these pages depict human life's shadow side, especially abuse of power and authority up and down the social scale, as unsparingly as voluminous documentation allowed. No one will mistake Stavenow lordship

for New Jerusalem. The evidence for this study's arguments and conclusions is much deeper and more far-ranging than any ever assembled
for the once regnant, relentlessly negative views, whose validity I was no
more inclined to doubt, upon embarking on this research, than other
liberal-minded historians. This study's discoveries, highlighting – among
other findings rehearsed in this conclusion – seigneurial authority's
limits, the Prussian state's largely autonomous and frequently construc-
tive actions, and the subject villagers' talent for insubordination and
self-defense, rise out of the archival depths like islands of solid rock. If
their implications for German history seem far-reaching, so they are
meant to be.

Bibliography

This bibliography includes sources and literature underpinning the present book as well as the author's articles on related themes.

UNPUBLISHED ARCHIVAL RECORDS

GEHEIMES STAATSARCHIV PREUßISCHER KULTURBESITZ (GStAPK), BERLIN

Provinz Brandenburg

Rep. 37: Gutsherrschaft Stavenow, no. 43. 728 folders
Rep. 2A: Gutsarchiv Kletze, no. 1
Rep. 2A: Kurmärkische Kriegs- und Domänenkammer. Domänenregistratur: Amt Eldenburg
Rep. 6A: Ältere Kreisbehörden: Prignitz, no. 11 (1808)
Rep. 16, no. 95: Amt Brüssow-Löcknitz: Kirchenregister von Rossow, 1651–96

I. Hauptabteilung

Rep. 22, Nr. 72a, Fasz. 11: Bauernunruhen in der Prignitz (1650s)
Rep. 22, Nr. 72a, Fasz. 14–15: Klagen der Ritterschaft in der Priegnitz gegen aufgewiegelte Untertanen, 1701–3 and related documents

BRANDENBURGISCHES LANDESARCHIV, POTSDAM

Provinz Brandenburg, Rep. 2, D. 42: Prignitz Kreis-Direktorium, 1786–94

PFARRAMT BLÜTHEN

Parish Register, 1694–1800, with accompanying statistical tables compiled by Pastor Karl Gross.

PUBLISHED DOCUMENTS, STATISTICS, AND REFERENCE WORKS

Behre, Otto. *Geschichte der Statistik in Brandenburg-Preussen bis zur Gründung des Königlich Statistischen Bureaus.* Berlin, 1905.

Bratring, F. W. A. *Statistisch-Topographische Beschreibung der gesamten Mark Brandenburg*, 3 vols. Berlin, 1804–9 (reprint: Berlin, 1968).

Breysig, Kurt. *Geschichte der brandenburgischen Finanzen in der Zeit von 1640 bis 1697: Darstellung und Akten: Erster Band*. Leipzig, 1895.

Enders, Lieselott, ed. *Historisches Ortslexikon für Brandenburg, I: Prignitz*. Weimar, 1962.

Fidicin, Ernst, ed. *Kaiser Karl's IV. Landbuch der Mark Brandenburg*. Berlin, 1865.

Friedensburg, Walter, ed. *Kurmärkische Ständeakten aus der Regierungszeit Kurfürst Joachims II (1535–1571)*. 2 vols. Munich, 1913–16.

Herold, Victor, ed. *Die brandenburgischen Kirchenvisitations-Abschiede und -Register des XVI. und XVII. Jahrhunderts*. Band I: *Die Prignitz*. Berlin, 1931.

Isaacsohn, Siegfried, ed. *Urkunden und Aktenstücke zur Geschichte des Kurfürsten Friedrich Wilhelm von Brandenburg. Zehnter Band. Ständische Verhandlungen. Zweiter Band: Mark Brandenburg*. Berlin, 1880.

Krug, Leopold. *Betrachtungen über den National-Reichthum des preußischen Staats, und über den Wohlstand seiner Bewohner*. 2 vols. Berlin, 1805.

Mylius, Christian Otto, ed. *Corpus Constitutionum Marchicarum*. 6 vols. Berlin, 1737–51.

Naudé, Walter. *Die Getreidehandelspolitik und Kriegsmagazinverwaltung Brandenburg-Preussens bis 1740. Acta Borussica: Die Getreidehandelspolitik*, 4 vols. Berlin, 1896–1931.

Novum Corpus Constitutionum Prussico-Brandenburgensium. Berlin, 1751–1801.

Rachel, Hugo. *Die Handels-, Zoll-und Akzisepolitik Brandenburg-Preussens bis 1713. Acta Borussica. Handels-. Zoll- und Akzisepolitik*. 3 vols. Berlin, 1911–28.

Riedel, Adolph Friedrich, ed. *Codex diplomaticus Brandenburgensis*. 41 vols. Berlin, 1838–69. Riedel's fifty-one documents on Stavenow (Series A, II), spanning the years 1263–1548, supplement the estate archive.

Schultze, Johannes, ed. *Das Landbuch der Mark Brandenburg von 1375*. Berlin, 1940.

Schiller, K. and A. Lübben. *Mittelniederdeutsches Wörterbuch*. 6 vols. Wiesbaden, 1969.

Stadelmann, Rudolph, ed. *Preussens Könige in ihrer Thätigkeit für die Landwirtschaft*. 3 vols. Leipzig, 1878–87.

Vogel, Werner, ed. *Prignitz-Kataster, 1686–1697*. Cologne/Vienna, 1985.

Wöhner, Paul Gottlieb. *Steuerverfassung des platten Landes der Kurmark Brandenburg*, 3 vols. Berlin, 1805.

LOCAL AND REGIONAL STUDIES OF BRANDENBURG-PRUSSIAN NOBLE LORDSHIPS, VILLAGES, AND CROWN ESTATES

Albrecht, Gerhard. "Die Gutsherrschaft Freyenstein." Dissertation, Pädagogische Hoschschule Potsdam, Historisch-Philologische Fakultät, 1968.

Brinkmann, Carl. *Wustrau. Wirtschafts- und Verfassungsgeschichte eines brandenburgischen Ritterguts*. Leipzig, 1911.

Geschichte des Geschlechts von Bredow: Herausgegeben im Auftrage der Geschlechtsgenossen. 3 vols. Halle, 1872–90.

Göse, Frank. "Zur Geschichte des neumärkischen Adels im 17./18. Jahrhundert – Ein Beitrag zum Problem des ständischen Regionalismus." *Forschungen zur brandenburgischen und preußischen Geschichte – Neue Folge* 7 (1997): 2–47.

Hahn, Peter-Michael. *Fürstliche Territorialhoheit und lokale Adelsgewalt: Die herrschaftliche Durchdringung des ländlichen Raumes zwischen Elbe und Aller (1300–1700).* Berlin, 1989.

Harnisch, Hartmut. *Die Herrschaft Boitzenburg.* Weimar, 1968.

Iida, Takashi. "Hof, Vermögen, Familie 1700–1820: Die brandenburgischen Dörfer Manker und Wustrau (Kreis Ruppin) im Vergleich." *Jahrbuch für brandenburgische Landesgeschichte* 50 (1999): 142–82.

Kaak, Heinrich. "Vermittelte, selbsttätige und maternale Herrschaft. Formen gutsherrlicher Durchsetzung, Behauptung und Gestaltung in Quilitz-Friedland (Lebus/Oberbarnim) im 18. Jahrhundert," in Jan Peters, ed., *Konflikt und Kontrolle in Gutsherrschaftsgesellschaften. Über Resistenz und Herrschaftsverhalten in ländlichen Sozialgebilden der frühen Neuzeit.* Göttingen, 1995: 54–117.

"Untertanen und Herrschaft gemeinschaftlich im Konflikt. Der Streit um die Nutzung des Kietzer Sees in der östlichen Kurmark 1792–1797," in Jan Peters, ed., *Gutsherrschaftsgesellschaften im europäischen Vergleich.* Berlin, 1997: 325–42.

"Brandenburgische Bauern im 18. Jahrhundert. Sozialgeschichtliche Untersuchungen in mikrohistorischer Perspektive," in Ralf Pröve and Bernd Kölling, eds., *Leben und Arbeiten auf märkischem Sand. Wege in die Gesellschaftsgeschichte Brandenburgs, 1700–1914.* Bielefeld, 1999: 120–48.

Kiekebusch, Werner von. "Geschichte des Klosters Heiligengrabe seit der Reformation." Unpub. ms., 1949, in GStAPK, Provinz Brandenburg, Rep. 16, no. 16.

Motsch, Christoph Josef. "Herrschaft und Untertänigkeit im Grenzgürtel der Neumark, Hinunterpommerns und Großpolens im 16. und 17. Jahrhundert." *Jahrbuch für brandenburgische Landesgeschichte* 48 (1997): 87–99.

Passow, Siegfried. *Ein märkischer Rittersitz.* 2 vols. Eberswald, 1907.

Peters, Jan, "Inszenierung von Gutsherrschaft im 16. Jahrhundert: Matthias v. Saldern auf Plattenburg-Wilsnack (Prignitz)," in J. Peters, ed., *Konflikt und Kontrolle in Gutsherrschaftsgesellschaften.Über Resistenz und Herrschaftsverhalten in ländlichen Sozialgebilden der frühen Neuzeit.* Göttingen, 1995: 248–86.

with Hartmut Harnisch and Lieselott Enders. *Märkische Bauerntagebücher des 18. und 19. Jahrhunderts. Selbstzeugnisse von Milchviehbauern aus Neuholland.* Veröffentlichungen des Staatsarchivs Potsdam, Bd. XXIII. Weimar 1989.

Pilsach, Christoph Freiherr Senfft von. "Bäuerliche Wirtschaftsverhältnisse in einem neumärkischen Dorf (Land Sternberg) vor der Regulierung der gutsherrlich-bäuerlichen Verhältnisse und der erste dortige Regulierungsversuch." *Forschungen zur brandenburgischen und preussischen Geschichte* 23:2 (1909): 127–91.

Rappe, Susanne. "'Wann er nicht bei seinem SchultzenRechte nicht bleiben könte.' Ein Dorfschulze zwischen Gutsherrschaft, Gemeinde und Selbstbehauptung im Gericht Gartow (Elbe) um 1700," in Jan Peters, ed., *Konflikt und Kontrolle in Gutsherrschaftsgesellschaften. Über Resistenz und Herrschaftsverhalten in ländlichen Sozialgebilden der frühen Neuzeit.* Göttingen, 1995: 287–314.

Roth, James L. "The East Prussian *Domaenenpaechter* in the Eighteenth Century: A Study of Collective Social Mobility." Ph.D. dissertation, University of California, Berkeley, 1979.

Sack, Joachim. *Die Herrschaft Stavenow.* Cologne/Graz, 1959.

Simon, Johannes. "Kloster Heiligengrabe: Von der Gründung bis zur Einführung der Reformation, 1287–1549." *Jahrbuch für brandenburgische Kirchengeschichte* 24 (1929): 3–136.

Vogler, Günter. "Die Entwicklung der feudalen Arbeitsrente in Brandenburg vom 15. bis 18. Jahrhundert. Eine Analyse für das kurmärkische Domänenamt Badingen." *Jahrbuch für Wirtschaftsgeschichte* 1 (1966): 142–74.

Wentz, Gottfried. *Das Wirtschaftsleben des altmärkischen Klosters Diesdorf im ausgehenden Mittelalter.* Berlin, 1922.

Wichmann, Max. "Die Höfe von Breddin (Prignitz) von der ersten Erwähnung bis zur Gegenwart." Unpublished ms., 1941, in GStA-PK, Provinz Brandenburg. Rep. 16, no. 97.

Wille, Ulrich. *Das Urbarium von Abbendorf und Haverland 1786.* Goslar, 1938.

LITERATURE ON THE BRANDENBURG-PRUSSIAN AND GERMAN EAST-ELBIAN NOBLE LORDSHIP–VILLAGE RELATIONSHIP, AND ON NOBILITY AND VILLAGERS IN GENERAL

Aubin, Gustav. *Zur Geschichte des gutsherrlich-bäuerlichen Verhältnisses in Ostpreussen von der Gründung des Ordensstaates bis zur Steinschen Reform.* Leipzig, 1910.

Bentzien, Ulrich. "Der Häker." *Deutsches Jahrbuch für Volkskunde* 11 (1965): 16–34.

Carsten, Francis L. *History of the Prussian Junkers.* Brookfield, VT, 1989 (German original: 1988).

Dickler, Robert A. "Organization and Change in Productivity in Eastern Prussia," in William N. Parker and Eric L. Jones, eds., *European Peasants and their Markets.* Princeton, NJ, 1975: 269–92.

Enders, Lieselott. *Die Uckermark. Geschichte einer kurmärkischen Landschaft vom 12. bis zum 18. Jahrhundert.* Weimar, 1992.

"Die Landgemeinde in Brandenburg. Grundzüge ihrer Funktion und Wirkungsweise vom 13. bis zum 18. Jahrhundert." *Blätter für deutsche Landesgeschichte* 129 (1993): 195–256.

"'Aus drängender Not.' Die Verschuldung des gutsherrlichen Adels der Mark Brandenburg im 17. Jahrhundert." *Jahrbuch für die Geschichte Mittel- und Ostdeutschlands* 41 (1993): 3–24.

"Emanzipation der Agrargesellschaft im 18. Jahrhundert – Trends und Gegentrends in der Mark Brandenburg," in Jan Peters, ed., *Konflikt und*

Kontrolle in Gutsherrschaftsgesellschaften.Über Resistenz und Herrschaftsverhalten in ländlichen Sozialgebilden der frühen Neuzeit. Göttingen, 1995: 404–33.

"Die Vermögensverhältnisse des Prignitzer Adels im 18. Jahrhundert." *Jahrbuch für brandenburgische Landesgeschichte* 47 (1996): 76–93.

"Bürgerlicher Kommunalismus zwischen Stadtherrschaft und Ratsobrigkeit in der Mark Brandenburg vom Ende des 15. bis zum Beginn des 17. Jahrhunderts, untersucht am Beispiel der Prignitz." *Jahrbuch für brandenburgische Landesgeschichte* 48 (1997): 37–68.

"Das bäuerliche Besitzrecht in der Mark Brandenburg, untersucht am Beispiel der Prignitz vom 13. bis 18. Jahrhundert," in Jan Peters, ed., *Gutsherrschaftsgesellschaften im europäischen Vergleich.* Berlin, 1997: 399–427.

"Nichts als Ehr', Lieb's und Gut's. Soziale Konflikt- und Ausgleichspotenzen in der Frühneuzeit," in Axel Lubinski et al., *Historie und Eigen-Sinn.* Weimar, 1997: 141–61.

Engel, Evamarie and Benedykt Zientara. *Feudalstruktur, Lehnbürgertum und Fernhandel im spätmittelalterlichen Brandenburg.* Weimar, 1967.

Görlitz, Walter. *Die Junker: Adel und Bauer im deutschen Osten.* Glücksburg, 1957.

Grossmann, Friedrich. *Über die gutsherrlich-bäuerlichen Rechtsverhältnisse in der Mark Brandenburg vom 16. bis 18. Jahrhundert.* Leipzig, 1890.

Hahn, Peter-Michael. *Struktur und Funktion des brandenburgischen Adels im 16. Jahrhundert.* Berlin, 1979.

"Adel und Landesherrschaft in der Mark Brandenburg im späten Mittelalter und der frühen Neuzeit." *Jahrbuch für brandenburgische Landesgeschichte* 38 (1987): 43–57.

Harnisch, Hartmut. "Die Gutsherrschaft in Brandenburg. Ergebnisse und Probleme." *Jahrbuch für Wirtschaftsgeschichte* 4 (1969): 117–47.

"Zur Herausbildung und Funktionsweise von Gutswirtschaft und Gutsherrschaft." *Jahrbuch für Regionalgeschichte* 4 (1972): 178–99.

"Klassenkämpfe der Bauern in der Mark Brandenburg zwischen frühbürgerlicher Revolution und Dreissigjährigem Krieg." *Jahrbuch für Regionalgeschichte* 5 (1975): 142–72.

Bauern – Feudaladel – Städtebürgertum. Untersuchungen über die Zusammenhänge zwischen Feudalrente, bäuerlicher und gutsherrlicher Warenproduktion und den Ware-Geld-Beziehungen in der Magdeburger Börde und dem nordöstlichen Harzvorland von der frühbürgerlichen Revolution bis zum Dreißigjährigen Krieg. Weimar, 1980.

"Bäuerliche Ökonomie und Mentalität unter den Bedingungen der ostelbischen Gutsherrschaft in den letzten Jahrzehnten vor Beginn der Agrarreformen." *Jahrbuch für Wirtschaftsgeschichte* 3 (1989): 87–108.

"Grundherrschaft oder Gutsherrschaft. Zu den wirtschaftlichen Grundlagen des niederen Adels in Norddeutschland zwischen spätmittelalterlicher Agrarkrise und Dreißigjährigem Krieg," in Rudolf Endres, ed., *Adel in der Frühneuzeit. Ein regionaler Vergleich.* Cologne, 1991: 73–98.

"Die Landgemeinde im ostelbischen Gebiet (mit Schwerpunkt Brandenburg)," in Peter Blickle, ed., *Landgemeinde und Stadtgemeinde in Mitteleuropa. Ein struktureller Vergleich.* Munich, 1991: 309–32.

Heinrich, Gerd. *Der Adel in Brandenburg-Preussen.* Darmstadt, 1965.

Kaak, Heinrich. *Die Gutsherrschaft. Theoriegeschichtliche Untersuchungen zum Agrarwesen im ostelbischen Raum.* Berlin, 1991.

Knapp, Georg Friedrich. *Die Bauernbefreiung und der Ursprung der Landarbeiter in den älteren Theilen Preussens.* 2 vols. Leipzig, 1887.

Die Landarbeiter in Knechtschaft und Freiheit. Leipzig, 1909.

Korth, Siegfried. "Die Entstehung und Entwicklung des ostdeutschen Grossgrundbesitzes." *Jahrbuch der Albertus-Universität zu Königsberg/Pr.* 3 (1953): 148–70.

Kratz, Gustav. *Geschichte des Geschlechts von Kleist.* 3 vols. Berlin, 1862–85.

Lennhoff, Ernst. *Das ländliche Gesindewesen in der Kurmark Brandenburg vom 16. bis 19. Jahrhundert.* Breslau, 1906.

Lubinski, Axel. "Die Realisierung von Gutsherrschaft und Erfahrungen mit Untertänigkeit. Das Beispiel Galenbeck in Mecklenburg (1719–1748)," in Jan Peters, ed., *Konflikt und Kontrolle in Gutsherrschaftsgesellschaften. Über Resistenz und Herrschaftsverhalten in ländlichen Sozialgebilden der frühen Neuzeit.* Göttingen, 1995: 201–47.

"Gutsherrschaft als lokale Gesellschaft und Konfliktgemeinschaft," in Axel Lubinski et al., *Historie und Eigen-Sinn.* Weimar, 1997: 237–60.

"Ländliches Kreditwesen und Gutsherrschaft. Zur Verschuldung des Adels in Mecklenburg-Strelitz im 18. Jahrhundert," in Jan Peters, ed., *Gutsherrschaftsgesellschaften im europäischen Vergleich.* Berlin, 1997: 133–75.

Mager, Friedrich. *Geschichte des Bauerntums und der Bodenkultur im Lande Mecklenburg.* Berlin, 1955.

Martiny, Fritz. *Die Adelsfrage in Preussen vor 1806 als politisches und soziales Problem.* Stuttgart, 1938.

North, Michael. "Untersuchungen zur adligen Gutswirtschaft im Herzogtum Preußen des 16. Jahrhunderts." *Vierteljahrschrift für Sozial- und Wirtschaftsgeschichte* 70 (1983): 1–20.

Peters, Jan. "Ostelbische Landarmut–Sozialökonomisches über landlose und landarme Agrarproduzenten im Spätfeudalismus." *Jahrbuch für Wirtschaftsgeschichte* 5 (1970): 97–126.

"Eigensinn und Widerstand im Alltag. Abwehrverhalten ostelbischer Bauern unter Refeudalisierungsdruck." *Jahrbuch für Wirtschaftsgeschichte* 2 (1991): 85–103.

Plaul, Hainer. *Landarbeiterleben im 19. Jahrhundert.* Berlin, 1979.

Rach, Hans-Jürgen and Bernhard Weissel, eds. *Landwirtschaft und Kapitalismus: Zur Entwicklung der ökonomischen und sozialen Verhältnisse in der Magdeburger Börde vom Ausgang des 18. Jahrhunderts bis zum Ende des ersten Weltkrieges.* 2 vols. Berlin, 1978–9.

Rosenberg, Hans. "The Rise of the Junkers in Brandenburg-Prussia, 1410–1653." *American Historical Review* 49 (1943–4): 1–22, 228–42.

"Die Pseudodemokratisierung der Rittergutsbesitzerklasse," in Hans-Ulrich Wehler, ed., *Moderne deutsche Sozialgeschichte.* Cologne, 1968: 287–308.

"Die Ausprägung der Junkerherrschaft in Brandenburg-Preussen, 1410–1618," in H. Rosenberg, *Machteliten und Wirtschaftskonjunkturen.*

Studien zur neueren deutschen Sozial- und Wirtschaftsgeschichte. Göttingen, 1978: 24–82.

Schilling, Renate. *Schwedisch-Pommern um 1700. Studien zur Agrarstruktur eines Territoriums extremer Gutsherrschaft.* Weimar, 1989.

Schultz, Helga. "Bäuerliche Klassenkämpfe zwischen frühbürgerlicher Revolution und Dreissigjährigem Krieg." *Zeitschrift für Geschichtswissenschaft* 2 (1972): 156–73.

Vogler, Günter. "Probleme des bäuerlichen Klassenkampfes in der Mark Brandenburg im Spätfeudalismus." *Acta Universitatis Carolinae: Studia Historica* (Prague) 11 (1974): 75–94.

Wernicke, Kurt. "Untersuchungen zu den niederen Formen des bäuerlichen Klassenkampfes im Gebiet der Gutsherrschaft." Diss. Phil., Humboldt Universität, Berlin, 1962.

Wille, Ulrich. *Die ländliche Bevölkerung des Osthavellandes vom Dreissigjährigen Krieg bis zur Bauernbefreiung.* Berlin, 1937.

Wunder, Heide. "Zur Mentalität aufständischer Bauern. Möglichkeiten der Zusammenarbeit von Geschichtswissenschaft und Anthropologie, dargestellt am Beispiel des Samländischen Bauernaufstandes von 1525," in Hans-Ulrich Wehler, ed., *Der Deutsche Bauernkrieg 1524–1526.* Göttingen, 1975: 9–37.

"Peasant Organization and Class Conflict in East and West Germany." *Past and Present* 78 (1978): 47–55.

Ziekursch, Johannes. *Hundert Jahre schlesischer Agrargeschichte.* Breslau, 1927.

WORKS ON BRANDENBURG-PRUSSIAN ECONOMIC AND AGRARIAN HISTORY, INCLUDING MONETARY AND METROLOGICAL SYSTEMS

Aubin, Hermann and Wolfgang Zorn, eds. *Handbuch der deutschen Wirtschafts- und Sozialgeschichte.* 2 vols. Stuttgart, 1971–6.

Bahrfeldt, Emil. *Das Münzwesen der Mark Brandenburg.* 3 vols. Berlin, 1889–1913.

Berthold, Rudolf. "Die Veränderungen im Bodeneigentum und in der Zahl der Bauernstellen, der Kleinstellen, und der Rittergüter in den preussischen Provinzen Sachsen, Brandenburg und Pommern während der Durchführung der Agrarreformen des 19. Jahrhunderts." *Jahrbuch für Wirtschaftsgeschichte* Sonderband (1978): 10–116.

Corni, Gustavo. *Stato assoluto e società agraria in Prussia nell'età di Frederico II.* Bologna, 1982.

"Absolutistische Agrarpolitik und Agrargesellschaft in Preussen." *Zeitschrift für historische Forschung* 13 (1986): 285–313.

Franz, Günther. *Der Dreissigjährige Krieg und das deutsche Volk.* Fourth edn. Stuttgart, 1979.

Goltz, Theodor Frh. von der. *Die Lage der ländlichen Arbeiter im Deutschen Reich.* Berlin, 1875.

Hagen, William W. "How Mighty the Junkers? Peasant Rents and Seigneurial Profits in Sixteenth-Century Brandenburg." *Past and Present* 108 (1985): 80–116.

"The Junkers' Faithless Servants: Peasant Insubordination and the Breakdown of Serfdom in Brandenburg-Prussia, 1763–1811," in Richard Evans and W. R. Lee, eds., *The German Peasantry. Conflict and Community in Rural Society from the Eighteenth to the Twentieth Centuries.* London, 1986: 71–101.

"Working for the Junker: The Standard of Living of Manorial Laborers in Brandenburg, 1584–1810." *Journal of Modern History* 58 (1986): 143–58.

"Seventeenth-Century Crisis in Brandenburg: The Thirty Years' War, the Destabilization of Serfdom, and the Rise of Absolutism." *American Historical Review* 94 (1989): 302–35.

"Der bäuerliche Lebensstandard unter brandenburgischer Gutsherrschaft im 18. Jahrhundert. Die Dörfer der Herrschaft Stavenow in vergleichender Sicht," in Jan Peters, ed., *Gutsherrschaft als soziales Modell. Historische Zeitschrift, Beiheft* 18 (Munich, 1995): 178–96.

"Glaube und Skepsis eines magischen Schatzgräbers. Ein Fall aus der Prignitz und Mecklenburg aus den 1760er Jahren," in Axel Lubinski et al., eds., *Historie und Eigen-Sinn.* Weimar, 1997: 175–86.

"Village Life in East-Elbian Germany and Poland, 1400–1800: Subjection, Self-Defense, Survival," in Tom Scott, ed., *The Peasantries of Europe from the Fourteenth to the Eighteenth Centuries.* London, 1998: 145–90.

"Prussia," in Joel Mokyr, ed., *The Oxford Encyclopedia of Economic History* (forthcoming).

Harnisch, Hartmut. "Statistische Untersuchungen zum Verlauf der kapitalistischen Agrarreformen in den preussischen Ostprovinzen (1811 bis 1865)." *Jahrbuch für Wirtschaftsgeschichte* 4 (1974): 149–83.

"Die agrarpolitischen Reformmassnahmen der preussischen Staatsführung in dem Jahrzehnt vor 1806/07." *Jahrbuch für Wirtschaftsgeschichte* 3 (1977): 129–53.

"Vom Oktoberedikt des Jahres 1807 zur Deklaration von 1816. Problematik und Charakter der preussischen Agrarreformgesetzgebung zwischen 1807 and 1816." *Jahrbuch für Wirtschaftsgeschichte* Sonderband (1978): 231–93.

Kapitalistische Agrarreform und Industrielle Revolution. Agrarhistorische Untersuchungen über das ostelbische Preußen zwischen Spätfeudalismus und bürgerlich-demokratischer Revolution von 1848/49 unter besonderer Berücksichtigung der Provinz Brandenburg. Veröffentlichungen des Staatsarchivs Potsdam, Bd. XIX. Weimar, 1984.

Helbig, Herbert. *Gesellschaft und Wirtschaft in der Mark Brandenburg im Mittelalter.* Berlin, 1973.

Hinrichs, Carl. *Die Wollindustrie in Preussen unter Friedrich Wilhelm I.* Berlin, 1933.

Hinze, Kurt. *Die Arbeiterfrage zu Beginn des modernen Kapitalismus in Brandenburg-Preussen, 1685–1806.* Berlin, 1927.

Jesse, Wilhelm. *Der wendische Münzverein.* Braunschweig, 1967.

Kaak, Heinrich. "Zum Jahresablauf in Dörfern am Rande des Oderbruchs," in Axel Lubinski et al., eds., *Historie und Eigen-Sinn.* Weimar, 1997: 175–86.

Kaufhold, Karl Heinrich. "Leistungen und Grenzen der Staatswirtschaft," in Manfred Schlenke, ed., *Preussen: Beiträge zu einer politischen Kultur.* Hamburg, 1981: 106–19.

Krüger, Horst. *Zur Geschichte der Manufakturen und der Manufakturarbeiter in Preussen.* Berlin, 1958.

Langelüddecke, Erich. "Zum Grundsatz der Entschädigung und des Loskaufs bei den Eigentumsregulierungen und Dienstablösungen der ostelbischen Bauern Preussens im 19. Jh." *Zeitschrift für Geschichtswissenschaft* 4 (1960): 890–908.

Melton, Edgar. "The Decline of Prussian *Gutsherrschaft* and the Rise of the Junker as Rural Patron, 1750–1806." *German History* 12 (1994): 286–307.

Mooser, Josef. "Preußische Agrarreformen, Bauern und Kapitalismus. Bemerkungen zu Hartmut Harnischs Buch 'Kapitalistische Agrarreformen und Industrielle Revolution.'" *Geschichte und Gesellschaft* 18 (1992): 533–54.

Müller, Hans-Heinrich. *Märkische Landwirtschaft vor den Reformen von 1807. Entwicklungstendenzen des Ackerbaues in der zweiten Hälfte des 18. Jahrhunderts.* Veröffentlichungen des Bezirksheimatmuseums Potsdam, Heft 13. Potsdam, 1967.

North, Michael. "Die Entstehung der Gutswirtschaft im südlichen Ostseeraum." *Zeitschrift für Historische Forschung* 26 (1999): 43–59.

Peschke, Werner. *Das Mühlenwesen der Mark Brandenburg. Von den Anfängen der Mark bis um 1600.* Berlin, 1937.

Rachel, Hugo, Johannes Papritz, and Paul Wallich. *Berliner Grosskaufleute und Kapitalisten.* 2 vols. Berlin, 1967 (reprint of original of 1934–8).

Saalfeld, Dietrich. "Zur Frage des bäuerlichen Landverlustes im Zusammenhang mit den preussischen Agarreformen." *Zeitschrift für Agrargeschichte und Agrarsoziologie* 11:1 (1963): 163–71.

Schäfer, Karl Heinrich. "Märkischer Geldkurs, Preise und Löhne in früheren Jahrhunderten." *Wichmann-Jahrbuch* 1 (1930): 74–90.

Schissler, Hanna. *Preußische Agrargesellschaft im Wandel. Wirtschaftliche, gesellschaftliche und politische Transformationsprozesse von 1763 bis 1847.* Göttingen, 1978.

Schulze, Hans K. "Die Besiedlung der Mark Brandenburg im hohen und späten Mittelalter." *Jahrbuch für die Geschichte Mittel- und Ostdeutschlands* 28 (1979): 42–178.

Treue, Wilhelm. *Wirtschafts- und Technikgeschichte Preussens.* Berlin, 1984.

WORKS ON GERMAN AND EUROPEAN ECONOMIC, SOCIAL, FAMILY, AND DEMOGRAPHIC HISTORY

Abel, Wilhelm. *Geschichte der deutschen Landwirtschaft.* Stuttgart, 1962.

Massenarmut und Hungerkrisen im vorindustriellen Europa. Hamburg/Berlin, 1974.

Die Wüstungen des ausgehenden Mittelalters. Stuttgart, 1976.

Agrarkrisen und Agrarkonjunktur: Eine Geschichte der Land-und Ernährungswirtschaft Mitteleuropas seit dem hohen Mittelalter. Third edn. Hamburg, 1978.

Strukturen und Krisen der spätmittelalterlichen Wirtschaft. Stuttgart, 1980.

Achilles, Walter. *Vermögensverhältnisse braunschweigischer Bauernhöfe im 17. und 18. Jahrhundert.* Quellen und Forschungen zur Agrargeschichte, Bd. XIII. Stuttgart 1965.

Landwirtschaft in der frühen Neuzeit. Enzyklopädie deutscher Geschichte, Bd. X. Munich, 1991.

Aston, T. H. and C. E. Philpin, eds. *The Brenner Debate. Agrarian Class Structure and Economic Development in Pre-Industrial Europe.* Cambridge, 1985.

Bath, B. H. Slicher van. *The Agrarian History of Western Europe A.D. 500–1850.* London, 1963.

Beck, Rainer. *Unterfinning. Ländliche Welt vor Anbruch der Moderne.* Munich, 1993.

Blackbourn, David and Richard J. Evans, eds. *The German Bourgeoisie. Essays on the Social History of the German Middle Class from the Late Eighteenth to the Early Twentieth Century.* London, 1991.

Blickle, Peter. *The Revolution of 1525: The German Peasants' War from a New Perspective.* Baltimore, MD, 1981 (German original: 1975).

Deutsche Untertanen: Ein Widerspruch. Munich, 1981.

"Begriffsverfremdung. Über den Umgang mit dem wissenschaftlichen Ordnungsbegriff Kommunalismus." *Zeitschrift für Historische Forschung* 22 (1995): 246–53.

Blickle, Peter, ed. *Aufruhr und Empörung. Studien zum bäuerlichen Widerstand im Alten Reich.* Munich, 1980.

Blickle, Renate. "*Hausnotdurft.* Ein Fundamentalrecht in der altständischen Ordnung Bayerns," in Günter Birtsch, ed., *Grund- und Freiheitsrechte von der ständischen zur spätbürgerlichen Gesellschaft.* Göttingen, 1987: 42–64.

Blum, Jerome. "The Rise of Serfdom in Eastern Europe." *American Historical Review* 62 (1957): 807–35.

The End of the Old Order in Rural Europe. Princeton, NJ, 1978.

Blum, Jerome, ed. *Our Forgotten Past: Seven Centuries of Life on the Land.* London, 1982.

Bogucka, Maria. "The Role of Baltic Trade in European Development from the XVIth to the XVIIIth Centuries." *Journal of European Economic History* 9 (1980): 5–20.

Bowman, Shearer David. *Masters and Lords: Mid-19th-Century U.S. Planters and Prussian Junkers.* New York, 1993.

Bräker, Ulrich. *Das Leben und die Abentheuer des Armen Mannes im Tockenburg.* Zürich, 1788.

Brakensiek, Stefan. *Agrarreform und ländliche Gesellschaft. Die Privatisierung der Marken in Nordwestdeutschland 1750–1850.* Forschungen zur Regionalgeschichte, Bd. I. Paderborn, 1991.

Braudel, Fernand. *Civilization and Capitalism 15th–18th Century.* 3 vols. New York, 1981–4 (French original: 1979).

Brose, Eric Dorn. *The Politics of Technological Change in Prussia: Out of the Shadow of Antiquity, 1809–1848.* Princeton, 1993.

Brunner, Otto. *Land and Lordship. Structures of Governance in Medieval Austria*, edited and translated by Howard Kaminsky and James Van Horn Melton. Philadelphia, 1984 (German original: 1939).

Adeliges Landleben und europäischer Geist. Salzburg, 1949.

Byres, Terence J. *Capitalism from Above and Capitalism from Below: An Essay in Comparative Political Economy.* London, 1996.

Chirot, Daniel, ed. *The Origins of Economic Backwardness in Eastern Europe. Economics and Politics from the Middle Ages until the Early Twentieth Century.* Berkeley, 1989.

Christiansen, Palle. *A Manorial World. Lord, Peasants and Cultural Distinctions on a Danish Estate 1750–1980.* Copenhagen, 1996.

Colburn, Forrest D., ed. *Everyday Forms of Peasant Resistance.* London, 1989.

Conrad, Christoph. *Vom Greis zum Renter. Der Strukturwandel des Alters in Deutschland zwischen 1830 und 1930* (Göttingen, 1994).

Cunningham, Hugh. *Children and Childhood in Western Society since 1500.* London, 1995.

De Vries, Jan. *The Dutch Rural Economy in the Golden Age.* New Haven, CT, 1974. *The Economy of Europe in an Age of Crisis, 1600–1750.* Cambridge, 1976.

Dewald, Jonathan. *The European Nobility, 1400–1800.* Cambridge, 1996.

Dillwitz, Sigrid. "Die Struktur der Bauernschaft von 1871 bis 1914. Dargestellt auf der Grundlage der deutschen Reichsstatistik." *Jahrbuch für Geschichte* 9 (1973): 65–109.

Dipper, Christoph. *Die Bauernbefreiung in Deutschland 1790–1850.* Stuttgart, 1980. "Übergangsgesellschaft. Die ländliche Sozialordnung in Mitteleuropa um 1800." *Zeitschrift für Historische Forschung* 23 (1996): 57–87.

Dülmen, Richard van. *Kultur und Alltag in der frühen Neuzeit.* 2 vols. Munich, 1990–2.

Elias, Norbert. *The Civilizing Process.* 2 vols. New York, 1978 (German original: 1938). *The Court Society.* Oxford, 1983 (German original: 1969).

Enders, Lieselott. "Weise Frauen – böse Zauberinnen: Hexenverfolgung in der Prignitz im 16. und 17. Jahrhundert." *Jahrbuch für brandenburgische Landesgeschichte* 49 (1998): 19–37.

Evans, Richard J. *Death in Hamburg. Society and Politics in the Cholera Years, 1830–1910.* London, 1987. *Rituals of Retribution. Capital Punishment in Germany, 1600–1987.* London, 1996. *Szenen aus der deutschen Unterwelt. Verbrechen und Strafen, 1800–1914.* Reinbek, 1997.

Franz, Günther. *Geschichte des deutschen Bauernstandes.* Stuttgart, 1970.

Frevert, Ute. *Women in German History. From Bourgeois Emancipation to Sexual Liberation.* Oxford, 1989 (German original, 1986).

Frey, Manuel. *Der reinliche Bürger. Entstehung und Verbreitung bürgerlicher Tugenden in Deutschland, 1760–1860.* Göttingen, 1997.

Flinn, Michael. *The European Demographic System, 1500–1800.* Baltimore, 1981.

Gagliardo, Joseph. *From Pariah to Patriot. The Changing Image of the German Peasant 1770–1840.* Lexington, KY, 1969.

Gleixner, Ulrike. *"Das Mensch" und "der Kerl". Die Konstruktion von Geschlecht in Unzuchtsverfahren der frühen Neuzeit (1700–1760).* Frankfurt/M., 1994.

Göttsch, Silke. *"Alle für einen Mann . . ." Leibeigene und Widerständigkeit in Schleswig-Holstein im 18. Jahrhundert.* Neumünster, 1991.

Gottlieb, Beatrice. *The Family in the Western World from the Black Death to the Industrial Age.* Oxford, 1993.

Gray, Marion W. *Productive Men, Reproductive Women. The Agrarian Household and the Emergence of Separate Spheres during the German Enlightenment.* New York, 2000.

Grießinger, Andreas. *Das symbolische Kapital der Ehre. Streikbewegungen und kollektives Bewußtsein deutscher Handwerksgesellen im 18. Jahrhundert.* Frankfurt/M., 1981.

Hagen, William W. "The German Peasantry in the Nineteenth and Early Twentieth Century: Market Integration, Populist Politics, Votes for Hitler." *Peasant Studies* 14 (1987): 274–91.

"Capitalism and the Countryside in Early Modern Europe: Interpretations, Models, Debates," *Agricultural History* 62 (1988): 13–47.

Harnisch, Hartmut. "Bevölkerung und Wirtschaft. Über die Zusammenhänge zwischen sozialökonomischer und demographischer Entwicklung im Spätfeudalismus." *Jahrbuch für Wirtschaftsgeschichte* 10 (1975): 57–87.

Heitz, Gerhard. "Bauernwirtschaft und Junkerwirtschaft." *Jahrbuch für Wirtschaftsgeschichte* (1964): 80–8.

"Zum Charakter der zweiten Leibeigenschaft." *Zeitschrift für Geschichtswissenschaft* (1972): 24–39.

Heitz, Gerhard et al. *Der Bauer im Klassenkampf.* Berlin, 1975.

Henning, Friedrich-Wilhelm. *Dienste und Abgaben der Bauern im 18. Jahrhundert.* Quellen und Forschungen zur Agrargeschichte, Bd. XXI. Stuttgart, 1969.

"Die Bestimmungsfaktoren der bäuerlichen Einkommen im 18. Jahrhundert." *Jahrbuch für Wirtschaftsgeschichte* 1 (1970): 165–83.

Das vorindustrielle Deutschland 800 bis 1800. Paderborn, 1974.

Hintze, Otto. "Zur Agrarpolitik Friedrichs des Grossen." *Forschungen zur brandenburgischen und preussischen Geschichte* 10 (1898): 275–309.

Hoch, Steven L. *Serfdom and Social Control in Russia: Petrovskoe, a Village in Tambov.* Chicago, 1986.

Höfler, Max. *Deutsches Krankheitsnamen-Buch.* Hildesheim, 1970 (reprint of 1899 original).

Hull, Isabel V. *Sexuality, State, and Civil Society in Germany, 1700–1815.* Ithaca, NY, 1996.

Jacobeit, Sigrid and Wolfgang. *Illustrierte Alltagsgeschichte des deutschen Volkes, 1550–1810.* Leipzig, 1986.

Jones, E. L. *Growth Recurring. Economic Change in World History.* Oxford, 1988.

Jones, E. L. and W. N. Parker, eds. *European Peasants and their Markets. Essays in Agrarian Economic History.* Princeton, NJ, 1975.

Imhof, Arthur E. *Die verlorenen Welten.* Munich, 1984.

Kellenbenz, Hermann. *Deutsche Wirtschaftsgeschichte.* 2 vols. Munich, 1977–81.

Klima, Arnost. "Agrarian Class Structure and Economic Development in Pre-Industrial Bohemia." *Past and Present* 85 (1979): 49–67.

Knodel, John. *Demographic Behavior in the Past: A Study of Fourteen German Village Populations in the Eighteenth and Nineteenth Centuries.* Cambridge, 1988.

Kochanowicz, Jacek. "The Polish Peasant Family as an Economic Unit", in Richard Wall et al., *Family Forms in Historic Europe.* Cambridge, 1983: 153–66.

"*La Théorie Economique . . .* Après Vingt Ans." *Acta Poloniae Historica* 56 (1987): 197–211.

Spór o teorię gospodarki chłopskiej. Gospodarstwo chłopskie w teorii ekonomii i w historii gospodarczej. Warsaw, 1992.

Kramer, Karl-S. and Ulrich Wilkens. *Volksleben in einem holsteinischen Gutsbezirk.* Neumünster, 1979.

Kriedte, Peter. *Spätfeudalismus und Handelskapital. Grundlinien der europäischen Wirtschaftsgeschichte vom 16. bis zum Ausgang des 18. Jahrhunderts.* Göttingen, 1980.

"Spätmittelalterliche Agrarkrise oder Krise des Feudalismus?" *Geschichte und Gesellschaft* 7 (1981): 42–68.

Kriedte, Peter, Hans Medick, and Jürgen Schlumbohm. *Industrialization before Industrialization: Rural Industry in the Genesis of Capitalism.* Cambridge, 1981 (German original: 1977).

Kula, Witold. *An Economic Theory of the Feudal System. Towards a Model of the Polish Economy 1500–1800.* London, 1976 (Polish original: 1962).

"The Seigneury and the Peasant Family in Eighteenth-Century Poland", in Robert Forster and Orest Ranum, eds., *Family and Society. Selections from the Annales.* Baltimore, MD, 1976: 192–203.

Measures and Men. Princeton, NJ, 1986 (Polish original: 1970).

Labouvie, Eva. *Verbotene Künste. Volksmagie und ländlicher Aberglaube in den Dorfgemeinden des Saarraumes (16.–19. Jahrhundert).* St. Ingbert, 1992.

Levi, Giovanni. *Das immaterielle Erbe. Eine bäuerliche Welt an der Schwelle zur Moderne.* Berlin, 1986 (Italian original: 1985).

Lubinski, Axel, Thomas Rudert, and Martina Schattkowsky, eds. *Historie und Eigen-Sinn. Festschrift für Jan Peters zum 65. Geburtstag.* Weimar, 1997.

Luebke, David. *His Majesty's Rebels. Communities, Factions and Rural Revolt in the Black Forest, 1725–1745.* Ithaca, NY, 1997.

Lütge, Friedrich. *Geschichte der deutschen Agrarverfassung.* Stuttgart, 1963.

Macpherson, Gordon, ed. *Black's Medical Dictionary.* 37th edn. London, 1992.

Małowist, Marian. "Über die Frage der Handelspolitik des Adels in den Ostseeländern im 15. und 16. Jahrhundert." *Hansische Geschichtsblätter* 75 (1957): 29–47.

Maurer, Michael. *Die Biographie des Bürgers. Lebensformen und Denkweisen in der formativen Phase des deutschen Bürgertums (1680–1815).* Göttingen, 1997.

Medick, Hans. *Weben und Überleben in Laichingen 1650–1900. Lokalgeschichte als Allgemeine Geschichte.* Veröffentlichungen des Max-Planck-Instituts für Geschichte, Bd. CXXVI. Göttingen, 1997.

Medick, Hans and David Sabean, eds. *Interest and Emotion: Essays on the Study of Family and Kinship.* Cambridge, 1984.

Melton, Edgar. "*Gutsherrschaft* in East Elbian Germany and Livonia, 1500–1800: A Critique of the Model." *Central European History* 21 (1988): 315–49.

Mitterauer, Michael and Reinhard Sieder. *The European Family.* Chicago, 1982 (German original: 1977).

Ogilvie, Shilagh and Bob Scribner, eds. *Germany: A New Social and Economic History, 1450–1800.* 2 vols. London, 1996.

Overton, Mark. *Agricultural Revolution in England. The Transformation of the Agrarian Economy 1500–1800.* Cambridge, 1996.

Perkins, J. A. "The Agricultural Revolution in Germany, 1850–1914." *Journal of European Economic History* 10 (1981): 71–118.

Peters, Jan. "Das unbarmherzige Dorf. Eine verhaltensgeschichtliche Studie aus dem südlichen Fläming (1728)." *Jahrbuch für brandenburgische Landesgeschichte* 42 (1991): 65–77.

"Eigensinn und Widerstand im Alltag. Abwehrverhalten ostelbischer Bauern unter Refeudalisierungdruck." *Jahrbuch für Wirtschaftsgeschichte* (1991/2): 85–103.

"Hexerei vor Ort: Erfahrungen und Deutungen in einer Kleingesellschaft der Prignitz. Saldernherrschaft Plattenburg-Wilsnack (1550–1700)." *Jahrbuch für brandenburgische Landesgeschichte* 49 (1998): 38–74.

Peters, Jan, ed. *Gutsherrschaft als soziales Modell. Historische Zeitschrift (Beiheft 18).* Munich, 1995.

Konflikt und Kontrolle in Gutsherrschaftsgesellschaften. Über Resistenz und Herrschaftsverhalten in ländlichen Sozialgebilden der frühen Neuzeit. Veröffentlichungen des Max-Planck-Instituts für Geschichte, Bd. CXX. Göttingen, 1995.

Gutsherrschaftsgesellschaften im europäischen Vergleich. Berlin, 1997.

Postan, M. M. "Economic Relations between Eastern and Western Europe," in Geoffrey Barraclough, ed., *Eastern and Western Europe in the Middle Ages.* London, 1970.

Rebel, Hermann. *Peasant Classes. The Bureaucratization of Property and Family Relations under Early Habsburg Absolutism, 1511–1636.* Princeton, NJ, 1983.

Robisheaux, Thomas. *Rural Society and the Search for Order in Early Modern Germany.* Cambridge, 1989.

Roeck, Bernd. *Lebenswelt und Kultur des Bürgertums in der frühen Neuzeit.* Enzyklopädie deutscher Geschichte, Bd. IX. Munich, 1991.

Rösener, Werner. *Peasants in the Middle Ages.* Urbana, IL, 1992 (German original: 1985).

Sabean, David Warren. *Power in the Blood. Popular Culture and Village Discourse in Early Modern Germany.* Cambridge, 1984.

Property, Production, and Family in Neckarhausen, 1700–1870. Cambridge, 1990.

Kinship in Neckarhausen, 1700–1870. Cambridge, 1998.

Schlumbohm, Jürgen. *Lebensläufe, Familien, Höfe. Die Bauern und Heuerleute des Osnabrückischen Kirchspiels Belm in proto-industrieller Zeit, 1650–1860.* Veröffentlichungen des Max-Planck-Instituts für Geschichte, Bd. CX. Göttingen, 1994.

Schulze, Winfried, ed. *Bäuerlicher Widerstand und feudale Herrschaft in der frühen Neuzeit.* Stuttgart, 1980.

Europäische Bauernrevolten der frühen Neuzeit. Frankfurt, 1982.

Scott, James. *Weapons of the Weak. Everyday Forms of Peasant Resistance.* New Haven, CT, 1985.

Scott, Tom, ed. *The Peasantries of Europe from the Fourteenth to the Eighteenth Centuries.* London, 1998.

Shanin, Teodor, ed. *Peasants and Peasant Societies: Selected Readings.* Oxford, 1987.

Spierenburg, Pieter. *The Broken Spell. A Cultural and Anthropological History of Preindustrial Europe.* New Brunswick, NJ, 1991.

Stuart, Kathleen. *Defiled Trades and Social Outcasts: Honor and Ritual Pollution in Early Modern Germany.* Cambridge, 2000.

Suter, Andreas. "Regionale politische Kulturen von Protest und Widerstand im Spätmittelalter und in der frühen Neuzeit. Die schweizerische Eidgenossenschaft als Beispiel." *Geschichte und Gesellschaft* 21 (1995): 161–94.

"Informations- und Kommunikationsweisen aufständischer Untertanen"; in Jan Peters, ed., *Gutsherrschaftsgesellschaften im europäischen Vergleich*, Berlin, 1997: 55–68.

Taylor, Peter K. *Indentured to Liberty. Peasant Life and the Hessian Military State, 1688–1815.* Ithaca, NY, 1994.

Theibault, John. *German Villages in Crisis: Rural Life in Hesse-Kassel and the Thirty Years' War, 1580–1720.* Atlantic Highlands, NJ, 1995.

Thirsk, Joan, ed. *The Agrarian History of England and Wales,* vol. v: *1640–1750. II: Agrarian Change.* Cambridge, 1985.

Thomas, William I. and Florian Znaniecki, eds. *The Polish Peasant in Europe and America.* 2 vols. New York, 1956. First edn. 1918–20.

Thorner, Daniel, ed. *A. V. Chayanov on the Theory of Peasant Economy.* Madison, WI, 1986.

Topolski, Jerzy. "The Manorial-Serf Economy in Central and Eastern Europe in the 16th and 17th Centuries." *Agricultural History* 48 (1974): 341–52.

"Continuity and Discontinuity in the Development of the Feudal System in Eastern Europe (Xth to XVIIth Centuries)." *Journal of European Economic History* 10 (1981): 373–400.

"Sixteenth-Century Poland and the Turning Point in European Economic Development", in J. F. Federowicz, ed., *A Republic of Nobles. Studies in Polish History to 1864.* Cambridge, 1982: 28–48.

Troßbach, Werner. *Bauern 1648–1806.* Enzyklopädie deutscher Geschichte, Bd. XIX. Munich, 1993.

Wall, Richard et al. *Family Forms in Historic Europe.* Cambridge, 1983.

Wallerstein, Immanuel. *The Modern World-System,* vols. I–II. New York, 1974–80.

Weber, Max. *Die Verhältnisse der Landarbeiter im ostelbischen Deutschland.* Schriften des Vereins für Sozialpolitik, Bd. LV. Leipzig, 1892.

"Capitalism and Rural Society in Germany" (1906) and "National Character and the Junkers" (1917), in H. H. Gerth and C. Wright Mills, eds., *From Max Weber: Essays in Sociology.* Oxford, 1946: 363–95.

Wehler, Hans-Ulrich. *Deutsche Gesellschaftsgeschichte,* Bd. I: *Vom Feudalismus des Alten Reiches bis zur Defensiven Modernisierung der Reformära 1700–1815.* Munich, 1987.

Deutsche Gesellschaftsgeschichte, Bd. II: *Von der Reformära bis zur industriellen und politischen "Deutschen Doppelrevolution" 1815–1845/49*. Munich, 1987.

Wiesner, Merry. *Women and Gender in Early Modern Europe*. Cambridge, 1993.

Wolf, Eric. *Peasants*. Englewood Cliffs, NJ, 1966.

Wrigley, E. A. and R. S. Schofield. *The Population History of England, 1541–1871*. Cambridge, MA, 1981.

Wunder, Heide. *Die bäuerliche Gemeinde in Deutschland*. Göttingen, 1986.

"Er ist die Sonn', sie ist der Mond." Frauen in der Frühen Neuzeit. Munich, 1992.

WORKS ON BRANDENBURG-PRUSSIAN, GENERAL GERMAN, AND EUROPEAN POLITICAL HISTORY, AND ON HISTORIOGRAPHICAL-METHODOLOGICAL QUESTIONS

Anderson, Margaret Lavinia. *Practising Democracy: Elections and Political Culture in Imperial Germany*. Princeton, NJ, 2000.

Asch, Ronald G. "Estates and Princes after 1648: The Consequences of the Thirty Years War." *German History* 6 (1988): 113–32.

Bassewitz, Magnus Friedrich von. *Die Kurmark Brandenburg im Zusammenhang mit den Schicksalen des Gesamtstaats Preussen während der Zeit vom 22. Oktober 1806 bis zu Ende des Jahres 1808*. 3 vols. Leipzig, 1852.

Baumgart, Peter. "Epochen der preußischen Monarchie im 18. Jahrhundert," in Otto Büsch, ed., *Das Preussenbild in der Geschichte. Protokoll eines Symposions*. Berlin, 1981: 65–96.

"Wie absolut war der preussische Absolutismus?" in Manfred Schlenke, ed., *Preussen. Beiträge zu einer politischen Kultur*. Reinbek, 1981: 89–105.

Baumgart, Peter, ed. *Ständetum und Staatsbildung in Brandenburg-Preussen*. Berlin, 1983.

Beck, Hermann. *The Origins of the Authoritarian Welfare State in Prussia. Conservatives, Bureaucracy, and the Social Question, 1815–70*. Ann Arbor, MI, 1995.

Behrens, C. B. A. *Society, Government, and the Enlightenment. The Experiences of Eighteenth-Century France and Prussia*. New York, 1985.

Bercé, Yves-Marie. *Revolt and Revolution in Early Modern Europe: An Essay on the History of Political Violence*. Manchester, 1987 (French original: 1980).

Berdahl, Robert M. *The Politics of the Prussian Nobility. The Development of a Conservative Ideology 1770–1848*. Princeton, NJ, 1988.

Birtsch, Günter. "Friedrich der Grosse und die Aufklärung," in Oswald Hauser, ed., *Friedrich der Große in seiner Zeit*. Cologne/Vienna, 1987: 31–92.

Blackbourn, David. *The Long Nineteenth Century. A History of Germany, 1780–1918*. Oxford, 1997.

Blackbourn, David and Geoff Eley. *The Peculiarities of German History. Bourgeois Society and Politics in Nineteenth-Century Germany*. Oxford, 1984.

Bonnell, Victoria and Lynn Hunt, eds. *Beyond the Cultural Turn. New Directions in the Study of Society and Culture*. Berkeley, CA, 1999.

Brandt, Peter, ed. *Preußen – Zur Sozialgeschichte eines Staates*, vol. III of *Preußen – Versuch einer Bilanz*. Reinbek bei Hamburg, 1981.

Brunschwig, Henri. *La crise de l'état prussien à la fin du XVIIIe siècle et la génèse de la mentalité romantique.* Paris, 1947.

Büsch, Otto. *Militärsystem and Sozialleben im alten Preussen 1713–1807.* Berlin, 1962.

Büsch, Otto, ed. *Das Preussenbild in der Geschichte. Protokoll eines Symposions.* Berlin, 1981.

Büsch, Otto and Michael Erbe, eds. *Otto Hintze und die moderne Geschichtswissenschaft. Ein Tagungsbericht.* Berlin, 1983.

Burns, Rob, ed. *German Cultural Studies: An Introduction.* Oxford, 1995.

Burschel, Peter. "Von Prügel und höherer Kultur. Über eine Quellensammlung zur Sozialgeschichte des preußischen Militärs." *Forschungen zur brandenburgischen und preußischen Geschichte, Neue Folge* 3 (1993): 251–4.

Carsten, Francis L. *The Origins of Prussia.* Oxford, 1954.

Deppermann, Klaus. "Der preussische Absolutismus und der Adel. Eine Auseinandersetzung mit der marxistischen Absolutismustheorie." *Geschichte und Gesellschaft* 8 (1982): 538–53.

Dinges, Martin. "'Historische Anthropologie' und 'Gesellschaftsgeschichte'. Mit dem Lebensstilkonzept zu einer 'Alltagskulturgeschichte' der frühen Neuzeit?" *Zeitschrift für Historische Forschung* 24 (1997): 179–214.

Dorwart, Reinhold. *The Prussian Welfare State before 1740.* Cambridge, MA, 1971.

Dülmen, Richard van. "Historische Kulturforschung zur Frühen Neuzeit: Entwicklung – Probleme – Aufgaben." *Geschichte und Gesellschaft* 21 (1995): 403–29.

Duplessis, Robert. *Transitions to Capitalism in Early Modern Europe.* Cambridge, 1997.

Dwyer, Philip G., ed. *The Rise of Prussia: Rethinking Prussian History, 1700–1830.* London, 2001.

Eley, Geoff. "Labor History, Social History, *Alltagsgeschichte:* Experience, Culture, and the Politics of the Everyday – A New Direction for German Social History?" *Journal of Modern History* 61 (1989): 297–343.

"Problems with Culture: German History after the Linguistic Turn." *Central European History* 31 (1998): 197–227.

Friedeburg, Robert von. "'Kommunalismus' und 'Republikanismus' in der frühen Neuzeit? Überlegungen zur politischen Mobilisierung sozial differenzierter ländlicher Gemeinden unter agrar- und sozialhistorischem Blickwinkel." *Zeitschrift für Historische Forschung* 21 (1994): 65–91.

"'Reiche', 'geringe Leute' und 'Beambte': Landesherrschaft, dörfliche 'Factionen' und gemeindliche Partizipation, 1648–1806." *Zeitschrift für Historische Forschung* 23 (1996): 219–65.

Fulbrook, Mary, ed. *German History since 1800.* London, 1997.

Gawthorp, Richard. *Pietism and the Making of Eighteenth-Century Prussia.* Cambridge, 1993.

Giesen, Bernhard. *Die Intellektuellen und die Nation. Eine deutsche Achsenzeit.* Frankfurt/M., 1993.

Hagen, William W. *Germans, Poles, and Jews: The Nationality Conflict in the Prussian East, 1772–1914.* Chicago, 1980.

"The Descent of the *Sonderweg.* Hans Rosenberg's History of Old-Regime Prussia." *Central European History* 24 (1991): 24–50.

Review essay on Hans Medick, *Weben und Überleben in Laichingen.* *Central European History* 32 (1999): 453–9.

Hahn, Peter-Michael. "'Absolutistische' Polizeigesetzgebung und ländliche Sozialverfassung." *Jahrbuch für die Geschichte Mittel- und Ostdeutschlands.* Berlin, 1980.

"Landesstaat und Ständetum im Kurfürstentum Brandenburg während des 16. und 17. Jahrhunderts," in Peter Baumgart, ed., *Ständetum und Staatsbildung in Brandenburg-Preussen.* Berlin, 1983: 41–79.

Hintze, Otto. *Die Hohenzollern und ihr Werk.* Seventh edn. Berlin, 1916.

"Preussens Entwicklung zum Rechtsstaat." *Forschungen zur brandenburgischen und preussischen Geschichte* 32 (1920): 385–451.

"Die Hohenzollern und der Adel," "Die Epochen des evangelischen Kirchenregiments in Preußen," "Preussische Reformbestrebungen vor 1806," in O. Hintze, *Regierung und Verwaltung. Gesamelte Abhandlungen zur Staats-, Rechts- und Sozialgeschichte Preussens,* ed. Gerhard Oestreich. 3 vols. Göttingen, 1967, vol. III, 30–55, 56–96.

Hinz, Bernhard. *Die Schöppenbücher der Mark Brandenburg, besonders des Kreises Züllichau-Schwiebus.* Berlin, 1964.

Hsia, Ronald Po-chia. *Social Discipline in the Reformation: Central Europe, 1550–1750.* London, 1989.

Ingrao, Charles. "The Problem of 'Enlightened Absolutism' and the German States." *Journal of Modern History* 58 (Supplement, 1986): 161–97.

Johnson, Hubert C. *Frederick the Great and his Officials.* New Haven, CT, 1973.

Johnson, Lonnie R. *Central Europe. Enemies, Neighbors, Friends.* New York, 1996.

Kathe, Hans. *Preußen zwischen Mars und Musen. Eine Kulturgeschichte von 1100 bis 1920.* Munich, 1993.

Kendall, Gavin and Gary Wickham. *Using Foucault's Methods.* London, 1999.

Kittsteiner, Heinz-Dieter. *Die Entstehung des modernen Gewissens.* Frankfurt/M., 1991.

Klippel, Diethelm. "Von der Aufklärung der Herrscher zur Herrschaft der Aufklärung." *Zeitschrift für Historische Forschung* 17 (1990): 193–210.

Koselleck, Reinhart. *Preussen zwischen Reform und Revolution: Allgemeines Landrecht, Verwaltung und soziale Bewegung von 1791 bis 1848.* Stuttgart, 1981.

Krieger, Leonard. *The German Idea of Freedom. History of a Political Tradition.* Chicago, 1957.

Kuper, Adam. *Culture: The Anthropologists' Account.* Cambridge, MA, 1999.

Levinger, Mathew. *Enlightened Nationalism. The Transformation of Prussian Political Culture, 1806–1848.* New York, 2000.

Lüdtke, Alf. *Police and State in Prussia, 1815–1850.* Cambridge, 1989 (German original: 1982).

Lüdtke, Alf, ed. *The History of Everyday Life. Reconstructing Historical Experiences and Ways of Life.* Princeton, NJ, 1995 (German original: 1989).

Luebke, David. "Frederick the Great and the Celebrated Case of the Millers Arnold (1770–1779): A Reappraisal." *Central European History* 32 (1999): 379–408.

MacDonogh, Giles. *Prussia. The Perversion of an Idea.* London, 1994.

Mączak, Antoni et al. *East-Central Europe in Transition: From the Fourteenth to the Seventeenth Century.* London, 1985.

Materna, Ingo and Ribbe, Wolfgang, eds. *Brandenburgische Geschichte.* Berlin, 1995.

McNeely, Ian. "Writing, Citizenship, and the Making of Civil Society in Germany, 1780–1840." Ph.D. dissertation, University of Michigan, Ann Arbor, 1998.

Megill, Allan. *Prophets of Extremity. Nietzsche, Heidegger, Foucault, Derrida.* Berkeley, CA, 1987.

Melton, James Van Horn. "Absolutism and 'Modernity' in Early Modern Central Europe." *German Studies Review* 8 (1985): 383–98.

Absolutism and the Eighteenth-Century Origins of Compulsory Schooling in Prussia and Austria. Cambridge, 1988.

Menge, Wolfgang and Emanuela Wilm. *So lebten sie alle Tage. Bericht aus dem alten Preußen.* Berlin, 1984.

Mirow, Jürgen. *Das alte Preußen im deutschen Geschichtsbild seit der Reichsgründung.* Berlin, 1981.

Mittenzwei, Ingrid. *Friedrich II. von Preußen. Eine Biographie.* Berlin, 1983.

Mittenzwei, Ingrid and Erika Herzfeld. *Brandenburg-Preußen, 1648 bis 1789: Das Zeitalter des Absolutismus in Text und Bild.* Cologne, 1987.

Moeller, Robert G., ed. *Peasants and Lords in Modern Germany: Recent Studies in Agricultural History.* London, 1986.

Moore, Barrington. *Social Origins of Dictatorship and Democracy. Lord and Peasant in the Making of the Modern World.* Boston, 1966.

Muir, Edward and Guido Ruggiero, eds. *Microhistory and the Lost Peoples of Europe.* Baltimore, MD, 1991.

Neugebauer, Wolfgang. "Zur neueren Deutung der preussischen Verwaltung im 17. und 18. Jahrhundert." *Jahrbuch für die Geschichte Mittel- und Ostdeutschlands* 26 (1977): 86–128.

"Zur Staatsbildung Brandenburg-Preußens: Thesen zu einem historischen Typus." *Jahrbuch für brandenburgische Landesgeschichte* 49 (1998): 183–94.

Niethammer, Lutz, et al. *Bürgerliche Gesellschaft in Deutschland.* Frankfurt/M., 1990.

Nipperdey, Thomas. *Deutsche Geschichte 1800–1866. Bürgerwelt und starker Staat.* Third edn. Munich, 1985.

Novick, Peter. *That Noble Dream: The "Objectivity Question" and the American Historical Profession.* Cambridge, 1988.

Obenaus, Herbert. "Gutsbesitzerliberalismus. Zur regionalen Sonderentwicklung der liberalen Partei in Ost- und Westpreußen während des Vormärz." *Geschichte und Gesellschaft* 14 (1988): 304–28.

Oestreich, Gerhard. *Neostoicism and the Early Modern State.* Cambridge, 1982.

Paret, Peter. *Yorck and the Era of Prussian Reform, 1807–1815*. Princeton, NJ, 1966.
Paret, Peter and Daniel Moran, eds. *Carl von Clausewitz: Historical and Political Writings*. Princeton, NJ, 1992.
Petersdorff, Heinrich von. "Otto Carl Friedrich, Freyherr von Voss." *Allgemeine Deutsche Biographie*. Leipzig, 1896, vol. XL, 352–61.
Pröve, Ralf. "Zum Verhältnis von Militär und Gesellschaft im Spiegel gewaltsamer Rekrutierungen (1648–1789)." *Zeitschrift für Historische Forschung* 22 (1995): 191–223.
Puhle, Hans-Jürgen and Hans-Ulrich Wehler, eds. *Preußen im Rückblick*. Göttingen, 1980.
Ribbe, Wolfgang, ed. *Geschichte Berlins*. 2 vols. Munich, 1987.
Rosenberg, Hans. *Bureaucracy, Aristocracy, and Autocracy. The Prussian Experience, 1660–1815*. Boston, 1958.
Roy, James C. *The Vanished Kingdom. Travels through the History of Prussia*. Boulder, CO, 1999.
Schieder, Theodor. *Friedrich der Große. Ein Königtum der Widersprüche*. Berlin, 1983.
Schlencke, Manfred, ed. *Preußen – Beiträge zu einer politischen Kultur*, vol. 2 of *Preußen – Versuch einer Bilanz*. Reinbek bei Hamburg, 1981.
Schlumbohm, Jürgen. "Gesetze, die nicht durchgesetzt werden – ein Strukturmerkmal des frühneuzeitlichen Staates?" *Geschichte und Gesellschaft* 23 (1997): 647–63.
Schmoller, Gustav. "Ueber Behördenorganisation, Amtswesen und Beamtenthum im Allgemeinen und speciell in Deutschland und Preussen bis zum Jahre 1713." *Acta Borussica*, Bd. I: *Die Behördenorganisation und die allgemeine Staatsverwaltung Preussens im 18. Jahrhundert*. Berlin, 1894: 79–143.
Schultze, Johannes. *Die Prignitz. Aus der Geschichte einer märkischen Landschaft*. Cologne, 1956.
Die Mark Brandenburg. 5 vols. Berlin, 1961–9.
Schultze, Johannes, ed. *Die Prignitz und ihre Bevölkerung nach dem dreissigjährigen Kriege*. Perleberg, 1928.
Schulze, Winfried. "Gerhard Oestreichs Begriff 'Sozialdisziplinierung in der Frühen Neuzeit.'" *Zeitschrift für Historische Forschung* 14 (1987): 265–302.
Scott, Hamish M., ed. "Prussia From Rossbach to Jena." *German History* 12 (1994): 279–394.
The European Nobilities in the Seventeenth and Eighteenth Centuries. 2 vols. New York, 1995.
Sheehan, James. *German History, 1770–1866*. Oxford, 1989.
Showalter, Dennis. "Hubertusberg to Auerstädt: The Prussian Army in Decline?" *German History* 12 (1994): 308–33.
Sperber, Jonathan. "State and Civil Society in Prussia: Thoughts on a New Edition of Reinhart Koselleck's *Preussen zwischen Reform und Revolution*." *Journal of Modern History* 57 (1985): 278–96.
Taylor, Charles. *Sources of the Self: The Making of the Modern Identity*. Cambridge, MA, 1989.

Thadden, Rudolf von. *Prussia: The History of a Lost State*. Cambridge, 1987 (German original, 1981).

Townsend, Mary Lee. *Forbidden Laughter: Popular Humor and the Limits of Repression in Nineteenth-Century Prussia*. Ann Arbor, MI, 1992.

Vetter, Klaus. *Kurmärkischer Adel und preußische Reformen*. Weimar, 1979.

Vierhaus, Rudolf. *Deutschland im Zeitalter des Absolutismus, 1648–1763*. Göttingen, 1978.

Vogel, Barbara, ed. *Preussische Reformen 1807–1820*. Königstein/Ts., 1980.

Vogler, Günter and Klaus Vetter. *Preußen: Von den Anfängen bis zur Reichsgründung*. Third edn. Berlin, 1974.

Wagner, Peter. *A Sociology of Modernity: Liberty and Discipline*. London, 1994.

Walker, Mack. *German Home Towns: Community, State, and General Estate, 1648–1871*. Ithaca, NY, 1971.

Wehler, Hans-Ulrich. *Das Deutsche Kaiserreich, 1871–1918*. Göttingen, 1973.

"Preußen ist wieder chic . . . Der Obrigkeitsstaat im Goldrähmchen," in H. -U. Wehler, *Preußen ist wieder chic . . . Politik und Polemik*. Frankfurt/Main, 1983: 11–18.

"A Guide to Future Research on the Kaiserreich?" *Central European History* 29 (1996): 541–72.

Weill, Hermann. *Frederick the Great and Samuel von Cocceji*. Madison, WI, 1964.

Weis, Eberhard. "Enlightenment and Absolutism in the Holy Roman Empire: Thoughts on Enlightened Absolutism in Germany." *Journal of Modern History* 58 (Supplement, 1986): 161–97.

Welskopp, Thomas. "Die Sozialgeschichte der Väter. Grenzen und Perspektiven der Historischen Sozialwissenschaft." *Geschichte und Gesellschaft* 24 (1998): 173–98.

White, Hayden. *Metahistory. The Historical Imagination in Nineteenth-Century Europe*. Baltimore, MD, 1973.

Willems, Emilio, *A Way of Life and Death. Three Centuries of Prussian-German Militarism. An Anthropological Approach*. Nashville, TN, 1986.

Würgler, Andreas. "Das Modernisierungspotential von Unruhen im 18. Jahrhundert. Ein Beitrag zur Entstehung der politischen Öffentlichkeit in Deutschland und in der Schweiz." *Geschichte und Gesellschaft* 21 (1995): 195–217.

Index